SEVEN DAYS BEFORE RICHMOND

McClellan's Peninsula Campaign of 1862 and its Aftermath

RUDOLPH J. SCHROEDER, III

iUniverse, Inc.
New York Bloomington

SEVEN DAYS BEFORE RICHMOND
MCCLELLAN'S PENINSULA CAMPAIGN OF 1862 AND ITS AFTERMATH

Copyright © 2009 Rudolph J. Schroeder, III

All rights reserved. No part of this book may be used or reproduced by any means, graphic, electronic, or mechanical, including photocopying, recording, taping or by any information storage retrieval system without the written permission of the publisher except in the case of brief quotations embodied in critical articles and reviews.

The views expressed in this work are solely those of the author and do not necessarily reflect the views of the publisher, and the publisher hereby disclaims any responsibility for them.

iUniverse books may be ordered through booksellers or by contacting:

iUniverse
1663 Liberty Drive
Bloomington, IN 47403
www.iuniverse.com
1-800-Authors (1-800-288-4677)

Because of the dynamic nature of the Internet, any Web addresses or links contained in this book may have changed since publication and may no longer be valid. The views expressed in this work are solely those of the author and do not necessarily reflect the views of the publisher, and the publisher hereby disclaims any responsibility for them.

ISBN: 978-1-4401-1407-6 (sc)
ISBN: 978-1-4401-1409-0 (dj)
ISBN: 978-1-4401-1408-3 (ebook)

Printed in the United States of America

iUniverse rev. date: 3/6/2009

For my loving wife, Sharon

Contents

Acknowledgements xiii

PART I	LINCOLN'S DECISION	 1
Chapter 1	A Plan Is Born	 2
Chapter 2	Approval	 10
Chapter 3	Changes and Preparations	 18

PART II	DEPLOYMENT	 27
Chapter 4	The Flotilla	 28
Chapter 5	Down the Bay	 30
Chapter 6	Fort Monroe	 37

PART III	PRELIMINARIES	 45
Chapter 7	Yorktown	 46
Chapter 8	Williamsburg	 58
Chapter 9	Eltham's Landing	 83
Chapter 10	Hanover Court House	 90

PART IV	SEVEN PINES	 97
Chapter 11	Seven Pines, Day One	 98
Chapter 12	Seven Pines, Day Two	 158
Chapter 13	Change of Command	 173
Chapter 14	Stuart's Ride Around McClellan	 186

PART V	THE SEVEN DAYS	195
Chapter 15	Oak Grove	196
Chapter 16	Mechanicsville	208
Chapter 17	Gaines's Mill	222
Chapter 18	Garnett's and Golding's Farms	255
Chapter 19	Savage Station	263
Chapter 20	Glendale	303
Chapter 21	Malvern Hill	358
Chapter 22	Journey's End	402
Chapter 23	Evelington Heights	415

PART VI	AFTERMATH	423
Chapter 24	Stasis at Harrison's Landing	424
Chapter 25	The Cost of Gallantry	435
Chapter 26	Redeployment	443

PART VII	CONSEQUENCES	451
Chapter 27	The Armies Go On	452
Chapter 28	The Significance of the Campaign	465

Epilogue 473

List of Illustrations 475

Appendix A 477

Appendix B 569

Appendix C 571

Appendix D 573

Notes 575

Bibliography 631

Glossary 675

Index 685

LIST OF MAPS

0.1	Area Map of the Campaign	xvi
5.1	Deployment, Army of the Potomac	32
7.1	Siege of Yorktown, April 5–May 3	50
8.1	Williamsburg, 10:00 A.M., May 5	60
8.2	Williamsburg, Afternoon, May 5	67
8.3	Williamsburg, Hancock's Advance, May 5	72
8.4	Williamsburg, Early's Charge, May 5	76
9.1	Eltham's Landing, May 7	85
10.1	Hanover Court House, May 27	92
11.1	Seven Pines, Johnston's Plan, May 31	103
11.2	Seven Pines, Actual, May 31	123
12.1	D. H. Hill's Attack, June 1	163
12.2	Seven Pines, Day Two overall, June 1	167
14.1	Stuart's Ride Around McClellan, June 12–15	191
15.1	Oak Grove, June 25	199
16.1	Mechanicsville, June 26	210
17.1	Advance to Gaines's Mill, June 27	225
17.2	Gaines's Mill, Initial Positions, June 27	229
17.3	Gaines's Mill, A. P. Hill's Attacks, June 27	233
17.4	Gainses's Mill, Ewell's Attacks, June 27	241
17.5	Gaines's Mill, D. H. Hill's Attacks on Sykes, June 27	244
17.6	Gaines's Mill, Whiting's Attack on Morell, June 27	247
18.1	Garnett's Farm, June 27	257

18.2	Garnett's & Golden's Farms, June 28	260
19.1	Lee's Plan of Pursuit, June 29	267
19.2	Allen's Farm, June 29	276
19.3	Savage Station, June 29	293
20.1	Lee's Revised Plan - June 30	305
20.2	White Oak Swamp and Brackett's Ford, June 30	312
20.3	Glendale, Longstreet's Attacks, June 30	331
20.4	Glendale, A. P. Hill's Attacks, June 30	350
21.1	Lee's Advance to Malvern Hill, July 1	368
21.2	Malvern Hill, 1st Attacks, July 1	384
21.3	Malvern Hill, 2nd Attacks, July 1	391
21.4	Malvern Hill, Final Attacks, July 1	396
22.1	Final Movements, July 2-3	414
23.1	Affair at Evelington Heights, July 3	418

ACKNOWLEDGEMENTS

Dan LaRose of Newport News, Virginia volunteered numerous hours of his time to assist in researching the order of battle appendix. His insight and diligence has made this part of the book much more complete and accurate than it might have been. His skill at editing several drafts of the book was essential to me.

Larry Gormley of Westford, Massachusetts provided me with frequent guidance and valuable assistance with maps. He also graciously gave of his free time to critically read a draft of the book and provide invaluable comment. An accomplished gentleman with a fine mind and an unmatched love of history, I am proud to count him as a friend.

Robert E. L. Krick, historian at the Richmond National Battlefield Park, generously provided me guidance on some hard to find sources on Georgia regiments.

Ken Peterson of Hampton, Virginia is a comrade from my airline days. His willingness to drop what he was doing and help me overcome numerous hardware and software difficulties allowed me to stay productive when I was too lazy to properly maintain my tools.

Patricia Richards of Williamsburg, Virginia helped me learn to navigate the rich sources of knowledge in Washington, including the Library of Congress and National Archives. This was an indispensable skill for me.

Bert Estes of Landenberg, Pennsylvania, an old comrade in arms, did me the great favor of braving the chaos that is downtown Philadelphia in order to send me copies of some hard to find newspapers from the Free Library of Philadelphia..

Alvin Reynolds of the Tidewater Genealogical Society allowed me to share his organization's bus transportation to and from the Library of Congress and the National Archives numerous times. You'll never know how much I enjoyed not having to drive and park in that confused city.

The Library of Congress staff, especially the men and women in Periodical Reading Room & Manuscript Reading Room, bent over backwards to see that I had productive days there. Their stellar reputations are richly deserved.

The Library of Virginia staff, especially Audrey C. Johnson, Senior Rare Book Librarian, showed great patience when I tried to hurriedly look at too many sources in a day trip. The professionalism of that staff was of great value to me on several occasions. This library is an extremely rich source of Civil War materials.

The College of William and Mary, Earl Gregg Swem Library Staff, especially Carole Conger at the circulation desk and Katherine McKenzie in Reference, were kind enough to help me on a number of occasions. This is one of the finest libraries in the nation.

Dr. John Coski and Ms. Teresa Roane, of the Museum of the Confederacy library were extremely diligent in helping me find several Civil War newspapers I was seeking. They run a first-class operation there.

Eleanor Mills and the staff of the Special Collections Library at Duke University were of tremendous help to me in locating a rare book. They are true professionals.

Mentioned last, but in importance assuredly first, is my wife, Sharon. She endured my irritation and frustration when I couldn't find answers diligently sought. She encouraged me when I passed through periods of discouragement. Lastly, she never once complained about the time I took out of our marriage to complete this project. Thank you, sweetheart.

None of these wonderful people are responsible for whatever errors you may find in this work. Those errors rightfully belong to me. The professionals mentioned above did their best. I only hope that I did also.

Jay Schroeder
Yorktown, Virginia
August, 2008

MASTER MAP LEGEND

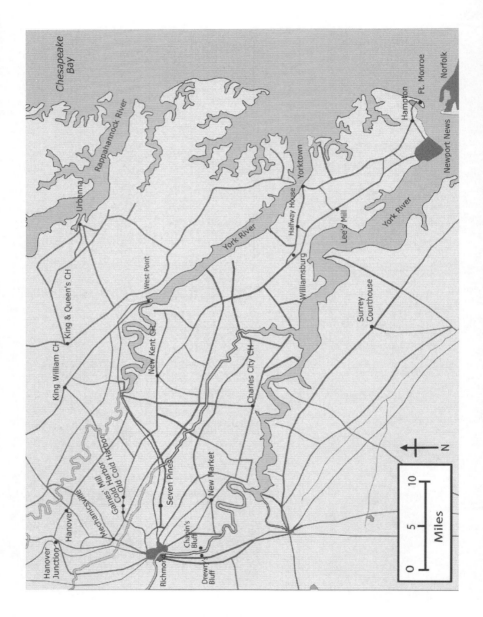

Area Map of the Campaign

PREFACE

There are a great many fine works on the American Civil War. What would be my motivation to write another? The short answer is that Civil War books are mostly written by people who love the incredibly rich history of that event, and write about it for no other reason than to further the study of it. Though I have no particular qualifications to undertake this project, I believe my twenty-five year military career and combat experience help me to understand the problems faced by leaders in the field. I hope that my passion for the subject matter, as well as my objectivity, will provide some small measure of enjoyment to a number of people who share my interest. My specific goal is to write a Civil War history book that can be read without the reader having to constantly take time out to search other documents and possibly the internet for information to assist in understanding the topic. This book is intended to be a complete work on the Peninsula Campaign. It has been researched and written over a five year period. It will attempt to answer the reader's questions or at least point to the answers. It will likely fall short of its goal. That is not the point. At least I tried.

McClellan's Peninsula Campaign of 1862 has for a long time been of great interest to me. As with a number of campaigns in this fascinating conflict, it allows the history enthusiast to ask why and what if. In this relatively short interval of time, so much occurred that could easily have turned out quite differently. Lincoln signed off on a campaign plan he really didn't like; the Confederate army changed leaders; McClellan retreated after each engagement, even those that were marginal Federal victories; and the Confederate capital city of Richmond remained untouched. Finally, General McClellan was permanently damaged and President Lincoln was left holding the proverbial bag. The stature of Robert E. Lee was greatly enhanced. The Confederate Army finally had a leader who could be respected and followed without question.

As to the ever-relevant matter of what to put in and what to leave out, this book will not attempt, as have so many others, to go back to the origins of the conflict, or even back to the firing on Fort Sumter. It will begin with an event relevant to the Peninsula Campaign, that being the development of the plan by which the Federal forces hoped to capture Richmond and put an early end to hostilities. It will end with the disposition of the opposing armies some months after the last shot of the campaign was fired, and the effect of the campaign on the two armies and their primary military leaders, Robert Edward Lee and George Brinton McClellan.

A vigorous attempt has been made to provide a sufficient number of high-quality maps of the critical time points of the relevant battles, and to specifically refer to the people and military units involved. I hope to make it easy for the reader to follow the narrative of the battles.

My use of footnotes may seem somewhat unorthodox. I have attempted to provide ample sources to the reader who seriously desires to gain a more comprehensive knowledge of the campaign. Not every reader has the time and monetary resources to travel to such research libraries as the Library of Congress and the National Archives. In addition to hard to access primary sources, I have tried to provide more modern and easily gained sources. This has obviously resulted in a great number of footnotes, but should make it possible for every reader to more easily pursue the subject to the depth desired.

The book also offers a glossary of military terms and archaic expressions, reprints of several documents relevant to the campaign, a thorough index, and an order of battle appendix down to the regimental and battery level. I desire that readers with no particular background in American Civil War history might be able to read this work, reasonably understand what transpired during the campaign, and why it was important to our nation's larger history. This goal will hopefully be accomplished because the book is as complete as is possible. The reader should not have to seek a number of other sources to understand what he or she reads in this one. On the other hand, it is hoped that the documentation in this work will assist the serious Civil War history enthusiast by providing direction to a variety of sources relevant to the campaign.

I've never read a perfect book, and this certainly will not be one. I will measure my success in the extent to which those who love Civil War history choose to read the book and consider the wonder and meaning of McClellan's Peninsula Campaign of 1862.

PART I

LINCOLN'S DECISION

"Does not your plan involve a larger expenditure of *time* and *money* than mine? Wherein is a victory more certain by your plan than mine? Wherein is a victory *more valuable* by your plan than mine? In fact, would it not be *less* valuable in this, that it would break no great line of the enemy's communication, while mine would? In case of disaster, would it not be more difficult to retreat by your plan than mine?"

President Abraham Lincoln [1]

CHAPTER 1

A Plan Is Born

To understand the events which led up to the Peninsula Campaign, we must skip about in time and location to put all the causative factors in perspective. Once we begin to deal with Lincoln's approval process of a concrete plan for winning the war, events will be laid out in a more chronological fashion.

The early months of 1862 included numerous Federal successes at arms. They were extremely fortunate in the West. At Mill Springs, Kentucky, an impetuous Confederate brigadier, Felix K. Zollicoffer, placed his brigade in the path of Brigadier General George Thomas, and paid with his life on January 19, 1862. Forts Henry and Donelson fell on February 6 and 16 to Brigadier General Ulysses S. Grant, giving the Federals access to the Tennessee and Cumberland Rivers. Fort Donelson was an especially bitter pill for the Confederates, as 12,000 men under General Simon B. Buckner were forced to surrender. The fall of Fort Donelson allowed the next domino to fall. Nashville became indefensible, and was occupied by Federal troops under Brigadier General William Nelson on February 25. The city was the first Southern capital to fall.

Also in February, Major General Ambrose E. Burnside captured Roanoke Island in coastal North Carolina, and in March, the town of New Bern, at the junction of the Trent and Neuse Rivers. This gave the Federals control of the northern end of the Outer Banks of North Carolina. The following month, Fort Macon at the southern end of the Outer Banks was taken, and the Federals had total control.

On April 6, General Albert S. Johnston attacked Grant's army at Shiloh. The camp was unfortified and the Federals were driven back to the banks of the Tennessee River at Pittsburg Landing. Darkness suspended the fighting before the battle reached a decisive conclusion, and Grant was reinforced overnight by Brigadier General Don Carlos Buell. The following day, a Federal counterattack reclaimed almost all the ground lost. Johnston was hit in the leg by a minie ball and bled to death on the battlefield. The Confederates withdrew, losing their best chance for a significant victory that winter. The Confederate retreat back to Corinth, Mississippi made it convenient for Henry Halleck, the overall Federal commander in the West, to combine Grant's and Buell's forces and prepare to move on Corinth.

At the same time as the battle of Shiloh, Brigadier General John Pope defeated Confederate forces at New Madrid, Missouri and at Island No. 10 in the Mississippi River. Now the Federals could operate on the Mississippi almost all the way downriver to Memphis. From the south, Rear Admiral Farragut fought his way up the Mississippi and forced the surrender of New Orleans, the largest city in the Confederacy, on April 28. The only remaining Confederate strong points on the Mississippi were Vicksburg, Fort Pillow and Port Hudson.

Federal successes at Pensacola, Apalachicola, Saint Augustine and Jacksonville in Florida, as well as Fort Pulaski in Savannah Harbor, made the importation of much needed supplies that much more difficult. Victories at Pea Ridge in Arkansas, and Glorieta Pass in New Mexico Territory rounded out the Federal good fortune in the far West and Trans-Mississippi. Everywhere Jefferson Davis looked, his men were outnumbered and outgunned.

Thus, those first months of 1862 indicated Northern momentum and possibly a short war. However, in March, Major General Thomas J. "Stonewall" Jackson's Confederate Army of the Valley alarmed Washington by attacking Federal forces at Kernstown, Virginia. Although Jackson's attack was repelled, he had the Federals' attention, and held it for months. He won at McDowell in May, then commenced to defeat two more Federal forces in sequence. This motivated President Lincoln to devise a plan to destroy Jackson's army.[1] The plan was singularly unsuccessful. Jackson made fools of the Federal generals in the Shenandoah until Lee recalled Stonewall and his men to the Virginia Peninsula in late June.

Although the preponderance of fighting seemed to be going in favor of the Federal forces, the victories were not concentrated in a particular area. They were scattered all over the map, and there was a felt need by many for a master plan for the conduct of the war. All the aged General-in-Chief Winfield Scott could manage to articulate was his "Anaconda Plan" which consisted of nothing more than closing the Mississippi River to the Confederates and putting in place a naval blockade of Southern ports. He wanted to squeeze the life out of the South, much as an anaconda constricts its prey. While the Anaconda Plan was a useful strategy that would have a decided effect on the South, a prey the size of the Confederacy could tolerate a great amount of squeezing and still fight on for some time. What was needed was a plan that would strike at Southern vitals.

McClellan had been made commander of the Army of the Potomac in the wake of the resounding Confederate victory at First Manassas (Bull Run). He assumed command on June 27, 1861. His mission was to take a young army, whose only real battle experience was their defeat at Manassas, and mold them into an effective, well armed force with the confidence to go on the offensive. A West Point graduate (1846), then an instructor there, veteran of the Mexican War, and then recipient of more military education as an observer of several European armies, McClellan was the right man to rebuild the Army of the Potomac.[2]

McClellan had a plan for defeating the rebellion. However, he had thus far kept it to himself. Neither his superiors nor immediate subordinates had any knowledge of what he was working out in his head. McClellan wanted to move his large army by water, down the Potomac, then the Chesapeake Bay, to land at the little town of Urbanna, Virginia on the lower Rappahannock River. McClellan believed such a movement would outflank the Confederate army of General Joseph Eggleston Johnston, presently dug in at Manassas Junction. McClellan felt that Johnston's position at Manassas Junction was too strong to take in a frontal assault. From Urbanna, McClellan would advance to Richmond, capture the city, and the rebellion would collapse.[3]

McClellan had restored discipline to the demoralized army routed at First Manassas, and had replaced incompetent officers. Equipment and arms kept rolling in, and the army was taking shape. There had been one tragic setback, however. On October 21, 1861, an ill-fated reconnaissance across the Potomac at Ball's Bluff had resulted in the death of Colonel Edward Baker, a personal friend of President Lincoln. More tragic were the deaths of hundreds of Federal troops under Baker's command. Baker, with no combat experience, was sent across the Potomac to attack a Confederate camp in the vicinity of Leesburg. Baker moved forward without benefit of reconnaissance. Failing to find the Confederates, he formed his men into a defensive position on the south bank of the river. Baker's men were attacked there by three infantry regiments and some cavalry under Confederate Brigadier General Nathan G. "Shanks" Evans. General Evans quickly enveloped the forces of the hapless Baker and drove them back into the river over a hundred foot high cliff. Many dove into the Potomac to escape, where they either drowned or were shot in the water.[4]

Rudolph J. Schroeder, III

Library of Congress

George Brinton McClellan

The massacre at Ball's Bluff had yet one more victim. Radical Republicans that controlled the Joint Committee on the Conduct of the War demanded that someone take the blame for the death of Lincoln's incompetent friend, Edward Baker. They couldn't call in and grill the dead Baker, thereby revealing him as the party responsible. Instead, they chose to scapegoat Brigadier General Charles P. Stone, a highly competent career officer with a track record of loyalty and integrity. Stone always treated civilians caught up in areas of fighting as well as he could, so they accused him of being a Southern sympathizer. Stanton ordered McClellan to strip Stone of his command and place him in arrest. Stone was arrested, by McClellan's order, at his quarters in the night, imprisoned without charges for months, and was refused a court of inquiry. McClellan, a friend of

Stone's took the coward's way out and failed to support Stone. Lincoln appeared to give political necessity priority over preventing an unwarranted imprisonment of a serving officer. The President was well aware of what was going on, and failed to stop it. Even after the Congress passed a law which guaranteed Stone would have to be charged or released, Stanton assured that Stone suffered just as long as possible. Finally, General Stone was released on August 16, 1862, but his career was essentially over.[5]

This debacle made it more difficult for McClellan to convince himself that his army was ready to take the offensive. He would initiate no further offensive moves that fall.[6] After declaring to a number of important people that he had no intention to put the army into winter quarters, McClellan did exactly that, and the winter of 1861–1862 went by too fast for him.

There was considerable political pressure on Lincoln to do something to carry the war to the enemy. Especially vocal was Horace Greeley and his New York *Tribune*. Greeley literally clamored for the Government to take some positive action. The Secretary of the Treasury predicted national bankruptcy soon.[7] No one in Washington wanted a long war; most didn't expect one. McClellan had spent a great deal of money and the greater part of the autumn and winter organizing and drilling his army, and constantly asking for more men, arms and supplies.

Many in Washington felt it was well past time to unleash the army on the Confederates. Before December ended, there were calls from Secretary of the Treasury Salmon Chase for Lincoln to dismiss McClellan. Chase was instrumental in the retirement of Winfield Scott, and was embarrassed by McClellan's inactivity. Chase and others wondered if McClellan might not be considering a presidential bid himself. McClellan had also used Senators Wade, Trumbull and Chandler to assist in General Scott's demise, and the powerful trio was likewise embarrassed. These three were Radical Republicans and the motive force behind the Joint Committee on the Conduct of the War. They were key members of a faction Lincoln was forced to accommodate to remain a successful President. McClellan's support base was rapidly dwindling.[8]

The Congressional Joint Committee on the Conduct of the War summoned McClellan to testify beginning on December 23 regarding the fight at Ball's Bluff. McClellan, however, was ill with typhoid fever, and wasn't able to appear. The general took to his bed for a period of two weeks. Neither Lincoln nor McClellan's senior generals knew the commanding general's plans. Lincoln became more frustrated with the situation, and began to talk to General McDowell and General Franklin, asking them how they would lead the army.

The President met with the two generals on January 10, 1862 with Chase and William Seward in attendance. Lincoln was distressed over the nation's situation, and complained of being "abused in Congress over the military inaction…" He told the two military men that he'd like "to *borrow* the Army of the Potomac for a few weeks and wanted us to help him as to how to do it."[9] McDowell favored an attack on the Confederate supply lines from the Occoquan River, east of Manassas. General Franklin preferred an attack from the shoreline east of Richmond.

By January 11, McClellan had learned of Lincoln's meetings with the General's subordinates. He forced himself out of his sick bed and resolved to defend himself from criticism. Appearing unexpectedly at a conference on January 13, McClellan, "looking exceedingly pale and weak," listened as Lincoln explained why he'd convened the meetings with Generals Franklin and McDowell. Chase tried to get McClellan to lay out his plans for the army. Chase had already been briefed on the plan by McClellan in early December. McClellan answered that he would only do so if Lincoln ordered it. McClellan then added a sharp remark to Chase, saying "No general fit to command an army will ever submit his plans to the judgment of such an assembly. There are many here entirely incompetent to pass judgment upon them;…no plan made known to so many persons can be kept secret an hour."[10]

Lincoln then pressed McClellan as to whether the general in fact had developed a plan. McClellan said that he had indeed. Lincoln then replied, "Then, General, I shall not order you to give it." Lincoln said at some point "I will hold McClellan's horse if he will only bring us success." Franklin later remarked that at least one person said that McClellan was a "ruined man" for responding the way he had.[11] McClellan had managed to avoid their probing questions, and went back to his accustomed inactivity.[12] However, he'd made a huge mistake. His rant had obviously insulted some of those present. There would be consequences.

It is difficult to understand why McClellan elected not to seek a one-on-one meeting with President Lincoln and candidly discuss his Urbanna plan with his superior. While McClellan might have made a valid point about the danger to operational security of discussing the plan in a large assemblage, a private meeting with the man who had to approve it in the final analysis surely posed no hazard. This was one of the major nails in McClellan's coffin. His eventual fall from grace was caused in great part by a series of such seemingly small errors.

At about this same time, on January 14 to be exact, Simon Cameron resigned as Secretary of War. He had been accused of running an administration guilty of malfeasance, patronage and corruption. The press had been dogging him for some time. The straw that broke the camel's back was a report Cameron released to the press that discussed arming slaves. Not withstanding the sensitivity of the issue, the report was released without the President being informed in advance. Lincoln then nudged Cameron into resigning his post and accepting that of Minister to Russia.[13]

Lincoln's surprising choice to replace Cameron was a Democrat. He was Edwin McMasters Stanton, a lawyer born in Ohio. He assumed the position of Secretary of War on January 15, 1862. Stanton had served as Attorney General under President James Buchanan, was a fairly new friend of George McClellan, and, privately, was not a fan of the Lincoln administration. Despite all this baggage, Stanton was recommended by Cameron, and Lincoln found Stanton to be a skillful administrator.[14]

On January 27, 1862, Lincoln, tired of waiting for McClellan to move, issued General War Order, No. 1. It read:

> *Ordered:* That the 22d day of February, 1862 be the day for a general movement of the land and naval forces of the United States against the insurgent forces.
> That, especially,
> The army at and about Fortress Monroe,
> The army of the Potomac,
> The army of Western Virginia,
> The army near Mumfordsville, Kentucky,
> The army and flotilla at Cairo, And a naval force in the Gulf of Mexico, be ready to move on that day.
> That all other forces, both land and naval, with their respective commanders, obey existing orders for the time, and be ready to obey additional orders when they are duly given.
> That the heads of departments, and especially the Secretaries of War and of the Navy, with all their subordinates, and the General-in-Chief, with all other commanders and subordinates of land and naval forces, will severally be held to their strict and full responsibilities for prompt execution of this order.
> Abraham Lincoln[15]

Lincoln then issued on January 31, 1862 President's Special War Orders, No. 1. It read:

> *Ordered:* That all the disposable force of the army of the Potomac, after providing safely for the defense of Washington, be formed into an expedition for the immediate object of seizing and occupying a point upon the railroad southwestward of what is known as Manassas Junction, all details to be in the discretion of the Commander-in-Chief, and the expedition to move before or on the 22d day of February next.
>
> Abraham Lincoln[16]

The release by Lincoln of these two orders forced McClellan to reveal his Urbanna plan. He immediately asked if Lincoln's orders were final, or if he could submit his objections to Lincoln's plan and submit his reasoning. Lincoln graciously agreed to hear the General out. McClellan came forward on January 31 with a twenty-two page proposal, touting it as a plan that would "save time, money, and lives."[17]

On February 3, Lincoln responded to McClellan's proposal, asking whether McClellan thought his plan would be cheaper, faster, cost less lives, better assure victory, result in a more valuable victory, or better facilitate a retreat if needed. McClellan's reply to Lincoln's one-page letter was a document of thousands of words, in which the general comprehensively discussed the military situation of the United States. He went back in time to the day, shortly after the rout of McDowell's army at Manassas, that he was appointed as Commanding General of all U. S. armies, offered his appraisal of the condition of the army, then described and defended in detail his plan for attacking Richmond.[18]

At this juncture, Lincoln was grateful for any sort of comprehensive war plan, and he obviously saw some logic in McClellan's arguments, though he still preferred his own plan. Lincoln, therefore, suspended his recent war orders. He was also careful to see that any plan adopted would assure an adequate defense of Washington. McClellan assured the President that he would leave behind enough troops to easily handle that mission. McClellan then began to work on fleshing out his Urbanna plan and gathering water transport for the deployment.[19]

All McClellan needed now was to secure Lincoln's approval for his modified Urbanna plan. Only Lincoln could make the plan a reality and allow McClellan to save the Union. Approval would come swiftly, and through a rather unusual decision process.

CHAPTER 2

Approval

On March 6, 1862, Lincoln summoned McClellan to a one-on-one meeting at the White House. The President had promised several days prior "to talk plainly" to his army commander. Lincoln kept his promise to himself and spoke sternly to McClellan. The President still had major reservations about McClellan's plan to move the Army of the Potomac down the Chesapeake Bay and operate up the Virginia Peninsula to Richmond. He felt compelled to discuss with McClellan the rumors about the capital speculating that McClellan had Southern sympathies and had the traitorous intent of moving the Army of the Potomac away from the city, leaving it defenseless. The mere mention of the matter, especially the term "traitorous," enraged McClellan. He was convinced that there was a conspiracy afoot to have him removed from command. He vowed to settle any doubts Lincoln might harbor.

A meeting was already scheduled for 10:00 A.M. the following day to deal with another matter. The meeting would be attended by twelve brigadier generals. McClellan told Lincoln that these twelve officers would now be a council of war, and he would let them deliberate the campaign plan, and decide by a vote all matters of "grand strategy." He, McClellan, would not even be present during the debate. Subsequently, he would have them bring their results directly to the President. This seemed to satisfy Lincoln.[1]

The promised meeting was hosted by army Chief of Staff Randolph B. Marcy at Army Headquarters. General Marcy laid out the question to be decided as a proposal by McClellan to change the base of the Army of the Potomac from Washington to Urbanna, Virginia. Instead of attacking the Confederate batteries on the lower Potomac, as previously envisioned, McClellan had decided to bypass them by deploying the army via the port of Annapolis, thereby making the Potomac River irrelevant to the campaign. Marcy then biased their consideration of the issue by communicating individually to them that McClellan's tenure was at stake. McClellan himself then joined the meeting and briefed the plan in detail using a large map. He then left the room, taking Marcy with him.

The twelve brigadiers, all of McClellan's division commanders, considered their commanding general's plan and voted for it, eight to four. Edwin V. Sumner, Irvin McDowell, Samuel P. Heintzelman and John G. Barnard were opposed. Barnard raised his objection based on his estimate that Joseph E. Johnston, as soon as he received word that McClellan's army was coming ashore at Urbanna, would take advantage of the Confederate rail system, and pull back to Richmond more quickly than McClellan could disembark his army and march to the Confederate capital. McClellan offered to use cavalry to cut the appropriate railroads along Johnston's withdrawal route, but Barnard was still unsatisfied and voted against the plan. Andrew Porter, Fitz John Porter, Louis Blenker, William B. Franklin, William F. Smith, Erasmus D. Keyes, George A. McCall and Henry M. Naglee, perhaps influenced in part by Marcy, voted in favor.[2] The dozen generals then went to the White House and reported their decision to the President.

President Lincoln seemed disappointed by their decision, but glad to have a decision at last. Secretary of War Stanton, joining the meeting, questioned the generals in detail. The Navy was called in to comment on their ability to support the plan. Assistant Secretary of the Navy Gustavus V. Fox assured the President that the Navy would assist in the campaign. The meeting was recessed for the night.[3]

At 10:00 A.M. the following morning, Saturday, March 8, the meeting was reconvened at the White House. McClellan was not present. Lincoln informed them that the modified Urbanna plan was approved, with conditions. He insisted that Washington be properly defended, and no more than two corps would be allowed to deploy down the Chesapeake Bay until the Confederate batteries on the lower Potomac were neutralized. He then announced the formation of five infantry corps, and the appointments of Sumner, McDowell, Heintzelman, Keyes and Banks as corps commanders.

All but Banks were to be part of McClellan's assault on Richmond. Banks' corps would remain to defend Washington. Lincoln told them he expected their full support for the offensive.[4] Lincoln could offer no further serious argument against the plan without substituting a plan for which he would have to assume total blame in case of its failure. He chose the former course of action.[5]

At last, McClellan had approval for a plan he had been developing over a four month period. McClellan was in fact capable of innovative planning. The Urbanna plan was an excellent example. His strategy was indeed innovative; the logistics considerations were given adequate attention. It was very ambitious, but appropriately so. After all, McClellan intended to have this one successful campaign, decimate the Confederate army, capture their capital and end the rebellion. Were he to be successful, he would spare the United States a long, costly, bloody war. Unfortunately, his intelligence estimates of Confederate strength were extremely inflated.[6]

At this point, Confederate movements invalidated much of the Federal planning. Specifically, the Confederate commander, General Joseph E. Johnston, took the course of action that John Barnard had been concerned about. Over the course of the war, Johnston became famous for his skill at retreat.

Over two weeks before McClellan was granted approval for the Urbanna plan, Johnston was called to Richmond to meet with President Davis. At that time, news was negative from everywhere in the Confederacy.

Johnston arrived at the Capitol on February 19, as Davis was conducting a Cabinet meeting to discuss the grim outlook. Johnston joined the meeting, and they began to discuss the Eastern theater. Johnston, almost as cautious and careful as his counterpart McClellan, had as his primary concern what he saw coming, not the unfortunate events that had already occurred.[7]

Davis stated his belief that McClellan was sure to go on the offensive with the arrival of spring. Davis favored a defensive strategy, and described his situation at Manassas as overextended and outmanned. He estimated that he had only 42,200 effectives, and believed he had to withdraw to positions closer to Richmond to better defend the city. Attorney General Thomas Bragg believed it would be a difficult maneuver to execute, owing mainly to the miserable condition of the roads in winter.

Johnston had doubts about the Orange and Alexandria Railroad being capable of hauling away the large amount of supplies and equipment presently near Manassas. Davis expressed concern about losing the materiel, then dismissed Johnston. He asked the general to give more thought to the matter and return the following day.

The following day, February 20, the Cabinet met again and spent hours attempting to find a way to safely withdraw the heavy guns from Manassas to Richmond. Johnston maintained that it couldn't be done until the roads dried, and that McClellan would likely attack Manassas before then.

After the conference, Johnston returned to his hotel, then took the train to Manassas the following day. Both at the hotel and on the train, he was asked by another passenger, a military officer, about things that were discussed at the Cabinet meeting. It was obvious to Johnston that details of the meeting were already close to public knowledge. Johnston wondered how he could carry off the safe evacuation of the army from Manassas with senior government officials so lax about keeping secrets. [8]

All Johnston could do was hope that the Federals hadn't concluded that he was going to withdraw soon, and he set about preparing his army for the move. In the entire war, this was probably the only time a Confederate army at the front was well supplied. The usually inept Confederate commissary department had amassed about three and a quarter million pounds of subsistence at Manassas. There was also a great amount of personal soldiers' baggage. Only fifteen miles south of Manassas, there was a Confederate meat-curing plant. It contained in excess of two million pounds of salted meat and bacon. The single track Orange and Alexandria Railroad had labored long and hard to carry all this treasure to the army. It now was able to save only a pitifully small percentage of it. As February slipped into early March, Johnston grew more and more apprehensive of what would soon happen.[9]

While railroad crews were hauling away supplies, a report reached Johnston that the Federals were crossing the Potomac at Harper's Ferry. Johnston felt he might have to withdraw before he was completely ready, but nothing came of the Harper's Ferry report. On March 5, Johnston became aware that there was "unusual activity" on the part of the Federal troops in lower Maryland. This was the tipping point for Johnston. He was now convinced that the poor security at the Cabinet meeting had resulted in a Federal move to flank him and hit his army in their withdrawal. He concluded that he had to withdraw right away, before the Federals could turn his flank. He sent out orders for an immediate withdrawal, directing his men to destroy what they couldn't carry with them. All weekend they slipped away to the south. Some were lucky enough to be marched to supply depots, where they were allowed to help themselves to anything they could haul away. This they did; several of them even managed to take turns carrying a 10 gallon keg of whiskey to the Rappahannock.

The rear guard, some of Johnston's cavalry, burned the depots and the meat-curing plant. The army became instantly demoralized when they saw the flames from their own burning supplies. The only bright spot for Johnston was that the Federals did not pursue them. In fact, it seemed that the Federals were either unaware or unsure the Confederate army was leaving.[10]

If McClellan were now to land his army at Urbanna, it would be farther from Richmond than Johnston's, and no flanking maneuver would be possible. An Urbanna landing no longer had any merit whatsoever. McClellan thus decided to modify his plan to land at Fort Monroe on the tip of the Virginia Peninsula, and use the James and York Rivers for

Federal gunboats and transports. He could land his troops near the fort and advance up the Peninsula to Richmond, and the campaign could still succeed.

About the same time that Johnston pulled back from Manassas Junction, and without his prior knowledge, a new Confederate weapon changed the balance of power in the vicinity of Fort Monroe. On March 8, the C.S.S. *Virginia*, the first Confederate ironclad, appeared out of nowhere and tore through the Federal warships anchored in Hampton Roads, near Fort Monroe. In a short period of time, the *Virginia* managed to sink the U.S.S. *Cumberland* and the U.S.S. *Congress* struck her colors. The *Minnesota* and the *St. Lawrence* were driven aground. The *Virginia* withdrew to Craney Island about 8:30 P.M., planning to come back on the morrow and finish the job.

Fortunately for Lincoln, the Federals had eye witnesses. Fort Monroe actually took the *Virginia* under fire. The 10,000 man garrison there was commanded by Major General John E. Wool.

The next morning, a telegram from Wool describing the damage reached Washington. Secretary of War Stanton was in a panic. Lincoln reacted much as he did when he was informed of the result at First Manassas. He envisioned the *Virginia* finishing off the blockading squadron at Fort Monroe, then shooting up Washington, New York and Boston. Widespread disaster was possible. At a minimum, the Urbanna plan would not be feasible now.

McClellan was less disturbed, but apprehensive. He sent orders to Annapolis to protect the transports he was massing there, and advised Wool that the plan for landing his army would probably change.

Stanton decided to make Secretary of the Navy Welles the object of his rage. Despite Stanton's rants, Welles remained calm and explained to Stanton that the first U. S. Navy ironclad, the U.S.S. *Monitor*, was due to arrive in Hampton Roads that very day. There would likely be no crisis. He related that his spies had been tracking the construction of the *Virginia* for months, and had thought the army would have taken the shipyard and eliminated the threat by now. Welles recommended that all remain patient until word reached them of the *Monitor's* arrival in Hampton Roads. Stanton was still in a panic and tried to arrange for the channel of the Potomac River to be blocked below Washington.[11] At Stanton's request, McClellan had ordered scows loaded with stone. Should the *Virginia* attempt to navigate up the Potomac, the scows could be quickly scuttled to block the channel. After more reports came in, the plan was wisely scrapped.[12]

On the very same day, Washington became aware that Johnston had withdrawn his army from the fortifications at Manassas. Shortly thereafter, more telegrams reported that the Confederate artillery batteries on the lower Potomac were gone. The men and guns had been withdrawn and the positions destroyed by explosives. Another report, this one from a fleeing slave who came into Washington from the west, related that Confederate troops had been observed leaving their positions at Manassas and Centerville all weekend. Tall columns of smoke were seen in the western sky from the burning supply depots.

McClellan rushed across the Potomac to see for himself. That evening, he sent a telegram back that he could confirm that the Confederates were indeed gone. Surprisingly, he promised to pursue them as far as possible the following day.

The shocking development in Hampton Roads effectively closed the York and James Rivers to Federal water transportation for a time. The final telegrams of note were from Assistant Secretary of the Navy Gustavus V. Fox, a former Naval officer who sent from Fort Monroe a report that the U.S.S. *Monitor* had appeared in Hampton Roads, met the C.S.S. *Virginia*, and battled her to a stalemate. Fox then sent a follow-up telegram that attempted to assure Washington that the *Monitor* was equal to the *Virginia*. Now McClellan was convinced that the *Virginia* could be neutralized, and that he could still safely land his army on the Peninsula.[13]

McClellan partially fulfilled his promise of the previous day. The Army of the Potomac did march out of Washington to the Confederate fortifications at Manassas and Centerville. When the Federals finally reached the scene, Johnston's men had been gone for a full day.

McClellan telegraphed Stanton from Fairfax Court House at 8:30 P.M. on March 11. He advised Stanton that he had ridden some forty miles around the area, and that the Confederate army was gone and had left behind a considerable amount of supplies and equipment. He believed the Confederates to be behind the Rapidan, holding Fredericksburg and Gordonsville.

While so much news was arriving in Washington in a very short period, McClellan seemed to keep a cool demeanor, as opposed to Secretary Stanton, and, to a lesser extent, President Lincoln. McClellan even found time on the 10th to again grouse at Stanton about the ordered formation of corps from the present division organization. He stated that he might have to delay offensive operations for the reorganization, and asked Stanton for the requirement for corps to be set aside. Stanton compromised and ordered McClellan to move the army and handle the reorganization just as soon as it could be effected without disrupting operations.[14]

McClellan characterized the Confederate fortifications as formidable, with those at Centerville superior to those at Manassas. A subsequent reconnaissance of the works at Centerville was made by Lieutenant Miles D. McAlester of the U. S. Engineers on March 14. This was followed by a similar survey of those at Manassas by the U. S. Coast Survey in April. McClellan felt these surveys validated his contention that the works were too formidable to be assaulted by his army, and that the Urbanna Plan was a better strategy for the Federals to implement.[15]

McClellan also told Stanton that the roads were terrible, and he intended to leave a part of Nathaniel P. Banks' command in the prepared Confederate positions at Manassas and Centerville, while "at once throwing all the forces I can concentrate upon the line agreed upon last week." That line, of course, was by water down the Chesapeake. McClellan stated that the arrival of the *Monitor* justified the course of action, and that he had already telegraphed to have the transports brought to Washington for the deployment down the Chesapeake. McClellan closed his message by offering Stanton an implied opportunity to veto the latest plan, and telling his superior that he might have to remain west of the city for a while. Forgotten was McClellan's recent promise to pursue Johnston's retreating army as far as possible.[16]

McClellan had received an urgent telegram from Marcy on March 11 to come into Washington that night. In the telegram, Marcy urged McClellan to keep the Administration informed as to his current actions and plans. He told McClellan that former Ohio Governor William Dennison, in reality a messenger from Lincoln, urgently wanted to see him before McClellan saw anyone else. For some reason, Dennison had been delegated to explain to McClellan that a decision had been made that day to essentially demote him to command only the Army of the Potomac while on campaign. Unfortunately for McClellan, he was too exhausted after a full day's efforts to ride back to Washington that night, and told Marcy so in a telegram sent from Fairfax Court House at 9:00 P.M.[17]

The manner in which McClellan became aware of his demotion was unfortunate, no matter what one's opinion of the need for the actual order. It was, however, not outside the ability of Lincoln and Stanton to humiliate people they were trying to control. In his own words, written much later, "While at Fairfax Court House on March 12, I was informed through the telegraph, by a member of my staff, that the following document had appeared in the *National Intelligencer,* of that morning." He then includes the document in his writings.[18]

On March 13, McClellan convened a second council of war. He met at his headquarters in Fairfax with the four major generals who now commanded his four corps: Irvin McDowell, Edwin Sumner, Samuel Heintzelman, and Erasmus Keyes. The meeting had the objective of discussing plans for the Peninsula campaign. In total consideration of the fact that the reorganization of the Army of the Potomac and the appointment of these four corps commanders was Lincoln's decision, not McClellan's, the General would have to sell them on the latest version of his plan.

The published results of this council of war were conditional. That is, if certain conditions could be met, the Urbanna plan should be implemented. If not, then the army should move against the enemy behind the Rappahannock at the earliest possible moment.

The conditions for implementing the Urbanna plan were:

1) That the Confederate ironclad *Virginia* be neutralized.
2) That sufficient transportation to move the army by water be available at Washington and Alexandria.
3) That a naval force be provided to silence the Confederate batteries on the York River.
4) That a force be left to defend Washington sufficient to "give an entire feeling of security for its safety from menace."

McClellan agreed with the findings of the council of war. They were not, by the way, unanimous, and McClellan forwarded them to the War Department.[19]

Several critically important considerations were discussed and major decisions taken. In light of Johnston's pullback to the Rappahannock River, Fort Monroe was chosen as a base of operations in lieu of Urbanna on the Rappahannock River. The naval requirements of the campaign were also a topic of discussion. The U. S. Navy would be required to contain the Confederate ironclad C.S.S. *Virginia*, as well as neutralize or at least suppress the Confederate batteries on the York. The York River was to be a vital line of communication, critical to the advance of the Federal army toward Richmond.[20]

CHAPTER 3

Changes and Preparations

Five major factors affected the need for final changes to George McClellan's campaign plan. They were:

1) the relative positions of the Confederate Army and the location of the debarkation point of the Federal Army relative to Richmond.
2) the adequate protection of Washington and its political ramifications.
3) the Confederate batteries on the lower Potomac.
4) the lift capacity of the flotilla.
5) the naval balance of power in Hampton Roads.

Consideration had to be given to each factor, and changes in that factor had to be adjusted for, if the campaign was to have a high probability of success. It should be noted that this chapter does not discuss events in chronological order, but rather by the factor to which they pertain. Some of these factors are discussed in later chapters, as they occurred during the campaign.

The primary factor was the relative positions of the Confederate army and the debarkation point of the expedition relative to Richmond. The essence of McClellan's strategy was to quickly put a large army on the ground closer to Richmond than Johnston's army. With Joseph E. Johnston's army in the vicinity of Manassas, landing the Federal army at Urbanna would allow that army to approach Richmond before Johnston could arrive there by land.

Lincoln was undoubtedly the greatest influence on McClellan's planning. Lincoln, in turn, was influenced by other politicians in Washington, each with their own agenda. Some of their fears could only be described as irrational. Nevertheless, Lincoln was a politician, in his first term, and always had in the back of his mind the desire to swiftly bring the war to a successful conclusion without making too many enemies. Ideally, he wanted the war behind him before beginning his reelection campaign in 1864.

When Johnston abruptly and stealthily withdrew his army from Manassas to positions behind the Rappahannock on March 8 and 9, the landing at Urbanna was no longer viable. Changes to the plan were imperative.

The adequate protection of Washington was a prerequisite for all planning. There was widespread fear of a Confederate attack. Lincoln's constant admonishments to McClellan to leave enough troops behind to adequately protect the capital affected the size of the force which would finally be sent on the campaign. Lincoln insisted that McClellan leave the capital "entirely secure" and must not depart on his campaign prior to arranging for said security.

As Lincoln did not quantitatively define his requirement, and McClellan failed to demonstrate its accomplishment in writing, the stage was set for a prolonged, unsolvable conflict between the two men. It was unsolvable because neither man could quite understand the other's thinking. Lincoln was unable to have McClellan comprehend the political significance of the security of the nation's capital. On the other side of the conflict, McClellan failed to convince Lincoln that the surest defense for Washington was to attack Richmond and force the Confederates to concentrate their army in their capital's defense.[1]

What McClellan did toward satisfying Lincoln's requirement could be construed as adequate and professional, or dismissed as devious, depending on whose side of the issue one resided. As described in the previous chapter, McClellan held a council of war prior to departing for the Virginia peninsula. At least one corps commander, Edwin V. Sumner, recommended a troop strength of 40,000 troops for the defense of Washington. McClellan added up the troops he considered at or close enough to Washington to participate in the defense of the city, and believed he had satisfied the requirement. He had assigned 22,000 troops in and around the city, and had posted others nearby at Manassas, Warrenton and on the lower Potomac River. All these troops in the aggregate, seemed to satisfy Lincoln's requirement.

By McClellan's math, he had provided 72,456 men and 109 pieces of light artillery. He further recommended that a force of 4,000 be brought down from New York to further reinforce those at and around the capital. He enumerated all of these alleged defenders of Washington in a letter to Brigadier General Lorenzo Thomas, the Adjutant General of the U. S. Army. He asked that Thomas lay the letter on Stanton's desk.[2]

A dispassionate observer of the issue could readily come to the conclusion that McClellan was giving little more than lip service to Lincoln's requirement that Washington be left "entirely secure." Some of the assumptions McClellan made were shaky at best. Some forces were double tasked. Others were even farther from Washington in terms of travel time than those deploying with McClellan.

What McClellan did not do was meet with Lincoln face-to-face and explain his rationale to his civilian superior. That might have satisfied Lincoln, or at least would have provided a basis for the two men to negotiate a settlement of the issue acceptable to both. All McClellan did was leave the aforementioned letter with Thomas and show a paper with the troop numbers on it to Ethan Allen Hitchcock, a military advisor to Lincoln, holding a position in the War Department. After leaving his numbers with Thomas, McClellan then departed for the Peninsula with his troops.

Edwin Stanton, newly installed as Secretary of War, was uneasy about the defense of Washington. He requested that Hitchcock and General James Wadsworth, commandant of the defensive forces in Washington, evaluate the defensive complement available for Washington and give Stanton their independent opinion. Hitchcock and Wadsworth agreed that McClellan had not faithfully fulfilled the President's requirement.

On April 3, while McClellan was still moving his army down the Chesapeake, Lincoln withheld McDowell's I Corps, a force of 30,000 men, and a long bickering dialogue between the army commander and the Lincoln administration began. The basic arguments of both men remained essentially the same throughout the campaign. McClellan kept inflating his estimate of the size of the Confederate army and requesting more troops. Lincoln kept telling the general to go on and do the job, as no more troops were available.[3]

Confederate artillery batteries on the lower Potomac influenced the choice of embarkation points. Lincoln did not want transports full of troops shot up on the way downriver to the Chesapeake. Much deliberation and planning was devoted to the problem of the Confederate batteries, but no concrete plan was ever approved to attack and neutralize them.

These bothersome batteries on the lower Potomac had been a concern to the leadership in Washington for some time. On March 8, Lincoln issued General War Order No. 3, which put restrictions on McClellan's deployment plans. The order stipulated that no more than two army corps would be allowed to deploy down the Chesapeake Bay until navigation there was freed from the Confederate batteries on the lower Potomac. It also ordered the army and navy to immediately cooperate in capturing those batteries.[4]

At one point in time, it was envisioned that Hooker's division could be put across the Potomac and take the offending batteries by force. This plan was discouraged by a report by Brigadier General John G. Barnard, the chief engineer. Barnard noted the lack of suitable naval forces to cooperate with Hooker's division, and felt the mission was thus unwise. Although the U. S. Navy had been advised as early as August 12 of the previous year of the need for a force of combat vessels to control the Potomac, they did not possess such a force in the spring of 1862.

Barnard's report essentially claimed that, had the Navy put capable vessels on the lower river the previous August, the construction of the batteries could have been prevented. Now that so many were in place, it was no longer possible to prevent the construction of more of them.

McClellan responded by modifying his plan to use Baltimore for his transports. While that would have avoided the Confederate batteries on the lower Potomac, there was a down side. Many of the troops and supplies earmarked to deploy for the Peninsula Campaign were at Aquia Landing, and would have to be transported to Baltimore, at a significant cost in time and dollars.

When the Confederates removed their guns and demolished their batteries on the lower Potomac in early March, McClellan again adjusted his plan. He finally decided on using three points of embarkation: Washington, Aquia Landing and Annapolis. As a footnote to the issue, an examination of the abandoned batteries confirmed the wisdom of Barnard's advice against Hooker's proposed mission.[5]

The lift capacity of the flotilla affected the rate at which the troops and their equipment could be moved down the Bay. The U. S. Navy did not own a fraction of the sea lift required to deploy an army of the size McClellan desired. Arrangements had to be made to charter private vessels to get the job done.

McClellan had been working for some time on arrangements for leasing transports for his campaign. The flotilla actually used consisted of vessels of a wide variety of sizes and shapes. In the end, the deployment was made in several trips.

The naval balance of power in Hampton Roads was a great concern to all Federal decision-makers. If the army could not be safely put ashore, the plan would not be viable.

The startling news on March 8 that the Confederate ironclad ram C.S.S. *Virginia* had partially destroyed the U. S. Navy's Northern Blockading Squadron in Hampton Roads prompted immediate, but temporary, changes in Federal planning. At first blush, it appeared that the overall plan for the campaign was no longer workable. Unarmed transports, especially chartered sailing vessels, would be sitting ducks for the *Virginia*.

Even if McClellan were willing to risk losing great numbers of troops on the voyage down the Bay, Lincoln would never have permitted it.[6]

The following evening, when reports came to Washington from Fort Monroe that the U.S.S. *Monitor* had arrived in Hampton Roads, engaged the *Virginia* that day, and fought her to a draw, the key players in Washington felt a sense of relief. Now it appeared that the army could be moved down the Bay, and only the choice of a landing point needed to be made.

All of these factors varied somewhat as the decision process ran its course and the time to actually move troops came closer. McClellan, to his credit, was unflappable and more flexible than Lincoln and his advisers. Each time a factor affecting the soon to be executed plan changed, General McClellan reacted in a professional manner and worked toward a reasonable solution. An exception might be McClellan's arrangement for the security of Washington, made prior to departing down the Chesapeake, where his math was in question.

Besides the five major factors mentioned above, there were other events which affected McClellan's preparations for the Peninsula campaign. Additionally, there were routine preparations underway, necessary to the deployment of such a sizeable force, that seemed to be unaffected by the dialogue between Lincoln, Stanton and McClellan.

Many of General McClellan's difficulties resulted from his failure to be forthcoming with his superiors. One frequent bone of contention was the Administration's claim that he never fully explained his plan for the campaign on the Virginia Peninsula. This, he finally did on March 14, after Lincoln had approved the plan.

On March 19, McClellan wrote a letter to Stanton, in which he outlined in detail his proposed operations for the Virginia Peninsula. He proposed to use Fort Monroe as his base of operations, then advance upon Richmond along the line of Yorktown and West Point, Virginia. He stated that Richmond was the objective point of the campaign, and believed the fall of Norfolk would facilitate the capture of the Confederate capital, which would precipitate the fall of the whole of Virginia.

McClellan thought the decisive battle of the campaign would occur somewhere between West Point and Richmond, owing to the fact that the Confederate government would realize that this campaign would determine the fate of their cause.

It would therefore follow that:
The Federal army should be concentrated, operate upon adjacent lines and maintain perfect communications.

No time should be lost in reaching the field of battle.

McClellan then proclaimed the unstated advantages of using the Peninsula as an avenue of approach to Richmond, and stated the importance of quickly reaching West Point, Virginia and using it as a supply depot. West Point would be the closest practical port to Richmond.

McClellan described the two possible methods of reaching West Point. They were:

1). By moving directly from Fort Monroe, by wagons up the roads, while simultaneously landing an infantry corps near Yorktown to turn Confederate lines south of there. This would likely involve a siege of several weeks to reduce Yorktown and Gloucester Point.
2). To make Yorktown the first objective of the campaign, by a combined land and naval attack. McClellan felt that this alternative would bring decisive results more quickly. However, it would require the navy to concentrate their firepower on the York River. After the Navy reduced the Confederate batteries at Yorktown, a strong corps would be brought up the river, and would attack West Point as soon as Yorktown fell. This would provide the logistics base needed, only twenty-five miles from Richmond. Even the north bank of the York could be used for the advance on the capital city. McClellan then reiterated the need for strong naval cooperation.

McClellan summarized by saying that rapid success required the Navy to "throw its whole available force, its most powerful vessels against Yorktown." He closed by asking for a prompt response.[7]

The first method would be slow and would not require much support from the Navy. The second would be quicker and likely less costly in casualties, but would require a much higher level of Navy participation.

McClellan's complex preparations continued. A few days before departing for the Peninsula, he met with Lincoln on a steamer in the Potomac. Lincoln told McClellan that there was pressure to take Blenker's division from McClellan and give it to Major General John Fremont, one of the Federal commanders in the Shenandoah. Lincoln stated that he had several good reasons not to do it. McClellan listened to the reasons and agreed with the President. On March 31, McClellan was surprised to receive a note from the President advising him that Blenker's division would in fact be going to Fremont. For whatever reason, Fremont had specifically asked for Blenker's division, many of them foreigners. Fremont was known to have an affinity for foreigners, and had a number of them assigned to his previous headquarters out West. Fremont had made Lincoln a proposition. Lincoln had been promised that Blenker would take Knoxville, if Lincoln would give him another 10,000 men.[8]

Before departing for the Peninsula, the War Department had issued an order putting Fort Monroe, manned by Major General Wool and a division of 10,000, under McClellan's command. McClellan was authorized to draw on Wool's command as he required. On April 3, McClellan was notified that Fort Monroe, General Wool, and the garrison had been taken from him by order of the President. No reason was ever given.[9]

The following day brought more bad news. McClellan received a telegram from Adjutant-General Lorenzo Thomas that the President had ordered McDowell's I Corps detached from the force under McClellan's immediate command. McDowell was to report to the Secretary of War. Now McClellan was deprived of about 50,000 troops, the largest corps in his army.[10]

One of McClellan's last orders issued before he departed for the Peninsula was to direct Lieutenant Colonel Barton S. Alexander, of the Corps of Engineers, to determine what defensive fortifications were necessary to hold the positions around Washington with a small force. He accomplished the study, but McClellan was relieved of responsibility for that area, and his successors failed to have the construction completed.[11]

One further fact deserves mention here, as it will pertain to the long, sometimes adversarial dialogue between Lincoln and McClellan over the issue of additional reinforcements for the Army of the Potomac. Shortly after he assumed command of the troops around Washington, McClellan organized what he called a secret service under his old friend and Chicago private detective, Allan Pinkerton, who also used the name Major E. J. Allen. Throughout McClellan's tenure, Pinkerton and his men spent their time procuring intelligence on the strengths, positions and movements of the enemy.

One of their primary sources were the variety of persons who came through the Federal lines from Confederate-held territory. They were a mixture of spies, "contrabands," refugee civilians and prisoners of war. McClellan claimed that all were thoroughly questioned, and some even provided statements under oath, as to what they had seen or heard.

Division commanders were tasked to personally interview these sources, then send them under guard to Washington. Once there, they would be taken to the provost-marshal-general of the army, accompanied by a written summary of the source's replies to the questions asked. The provost-marshal-general would then send the source and paperwork to the Chief of Staff of the Army of the Potomac, who would make the final determination of what examinations were necessary. Additionally, division commanders were directed to share applicable intelligence gained from sources passing through their hands.

From these sources, McClellan reached an estimate of Confederate strength around Washington and the Shenandoah Valley of 115,500 men, about 300 field guns and 26–30 siege guns. Obviously, these were inflated figures, but they were what the general had to work with.[12]

Thus, McClellan departed Washington for the Virginia Peninsula with a powerful army still in excess of 100,000 men, although Washington had diminished it by over 50,000 men. He had the additional concern that the President lacked confidence in him and the Secretary of War was plotting his downfall. The last major problem, that of Pinkerton's grossly inaccurate intelligence on the Confederate army, was still unknown to him. It would assure George McClellan's professional demise.

PART II

DEPLOYMENT

"Soldiers of the Army of the Potomac! For a long time I have kept you inactive, but not without a purpose; you were to be disciplined, armed and instructed; the formidable artillery you now have, had to be created; other armies were to move and accomplish certain results. I have held you back that you might give the death-blow to the rebellion that has distracted our once happy country. The patience you have shown, and your confidence in your General, are worth a dozen victories."

Major General George B. McClellan[1]

CHAPTER 4

The Flotilla

McClellan wanted the army moved to Fort Monroe as quickly as possible, in order to get an advantage on Joseph Johnston. General Johnston's surprise withdrawal from Manassas had motivated McClellan to get his Peninsula Campaign underway immediately. McClellan's plan had finally been approved by Lincoln, and the general spent March 13 and 14 sending the many telegrams necessary to getting the army moving. McClellan intended to move the Army of the Potomac to Alexandria as soon as possible, load them upon transports, then promptly get underway down the bay.

McClellan had originally planned for the flotilla to depart from Annapolis. Now that Johnston's army had withdrawn from Manassas, and the Confederate guns on the lower Potomac had been withdrawn and their works destroyed, moving the massive army all the way to Annapolis for embarkation was no longer necessary. It would be more efficient to gather the transports at Alexandria, and depart from there.[1] McClellan's exact words in his report on the campaign, not filed until August, 1863, were, "In the arrangements for the transportation of the army to the Peninsula by water the vessels were originally ordered to rendezvous mainly at Annapolis; but upon the evacuation of Manassas and the batteries of the Lower Potomac by the enemy it became more convenient to embark the troops and material at Alexandria, and orders to that effect were at once given."[2]

McClellan now directed that all the available transports be immediately marshaled at Alexandria. Assistant Secretary of War John Tucker, a former railroad president from Pennsylvania, was the official responsible for gathering the flotilla. Tucker had chartered everything available on the East coast that would float. The vast majority of the vessels were chartered from business enterprises or individual owners. According to records of the movement, 113 steamers were chartered at an average daily cost of $215.10, some 188 schooners were also contracted at an average daily cost of $24.45, and 88 barges at a daily average of $14.27. This put the cost at about $24,300 per day. The total size of the flotilla, composed of steamers, brigs, schooners, sloops, ferryboats, canal boats and barges, was in excess of 400 vessels. A number of these vessels made the entire voyage to Fort Monroe under tow. This was the biggest combined naval and ground force operation in the nation's history. Nothing even close to it had ever occurred before in North America.[3]

Despite the best efforts of Tucker and McClellan's large and able staff, the actual flotilla assembled was not capable of meeting the army's requirement. Although McClellan had been promised transport capability for 50,000 men, only about 25,000 men could be moved in the first trip of the flotilla down the bay. Amazingly, the first troops were underway only four days after the campaign plan was approved. It took numerous trips and about 20 days to move the entire army. The naval support vessels that augmented the civilian transports were based at Annapolis, and took longer than McClellan had expected to arrive at Alexandria and load their passengers and cargoes. These facts severely annoyed McClellan.[4]

Those escort vessels also had to return to Alexandria to escort each subsequent trip of the flotilla. For example, on March 20, Assistant Navy Secretary Gustavus V. Fox messaged Flag Officer Louis Goldsborough, ordering him to "Send back to the Potomac immediately the vessels of the flotilla that convoyed the army transports of Heintzelman's division to Old Point, as they will be needed to convoy another detachment. They are the *Anacostia*, *Freeborn*, and *Island Belle*."[5]

In retrospect, the deployment of McClellan's army was arguably the most professional facet of the Peninsula Campaign from the Federal perspective. Once in the campaign area, Federal professionalism became a bit more scarce.

CHAPTER 5

Down the Bay

To inspire the soldiers who so worshiped him, McClellan gave them a rousing speech within a day of the President's approval of his Peninsula campaign. Printed on the general's portable printing press and widely distributed to the army, the speech explained that he had held them back thus far, in order that they might be fully prepared to end the rebellion by delivering a crushing blow to the enemy. He reassured them that they now had the training, arms, and discipline to be capable of success in their mission. The general told them, "I shall demand of you great, heroic exertions, rapid and long marches, desperate combats, privations perhaps." McClellan promised to share the dangers and hardships of the campaign, and care for them as a father for his children. He promised them that they, in the future, would be proud to have been members of the Army of the Potomac. He assured them that "we will share all these together; and when this sad war is over we will all return to our homes, and feel that we can ask no higher honor than the proud consciousness that we belonged to the ARMY OF THE POTOMAC."[1]

Some Northern newspapers, such as the *St. Louis Republican* and the *New York Herald*, gave McClellan rave reviews on his speech. The General's men now loved him even more. The Radical Republicans, however, did not, and the speech, in which McClellan used the term "this sad war," caused the Radicals to intensify their efforts to assure his undoing. The Joint Committee on the Conduct of the War had walked the ground at the Confederate camps near Manassas and returned in a fury. They had discovered the Quaker guns left behind by Johnston's army and had been told that Johnston had been slipping men and equipment out of Manassas for weeks without the Federals discovering his trick. The Committee believed what they were told and jumped to the conclusion that McClellan was a loser that needed to be relieved of command.

After all, McClellan was a Democrat who didn't share their radical politics. He believed in preserving the Union, but saw no merit in fighting a civil war over the issue of slavery. The Radicals came to believe that General McClellan couldn't be trusted in such a sensitive position. McClellan's speech to his troops particularly offended them. On March 17, they initiated a vote in the U. S. Senate to censure and dismiss him. It failed by a single vote. They then searched for a way to persuade Lincoln to fire the general.[2]

McClellan had originally planned to embark McDowell's large I Corps first, move it as a unit to a point named "the Sandbox," just downstream of Yorktown, thereby flanking all Confederate troops between there and Fort Monroe. If that plan was not deemed feasible for any reason, McDowell's corps would be landed on the opposite bank of the York River, in order to move on West Point. When the transports began to dribble into Alexandria slowly, McClellan felt the need to again change his plan. He began to load the troops by division, while attempting to keep infantry corps together.[3]

McClellan's army began embarking at Alexandria on the evening of March 16, 1862 with much fanfare. The dreary, red-bricked wharf area of Alexandria was that day a festive place. It was a clear, sunny day. Military music helped to raise spirits. Bright, waving flags and throngs of interested spectators made the scene more like a holiday celebration than the occasion of tens of thousands of men going off to engage in a deadly struggle.[4] Charles Hamilton's division of Heintzelman's III Corps was the first to load, followed five days later by Fitz John Porter's division. Once these two divisions were underway, the remainder of the army had to await the return of the transports, before they could be loaded and moved to Fort Monroe.[5] The rate of deployment after those first two divisions was approximately one division per day. The Potomac and the Chesapeake were full of vessels for almost three weeks, going southbound heavily laden, returning northbound empty, riding high in the water.[6]

On the day his III Corps division embarked at Alexandria, Hamilton received orders to report to General Wool upon his arrival at Fort Monroe, for the purpose of securing an assigned campground for his men. Hamilton was also ordered to follow Wool's orders should the fort be attacked and General Wool determine a need for Hamilton's men to assist in the common defense.[7]

Samuel P. Heintzelman, corps commander of Hamilton's and Porter's divisions, received more detailed orders from McClellan on March 22. McClellan directed Heintzelman to move his two divisions some three or four miles from the fort, try to position them so as to straddle the two main roads to Yorktown, but maintain a good defensive position. This, Heintzelman was to do only if the terrain allowed "easy communication and mutual support between the two divisions." McClellan also suggested that Heintzelman not move too far from the fort, the object being to make the Confederates believe that the main object of the Federal army was Norfolk, not Yorktown. McClellan promised to send Heintzelman his third division, that of Brigadier General Joe Hooker, as soon as possible.

Seven Days Before Richmond

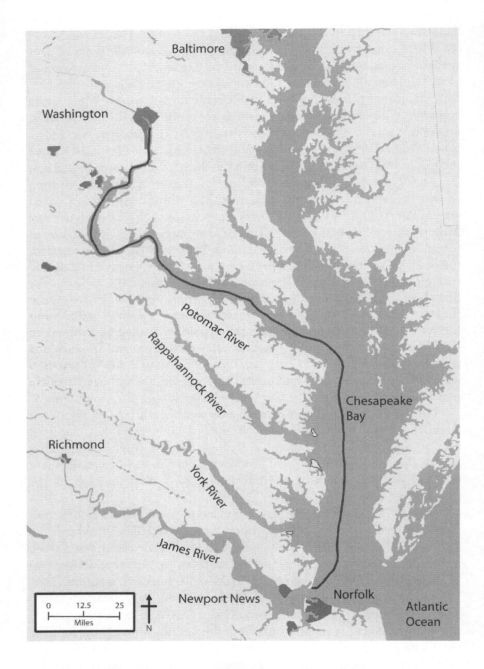

Map 5.1 — Deployment, Army of the Potomac

Heintzelman was required to maintain a strong reconnaissance of the Confederates up the Peninsula. McClellan also advised Heintzelman that detailed instructions were being sent to the quartermasters of the corps from Brigadier General Stewart Van Vliet, the Quartermaster-General of the Army of the Potomac.

McClellan also promised to send extra clothing, ammunition, etc. to Fort Monroe to make up any shortages Heintzelman might have. McClellan closed the order with the requirement that Heintzelman report frequently and fully the conditions on the field and any intelligence gained. He also suggested that Heintzelman immediately engage local guides and attempt to employ spies.[8]

As the second half of March passed, Confederate signal stations reported the progress of McClellan's army down the Chesapeake Bay. They soon discovered that the point of debarkation was Fort Monroe.[9] The Confederates were not too sure, however, of the ultimate objective of this large Federal deployment. Possible targets of the expedition were Richmond, Norfolk and Eastern North Carolina.

On March 18, Wool sent a message by boat to Stanton, revealing that the Confederates seemed to believe the target of the expedition was Norfolk. It read: "All is quiet, and from appearances the enemy are anticipating the expedition now preparing for this place to be intended for an attack on Norfolk, and consequently troops are concentrating at and near that place. Sewell's Point is being re-enforced, and new batteries are being erected between that point and Lambert's Point, at the mouth of Elizabeth River. Stores of every description are arriving.[10]

After the war, General Joseph E. Johnston wrote:

> From the 25th to the 29th of the month, our scouts observing the Potomac reported steam transports, loaded with Federal troops and military material, passing down the river continually. By their estimates of the number of men carried by each boat and their count of the number of trips, an army of one hundred and forty thousand men was conveyed in this way to some point beyond the mouth of the Potomac, probably Fort Monroe, as no reports of such vessels entering the Rappahannock were received. Reports of the Adjutant-General of the United States Army, published subsequently, show that it amounted to one hundred and twenty-one thousand men, and two hundred and forty field-pieces; it was joined, not long after, by a division of twelve thousand men.[11]

In Richmond, President Davis was uncertain whether all these Federal troops were moving to Fort Monroe to march up the Peninsula and attack Richmond, or were being sent to North Carolina. His immediate reaction was to direct General Johnston to order John G. Walker's brigade from Fredericksburg to reinforce the Confederate troops in North Carolina, and the brigade of Cadmus M. Wilcox from the Rapidan to join Magruder's forces near Yorktown.[12]

By April 5, Richmond determined that McClellan's army was advancing on Yorktown from Fort Monroe. Johnston then transferred the divisions of D. H. Hill, D. R. Jones and Jubal Early to the Peninsula. This left only the divisions of Jackson, Ewell, Longstreet and Gustavus W. Smith in Northern Virginia.[13]

Magruder's reports to Richmond convinced Davis that McClellan's strategy was to move on Richmond by way of the Virginia Peninsula with his entire army. He therefore ordered Johnston to start the remainder of his army on the way to the Peninsula, then come to Richmond for orders. There were some exceptions. Ewell's division and a single regiment of cavalry was left to keep watch on the upper Rappahannock, and Jackson was left in the Shenandoah, with the authority to call on Ewell for assistance as necessary. Gustavus W. Smith was ordered to leave a brigade equivalent in the Fredericksburg area, then move toward Richmond with the rest of his command.[14]

McClellan and his staff embarked on April 1. He had Heintzelman in place and in charge of that part of the army already at their destination, but McClellan was anxious to arrive at Fort Monroe, take personal charge and lead it to victory.

As the vessels of the flotilla departed from the crowded docks at Alexandria, a best effort was made to give them a proper send-off. The many military bands on hand played the appropriate martial music, and salutes were fired from the nearby naval yard. Passing Mount Vernon, ships' bells tolled, and the soldiers were given pause to think about that first great American leader, who fought to create the Union they were now asked to preserve. Fort Washington fired salutes in honor of the departing army as it sailed past. Beyond that point, there was little to see of interest, save a few grand homes, as the flotilla made its way down the widening Potomac.[15]

The troops were generally in high spirits. They were glad to finally be out of their cold, wet, crowded, winter quarters. They had been miserable in the rain, mud and snow, continually irritated and unable to get through a day without swearing at each other. Their winter was characterized by diseases such as typhoid fever, pneumonia and diarrhea. The disease rate among the soldiers was reported at around 10%. Surgeons had little to work with in keeping the army healthy. The treatment for diarrhea, for example, consisted of nothing more than administering oak bark tea and opium.[16]

Now the men believed they were off on a campaign that promised them adventure and glory. Soldiers typically do not tolerate inactivity well, and McClellan's men were no exception. The voyage itself was to them an adventure. They were enjoying the bands, the cheering crowds, and the overall patriotic atmosphere of the sailing. At least one barrel of whiskey found its way aboard a transport with the help of the 37th New York (Irish Rifles), and materially improved morale until a fight broke out between regiments from two different states. The disorder was physically settled by Colonel Orlando M. Poe, commander of the 2nd Michigan.[17] Other troops did not enjoy the voyage at all. They complained that the transports were dirty, foul-smelling and overcrowded, and they were forced to drink "miserable whiskey."[18]

A notable exception to the visual boredom of the lower Potomac River was the view of the now unoccupied Confederate works at Aquia Creek, where the guns that were so irksome to Lincoln had been. These once-feared positions were now seen to have been quite meager, though their relatively small number of guns had been effective in stopping up transport on the Potomac for months.[19]

The flotilla spent the entire first day navigating down the Potomac River, and the generally good weather allowed the men to sleep peacefully on deck that night. The chaplains on board made good use of the captive audience, and many vessels conducted worship services, consisting of singing, prayer and sermons of encouragement. The relaxed atmosphere and pleasant weather added to their enjoyment. The next morning saw the lead vessels of the flotilla arriving off Fort Monroe. Some vessels were able to go right in to the docks, but the majority were compelled to anchor off the Fort, awaiting their turn to unload their restless passengers and their cargoes. Some of the men were even treated to a look at the brand-new U. S. Navy ironclad, the U.S.S. *Monitor*, waiting off Fort Monroe for her Confederate counterpart, the C.S.S. *Virginia*, to come out of Hampton Roads and do further battle. To the soldiers on the arriving transports, the *Monitor* seemed a curious-looking vessel for a warship, and some of the men laughed and made jokes about the little ship's unorthodox appearance.

The deployment went on for twenty days, and not all the flotilla's transports arrived at Fort Monroe in good weather conditions. There were cases of vessels arriving at their destination in stormy weather, or enduring stormy conditions after they had arrived and anchored off the fort. Transports were bounced off neighboring vessels, occasionally cables parted, and a vessel or two became temporarily adrift with their horrified passengers still aboard. Seasickness was sometimes in evidence.[20]

The movement of the Army of the Potomac down the Chesapeake Bay was relatively uneventful from a military viewpoint, despite the impressive size of the move. U. S. Navy gunboats patrolled up and down the Bay, looking for any potential Confederate threat. They feared a sudden strike into the unarmed transports packed with troops. It just didn't happen. The Federal gunboats found no opponents to engage.

Assistant Secretary Tucker estimated that, there were 389 vessels in the flotilla. He reported that 121,500 men, 14,592 horses and mules, 1,150 wagons, 44 artillery batteries and 14 ambulances were moved to Fort Monroe. Another authoritative source (Cullen) puts the numbers at over 100,000 men, 25,000 horses and mules, 3,600 wagons, 300 pieces of artillery, and 2,500 head of cattle. Additionally, pontoon bridges, telegraph equipment, and the many other items needed by a large army in the field were moved. The headquarters baggage wagons even included McClellan's portable printing press, carried along for the ostensible purpose of mass printing copies of official orders and McClellan's speeches to the troops. It is interesting to note that, in all the chaos of the several Federal retreats late in the Peninsula campaign, which saw many millions of dollars of Federal equipment and supplies burned or abandoned to the Confederates, McClellan was able to hold on to his printing press.

Amazingly, no human lives were lost in this deployment, even though some of the vessels weren't particularly suited for the purpose or especially seaworthy. The only deaths recorded were eight unlucky mules gone overboard and drowned. This occurred when nine barges under tow were driven ashore in a storm, only a few miles from their destination. Other than the mules, their cargoes were saved.[21]

Tucker was justifiably proud of the results of his efforts in gathering the mighty flotilla. He commented that "for economy and celerity of movement, this expedition is without parallel on record."[22] In truth, Tucker was not boastful. No prior nor subsequent event of the American Civil War compared in sheer size and organization to this deployment.

CHAPTER 6

Fort Monroe

As to be expected in such an endeavor, there was great congestion and chaos as the many vessels of the flotilla attempted to unload their troops, livestock and supplies. The docks in the fort's small harbor were never designed to accommodate a flotilla of 400 vessels, and they could not be made adequate in a short period of time. Troops, livestock and supplies were waiting on ships for days in some cases. A few captains lost patience and made their own landings out of turn.[1]

As the many transports offloaded their payloads onto the docks, the confusion ashore grew by leaps and bounds. Concentrated masses of infantry, artillery trains, and formations of cavalry all combined to create chaos. The noise was overwhelming, made up of shouting men, animal noises, and the cacophony of sounds made by wagons, limbers and caissons. It was a grand scene.[2] The port congestion was not limited to Fort Monroe, but also to Newport News, and it continued throughout the deployment. For example, on March 30 the Vice President came down on a tug, and was unable to land at Newport News. The tug had to divert to Hampton to put the gentleman ashore. That afternoon, a Confederate steamer briefly shelled the port.[3]

As they arrived, the men were marched to an encampment near the ashes of the town of Hampton, a once beautiful village just west of Fort Monroe. Hampton had been burned by the Confederates the previous year to keep it from falling into Federal hands intact. Heintzelman, whose divisions camped there, felt that Magruder had burned Hampton for no good reason.[4]

On March 27, Butterfield's brigade of Porter's division was sent on a reconnaissance to Big Bethel. Butterfield's force consisted of the 12th, 17th and 44th New York, the 83rd Pennsylvania, the 16th Michigan, part of Berdan's Sharpshooters and Griffin's battery. Early in their march, they almost collided with George W. Morell's brigade at a road intersection, the very same intersection where two Federal forces had collided a year earlier. Fortunately, this time the two forces properly identified each other before shots were fired. Morell's brigade was allowed to pass first through the intersection.

Near Big Bethel, Butterfield's men found the Confederate works abandoned. The brigade sent a section of Griffin's battery and three regiments, the 12th New York, 83rd Pennsylvania, and the 16th Michigan, about three miles farther up the road, then returned to Big Bethel. The only Confederates encountered were a party of five mounted pickets at Heath's Corners. The pickets were chased for a distance, but returned to shadow the brigade's rear guard as the Federals withdrew later in the day.[5]

Heintzelman believed there were probably about 200 Confederate cavalry in the vicinity, though none offered battle.[6] This reconnaissance seemed to be in consonance with the orders Heintzelman received from McClellan on March 22, described in Chapter 4. It sought to develop the enemy's presence and works, but did not disabuse the Confederates of the notion that the target of McClellan's army was Norfolk, rather than Richmond.

In less than three weeks, an incredible number of men, animals, wagons and ambulances, artillery batteries, and a tremendous amount of supplies had arrived at Fort Monroe. An observer from the British military called the amazing deployment "the stride of a giant."[7]

Heintzelman arrived there on March 24, about 10:00 A.M. He first took his entire staff and called on General Wool, who took Heintzelman, Hamilton and others for a tour of the U.S.S. *Monitor*. Heintzelman was impressed with the little ship. After surveying the minor damage inflicted on the unusual ironclad by her extended fight with the C.S.S. *Virginia*, Heintzelman stated that, "she appears to be perfectly invulnerable."[8] Heintzelman stayed very busy, seeing to the preparations necessary for his III Corps to commence combat operations, as well as doing everything he could to facilitate the completion of the deployment.

McClellan and his staff arrived at Fort Monroe on the afternoon of April 2, aboard the steamer *Commodore*. Almost immediately, he went aboard the *Minnesota* and met with the local U. S. Navy commander, Commodore Louis Goldsborough, who again explained to McClellan how the Navy planned to neutralize the C.S.S. *Virginia*. Goldsborough was jealous of his rank, and later took exception to the tone of some of the dispatches he receive from McClellan and staff.[9]

There was an in-depth discussion between the two leaders of what part the Navy's gunboats could play in McClellan's planned capture of Gloucester Point and Yorktown. Goldsborough came away from the meeting believing that McClellan was totally satisfied and had expressed such. McClellan outwardly professed to be upbeat about his situation. He telegraphed his wife, "The grass will not grow under my feet."

McClellan, however, subsequently wrote about that point in time in a very different manner. He stated in his report:

> On my arrival at Fort Monroe the James River was declared by the naval authorities closed to the operations of their vessels by the combined influence of the enemy's batteries on its bank and the Confederate steamers Merrimac, Yorktown, Jamestown, and Teaser. Flag-Officer Goldsborough, then in command of the United States squadron in Hampton Roads, regarded it (and no doubt justly) as his highest and most imperative duty to watch and neutralize the Merrimac, and as he designed using his most powerful vessels in a contest with her, he did not feel able to detach to the assistance of the army a suitable force to attack the water batteries at Yorktown and Gloucester. All this was contrary to what had been previously stated to me and materially affected my plans. At no time during the operations against Yorktown was the Navy prepared to lend us any material assistance in its reduction until after our land batteries had partially silenced the works.[10]

Goldsborough's position made McClellan's master plan a lot less viable. He could no longer depend on Goldsborough's gunboats to reduce any of the Confederate batteries on the James River or provide cover for his left flank. Nor could the gunboats be relied upon to reduce the Confederate batteries at Yorktown and Gloucester Point. Goldsborough's level of offered support was a far cry from what Assistant Secretary Fox had promised in Washington. This Navy shortfall in support would make it difficult, almost impossible, to move transports up the James to flank Yorktown. McClellan's master plan would need yet further revision.[11]

The batteries at Yorktown and Gloucester Point were critical to McClellan's plans. They covered the York River at a narrows, where the channel was only 1,000 yards across. Both sets of batteries had to be defeated to safely move troop transports farther up the river.[12]

There is some evidence that McClellan was somewhat aware of the possibility of limited support from the Navy, even before he sailed from Alexandria. After his meeting with Goldsborough, McClellan returned to the *Commodore*, and sent for Heintzelman and several of his other generals who had previously arrived. Understandably, they conferred on board the *Commodore* at length. Some of them stayed up until 2:00 A.M.[13]

The plan agreed upon was for an advance on the morning of April 4, with Heintzelman moving via the Great Bethel (Yorktown) Road with the divisions of Hamilton, Porter and Sedgwick. Porter's division would be in the lead. Keyes would move in parallel on the Lee's Mill road with the divisions of William F. Smith and Darius Couch. Smith's division would lead. McClellan would follow Heintzelman with the reserve. The objective for the first day's advance was Howard's Creek.[14]

McClellan immediately identified and attacked a number of logistical problems. One of his first actions to relieve the port congestion was to telegraph Assistant Secretary Tucker and request ten more tugs and six light draft ferry boats. He also told Tucker he could use many more tugs. McClellan had respect for Tucker's abilities and welcomed his advice.[15] Tucker responded the same day, promising to promptly send the requested vessels if he could obtain them.[16]

Due to the delayed arrival of the horse transports at Alexandria, little cavalry was present at Fort Monroe by the time McClellan arrived. He had available only the 3rd Pennsylvania Cavalry and the 5th U. S Cavalry. The 1st U. S Cavalry was in the harbor, but not yet ashore. Another problem was the lack of wagons. This deficiency prevented Casey's division from moving out for several days after they were ashore.

A particularly vexing problem for McClellan was the poor maps provided him and his staff. This problem would hound the Army of the Potomac throughout the campaign. The maps provided by General Wool's staff were the cause of much distress. McClellan complained that the mapmakers couldn't even fix the course of the rivers in the area. In the case of the Warwick River, the maps had its course so wrong, that it totally changed the tactical importance of the stream. The faulty maps showed the Warwick River coming down from the vicinity of Mulberry Island on the James, rather than originating much farther east, very close to the York River. In its true course, the Warwick provided a natural barrier to an invading army, and made Magruder's defensive situation somewhat less difficult. This was an important item of information for McClellan to know as he planned his advance up the Peninsula.[17]

General Wool had a Colonel Cram of the U. S. Topological Engineers attached to his staff. Cram provided McClellan a map detailing the defenses at Yorktown. McClellan examined it and concluded that Magruder could be rapidly reinforced, and that the fortifications at Yorktown were indeed formidable. McClellan determined that he needed to take Yorktown as soon as possible, before it could be reinforced. Since McClellan knew that McDowell's corps would not be arriving for some days, it would no longer be feasible to flank Yorktown by moving up the opposite bank of the York

River. All factors considered, it was becoming a matter of urgency to move on Yorktown with celerity.[18]

McClellan's other significant problem was the abysmal quality of the intelligence available on the Confederate army in the area. In McClellan's own report, he complained,

> As to the force and position of the enemy, the information then in our possession was vague and untrustworthy. Much of it was obtained from the staff officers of General Wool, and was simply to the effect that Yorktown was surrounded by a continuous line of earthworks, with strong water batteries on the York River, and garrisoned by not less than 15,000 troops, under command of General J. B. Magruder. Maps, which had been prepared by the topographical engineers under General Wool's command, were furnished me, in which the Warwick River was represented as flowing parallel to but not crossing the road from Newport New to Williamsburg, making the so-called Mulberry Island a real island; and we had no information as to the true course of the Warwick across the Peninsula nor of the formidable line of works which it covered.[19]

As early as March 12, Wool had telegraphed a report to Washington, specifically to U. S. Army Headquarters, providing an estimate that Magruder had from 15,000 to 18,000 men, extending from the James River to Yorktown. The numbers were fairly accurate, but the estimate didn't mention the line of works behind which these defenders were deployed. The primary reason for this omission was that the source was a spy sent to enlist in a Confederate regiment. He gathered his information, then deserted, returning to provide it to the Federals. Unfortunately for the Federals, the turncoat private was posted in an advanced position and never saw the line of Confederate works close behind him.[20]

Although many capabilities of McClellan's army improved throughout 1862, "the intelligence service was bad, and was little improved during the time he was in command of the Army of the Potomac." One of several deleterious results of the poor intelligence service was McClellan's consequential lack of knowledge of the terrain in the campaign area. This was not uncommon for Federal generals at this point in the war, but McClellan was a details man, and might have made a greater effort to secure the accurate topological data he needed.[21]

McClellan had estimates that Magruder had 15,000 to 20,000 men in the Peninsula defense, and that Major General Benjamin Huger had another 15,000 at Norfolk. McClellan was concerned that Huger would be able to detach some of them to aid Magruder as the Federals attacked up the Peninsula. These numbers, provided by Allan Pinkerton, would later be seen to be slightly inflated. There were also intelligence reports that there existed at Williamsburg, another line of fortifications.[22]

Heintzelman spent much of April 3 dealing with the preparations for his corps' advance, scheduled for the next day. He complained that the supplies he needed for his troops and their imminent operation were not present. He blamed this lack of supply support on neglect in the Quartermaster's Department. Heintzelman was no fan of the Quartermaster's Department, and believed that several other senior officers had spoken to McClellan about the lack of efficiency of General Van Vliet. Jokingly, Heintzelman related that the consensus recommendation for Van Vliet was decapitation, but that there was a shortage of axes and grinding wheels.[23]

Around 1:30 P.M. on April 3, McClellan found time to write a letter to his wife, Ellen. In it, he reported that he'd been incredibly busy since his arrival, meeting with Goldsborough and Generals Heintzelman, Smith, Porter and Wool. He then related in detail his plan to move the following day toward Yorktown. McClellan also complained about the lack of wagons, the crowded harbor at Fort Monroe, and the poor performance of Van Vliet. He closed by expressing hope that he could take Yorktown in a couple of days and make the York River his line of communications. He restated his belief that the campaign would turn on a great battle near Richmond.[24]

McClellan then sent a note to Goldsborough in which he detailed his plans for the immediate future. He began by informing Goldsborough that the army now had sufficient wagons to move most of his army and was beginning his forward movement.

He proposed to be in the rear of the Ship's Point Battery by 2:00 P.M. the following day and take it no later than 3:30 P.M. On April 5, McClellan intended to invest Yorktown, putting a sufficient blocking force above it to prevent escape of the defenders. Due to a lack of transports, McClellan had abandoned the idea of putting troops on the far bank of the York.

McClellan then requested a brace of gunboats, more if available, to be near Ship's Point on the 4th, hoping their assistance would help make short work of the enemy positions. Ideally, McClellan wanted to get his blocking force above Yorktown before the gunboats commenced fire.

McClellan proposed communicating with Goldsborough at Howard's Bridge at noon on April 4. Alternatively, he expected to be able to have telegraphic communications with his headquarters by evening. He promised to make a personal visit to Goldsborough on the evening of the 3rd, if possible. In any case McClellan asked Goldsborough to answer as to whether or not the gunboats would be forthcoming.[25]

McClellan discovered during the night of April 3 that General Wool, Fort Monroe and its 10,000 man garrison had been removed from his command. He complained that this left him with no base of operations under his control. The order also forbade McClellan from detaching any of the garrison troops without Wool's concurrence. On the morning of April 4, McClellan ordered that portion of his force that had already disembarked and was properly equipped to move out. This amounted to about 58,000 men and 100 guns. Left behind was Casey's division, which had not received their wagon train as yet.[26]

McClellan sent one more telegram that day. It was to Secretary Stanton, and simply informed Stanton that the army would advance on Yorktown the following morning and expected to find resistance from 15,000 entrenched Confederates. McClellan also mentioned that there had been no sighting of the *Virginia* as yet, but that Goldsborough was confident of being able to sink the Confederate ironclad when she ventured out.[27]

McClellan, in the short span of four days, had suffered a string of serious setbacks to his Peninsula campaign. First, Blenker's division had been taken away by Lincoln. Second, the Navy, through Goldsborough, then revealed its gunboats would not be able to support McClellan's advance up the Peninsula. Finally, Wool's 10,000 man garrison was removed by Lincoln from McClellan's command. McClellan had planned to attach Wool's division to McDowell's I Corps. This last loss occurred, despite Lincoln's promise on March 31 that Blenker's men would be the last troops McClellan would lose.

Still, McClellan put a good face on the situation, sending an ingratiating note back to Lincoln. McClellan then attempted to adapt to the new situation and move forward. In his report, he wrote concerning Yorktown, "I had therefore no choice left but to attack it directly in front, as I best could with the force at my command."[28] There would soon be still more bad news in General McClellan's immediate future.

On April 4, Goldsborough ordered the *Penobscot, Marblehead, Corwin, Octorara, Victoria, Currituck* and *Wachusett* to assist the army by undertaking, among other tasks, the reduction of Yorktown and Gloucester Point. He informed Commander Missroon aboard the flagship *Minnesota* of the order.[29]

At 8:30 P.M. on April 4, McClellan sent a telegram to Goldsborough from Big Bethel. The general relayed to Goldsborough that he believed the

Confederates were being reinforced from both Richmond and Norfolk. McClellan anticipated a fight the following day, and asked for gunboats off Young's Mills in the morning.[30]

There was one bright spot to which McClellan could look forward. Stanton had held out a carrot to the beleaguered general. McDowell's large I Corps would join the rest of McClellan's army as it neared Richmond, in time for the culmination of the campaign. His strategy would now be one of steady, careful advance to the vicinity of Richmond. He would be reinforced there by McDowell, then fight the expected major battle for the Confederate capital.[31]

PART III

PRELIMINARIES

"No one but McClellan could have hesitated to attack."
General Joseph E. Johnston[1]

CHAPTER 7

Yorktown

(April 5–May 3)

On April 4, McClellan ordered most of the forces already ashore to move out from the Fort Monroe area and advance up the Peninsula. His objective was to capture Yorktown, where he knew a Confederate force of infantry and artillery awaited him in prepared positions. He also knew that the Confederate ironclad *Virginia* covered the mouth of the James River, and that Confederate shore batteries prevented the U. S. Navy from operating very far up the York. He hoped to take Yorktown quickly by maneuver, but was willing to patiently lay siege to the town if necessary.[1]

The combat elements of McClellan's force consisted of: III Corps under Heintzelman; IV Corps under Keyes; Sykes' Regular infantry brigade; some cavalry under George Stoneman and William Averell; as well as Hunt's reserve artillery of about 100 guns. They were followed by a large headquarters element.[2]

The initial forces of McClellan's advance on Yorktown moved up the peninsula along two axes. Only two roads were available, and neither was in very good shape, owing to the spring rains. The roads were extremely muddy and the advance was slower than McClellan desired or planned for. The movement was also hampered by hostile local inhabitants and very poor maps. Incredibly, McClellan failed to do adequate reconnaissance in his front. This point in time might have been McClellan's best chance of defeating his Confederate adversaries, but he failed to take advantage of the opportunity.[3]

III Corps under Heintzelman was on the right, moving up the Yorktown road. Heintzelman had with him the divisions of Porter and Hamilton, as well as the II Corps division of Sedgwick. Sedgwick was to move with the reserve at first and take orders directly from McClellan. Heintzelman also had the services of Averell's 3rd Pennsylvania Cavalry.

On the left was Keyes' IV Corps, advancing up the Lee's Mill road. Keyes commanded the divisions of William F. "Baldy" Smith and Darius N. Couch, and the attached 5th U. S Cavalry. Casey's division, although of IV Corps, had arrived at Fort Monroe and come ashore, but was left in camp at Newport News awaiting its transportation.[4] McClellan followed behind with the reserve, comprised of Sedgwick's division, Sykes' brigade of Regular infantry, the army's reserve artillery, and a large headquarters guard.[5] Sumner's III corps would move up later, and Franklin's division would be held near the York River to provide a flanking capability by water.

About noon on April 5, Keyes' force made contact with the first Confederate skirmishers. Some Confederate artillery fire was also received by the lead elements of the column. The fire came from three guns across the Warwick River near Lee's Mill, and continued more or less all afternoon. Keyes complained about the roads. He stated that they would not permit his artillery to advance with his infantry. He was also waiting for his reserve ammunition wagon to come up. Instead of a reconnaissance in force to develop the enemy's position and strength, McClellan, in his typical non-aggressive style of battlefield command, timidly probed the Confederate works. Even though he'd made contact with little more than a skirmish line and less than a battery of artillery, McClellan decided he was up against a strong Confederate force, and sent back to Fort Monroe for his siege train.[6]

At this critical moment in McClellan's day, he was handed a telegram that dramatically changed the military balance of power on the Peninsula. Sent by Lorenzo Thomas and addressed to McClellan, it read: "By direction of the President General McDowell's army corps has been detached from the force under your immediate command, and the general is ordered to report to the Secretary of War. Letter by mail."

This order had the effect of denying McClellan the use of McDowell's I Corps, the largest in the army. This deduction of 37,000 troops, on top of the 10,000 of Blenker's division already lost to Fremont, had reduced his army by about a third.[7]

McClellan and his staff were stunned. In a conversation with McClellan just a few hours after taking Blenker's division for service with Fremont, Lincoln had promised McClellan that there would be no further deductions from his army. This message, coming at the same time as meeting Confederate resistance, seeing the natural and man-made impediments to assaulting the Confederate positions, and being rained on all day, helped push McClellan toward the conclusion that a siege was the right course of action.[8]

McClellan actually seemed to believe at one point in time that Lincoln's withdrawal of McDowell's I Corps was part of a conspiracy by McClellan's enemies in Washington, designed to assure his failure by making his army too small to carry out the approved campaign plan.[9] An hour past midnight on April 6, McClellan wrote his wife regarding Lincoln's decision, stating that "it is the most infamous thing that history has recorded." He closed by promising to tell the next day "exactly what I intend doing."[10]

McClellan had another significant problem, over and above the loss of the 50,000 troops taken by President Lincoln. That problem was the lack of cooperation by the United States Navy. Before McClellan departed Washington, he had formed the opinion that the Navy would cooperate with his campaign on the Peninsula. At the outset, McClellan was assuming a combined land and naval attack upon Yorktown, the first tactical objective of the campaign. McClellan wrote to Secretary of War Stanton on March 19 that:

> To accomplish this, the navy should at once concentrate upon the York River all their available and most powerful batteries; its reduction should not in that case require many hours. A strong corps would be pushed up the York, under cover of the Navy, directly upon West Point, immediately upon the fall of Yorktown, and we could at once establish our new base of operations at a distance of some twenty-five miles from Richmond; with every facility for developing and bringing into play the whole of our available force on either or both banks of the James. It is impossible to urge too strongly the absolute necessity of the *full cooperation of the navy* as a part of this programme.

McClellan was fixated on this point. The same evening he telegraphed Stanton again, asking for an immediate answer on the subject of Navy cooperation. Stanton came back with a request by Lincoln for McClellan to meet with the President at Alexandria immediately. There is no record of the proposed Alexandria meeting. It may or may not have taken place, but McDowell, from Washington, wrote McClellan that the plan had been favorably received. He also told McClellan that it was questionable whether the Navy would be able to cooperate adequately. He recommended that McClellan continue moving troops south in order to keep the flotilla occupied.

As late as the March 17, Assistant Secretary Fox had told McDowell that the Navy would fully cooperate. McDowell asked Commodore

Goldsborough and Colonel Woodbury of the engineers to confer on the ongoing plan.[11]

It appears that the appropriate guidance never made it down through Navy channels from the Secretary and Assistant Secretary to the operational commanders who would have to support McClellan. It also appears that McClellan wanted more support than the Navy could provide.

That same day, Navy Secretary Welles did order the commandants of the navy yards at Boston and New York to send what gunboats they could to Hampton Roads. Barnard also went to see Goldsborough at Hampton Roads, but there is no clear record of their meeting.

We cannot accuse McClellan of failing to devote sufficient effort to securing naval cooperation. He appears to have done all he could. The question of what happened on the Navy side is very murky. The most likely explanation of the matter is that McClellan expected too much and the Navy provided too little.

Specifically, the Navy would not reduce the Confederate fortifications at Yorktown by naval gunfire, nor run past them. The Navy explained that the batteries at Yorktown were situated on a bluff, and up too high for the Federal gunboats to take them under fire.

McClellan should have been fully aware of the role the Navy was willing to play as early as April 2. Upon his arrival at Fort Monroe on the afternoon of April 1, the first person he went to see was Flag Officer Louis M. Goldsborough. Goldsborough made McClellan aware that the James River was closed to Federal naval operations due to the threat of Confederate shore batteries and the Confederate steamers *Virginia, Yorktown, Jamestown* and *Teaser*.[12]

Goldsborough went on to explain to McClellan that containing the *Virginia* was his primary mission, and he needed all his more capable vessels to do so. He just would not be able to detach sufficient force to reduce Yorktown. McClellan later complained that Goldsborough's position was in direct opposition to that which he had been previously told.[13]

This lack of naval cooperation, as perceived by McClellan, coupled with the loss of McDowell's I Corps, forced McClellan to resort to a conventional siege of the Yorktown line. He felt he had no other attractive option at that point in time.

The Confederate force manning the defensive line extending from Yorktown across the Peninsula consisted at this time of no more than 11,000–13,000 men. It was commanded by Major General John Bankhead "Prince John" Magruder.[14]

Seven Days Before Richmond

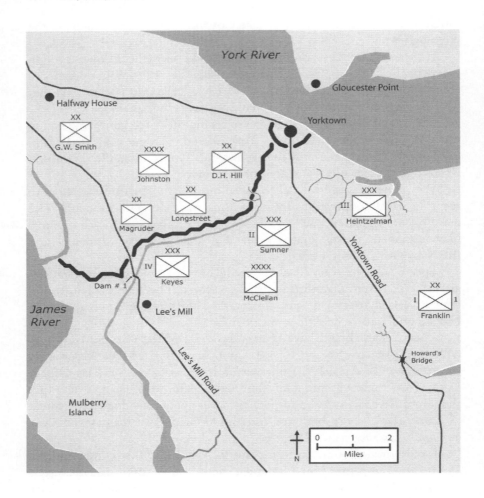

Map 7.1—Siege of Yorktown, April 5–May 3

Magruder's situation was tenuous. He didn't have nearly enough troops to properly man a line some twelve miles long. Although anchored on his left by substantial fortifications at Yorktown, the remainder of the line depended on meager works and some beneficial topological features. Continual efforts were made to improve the defenses.

Magruder had no illusions about being able to defend his line for very long against the approaching Federal divisions. His mission was simple. He was to hold on until he could be reinforced. Since he couldn't defeat the approaching threat, he devised a deception plan to deter them from a serious attack on his thinly manned lines. It consisted of moving the same troops around behind his lines, but in sight of the Federal pickets and observation balloon. With shouted orders and bugle calls, he simulated the noise and commotion of a much larger force in the process of tweaking its defensive posture. The ruse apparently worked, but Magruder worried about the Federal observation balloon discovering his deception. Magruder used his artillery to motivate Lowe to keep his balloon a safe distance behind Federal lines. This made it less likely that Magruder's deception plan would be discovered.[15]

McClellan, deluded by Pinkerton's inflated reports, believed the Confederates had 180,000–200,000 troops that could be brought to bear on his army. He soon decided on a siege and sent for his siege train of heavy field pieces and mortars. Thus began a great and protracted labor to move the heavy guns and their support equipment into position.

McClellan cannot be accused of not having a plan for taking Yorktown. He had a concrete strategy for doing so, and it was based, in part, on a detailed report made by Brigadier General Barnard, McClellan's Chief Engineer. Barnard's report discussed the topology of the area, the natural barriers to an attacking force, the fortifications he could observe, the effect on the local roads from the recent rains, and many other things. Barnard seemed to agree with McClellan that the defenses were too hard to successfully take by frontal assault, and that a siege was the more appropriate strategy. In his report, he stated,

> If we could have broken the enemy's line across the isthmus, we could have invested Yorktown, and it must, with its garrison, have soon fallen into our hands.
> It was not deemed practicable, considering the strength of that line, and the handling our forces (owing to the impracticable character of the country), to do so.
> If we could take Yorktown, or drive the enemy out of that place, the enemy's line was no longer tenable. This we could do by siege operations. It was deemed too hazardous to attempt the reduction of the place by assault.

McClellan did share excepts from Barnard's report with Washington. On April 5, McClellan sent a telegram to Lincoln that described the Confederates as being in "large force" and "intend to make a determined resistance." He then related the reconnaissance conducted by John Barnard, describing the Confederate works as extending across the Peninsula from Yorktown to the mouth of the Warwick River. The works are described as formidable. Lastly, McClellan related that deserters have reported the

Confederate defenders as being reinforced daily from Richmond and Norfolk.

From that point on in the telegram, McClellan reverted to complaining about his perceived shortage of troops and begging Lincoln to reconsider the detachment of McDowell's I Corps from the campaign. As a fallback position, he asked Lincoln to at least give him General Franklin's division.

The strategy that McClellan adopted for his siege was to build a parallel as near as feasible to the Confederate works and populate it with guns and supporting infantry, from the York to the James rivers. Roads and bridges were constructed as necessary to move up guns and provide for adequate resupply of the army. The guns would suppress the enemy's guns and allow trenches to be dug even closer. This action would culminate in an assault on Yorktown and the resultant collapse of the enemy's line.[16]

Unbeknownst to Magruder, he would only have to hold on with his meager force for a few more days. Events in Richmond would save him. The Confederate army at Yorktown would be reinforced within a few days by Joseph E. Johnston's command. Subsequent to April 12, Huger and his command from Norfolk joined the forces at Yorktown. General Johnston assumed overall command of the combined army. Even more reinforcements were sought by Richmond.[17]

Johnston was called to Richmond, and met with Jefferson Davis on the morning of April 14. Johnston told the President that Yorktown couldn't be held, and that it was too risky to try to do so. He wanted to retreat immediately to the outskirts of Richmond and concentrate all available forces there. He urged calling troops from Norfolk, the Carolinas and Georgia, adding them to those of Johnston's army and Magruder's, and meeting McClellan's army just outside of Richmond. He even considered that an offensive opportunity might then arise if Confederate forces were well concentrated.[18]

Davis decided to call a council of war. It convened at 10:00 A.M on April 14, and met almost continuously until after midnight. Attendees were President Davis, Robert E. Lee, Joseph E. Johnston, James Longstreet, Gustavus W. Smith and Secretary of War George W. Randolph. All of the attendees had prior personal knowledge of George McClellan.

Lee preferred a strategy of having Johnston make the longest possible delay for the Federals along the Yorktown line. Most likely, Lee's recommendation was based on his knowledge of McClellan's cautious nature, and the relative strength of the forces on the Peninsula.

Johnston reiterated what he had told Davis in his prior one-on-one meeting. Only a concentration of all available Confederate forces closer to Richmond would minimize the risk of disaster. Johnston then posed an off-the-wall alternative. They could leave Magruder to delay McClellan, while marching all other forces north to threaten Washington. The object of the plan would be to force McClellan to rush back to the defense of his own capital. Longstreet thought McClellan wouldn't attack the Yorktown defenses until the first of May. Smith supported Johnston's plan, and urged the more ambitious strategy of invading the North.

Randolph and Lee combined to oppose the others. They pointed out that losing Yorktown would also mean losing Norfolk, the naval yard there, and the ironclads under construction. It would also mean losing the base for the C.S.S. *Virginia*. Lee also made the powerful argument that every day they held Yorktown was a day that could be devoted to building an army that could wage a protracted struggle. Their present volunteer army of one-year volunteers assured defeat. A conscription bill was working its way through the Confederate Congress, and it needed time to be born. That bill was passed by Congress on April 16. Lee also made note that taking defensive troops out of North Carolina, South Carolina and Georgia could result in the loss of the important ports of Savannah and Charleston.[19]

After the marathon debate, Lee's strategy was adopted, and Davis ordered Johnston to make the delaying action at Yorktown. Johnston made no protest of Davis' decision, as knew that Yorktown could only be held for a relatively short time, and then he could withdraw the army to positions more to his liking.[20]

On April 15, Johnston went to Yorktown, taking Smith's and Longstreet's divisions with him. There were now 55,633 Confederate troops defending Yorktown.[21]

McClellan conducted his siege of Yorktown from April 5 through May 3. Both sides were reinforced throughout the siege, with the total number of troops involved approaching 170,000 by the end. The final numbers gave the Federals almost a two-to-one advantage in troops and a huge advantage in artillery. Using slave labor from nearby plantations, the Confederates improved their works. They enjoyed an advantage, in that they made use of some of Cornwallis' works dating from 1781 during the Revolutionary War. The Federals were starting from scratch, and had no slave labor. McClellan made their task even more difficult, when he decided to build emplacements into the works for 111 very large siege guns. The task faced by the Federals of improving roads up to the front was formidable. On their left wing, roads had to be corduroyed, bridges built and heavy siege guns slowly moved forward.[22]

It was miserable duty for the men of both armies, especially for the Confederates in their earthworks. They were wet and muddy for a month. The weather was often rainy, and the trenches drained poorly. Besides coping with the mud and the rain, there was a paucity of vegetables and meat, other than salted beef. Some of the soldiers of both armies had the dangerous assignment of picket duty, which was described as "exceedingly vicious wherever pickets or lines could see each other." Occasionally, firefights between pickets escalated as artillerists pitched in. As the Federals crept closer and closer to the Confederate works, picket duty became more dangerous and more miserable for men of both sides. The Federals tried to combat the misery and spread the danger around by scheduling individual companies for duty tours of 24 hours on and 48 hours off.[23]

The soldiers faced a constant dilemma. Down in the bottoms of their trenches, they were fairly safe from the Federal sharpshooters, but were partially immersed in the water pooled there. Getting up out of the water exposed them to accurate sharpshooting. Initially, the Federals enjoyed the advantage of having Hiram Berdan's 1st U. S Sharpshooters in their lines. Berdan's Sharpshooters were an elite regiment of Federal infantry. Their weapons were Sharps breechloaders fitted with telescopic sights and were designed to put every round into a 10 inch circle at 200 yards. Volunteers were made to demonstrate their skill as marksmen before being accepted by Berdan. The men wore distinctive dark green uniform coats, earning them the nickname of "green breeches." This unit's mission was to kill Confederate pickets and any other soldiers who got careless and exposed themselves.

With the arrival of John Bell Hood's Texas brigade, many soldiers of which were equipped with Enfield rifles, the sharpshooting capabilities of the two armies were more equal. Hood's sharpshooters weren't on the line continually, but were slipped into the line unannounced when there were reports of Berdan's men getting too bold. Hood's job was to drive the Federal sharpshooters out of their tree perches or similar hiding positions and make that section of the line a little safer.[24]

Although the majority of the month-long siege was little more than protracted misery and boredom for the Confederates and back-breaking work for the Federals, a few notable engagements did occur. The most violent and significant of these contacts was the fight at Dam No. 1, which occurred mid-way through the siege.

On April 16, McClellan made his first aggressive move since the siege began. He was told that at a place on the Warwick River called Dam No. 1, the Confederates were beefing up their defenses. This piece of intelligence was uncovered by subordinates of Baldy Smith, who added that he thought this was the weakest point in the Confederate line. McClellan ordered Baldy Smith to prevent the Confederates from making their improvements. This was not the first attention paid to Dam No. 1. It was the "weak spot" that Brigadier General Winfield S. Hancock had suggested be taken ten days prior. McClellan had not chosen this location for his artillery to destroy, but ordered Smith to attack, with the proviso that he was not to bring on a general engagement. McClellan told Baldy Smith to "confine the operation to forcing the enemy to discontinue work." Smith began by moving forward his division artillery and his 1st brigade, as close to the dam as he could. The brigade, composed of the 2nd, 3rd, 4th, 5th and 6th Vermont regiments, was there to support the batteries. The artillery banged away all day, as did the skirmishers, targeting the Confederates across the millpond.

The Confederate officers told their men to take cover, and soon there were no visible targets for the Federal artillerists. A brave, perhaps foolish, Federal officer, Lieutenant E. M. Noyes, an aide to General Brooks, waded across the millpond, approaching within fifty yards of the Confederate pickets. McClellan rode up while Noyes was performing his risky reconnaissance. Noyes reported directly to the commanding general that the pond was only waist-deep. He had been undiscovered by the Confederates, and suggested the position could be carried.

A reconnaissance in force was then conducted by four companies of the 3rd Vermont under Captain Harrington. The waist-deep water forced the infantrymen to cross in the vulnerable position of muskets and cartridge boxes above their heads. Four companies coming across the pond was all the force needed to scatter the Confederate pickets. The pickets were from the 15th North Carolina, commanded by Colonel Robert M. McKinney. As McKinney gathered up the rest of his regiment to counterattack, he was killed and the counterattack failed. The wet Federals hastened into the Confederate rifle pits, where they began to fire into the woods. Now a decision had to be made as to the appropriate next step.[25]

Baldy Smith was in the middle of experiencing a personal problem. He had just been thrown from his feisty mount for a second time. His head was not yet clear, and he failed to see the opportunity the crossing presented. McClellan rode up to observe, but left without offering assistance or advice. The Federal senior leadership failed to issue any orders of support for the vulnerable Vermonters in the rifle pits, and the inevitable happened. After forty minutes, the Confederates counterattacked with a brigade of Georgians and Louisianians under Howell Cobb. Captain Harrington and his Vermonters recrossed the millpond in a hurry. Eighty-three of the original 192 Federal infantrymen were casualties. The 15th

North Carolina lost 12 killed and 31 wounded. Total casualties on the Federal side were 165, and the Confederates suffered 43. The affair was over by 4:00 P.M.[26]

Now the Federal generals believed that it was possible to effect a lodgment on the far side of the millpond, and made a second attempt late in the day. The second effort was made by four companies of the 6th Vermont under Colonel Nathan Lord, Jr. The crossing was attempted at the same point as Harrington's earlier foray. Simultaneously, four companies of the 4th Vermont under Colonel Edwin H. Stoughton, would attempt to cross atop the dam, under the covering fire of the division's 20 artillery pieces. The Confederates were now fully alert to the threat of crossings of the millpond, and Lord's force was stopped short of the rifle pits. Stoughton reached the dam, but Baldy Smith recalled him, and Lord followed suit. The Vermont brigade would make no further attempts to take and hold ground on the Confederate side of the millpond.[27]

On May 1, McClellan increased the lethality of the bombardment by introducing his 100 pounder rifles to the bombardment. His siege batteries had a complement of 71 heavy guns, including two 200-pounders and five 100-pounders. Several 13 inch mortars were also being set up. His goal planned to have all his siege guns and heavy mortars operational by May 6.[28]

Johnston had no intention of keeping his army in place and enduring a protracted siege. Just after sundown on the Saturday evening of April 3, Johnston had his artillerists commence a great bombardment, all along his lines. After a lengthy display of red fuses flying across the night sky and tremendous sounds of exploding shells, all was quiet by midnight. At daybreak, Heintzelman and self-proclaimed Professor Thaddeus Sobieski Lowe went aloft in the balloon *Intrepid*. Lincoln had appointed Lowe as Chief of Aeronautics and paid him as a colonel. All Heintzelman and Lowe could observe to the north were the abandoned tents of the Confederate army. All the men, animals and artillery, other than those guns spiked and abandoned, had melted away in the night. Heintzelman and Lowe shouted the news down to their colleagues. Just as at Manassas eight weeks before, Johnston had stealthily withdrawn his army under cover of darkness.[29]

However, the Confederate retrograde was not exactly an example of military perfection. There were at least a couple of security leaks, but it appears that Washington did not take them seriously. Johnston, as at Manassas, had to sacrifice arms and materiel to save men. At Yorktown and Gloucester Point, the Confederates left behind 77 artillery pieces. They were mostly old, smooth-bore ship's guns and were simply too heavy to be hauled away in a hurry. These guns had been taken from the Federal navy yard at Norfolk early in the war, and their military usefulness was limited.[30]

Several months prior, Magruder had selected a defensive line of battle near Williamsburg. It was 4–5 miles long, and some slight entrenchments had been built. The centerpiece of the position was Fort Magruder, a fully completed enclosed fort.[31]

As the Confederates cleverly retired just before Federals launched their long-planned attack, all of McClellan's siege effort was essentially wasted. His excessive caution denied him a golden opportunity for a breakthrough. This same excess of caution would be his undoing as the campaign went on. The Northern press had mixed opinions of the significance of events at Yorktown. While some papers, such as the *New York Tribune*, proclaimed a brilliant victory, others, as the *New York Evening Post*, felt that McClellan had once again let the wily Joseph Johnston and the enemy army escape unscathed.[32]

The frustrated McClellan was determined to aggressively pursue the withdrawing Confederates. Federal cavalry under Stoneman, accompanied by four batteries of horse artillery, were the first to give chase along the Yorktown and Williamsburg roads. Heintzelman was ordered to send Hooker's division after Stoneman in support. Baldy Smith was ordered to take his division up the Lee's Mill and Williamsburg road, also to support Stoneman. Shortly thereafter, Philip Kearny's division was sent up the Yorktown road.

The divisions of Couch and Casey were sent up the Lee's Mill road. Sumner was then ordered forward to assume overall command of the pursuit until McClellan arrived.[33]

CHAPTER 8

Williamsburg

(May 5)

The rear of the retreating Confederate column reached Fort Magruder on the afternoon of May 4. McClellan's cavalry was close on their heels. The Federal horsemen had caught up with Jeb Stuart's cavalry, the Confederate rear guard, about eight miles south of the fort.

The man tasked to support the cavalry was Paul Jones Semmes. Semmes' fatigued brigade was ordered to double-time back to meet the Federal horsemen. Sharp skirmishing occurred before sundown. McLaws, the division commander, then sent Joseph Kershaw's brigade and two batteries back to reinforce Semmes. One Federal gun was captured when it became stuck in the mud. After nightfall, Longstreet directed Richard Anderson's and Pryor's brigades to relieve Kershaw and Semmes.[1]

As early as 2:00 A.M. on the morning of May 5, Johnston continued his retreat. Even before he began his withdrawal from Yorktown, he anticipated McClellan's attempt to cut off the Confederate retreat with a flanking movement by the York River. Johnston ordered his leading divisions on the road very early, hoping to get them in position to confront what he expected to be a landing around West Point.[2]

Longstreet's large division, comprised of the brigades of A. P. Hill, Richard H. Anderson, George E. Pickett, Cadmus M. Wilcox, Raleigh E. Colston and Roger A. Pryor, was left in its entirety as the rear guard. Pryor and Anderson made the initial contact with the advancing Federals just after dawn on the 5th.

Hooker's and Smith's divisions reached the area of the Confederate defenses just after dark on the 4th. By about 5:30 A.M. the next morning, the first infantry of Hooker's division moved into position in front of Pryor and Anderson. Hooker himself rode along the lines and evaluated the defenses. He noted the thick woods masking the defenses and a deep abatis of felled trees along the road.[3] Hooker's problem was that his infantry would have to traverse the woods, the abatis, a ravine in front of the works, and 600–700 yards of ground without cover just to get at the Confederates. He decided to attack immediately, as the Confederates would likely be putting more defenders in place. He did not consult the corps commanders. By around 6:00 A.M., his skirmishers had crossed through the woods and the abatis, and had driven in Anderson's pickets.

Anderson reacted to the situation of his pickets by adding several more companies forward. Finding this action ineffective, Anderson ordered all his pickets to pull back into his redoubts. This allowed the Federal infantry to form a line of battle astride the road.[4]

By 7:00 A.M., Hooker's artillery had begun to arrive. There were four six-gun batteries under Major Charles S. Wainwright. Wainwright's men had labored hard to advance up the Hampton Road, the road that Baldy Smith thought was unusable for artillery. It was still raining hard, and the first battery to arrive, Battery H, 1st U. S. Artillery under Captain Charles H. Webber, began to unlimber and set up in a clearing. The site was picked by Wainwright and Hooker, and was only about 700 yards from Fort Magruder. Anderson's guns in Fort Magruder and the nearby redoubts took Webber's men and horses under fire immediately. The savage fire caused instant casualties, and the gun crews fled without returning fire. Wainwright and Webber were unable to prevent the rout. Enough men were rallied to man only two guns.

Very soon, Captain Thomas W. Osborn's Battery D, 1st New York Artillery arrived and Wainwright had them man four of Webber's unmanned guns, rather than unlimber and set up their own. They were able to establish a return fire on the Confederates by about 8:00 A.M. Eventually, Captain Walter M. Bramhall's battery, the 6th New York Independent Artillery, arrived and pitched in, and two of Osborn's guns were manned. All of the guns were placed close on the right of Webber's guns. All of this Federal artillery was focused on a mere half dozen Confederate guns in Fort Magruder and a nearby redoubt.[5]

Despite the problems associated with directing artillery in a driving rain, the Federal artillerists were doing some real damage. In Fort Magruder, they were feeling the effects not only of Wainwright's artillery, but of the sharpshooters leading Hooker's infantry. Many Confederate artillerists were killed, but infantrymen replaced them and kept up the fire from the fort.

On a side note, Stuart's cavalry attempted a reconnaissance by the 4th Virginia Cavalry down the Hampton road early in the morning. They quickly withdrew after taking fire from the cover along the road. Stuart then placed them in the rear of Fort Magruder for most of the day, using them for couriers, escorts and similar tasks. Stuart himself stayed busy directing artillery and assisting Richard Anderson in managing the battle.[6]

Seven Days Before Richmond

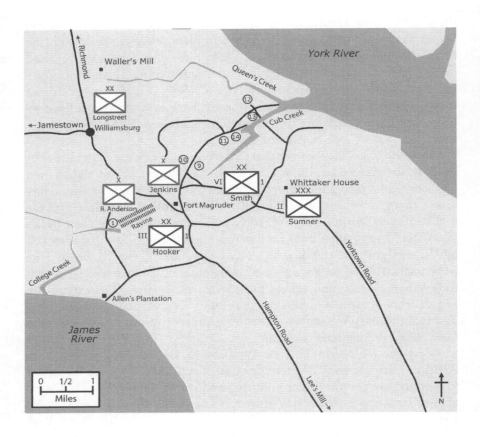

Map 8.1—Williamsburg, 10:00 A.M., May 5

It was still relatively early in the morning when Hooker was ready to attack with two brigades. Hooker put Patterson's 3rd brigade in the woods left of the Hampton road. Grover's 1st brigade was to the right of the same road.

Each brigade fielded about 2,600 men. Hooker planed to move forward through the woods and the abatis to the edge of the open field. Using the cover of the felled trees making up the abatis, the two brigades would use musketry to force the Confederates from the rifle pits that dotted the open area, them move into them. Artillery fire would continue throughout, pounding Fort Magruder and the adjacent redoubts. Approximately 7:00 A.M., Hooker's infantry moved forward with the artillery duel in progress.[7]

On the Confederate side, Longstreet and Anderson were making plans to counter Hooker's attack. Anderson wanted to flank Hooker on the right. To do that, he planned to extend his lines, and counterattack from behind Redoubts 1–4. Longstreet was at his headquarters at the College of William and Mary, and started to release the remainder of his brigades to Anderson. Even before Hooker's infantry attack began, Wilcox's brigade, retreating through Williamsburg, was ordered to countermarch back to Anderson's lines. By 9:00 A.M., they were engaged.

Anderson asked Pryor to move part of his brigade to his right to better support Wilcox. This Pryor did, shifting the 8th and 14th Alabama, as well as part of the 14th Louisiana.[8]

Anderson had been running his part of the battle from Fort Magruder. He now decided to get out with the brigades on his right and personally oversee their attempt to flank Hooker. Before he did so, he sent a courier to Longstreet, asking for the brigades of A. P. Hill and George Pickett as support for his counterattack. Anderson, before he left the Fort, placed Colonel Micah Jenkins in local command of Anderson's brigade and the rest of Pryor's brigade.[9]

Hooker had decided on an almost immediate attack on the Confederates in the vicinity of Fort Magruder, because he felt that to wait was to allow more defenders to show up.

Unfortunately for Hooker, this meant the only intelligence he had of the Confederate defenses in his front was what he personally gathered earlier in the morning. He did know a few other things that were relevant. He was sure that Baldy Smith's division was somewhere on his right, on the Yorktown road. There were flooded woods over there, and Hooker had to wonder if there were Confederate troops in them. He also wanted to know how far the Confederate right extended relative to the Federal left.

To get the answers he needed, Hooker sent the 11th Massachusetts and 26th Pennsylvania to his far right flank, with orders to determine whether it was possible to reach the Yorktown Road. Shortly thereafter, Emory's cavalry brigade arrived, and Hooker ordered them to his extreme left to observe the Confederates there. Emory's brigade consisted of the 3rd Pennsylvania Cavalry and the 8th Illinois Cavalry.

Earlier that morning, Hooker had received the services of Lieutenant Miles McAlester, a topographical engineer. Hooker had told the young officer that he wanted to know the extent of the Confederate lines on his far left, as well as the best route for moving his troops up to meet them. Major Wainwright, Hooker's chief of artillery, had already asked Hooker about how to get his guns to the head of the ravine. The artillerist wanted to put some guns there to prevent the enemy from using it to their advantage. McAlester, given a daunting and important task, set off to find answers for his general.[10]

When the fight began, both opponents were in lines less than a mile long, with about 5,000 troops each committed by Hooker and Anderson. With each side controlling a part of the battlefield, the fight was carried back and forth through the felled trees. Artillery from both opponents played an effective role. Little ground changed hands. The infantry fight was hampered by the rough ground and man-made obstructions. Regiments could not maintain lines of battle, so effective attacks were all but prevented. These small-unit firefights produced a high number of casualties, including the death of Colonel Christopher H. Mott, commander of the 19th Mississippi.[11]

Wainwright was not able to move his guns to the edge of the ravine. Then McAlester returned and confirmed that too many trees were in the way of Wainwright's proposed move. McAlester recommended to Hooker that troops could best be moved by way of the Hampton road or alongside it. McAlester also reported the Federal line extending beyond Redoubt # 2, but felt a flanking maneuver could succeed there.[12] Hooker also heard from Colonel Blaisdell, commander of the 11th Massachusetts, that the way to the Yorktown road was clear of Confederates. His regiment had reached the road and Blaisdell had encountered General Hancock there.

Thinking Heintzelman was at Sumner's headquarters, Hooker sent a note suggesting that the two wings of the army be linked into an unbroken front. In the note, Hooker told Heintzelman that Hooker's way to the Yorktown road was clear, and that putting the army together would allow them to "whip the enemy." Heintzelman was not at Sumner's, but the senior officer there read it and returned it to Hooker marked "opened and read."[13]

By 11:00 A.M., Hooker was no longer so optimistic. Fresh Confederate troops appeared on his left flank, the musket fire from the rifle pits was intense, and the artillery fire from Fort Magruder and the nearby redoubts continued to take a toll. He was about to commit his last reserve brigade.

In Sumner's camp at the Whittaker House, less than a mile away, there was no desperation. In the hard rain, they were unhurriedly planning the day's strategy. Outside, the men were enjoying their fresh rations. Two members of McClellan's staff had hurried down to Yorktown to bring him forward, as some were concerned about the idea of attacking entrenched Confederates without the commanding general being present.[14]

Rudolph J. Schroeder, III

Library of Congress

Joseph Hooker

Sumner, Keyes, Heintzelman and Smith were at Whittaker House, and were aware that Hooker was in a fight. Despite the heavy cover, the sounds reaching the four generals definitely indicated a large engagement. Much earlier that morning, Sumner had ordered Kearny to move his division up behind that of Hooker. On the right, Couch and Casey were on the Yorktown road behind Baldy Smith. Some intelligence was being received at the Whittaker House. Local Negroes had come in and related that the works on the Confederate far right weren't manned. Envisioning the possibility of a successful attack there, the generals decided to send out scouts to verify or discount these questionable reports. Concluding their meeting, Heintzelman and staff rode out to find Hooker. Meanwhile, Baldy Smith's division remained idle astride the Yorktown road. Hooker held on, waiting for Kearny.[15]

Edwin Vose Sumner

Around 11:00 A.M., Hancock was summoned to the Whittaker House to meet with Sumner. Baldy Smith, Hancock's division commander, was present. Sumner told Hancock that there were reports that some redoubts on the far right were unmanned. Hancock was ordered to take his brigade, part of Davidson's third brigade, and a battery to occupy them. Smith's Vermont brigade, commanded by Brigadier General W. T. H. Brooks, was made available to support Hancock if needed. It was just then that Hooker's courier arrived with his message to Heintzelman, who had departed. Sumner read it, marked it as read, then returned it to the courier.

Sumner likely believed that Johnston's entire army was behind the Warwick works, and he wasn't overly concerned about Hooker's problem. There would be many other problems to deal with. This analysis by Sumner would have been a poor one, inaccurate in judging the size of the Confederate force and their plans.[16]

Johnston had made his headquarters in the Vest house on Duke of Gloucester Street in Williamsburg. He commanded from there on the 4th and 5th of May. This headquarters was only about two miles from Hooker's fight near Fort Magruder. There was also a lot of chaos in Williamsburg as the rest of Johnston's army passed through the soggy streets on their way toward Richmond. Many panicked civilians were attempting to do the same thing. Johnston would leave at noon for Richmond.

Wounded soldiers from the Warwick line were arriving in Williamsburg by then. Those able to travel joined the army bound for Richmond. The less fortunate, not strong enough to be moved, were left in a rudimentary field hospital, in the care of local citizens.

Federal prisoners were also being marched through the town, on their way to prisons in Richmond. They were confronted by angry citizens, who brandished weapons and threatened the Federals. No violence to prisoners was recorded.[17]

By midmorning, over 10,000 troops were in the fight in front of the ravine. A. P. Hill and Pickett arrived with their brigades and entered the fray. Hill formed up behind the redoubts on the right of Fort Magruder, and Pickett's men went in on Hill's right. Now, Anderson was in great shape. He had more men in the fight than Hooker, and had extended the Confederate line farther to the right. Anderson now hoped to turn Hooker's left and drive him back.

This was the first real battle experience as a brigade commander for A. P. Hill, and for his men as a brigade. At Williamsburg, he proved he was a great personal leader. At one point in the fighting, the 7th Virginia regiment, daunted by the intensity of the fire they were experiencing, would not continue their advance, despite the urgings of their commander, Colonel James Kemper, A. P. Hill appeared on foot, waved his revolver over his head, urged the men forward, and the advance resumed.[18]

As noon drew near, the list of combat assets began to favor the Confederates. Fresh infantry and more artillery arrived and went into the fight. Two of Hooker's brigades, those of Francis Patterson and Cuvier Grover, were being steadily worn down. Hooker committed his last reserve, Daniel Sickles' Excelsior brigade, presently commanded by Colonel Nelson

Taylor. The brigade was comprised of the 70th, 72nd, 73rd and 74th New York.

As the four regiments of Taylor's brigade moved forward, they began to shoulder the load of the fighting from those troops who'd been in contact all morning. On the Confederate side, A. P. Hill's brigade was doing much the same. Taylor's New Yorkers and Powell Hill's Virginians suffered more than their share of casualties near the ravine that day.

The rough terrain and felled trees made formations hard to maintain, and regimental tactics devolved into small unit fights. Foliage and the normal smoke produced by black powder muskets reduced the visibility dramatically. Impacting artillery rounds shredded the felled trees and stumps and altered the battlefield minute by minute. Many musket shots were taken in the blind, and friendly fire took a toll.

Hooker earned the sobriquet "Fighting Joe" for his bravery at the battle of Williamsburg. Despite having a horse shot out from under him, he took another and continued to lead from the front.[19]

Heintzelman rode up to Hooker's headquarters about 1:00 P.M. He quickly learned about Hooker's earlier dispatch, Sumner's scribbled, uncommunicative response, and the disturbing fact that Hooker had committed the last of his reserves (Taylor's brigade). Heintzelman immediately took action. He messaged Sumner for reinforcements, directed Kearny to expedite his division up the Hampton road, and discussed with Hooker their next moves. Lieutenant McAlester was then sent out on a second scouting sortie, as the young officer's first report had stated that the Confederate right flank could be turned. Heintzelman was heartened by the effects of putting the Excelsior brigade into the fight. The New Yorkers were creating stability in the line, although ammunition would soon become a problem. At least the Confederate advance was slowed.[20]

By noon, Johnston had concluded that the rear guard would have to hold off their pursuers until nightfall, and returned to the front line. He took advantage of the fact that D. H. Hill's division, made up of the brigades of Rodes, Featherston, Jubal Early and Rains, was not very far away, and Johnston ordered it back as a reserve for Longstreet. Jubal Early's brigade was split in two parts, with two regiments added to the fight on the Confederate right, and the other four placed in an observation role beyond the Confederate left. Both D. H. Hill and Jubal Early went with the left force.[21]

Also around 1:00 P.M., Keyes was at his headquarters at the Whittaker house, and received word that Couch's division was nearing the front. In fact, the lead brigade, under John Peck, was already arriving.

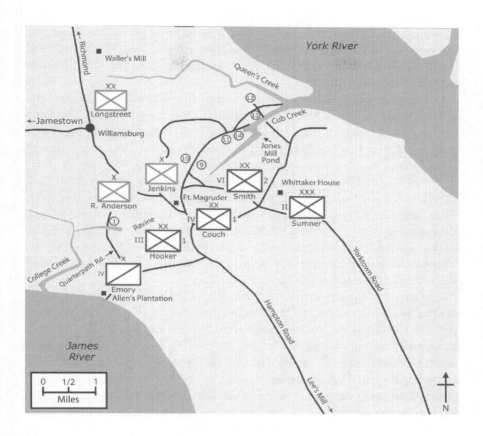

Map 8.2—Williamsburg, Afternoon, May 5

These were the first Federal reinforcements to arrive. After a hasty conference, Peck's brigade was sent via the Yorktown road into the line on Hooker's right. The plan was for Couch's other two brigades to move into line between Hooker and Baldy Smith's divisions. Couch would command this part of the line. Apparently, Sumner was at last aware of Hooker's predicament, and was preparing to bail Fighting Joe out.[22]

Peck's brigade went into the line straddling the Yorktown road, right in front of Fort Magruder. The brigade's front line was the 55th New York on the left and 102nd Pennsylvania on the right. The second line was the 93rd Pennsylvania on the left and the 94th Pennsylvania on the right. Grover's brigade of Hooker's division was on Peck's left, but not linked up. Wainwright's batteries were also to the left of Peck. In Peck's front was Jenkins.

Jenkins had been put in temporary command in the Confederate center by Anderson, before he left Fort Magruder to personally direct the fighting on the Confederate right. Anderson gave Jenkins his brigade and the mission of holding Fort Magruder and the ground around it. This was exactly where Peck attacked.[23]

Jenkins had five infantry regiments and part of another. They were the 4th, 5th, and 6th South Carolina, the Palmetto Sharpshooters, the Louisiana Foot Rifles, and part of the 14th Louisiana. Jenkins had artillery, but it was presently supporting the fight near the ravine. When Peck's brigade moved up in Jenkins' front, it represented a formidable challenge to Jenkins.

Peck began his attack in orthodox fashion, with the 55th New York and 102nd Pennsylvania advancing line abreast across open ground with no flank support. As might be expected, Jenkins' sharpshooters and artillery, all dug in, took a toll on the Federals. The Federal attack was repulsed, and Peck's regiments withdrew into the cover of the woods. It is questionable whether Peck's attack gave any help to Hooker.[24] What Hooker needed was an infusion of fresh troops at the ravine.

When Longstreet arrived on the field a little after midday, he was pleased with his situation. On the right, Anderson was on the verge of turning Hooker's left. In the center, Jenkins was holding the line. Since Longstreet had added Pickett's and A. P. Hill's brigades to Anderson's force, Hooker was in difficulty. Not only were the Federals outnumbered around the ravine, but ammunition was becoming a problem for them. Hooker began a somewhat controlled withdrawal. To Hooker's right, Couch continued to move his other two brigades into line.

As Hooker's infantry withdrew, they put Wainwright's batteries in jeopardy. Normally, the guns could have been withdrawn safely, but the muddy conditions made that impossible. Some of the guns were stuck in the mud and couldn't be moved on short notice. Also, many of the artillery horses had been killed by that point. The infantry support for the batteries was the 5th New Jersey. Now, they faced the onrushing Confederate attackers, and tried to slow them down. Bramhall's battery kept firing until it was about to be overrun. The gunners then fled for their lives. The 5th New Jersey made a gallant fight against overwhelming numbers, and paid a huge price. Eventually, two of Wilcox's regiments, the 9th Alabama and 19th Mississippi captured the guns. Unfortunately, these regiments took some friendly fire from the redoubts until they could plant their colors and be seen through the smoke.[25]

Unlike Heintzelman, who could think of nothing more useful at this critical point than to gather up his bands and have them play martial music, Hooker calmly and coolly sent for Emory's cavalry. He put the horsemen across the Hampton road to prevent able-bodied soldiers from fleeing the battlefield. Hooker then joined with Grover to form a new line of defense. In it, they put the 5-gun battery of Captain Smith (4th New York Independent Light). Hooker personally rallied his men, riding up and down the line, exhorting the soldiers to hold their ground. When two Confederate regiments closed to 150 yards, Smith's guns opened on them with triple-shotted canister and dispersed the attackers. Grover credited Smith's battery as the most decisive action leading to the successful defense of the position.[26] Heintzelman, however, credited his idea of martial music, writing later that "it saved the battle."[27]

Although Smith's volley of canister dispersed the two attacking Confederate regiments, and inflicted many casualties on them, the remainder of those regiments set up in the woods and began firing at the gunners who were very exposed. Wainwright sent his artillerists to hide in the woods until he could find some infantry support for the battery. Wainwright found Grover and then Hooker. Both generals promised help, but none arrived. After hearing that Kearny was drawing near, Wainwright set out to find him and ask his help. Kearny instantly ordered a company of the 1st Michigan to accompany Wainwright back to his battery and do whatever the artillerist ordered. That solved Wainwright's problem.[28]

Stuart attempted to employ his mostly idle cavalry at this point. Seeing the Federals retreating, he wrongly expected them to break, and he wanted to pitch into their rear with his cavalry and horse artillery. Although lukewarm to the idea, Longstreet permitted Stuart to try his luck. Stuart moved forward without resistance to the abandoned Federal guns, then the horsemen were driven back by musketry from the woods. The horse artillery remained there, supported by infantry. Stuart's attack seemed to affect nothing, and there were few casualties.[29]

Hooker's salvation was now at hand. Kearny's first regiment reached Hooker's lines some time between 2:00 and 2:30 P.M., to the cheers of Hooker's men and the music of Heintzelman's bands. The lead element was Berry's 3rd Brigade.

Berry's brigade was followed by Birney's 2nd Brigade. These brigades added 5,000 to 6,000 Federal soldiers to the fight. Kearny and his two brigadiers immediately met with Hooker and decided that Kearny's division would go on the offensive. Neither division commander met with Sumner or his staff.

The 3rd and 4th Maine from Birney's brigade and the 3rd Michigan from Berry were sent to Emory over at Allen's Plantation. Emory had been there for some time observing the Confederate far right. The rest of Kearny's regiments were put into Hooker's line, the 2nd and 5th Michigan, and the 37th New York went in left of the road, and the 38th and 40th New York on the right. Wainwright was finally given a single company of infantry to support his batteries.[30]

Kearny's regiments moved forward toward the ravine, but too slowly. Hooker's exhausted troops, short on ammunition, fell back through Kearny's regiments. As the advancing Federals neared the ravine, they observed the dead and wounded all around them. Kearny was riding along the line, sometimes in front of the regiments, inspiring confidence and urging the men on. Even old General Heintzelman was there, waving his hat in the air.

The lack of celerity of the Federal advance was costly in casualties, and diminished chances of success. The Confederates had brought in Colston's and D. H. Hill's brigades, and their defense became more determined. The slow Federal advance had resulted in the 5th Michigan losing about a third of the regiment while moving through the woods and the abatis. They persevered, however, and by the end of the day had taken some of the Confederate rifle pits in the open area. Colonel Poe's 2nd Michigan had a casualty rate of around 20%. Although Williamsburg was a smaller battle than several others in the Peninsula Campaign, some participants thought it might have been the hardest fought.[31]

Longstreet put in his last reinforcements early in the afternoon. D. H. Hill's brigades had received orders to countermarch, and were passing southbound through the town of Williamsburg. Hill and Johnston met with Longstreet in the field. Johnston gave tactical command to Longstreet and departed after a while. Longstreet decided to use the arriving regiments of D. H. Hill's brigades piecemeal, wherever they were needed. The 2nd Florida and the 12th Mississippi (from Rodes' brigade) were put in on the right to reinforce Anderson. The 24th and 28th Virginia (Rodes' brigade) and the 5th and 23rd North Carolina (from Jubal Early's brigade) were put in on Jenkins' left, east of Fort Magruder. Harvey Hill's remaining regiments were placed behind Jubal Early on the left as they arrived.[32]

As the latter part of the afternoon wore on, the front became more stable. Although the fight near the ravine and by Fort Magruder, fueled by the fresh regiments put in by both armies, continued on, Longstreet thought he had accomplished his mission. With two divisions, he had held back the Federal pursuit by five divisions, so that Johnston could safely withdraw the rest of the army and its trains. He would withdraw after nightfall, and all would be well. By nightfall, the lines would be just about where they had been at sunrise.

Most of the day, Emory and his cavalry had been waiting in the rain near Allen's Plantation for reinforcements. Finally, around 3:30 P.M., the promised forces arrived. First came the three infantry regiments from Kearny's division, then an artillery battery. A while later, Lieutenant McAlester arrived on the scene. McAlester was a bit surprised that there were only 2,000 infantry and only one battery in the force. The reason was likely the plan hastily contrived by Hooker, Kearny, Berry and Birney. It envisioned that Hooker would do nothing more than hold his ground, while Kearny's main force moved to the Plantation for a flanking movement. Unfortunately, Hooker was in no shape to hold his ground. His division was spent, and had to be replaced by Kearny. That left only this small force under Emory to attempt to turn the Confederate flank.

Emory decided to get on with the attempt, formed up his forces and moved up the Quarterpath road. The Federals cautiously advanced past a millpond, then past unmanned Confederate defenses around Redoubt No. 1. Emory decided to halt the advance there, due to the terrain, the late hour and the lack of a guide. Perhaps in the back of Emory's mind was the same thought as Lieutenant McAlester, that the force was insufficient for the mission. Emory did believe that a strong attack should have been attempted from Allen's Plantation earlier in the day. Such an attack would have likely prevented the bitter contest at the ravine.[33]

As one might expect, Emory was criticized by some for an excess of caution. Most agreed that he acted wisely. Little success could have come from an attack by a too small, thrown-together force moving without guides and attacking so late in the day. An example of the opposite decision would be forthcoming before May 5 was over.

Hancock had been assigned the mission of moving to the extreme Federal right and the redoubt overlooking the dam on Cub Creek., if it was unoccupied. He was authorized to move a little farther, then send for reinforcements. Hancock's force was comprised of the 5th Wisconsin, 6th Maine and 49th Pennsylvania of his own brigade, as well as the 7th Maine and 33rd New York of Davidson's brigade. Hancock's artillery support was the 1st New York Independent Light battery of 6 guns under Lieutenant Andrew Cowan. The only cavalryman along was one Lieutenant George A. Custer. The total force amounted to about 2,500 men.

Hancock had thus far not had an opportunity to distinguish himself in the current conflict. May 5 would change all that, making Hancock known throughout the United States Army and the nation, and bringing out the extent of his military talent.[34] Hancock's force neared Cub Creek without making contact with or even observing any Confederate troops. In sight was the dam, a narrow structure about 75 yards long. On the other side of the creek, Redoubt No. 14 was in sight. General Keyes and his staff rode up from Hancock's rear, so Hancock called a halt and conferred with Keyes.

Seven Days Before Richmond

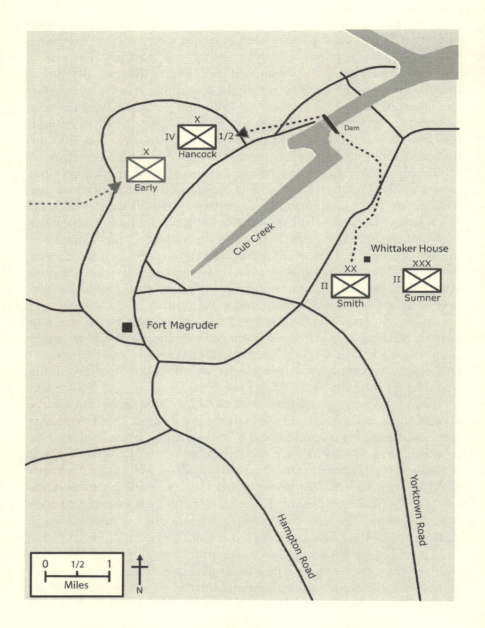

Map 8.3—Williamsburg, Hancock's Advance, May 5

Hancock reviewed his orders and asked for cavalry support. Keyes replied and promised to go to the rear and secure it. Hancock put together a force from the 6th Maine and 5th Wisconsin to cross the dam. Simultaneously, he deployed the rest of his infantry along the road. Lieutenant Custer was given the assignment of leading the party across the dam, and reported that it was unoccupied. Custer was surprised, in that he felt a small force of defenders put into the redoubt could have easily defended against any crossing of the dam by a division-sized force.[35]

Based on Custer's report, Hancock crossed his entire command across the dam, placed a small covering force in Redoubt No. 14, then advanced with his main force to the empty Redoubt No. 11. Realizing that Redoubts 12 and 13 were now in his rear, he sent a courier back to Baldy Smith, asking for another brigade to occupy them.

At this juncture, Hancock had turned the Confederate left flank without firing a shot. He was only about a mile and a half northeast of Fort Magruder. Between Hancock and Fort Magruder were Redoubts 9 and 10, then Micah Jenkins' command. The terrain in Hancock's front was generally an open grassy plain. There was a dense wood on Hancock's right and a smaller clump of trees on his left. Queen's Creek road ran right from Hancock's position to Fort Magruder. There was high ground at Redoubt No. 11, and a picket fence 100 yards in front of the crest. Hancock set up his infantry and artillery there for a time.[36]

Still, Hancock observed no Confederate activity in his front, so he posted the 33rd New York in Redoubt No. 11 and the 7th Maine was tasked to cover the woods on the right. He then moved the other three infantry regiments and his guns forward about 600 yards. He protected his flanks with skirmishers, as he still had no cavalry.

Hancock's forward position had the benefit of ten guns. Cowan's battery had been with Hancock from the start of the mission, and four more guns under Captain Charles C. Wheeler joined them en route. Hancock put the 5th Wisconsin on the right of the guns and the 6th Maine and 49th Pennsylvania on the left. He then sent skirmishers ahead to scout toward Redoubts 9 and 10, straddling the Queen's Creek road, hoping to develop the Confederate position.[37]

Jenkins, put in command of the Confederate center by Longstreet, had been attacked from the southeast earlier by Peck, and had subsequently deployed his forces to repel another similar attack. His infantry was positioned in Fort Magruder and Redoubts 7, 8 and 9. A part of the 6th South Carolina, under Colonel John Bratton, was in reserve behind the fort. Redoubt No. 10 was unoccupied when the fight began.[38]

Jenkins was apparently unaware that Hancock's force was across Cub Creek and close on his left rear. From only 300–400 yards away from the nearest of the Confederate redoubts, Hancock's guns opened on Fort Magruder, the adjacent redoubts and the reserves of Colonel Bratton. It is likely that Jenkins was caught unawares because he was fixated on another attack from the southeast. He did react immediately, however, and rode over to his left to confer with Bratton there. Jenkins assumed that Hancock's artillery barrage was a prelude to an attack by a major force, and directed Bratton to put his reserve force into Redoubts 9 and 10, hold them there, and await reinforcements.[39]

Bratton promptly began to move toward the two redoubts, aware that the Federals appeared to also be moving toward Redoubt No. 10. Bratton expedited some of his men over there and occupied it before the Federals could arrive there.[40] The two redoubts now provided a buffer between the attacking Federals and Jenkins' left flank. Jenkins must have been aware of the importance of Bratton's positions, as Jenkins found three companies of the 14th Alabama and three batteries to send to the redoubts.

A rather intense artillery exchange began between Hancock's ten guns and some of Baldy Smith's guns on the Yorktown road, and Confederate guns in Fort Magruder, the redoubts and the woods. The artillery duel continued for several hours.[41]

Hancock was still hoping to initiate an attack, and was waiting for the brigade he'd requested as reinforcements. At 2:30 P.M., he received a reply to his request. To his amazement, Sumner had ordered a withdrawal back to Hancock's earlier position. Hancock was to hold there.

Hancock was furious and went into a rant of profanity. He did not obey Sumner's order. He shared with Custer his intention to remain right where he was until 4:30 P.M. If no help came by then, he would withdraw as ordered. Hancock was probably lucky that the rest of the afternoon went well for him. Sumner could have been very hard on the brigadier. Custer later wrote that he thought Hancock was taking a big risk and betting on events to justify his actions.[42]

As to be expected, message traffic between Sumner, Smith and Hancock sharply increased. Hancock persevered in begging Sumner for reinforcements, and both Keyes and Smith supported Hancock. Sumner dithered, wanting to wait for the first regiments of Casey's division to arrive via the Yorktown road. Indecision seemed evident. Brooks' brigade was ordered twice to go forward to aid Hancock, then ordered back.[43] While the senior general dithered, the artillery duel continued, and the weather worsened. Hancock waited until 5:00 P.M., thirty minutes later than he had planned, then still failed to obey Sumner's orders. Instead, he made a decision to pull his men and guns from their advanced position back to the area just in front of Redoubt No. 10. Hancock was still clinging to the hope of receiving reinforcements.[44]

The sky was getting darker and there was heavy rain. Hancock delayed a few more minutes, hoping the lowering visibility would help to cover his pullback.[45] Hancock waited too long. He had just given the order, and the men were just beginning to pull back, when he observed Confederate infantry coming from the tree line on the right. They came right toward Hancock's position, which was totally exposed on the grassy field.[46]

Those Confederate troops were from the 24th Virginia of Jubal Early's brigade, and they were in the process of poorly executing a risky plan devised by D. H. Hill and Jubal Early. As mentioned previously, they had been sent by Longstreet in early afternoon to a position on the Confederate far left. The troops with the two Confederate generals were the 24th and 38th Virginia and the 5th and 23rd North Carolina. These four regiments were gathered in a field west of Hancock's position, screened by a line of dense woods. Early was aware that Hancock was there, and he could hear the artillery exchange. He knew the Federal guns were just beyond the line of trees.

Jubal Early, though having limited visibility from his position on relatively low ground in the trees, decided he wanted to attack. His idea was to outflank the Federal guns and capture them. Hill concurred, but referred the decision to Johnston, who bucked it back down to Longstreet, his tactical commander for the rear guard. Longstreet refused permission for the attack, reminding the two aggressive generals that their mission was a rear guard action, nothing more. He did not believe the attack was necessary to assure the safe retreat of the Army up the Peninsula. When Hill received General Longstreet's message, he went in person to Longstreet and appealed the decision. Longstreet at last acquiesced.[47]

While all this was happening, Rains' brigade had been brought up behind Jubal Early's, and those assets were available to defeat Hancock and run him off the field. Unfortunately, Harvey Hill was in a hurry and did not wait for reinforcements. He formed the four regiments from Jubal Early's brigade into a line of battle, with the 24th Virginia on the left, then the 38th Virginia, the 23rd and 5th North Carolina in that order. Early led the left two regiments into the woods, and Hill the right two. The regiments had to traverse about a half mile of woods, swampy, with tangled undergrowth. It was by then 5:00 P.M. and it was getting dark in the woods. The force soon irretrievably lost its alignment.

Seven Days Before Richmond

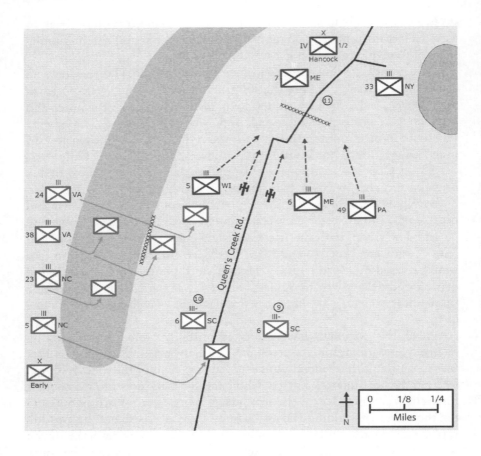

Map 8.4—Williamsburg, Early's Charge, May 5

The first regiment that came out of the woods was the 24th Virginia. They were surprised to find that they were not positioned in the Federal rear as envisioned. They weren't even on the enemy flank; they were a quarter of a mile in front of Hancock's guns. The nearest Federal troops to the Virginians were the 5th Wisconsin under Colonel Amasa Cobb, near some farm buildings. Jubal Early let his zeal override prudence, and charged them with his single regiment. He sent a message to Hill to bring the other three regiments in a hurry. He intended to blow through the Wisconsin regiment and advance on the redoubts. The 5th Wisconsin did an excellent job of executing a fighting withdrawal, while Hancock's artillery was withdrawn to the vicinity of Redoubt No. 11.[48]

Early's charge was welcomed by Hancock, who was just about to finally obey Sumner's order to withdraw to Cub Creek. In fact, Hancock's skirmishers and artillerists had already begun to withdraw when Early attacked. The next surprise for the 24th Virginia was that Hancock's men were not fleeing, but rather increasing their fire. The Virginians began to take casualties, including General Early. Shot through the shoulder and suffering from shock, he went to the rear.[49]

Hancock, a talented commander, calmly set about optimizing his defenses. As soon as his batteries completed their withdrawal from their forward position, he placed them on the flanks of his earthworks and had them open fire on Fort Magruder and the Confederate-occupied redoubts. Then, as the 49th Pennsylvania and 6th Maine arrived, he put the 6th Maine into the redoubt, pulled the 33rd New York from the redoubt and put it in line on the right, next to the 7th Maine. He then put the 49th Pennsylvania on the left of the redoubt. The center was left for the 5th Wisconsin after their well executed withdrawal.[50]

While Early and the 24th Virginia were charging Hancock's position, the 5th North Carolina came out of the woods. Their commander, Colonel Duncan McRae, aligned the regiment to face Hancock's men and extended the Confederate line.

Some of Hancock's artillery soon took the 5th North Carolina under fire. Hill came out of the woods and was also shocked to find he was even further off in his navigation. The 24th Virginia was on Hill's left and the 5th North Carolina was on his right, 800–900 yards in front of Hancock's men and much too far away from Early's men to allow mutual support. At this point in time, the 38th Virginia and the 23rd North Carolina, who should have been in the gap between Early and Hill, were nowhere in sight. Hill then received Early's plea for support. Bratton also sent Hill a message asking for orders, as he was unsure which redoubt should be his initial objective.

Hill then knew for sure that his plan was no longer intact. The tangled woods had seen to that. He didn't feel he could wait for the two missing regiments. The 24th Virginia could not be left to fight Hancock's men and guns all alone. Hill's response to McRae was to charge Redoubt No. 11, which was firing at them. To answer Early's request for help, Hill went back into the woods and managed to find the two missing regiments, the 38th Virginia and the 24th North Carolina. Hill ordered them to move north through the woods to cover the left flank of the 24th Virginia, clear the woods of any Federals there, and put themselves in position to take Hancock's men in flank or rear. Early's men were taking casualties, so McRae wheeled the 5th North Carolina left and charged.[51]

Hill then rode quickly to Redoubt No. 10, where he found Lieutenant Early, Jubal Early's aide, and Colonel Bratton. Lieutenant Early told Hill that General Early had been wounded, and informed Bratton that two regiments were missing and the attack was to be continued anyway.

Bratton was furious. As commander of Jenkins' left flank, no one had even informed him of Hill's planned attack. He even related that, seeing McRae's 5th North Carolina emerge from the trees and move toward his position, he momentarily considered the possibility that they were Federals. Bratton also expressed his desire to have his 6th South Carolina join in the attack, and told Hill that Jubal Early had approved that action before leaving the field. Harvey Hill concurred, and the 6th South Carolina made ready to move forward.[52]

As the 5th North Carolina moved forward, the light was fading, the rain was very heavy and the advance was slowed by soft ground and thick, wet grass. To complicate matters, the regiment had to angle from right to left, in order to close with the 24th Virginia. This lengthened their exposure to Hancock's fire. By now the 5th Wisconsin had completed its withdrawal to the center of Hancock's position and enjoyed the flank support of several other regiments.

The 24th Virginia had reached a rail fence only a hundred yards from the Federals. It had taken them 10 to 15 minutes to get to that meager protection. The Confederates were taking fire both from Hancock's main position and from the woods on the Confederate left. Canister from Hancock's guns was also a great threat.[53]

The 5th North Carolina eventually joined the Virginians behind the fence, but directly in Hancock's front. The other two Confederate regiments were still not of any help to Hill's attack. The 38th Virginia, commanded by Lieutenant Colonel Powhatan B. Whittle, was still in the woods and far from the fight.

The 38th was split into two parts. Several companies, as ordered personally by General Hill, changed direction and marched north through the woods. Other companies continued east, came out into the plain, then turned north toward the fight. The 23rd North Carolina, under Colonel John Hoke, continued north in the woods, eventually making contact with the 33rd New York, which was covering Hancock's right flank.[54] The New Yorkers stopped the Confederates there.

Both charges were destined to fail, as Hancock now had all five regiments, well over 3,000 muskets and eight guns massed on a slight ridgeline. The two Confederate regiments making the attack numbered no more than 1,200 men. Hill made the prudent decision to call off the attack.

As the Confederates began to fall back, Hancock ordered a counterattack. The Confederates were very close to Hancock's lines when the counterattack was initiated. One regiment, the 7th Maine, even fixed bayonets, but the weapon of choice was the musket.[55] The Federals fired several volleys, then were ordered to halt. Hancock, excited, shouting and cursing, urged his men to "aim low" as they fired on the retreating Confederates.[56] It cannot be determined with certainty whether the Confederates retreated based primarily on the fire they were receiving, or because of Harvey Hill's order. Reports are conflicting.

Colonel McRae had been left in charge of Early's brigade when Early left the field after being wounded. McRae was aware that he had insufficient combat power to assault Hancock's position. He sent a courier to Hill, asking the rest of the brigade come up to help. McRae also suggested that the two regiments already engaged hold their positions until reinforcements arrived. He hoped that the attack would then be resumed. McRae, for some unknown reason, believed Hancock's men were disorganized, and noted that their fire had slackened. Hill replied with the order to pull back immediately. McRae, furious, obeyed promptly, passing the order to Major Richard L. Maury, now in command of the 24th Virginia. It was a difficult and dangerous order for McRae to carry out. His men, on the ground and behind a fence, now had to expose themselves in order to retreat. Although Hancock did order a counterattack, he did not allow his men to pursue the retreating Confederate regiments very far.

The 24th Virginia, having little distance to run to reach the safety of the woods, did so with few additional casualties, but Colonel Terry and Lieutenant Colonel Hairston were severely wounded, and command devolved on Major Richard L. Maury.

Some 66 men of the regiment were captured by the 33rd New York, when they attempted to use the cover of the woods for their retreat. The regiment suffered 190 total casualties.[57]

The 5th North Carolina, however, was way out in the open field, and was badly mauled while making their way to safety. The regiment suffered an amazing 302 total casualties, including Lieutenant Colonel Badham killed. Jubal Early's brigade lost 508 men overall. Hancock lost about 100.[58]

The 6th South Carolina and part of the 38th Virginia were just starting their advance, and weren't a factor in the fight. The 24th North Carolina also contributed little to the Confederate effort.

It is important to remember that Hancock's local success was not exploited. Sumner failed to provide the reinforcements that Hancock had requested fairly early in the afternoon.[59] Had Sumner reinforced Hancock, the situation at the end of the day might have been considerably different. So the essential question is why did Sumner withhold reinforcements from Hancock? After the fight, Hancock was joined by Baldy Smith and the 3rd Vermont. Even later, Davidson's and Naglee's brigades arrived, bring the total Federal manpower there to 6,500 men.[60]

On the Confederate side, why didn't D. H. Hill reinforce the exposed regiments with one of his two other brigades? He never really made good use of the 6th South Carolina or the 38th Virginia, nor the two brigades he had on the other side of the tree line. The post-war writings of Major Maury and Colonel McRae both criticize Harvey Hill for his lack of support, and especially for ordering the two exposed regiments to retreat under fire. Those troops could have easily held their positions until nightfall and retreated with a much lower number of casualties.

Hill's defense of his decision was simple. He pointed out that the action lasted some 23 minutes, and Hill had been ordered not to delay the army's march northward after dark. There simply wasn't time to bring up two fresh brigades. He also knew that Hancock would soon be reinforced in his prime position.[61]

When Baldy Smith arrived at Hancock's position, he took command and began preparing for the next morning, which many Federals thought would be a continuation of the day's fighting. Simultaneously, the Federals began burying their dead and aiding the wounded.

McClellan arrived at Sumner's headquarters on the Yorktown road about the time of Early's repulse, around 5:00 P.M., and was greeted by cheers from the officers and men there. He set up his own headquarters and summoned Sumner to report there. In a lapse in judgment, Sumner replied that he was busy, and asked if he could come a bit later. An irate McClellan showed up at Sumner's Whittaker house headquarters twenty minutes later, had a conversation with Sumner, and General McClellan and his staff then went on a reconnaissance of the of the Federal lines. Sumner sort of faded from sight. Later McClellan wrote that Sumner was a fool and Heintzelman and Keyes were guilty of "utter stupidity and worthlessness." McClellan also modestly added that he was able to "save the day."[62]

McClellan did take a few actions of significance. He sent Smith and two brigades to reinforce Hancock, attempted to set up direct communications between the two wings of the army (unsuccessfully), and redirected two fresh divisions on the way to the front to Yorktown and West Point.[63]

This was just the first of numerous occasions during the Peninsula Campaign when McClellan arrived after the battle was over. In this case,

McClellan chose to oversee the loading of General Franklin's division on transports at Yorktown. This was most certainly not a task beyond the capability of Franklin, a highly competent officer. As early as 9:00 A.M., McClellan heard heavy firing from the battlefield and reported same to Washington via telegram. Baldy Smith sent several messages to McClellan asking him to come to the front.[64]

The overall casualty figures demonstrate that the battle of Williamsburg was a rather bloody affair. About 12,000 Federal and 9,000 Confederate troops were actually engaged in the fighting. Total Federal casualties were 2,239 (456 killed, 1,410 wounded and 373 missing) and they lost twelve guns to the enemy about 400 Federals were captured. The Confederates sustained 1,560 casualties, including Jubal Early wounded. The regiments hardest hit were the 70th New York and the 5th North Carolina. For more information on casualties, see Appendix B.[65]

McClellan, always the logistician, mentions in his writings of 1864 that it was important that he resupplied his army on May 5 with ammunition, rations and forage. He was aware that his men were short of all of these, as the supply trains had been forced off the roads to allow troops and guns to move up.[66]

The Federals improved their lines during the night. Kearny's relatively fresh division replaced Hooker's battered one on the left. Kearny also brought up all his assigned artillery and reclaimed the regiments he had detached to Emory on the far left. Couch still commanded the Federal center, and moved up brigades from his own division to reinforce the line there.

Pickets reported about 3:30 A.M. on May 6 that the Confederates had withdrawn from their lines. By first light, the 7th Massachusetts had entered Fort Magruder and adjacent earthworks. Federal infantry checked other works. All were devoid of Confederates.

The Confederates had used Fort Magruder as a hospital, and Hancock used Redoubt No. 11 as a field hospital for Confederates left in the grassy field. Some of the wounded were brought into Williamsburg, filling up many public buildings and private homes. Because of their need to withdraw immediately, the Confederates were forced to leave all their dead and many of their wounded on the battlefield. McClellan's men would spend days burying the dead and picking up the battlefield. Most of the Confederate dead were buried on the battlefield. As was common, the dead were scavenged for whatever on their persons was valuable or useful. Some of the wounded lay in the felled trees, and some of them were burned alive when the trees caught on fire.[67]

Seven Days Before Richmond

The battle of Williamsburg was a battle that neither commanding general had intended to fight. Johnston desired to retreat to Richmond unmolested. McClellan intended to interdict that retreat by way of an amphibious movement at Eltham's Landing. The Federal pursuit from Yorktown was too efficient for Johnston to get away clean, and the rear guard fight at Williamsburg resulted. However, the planned interdiction at Eltham's Landing would clearly not take place, and the Confederates withdrawal to Richmond would continue in a fairly orderly manner.

Williamsburg was also a bit unusual in that neither commanding general spent a significant part of the day anywhere near the front lines, nor exerted much tactical control over their forces. McClellan left tactical control to Sumner, who mostly dithered. Johnston left the battle in the hands of Longstreet, who was also indecisive. In reality, the battle was most influenced by Hooker and Anderson. Hancock, although he showed great initiative and skill in flanking the Confederate left and occupying Redoubt No. 11, didn't materially affect the outcome, other than the casualty count. Likewise, Jubal Early's and D. H. Hill's abortive charge against Hancock did little but run up the Confederate casualty count.[68]

As was usual in the Civil War, both sides claimed victory—the Federals, because they ended up in possession of the battlefield, the Confederates, because they accomplished their objective of a successful rear guard action. McClellan, however, believed that Hancock was "magnificent," and "superb." McClellan's opinion was not well received by Hooker and his division, who had borne the brunt of the fighting on the Federal side, and were barely credited for their valor.

CHAPTER 9

Eltham's Landing

(May 7)

As the sun rose on the morning of May 6, the rain had finally stopped. Federal troops had already poured through the Confederate works of the Warwick Line, and now McClellan's men started to enter the town. As expected, the town was in shoddy shape, reflecting the retreat of Johnston's army through it. The townspeople had removed all their wagons and stock from view, and silently watched the Federals pass by. The only celebrants were some slaves that now rejoiced in their newly-found freedom. Many others had packed up and left. There were numerous seriously wounded Confederates around the town. Every building, public or private, being used as a hospital was marked with a yellow flag. The whole town seemed to be cooperating in the care of the wounded.

The Vest house was now empty, and McClellan set up his headquarters there and went to work on a variety of problems. Since his army was somewhat scattered and his logistical situation was less than good, he decided not to pursue Johnston right away. The roads were a muddy mess, preventing sufficient resupply by wagons, so wharfs were being built along Queen's Creek to allow resupply by water.[1]

By May 10, McClellan was ready to move the remainder of his army out of Williamsburg in pursuit of the retreating Johnston. The Federals left behind only the 5th Pennsylvania Cavalry as a garrison. McClellan, always image conscious, had his army in presentable condition as it rumbled through Williamsburg. The huge force took two days to clear the town.[2]

McClellan was always asking for reinforcements, and Franklin's division (part of McDowell's Corps, the remainder of which had been detached from the Army of the Potomac) was returned to him, arriving off Fort Monroe on April 22. They were held on transports for 10 days, then finally allowed ashore after General Franklin complained of the long period of inactivity imposed on his troops. The division was not ashore long.

McClellan's original plan called for the division of Franklin, followed by the divisions of Porter, Sedgwick and Richardson to move by water to West Point on the York River. There they would be in the rear of Johnston's army. The four divisions would move across the Peninsula and cut the main roads. The Confederates would be unable to retreat to their works at Richmond, and would have to fight in the open, with Federal forces on two sides of them and the Federal navy on the other two. It was a plan which could have resulted in the decimation of Johnston's army.[3]

McClellan had reloaded Franklin's division onto transports on May 5. Although they were ready to head upriver that evening, it was decided preferable to make the trip in daylight the next morning. McClellan had intended for both Sedgwick's and Richardson's divisions to go along, but the fighting that broke out on the 5th made McClellan cautious, and he rode to the front, taking both divisions with him.[4]

Early on May 6, Franklin's division sailed up the York, in an attempt to cut off the retreat of most of the Confederate army. The idea now was to get behind Johnston and attack his wagon trains as they withdrew, but Johnston had seen this possibility and detached Whiting's division of Gustavus W. Smith's command. In fact, McClellan's flanking movement by water was a good plan, it was just executed about two days too late to be successful.[5]

Franklin's division arrived at Eltham's Landing, near West Point on the Pamunkey, about 1:00 P.M. on May 6 and immediately began to disembark. There was shallow water off the landing, and the men had to come ashore in pontoon boats. It was not a totally uncontested landing. A trooper of the division named Adams recounted:

> Our light draught steamers and sailing vessels deployed along this broad plateau, some of them within one hundred yards of the shore, and prepared to land the troops, while the gunboats took position to cover the landing.... In less than an hour from the time we had taken position the water swarmed with all sorts of odd craft, from pontoons to canalboats.... But the enemy was not inclined to let us do this work in peace. As soon as the first fleet of pontoons started to make a landing, the enemy opened from a battery concealed on the lower end of the ridge I have before described. His shells and round shot flew thick and fast, some of them exploding among the pontoons, others paying their compliments to the fleet. The pontoons kept steadily on towards the shore, which the men reached with cheers.[6]

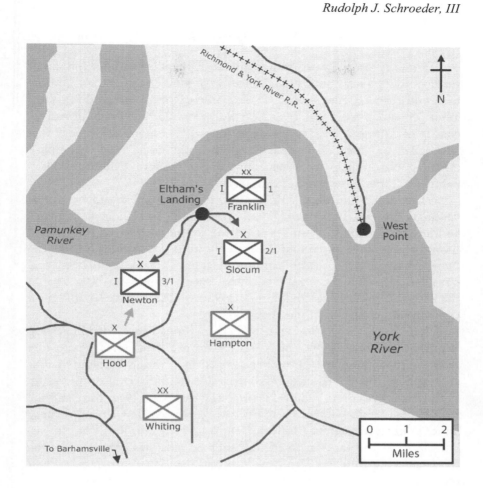

Map 9.1—Eltham's Landing, May 7

After some delay in finding water deep enough to get within range, the Federal gunboats did manage to take the offending Confederate guns under fire and silence them. By sundown, an infantry brigade, three artillery batteries and some cavalry were landed. Even Professor Lowe was up in his balloon, but provided no concrete information.[7]

By nightfall, the Federals had put together a 400 foot long floating wharf, made from the pontoon boats, some canal boats and planking. Franklin quickly sent the transports back to Yorktown to bring up Sedgwick's division. It was a fortunate thing for the Confederates that McClellan only had enough transports to move one division at a time. Franklin's men worked all night by torchlight, getting the whole division and its equipment ashore by dawn. It was a great piece of work, but was two days late.⁸

Franklin's orders were to remain at Eltham's Landing and await further orders. They contained no mention of moving across the Peninsula to cut off the Confederate retreat.⁹ The orders were sound, in that almost all of Johnston's army was at or near Barhamsville, and Franklin had no chance of cutting off their movement toward Richmond. It is likely that McClellan did not believe that Franklin could successfully accomplish anything without help. It was necessary for Sedgwick to reinforce Franklin before attacking Johnston's retreating army.

That evening, Gustavus W. Smith sent word to Johnston at Burnt Ordinary that "a large body of United States troops had landed at Eltham's, and nearly opposite to West Point, on the southern shore of York River." Johnston was made aware that the Federals were in a thick wood between New Kent road and Eltham's Landing. He knew they needed to be pushed out of there so his army could withdraw safely. Smith was tasked to do the job. Johnston believed that Smith performed the task well, with minor casualties, as compared to the Federals.¹⁰

By early the next morning, May 7, Franklin had succeeded in getting his entire division ashore and put it in an excellent defensive posture around the landing site. The water assisted in covering Franklin's flanks and even part of his front. Franklin put Newton's brigade on the right. His brigade was comprised of the 18th, 31st and 32nd New York, and the 95th Pennsylvania. Newton's artillery was Battery A, New Jersey Artillery, under William Hexamer.

Slocum's brigade was on the left. His brigade was composed of the 5th Maine, the 16th and 27th New York and the 96th Pennsylvania. Their artillery was the 1st Massachusetts Battery, under Josiah Porter.

Later in the morning, Dana's brigade of Sedgwick's division arrived. More reinforcements followed.

Smith's initial plan was to put virtually no Confederate troops in Franklin's front, hoping to entice him to move inland, away from the protection of his gunboats. Franklin's orders kept him from taking the bait. Instead, the Federals were digging in. On the morning of May 7, Smith decided to alter his plans. He ordered an attack by Whiting's men on Newton, hoping to drive him close enough to the river that Confederate artillery might engage the gunboats. Around 9:00 A.M., the Confederates arrived in force, under the overall command of Smith. The troops chosen to lead the attack were the brigade of John Bell Hood. They were the 1st, 4th and 5th Texas, and the 18th Georgia. The brigade had the support of a single battery. This was a well-led brigade with high morale. The

Texans had nicknamed the assigned 18th Georgia as the "3rd Texas." Wade Hampton's brigade, composed of the 14th and 19th Georgia, the 16th North Carolina, and Hampton's South Carolina Legion, was there in support of Hood. Hampton's artillery support was George Moody's Madison (Louisiana) Battery.

Whiting's two brigades launched an attack on Newton's brigade. By 11:00 A.M., the Confederates had driven in Newton's skirmishers. Hood's brigade pushed into the woods, driving the Federal skirmishers until they ran up against the main line of Federal infantry in brigade strength. After several attacks and counterattacks, some of the Federal regiments, unable to see very far in the woods and fearing for their flanks, broke toward the open ground near the river and the covering fire of Federal gunboats. After a retreat of almost a mile, the line was reinforced and was held there. Hood saw no value in continuing the fight, as he'd already carried out Johnston's orders. He broke off the fighting at that point. Some firing lasted until about 3:00 P.M., when Whiting's division retired.[11]

Franklin reported his casualties as 49 killed, 104 wounded, and 41 missing, for a total of 194. He noted the high proportion of officers as casualties.[12] Hood's brigade had sustained only 37 total casualties. Total Confederate casualties were 8 killed and 40 wounded. It could have been worse for them, as Hood stumbled into a group of Federal pickets in a clearing, and was nearly shot at close range.[13]

Franklin was the least aggressive of the four division commanders that McClellan had to choose from to be the first ashore at Eltham's Landing. While Franklin did a fine job of setting up a defensive posture there, he did little else of which to be proud. Although he was reinforced heavily within 24 hours and had 25,000 troops at his disposal, Franklin seems to have bought into the myth that Johnston had an army of 80,000 to 120,000 nearby. Therefore, Franklin took the conservative option. He sat and waited on the Pamunkey while Johnston and his army passed by, marched to Richmond, and prepared for the real fight that was to be the Seven Days.[14]

The fight at Eltham's Landing was not an important engagement in terms of ground gained or lost, high casualty counts, or one side fleeing the field. None of that happened. Some call it a heavy skirmish, rather than a battle. It was important, however, but for other reasons. McClellan's goal was to interrupt the Confederate retreat and trap Johnston's army between two large Federal forces. Measured against that goal, Eltham's Landing was a complete Federal failure. As was his wont, McClellan attempted to put a positive spin on the results of the fight. He took pride in gaining the site for a logistics base deemed critical to the drive on Richmond.

West Point, just across the river from Eltham's Landing, was at the end of the Richmond and York River Railroad, which would be of great value to McClellan in the near future. He was especially pleased to have gained possession of the railhead without having to fight a full-scale battle to do so. The irony was that Johnston had no intention of trying to deny White House Landing to McClellan. Johnston knew he did not have the logistics to hold it if he desired. It was exposed and too far from Richmond.

Johnston had no desire to precipitate a major fight at Eltham's Landing. His intent was merely to check the Federal force near the river long enough to let his generals get their trains past without damage. Hood, who actually loved combat, was typically overaggressive on that day. Johnston, who had asked Hood merely to feel the enemy gently, then fall back, had a question for Hood. He inquired what Hood's Texans would have done if they'd had orders to charge the Federals and drive them. Hood replied, "I suppose, General, they would have driven them into the river, and tried to swim out and capture the gunboats."[15]

It is interesting to note that neither commanding general was on the battlefield, personally managing their side of the battle. In the case of Johnston, he just didn't get to the battlefield in time to affect the battle. For McClellan, his absence was to become a common occurrence in the Peninsula Campaign, a habit for which he was much criticized in post-war writings.

More wounded were brought into Williamsburg as they were discovered in the tangle of the abatis and the woods there. The situation just became more difficult each day. McClellan asked for a truce with Johnston's rear guard, requesting that Confederate surgeons be sent back to assist the Federal medics in caring for the wounded. The Confederate doctors soon arrived, and were given unrestricted movement in the town. Some Federal officers were annoyed by that fact, as they had some restrictions on their movement. Despite what the Federal officers considered "indecent rudeness" on the part of the local ladies to the occupying soldiers and officers, the Federals claimed to have behaved well. One notable exception was an act of "brutal violence" committed by a colored servant of a New York regiment on the person of a widow. The Federals forced the criminal to dig his own grave, then shot him for his crime.[16] The doctors of both armies did work together for several days, in an attempt to save the lives of the soldiers of both armies. The amputated limbs piled up, and the chaplains sometimes took over when the surgeons gave up.[17]

Although doctors in blue and gray worked together in a common cause in those makeshift operating rooms, outside in Williamsburg, it was not an pleasant atmosphere. The vast majority of the townspeople were extremely unhappy to come under Federal occupation. They were as defiant as they could be, and as rude to their occupiers as they dared to be. The Federals, as the occupiers, imposed harsh martial law. Despite McClellan's orders to the contrary, some Federal troops were guilty of confiscating and destroying private property. The Federals required loyalty oaths of the citizens and shut down the local newspaper. As it turned out, Williamsburg would be under Federal control for the remainder of the war.[18]

In the wake of the fight at Eltham's Landing, the Confederates continued their withdrawal toward their works near Richmond, arriving on the north bank of the Chickahominy on May 9. The Federals waited for McClellan and the rest of his army to come up from Williamsburg; they then gathered and organized themselves. On May 10, they continued their advance to the Chickahominy River. The army departed Williamsburg in grand form, with flags flying and their musicians playing. The townspeople had to be impressed with an army so immense that it took two days for the last of it to pass through the town.

The Federal army, save the small garrison left behind, was gone from Williamsburg, but the harsh living conditions would be there in Williamsburg for years. A further indignity was suffered when the main building of the College of William and Mary was burned, just in the wake of a Confederate cavalry raid. The townspeople believed that the Federals set the fire in retaliation for the especially effective raid.[19]

It would be some two and a half weeks before the two great armies would fight again. Neither opponent considered this period idle time. Both sides were working hard to prepare for the desperate conflict that they knew was forthcoming.

CHAPTER 10

Hanover Court House

(May 27)

After the fight at Eltham's Landing on May 7, the Federal troops there moved over to the main road, rejoined the main body, and the Army of the Potomac continued their march to the Chickahominy in pursuit of Johnston's army. Their trek had started at Williamsburg, passed through Barhamsville, New Kent Court House, Baltimore Crossroads and close to Bottoms Bridge. There, Keyes' IV Corps crossed the Chickahominy and moved upstream just south of the railroad to the area of Seven Pines. The remaining four corps moved up the north bank, almost to Mechanicsville. McClellan began a flurry of bridge building. When he was ready, he crossed Heintzelman's III Corps to the south bank of the river, where it backed up Keyes' IV Corps.

McClellan now had about a third of his army south of the Chickahominy. His general plan was to inch them forward on the south bank, thereby uncovering more crossing sites. He would then build more bridges, enabling him to rapidly cross his forces as necessary. If he could put most of his army on the south bank, the Richmond and York River Railroad would be used to bring up his heavy siege guns within range of Richmond. He would simply use the railroad as the axis of advance for the bulk of the army. The railroad would also allow him to resupply his army handily from his port at White House Landing.

McClellan was informed that a Dr. Pollock had been heard to say that a Confederate force of about 17,000 men had moved to Hanover Court House, a point on the Virginia Central Railroad, some fourteen miles north of Richmond, essentially in McClellan's right rear. For some reason, McClellan attached great credibility to that single source intelligence and ordered a cavalry reconnaissance of the location. His concern was that Confederates at that location could threaten his communications and would be in position to either reinforce Jackson or impede McDowell's junction if he ever came south. The cavalry report confirmed the doctor's statement, but refined the number of Confederates there down to approximately 6,000. McClellan found the presence of that many Confederate in his rear unacceptable and took action right away.[1] On the same day, McClellan became aware of another Confederate force moving south from the vicinity of Fredericksburg. This was likely the brigade of J. R. Anderson, which was on its way to join Branch at Hanover Court House.[2]

McClellan gave his favorite corps commander, Fitz John Porter, the task of driving the Confederates out of Hanover Court House. On the evening of May 26, McClellan wrote his wife about the mission he'd given Porter to accomplish the following day. He described to her the object and importance of the mission, writing, "the object being to cut off & disperse a force of the enemy threatening my right & rear—also to destroy the RR bridges—when this is done I will feel very comfortable in that direction & shall be quite ready to attack."[3]

Porter's command consisted of Morell's division (the brigades of John H. Martindale, James McQuade and Daniel Butterfield), a provisional brigade under Gouverneur K. Warren, a thrown together advance guard under William H. Emory, consisting of detachments of the 5th and 6th U. S Cavalry, Berdan's 1st U. S Sharpshooters and the 2nd U. S. Artillery, Battery M (horse artillery).

Martindale's brigade consisted of the 22nd Massachusetts, the 2nd Maine, the 25th New York, the 44th New York, and Battery C, Massachusetts Light Artillery.

McQuade's brigade was made up of the 14th New York, the 4th Michigan, the 9th Massachusetts, the 62nd Pennsylvania, and Battery E, 5th Massachusetts Artillery.

Butterfield's brigade was composed of the 16th Michigan, the 12th New York, the 17th New York, the 83rd Pennsylvania under Colonel John W. McLane, and Battery D, 5th U. S. Artillery.

Warren's provisional brigade was made up of the 5th New York, the 13th New York, the 1st Connecticut Heavy Artillery, the 6th Pennsylvania Cavalry (2 regiments), and the Rhode Island Battery.[4] All together, there were six artillery batteries in Porter's command.

Brigadier General Lawrence O'B. Branch was the commander of the Confederate force near Hanover Court House. His mission was not, as McClellan feared, to attack the rear of McClellan's army, but to guard the Virginia Central Railroad. It was the principal link between Richmond and the fertile Shenandoah Valley. Branch was grounded in congressional politics, not a trained military officer. His combat experience was limited to the losing end of the fight for New Bern, North Carolina, where he had been severely outnumbered.[5]

Seven Days Before Richmond

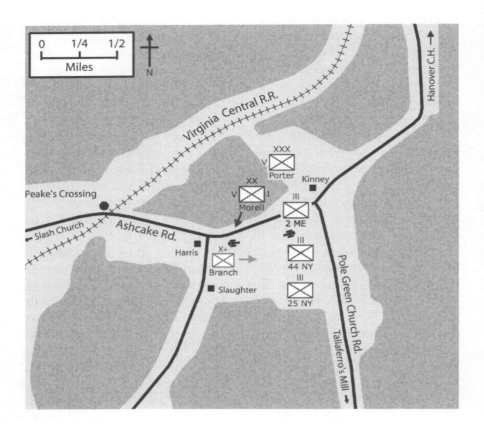

Map 10.1—Hanover Court House, May 27

Branch had only a modest force under his command. It was a reinforced brigade of seven infantry regiments, about 4,000 men. They were the 7th North Carolina, the 12th North Carolina, the 18th North Carolina, the 28th North Carolina, the 33rd North Carolina, the 37th North Carolina, and the 45th Georgia. They were supported by the Branch (North Carolina) Artillery and the 4th Virginia Cavalry. Branch also had reporting to him Company H, 9th Virginia Cavalry. Anderson's brigade was expected to join Branch near Hanover Court House on May 27, but was late moving there. Anderson's tardiness produced a terrible consequence for Branch.[6]

Porter's command moved from New Bridge, through Mechanicsville, then toward Hanover Court House along a road of foot-deep mud. The rain ceased mid-morning, but the mud was there all day, making the eighteen mile trek to the battle very tiring for the men. By the time the first shots were fired near an outpost south of the court house, it was noon and the Federals were already feeling tired. Near Dr. Kinney's house, troops from Branch's brigade, along with two guns, tried to stop the Federals from advancing along the road to Hanover Court House.[7] The lead infantry regiment, marching right with the cavalry was the 25th New York, and they were stung hard by the Confederates before Porter's main body could slog through the mud to support them. After about an hour of fighting in a woodlot and near Dr. Kinney's house and barn, the Confederates withdrew. Most went north towards Hanover Court House, and Porter gave chase, leaving behind three regiments to secure the crossroads. One of those regiments was the cut up 25th New York.[8]

The real fighting was preceded by mistakes by both commanders. Porter had convinced himself that Branch would be at Hanover Court House, and marched right past the Confederates. Branch was actually at Peake's Crossing, about four miles to the south. Branch made a more serious mistake by giving battle at all. Had he correctly assessed the strength of Porter's command, Branch should have immediately retreated from the area. However, he believed what he was told by a local, who reported the Federal force as small, and committed five regiments against the three regiments of Porter's rear guard.[9]

The situation at the crossroads was bleak for the Federal rear guard, consisting of the 2nd Maine, the battered 25th New York, the 44th New York and a section of artillery. The Federals were commanded by Martindale. Staff officers went up the road to find Porter and get help. The 18th North Carolina charged the Federal artillery with bayonets fixed, but was repulsed. The fight then degenerated into a close-up fight along a hedgerow. The opposing infantry were so close that they literally were poking their muskets through the hedge, attempting to get a shot at the enemy. The desperate fight went on so long that muskets became overheated and the Federals began to run short of ammunition.

The Federal musket fire began to slacken, and the Confederates were able to drive the Federals from their guns, and Martindale saw the center of the Federal line began to break. Some of the Federals took cover in the woods.[10]

In the nick of time, Porter reached the scene. Thousands of Federals quickly drove the Confederates from the field. Branch had no option but to withdraw quickly. Darkness soon made a halt to the fighting. Porter reported to McClellan that he killed many Confederates and took a "great many prisoners."[11]

Regiments on both sides incurred serious numbers of casualties. Totals of killed and wounded were about the same for both opponents. The Federal killed and wounded totaled 285, most from the New York and Maine regiments who fought at the crossroads before Porter returned. Confederate losses can only be estimated at about 300 or a little less. The Federals, however, captured 731 of Branch's men, while Branch captured only 70 Federals. Many of the Confederates taken prisoner were collected by Federal cavalrymen as they straggled during the retreat from the battle area.[12]

A definite plus for Porter's cavalry was that they were now free to damage the Virginia Central Railroad without interference. They burned a number of rail bridges and captured a trainload of military supplies. The soldiers were personally rewarded by taking possession of a boxcar loaded with tobacco, which they enjoyed immensely upon their return to camp.

McClellan toured the battlefield and was greatly pleased by Porter's success. All of the Federal objectives of the expedition were accomplished. Great destruction was inflicted upon the bridges and railroads as far as Ashland on May 28 and 29. Specifically, on May 28, part of the 6th U. S. Cavalry under Major Lawrence Albert Williams, destroyed the road bridges over the Pamunkey River and the Virginia Central rail bridge over the South Anna. On the 29th, the same troopers destroyed the Fredericksburg, Richmond & Potomac rail bridge over the South Anna and the turnpike bridge over the same. Also on May 29, part of the 6th U. S. Cavalry rode into Ashland, chasing out a few Confederates and destroying the rail bridge over Stoney Creek, and damaging the railroad and telegraph. Warren entered the town afterwards and took a number of prisoners. Porter's ad hoc command returned to their previous camps late on May 29.[13]

Typical for McClellan, he reported to Washington that the Battle of Hanover Court House was another "glorious victory over superior numbers." He went on to become carried away in praising his favorite subordinate, calling the expedition "one of the handsomest things of the war...."[14] Typically also, McClellan was convinced that the powers in Washington did not adequately understand the significance of Porter's victory or the magnificence of his performance. He even went to the extent of writing Secretary Stanton on May 30, complaining about the "tone" of Stanton's and Lincoln's dispatches regarding the matter.[15]

What McClellan failed to mention was that the expedition to Hanover Court House had caused him almost a week's delay in crossing more of his army across to the south bank of the Chickahominy. McClellan had refused to cross any more troops until Porter returned and the Army had an adequate reserve. In fact, McClellan told Porter before launching him on the expedition that there was a risk involved in the expedition. McClellan actually incurred an even greater risk by delaying the crossing of more of his army. In just a few days, he would pay a hefty price for his caution.[16]

Branch's bloodied command withdrew to the south, toward Joseph Johnston's lines. Later that same day, Branch's brigade and that of Joseph R. Anderson were assigned to a new division under the newly promoted Major General A. P. Hill.[17]

At this point in time, McClellan needed to be an extremely active leader. He should have been moving all his corps to their appropriate positions for a concerted offensive against Richmond. Instead, he decided to wait until the Confederates were driven out of Hanover Junction before making any offensive move. He became passive, and let Johnston temporarily assume the initiative.[18] McClellan seemed unable to take any decisive action. Rather, he spent much of his time pleading with Lincoln and Stanton for more and more reinforcements to counter many thousands of imaginary Confederate troops, as well as writing letters to his wife describing how everyone in Washington was out to get him. He couldn't bring himself to think offensively, preferring instead to be doubly sure he was covered against a disaster.[19]

As fortune would have it, on the same day as the Battle of Hanover Court House was fought, the Confederate War Office in Richmond became aware that Irvin McDowell and his large and powerful I Corps had moved south to Guiney's Station on the Richmond, Fredericksburg & Potomac Railroad. This put McDowell only twenty-five miles from Porter at Hanover Court House. The Confederate leaders in Richmond wrongly interpreted McDowell's movement as the long-feared linkup with McClellan's other five corps, a linkup which could possibly occur in a matter of only a day's march. This was not the case. McDowell was only conducting an exercise with his command. However, Johnston was motivated to promptly attack that part of McClellan's army isolated south of the Chickahominy River, namely the III Corps of Heintzelman and the IV Corps of Keyes. A quick reconnaissance by Jeb Stuart's cavalry was conducted, and indicated, however, that McDowell was not coming down to join the main body of the Army of the Potomac after all. Despite Stuart's report, the decision-makers in Richmond felt that time was of the essence, and the secret planning for the Battle of Seven Pines began.[20]

PART IV

SEVEN PINES

"Charge 'em like hell, boys: show 'em you *are* damned Yankees."
Colonel E. E. Cross [1]

CHAPTER 11

Seven Pines, Day One

(May 31)

Understanding why Seven Pines happened when and as it did requires us to appreciate the nature of the mood in the Confederacy, as well as the history between the key players in the battle. Some of this history created motivations and limitations on their actions.

As May of 1862 moved into its second half, the mood in the Confederacy, especially in Richmond, could best be described as that of somber desperation. The sense of fear and panic enveloping Richmond was manifested in several ways. On the roads leading south and west from the capital, wagonloads of refugees streamed away from the city in search of a safer place for their families. In the capital, the cabinet was planning for the contingency of abandoning Richmond. Some commodities, such as tobacco, were burned down at the docks. Politicians made brave speeches or visited the troops, urging them to save their capital city.[1]

Against this backdrop, Johnston certainly had to feel immense pressure to act. Robert E. Lee, Chief Military Advisor to President Davis and *de facto* commanding general of the Confederate armies, sent his military secretary, Colonel Armistead L. Long, to visit Johnston at his headquarters and determine what the general's plans were for the defense of the capital. The fact that Lee sent a colonel to meet with Johnston at this critical juncture, rather than make the five mile ride himself and ask Davis to accompany him, is likely the result of the lack of trust and confidence the President and Lee had in Johnston.

The bad feelings between Davis and Johnston came from a number of events in their common past, and involved several other key members of the Confederate military and civilian leadership. The earliest problem went back to the relative ranking between Joseph Johnston, Albert Sidney Johnston (no relation), Robert E. Lee and Samuel Cooper.

Joseph Johnston believed he should outrank the others because he served as a brigadier general as a quartermaster in the U. S. Army, while the others were line colonels. Davis used the statutes available, elected to use Johnston's line rank as lieutenant colonel of cavalry, thus making him the junior of the four men. A letter of protest written by Johnston in anger and a reply by Davis, written while ill, made the situation one which was never totally overcome by the two key men.[2]

Both gentlemen did make honest attempts to put their differences behind them, but Secretary of War Judah P. Benjamin, seemed to keep the rift alive with petty and sometimes unjust administrative complaints about Johnston. The general appealed to Davis to set the record straight, but his appeal fell on deaf ears. Fort Donelson had just fallen, and the President had bigger fish to fry. Benjamin was an old friend of Davis', and Davis cleared the complaints from his desk without any investigation. He simply went with Benjamin's allegations and censured Johnston. General Johnston was all the more angry because he knew the criticisms from Benjamin were unfounded.[3]

The rift had been exacerbated by the particular nature of Johnston's withdrawal of his army from its positions near Manassas, mentioned above. Although the withdrawal had been discussed at a cabinet meet some weeks before, Davis felt that he had made it clear to Johnston that he wanted to have a second discussion about the potential withdrawal before the final decision was made. Johnston, on the other hand, believed that he had been given authority to implement the movement of the army to positions south of the Rappahannock River when he felt the circumstances so dictated. In early March, Johnston moved the army south without informing Richmond, and maintained a communications blackout during the move. In Johnston's mind, operational security demanded no less. His experience was that the civilian leadership in Richmond could not keep a secret, and he dare not risk compromising his move. Davis regarded the sudden and unannounced withdrawal as willful disobedience of his directions to Johnston, poor management of the army, and, as mentioned previously, a waste of critical war materials.[4]

As if all the aforementioned problems between the two men weren't sufficient, they could not seem to agree on the strategic deployment of the Confederate army in the East. Johnston had a specific strategy in mind to deal with the threat of McClellan's invading army. He would not have moved the army down to Yorktown and withstood the siege. Instead, he would have robbed the commanders in North Carolina of sufficient troops to gather a large army in the vicinity of Richmond. There he would fight McClellan far enough inland to take the Federal gunboats out of the fight. This strategy depended in part on using the few troops already down near Yorktown to employ delaying tactics against McClellan until the main Confederate army could be assembled near Richmond.

Lee was opposed to Johnston's strategy. He favored contesting every foot of ground with McClellan, and weighed in with Davis on the issue. Davis ordered Johnston to conduct a foot-by-foot defense of the Peninsula, and left Johnston in nominal command of almost all of the forces in Virginia. Davis did allow Lee to call the shots for the Confederate troops operating in the Shenandoah Valley, the central part of the state, and in the vicinity of Norfolk.

This Lee did without consulting Johnston, which precipitated even worse relations between them. The Shenandoah Valley campaign was conducted by Stonewall Jackson, and was brilliantly successful. It had the effect of forcing Lincoln to withhold McDowell's I Corps, the largest in the Army of the Potomac, from McClellan's campaign on the Peninsula. The bottom line was that the Confederate high command was divided in preferred strategy and there was significant mistrust between the key players. Johnston went so far as to state that his authority didn't extend beyond those troops immediately around him.[5]

Davis had also come to feel that Johnston didn't run a very tight organization. As the army retreated closer to Richmond, Davis noticed stragglers roaming the streets of the capital. On one occasion, Davis rode out towards Mechanicsville to visit Johnston. Unable to find Johnston or his headquarters, he encountered Brigadier Generals Jeb Stuart and Howell Cobb. Neither could tell their President where Johnston's headquarters was situated, nor what enemy force was in their front. As it was, Davis had more tactical intelligence of that part of the front than the two brigadiers. Davis was concerned that his information indicated a Federal division, that of Franklin, was opposed only by Cobb's brigade and Stuart's cavalry. Davis had a real concern that Franklin would become aware of the thin defenses in his front and roll right into Richmond.[6]

Already of the opinion that Johnston was remiss in instilling discipline in his army, President Davis set out on May 29 to observe what he had been advised would be an assault on the left flank of McClellan's invading army. No one thought to inform the President that the operation had been cancelled due to intelligence that the Federals were stirring up along the Rappahannock. Another factor in the cancellation was the timidity of Gustavus W. Smith, who really didn't want to attack across Beaver Dam Creek, a natural defensive line. Davis encountered Howell Cobb and John Bell Hood. Cobb, commanding a Georgia brigade and Hood a Texas brigade, were forced to admit they had no idea of Johnston's plans. Davis returned to his office, his faith in Johnston's ability to lead the army yet further eroded.[7]

Despite the strains put by the war upon the friendship between Lee and Johnston, their views as to the proper strategy for the Confederacy began to slowly become more similar. Specifically, each man began to appreciate some of the other's ideas. Johnston began to see the value of Lee's operation under Jackson in the Shenandoah Valley, appreciative of the difficulty it made for Lincoln whenever he thought to reinforce McClellan. Lee had wisely begun the process of creating the huge army that Johnston had envisioned for the defense of Richmond. Lee had augmented Johnston's artillery by nine batteries, had converted fourteen companies of men from heavy artillery units to infantry, and had added seventeen companies of infantry from the remains of the Wise Legion. Lee also brought in the division of Major General Benjamin Huger, some 7,400 men, from Petersburg and Norfolk. There was also a newly organized division of 10,000 men, under A. P. Hill, moving south from Hanover Junction. Lee went so far as to cast about in North and South Carolina for brigades that could be spared, as well as gleaning some troops from the Richmond garrison. This added almost another 10,000 troops. By May 30, Johnston had 94,813 present for duty. McClellan could only manage to field 103, 382. This was as close to parity in size the Confederates had ever come thus far.[8]

Lee and Johnston were also moving closer in their view of appropriate operational strategy to be applied against McClellan. The two generals met with Davis on May 14 at Johnston's headquarters. The meeting took place on the bank of the Chickahominy, and the river and its swampy littorals were principal elements in the discussion. They agreed that there was a possibility that McClellan would elect to straddle the river with his army, and if that occurred, they would take advantage of the situation and offer battle. A few days after the meeting, McClellan provided the opportunity sought by the Confederate leadership by sending Heintzelman's III Corps and Keyes' IV Corps south of the river. The remaining three corps he deployed in a slight arc along the north bank. Although the President was likely impatient and frustrated, the two generals were now at last working well together. Lee kept channeling all the reinforcements he could find to Johnston, and Johnston kept watching McClellan's movements, waiting for the right moment to attack him.[9]

The ostensible purpose for Colonel Long's visit to Johnston's headquarters was to inform Johnston that Roswell Ripley's brigade, summoned by Lee from South Carolina, had reached Richmond and would shortly be joining Johnston's forces. Such a message, while important, could have easily been delivered by a courier of much lesser rank. In reality, Colonel Long was sent to Johnston to inform the general that General

Lee would be "glad to participate in the battle." Lee's message to Johnston was clear. He would not interfere with Johnston's exercise of command, but would assist him in any manner possible.[10]

Johnston and Lee had been friends for many years, and Johnston knew that Lee was a man of his word. He was likely not concerned about Lee participating as an observer and attempting to give commands to some of Johnston's troops. There was, however, the possibility that there would be another Confederate victory, such as the one at Manassas, and that the press would credit Lee rather than Johnston. After all, hadn't they given the lion's share of the credit for the great victory at Manassas to Beauregard? Johnston was reluctant to reject Lee's offer of help, and did not. Long rode back to Lee's office, arriving in the rain, satisfied that he had accomplished his mission. Johnston had revealed that the attack would take place the following day, but did not share the specifics of his battle plan. Long made note that "General Johnston expressed gratification at this message, and the hope that General Lee would ride out to the field, with the desire that he would send him all the reinforcements he could."[11]

The target of the Confederate attack on May 31 was that portion of McClellan's army seemingly isolated on the south side of the Chickahominy River. This force consisted of Keyes' IV Corps and Heintzelman's III Corps. Keyes' corps consisted of the divisions of Casey and Couch. Casey was positioned less than a mile west of Seven Pines, with Couch's division just east of Seven Pines. The place was little more than a road intersection, where the Nine Mile road met the Williamsburg road. It was named for seven large pine trees there.

Casey's division was composed of the brigades of Naglee, Wessells and Palmer. The regiments positioned to the west would be the first to make contact with the attacking Confederates.

Couch's division, just east of Seven Pines, was deployed near the Williamsburg road, and consisted of the brigades of Peck, Abercrombie and Devens. The regiments were all from New York, Pennsylvania and Massachusetts. These brigade commanders were key players on the Federal side of the battle and bore the brunt of the Confederate attack on May 31.

Casey, soon to be the focus of a vicious Confederate attack, was a frustrated and angry officer that morning. Casey had remained a brigadier general while officers junior to him were advanced to positions above the division commander level. Perhaps Casey's lack of political connections were the cause of his lackluster progress to that point. This unfortunate career situation was extremely frustrating to him.[12]

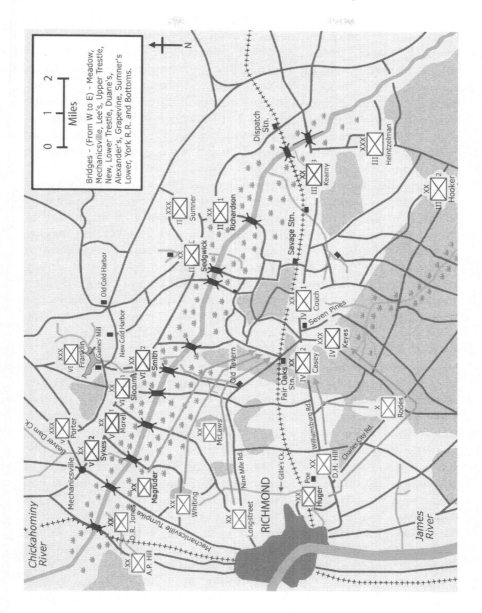

Map 11.1—Seven Pines, Johnston's Plan, May 31

In recent days, anger was generated as McClellan, through Keyes, the IV Corps commander, had formally asked Casey why his division was slowly losing strength. McClellan had used Casey's division as a training command. New recruits arrived in Washington, were shipped to Casey's division, trained, then transferred to other combat units. They were then replaced by more green troops. When McClellan was trying to field the large expedition to the Peninsula, he was essentially forced to create Casey's division and deployed them with the rest of the army, but they were the least experienced and least trained division in the Army of the Potomac. Some of Casey's soldiers had only been in Washington a few days when they were marched onto steamers for the Peninsula. Some had received their weapons on the docks. Casey was afforded no reasonable opportunity to weed out incompetent officers and ask for replacements.[13]

Casey had other problems. Upon arrival at Fort Monroe, he discovered that his supply trains had been left behind in Washington. The division marched to Yorktown, and assumed a daily regimen of attempting to master the drill manual, while hauling their own supplies and digging fortifications for McClellan's siege. By scrounging around, Casey managed to procure a few cast off wagons and horses to ease the problem of hauling supplies to his men. The fatigued and weakened men of Casey's division easily fell victim to sickness, mainly dysentery. To add insult to injury, one of his largest regiments, the 93rd New York, was transferred out of the corps. By May 22, his division, which had once numbered 10,000, was down to 3,577.[14]

Thus, the feelings of frustration and anger in Casey were fully justified in those last days of May. His feeling of isolation was physically as well as psychologically valid. Here was a severely weakened, under strength and poorly trained division, and the army commander chose to place it in a forward and exposed position where it would be attacked first by a Confederate army thought by McClellan to be larger than his own. The position Casey occupied was closest to Richmond, and his flanks were in the air. He had no cavalry support and his nearest infantry support was over a mile away. He was a sitting duck and he knew it. Why McClellan positioned Casey where he did cannot be explained.

Casey's division was not the only Federal unit in a less than excellent position. The deployment of the army as a whole was poor. There were three corps positioned along the north bank of the Chickahominy. Their right flank was behind Beaver Dam Creek, an excellent defensive feature with its high banks, and thus they were not easy to attack from their right. Porter's V Corps had the right end of the line, Franklin's VI Corps held the center, and Sumner's II Corps had the left end of the line, a little over two miles upstream from where the Richmond & York River Railroad crossed the Chickahominy. Just south of that crossing was Heintzelman's III Corps.

Incredibly, the remaining corps south of the river, IV Corps, was pushed forward almost three miles west of Heintzelman, their nearest support. That brings us back to the internal deployment of IV Corps. The two divisions were not positioned well for mutual support. For Casey, the bottom line was that a sufficiently powerful Confederate attack could easily turn either of his flanks or push him back into Couch's division. Couch would then have to try and stop the momentum of the Confederate attack while Casey's men retreated through Couch's lines.

Two other factors made the situation worse for the Federals. First, the Confederates would enjoy excellent roads to use as they moved forward from Richmond. Second, the lack of adequate bridges across the Chickahominy made support from Porter, Franklin or Sumner problematic. The difficulty of crossing that river depended on the quantity of recent rainfall. The Federal troop deployment could have hardly been worse.[15]

There had to be a reason why an army full of West Point generals would find itself in this position. The answer to the question is as strange as the need to ask it. There were several factors which had an effect on how McClellan operated on the Virginia Peninsula. They were: President Lincoln's involvement in the operational control of the Army of the Potomac, McClellan's view of correct strategy for the campaign, and the political turmoil within the Army of the Potomac.

Lincoln's personal involvement in the Peninsula Campaign stemmed from his near paranoia about a Confederate assault on Washington. Because he so feared that event, he placed limits on what McClellan could and could not do with the Army. This resulted in the Federal army moving north of the Chickahominy, placing themselves in a better position to cut off Lee if he moved a significant part of his army northward, closer to Washington.[16]

McClellan's view of correct strategy forced him to put the major portion of his army on the north side of the Chickahominy. Lincoln told McClellan at one point that when McDowell's large I Corps was finally released to McClellan's control, it would join him overland, keeping itself between Washington and the Confederates. He, therefore, had to extend his deployment to the northwest to facilitate a linkup with I Corps.[17]

The political turmoil within the Army of the Potomac is relatively easy to understand. McClellan had his favorites and others of which he had a low opinion, and made decisions based on those criteria.

As to which forces would be left south of the river, McClellan had been sadly disappointed by the failure of Heintzelman and Keyes to break the Confederate defenses at Yorktown, precipitating, in McClellan's mind, the need for a month-long siege. He acted to reduce the responsibility of the two lackluster generals by creating two provisional corps, V Corps under Porter and VI Corps under Franklin. These two officers were favorites of McClellan, and he wanted them positioned where he thought the hard fighting would take place. He deployed them north of the river, and left Keyes and Heintzelman on the south side in blocking positions.[18]

Johnston spent the late afternoon of May 30 examining his options for destroying the Federal IV Corps. He considered Casey's isolated position around Seven Pines, then studied his own deployment. The seven Confederate divisions were in an arc from just south of Beaver Dam Creek to Drewry's and Chaffin's Bluffs on the James River. (*See* map 0.1) The line was nearly continuous. He also had good options as to axis of attack. There were several roads leading east out of Richmond. The Williamsburg road ran east, right through Seven Pines. The Nine Mile road ran parallel, just two miles to the north, then veered southeast to Fair Oaks, a station on the Richmond and York River Railroad, then down to Seven Pines. By using these two roads, Johnston could easily mount a converging attack on Casey. There was another road that ran southeast from the capital, the Charles City road. It had potential as a way to move troops in a flanking movement around the Federal left.[19]

Johnston also had to consider which of his generals were to play key roles in the forthcoming battle. The army had been reorganized just two days prior into "wings," as Confederate law did not permit formal corps organization. Each wing had two divisions, with the Right Wing (11 brigades) under Longstreet, the Centre under Smith (9 brigades), and the Left Wing (6 brigades) under Magruder. There were also forces which were not part of any of the three wings. They were Huger's division, Stuart's cavalry brigade, Pendleton's artillery reserve, and various troops around Richmond.[20]

The new organization looked more tidy on paper than it was in reality. There was a real shift in power among the generals subordinate to Johnston, and there were a number of reasons that he made that shift take place. Smith was second in seniority to Johnston, with Longstreet next in line. Smith had moved up the pecking order simply by not moving around while others were transferred to other theaters.

Johnston did rely heavily upon Smith to help direct the army in Northern Virginia. The tactical situation was such that the Confederate forces had to be split into two large groups, and Smith commanded those nearer the Potomac. Johnston took the step of writing Davis and requesting that Smith's impending reassignment to Knoxville be cancelled.

There were problems, however, with Smith's health. This was a problem that could only grow in Johnston's mind. On three occasions earlier in 1862, Smith, who was supposedly suffering from an ill-defined neurological ailment, became bed-ridden just at the point when his leadership was most needed. On each occasion, Smith's inability to perform his duties had caused embarrassment to Johnston. The first was a conference in February with President Davis, which had to be postponed. The second was a debate in April over defending Yorktown. The third was Smith's illness during the retreat from Williamsburg.[21]

Smith had problems other than his health. He was unable to work well with John Magruder, and Magruder's promotion to command the Left Wing was likely Johnston's way of getting Magruder away from Smith, rather than any sanction against Smith. By creating the Left Wing, giving it to Magruder, and dividing the six brigades of Magruder's division into two small divisions, a position was also created for McLaws, who had just been promoted to major general. The other small division was given to David R. Jones. No one failed to notice what Johnston had engineered.[22]

The event which finally caused Johnston to lose confidence in Smith occurred on May 29. Smith was tasked to begin the battle by attacking the Federal right flank across Beaver Dam Creek. Smith did not initiate the attack, concerned that "it would be a bloody business." Smith had decided the objective wasn't worth the men it would cost. As it happened, this was the day of President Davis' second disappointing visit to Johnston's army that week.[23]

That evening, Johnston held a meeting of his wing commanders. Smith espoused a conservative approach and Longstreet objected. Later in the evening Johnston confided in Longstreet that Smith was the wrong officer for the task he had been given, and stated that his faith in Smith had dwindled.[24]

As Johnston's confidence in Smith diminished, he began to place more faith in Longstreet. Johnston considered Longstreet to be strong as an administrator and tactician, and, mistakenly thought he had performed well at the battle of Williamsburg. When Johnston finally arrived at Williamsburg that day, Longstreet had finally gotten the situation under control, and Johnston let him remain in tactical command. Johnston's subsequent report of the battle lavished praise on Longstreet. Smith's inaction at Beaver Dam Creek also pushed Johnston to rely more on Longstreet.[25]

On the afternoon of May 29, Johnston summoned Longstreet and showed him a report from D. H. Hill which claimed that the Federals were still at Seven Pines, and that their left flank was in the air. Johnston had sent a note back to Harvey Hill, in which he informed Hill that an attack would commence in the morning. The note also directed Hill to take orders from Longstreet.[26]

Longstreet noted that Smith was not present at the meeting, although he was second-in-command of the Army. His puzzlement went away when Johnston briefed the plan for the following day's battle. The plan called for putting the two "Left Wing" divisions in two different parts of the battlefield. A. P. Hill's division would remain across from Beaver Dam Creek. It would not attack, but simply observe the Federals there. Smith's division, under Whiting, would have only a supporting role. Smith was essentially without a role to play in the next day's fighting.

Johnston's idea was to mount a converging attack on Casey by using three brigades, about 10,000 men, of D. H. Hill's division on the Williamsburg road, augmented by Rodes' brigade, presently on the Charles City road. Longstreet likely suggested bringing Huger's division from Drewry's Bluff over to the Charles City road to free up Rodes' men. Longstreet knew from personal inspection that a small force of only a thousand men could defend Drewry's Bluff from Federal gunboats after Huger departed.[27]

With the addition of Rodes' brigade, D. H. Hill would surely have enough combat power to break Casey's lines, and Huger's division on the Charles City road could even be used in a flanking attack if necessary. Johnston instantly agreed to Longstreet's proposed solution.[28]

Johnston wanted to further strengthen D. H. Hill's attack, and to that end, they explored the possibilities. There were three other divisions tagged to participate in the battle, those of Longstreet, Whiting and McLaws. They were all encamped along the Nine Mile road or along the Chickahominy. There was a problem in using all of these troops in the attack, however. The terrain was not open enough for all of the fifteen brigades to move simultaneously. Shifting one division to the Williamsburg road would help the situation. Johnston knew Longstreet's division was the best choice. McLaws was presently involved in a covering position on the river, and would take too long to move to the Williamsburg road. It would possibly tip off the Federals that a major attack was imminent. If Whiting were sent, there was the danger that Smith would reclaim command of Whiting's division and take overall charge of the attack on the Williamsburg road.[29]

As the plan stood, the attack would begin with nine brigades on the Nine Mile road, ten on the Williamsburg road, and three more on the Charles City road. The glitch was in the logistics of moving a large number of troops before the next morning. Huger's three brigades would have to use a part of the Williamsburg road in their movement from Drewry's

Bluff to the Charles City road. Longstreet's six brigades would also need to use the Williamsburg road to move from their camps to the battlefield. The planned dawn attack meant that this sharing of a road between nine infantry brigades and their support would have to be managed in the dark. Johnston had no choice but to veto the plan in its current form.[30]

The next idea considered was to split Longstreet's division into two equal parts, with three brigades moving down the Nine Mile road and the other three down the Williamsburg road. While that would eliminate the road congestion problem, it begged the question as to which road Longstreet himself would actually travel. If Longstreet stayed on the Williamsburg road, the Nine Mile road force would be led by Smith, McLaws or Whiting. If Longstreet chose to stay on the Nine Mile road, D. H. Hill, a known aggressive fighter, but known to be impulsive, would be unsupervised on the Williamsburg road, opening the battle with seven brigades. Johnston and Longstreet remembered Harvey Hill's bloody charge on a battery at Williamsburg. They also felt seven brigades were more than Hill could manage in battle.[31]

Johnston had reached the point where he had to make a decision, and he chose a plan that seemed to him the simplest of the lot. The final plan called for Huger to make a night march down the Charles City road and relieve Rodes' brigade. Rodes would then begin his move northward and reunite with D. H. Hill's division on the Williamsburg road. Hill would know from Rodes that Huger was in place and protecting Hill's right flank. The attack could then begin. Hill was to fire signal cannon to communicate to Longstreet on the Nine Mile road that the fight was on. Johnston, aware of how aggressive Harvey Hill could be, put language into Hill's orders that limited his options for his attack. The language stated that "abatis and entrenched positions were ordered to be taken by a flank movement of the brigade or brigades in front of them."[32]

Upon hearing D. H. Hill's signal, Longstreet would attack with six brigades down the Nine Mile road. Longstreet would be supported by Chase Whiting. Johnston would remain near an old house where the Nine Mile road makes its turn to the southeast. He would monitor the battle from there, send reinforcements to Longstreet as necessary, and guard against Federal reinforcements crossing the Chickahominy to aid Keyes. Johnston had McLaws' division to use for the latter purpose.[33]

Johnston's last remaining important task was to coordinate the efforts of all his subordinate commanders. He went about this in a less than thorough and diligent manner. Longstreet had gotten his instructions from Johnston personally. Longstreet knew he was to supervise D. H. Hill, so Johnston sent no further word to Hill. Johnston sent brief notes to

Smith and Chase Whiting, simply stating that an attack on the enemy would take place in front of D. H. Hill. Johnston assumed that Smith would inform A. P. Hill.

For reasons which cannot be explained, Johnston appears to have failed to notify neither Magruder nor McLaws concerning the planned attack. While it is possible that he did so, Johnston's report makes no mention of any communication with those two generals.[34] Even worse, his orders to Huger were confusing and helped cause the plan to go awry.

This was Huger's first combat operation under Johnston. Unfortunately, the development of the battle plan, as described earlier, was less than ideal. Huger ended up with two important tasks. First, his relief of Rodes' brigade on the Charles City road was a precondition for the battle to begin. Second, his ability to move his division from the Charles City road to mount an attack on Keyes' left flank might become critical to a successful final outcome of the day's fighting.

Johnston did send two notes to Huger during the night. The first note never really said there was going to be a battle the following morning. Johnston simply stated that Hill's reports had led Johnston to conclude that there was considerable Federal force in Hill's front, and that it seemed necessary to match it. This he followed with orders for Huger to "concentrate the troops of your division on the Charles City road..." The last sentence alone mentions the possibility of fighting on the following day. He wrote, "Be ready, if an action should begin on your left, to fall upon the enemy's flank."[35] Despite the specific taskings given to Smith and Whiting, Johnston had given Huger an ambiguous message that was virtually impossible to clearly understand and act upon.

Later in the night, Johnston had become confused by his own communications. He could no longer recall what he'd sent to Huger, and couldn't locate a copy. He thus felt the need to send another note to Huger. It read:

> GENERAL: I fear that in my note of last evening, of which there is no copy, I was too positive on the subject of your attacking the enemy flank. It will, of course, be necessary for you to know what force is before you first. I hope to be able to have that ascertained for you by cavalry. As our main force will be on your left, it will be necessary for your progress to conform to that of General Hill. If you find no strong body in your front, it will be well to aid General Hill; but then a strong reserve should be retained to cover our right.[36]

This second note to Huger both cleared up some ambiguities and created more. It had to tell him that Johnston was in fact going to attack the Federals at Seven Pines the next day. It created more ambiguities, in that it did not tell him that he was to hurry over to the Charles City road, that he was to free up Rodes' brigade to rejoin D. H. Hill on the Williamsburg road, or that no attack could start until Rodes rejoined Hill. It also failed to mention anything about Longstreet's role in the plan. He also couldn't know from either message whether he would have any help finding his way to the right position on the Williamsburg road.

Huger was a man of plodding intellect, lacking in imagination. He was old, nearly deaf, and not well regarded by Johnston or Jeff Davis. As he had an artillerist background, he had been assigned to command the Norfolk area, and was tasked to recover the heavy artillery from the Gosport Navy Yard. He had not performed well in that assignment. Lee had taken part of his division for operations in northern Virginia, and Huger and the remaining three brigades were assigned to garrison Drewry's Bluff.[37]

Although Huger sincerely wanted his first combat experience as a commander to be noteworthy, his orders from Johnston were so nebulous as to make that outcome difficult. The old general didn't really have the intellect to make anything happen from such unclear tasking.

That night, Johnston was confident that the force of twenty-three brigades against the Federal IV and III Corps south of the Chickahominy would give him a decisive victory. McClellan's nearest safe haven was Fort Monroe, almost a hundred miles away. Seven Pines was planned to be just the start of the defeat and ultimate destruction of McClellan and his invading army.[38]

Unfortunately for Johnston, the success of his battle plan depended on the competent performance of several of his generals. As his successor, Lee would also discover that even relatively simple plans can be thwarted by one or two generals with a shortage of competency or a superabundance of ego or ambition. In the specific case of Johnston's plan for Seven Pines, there was a good amount of complexity. Huger had to promptly move up to the Charles City road and relieve Rodes, who then had to move smartly up to the Williamsburg road and rejoin D. H. Hill's division. D. H. Hill had to launch the attack on time, firing two signal guns to inform Longstreet and others on the Nine Mile road. Hill's signal guns had to be audible on the Nine Mile road. Lastly, the Chickahominy crossings had to be kept under observation, and any Federal attempt to cross more troops to the south side of the river had to be prevented or at least hotly contested. There were too many ways the plan could go awry.

The opening sentence of Johnston's late night second note to Huger reveals that perhaps he wasn't as confident as he later believed he was. Johnston had little confidence in Huger, almost none in Smith, and had some concern about the impetuosity of D. H. Hill. The general in which Johnston had almost total confidence was Longstreet. The commanding general was later to be keenly disappointed in his favorite.[39]

Longstreet was one of the more interesting personalities of the Civil War. Lee referred to him as his "warhorse." In the course of the war, Longstreet acquired a reputation as a tough general, always capable of maintaining a stiff defense and mounting a grinding, almost unstoppable offense. Many, however, came to believe that Longstreet wasn't suitable for independent command. He functioned best when serving under a talented leader such as Lee. Longstreet's post-war political conversion to the Republican party and subsequent criticism of Lee created a storm of controversy, and is beyond the scope of this work.[40]

Longstreet was also ambitious, much more so than he was later willing to admit. His claims that he sought only a commission as a paymaster are not believable. The facts were that he worked hard to secure a high post in the Confederate States Army, despite his protestations to the contrary.[41]

Longstreet moved up through the Confederate general officer seniority list through the natural attrition of generals during the winter of 1861–1862. By April of 1862, he had become Johnston's most trusted subordinate. Longstreet worked hard to earn that position. One evidence of his dedication was the fact that, after fever killed three of his children in the last few days of January, 1862, he took only enough leave to go to Richmond and bury them, then returned to his post.[42]

On his return to the field, Longstreet was a different person. His personal loss had made a major change in his personality and behavior. Where he had previously been the life of the party when time allowed it, engaging in poker games, and enjoying liquor and cigars, he gave all that up. Subsequent to his return, he was very moody, in an extended period of mourning. He even turned to religion for comfort, joining the Episcopal Church.[43]

Longstreet seemed to keep his own counsel, making the war his whole life. In reality, he also was keenly interested in his own advancement and taking care of selected subordinates. Longstreet wasn't the only ambitious officer in the war. They were all too common. The difference between Longstreet and many others was that he was a brave, competent and experienced combat leader, not a politician or lawyer who got involved in the war as an opportunity to further a previous career afterwards.

Rudolph J. Schroeder, III
Library of Congress

James Longstreet

In actuality, Longstreet was not a very talented politician. Early in the war, he wrote letters to politicians, attempting to get them to use their influence in specific situations, but had little skill in writing. His attempts to secure advancement for favorite subordinates, were not subtle and largely unsuccessful.[44]

Longstreet also had difficult dealing with his peers in a diplomatic manner. On one occasion in early April of 1862, when both Johnston and Smith were away from the army, Longstreet was left in temporary command. He sent a letter to Jackson out in the Shenandoah, suggesting Longstreet join Jackson with reinforcements adequate to strike a heavy blow and force a different course of action on the part of McClellan. Since Jackson did not desire to have Longstreet, his senior, present in the Valley district, Longstreet dropped the scheme. Were Longstreet's motives coming from a desire to prosecute the war, with no regard for personal glory, he could have sent reinforcements to Jackson under a more junior officer. Jackson was probably wise to respond in the manner he did.[45]

Longstreet was also blatant at times in blowing his own horn and audaciously recommending his own advancement. A couple of examples make the case quite easily. First, during the retreat from Yorktown, Johnston had put Longstreet in temporary command of his and D. H. Hill's divisions to fight a rear guard action at Williamsburg. Longstreet mismanaged the fight and the Confederates suffered about 1,500 casualties, much more than they should have. Johnston arrived near the end of the fight, when Longstreet finally had matters under control. Longstreet, in his report, described himself as "commanding Second Corps." This despite the fact that Confederate law did not acknowledge the existence of corps. The second and most outrageous example of Longstreet's attempts at self-promotion was his letter of May 9, 1862 to General Samuel Cooper, Adjutant and Inspector-General of the Confederate Army. In said letter, Longstreet suggested that Brigadier Generals Richard H. Anderson and A. P. Hill be promoted to the rank of major general immediately. Longstreet then audaciously suggest that his own large division be divided into two divisions of three brigades each. He then suggested that adding D. H. Hill's division would make him a true corps. Beyond this, he hinted that he could be promoted to the rank of general. There was no rank of lieutenant general at the time. Cooper, as appropriate, did not reply to the letter, but sent it to Lee. Always the gentleman, Lee let Longstreet's ungentlemanly behavior pass, and responded in writing that he appreciated the recommendations on Anderson and Hill, and reminded Longstreet that his proposal was not legal. It is worth a look at the civility and sensitivity to the egos of his subordinates exhibited by Lee in handling Longstreet's unreasonable request. The final paragraph of Lee's response read, "Whilst the President has every desire to comply with your wishes, he does not feel at liberty to go beyond the law which limits the number of appointments to those actually demanded by the service, and can only appoint general officers in proportion to what may be required by the number of troops."[46] Lee's subtle rebuff was likely still on James Longstreet's mind on the eve of the battle of Seven Pines.

The American Civil War had no shortage of political generals. While a good politician posing as a general is generally a useless individual and a hazard to his men, a competent fighting general who was a lousy politician, such as Longstreet, might be well accepted, had he no other character flaws. Unfortunately, Longstreet had a significant flaw. He had a marked tendency for deception. He was not hesitant to deceive his superiors in his constant effort toward self-advancement. More tragic was his tendency to deceive himself. He tended to remember events as he wished they had been, rather than how they had actually occurred. This did not first appear as a manifestation of advancing age, as reflected in post-war writings. It began as early as 1862. Although Longstreet's actions along this line at Gettysburg have been well documented, they occurred in the Peninsula Campaign as well.

An example from the Peninsula Campaign of Longstreet's flaw was the rear guard action at Williamsburg after the abandonment of the Yorktown line. Joseph Johnston had nothing but praise for Longstreet's performance, but only because he rode back to the rear and arrived at the battle area after the fighting was essentially complete. He assumed that Longstreet had managed the fight well, whereas he had not. Only the aggressive D. H. Hill had prevented a rout. Poor generalship on the Federal side also provided Longstreet a lot of help. There were few official reports of the engagement written in a timely manner, and Johnston took Longstreet's report as valid. D. H. Hill's report wasn't written until the following January. In fairness to Johnston, the Federal landing at Eltham's Landing was his primary concern at that time.[47]

This background brings us back to the evening of May 30, as Johnston and Longstreet were finishing up the planning for the battle of Seven Pines. Johnston made yet one more mistake that would come back to haunt him the next day. He unfortunately made an offhand remark that was interpreted by Longstreet as giving him a blank check in revising the next day's battle plan as he saw fit.

It was Johnston's leadership style to allow his subordinates sufficient latitude to exercise their judgment on the battlefield as circumstances dictated. In April, Johnston had left Ewell and Jackson on their own in Northern Virginia to decide when and where attacks were to be made. He understood that his generals on the field might have to make decisions when there wasn't time to consult headquarters. Although this was a common practice of commanding generals on both sides, it often resulted in unforeseen negative consequences. In the case of Seven Pines, it utterly negated Johnston's battle plan for May 31.[48]

Longstreet returned to his headquarters and began the last minute preparations for sending his division into battle. He ordered the men to cook rations, load their wagons and gave marching orders to the regiments. As he performed these mundane tasks, he began to think ahead about the results of the upcoming battle. Since the plan called for a converging attack, with Hill attacking from the Williamsburg road and Longstreet from the Nine Mile road, credit for the almost certain victory would likely be shared with Hill. Harvey Hill might even get the majority of the credit if the Federals in Hill's front broke first. Longstreet's ambition forced him to seek a way to come out the brilliant combat leader.

The only sure way to take major credit for the victory would be to move his division over to the Williamsburg road, assume overall command as the senior officer, and lead the combined force to victory. Longstreet knew the logistics of moving his division over to the other road would be difficult, but determined to do it any way. He began to rationalize, looking for military reasons for doing what his ambition required him to do.

Concepts such as a lack of unity of command, the insufficiency of Hill's command, and Hill's reputation for impetuous action likely came to his mind. Lastly, his ultimate rationalization was that the heavy rain was washing away the bridges across the Chickahominy, thus taking away the threat of reinforcements. If true, then the remaining troops near the river, those of McLaws and Whiting, would be able to handle the situation without Longstreet's division.[49]

Having convinced himself that what he was about to do was the militarily correct course of action, Longstreet sent a courier cross country to deliver a message to Hill. Harvey Hill stated, "I was directed by General Longstreet to move with my whole division at dawn on the Williamsburg road and to lead the attack on the Yankees."[50] Longstreet would follow Hill with his six-brigade division and would be in overall command. The plan was now what Longstreet's ambition required, and no longer resembled Johnston's final plan.

Rudolph J. Schroeder, III

Library of Congress

Thomas Jonathan Jackson

Longstreet's revised plan might have succeeded, as it was one option that had been seriously considered. Longstreet inadvertently made success impossible by neglecting to notify Johnston that he had completely changed the plan. Therefore, Johnston could not be of much help to Longstreet if the fighting did not go well.[51]

The battle of Seven Pines was supposed to begin at dawn on May 31. By then, Huger's division was supposed to have arrived on the Charles City road and relieved Rodes' brigade. Rodes should have then marched north and rejoined D. H. Hill's division on the Williamsburg road. Those actions being complete, Hill was to fire two signal shots to inform the troops on the Nine Mile road that he was initiating the day's fighting.

Hill's other three brigades, under Rains, Anderson and Garland waited impatiently in the trees alongside the road. The two cannon to be used for the signal were prepped and ready.

Dawn came and went, the sun rose higher, the fog burned away, but there was no sign of Rodes and his brigade. Harvey Hill took the logical step of sending couriers to find out what had happened to Rodes. It took until 9:00 A.M. simply to find out that Huger's division had not relieved Rodes on the Charles City road. Huger had not as yet turned onto the Charles City road. Hill also was told that there was a snarl on the Williamsburg road, a bit east of the Charles City turnoff. He decided to personally ride back there to see the situation for himself.[52]

Hill only had to ride as far as the Poe, house to see the cause of the delay. He was surprised and disturbed to see Longstreet's troops rather than Huger's. Hill had received Longstreet's late night message totally changing General Johnston's battle plan, but Hill expected Huger's men to use the road first, as their march was a precondition to the initiation of the battle. It made no sense whatsoever.[53]

The snarl was not caused solely by the troops and their generals. Mother Nature, as she often does, played an important role. The night had been punctuated by a series of extremely violent thunderstorms. Soldiers of both armies have commented on the storms, especially the lightning and the flooding resulting from the downpours.[54]

Johnston, in later years, maintained that this storm provided the best chance to destroy half of McClellan's army. The claim may not have been as far-fetched as it seems.[55] The effects on the Federal troops were terrible. The rifle pits they had labored so hard on quickly filled up with water. The sand and clay roads became slick and too muddy to support traffic. Creeks and streams overflowed their normal banks and minor bridges were swept away. Even substantial logs, put down to corduroy the road from Sumner's II Corps to the Chickahominy, started to loosen and move.[56]

This deluge greatly diminished the mobility of the Federals. For an army spread out and straddling a now wild little river, the ability to retreat or to concentrate troops in mutual support was much reduced. The effects on Johnston's army were, of course, similar. Rodes would have to cross White Oak Swamp, which was now four to five feet deep. The two roads, Williamsburg and Nine Mile, along which the attack was to be made, were now like jelly. The bridge across Gillie's Creek, required by both Huger and Longstreet, was gone. Despite the fact that Huger had his troops on the march at 3:00 A.M., Longstreet's division arrived at the washed out bridge first. Longstreet's men quickly improvised a bridge across the creek with a wagon and planking. This allowed them to cross dry, but they were required to cross single-file to do so. The 10,000 man division began to slowly cross. They could have saved a great deal of time by crossing four-abreast with cartridge boxes and haversacks slung on their muskets. Huger's lead brigade arrived as Longstreet's men were crossing.[57]

Huger was feeling a great deal of pressure at that point in time. His operation at Roanoke Island was a failure, and he knew he very much needed to do well in the forthcoming battle. Should he fail to get his division up to relieve Rodes, he might be stripped of his field command.

He asked directions to Longstreet's headquarters, went there and found Longstreet and also D. H. Hill. Huger and Longstreet, both hard of hearing, were likely conversing in shouts. Hill, the junior man, said little. Huger claimed the need to cross first, stating the need to get to Rodes quickly. Longstreet refused, probably not willing to admit that his revision of Johnston's plan caused the snarl at Gillie's Creek. Longstreet claimed to have orders from Johnston to command the right wing of the army. Huger asked to see the orders, but Longstreet replied that they had been verbal orders.

A further complication was that Lieutenant Robert Beckham of Johnston's staff had arrived before Huger and Hill and relayed Johnston's questions to Longstreet. Johnston wanted to know why Longstreet and his division weren't marching down the Nine Mile road, according to Johnston's plan. Johnston also wanted to know why Longstreet thought he had the authority to completely revise the commanding general's battle plan.

Longstreet did have some wiggle room in the situation. First, it is usually easy for a major general to intimidate a lieutenant. Longstreet assured the young staff officer that all was well and on plan. Beckham became confused and rode off before the other two generals arrived.[58]

Now Longstreet was feeling more pressure. He concluded that he had to initiate an attack very soon, before Johnston fully understood the situation and sent new orders. Since part of Longstreet's division was already across the creek, he ordered Huger to have his men move aside and wait until Longstreet was finished with the makeshift bridge.

Huger would not give up. He decided to determine the issue on date of rank. After concurring that their last two promotions were on the same dates, the contest came down to the dates of their original commissions. Longstreet succeeded in bluffing Huger, even though Huger was really the senior officer by a few days. Huger gave up the fight, rather than accuse Longstreet of dishonesty.[59]

It was "then possibly 10 A.M." After that time "Huger's movements were directed by Longstreet." Incredibly, Longstreet again changed the battle plan. By now it would have been hard for Johnston to recognize it. Longstreet's latest change divided up his large division into three forces and spread them across three axes of attack. Specifically, he sent Wilcox with his own plus Colston and Pryor's brigades down to the Charles City road to support Huger. Longstreet thought this would satisfy Huger, as it doubled his force. Longstreet then sent Richard Anderson, with his own plus James L. Kemper's brigade, along the Williamsburg road in support of D. H. Hill, the originally intended route for these troops. Lastly, Pickett's brigade was sent alone east along the Richmond and York River Railroad. This seemed to be an attempt, feeble though it was, to fill the gap between D. H. Hill's left flank, and the right flank of the troops on the Nine Mile road.[60]

Obviously, this major repositioning of large numbers of troops was immensely time-consuming. Strangely, a major effect was the dilution of what Longstreet had hoped to accomplish by moving his division down to the Williamsburg road. Keeping in mind the sham pulling of rank by Longstreet to cross Gillie's Creek first, what then happened was ironic. Huger's division, sitting along the road west of Gillie's Creek, watched while all six of Longstreet brigades crossed the makeshift bridge. After Longstreet's men were across, they took their turn sitting next to the road while Huger's division crossed and marched by on their way to the battle. They were then followed by the brigades of Wilcox, Colston and Pryor. Longstreet had succeeded in reducing the number of brigades which were to attack the Federals at Seven Pines to six of his brigades, down from thirteen.

Harvey Hill was becoming more impatient. Now he was informed that there would be a further delay in initiating the attack, and that he was only receiving two brigades of reinforcements, those of Richard Anderson and James L. Kemper. Hill rode back to his headquarters in disgust, and decided, in his characteristic fashion, to take action. He sent orders to Rodes to rejoin the division, not waiting for Huger to relieve him. Rodes put his brigade in motion immediately, but the rain-swollen swamp made the march slow and dangerous. Only the lead elements reached the Williamsburg road by 1:00 P.M.[61]

Although Hill had not been relieved by Longstreet of the requirement to have Huger in position prior to starting the battle, he could wait no longer. Hill began to put his men into line of battle. He positioned Garland's brigade north of the road. Garland's men were supported there by the brigade of G. B. Anderson.

On the south side of the road was Rodes' brigade. Rodes had only a few skirmishers present when the division went into battle formation.

Unreasonably, Hill expected Rodes' men to join the formation, regiment by regiment, as they emerged from the swamp. Rodes' brigade was supported by Rains.

The plan was for the two brigades to attack together south of the road. Just after 1:00 P.M., Hill fired his two signal guns. Without orders and seven hours late, the attack on Casey's division at Seven Pines was at last underway.[62]

In the Federal camps at Seven Pines, Casey's division was unaware of the impending attack. Many in this inexperienced division did not fully appreciate the vulnerability of their exposed position. They were more concerned about the problems visible all around them. They were covered in mud, their trenches were water-filled, and their makeshift commissary train had not arrived. They ate what cold food they could find. Adding to the misery of one regiment, the 101st Pennsylvania discovered their commander, Colonel Joseph H. Wilson, had died of disease in the night.[63]

Despite the fact that the men of Casey's division were wet, tired, hungry and in less than great spirits, they were ordered to work after their cold breakfast. Casey determined that they must construct field works sufficient to withstand a Confederate attack for 2–3 hours before they could expect help from other Federal troops. They had previously constructed a formidable abatis near Seven Pines. When they were repositioned forward the next day, Casey resolved to dig rifle pits and construct a redoubt as their first order of business. As the sun burned off the fog and began to dry the landscape a bit, the sound of axes in use could be heard west of the Federal camp. More trees were needed for another abatis.[64]

The Federals were building this second abatis on the eastern edge of a narrow woods, about 400 yards wide. Casey sent several companies of skirmishers to observe Confederate movements. The skirmishers moved to the western edge of the woods and attempted to look west across a field which was no longer in cultivation and was now covered in dense scrub growth. There were a few clear spots in the field, as well as a few scattered small trees. Unfortunately for the Federals, the combination of undergrowth and fog prevented observation of D. H. Hill's troops.[65]

Casey was beginning to suspect that he would be attacked very soon. He had reports of heavy traffic on the railroad. Although this had nothing to do with D. H. Hill preparing his brigades to assault Casey's camps, Casey accidentally reached the right prediction. Another piece of evidence, more perplexing than informative, was the capture of a Confederate staff officer, Lieutenant J. Barrol Washington, who carelessly rode into the lines of the 100th New York on the Nine Mile road. The capture was adroitly handled, and Washington was unable to destroy any of the papers he carried. Washington did not break down under questioning, but his mere presence made Casey more sure that an attack was imminent.[66]

A little before noon, Casey received final confirmation of the impending Confederate attack. A vidette rode back from the west edge of the woods with the word that he had observed through a glass, soldiers forming ranks and officers mounting up. The vidette had been sent by a Captain Townsend of the 85th Pennsylvania to tell Casey that the captain thought an attack was imminent.[67]

Casey concluded that Captain Townsend was correct, and took action to prepare to receive the attack. He ordered the 103rd Pennsylvania to abandon their work and move forward to reinforce the division's pickets. This one action would pay great dividends. For some unknown reason, Casey took some time in completing his next actions. About an hour later, he brought the rest of his regiments back from their fatigue duties and put them under arms and had the artillerists harness their horses. This he did after first reports of firing, and after D. H. Hill's two signal guns had been fired.[68]

The 103rd Pennsylvania was under the command of thirty-six year old Major Audley W. Gazzam, a former Pittsburg lawyer. He was the only field officer left available after the local diseases had taken their toll on the regiment. For the same reason, some of his companies were now commanded by lieutenants. The inexperience of the regiment's officers had a telling effect, especially in the opening minutes of the battle.

A simple description of the actions of the 103rd Pennsylvania in the first hour of the battle serves to demonstrate what inexperienced leadership can do to an infantry regiment in their first real combat. Company C was on picket duty when the attack began. It appears that the company commander was unaware that the remainder of the 103rd had also come up. Major Gazzam failed to reclaim Company F from their fatigue duties, and also left Company I in camp, rather than sending them forward as ordered by Casey. Possibly Gazzam didn't appreciate that a major attack was underway. He appeared to be allowing Company I to rest, as they were scheduled to assume picket duty next. Neither Company F nor I was ever able to rejoin the 103rd, but later fought with the 96th New York. Gazzam, now short two companies, moved forward with seven companies, reached the woods, and sent Companies B and G south of the road. The foliage was thickest there, and Gazzam promptly lost control of B and G companies. With only five companies left under his immediate command, Gazzam tried to form a line some fifty yards behind the picket line. With only 430 men to work with, Gazzam was understandably unsuccessful.[69]

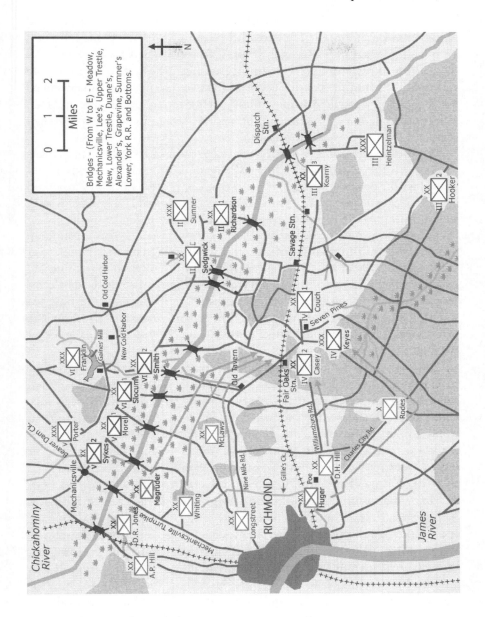

Map 11.2—Seven Pines, Actual, May 31

On the Confederate side, D. H. Hill had two brigades north of the Williamsburg Road. In the lead was the brigade of Samuel Garland, Jr., a brigadier with one week in grade. Garland's brigade had been reinforced for this battle, and he had under his command the 2nd Florida, the 2nd Mississippi Battalion, the 5th and 23rd North Carolina, and the 24th and 38th Virginia, about 2,065 men total. Garland pushed forward the 2nd Mississippi Battalion, 300 men strong, as skirmishers, directing them to stay out in front of the brigade some 150 yards or more. Garland advanced his five infantry regiments line abreast, trying to stretch his line as much as he could. He knew this left him no reserve, but Anderson was to follow him, and the risk should be manageable.[70]

Garland's advancing Confederates were soon observed by the pickets of the 85th Pennsylvania of Wessells' brigade. The pickets quickly noted that Garland was extending his line ever more northward, and attempted to outflank the Federals. The 85th's commander, Colonel Joshua B. Howell, sent a courier to the rear with this critical bit of intelligence.

The courier rode through the 103rd Pennsylvania as it was forming up in the trees. At just this moment, D. H. Hill's two signal cannon fired over their heads.[71] At Hill's signal shots, the 2nd Mississippi Battalion, led by Lieutenant Colonel John G. Taylor, started across the field, the troops wending their way through the underbrush. The Federals could now see the attacking troops, and opened on them with muskets. As casualties were taken, Taylor's men hesitated and the main body of the brigade began to catch them up.[72]

Inevitably, the few Federal skirmishers could not withstand the intensity of Garland's attack. Outnumbered ten to one, they were forced to fall back through the five company portion of Gazzam's 103rd Pennsylvania. Confusion reigned in the woods, then the Confederates arrived. Even worse for the Pennsylvanians, Federal artillery dropped rounds short of the advancing Mississippians, into Gazzam's position. Although no clear targets were yet visible to him, Gazzam ordered his men to open fire.[73]

In a matter of minutes, Garland's men were wrapping around both of Major Gazzam's flanks. Gazzam wisely ordered his men to fall back. Although his report puts this point in the fight in a better light, chaos was present in the woods. The regiment scattered in several directions. Even companies fragmented. As the fleeing Federals fought to cross back through their own abatis, the chaos became worse. Gazzam himself was unhorsed by a tree limb in the face and landed on a log, stunning him for a moment. He got to his feet and managed to retrieve his mount, but too late. His regiment as such was gone. Gazzam rode from the woods and soon determined that his men had scattered.[74]

Garland's troops found the terrain tougher to deal with than the poorly led and ill-prepared Federals. This changed, of course, when the attackers reached the abatis. The heavy rains had flooded part of the woods and created hip-deep mud in places. Wounded men were said to have sunk into the mud and drowned. The skirmishers were caught up by the five regiments, which were not really advancing in parallel lines. It was a less than orderly attack at that point in time.[75]

Now that they had driven the Federals from the woods, Garland's brigade began to tackle the abatis. It was a formidable obstacle, and Casey had devised a clever way of using it in defense. He positioned his men about 200 yards in the rear of the abatis, and had them direct their musket fire into it, even if they couldn't clearly see individual Confederate soldiers. When he first alerted the division to the impending attack, Casey looked for Henry Naglee, but couldn't find him. Naglee was on the extreme right flank, looking at the construction of defensive works.[76] In the absence of Naglee, Casey personally ordered the men into line of battle.

Casey was placing great reliance on Spratt's Battery H, 1st New York. Casey was expecting the battery to open fire any time. Spratt was ordered to target the Confederate artillery, as soon as it revealed itself by opening fire. Casey preferred this use of the battery to having it fire blindly into the abatis at Garland's infantry. Before long, Casey added the woods as an authorized target.[77]

Similar to D. H. Hill, Casey used the Williamsburg road as the boundary between brigades. From Palmer's brigade, Casey deployed the 92nd and 98th New York south of the road. Palmer's other two regiments, the 81st and 85th New York, were back about 200 yards, holding the rifle pits and division left flank. Naglee had one regiment south of the road, the 100th New York. Naglee's other four regiments were north of the road. In line with the battery were the 11th Maine and 104th Pennsylvania. The 52nd Pennsylvania was on picket on the Nine Mile road, and the 56th New York was positioned along the railroad towards the river. Casey's third brigade, commanded by Henry Wessells, had already lost the use of the 103rd Pennsylvania in the initial attack on the woods. His other three regiments, the 85th and 104th Pennsylvania and the 96th New York, were placed north of Palmer's brigade, and held the rifle pits there.

Casey had decided to spread out his artillery. He placed Battery A, 1st New York in the redoubt, the 7th New York Independent Light supported the right end of the rifle pits, and the 8th New York Independent Light was to the rear of the redoubt.[78]

Casey believed he was now ready to fight Hill's attacking division, but he had an unrecognized problem. In his deployment of his division, he had made a major mistake which would cost him in the next hour. He had deployed regiments in a manner to preclude his brigadiers from commanding their troops as brigades. Any counterattacks the Federals would initiate would be of regimental size. This was true of Palmer's and Naglee's brigades only. Wessells still had his command concentrated and intact, except for Gazzam's 103rd Pennsylvania, which had been scattered early on the fight for the woods.

On the Confederate side, Harvey Hill had his own problems. He had command and control problems, also. Garland hadn't lost a great number of men in the fight for the woods, but he had lost some key people. The colonel of the 5th North Carolina, Duncan McRae, had the assignment of keeping the brigade's right flank on the Williamsburg road. He had returned prematurely to his unit after a wound, and had to leave the field due to exhaustion. This occurred as the 5th was approaching the abatis near the Williamsburg road. Garland became aware that McRae had gone, and personally went to handle that part of the line. While Garland was busy on the right flank, the 23rd North Carolina mistakenly responded to voice commands given to the 38th Virginia and retreated unnecessarily. At almost the same instant, the only remaining field officer of the 24th Virginia, Major Richard Maury, was hit by a bullet, causing that large regiment to be temporarily in disarray. The ongoing problem of small parties of men from the 2nd Mississippi Battalion mixing in with the other regiments added to the confusion.[79]

Garland was just now realizing that his supports were not where they were supposed to be. G. B. Anderson's brigade was supposed to have followed Garland's men into the woods, but they weren't anywhere to be found. Garland was also concerned about his right flank. There, just across the Williamsburg road, Rodes' skirmishers were supposed to be keeping pace with Garland's brigade. Garland wanted to send a staff officer to Anderson and tell him to hurry, but no one was available to make the trip. Garland would just have to depend on Anderson's instincts as a professional soldier.[80]

Anderson showed the professionalism that Garland had expected. Anderson's brigade was assigned four infantry regiments, the 27th and 28th Georgia, the 4th North Carolina, and the 49th Virginia, about 1,865 men. For this operation, he had been reinforced by the Palmetto Sharpshooters and the 6th South Carolina. Both of the reinforcing units were under Colonel Micah Jenkins of South Carolina. As with all situations where a combat unit is reinforced just before a combat operation, some level of confusion results. So it was with Anderson's brigade. The swampy terrain and foggy morning were likely the reasons that Lieutenant Colonel Zachry's 27th Georgia became disoriented in the woods and inadvertently moved from the left to the right flank of the 49th Virginia. A fifteen minute pause in the advance north of the road was made to reorganize the Confederate attack.[81]

The pause was worthwhile, as it provided enough time for Rodes to advance on the south side of the Williamsburg road. Hill had fired the signal guns as Rodes' men were still coming out of the swamp. Only the 6th Alabama under Colonel John B. Gordon and the12th Mississippi under Colonel William H. Taylor were in proper position to begin the attack.

Rodes had already advised General Hill that it would take another 15–30 minutes to form his entire brigade. Rodes was a master of small unit tactics, and had a definite plan for his men. On the signal gun, he sent the 6th Alabama forward as a skirmish line, and the 12th Mississippi as the same, about 150 yards behind. He planned to sent the remaining regiments behind them as they exited the swamp. When all of the brigade was present, Rodes would have them reform in line of regiments abreast. This would have to be done in complete view of their Federal opponents.[82]

The plan for Rodes' brigade was chancy at best. The fact that Garland had cleared the Federals from the woods spared Rodes a lot of casualties. Before Hood's 6th Alabama, the two separated companies of Gazzam's 103rd Pennsylvania had pulled back. Gordon entered the woods and pressed immediately forward to the abatis. Gordon leaped his horse over part of the obstacle and urged the regiment forward. Despite his exposure to enemy fire, he was not hit.[83]

Coincidentally, the 6th Alabama rushed out of the trees south of the road just as Garland and Anderson's brigades finished their reorganization and resumed their advance north of the road. This gave a combined strength in excess of 5,000 men. Casey quickly realized he would be overlapped on his right flank. This was his intermediate line of defense, and it wouldn't hold more than a few more minutes. He needed to retrograde to his rifle pits and redoubt, where he planned to hold on until Keyes sent up help. Spratt's battery was a problem. It was vulnerable, and some number of minutes would be needed to harness Spratt's horses, hook up and pull the four guns out of harm's way. Casey really didn't want to abandon the guns. Just then, Naglee rode up and asked Casey for orders. Casey told him to counterattack with his three regiments, slow down the Confederate attack enough to save the guns. The counterattack was made more desperate because two of the regiments, the 11th Maine and the 104th Pennsylvania, did not have all their companies in line at that point.[84]

The 11th Maine was in the least prepared condition to launch a counterattack, having only three companies in line. Colonel William W. H. Davis of the 104th Pennsylvania led them in the attack.

The 100th New York, with all companies in line, charged under the leadership of Colonel James M. Brown. The unexpectedness of this charge of less than a thousand men caught the Confederates by surprise.[85]

In 1863, Casey told a congressional committee that "I never saw a handsomer thing in my life than that charge was." The 4th North Carolina, which received much of the fury of Naglee's counterattack, described it as "fearful" and as plowing up the ground and tearing up the foliage. There was an irony about the counterattack, in that, although launched by Casey to buy time for the extraction of Spratt's battery, it had the unfavorable result of destroying much of the protective abatis. For a few minutes, though it must have seemed to the soldiers as much longer, both sides stood without cover and fired continuously.[86]

Spratt's Federal battery was already in trouble. Both Spratt and his first lieutenant were wounded, and the battery was now being commanded by Second Lieutenant C. E. Mink. He was able to bring off three of the guns, but the infantry paid heavily to save them. Colonel James M. Brown, commander of the 100th New York, was killed. Ironically, he had earlier confided to his major that he thought the counterattack idiotic. The 85th Pennsylvania was hit hard, losing all their field officers. G. B. Anderson, unwilling to continue trading musket fire with the Federals at close range with no cover, ordered a charge. The fighting then became hand-to-hand, with bayonets and clubbed muskets the weapons of choice. Naglee's men, after their casualties reached the fifty percent mark, finally broke. Although a few of them reformed in the rear of the rifle pits, most of the brigade was lost to the battle for the day.[87]

Casey was now down to nine regiments, having essentially lost four. The two regiments of Wessells' brigade pulled back with few casualties. This left Casey with seven regiments and three batteries in fighting condition on the main line of defense. He felt he could hold in place against a frontal attack, but had no help for his flanks. To stay and fight was futile in the long run, unless Keyes sent him Couch's division as reinforcements. Casey hadn't received any communication from Keyes since the fighting began an hour ago. Casey was beginning to wonder if his division had been deserted.[88]

General Keyes, commander of IV Corps, knew the battle was beginning when Confederate Lieutenant Washington of Johnston's staff was captured. Escorted to Keyes' headquarters, Washington provided little intelligence to Keyes. The captive was even cool enough to claim his identity to be "Lieutenant B. C. Chetwood."⁸⁹ Confident that "Chetwood" was a waste of his time, Keyes left for the front.⁹⁰

Keyes had more in common with his Confederate adversary, James Longstreet, than he knew. Both men felt they were deserving of promotion, that the impending battle would be a catalyst for such advancement, and both were ambitious enough to let their personal desires distort their military judgment. This impaired judgment resulted in mistakes by Keyes that could have destroyed his corps.

Keyes had a good, but not special, record in the pre-war army. He was a colonel when hostilities began, and advanced to brigade command prior to Bull Run. He then replaced his division commander, when that officer was transferred to the West. When Lincoln decided to create corps, Keyes was a senior division commander, and was selected to command IV Corps.

Keyes was from New England and a Lincoln supporter. Though he didn't believe Lincoln to be a radical abolitionist, Keyes did believe that Lincoln's election would lead to war. Keyes personally would not qualify as an abolitionist, as he had once purchased a female slave for $350 as a cook for his wife.⁹¹

Keyes believed that a number of entities were to blame for his career not being further along than it was. He believed that his performance at Bull Run deserved better press than it had received. His contemporaries also failed to appreciate him. He also believed that McClellan disliked him and had definitely opposed appointment of Keyes as a corps commander. McClellan was accused of slighting Keyes, failing to ask his opinion when appropriate, even excluding him from meetings. At Yorktown, Keyes claimed McClellan gave orders directly to a IV Corps division commander.⁹² Due to all of his beliefs described above, Keyes came to the conclusion that it was no accident his corps was deployed south of the Chickahominy River. No, it was a conscious effort by McClellan to destroy Keyes' career.

All this emotional baggage, this delusion and pouting, led Keyes to where he was right now, on the way to fight the battle of Seven Pines, determined to do it in such a manner as to share the glory with no one, neither superior nor subordinate. This decision, born of personal ambition, caused Keyes to make his first tactical mistake, the failure to communicate with subordinates and superiors alike during combat. Specifically, he ordered troops around the battlefield without telling their commanders why and what for. He also kept his plans from his superior, George McClellan.⁹³

As to Casey's concern that Keyes and others had forgotten and/or abandoned him, appearances were deceiving. The fact was that Keyes was trying to help Casey, but his attempts thus far were inept at best. Keyes divided Couch's division, his corps reserve, into several smaller formations. He did worse, he assembled groups of regiments across brigade lines, destroying effective command and control. To top off the day's fiasco, Keyes sent the fragmented division into the fight without informing Casey that help was on the way.

Keyes had, in fact, sent Peck's brigade of Couch's division to reinforce Casey on his extreme left flank. Peck commanded a brigade of five regiments and a section of guns, some 2,000 men. He sent out several probes in all directions, but were never able to link up with Casey. Sadly, no one ever informed Casey that Peck was out there. Throughout the fight, Casey believed his left flank was vulnerable.[94]

The 93rd Pennsylvania of Peck's brigade, was ordered out front of the brigade, effectively taking it from Peck's command. Just about the time of Naglee's counterattack, Keyes took the 55th New York, sent it across the rear of Casey's division, and put it in support of the artillery battery placed on the right of the rifle pits. Keyes then personally led the 62nd New York from Peck's brigade to the far right flank of the corps, near the intersection with the Nine Mile road. There the 62nd joined three regiments from Abercrombie's brigade (67th New York, 61st and 93rd Pennsylvania), as well as the 7th Massachusetts of Devens' brigade. Keyes put Couch in command of this force.[95]

Keyes had committed the same sins as Casey. He had destroyed the command and control structure of Couch's division by scattering Couch's regiments willy-nilly across the battlefield, and he had communicated almost not at all. Although Keyes later claimed that he had sent Casey all the reinforcements he could spare, eight of Couch's fourteen infantry regiments, he had not adequately reinforced Casey.[96] General Casey wasn't aware of the locations of the reinforcements, and therefore couldn't integrate them into his defense. Peck was now far on the left of the corps with only two regiments left. Only five regiments held Couch's main defensive line, two of Abercrombie's and three of Devens'.

On the Confederate side, Harvey Hill was making ready to assault Keyes' main line of defense. He had the advantage of better tactical intelligence than had Keyes. Hill knew more about the positions of Federal troops on their corps flanks than did Casey. Hill wisely extended his line of battle to reach both Couch on the Federal right and Peck on the Federal left. At the same time, Hill would attack the rifle pits in the center of the Federal line. The Federal left under Peck was covered by the brigade of Gabriel Rains, as yet uncommitted. The Federal right under Couch was met by Richard Anderson and two regiments under Micah Jenkins. Jenkins was ordered to move east, paralleling the movements of Garland and G. B. Anderson in the center. This allowed them to meet Couch's five regiments head on.[97] Although Casey was unaware of it, the time taken by Hill to position his forces on the flanks, provided a brief respite for Casey's men in the center subsequent to Naglee's repulse.

On the far Federal left, the 93rd Pennsylvania, under Colonel James M. McCarter, slogged through the wet terrain to its assigned position. No sooner had it arrived than Rains' Confederate brigade of four regiments arrived in the 93rd's front. Both commanders gave the order to open fire at the same time and there followed an intense fifteen minute period of musketry. Rains later stated that it was the most prolonged and continuous volley he had experienced thus far in the war. Close to a hundred of Rains' men broke, but Rains personally rallied them. The Federal fire was so effective that some Confederates laid down, let the minie balls pass over them and fired from a kneeling position.

Though the Federals put up a stout fight, they were outnumbered severely, and McCarter, having had his mount killed under him, ordered the regiment to pull back in stages. This had the effect of allowing Rains to turn left and attack Casey's rifle pits from the left rear.[98]

On the north end of the battlefield, Jenkins and Couch skirmished for a brief twenty minutes. Although reports are less than definitive, it seems likely that Jenkins' two regiments made contact with the 23rd Pennsylvania. The 23rd's commander, Colonel Thomas H. Neill, stated that he had to retire in order to avoid losing his colors and having many of his men captured. Jenkins praised the stubbornness of the Federal defense, but turned right to attack the north end of Casey's defenses. This suggests that Jenkins was little worried about Neill's battered regiment attacking his flank.[99]

The net effect of the attempt by Casey to extend his line to match the Confederates was a true disaster. He had sent five regiments to the north end of the line, but only one was able to engage the attacking Confederates. On the south end, only one regiment of four got into the fight. Both of these Federal regiments were easily driven out of the way, and the forces of Jenkins on the north and Rains on the south were able to attack Casey's center at the rifle pits from both flanks. The Federals didn't even retreat in an effective manner, but scattered, taking themselves out of the fight.

Casey was now left to defend the rifle pits with the remainder of his division. He had only six regiments and three batteries to work with, and his troop placements were also poor. The linchpin of Casey's defensive arrangement was a redoubt in the center of his line. It was manned by Company A, 1st New York Artillery. The battery employed six twelve-pounder Napoleons and was commanded by Major Guilford D. Bailey. Bailey, a West pointer and experienced artillerist, and was highly regarded by Porter Alexander. The battery had a clear field of fire.[100]

Casey had only two other batteries, the 7th New York Independent Light under Captain Peter C. Regan and the 8th New York Independent Light under Captain Butler Fitch. They were poorly placed. The 7th had been placed at the north end of the line of rifle pits, but behind the main line of infantry regiments. It, therefore, could not fire to the west without firing over the heads of its own infantry supports. The 8th set up directly behind the redoubt, again having no clear field of fire. Neither battery could effectively assist in the defense of the rifle pits. They could only be used in a rear guard action if the pits fell. Whomever placed the artillery for Casey had effectively cut his artillery support by two-thirds.[101]

The Federal infantry had no difficulty understanding that all was not well. After a stormy night of no sleep, little or no breakfast for some of them, witnessing the fighting earlier in the day, and looking around at their immediate situation, they observed the rout of the skirmish line, the repulse of Naglee's counterattack, and the loss of part of Spratt's battery. They hoped to soon be able to fight the Confederates themselves.

They had enjoyed the respite while Harvey Hill had sent Rains and Jenkins to clear the woods on his flanks of significant opposition. Next, Hill's full weight would fall upon the defenders of the rifle pits. Now the green troops of Casey's center waited for their comrades to retreat through their lines to clear their field of fire.

Casey had some problems with the placement of his infantry, not just his artillery. With the redoubt in the line, he had four regiments to the south of it and only two, the 85th and 101st Pennsylvania to the north. Of these two, only part of the 85th was south of the Williamsburg road. To add to the command and control problem, Casey had mixed in regiments of Palmer's and Wessell's brigades. This had the effect of causing officers not to know where to find their immediate superiors when they needed to.

Harvey Hill's plan of attack would be relatively simple. South of the road, Rodes' large brigade would lead, and on the north side, it would be the brigades of Garland and G. B. Anderson. The problem Hill had was that it was already 3:00 P.M., and his troops were getting tired and had lost many men in the woods and crossing the abatis. Their spirits, however, were extremely high. They had driven the Federals from the woods, taken their abatis, and wanted very much to finish the job. Hill added a little insurance by having five guns of Captain Thomas H. Carter's King William (Virginia) Artillery brought forward to provide direct artillery support.[102]

With Hill's attack plan set and Casey's defensive alignment in place, the only major variable left was the tactics to be employed. In this area, the Confederates came up with the superior choice. Colonel Bailey ordered his batteries to target advancing infantrymen, while Carter had his guns pointed toward the Federal artillery. Bailey opened fire, caused some casualties among Confederate infantrymen, and was shortly silenced by Carter's guns. By the time Bailey understood his mistake, he knew it was time to get out of harm's way. He ordered his guns out, but his artillery horses were already taken out by the Confederate fire. He ordered his guns spiked, and was killed by a musket ball in the process of spiking them. At this point, the redoubt was no longer firing, and the 8th New York Independent Light, set up directly in the rear of the redoubt, opened fire. This resulted in several Federal soldiers killed and wounded by friendly fire. Nothing could have had a worse effect on morale.[103]

The view from the rifle pits was one of a target-rich environment. The Confederates came on 8–10 ranks deep, taking casualties, but still coming, relentlessly. The Federal troops in the rifle pits knew how the contact had to end.[104] The Federals were exacting a heavy price, however. The 4th North Carolina closed to 50–60 yards of the rifle pits, and was sustaining heavy casualties. They took temporary cover behind a rail fence, and waited for Rodes' men on their right flank to catch up. All of them knew they couldn't endure the Federal fire much longer. Their lieutenant caught sight of the last field officer in the regiment, Major Bryan Grimes, sitting on his horse.[105]

Grimes was likely trying to figure out his next move. This was his first real battle, and his background was as a lawyer, not a soldier. Just then, an adjutant came up and suggested that the regiment couldn't survive the current situation, and further suggested that they charge the works. Grimes readily assent and shouted, "Charge them! Charge them!"[106]

As the 4th North Carolina charged the rifle pits, the Federal defenders were already breaking. On the north end of the redoubt, the 85th Pennsylvania decided to retreat when they saw the artillerists spiking their cannon. The 85th needed no further motivation to leave.[107] South of the redoubt, the 85th New York, had already been hit by friendly fire, and witnessed the commander of the 92nd New York, on their flank, shot from his horse, falling wounded to the ground. Palmer rightly concluded that Rodes' brigade would not be stopped, and he heard firing on his left flank and his rear. He rode quickly to find Casey, hoping to receive clear orders.

Palmer found his corps commander before his division commander. Keyes was busy guiding the 10th Massachusetts to a new position across the field. Palmer pleaded for reinforcements, but Keyes responded that he was forming a new defensive line to the rear. As Palmer hurried back to his command, he realized that Keyes had written off Casey's entire division, and that the rifle pits had been taken even more quickly than the abatis.[108]

The Confederates were now in possession of the rifle pits, but had paid a heavy price, despite Casey's less than adroit positioning of his forces. Hill's division was showing the effect of the Federal fire they had weathered. The lead regiment, the 4th North Carolina, was diminished, tired and spooky. They even abandoned the redoubt and the captured artillery momentarily, spooked by unidentifiable noises and unable to see through the smoke.[109] Rodes, normally an aggressive brigade commander, became convinced that Casey's division would mount a counterattack, and decided not to pursue immediately. Instead, he waited for Carter to bring his guns forward. Fortunately for the Confederates, D. H. Hill rode up with the first of Carter's guns, and reassured Rodes.[110]

The only threat of a counterattack was not from Casey himself, but from Colonel Joshua B. Howell, commander of the 85th Pennsylvania of Wessells' brigade. Although his men would not stay in the rifle pits to meet the Confederate charge, despite their colonel's cool demeanor, Howell was able to reform the majority of them in the second abatis. Gathering up a few men here and there from other regiments, he marched the party of only a few hundred soldiers toward the front, between Casey's and Couch's lines. They engaged Rodes' advancing skirmishers briefly, until ordered to withdraw by a staff officer with less audacity and more common sense.[111] Howell's insane little attempt at a counterattack had only one real effect. It led Hill and Rodes to consider whether or not there was still some fight left in Casey's division. Hill paused to assess their strength before resuming their advance. There was still Couch's division to deal with.[112]

To this point in time, the battle of Seven Pines had only involved a single division from each army. They had slugged it out half the afternoon with Hill's Confederates severely defeating Casey's green, poorly led regiments. Neither division commander had received any effective help from his immediate superior, and the commanding generals had little current knowledge of where the battle stood.

On the Confederate side, Longstreet had only provided the brigade of Richard Anderson and Dearing's Latham (Virginia) Battery. Longstreet certainly had enough troops to spare. Besides his own remaining five brigades, he controlled Huger's division of three brigades. Longstreet, whose primary objective for the battle was to advance his own reputation, was mysteriously cautious. He wasted the day for most of his troops by marching them between the Williamsburg and Charles City roads, and he was hardly seen on the battlefield.[113]

Keyes, Casey's immediate superior, tried a lot harder than Longstreet to aid his division in the fight, but was not effective. Keyes failed to employ his divisions as divisions, and was non-communicative throughout the day. He employed Couch's division piece-meal, while Casey's was being decimated, and failed to even tell Casey where his reinforcements were. Keyes also failed to inform his immediate superior, III Corps commander Samuel Heintzelman, of the situation. Heintzelman heard the sounds of combat as early as 1:00 PM, but never received a message from Keyes.[114]

Heintzelman impressed several important people as an excessively cautious officer. One writer described him as "one of the failures" of the U. S. Army's seniority system. Others credited Heintzelman with bravery, experience and devotion to duty, but lacking in initiative and imagination. He was widely thought to lack the leadership skills required of a corps commander.[115] Examination of Heintzelman's total war record, from Bull Run through Malvern Hill supports the opinions expressed above. Heintzelman probably didn't need much initiative or imagination to do his duty at Seven Pines. The courage and the common sense expected of all officers, regardless of rank, should have sufficed. He did not exhibit those traits on May 31, 1862.

Although Heintzelman heard gunfire about 1:00 PM, he squandered an hour, waiting for a message from Keyes. That message never came, so Heintzelman sent two aides to see whether that faint sound of musket fire was a mere skirmish or something more significant. By 2:00 PM, the aides had not yet returned, but a message arrived from a lieutenant on Keyes' staff, one Oswald Jackson, that conveyed that the enemy was pressing them hard, and asked for two brigades of reinforcements, if the troops could be spared. The message hardly reflected the beating that Hill's division was giving to Casey. The lieutenant even made the error of representing the axis of attack as being along the Richmond and York River railroad, rather than the Williamsburg road.[116]

Heintzelman, through his innate cautious nature and unhappiness over Casey's weak division being placed in the most exposed position in the army, had prepared two of Kearny's brigades and, with McClellan's assent, sent them forward to the vicinity of Savage Station. Nevertheless, Heintzelman was not prepared to give up these two brigades on the basis

Seven Days Before Richmond

of a message from a lieutenant of Keyes' staff. Instead, the cautious general sent a message to Kearny, that ordered Kearny to move one brigade toward the railroad. Heintzelman's next order brought the remainder of his corps close at hand. A third message went to General Sumner, the II Corps commander, presently on the opposite bank of the swollen Chickahominy.[117]

Finally, a senior Federal general was putting together a coordinated attempt to respond to D. H. Hill's assault. Heintzelman, cautious but by the book, was planning to employ his corps by divisions. He had the advantage of two of the best division commanders in the Federal army, Joseph Hooker and Philip Kearny. It is arguable whether these orders by Heintzelman or Sumner's later actions deserve the major credit for saving the left wing of McClellan's army.

Finally, Heintzelman's two staff officers returned from their mission. They had finally located Keyes, who had told them that his front line, Casey's division, had been driven in. Heintzelman hardly needed this report, as he could see the stragglers from the abatis passing by his headquarters. Heintzelman mounted up and rode for the front.[118]

Heintzelman's orders issued before he rode forward from his headquarters were sound, but events didn't follow them exactly. The first order called for Kearny to send a brigade toward the railroad. Kearny selected Birney's brigade, which didn't receive their orders until almost 3:00 PM. By that time, Casey had been driven back on his rifle pits. Birney got his men on the march in a matter of minutes, but Kearny rode up just then and ordered Birney to reverse march to the Williamsburg road and help man the rifle pits recently thrown up just northeast of Seven Pines.[119]

Kearny personally positioned Birney's brigade in the new rifle pits, which were likely the old rifle pits that Casey had used two days ago. Kearny then had second thoughts and moved two of his regiments, the 3rd Maine and the 38th New York, toward the railroad. Birney queried Kearny about the repositioning and Kearny again repositioned the brigade, moving all his men but a line of skirmishers back from the railroad. At last, Kearny was pleased with Birney's position, now on the right flank of Couch's division, where the brigade suffered very few casualties the rest of the afternoon. Heintzelman considered them "not engaged" for his report.[120]

Birney continued to receive orders throughout the afternoon. They came from Kearny, as he interpreted the concept given him by Heintzelman at 2:00 PM. Unfortunately for the Federals, Kearny did a poor job of implementing the corps commander's concept for defense. Kearny never should have ordered Birney to reverse march. Had Birney continued on his way, he would have been able to support Couch's makeshift brigade on Casey' far right. This would have given the Federals seven or eight regiments equivalent. While that force could not have held out against the Confederates indefinitely, it likely would have bought sufficient time to reinforce Casey at the rifle pits, before the full weight of the Confederate assault arrived.

An oddity of the Federal III Corps was the combination of a cautious corps commander and two aggressive division commanders. A point they had in common was that all three generals were not liked by McClellan. This is the most probable explanation for their placement at the rear of the army, while McClellan always seemed to lead with his favorite, Fitz John Porter.[121]

"Little Phil" Kearny was a combat-experienced officer, who was not above bragging about his military accomplishments.[122] Kearny had the right instincts to be a combat leader. He was a brave, hard-charging officer who led from the front, sometimes to the criticism of his superiors. What he lacked was the ability to convince his superiors that he had the temperament to be a leader of a large command. He also had a problem keeping his opinions to himself. McClellan and Kearny shared a mutual disrespect for each other.[123]

Hooker's story was somewhat different. He was also brave and aggressive, but did have political skills. Unfortunately, he had trouble getting along with almost everyone, and his political scheming usually hurt his career. Hooker could not stand the sight of McClellan. The only reason he commanded a division was political patronage. His guardian angel was Treasury Secretary Salmon P. Chase.[124] Despite all of his personality shortcomings, the aggressive Hooker was valuable enough as a combat leader to be given a division to command. Upon receiving Heintzelman's orders around 3:00 PM, Hooker instantly put his brigades in column and marched toward Seven Pines.[125]

Hooker's lead brigade was under the command of Colonel Samuel H. Starr of the 5th New Jersey. The regular brigadier was Francis Patterson, who was ill. The brigade was short two regiments, as the 7th and 8th New Jersey had been detailed to cover Chickahominy crossings. Thus, Starr had only the 5th and 6th New Jersey to call a brigade and lead the division into the fight.[126]

The traffic past Keyes' headquarters from the division of Silas Casey was now getting heavy. Reports indicate that remnants of infantry regiments, wagons, and artillery pieces were all racing for the rear. Starr ordered the fugitives out of the way of his regiment, but in their panic, they ignored him. Starr was tasked to lead Hooker's division to the front, and Starr's brigade commander, Francis Patterson was watching him close by. Starr drew his saber, ordered his men to fix bayonets, and waded into the fleeing mob. He was able to part the mob somewhat, and Hooker approved. However, the lead element of the division never reached the battlefield until sundown. The fighting at that location was finished by then.[127]

Despite the fact that Heintzelman's orders to III Corps were adequate to put his six brigades into the fight, only two of them made it to the battlefield in time. Kearny's orders to Birney essentially took Birney out of the equation, and Hooker's three brigades were victims of the road being clogged by refugees from Casey's division. The forces that were left to the Federals were Kearny's other two brigades, under Jameson and Berry. These two brigades were joined by the troops of Couch's division under command of Abercrombie and Devens.

These troops had not yet become engaged. Heintzelman was less than totally aware of the tactical situation. After 3:00 P.M., he found Keyes between Casey's and Couch's lines, such as they were. Keyes made Heintzelman fully aware of what a disaster the afternoon had been. Yet as bad as things seemed to the two Federal generals, neither at that point knew that Casey's position at the rifle pits was being turned on both flanks.

Heintzelman assumed personal command and allowed Keyes to resume his task of positioning individual regiments. Both Keyes and Heintzelman noticed a lull in the fighting around 4:00 P.M. Although neither general knew why, it was because Howell's feeble counterattack had caused Hill's men to pause and regroup. Heintzelman prudently tried to make good use of the lull. He was sure that Abercrombie and Devens couldn't hold their positions for long unaided, so he took steps to reinforce them. Heintzelman believed that Birney was already on his way, although he wasn't, and ordered Kearny to bring forward another brigade from Savage Station right away, and hurry up his third brigade from the camp near the Chickahominy. Couch had been ordered off to another location on the field, so now Heintzelman assumed the duties of a division commander.[128]

On the Confederate side, Hill's division was just about out of momentum. They had shattered Casey's division in three successful attacks, but had suffered heavy losses. Garland's and G. B. Anderson's brigades reported over 40% casualties. Both brigades had to be put into the reserve until they could be reorganized.[129] Longstreet, on Hill's left, had two regiments of Richard Anderson's brigade, which had also suffered casualties, but were better off.

Hill had only the brigades of Rodes and Rains, as well as Carter's battery. About 4:00 PM, Longstreet reinforced them with Dearing's battery. At last, Longstreet elected to reinforce D. H. Hill with three brigades, those of Colston, Kemper and Wilcox, under overall command of Wilcox. Unfortunately for the Confederates, these three brigades were over on the Charles City road, behind Huger's division. Wilcox had for hours heard the fight in the distance to his left front. After receiving written orders from Longstreet to march his three brigades over to the Williamsburg road, he found the task more difficult than envisioned. He later explained that the terrain between the two roads was low and flooded. In places, his men waded through waist deep flooding. It was 5:00 P.M. when Wilcox's first brigade reached the Williamsburg road. Longstreet personally hustled each regiment down the road to Harvey Hill. The net effect of the movement was that, of three brigades, only three companies of the 11th Alabama saw any combat that afternoon. The similarity to what happened to Hooker's troops is amazing. Six brigades, three of each army, failed to affect the outcome of the day's battle.[130]

The key question concerning this point in the fight is the remaining combat power of Rodes' and Rains' brigades. Given all the casualties the two brigades had already sustained, how many men were still able to assault the Federal defensive line? Stephen H. Newton crunched the numbers and concluded that Rodes started the day with 2,200 men, started the last assault with about 1,600, and ended the day with about 1,100. Rains began the day with 2,870, began the final assault with 2,400, and ended the day with 1,990. In aggregate numbers, D. H. Hill began the day with about 9,000 men, but could only commit about 4,000 to the final assault of the day. All of those 4,000 came from south of the Williamsburg road.[131]

Strangely, the weakness of D. H. Hill's division, which forced him to make his final assault south of the Williamsburg road, had an unanticipated effect on Federal actions. Keyes had estimated that the Confederate attack would come north of the Williamsburg road, where Abercrombie and Devens were positioned. When Heintzelman assumed personal command, he discovered that the line was very weak south of the Williamsburg road. There were only the two regiments under Peck, and they were separated from the rest of the line by several hundred yards of heavy forest. By sheer chance, Rodes hit that gap in the Federal line.[132]

Heintzelman acted immediately to fill the gap in the Federal line. His first thought was to use some of Kearny's men, and sent a courier back to order Kearny to bring up one of his brigades. Concerned that it might take too long to fill the gap that way, Heintzelman took Keyes with him and rode toward Peck's position, thinking he might be able to contract the line by drawing in the left flank a bit. Heintzelman reached Peck by 4:30 PM, and finally had an accurate appreciation of Peck's isolation. Heintzelman could hear gunfire to the north. That could be a threat to the main line, and could mean capture of Peck's command. Heintzelman at that point ordered Peck to double-quick his men to join on the main line.[133]

Kearny and Casey met by accident on the Williamsburg road. Casey was all fired up and desirous of gathering up enough troops to retake his camps. He had seen the effect on the Confederates of Howell's token counterattack, and was trying to regroup as much of his division as possible. As Kearny came up, traveling with the head of Berry's brigade, Casey offered him a proposition, "If you will regain our late camp the day will still be ours."[134]

The aggressive Kearny was game for the attempt, although he only had with him the 3rd Michigan and a thrown-together company of sharpshooters. It wasn't helpful that the terrain was mostly dense woods, containing the abatis, rifle pits and flooded areas. Smoke reduced visibility in places. The conditions could hardly have been worse. The Federals were able to advance just to the eastern edge of Palmer's recently abandoned camps, when they were stopped by heavy fire.

Kearny left to bring forward another regiment, the 5th Michigan, commanded by Colonel Henry D. Terry. Terry asked Kearny where to put his men into the woods, and Kearny told him that anywhere would do, as there was "lovely fighting all along the line." As the 5th Michigan joined the 3rd in the woods, Kearny again went back, this time to bring up the 37th New York.[135]

Peck attacked from the southwest with the 93rd and 102nd Pennsylvania. The attack struck Rodes' brigade in the right flank. Most of the contest was conducted in dense foliage, but Peck's troops did cross an open field and received heavy artillery and musket fire. Both regiments hit the ground, attempting to hold position, but minimize their exposure. After about a half hour, matters became worse for Peck's regiments. Their ammunition began to run low, Peck's horse, previously wounded, collapsed and dumped him on the ground. More Confederates could be seen in the distance, coming onto the field. Peck, unavoidably, had to give the command to fall back.[136]

Too bad that Heintzelman was unaware that Peck and Kearny had blunted Hill's attack. Had he held on until Hooker's division arrived, the Federals at least would have had a chance to hold Seven Pines until nightfall. Peck had some success against Rodes because he struck the 6th and 12th Alabama in their exposed right flank. This was mainly because Rains' brigade, on Rodes' right, was again lagging behind in the attack.

The commander of the 6th Alabama, Colonel John B. Gordon complained that all his field officers as well as his adjutant were dead. So were all the officers' horses. He claimed that at least half of his command were casualties.[137]

This was a most opportune time for Rains to move rapidly forward. Peck's attack on Rodes' right flank (6th and 12th Alabama) made Peck's left flank very vulnerable to Rains. An attack then and there by Rains would have ended all Federal efforts to defend on their left. Rains' brigade was close enough to Rodes for him to see them and grow more angry by the minute. Rains' report of Seven Pines sheds no light on the final attack of the day. It is possible that discipline broke down in Rains' brigade, and the men elected to glean the overrun Federal camps rather than continue forward to support their sister brigade.[138]

The troops on the left side of Rodes' brigade weren't faring too well, either. Rodes had put the 4th Virginia Heavy Artillery Battalion in the lead on the left flank, mainly because they were relatively unscathed to this point. The 4th was a heavy artillery outfit that had been recently converted to infantry. Behind them, Rodes placed the 5th Alabama. These two units were trading shots with Michigan regiments of Kearny's division. When the 4th Virginia collided with the 3rd Michigan, the Virginians, green as infantrymen, laid down, and a good many broke for the rear. The 5th Alabama then started taking fire and sustaining casualties. It was a bad situation for the Alabamians, in that they were reluctant to fire over their own troops. Over 100 casualties were taken at this point by the 5th Alabama. The center of Rodes' brigade was the 12th Mississippi. They had no Federal infantry opponents, but observed a battery setting up in their front.[139]

Rodes' attack had ground to a halt. It was evident that Heintzelman only had to hold for another three-quarters of an hour to be saved by nightfall. Help was arriving for the Federals. Three more regiments of Jameson's brigade had finally forced their way though the fugitives on the Williamsburg road and reported to Kearny. The numerical superiority of the Confederates had now vanished, but Heintzelman was unaware of it. Had he known the true situation, a vigorous counterattack with Jameson's three fresh regiments could well have had a most beneficial effect on the Federal line.

Heintzelman was not Kearny, however. The prudent corps commander made logical troop dispositions, but they accidentally assisted the Confederates. Heintzelman split off the 87th New York to reinforce Peck's command. Peck, unbeknownst to Heintzelman, had already withdrawn. Jameson's other two regiments, the 63rd and 105th Pennsylvania, were sent into line behind and to the right of Kearny's other brigade.[140] There was nothing unsound about beefing up the line south of the road, but now there was no readily accessible reserve, as Hooker wasn't going to get there in time. If a break in the line occurred anywhere, there was no quick salvation for the Federals.

As it happened, the break occurred on the right of the Federal line, at a point where Hill wasn't even attacking. The particular point of the break was relatively well defended by the major part of Devens' and Abercrombie's brigades, supported without their knowledge by Birney. The line should have held at that location. Hill should not have been able to project enough combat power that late in the day.

Keyes, however, was still racing around the battlefield, moving regiments to and from tasks known only to him. When Hill's men closed in on the Federal camps, Keyes mounted a feeble and unsuccessful counterattack. Taking the 23rd and 61st Pennsylvania from Abercrombie's brigade, Keyes tasked them to assault the Confederate left. The two Pennsylvania regiments attacked Garland, G. B. Anderson and Richard Anderson in the process of reorganizing. The attack was a total failure. The Pennsylvanians ran into the Palmetto Sharpshooters, the 6th South Carolina and the 28th Georgia, all three units under the command of Jenkins. The Federals were easily turned back. Jenkins even contemplated making an attack of his own.[141]

Keyes' failed counterattack hadn't really caused much of a problem to the overall Federal cause. Unfortunately, he was likely feeling the presence of his superior, Samuel Heintzelman, on the battlefield and felt compelled to make something happen. His next caper was to take the 7th Massachusetts and the 67th New York out of the line to beef up the attack. He probably didn't inform Heintzelman of this latest robbery from his defense. Then matters became even stranger. Instead of the four regiments attacking, all four exited the fight, retreating north, not east. They ended up near Fair Oaks, encountering those detached regiments under Couch. All of these regiments were from Couch's division, and cheerfully rejoined their rightful commander. Couch, by this time, was involved in the fighting at Fair Oaks, and now the defenders on the Williamsburg road at Seven Pines were short four regiments.[142]

Devens, another of Couch's brigade commanders, wasn't even informed that Keyes had taken away the 7th Massachusetts. Devens had already lost the 2nd Rhode Island and Keyes had taken the 10th Massachusetts about 1:30 P.M., in an effort to reinforce a line just behind the rifle pits. The commander of the 10th, Colonel Henry S. Briggs, had a tense afternoon, just trying to keep his regiment of 500 alive and concentrated. Finally

Briggs found Devens, who ordered the frazzled colonel to pull back to the main defensive line, and position himself to the left of the 36th New York.[143]

The late afternoon of May 31 was a bitter one for Briggs and the 10th Massachusetts. Briggs had gone forward with only seven companies. When Devens directed him to fall back to the main defensive line, Briggs had already lost two captains. While maneuvering his regiment, Briggs unfortunately found himself at a place where he was taking both Confederate and friendly fire. He was hit in both upper legs simultaneously. To make matters even worse, he could find neither his lieutenant colonel nor major. Captain Ozro Miller assumed command, and while losing control a number of times, managed to get 200 men of the retreating regiment into line with the 36th New York.[144]

Then came the sequence of events that clearly revealed to Devens that he was in trouble. Devens observed the arrival of the 63rd and 105th Pennsylvania of Kearny's division on his left, likely relieved that his flank was protected. Almost immediately, Devens heard a lot of firing to his right. Assuming the 7th Massachusetts, the regiment linking him to Abercrombie's command was engaged, Devens rode over there. It was then revealed to him that the 7th Massachusetts was gone.[145]

Abercrombie was also gone. Due to Keyes' uncoordinated actions, there was now a giant gap in the left side of the Federal line. Again, the Confederates happened into the gap. A short while after turning back Keyes' counterattack, Jenkins took possession of the 5th South Carolina and the 19th Mississippi. Jenkins, probably confident after his repulse of Keyes, decided to attack through the just discovered gap with all five regiments under his command.[146]

Jenkins quickly found out that there were no Federals to fight on his left. The full weight of the Confederate assault fell upon the hapless and shaky 10th Massachusetts. Captain Miller did his best, but the regiment broke, men fleeing to the rear. The 36th New York was flanked and withdrew in an orderly but rapid fashion. By 5:00 PM, McClellan's army had no line whatsoever north of the Williamsburg road.[147]

Now the Federal troops south of the Williamsburg road began to melt away. They were not being attacked directly, but they were aware of the collapse north of the road, and they could see the three brigades under Wilcox arriving in their front. Rodes was personally guiding James L. Kemper's brigade forward through his lines. A stray minie ball hit Rodes in the arm, and he had to relinquish command. Gordon took command after Rodes had briefed him on terrain and the enemy in his front.[148]

The daylight was rapidly fading. Kemper hurried his regiments forward, but the Virginians were too late to attack the Federals in their front, as those Federals were fleeing. Senior officers here and there rallied a hundred or two, but the effort was hopeless. The men just could not be made to hold their position in the gathering darkness with an unknown number of Confederates in the woods to their front. Jenkins reported that at 7:40 P.M. his day of fighting was over, and all he could see of the enemy was small groups in the distance, on the other side of a wheat field.[149]

The day could have been an even greater disaster for the Federals. Nightfall, as in many Civil War battles, saved the vanquished from becoming the annihilated. Also helpful was the relatively calm demeanor of Heintzelman, Hooker, Kearny and Peck. Hooker's division met the bits and pieces of retreating III and IV Corps troops about a mile east of Seven Pines. Hooker's men, under Heintzelman's orders, were in the process of completing some unfinished rifle pits. In the darkness, Heintzelman was trying to construct yet another defensive line. There was still a potent force available. Hooker's division was intact, with about 5,000 men. A couple of Kearny's regiments had not fought and were intact, and the majority of Jameson's and Berry's regiments were still in fighting shape. Of the remnants of Keyes' IV Corps, about 1,800 men had been rallied.[150]

Heintzelman could likely field about 10,000 men the morning of June 1, over half of them fresh troops. Heintzelman and Keyes later learned that six regiments of Couch's division and Birney's brigade had escaped to the north. For the present, Keyes' IV Corps was not combat effective, and Heintzelman's own corps had also taken a beating. There was concern about what the morning would bring.

On the Confederate side of the line, D. H. Hill was taking stock and beginning to bury the fallen. Hill was less concerned about the morning, as Longstreet's division has passed through Hill's and assumed the front line. Hill reported a comfortable night in Casey's camp.[151]

At 4:00 P.M., Johnston was on the Nine Mile road. He had been waiting for some time for a message from Longstreet as to the progress on the Williamsburg road. Unfortunately for Johnston, from early morning on, more and more persons arrived to look over his shoulder. Almost all of them he could have easily spared. The first to arrive were G. W. Smith and his staff, who rode up shortly after first light. Then came Robert E. Lee with Major Armistead Long, then President Davis, followed by Postmaster General John Reagan. A bit farther away and even less welcome were Brigadier General John Floyd, and editor John Daniel of the Richmond *Examiner,* a newspaper very opposed to the Davis administration. These unwelcome rubberneckers didn't even get along with each other.[152]

When Longstreet's message arrived, Johnston had mixed emotions. He obviously welcomed the news that the Confederates on the Williamsburg road had been successful, but Longstreet also complained about the lack of support from the troops on the Nine Mile road. Now Johnston had to decide what to do next, and didn't relish having to perform that task with so many onlookers.

Longstreet, in his message, claimed credit for the success on the other road, and while disappointed that he hadn't been properly supported, believed that one more assault might drive the enemy into the Chickahominy. He also mentioned that little time remained in which to act.[153]

As previously mentioned, the first unwelcome onlooker to arrive was G. W. Smith. He arrived at first light on May 31, when nothing as yet had gone awry. Johnston really didn't want Smith there, for two principal reasons. Johnston had little confidence in his second-in-command and he didn't want to split the credit for the expected success of the battle with Smith. Johnston had hoped that, by naming Smith as commander of the "Left Wing" of the army, Smith might go elsewhere and attempt to be seen as in command of his own and A. P. Hill's divisions. Smith chose, instead, to be with Johnston on the Nine Mile road. His rationale was that it wasn't right for him to assume command of his own division after it had been passed on to Whiting. His stated purpose was to be with the army commander to offer assistance as needed.[154]

Johnston could find no polite way to deny Smith the privilege of remaining at army headquarters. As the day went on, Johnston was more and more unhappy with Smith's presence, as Smith was perfectly positioned to record every message received from the field, as well as every little mistake Johnston made, especially his indecision at critical points.

One of the first messages revealed that Longstreet was moving south to the Williamsburg road, rather than east along the Nine Mile road. Smith recorded in accurate detail Johnston's inability to choose an appropriate response. Johnston had several options. He could cancel the attack, which was out of control before it began. He could send an order to Longstreet to countermarch and return to the agreed upon plan. He could let Longstreet continue down to the Williamsburg road, and order McLaws and Whiting to attack down the Nine Mile road with the two divisions already in position there.

Johnston was unable to make the needed timely decision. He was aware the battle was at the moment out of control, but couldn't seem to choose a revised plan to regain control. He even seemed to try and convince himself that all was going well, and sent Lieutenant Washington riding east down the Nine Mile road, looking for Longstreet, where all knew Longstreet was not. As you will recall, the result of that fool's errand was the capture of the young lieutenant by the Federals. All the while, Smith, with poker face, was taking it all in, especially the moment just prior to 11:00 A.M., when Johnston came close to aborting the whole operation. Johnston was heard to make the comment to Major French of Smith's staff that "he wished the troops were back in their camps."[155]

Johnston's likelihood of canceling the battle plummeted with the arrival of his next guest, General Lee. Accompanied by Major Long, Lee came out to observe the battle. True to his earlier promise, Lee was not there to meddle, but simply couldn't remain in the confines of his office while the fate of the Confederate capital hung in the balance.[156]

Johnston likely regarded Lee as another unneeded and unwelcome observer. The battle had to go forward now. Johnston could hardly tell Lee he had already lost control of his forces, just as the fight was beginning. He decided to press on and tell Lee nothing. Lee, true to his previous word, didn't meddle or pry. Once, during the afternoon, Lee mentioned to Johnston that it sounded like there was musket fire in the distance, perhaps from Seven Pines, Johnston replied that he thought it was merely an artillery exchange. Johnston was likely hoping that the battle never fully developed. It was too late in the day for a real success, and anything less would kill all chance of surprising the Federals the following day. In his agitated state, all Johnston could think to do was ignore the clues he was receiving and hope the day would end without battle.[157]

This tactic of denial worked well enough until Longstreet's note arrived via Major Whiting at about 4:00 P.M. The note was *prima facie* evidence that the battle had been in progress for several hours already.[158] It also caused Johnston to believe that victory was still obtainable if he acted decisively. Just then, he was informed that President Davis was arriving to observe. Johnston had no desire to explain to the President why his largest army had done nothing all day, so he acted instantly.

Johnston had troops immediately at hand which he could set in motion without delay. Three of Whiting's brigades, those of Hood, Pettigrew and Pender, were right at the headquarters. Just a few hundred yards to the west were the brigades of Robert Hatton and Wade Hampton.

These five brigades, under the approved plan, had been tasked to be the reserve for Longstreet's division, which should have marched past the headquarters and attacked down the Nine Mile road. More specifically, Whiting's men were to prevent Sumner's II Corps from crossing the Chickahominy and reinforcing the III and IV Corps.[159]

The frantic need for immediate action took over Johnston's thought processes, and he gave no weight to niceties such as chain of command. After the briefest of searches for Chase Whiting, Johnston ordered Smith to reassume command of his old division to go back and bring forward the last brigades. Johnston took *de facto* command of Whiting's men, sending orders directly to the three brigade commanders to form in line of battle. The commanding general took the fate of the day's combat directly into his own hands.[160]

If the fates had conspired to force Johnston to act, they further conspired to change the character of his opponent. On the north side of the swollen Chickahominy River, Sumner and his II Corps waited for a part in the big fight. Many adjectives could be used to describe this unique officer. He was old, experienced, unimaginative, stubborn and brave. His nickname was "Bull," allegedly because a spent musket ball once bounced off his head.[161]

Now the fate of III and IV Corps and perhaps the whole campaign rested on the actions of one officer, Edwin Sumner. McClellan had sent a message to Sumner about 1:00 P.M., just after D. H. Hill attacked, to "be in readiness to move at a moment's notice." Sumner's two divisions were commanded by Brigadier Generals Richardson and Sedgwick. Upon receipt of McClellan's message, Sumner ordered his division commanders to leave their camps and move close to two newly built bridges across the Chickahominy. Within ninety minutes, Sumner ordered Sedgwick, then Richardson to cross. Both Richardson and McClellan said that the orders to cross came from McClellan, but Sumner's report was a bit more vague. He may have decided to cross on his own, and McClellan backed his successful move later.[162]

In retrospect, the most difficult part of the day for II Corps was getting safely across the Chickahominy, which was out of its banks after the night's hard rain. Sedgwick's men crossed on a bridge dubbed "the Grapevine" for the use of grapevines when the available rope was exhausted. The bridge wobbled and swayed as the division began to cross, and the approaches were under a foot and a half of water. The logs used to corduroy the approaches began to work loose in the water, and threatened to float away.[163]

The five regiments of Gorman's brigade were the first of Sedgwick's division to cross the shaky bridge. Various officers of the five regiments described the crossing of Chickahominy Swamp as taking two hours, tedious, trying, having waist-deep water, etc. The troops were also credited with being without hesitation and cheering as they went. Fortunately, the planking of the bridge seemed to become more stable as more weight moved onto it.[164]

Following Gorman's infantry was Edmund Kirby's Battery I, 1st U. S. Artillery. The crossing of the weighty guns was a much more difficult prospect than that of the infantry. Horses, cannon and caissons all sank into the mud. Kirby was up to the task. He had the horses unharnessed and led across the river, then his artillerists and teamsters waded into the water and man-handled the pieces across one at a time. The process was slow but successful until one gun splintered the corduroy logs just short of the bridge, dropped into the mud, and could not be extricated.[165]

William Burns' brigade, now approached the bridge. The lead regiment, the 72nd Pennsylvania, detoured around the mired guns and disgusted artillerists. The infantrymen were grim-faced, likely thinking they might be going into battle without artillery support. As General Burns rode up, he was also thinking about the prospect of fighting short of artillery. He quickly ordered the 106th Pennsylvania to leave the road and assist Kirby's men in moving their guns.[166]

The men of the 106th jumped into the muck, levered out the gun, and literally carried it across the Grapevine Bridge. They immediately went back across for a second gun. This drill took about an hour, and up ahead, Bull Sumner noticed that Burns' brigade was no longer right behind Gorman's. He sent staff officers back to investigate. They insisted, on Sumner's authority, that Burns move his brigade immediately, without regard for Kirby's problem. Burns refused to move until two guns were safely across the Chickahominy. With the delay, it was now just after 4:00 P.M.[167]

Down at Fair Oaks Station, Couch was in command of an improvised brigade. Couch had been isolated there for over two hours, and came to his present situation through a relatively strange sequence of events. Couch had been posted on the far right of Keyes' line, with two regiments, the 65th New York and 31st Pennsylvania, along with Battery H, 1st Pennsylvania Light. After the failure of Keyes' weak attempt to recover Casey's rifle pits, Couch took command of two additional regiments, the 23rd and 61st Pennsylvania, after they retreated north rather than east. During that confused retreat, they brought along a part of the 7th Massachusetts and 62nd New York. Now Couch had a good-sized command, but it was a thrown-together brigade and some parts of it had to be somewhat demoralized after their earlier repulse and confused retreat.[168]

Couch had some serious concerns at that point. He was angry about the way Keyes had taken apart his division earlier in the day. His report on this day's action would be blunt about Keyes' actions. By the sounds of battle coming from the vicinity of Seven Pines, Couch rightly assumed he was cut off from the rest of his corps. Adding to his concern was a report from his pickets that the Confederates were moving on the Nine Mile road.[169]

Couch began to explore his options. He first made a tentative attempt to cut his way through to the main body of the corps, and quickly concluded that it was a suicidal course of action and abandoned the attempt. He favored digging in at his present position, but was prevailed upon by Abercrombie to attempt to get the command out of their present danger. Couch prudently gave great weight to Abercrombie's considerable advantage in age and military experience.[170]

Couch was thinking clearly now, and sent a staff officer to inform Sumner that he was retreating toward the Chickahominy, specifically toward the Grapevine Bridge, and set his brigade in motion. Couch never made it to the river. If he had, it might have been a great boon to the Confederates. The path would have been clear for Whiting to continue past Fair Oaks Station down the Nine Mile road and hit Heintzelman's right flank. It could have made the day a great Confederate victory. Captain van Ness, Couch's courier, met Sumner's van on the road, and was sent back to Couch with the great news that reinforcements from II Corps were on the way. Couch soon saw them in the distance.[171]

Sumner, never one to lead from the rear, rode up at a gallop several minutes in advance of his lead unit. Couch had already put his makeshift brigade into line of battle near the Adams House. He had shrewdly put his infantry in the trees north of the Nine Mile road, and had been able to cover his left with a section of a Pennsylvania battery. He was, however, quite concerned about his right flank, if the Confederates attacked from the east. Sumner was sympathetic and authorized Couch to take the first regiment that arrived to secure the right flank. That regiment was Sully's 1st Minnesota, which arrived a few minutes later and was quickly put into position.[172]

Johnston sent Whiting's division down the Nine Mile road in a state of near ignorance. They were to pass through Fair Oaks Station and advance to Seven Pines. Johnston was not aware that Couch's brigade was in the trees to the left of the road, and also didn't know that Sumner had crossed a major force to the south side of the river. He never expected to encounter Federals this far west. Johnston had committed his reserve division, and had set it up for severe punishment.

Johnston made another foolish move. He sent Hood's brigade into the dense woods, far to the right of the Nine Mile road. They were supposed to link up with D. H. Hill's left. Hood and his men spent most of the afternoon in the woods. Pender and Pettigrew put their brigades into line of battle. Pender's right was resting on the Nine Mile road. Johnston was waiting for Smith to bring the other two brigades forward, and planned to use Hampton's brigade to extend the line. Hatton's brigade would be kept in reserve. This was a fairly sensible troop deployment.[173]

Johnston's relatively logical deployment did have a few problems. First, without knowing where Hill's left flank was, it wasn't wise to put Hood and his men into the woods. A more serious flaw in the deployment was Johnston's corruption of the command and control structure of the army. He failed to do his job as commanding general, and instead took the duties and responsibilities of Smith and Whiting. He gave Smith tasks that a courier could have completed, then Smith took over control of three brigades. Chase Whiting remained beside Johnston and served only as a figurehead.

Johnston really wanted to finish off the Federals at Seven Pines. So much so that he was blind to the signs of Couch's presence beside the Nine Mile road. Pender's skirmishers reported the enemy in significant numbers in the tree line, and forwarded the intelligence to Whiting. Whiting believed the report and tried to persuade Johnston to sweep north and clear the woods. Johnston was close-minded to the suggestion and said, "Oh! General Whiting, you are too cautious."[174]

Couch's sole artillery support was Battery H, 1st Pennsylvania Light Artillery under Andrew Fagan. It took Pender's men under fire with its two twelve-pounders just as Johnston was admonishing Chase Whiting. The range was minimal and the artillery section seemed like a couple of batteries. Pender attempted to attack Couch's men in the trees. Running low on canister, Fagan fired whatever he had left—spherical case, solid shot, etc. Pender's men could not endure the fire and went into the trees next to the road.[175]

Dorsey Pender wasted no time in regrouping his men. Just then, Whiting sent directions for Pender to scout the Federal position carefully. It went on to say that a second assault could be attempted only if Pender was sure the Federal guns could be taken. Before Pender could mount a scouting operation, an unknown officer galloped past the brigade and shouted "Charge that battery!" The angry Confederates went forward to attack anew.[176]

By coincidence, the brigades of Hampton, Hatton and Pettigrew on Pender's left advanced at the same time. To the Federals, it looked like a well coordinated attack of division strength. The three left-hand brigades were attacking on Smith's orders. He had witnessed Pender's first attack and was trying to enlarge and extend and turn the Federal right flank.[177]

Smith had eleven regiments committed to the fight, and they were making their way through the woods at a slow pace, organized into six distinct lines. The Federals at first only had the 65th New York (1st U.S. Chasseurs) and the 1st Minnesota, supported by the two guns of Battery H, 1st Pennsylvania Light. About 30 minutes later, the 69th and 72nd Pennsylvania of Burns' brigade extended Couch's line a hundred yards to the left, but the brunt of the fighting was still borne by the 65th New York under Colonel John Cochrane and the 1st Minnesota under Colonel Alfred Sully.[178]

The fight was conducted at very close range, and called more for courage than knowledge of tactics. Cochrane was impressed by the courage of the charging Confederate soldiers. Sully stated in his report that "the enemy were slaughtered in great numbers within a very few yards of our line."[179]

The Federals were crouched behind a rail fence, and had both flanks covered. They had no problem seeing the charging Confederates in the setting sun. The two Federal regiments held off three brigades for almost two hours, inflicting heavy casualties on Smith's men. The Confederates lost over 1,200 men. The leadership was hit hard. The Hampton Legion lost 141 killed or wounded. Hatton was killed instantly while leading his brigade. Pettigrew was wounded and captured. Hampton was hit in the foot with a musket ball, but refused to leave his command. Instead, he stood on one leg while the surgeon removed the ball.[180]

The Confederate casualties were so high partly because of the tangled undergrowth through which they were advancing. Visibility was limited. It made it almost impossible for the officers to control their troops. Of even greater effect was the fact that at least some of the troops were ordered to charge with empty muskets, so as not to fire until ordered. When they were not able to close the Federal lines with bayonets, they stopped, stood, loaded and fired. They were extremely vulnerable during that time. The end result was that the two Federal regiments were still in place at nightfall.[181]

Pender's brigade was suffering as well. When Pender commenced his second attack, precipitated by the unknown rider, Couch was just beginning to be reinforced by three regiments from Sumner's II Corps, the 15th Massachusetts, 34th and 82nd New York. Of more importance, Lieutenant Kirby had finally gotten the first of his guns to the battle. Pender's men were now opposed by six regiments and four or more guns. Two of the regiments were able to provide enfilading fire. The second attack was a bigger failure than the first.[182]

Sumner rode numerous times back to the Chickahominy to urge the trailing part of his corps to expedite their crossing. He was becoming more confident that he had enough combat power in his line to hold his ground. He did put two more regiments, the 7th Michigan and the 20th

Massachusetts from Dana's brigade into the line. Sumner then received the bonus of two more of Kirby's guns, giving him a battery complement of six guns in the center of his line. Sumner then positioned the 71st and 106th Pennsylvania of Dana's brigade and the 69th and 72nd Pennsylvania of Burns' brigade just behind his artillery as a close reserve. Sumner, pleased that his far right was holding its ground despite the numbers there, was considering a counterattack if the Confederates attacked his guns again.[183]

At dusk, Pender's brigade attacked for a third time. By then, it seems that Johnston had departed the area. Sometime later, he claimed that he had left General Smith in command and gone south to find Hood's brigade, as well as to confer with Longstreet. Johnston never located Longstreet, but found Hood's command waiting in waist-deep water for orders. They had located none of the enemy, but had seen Hatton's horse race across the 4th Texas' rear.[184]

On the face of it, it appears that Johnston impulsively put a division into battle, then tried his best to distance himself from the bad result. His report on the battle, as well as his memoirs, attempt to convey that he thought Smith's men were only up against the remnants of Casey's division at Fair Oaks, and didn't need the help of Hood's brigade. Therefore, rather than have Hood strike northeast and bail out Smith, Johnston chose to have Hood wade eastward in hopes of joining up on Longstreet's left and attacking the Federals left at Seven Pines.[185]

This order by Johnston to Hood took away the last chance for a significant Confederate victory. The ironic part of Johnston's choice was that there wasn't really an objective for Hood's brigade at Seven Pines. Casey's defense of the rifle pits had already failed. Casey was shattered and had no flank for Hood to fall upon. Hood ended up looking unsuccessfully for his non-existent objective in the twilight, while the option not chosen by Johnston, Sumner's left flank, was left unthreatened. Meanwhile, Smith was vainly attempting to reorganize Hampton's, Hatton's and Pettigrew's brigades after their earlier losses. This left Whiting, with Pender's brigade as his sole asset, to try a third time to crack the Federal center. It is not totally clear exactly who ordered that attack. It is interesting to note that neither Whiting nor Pender filed an official report on the battle.

Pender's four regiments, though tired, moved smartly to the attack. Their initial approach was shielded by a strip of trees protruding from the woods. The attackers were able to get within scant yards of their objective in the poor light. At that point, muskets and twelve-pounders lit up the field. Pender's men were caught in a crossfire between Kirby's guns and four of Sedgwick's regiments on their flank.

Despite the fierce Federal fire, the outcome was in doubt for a few moments. The opposing forces were close enough to allow a Federal cannoneer to use a sponge to strike a Confederate officer. The guns continued to fire, despite the attackers and the soft soil.[186]

Pender's men had had enough. By now Sumner had resolved to end the fight. He ordered all available regiments of Sedgwick's division forward in a general advance. The advance turned into a pursuit of Pender's fleeing brigade. Although Pender tried valiantly to rally his men, they were badly outnumbered, and thanks to the lack of Hood's brigade, outflanked. Pender retreated almost to the Nine Mile road. The Federals stopped their pursuit at the edge of the woods.[187]

It was now almost totally dark. Johnston had returned, unsuccessful in locating Longstreet. Johnston was accompanied by a small number of nervous staff officers and couriers. The reasons for their apprehension were sound. Visibility was dropping, Whiting's center was in turmoil and the possibility of the sudden appearance of Federal troops was very real. There was still some musket fire in the area. They really wanted their general out of there.

Johnston seemed unconcerned about the danger of his present location. He also seemed to be unaware of how poorly he had fought his army that day. In his mind, the fight at Fair Oaks was more or less a draw, and he knew Longstreet had been successful at Seven Pines. He was hoping that Longstreet's day had been so thoroughly successful that Johnston could justify a renewal of the battle in the morning. He made a statement to his staff officers. "So I announced to my staff officers that each regiment must sleep where it might be standing when the contest ceased for the night, to be ready to renew it at dawn the next morning."[188]

Johnston was aware that some of his staffers were nervous about their location, but he was not. He even attempted to calm one of his colonels by making light of the situation. At that moment, a partially spent musket ball struck Johnston in the shoulder. The wound was not serious, and should not have caused him to dismount. Unfortunately for Johnston, his luck was getting worse by the second. Only a few moments later, one of Kirby's last shots of the day burst nearby, and shell fragments struck the General, penetrating his chest and thigh and knocking him from his horse. Drury Armistead, a courier, gathered his general in his arms immediately, carrying him several hundred yards to what seemed to the lieutenant to be a safer place.[189]

The group of unwelcome onlookers which had annoyed Johnston all day by their mere presence now took as their foremost concern Johnston's physical well being. The severely wounded general was placed in an ambulance, and for a short while, old animosities were forgotten and blame for recent poor decisions were no longer issues. Johnston later wrote "The President, who was with General Lee, not far to the rear, had heard of the accident, and visited me, manifesting great concern, as he continued to do until I was out of danger."[190]

Once the ambulance had departed, the staff's attention shifted to the whereabouts of Smith. His last known position on the battlefield was north of the Nine Mile road, directing the movements of the brigades of Hatton, Hampton and Pettigrew. Couriers were sent to inform him that Johnston had been wounded, and that he, Smith, was now the commanding general.

Smith wasn't easy to find in the darkness, amid the chaos of the waning gunfire. At last, Colonel Benjamin S. Ewell located Smith in a small farmhouse, stretched out on a couch. The stress of the day's battle had aggravated his nervous ailment, and the general was semi-conscious. Benjamin S. Ewell labored to get him up and inform him about Johnston. Smith, with great effort, arose and went to see President Davis.[191]

The meeting between the ailing general and the President was less than enjoyable for either man. Davis began by reviewing the fact that Smith was now in command, and asked what the general's plans were. General Smith, even had he been in perfect health, would have found it difficult to satisfy Davis. Smith began by stating that the battle had been poorly fought, and gave Johnston full credit for the poor leadership. Smith briefed the original plan, characterized Longstreet's behavior as a "misunderstanding," and said that there was a "delay on the latter road, in commencing the attack." Smith was able to describe in detail the actions of Whiting's division, and spun the report of that action as having stopped the Federal reinforcements from reaching Longstreet's left flank. He then inquired of the President whether he knew the results of the day's fighting by Longstreet's command since 4:00 P.M.

In fact, there had been no further messages from Longstreet. The battle on the Nine Mile road made it impossible to tell what had been going on with Longstreet at Seven Pines. An impatient Davis again asked the new army commander what his plans were. Smith stalled, reminding Davis that he had not been a part of developing Johnston's battle plan nor executing it. Smith could only finish by saying that he couldn't know what to do until he knew what had happened with Longstreet's right wing.

Joseph Eggleston Johnston

Davis was not hearing anything in which he could take heart. The President came away from the meeting, conducted with the wounded passing by, with no good news. His new army commander was ill and exhausted, had criticized his wounded superior, fought a stalemate at best, and didn't have a clue about the fate of half the army. On top of that, he admitted he didn't know what to do next. Smith was aware that Davis was unimpressed.[192]

There was a paucity of happiness on the Federal side of the lines as well. Although Sumner and Couch had held their positions with their thrown together force at Fair Oaks Station, the Federal generals were burning the midnight oil. McClellan had finally come to the battlefield, and expressed his horror at the lack of artillery support in place. Sumner was busily trying to straighten his lines, McClellan ordered his chief of engineers to commandeer troops to assist in getting the rest of Sumner's artillery across the Chickahominy. Additionally, McClellan demanded that "It is absolutely necessary that several bridges be practicable for Artillery in the morning." The engineers would have a busy night.[193]

Crossing the artillery and improving the bridges was a miserable experience. The initial crossing of Kirby's battery had made the road to Grapevine Bridge even more of a quagmire. Horses were unharnessed and led across, and each cannon was manhandled to the bridge. It is hard to fully appreciate the rain, the mud, the exhaustion and the confusion that must have been the lot of those men who carried out McClellan's orders that night. Near the front lines, there were dead and wounded lying about and there were the sounds of men shrieking and groaning.[194]

On a higher plane, McClellan, as Smith, had much the same answers to seek. He wasn't sure about the condition of his III and IV Corps. He'd had no word of them subsequent to being informed that they had been pushed out of Seven Pines. Since it was already fully night when McClellan returned to the battlefield, he had a less than perfect appreciation for Confederate strength or their losses. He really had one big decision to make. Was the next morning an opportunity for a successful Federal attack or should he assume the defense? On a personal level, he had to consider how to report the day's fighting and current situation to his superiors in Washington.

McClellan needed very little time at all to decide how to handle Washington. He would wait until morning to shed more light on the situation. He desired to find someone to blame for the defeat at Seven Pines. before communicating with Washington. He delayed that communication until noon, and laid all the blame on Casey's division.[196]

McClellan's picture of what really happened to III and IV Corps came largely from a meeting with Heintzelman at headquarters late in the evening of May 31. Heintzelman, exhausted and depressed, met with McClellan north of the Chickahominy and reported on the condition of III and IV Corps. Understandably, he stressed the rout of IV corps and the relatively good condition of his own III Corps. One can only think that Keyes was the primary source of the exaggeration of the rout of Casey's division. Keyes was likely attempting to escape blame for his poor leadership. The meeting between Heintzelman and McClellan concluded with the resolution that III and IV Corps should not be asked to do more than hold their ground in the morning.[197]

CHAPTER 12

Seven Pines, Day 2

(June 1)

McClellan also decided to keep Sumner's II Corps in a defensive posture for a while. This would serve to repulse any further Confederate assaults around Fair Oaks. Sumner continued to bring the rest of his corps into line during the wee hours, although he received no specific orders from McClellan. By 3:00 A.M., all of Sumner's II Corps, the divisions of Richardson and Sedgwick with eight supporting batteries, were in line. McClellan likely thought about a possible attack toward Fair Oak Station.[1]

Gustavus W. Smith, the new commanding general of the Army of Northern Virginia, had just finished meeting with James Longstreet. These two officers had been Joseph Johnston's principal subordinates. Now that he was gone, their differences overcame their desire to cooperate in the common cause. Although G. W. Smith was technically senior, Longstreet felt he should be commander of the army, and wasn't ready to defer to Smith. This fact alone was a severe detriment to the Confederates. Their accounts of the meeting differ substantially. The only area of agreement was that the meeting lasted from 1:00 A.M. until 3:00 A.M, and took place at Smith's headquarters. Both men claim to have initiated the meeting.[2]

Smith had already received a number of messages from his left wing, telling him that the Federals were putting heavy reinforcements opposite Whiting's line near Fair Oaks Station. McLaws passed on a report from his videttes that the Federals were seen throwing "heavy objects" in the river. These were, of course, pontoons. McLaws advised Smith that perhaps the Federals were going to try to outflank the Confederates above Richmond.[3]

When Longstreet heard McLaws' conjecture during his meeting with Smith, he dismissed it out of hand. The meeting then moved on to discuss the possibility of an attack after dawn. Smith believed that Longstreet was telling him that D. H. Hill's division was somewhat beat up, Longstreet's division was still pretty fresh, and Huger's men had not fought at all. Smith already had a rough idea of what his attack plan would be. The Federal III and IV Corps seemed to Smith to be unable to effectively fight offensively until they could be reorganized, so he saw Sumner's II Corps as the place to attack. Smith's idea was to have Longstreet use Hill's battered division to hold the line east of Seven Pines, while Longstreet attacked Sumner's left flank by striking north with Longstreet's six brigades, supported by Huger's three. Once the attack developed momentum, Whiting's division could pitch in. Lastly, if Longstreet's attack motivated McClellan to abandon the idea of forcing one or more river crossings in front of McLaws and Magruder, then those two divisions could also join the attack.[4]

Longstreet knew that G. W. Smith was developing an attack plan based on a major incorrect assumption. That bad assumption was the poor condition of the Federal III and IV Corps. Longstreet, in a fashion common to him, had much exaggerated his defeat of IV Corps and his damage to III Corps. He complained to Smith that for his and Huger's divisions to attack north would leave III and IV Corps to attack from the rear as soon as the attack got underway. Longstreet went so far as to accuse Smith of a loss of nerve. Longstreet likely told Smith he didn't like the plan, but Smith persisted, and ordered Longstreet to follow the plan, and to send Whiting a brigade from Huger's division. Longstreet was told to attack as soon as possible after daybreak.[5]

G. W. Smith, after ordering Longstreet to obey and execute the plan for the morning, sent messages to Whiting, Magruder, McLaws and A. P. Hill, telling them what he needed them to know prior to the dawn attack. G. W. Smith had been ill, was now still exhausted, and obviously not at his best. Had he been, he might have been a bit skeptical about just what Longstreet was going to do in the morning. One must remember, Smith was quite aware of how Longstreet wrecked the plan for the previous day. And that deliberate act by Longstreet was perpetrated against Joseph E. Johnston, a man for which Smith had great respect. Now, the orders that Longstreet was expected to obey came from Smith, the man whose position Longstreet's ambition demanded he obtain. But Smith was all done for the day. He finished sending his messages and attempted to get a few hours of badly needed sleep before the dawn attack. He really believed that Longstreet would be a good soldier and obey his orders.[6]

Longstreet appears to have had no plan to follow G. W. Smith's orders. In his report on Seven Pines, he doesn't refer to Smith's attack order, only defending the position his division held when firing ended the previous night. In his memoirs, Longstreet was even more candid. He made the claim that Smith's plan would only work if Magruder came in at the pivotal point without orders from his commander. Longstreet had no faith that such an action would take place. Therefore, Longstreet wasn't willing to follow

Smith's orders. Instead, Longstreet found D. H. Hill and directed him to advance along the Williamsburg road, develop the enemy's front along the railroad, and use artillery on the Nine Mile road against the Federals.[7]

Longstreet did almost nothing that G. W. Smith, his superior, had ordered. Longstreet even failed to initiate a probe of the Federal position. Instead, he found Hill and told him several items which contradicted Smith's desires. Longstreet told Hill that he had certain knowledge that they had three Federal Corps (II, III & IV) in their front. This Longstreet did despite the fact that he knew that Sumner's II Corps was in Whiting's front, some miles away. Next he gave Hill tactical control of Longstreet's division and told Hill to appropriate troops from Huger if he needed them. This clever action put some distance between Longstreet and the actions which would unfold on June 1. It also took Huger out of the command structure. When Hill asked Longstreet for guidance, Longstreet answered with "You have taken the bull by the horns and must fight him out." Longstreet then quickly rode away before Hill could ask for clarification. This left Hill to his own initiative in ordering an attack, and with no knowledge of the army commander's plans. Now G. W. Smith was going to endure what Johnston had on the previous day, waiting in futility for Longstreet to begin an ordered attack.[8]

Even the aggressive Hill wasn't keen on initiating a large attack at this point. He had suffered over 3,000 casualties the previous day at Seven Pines, and had been told by Longstreet not to anticipate receiving reinforcements from G. W. Smith or anyone else. Hill decided to concentrate his forces around the captured Federal camps, and hope they would try to retake them. But now with Longstreet's division of five brigades available to him, he couldn't force himself to stay totally defensive.[9]

Hill had been informed that Federal skirmishers had been observed in Pickett's front, and Hill decided to attack them before they could attack Pickett. What Hill intended was a small, quick, sharp blow. Pickett erroneously assumed that the attack order he received had also been given to all the other brigadiers. In fact, only Armistead and Mahone, both to Pickett's left, had been ordered to support the attack. On Pickett's right, Pryor and Wilcox remained in a defensive posture. It was ironic that, on June 1, while Smith was waiting for a huge assault by at least eight brigades commanded by Longstreet, a junior division commander, Harvey Hill, on his own initiative, commenced a small attack of only three brigades from two different divisions, neither of them Hill's.[10]

Pickett's attack had the potential for real success, because the Federal line in his front happened to have a sizeable gap between two brigades of Richardson's II Corps division. That division had arrived in the night and had not adequately scouted the area. The commander of the 5th New Hampshire, Colonel Edward Cross, found that his regiment and the Confederates had slept only a hundred yards apart. At dawn, General French, commander of Richardson's 3rd brigade, discovered "an uncovered space of three-fourths of a mile in my left...." Confederate cavalry had been observed along the front, so both French and Richardson had cause to be worried about an attack there. French side-stepped his regiments to the left, and Richardson sent up the 81st Pennsylvania of Oliver O. Howard's brigade to fill the gap.[11]

Colonel James Miller of the 81st Pennsylvania had just finished placing his companies in line when the 3rd Alabama came through the trees. One of their first shots killed Miller. The 3rd was the lead regiment of Mahone's brigade. This was their first fighting in the battle so far. They began their work just after midnight on the 31st, but were squandered by being marched and countermarched with Huger's division. They were frustrated by hearing the sound of musket fire and not allowed to fight. After nightfall, they marched north from Charles City road to Williamsburg road, and were put into line on the far left of Hill's and Longstreet's divisions. They only had a few hours to rest there, along with the 12th and 41st Virginia.[12]

Mahone reported to Harvey Hill and was told to put his brigade into the woods to the left of Armistead and Pickett. Mahone instantly ordered the 3rd Alabama and 41st Virginia to charge the woods. Mahone's third regiment, the 12th Virginia, brought up the rear. Unfortunately for Mahone, the 41st became disoriented in the foliage, and started moving parallel to the Federal lines. At that point in time, Mahone's only regiment in the fight was the 3rd Alabama.[13]

Although the 3rd Alabama was the sole regiment of Mahone's brigade attacking the Federals, it had an able leader, Colonel Tennant Lomax.

The 3rd was doing well, striking the 81st Pennsylvania before it could get oriented. The 81st fell back in two directions, dividing into two parts. Even though they were forced to retreat, the men of the 81st did great damage to the 3rd Alabama. The Pennsylvanians took 91 casualties, including their colonel, and the Alabamians suffered 175 casualties, including their colonel, who was killed in the contact.[14]

Other than the 3rd Alabama, Mahone's brigade had little effect on the fight. The 41st Virginia, when it finally emerged from the tangled undergrowth, launched an ineffective attack against the 52nd New York. It petered out in a few minutes. The last regiment, the 12th Virginia, never attacked the Federal lines at all. By the time it reached Mahone, it came under a steady fire, became confused, and thought it had been ordered to retreat. The confusion had a price of 52 casualties, and angered Mahone. He disgustedly reformed the brigade "on the line of the main road."[15]

To add to the Confederate confusion, Harvey Hill happened to be riding by when the 12th Virginia retreated, and erroneously concluded that Mahone's whole brigade had been repulsed. He wheeled about and galloped back to his camp, meaning to find another unit to replace Mahone's, which he referred to as "cowardly Virginians." Near the Williamsburg road, he encountered Colonel Alfred M. Scales and his 13th North Carolina of Colston's brigade. Hill ordered the 13th to go and replace Mahone's men, personally guiding them to their new position. When Hill paused to berate some of Mahone's troops for cowardice, Mahone came up and shouted at Harvey Hill: "You should not abuse my men, for I ordered them out of the fight." Mahone then assumed all blame for the retreat of his one confused regiment. Hill was too angry to sort out the facts, he apologized to the men, then turned on Mahone, accusing him of not obeying orders. Mahone was so furious that he challenge Harvey Hill to a duel, but it never took place.[16]

No matter how angry Hill became and how vehemently he railed at his subordinates, he could not change the outcome of the fighting. To the right of Mahone's brigade, Armistead's three regiments were also repulsed by four regiments of French's brigade. Although there are no reports from Armistead or the three regimental commanders, French's regimental commanders reported that the 9th and 14th Virginia attacked three or more times, coming within 50 yards of the main Federal line. Armistead's other regiment, the 53rd Virginia, had been held back in division reserve. It spent several hours wandering about without engaging in any serious fighting. Colonel Tomlin reported that there was much to fear from friends as enemies, due to the intermingling of the two sides.[17]

Pickett's brigade was to the immediate right of Armistead's. Pickett described the repulse of Armistead as a rout. At one point, Pickett said that he saw nothing between the railroad and himself but Armistead himself. Pickett sent couriers to Hill right away, requesting help, telling Hill that his attack was going well, and, with reinforcements and more ammunition, he could drive the Federals across the Chickahominy.[18]

Pickett couldn't have been more wrong. His men had not, as he mistakenly believed, overrun two heavily defended abatis and defeated a large Federal force. In fact, they had luckily hit the seam between Birney's and Patterson's brigades. The abatis was at the northern end of Casey's original line which ran through Seven Pines. It was now manned lightly. Pushing through that light resistance, Pickett had put himself between the fresh troops of two Federal brigades.[19]

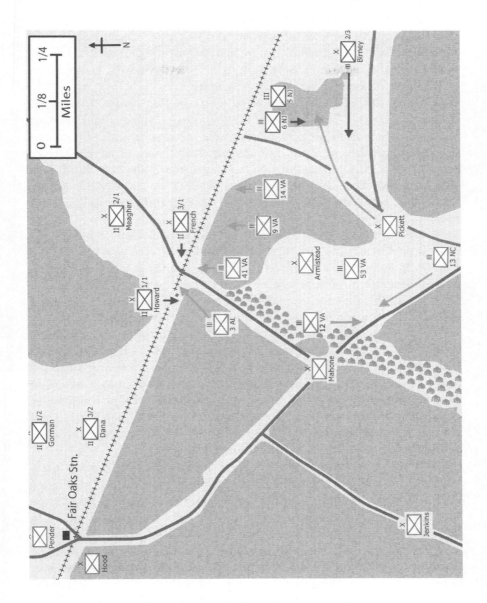

Map 12.1—D. H. Hill's Attack, June 1

Birney was not in command of his brigade that morning. He had been summoned to III Corps headquarters, and had left Colonel Ward of the 38th New York in command. Birney had sent word back to Ward to put skirmishers out and not provoke an attack. Ward followed those orders and ignored Pickett's move through the abatis.[20]

Hooker did not ignore Pickett's advance. Just before 7:00 A.M., Hooker began to hear considerable musketry. Hooker had thirteen regiments assigned to his division, but only seven were under his control this morning. They were the 5th and 6th New Jersey of Starr's brigade and Daniel Sickles' brigade of five regiments, the 70th, 71st, 72nd, 73rd and 74th New York. His brigade was part of Hooker's division on the Peninsula. Hooker's artillery tried to follow the infantry, but could not due to the muddy conditions.[21]

Starr's two New Jersey regiments led Hooker's division into the fight. They moved across Hobart Ward's front and made contact with Pickett's 19th Virginia. Pickett smartly refused his flank, then sent another appeal to Hill for reinforcements. Pickett reported being pressed by "brigade after brigade," and his four regiments had to go on the defensive, falling back to the recently captured abatis. There, Pickett intended to make a stand.[22]

If Hooker had put all seven of his regiments into the fight, he likely could have prevailed, but some of them had gone. Heintzelman had just ridden up, felt concern about the breadth of the enemy's line, and took Hooker's second brigade. These troops he made into a defensive line. Although the decision was perfectly logical as a corps commander, he failed to inform Hooker. The end result of Heintzelman's action was Hooker fighting four Confederate regiments with only two of his own, and not aware of where his second brigade had gone.[23]

Hooker was getting pretty concerned at this point, and wrote a hasty note to Ward asking for help. Ward, hearing the fight, had already realigned his line toward the fight. Hooker's note motivated Ward to fire on the enemy and charge their lines, despite his brigade commander's desire to stay on the defense. A brutal and chaotic fight ensued.

Pickett's spin was that the 18th and 19th Virginia, firing from the abatis, took a heavy toll on Ward's men. Colonel Henry Staples, commander of the 3rd Maine and leader of the attack, claimed that his men chased the Confederates a mile through the woods and swamps, until stopped by a large Confederate reserve force.[24]

Neither of these reports were accurate, of course. In truth, Pickett's men defended the abatis for almost an hour, then pulled back about 400 yards. Then, Colston's and Mahone's brigades covered Pickett's flanks, and the three brigades held their positions for the remainder of the day. Pickett's men were not routed, and lost about 350 men of the 1,700 that entered the fight. Pickett's report of the murderous volleys fired from the abatis was also much overblown. There were six Federal regiments in the fight, about 2,200 men, and they lost only 286 men killed and wounded. According to Federal reports of the contact, they took most of their casualties after Pickett retreated.[25]

Aside from a bit more skirmishing and sniping that occurred throughout the remainder of June 1, the significant fighting at the battle of Seven Pines was over. Despite a number of overblown reports of the fighting, the facts support only a brief, intense musketry exchange between about five brigades on each side. Little or no territory changed hands.

In both armies, the commanding generals and their key subordinates had the common experience of not being active where and when their respective armies needed them most.

McClellan made an appearance at Sumner's headquarters while Richardson's division was under attack, blessed Sumner's actions, and left.[26] Sumner delegated his authority to Richardson and hardly mentioned it in his report on the battle. Heintzelman did little all day, except diverting one of Hooker's brigades from the Federal attack on Pickett to other duty. Essentially, the Federal army was run almost entirely by two division commanders, Hooker and Richardson.

On the Confederate side, neither G. W. Smith nor Longstreet ever ventured close to the gunfire. Harvey Hill again had tactical control. This, despite the fact that the Confederate troops in the fight were not from Hill's division. They seemed to spend most of the day exchanging notes. The notes did not reflect reality.

As you may recall, Smith had ordered Longstreet to begin a dawn attack northward toward Fair Oaks Station. At 8:30 A.M., Smith's headquarters received a brief note from Longstreet, which read "I have ordered a brigade of General Huger's, as agreed upon, to the support of General Whiting. Please send a guide for it." Longstreet failed to mention the attack he had been ordered to conduct. Over the next sixty minutes, Smith received intelligence from McLaws and Whiting that Sumner was still crossing troops over the Chickahominy. Nothing more from Longstreet. By 10:30 A.M., the fight between Hooker and Pickett was ending and Smith messaged Longstreet that "The enemy are, from all accounts, crossing the river and concentrating below on this side. I have as yet heard nothing of Ripley's brigade or that from Huger's division." Smith went on to tell Longstreet to "ask Stuart if he cannot devise means for keeping your left and Whiting's right in communication with each other." Smith gave his reason. "I have directed Whiting to take closer defensive relations with Magruder's troops...." Smith ended by stating that the action "was absolutely necessary to enable a good defence to be made whilst you are pivoting on Whiting's position."[27]

The pace of message traffic then increased. G. W. Smith almost immediately received another missive from Longstreet. It stated that the brigade in question could not be spared. He claimed that all but one of his brigades were already fighting. It went on to mention that Smith was not presently fighting, so the brigade would not be sent, unless the situation changed. Another message from Longstreet arrived on the heels of the previous one. In this one, he went so far as to suggest that the entire Federal army was in his front, and requested a diversion be made by Smith to help Longstreet's men hold their ground. Longstreet also complained about his ammunition supply running out too quickly. Longstreet subsequently claimed that there was also a statement that "with the aid of his (Smith's) troops the battle would be ours." Smith made no acknowledgement of that postscript.[28]

Now Smith could appreciate what Johnston had suffered through the previous day. For the second day in a row, the Confederate commanding general had delegated a critical part of the battle plan to Longstreet and then waited miles away for that critical action to be executed. Again, Longstreet had disregarded his orders and totally changed the battle plan for the worse. And again, the commanding general, this time Smith, had to wait impotently for news from Longstreet. Smith, likely remembering Johnston's earlier remark about wishing the troops were back in their camps, called a council of war. Attendees were Whiting, McLaws and the chief engineer, Major Walter H. Stevens. While this council was in session, another Longstreet message arrived, urgently appealing for reinforcements. Longstreet was sticking with the assertion that the entire Federal army was attacking him. Smith was beginning to believe that Longstreet's situation was more serious than he originally believed.[29]

Smith made a decision. He sent McLaws to personally inform Longstreet that Ripley's brigade, coming from Richmond, as well as 5,000 other troops were hurrying to Longstreet's aid. McLaws also was to assure Longstreet that all of the Federals were not on his front. Longstreet was told not to retreat, but to take the reinforcements and attempt to drive the Federals back to their original positions. Smith's action essentially ended the day's fighting. It was extremely unlikely that Longstreet would attack, regardless of how many reinforcements he received.[30]

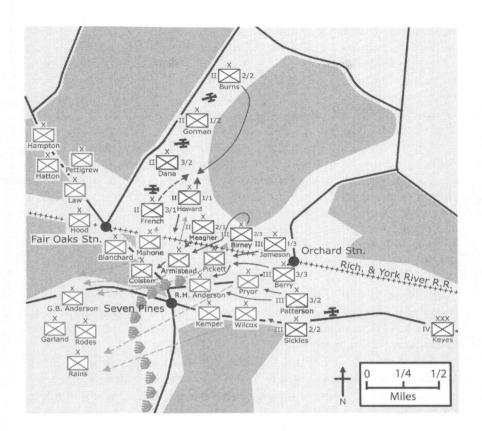

Map 12.2—Seven Pines, Day Two Overall, June 1}

About 1:30 P.M., Davis returned to Smith's headquarters, asking where he could find General Lee. Smith was surprised at the question. He asked Davis if he had a particular reason for believing that Lee would be there. Davis candidly responded that he had told Lee earlier that day to assume command of the Army of Northern Virginia. Smith attempted to put a good face on, and responded with "Ah, in that case he will probably soon be here…." Smith later recalled that he and the President walked for half an hour and chatted on a number of subjects, but not on the situation on the battlefield. At 2:00 P.M., Lee rode up and assumed command.[31]

About 9:00 P.M. on June 1, D. H. Hill authorized a general withdrawal to the vicinity of Seven Pines. About twenty minutes later, Federal forces along the Williamsburg road gave up their pursuit.[32] June 2 was a day of quiet around both Seven Pines and Fair Oaks. Neither McClellan, nor the newly appointed Robert E. Lee was motivated to resume the fighting. Lee was sure that McClellan would now significantly build up his forces south of the Chickahominy. Due mainly to the poor placement of his forces in late May, McClellan's army had suffered heavy losses. These losses reinforced his erroneous belief that he was facing a Confederate army much larger than his own. He also knew that Johnston was a defensively oriented general. For Johnston to initiate the attack on Seven Pines on May 31, McClellan felt he must have had a superior force.[33]

On the night of June 3, the first brigade of Hooker's division, commanded by Brigadier General Grover, reoccupied the battlefield near Seven Pines after the Confederate withdrawal two days prior. The pickets were exhorted to be especially watchful, as the Federals expected a follow-up Confederate attack.

The advance guard for the brigade was the 11th Massachusetts under Colonel Robert Cowdin. When they awakened at dawn, they discovered they had slept amongst the hastily buried and unburied dead, as well as numerous horses. The corpses were black and swollen, and there were maggots everywhere. The bodies had been there for several days, and the repulsive little worms were all around the troops. The maggots invaded all of the personal possessions of the men of the 11th Massachusetts. Most of the soldiers passed on breakfast.[34]

The Army of the Potomac sustained 5,031 casualties at Seven Pines, and the Confederates 6,134. Thus far, this was the deadliest fight in the Eastern theater. Compared to Shiloh in the West, the casualties at Seven Pines were minor. What was unique about the battle, though, were the subsequent controversies, assaulted and ruined military reputations, and long-lived misconceptions. In that respect, Seven Pines ranked up there with Gettysburg.[35]

The reports of both commanding generals had much in common. As might be expected, given their personalities, they claimed victory, glossed over their lackluster personal performances, and blamed their inept subordinates for the less than desirable outcome. McClellan, in rosy prose, claimed to have inflicted great losses on the Confederates, and was now within four miles of Richmond. He went on to tell Washington that "I only wait for the river to fall to cross with the rest of the force and make a general attack...." Where McClellan mentioned setbacks at all, he picked Silas Casey as his scapegoat. McClellan went so far as to recommend that Casey's division be broken up and the usable parts of it transferred to other divisions. McClellan never acknowledged that his terrible troop dispositions had made it impossible for Casey's division to hold very long against the Confederate attack.[36]

Casey, quite naturally, strenuously disagreed. In his report, he maintained that his division put up a stubborn resistance, held their position for over three hours against a much larger Confederate force, and was not reinforced. During this defense, Casey's division took 30% casualties, and represented about a third of all Federal casualties in the battle. Casey ended his report by urging his superiors not to blame his men for all the Federal mistakes at Seven Pines.[37]

Casey, as a division commander, had to route his report through his corps commander, Erasmus Keyes. General Keyes, who was primarily responsible for the drubbing the Federals took at Seven Pines, was set on sacrificing someone else to deflect criticism from himself. Keyes had to be careful about how he criticized Casey. Keyes couldn't bludgeon someone who had lost a third of his men. Keyes shrewdly avoided any criticism of Casey's tactical management of his division. Instead, he disagreed with Casey's assertion that he had not been reinforced. Keyes explained that he continued to send reinforcements to Casey, as long as there were troops to spare. The egotistical Keyes also made ambiguous references to "the men who left the ranks and the field, especially the officers who went away without orders." All who read it understood that Keyes was referring to Casey's men.[38]

Heintzelman was not above piling on Casey. Heintzelman told McClellan that a III Corps officer had visited Casey's camp, and that "he found more men bayoneted or shot within their shelter-tents than outside of them." This would indicate cowardice, and that Casey was attempting to protect such men. Heintzelman essentially accused Casey of knowing which regiments behaved badly, but would not reveal them.[39]

McClellan eagerly joined the conspiracy to scapegoat Casey. On June 5, Casey received McClellan's findings on the battle. The rout was blamed on "defective disposition of pickets and inefficiency of officers together with bad discipline...." McClellan reported to Secretary of War Stanton that Casey displayed personal courage, but asserted that he did not have the confidence of his troops. The long-term course of action was to promote Casey for his bravery, and reassign him to Washington. Casey never again commanded troops in the field. McClellan, after he had been fired and retired, helped to remove the stigma from Casey and his division, but it was too late for Casey's military career.[40]

The Confederate commander was no less averse to finding a scapegoat. Convalescing from his wounds, Johnston read Longstreet's report and seemed to place great stock in it. When Johnston wrote his own report, he blamed Huger for almost everything that went awry on the Confederate side. He claimed on June 24 that the fact that Huger's division wasn't in position to attack when G. W. Smith, Longstreet and D. H. Hill's men moved out was the reason that Keyes' IV Corps was not destroyed, only defeated. He added that an attack by Huger as late as 4:00 P.M. would have made for a more thorough defeat of Keyes. Then Johnston crossed the line. He willfully tried to protect Longstreet by vilifying Huger. Johnston told the giant lie that Longstreet faithfully executed the master plan for the battle, when in fact he made a hash of it in pursuit of greater glory for himself. Johnston then got Smith to delete several sentences from his report that would embarrass Longstreet by exposing his failure to follow orders. Unfortunately for Smith, he had not, at that point come to realize that Longstreet had made a fool of Smith on the second day of the battle.[41]

Huger, as did his Federal counterpart Casey, protested loudly. Neither man secured any satisfaction. Huger could not get neither Longstreet nor Johnston to revise their reports to make them more truthful, nor would Johnston order a court of inquiry. Huger finally requested a court-martial, citing Johnston's indisposition to investigate the matter.[42]

By the time Huger saw the reports in August, 1862, many things had changed. Longstreet's performance during the Seven Days had led Lee to deem him indispensable. Conversely, Lee had come to desire that Huger serve elsewhere in the war. By then, Lee had given Huger's division to Richard H. Anderson, and had Huger transferred to the Trans-Mississippi in a non-leadership role.[43]

Interestingly, only Casey and Huger wrote reports which placed criticism where it belonged. Longstreet's disobedience of the army commander's orders two days in a row has monopolized the study of Seven Pines, to the point where Keyes' part in the defeat of IV Corps has decidedly taken a back seat. Longstreet's guilt was not made public until many years later, when Smith became a prolific writer on the subject. Even then, the emphasis was on the "wrong road" aspect of the battle, not Longstreet's neglect of tactical control of his forces on either day.

Despite his complaints to the contrary, Smith did not have his reputation ruined by Seven Pines. In truth, his fortunes declined slowly and steadily, as it became apparent that he was not capable of field command. His nervous ailment alone should have taken him out of the field long before Seven Pines.

Many historians have given great credit to Sumner for crossing his divisions over tenuous bridges and coming to the aid of Heintzelman and Keyes. It was widely agreed that this was more a reflection of his personal soldierly qualities of tenacity and determination, rather than an appreciation of optimum tactics. This popular act by Sumner made the efforts of Heintzelman to slow the Confederate advance seem much less important. There was no glory whatsoever for the division commanders involved.

On the Confederate side, D. H. Hill performed at a level that should have deserved notice by historians. Despite the fact that he lacked sufficient staff to properly control the number of troops assigned to him at times, had scant assets for scouting the enemy, and didn't really know what the army commander wanted done, he stuck to the attack on May 31. The following day, he launched a morning attack, which was repulsed, then reinforced his main line, holding it all day. This was at the time when Longstreet was sending panic-laced messages to Smith.[44]

A look at the tactics employed by both sides reveals a typical difference between the two armies in the east during 1862. The Confederates, by and large, employed their troop using the command structure of divisions and brigades. The Federals, on the other hand, seemed prone to destroying their command structure and maneuvering by regiments. The best example is that of D. H. Hill, who kept his division as concentrated as possible, and enjoyed great success on May 31 against Casey, then Couch. Hill never succumbed to the temptation of stealing a regiment from one brigade and personally placing it somewhere else to meet a suddenly noticed need. Keyes is the best case of the opposite. Keyes, a corps commander, meddled in the command structure all the way down to the regimental level. He split his forces into four small commands, most a mixture of men from different brigades. Keyes failed to communicate adequately with Heintzelman, his superior, as well as with his division commanders, Casey and Couch. This difference in tactics can be seen throughout 1862 and the first part of 1863 in the East.

No battle can be analyzed without discussion of who won and who lost. On May 31, Hill defeated Keyes' IV Corps, capturing several guns, and driving them out of Seven Pines, despite their reinforcement by Kearny's division from III Corps. Hill's spoils were the tiny village and the camps of Casey's division. On June 1, Sumner and Couch repulsed an attack by Whiting near Fair Oaks Station. Whiting paid heavily, but his division remained combat effective. Overall, the Confederates were the tactical victors.

Seven Pines was a strategic draw. D. H. Hill was ordered to withdraw from Seven Pines the evening of June 1, and McClellan's army remained in essentially the same position, very close to Richmond. The loss of 5,000 men was not a crippling event for McClellan.

For the Confederates, while it was likely that the battle was a morale builder, it cost over 6,100 casualties and failed to push McClellan back from Richmond. They suffered from a serious internal power struggle which squandered their opportunity for a real victory, and cost lives. Perhaps their greatest gain was getting rid of Johnston as commander in the East. Although Lee was still feeling his way during the Seven Days battles, leaving Johnston in command might well have resulted in the fall of Richmond and the demise of the Confederacy in 1862. However, Jefferson Davis would likely have relieved Johnston and replaced him with Robert E. Lee before that would have occurred.

It is worthwhile to study the battle of Seven Pines for the issue raised earlier, the disparate manner in which the two armies fought the battle. Armed with an appreciation of the deleterious effects of dispersing one's forces and breaking down the command structure, we can better understand subsequent, more important battles.

At Seven Pines, the generals squabbled and blundered, and the soldiers fought bravely. There were many heroic acts by regimental or smaller parties during this battle. It is a testament to the common soldier and the officers at the company and regimental level, that they could fight so hard with such pathetic senior leadership.

CHAPTER 13

Change of Command

On the afternoon of June 1, the Army of Northern Virginia received a new commander. General Robert E. Lee rode out from his office in Richmond on his gray mount Traveller, and at 2:00 P.M., relieved Major General Gustavus W. Smith.

Lee's assumption of command had a number of effects on the Confederate Army. Besides the obvious results obtained from placing the army under a more competent commander, there were also several not so visible benefits. Perhaps the most important of these was the enhanced relationship between the new commander of the Army of Northern Virginia and the Confederate President. More about that effect later.[1]

General Lee arrived at his field headquarters just at the end of the two-day battle of Seven Pines, passing on his ride, a stream of casualties being transported to Richmond. It had been a costly contest, with over 11,000 men of both armies killed, well over 8,000 wounded, and over 1,000 captured/missing. For over 20,000 casualties, the two armies gained nothing. The small amount of ground taken by the Confederates near Seven Pines on May 31 would soon be given back.

Lee had to know that his first priority had to be to regroup and reorganize his army. The Southern soldiers had fought hard, despite the incompetent performance of the majority of their generals. Lee needed to make leadership changes, reorganize units, secure more reinforcements, and replenish supplies and equipment. These actions would take a bit of time, but there were some immediate concerns that had to be dealt with. After all, he had an invading Federal army of over 100,000 men in his front, and little maneuver room between his army and his nation's capital. Lee also had to tend to the process of evacuating the remainder of the wounded back to Richmond, removing the dead from the battlefield, and gathering up discarded weapons, equipment and supplies that remained on the field. He needed to collect and study the reports of his subordinate commanders, and replace wounded or deceased officers. His plate was full.

The sheer amount of wounded men involved put a great strain on the Confederate government. Richmond had some experience in dealing with wounded, but nothing to compare with the current problem. After the battle of First Manassas, the city took care of 1,500 wounded, but now there were three times that number, and medical facilities around the city were stretched thin. They filled all the normal military hospitals, then the civilian ones, then began to place them in public buildings and private homes. Inevitably, official efforts were inadequate, and private citizens, mainly women, intervened. According to Sallie Putnam, "Their wants were supplied in a few hours by the citizens, who cooked and sent refreshments, beds, pillows and blankets, water, soap, and all that could for the time relieve the helpless sufferers."

The dead were another sort of problem. Their rigid bodies were stacked like firewood and hauled to the capital by overloaded wagons. The citizens of Richmond anxiously and fearfully sought word of their loved ones. They mostly stood around the public bulletin boards, waiting for the latest casualty updates to be posted. Seven Pines served to make the threat of McClellan's nearby army more real. It was a sad city in those times.[2]

The Federal wounded fared even worse than their Confederate peers. The Medical Director of the Army of the Potomac was Charles Stuart Tripler. He was better at red tape than providing for the wounded soldiers of McClellan's army. Even though the Federals had fewer killed and wounded, Tripler could not handle the problem. His ambulance corps was wholly inadequate, and his field hospitals were already occupied caring for the many soldiers ill from their time in the Chickahominy Swamp. He had kept the ill in his field hospitals, rather than transporting them to the North for care. Now he had thousands of wounded soldiers and nowhere to care for them. The Federals had the female nurses of the U. S. Sanitary Commission to care for their wounded men. The civilian Commission had staffed a flotilla of hospital ships, but Dr. Tripler disapproved of their organization. Nevertheless, some of the ships were at White House Landing, and were literally lifesavers for the Federal wounded.

The Richmond & York River Railroad was used effectively by both sides. The Confederates used the western half to help move wounded to Richmond, and the Federals used the eastern half to move their wounded to White House Landing. Jammed tightly into freight cars, they arrived together—the dead, the wounded, the maggots. They were laid on the ground in the rain until they could be provided space on a hospital ship. No sooner than the doctors and nurses would feed, wash and dress the worst wounds of their charges than another train would arrive with more. It was a horrific experience for the wounded as well as the nurses and doctors.[3]

Rudolph J. Schroeder, III

Library of Congress

Robert Edward Lee

All the while, the task of cleaning up the battlefield went on. Arms dropped by friend and foe alike were gathered up, and equipment found to be serviceable was sent where it could be of use. Confederate troops which had gained ground during the battle received orders by Lee to move back on the evening of June 1 to their pre-battle camps.

After a while, Federal troops of Hooker's division reoccupied those camps. Some of them remarked on the extent of the carnage, the sight of poorly buried corpses, washed up by the recent rains. Others had not been buried at all. The stench of burned horses was sickening at first, but the men soon adapted to it. The trees were riddled with musket balls. The overall effect impressed many of the green troops.

They found their camps now contained almost nothing of use. They did find one curious prize, a double-decker bus from Richmond with Exchange Hotel painted on the side, used in a pinch by the Confederates as an ambulance, now stuck in the mud. The industrious Federals dug it out and entertained themselves by riding around in it.[4]

In his customary fashion, McClellan proclaimed Seven Pines a great Federal victory. The portable printing press (more to be said about that later) that was a cherished part of his headquarters equipment, cranked out an address to the troops on June 2. It spoke of his fulfillment of the first part of his promise to them. It reminded them that they now were face to face with the enemy before the enemy capital, and that "The final and decisive battle is at hand." It went on to urge the army to crush the rebellion here and now, and to restore peace to the union. The address was well received by his dedicated troops.

McClellan had been lucky so far. Seven Pines, with any kind of competent Confederate generalship, could have resulted in the destruction of the III and IV Corps. Luckily, Sumner was thinking clearly that day and had crossed the Chickahominy in time to reinforce the two isolated corps. McClellan had contributed little to the battle, other than direct Sumner to try to reinforce Keyes and Heintzelman. McClellan did give brief thought on June 1 to moving on Richmond with the two uncommitted corps north of the river. The corps commanders, Porter and Franklin, advised McClellan that it was an impracticable idea.

Such a move on Richmond was only possible if McClellan were to change his view of his situation on the Peninsula. He had always insisted that Lee's was a larger, more powerful army. He was convinced that he had to move with caution from this point on. Such a view was wholly inconsistent with a risky attack on Richmond with only two corps.[5]

In Richmond, the opinion of the battle of Seven Pines was much different than that on McClellan's portable printing press. It was considered a Confederate victory, emphasizing the sound defeat of Casey's division on May 31. This elation was well tempered by the grief over losing more than 6,000 Confederate soldiers. The certain fact was that both armies were exactly where they were before the battle, just a bit smaller.

No one in Richmond understood that Johnston had conceived a well thought out battle plan, or that it had gone totally awry. No one wished to criticize a general in the hospital with serious wounds. Longstreet, who should have been blamed for what went wrong, was able to lay it all off on the hapless Huger. Try as he might, Huger could not convince the Confederate government to convene a court of inquiry. Huger was deemed guilty by the press of shirking his duty. President Davis, as do all politicians, put a positive spin on the lack of a decisive victory, and said, "The opportunity being lost we must try to find another."[6]

Lee's thoughts became directed at creating another chance to get at McClellan's army in the field. He knew that if he backed his army into the works at Richmond and allowed McClellan to lay siege, the Federal heavy guns and logistical superiority would ultimately cause the city to surrender. He had to fight the Federals in the open, where maneuver could possibly counter the size advantage of the Federals. Lee believed in taking the initiative. The question was how to seize the initiative both strategically and tactically. Lee could not have been more different than Joe Johnston.

Lee began by calling together his generals on June 3 at a house called the Chimneys on the Nine Mile road. Instead of telling them his plans, he asked his subordinates what their thoughts were concerning the army's condition and position. The generals spoke freely and openly, happy to be consulted, after serving under the mysterious Johnston. The mood, a little tense at first, improved, and there was even a little humor injected by D. H. Hill. There were a variety of opinions. Concerns were voiced about McClellan's big guns and doubt about being able to defend Richmond against such a large Federal host. Lee reassured them, telling them he intended to fight for the nation's capital, but gave them little in the way of details. Most left the meeting reassured.[7]

Although he chose not to shower his generals with details, Lee had already begun to plan the reorganization of the army, and plan, in general concept, his next battle. Richmond had received a telegram on June 1 from Alexander R. Boteler, a Confederate Congressman and staff officer to Jackson. Boteler's message detailed the threat to Jackson's army of the several Federal columns in the Shenandoah, and passed on Jackson's urgent need for reinforcements. All Lee could do for the present was order scattered garrison troops from the upper part of the Valley to march to Jackson immediately. When Boteler reached Richmond, Davis,

Lee and Boteler met to discuss the future of the Army of the Valley, as it was called.

Jackson sent Boteler to Richmond with a proposal to reinforce the Army of the Valley. It would be brought up to 40,000 men and invade Maryland and Pennsylvania. Lee saw the advantage of that move, but thought it feasible only if Georgia and the Carolinas would offer their garrison troops. Just as quickly as Lee embraced Jackson's idea, he dropped it. He probably thought it would result in McClellan's recall, and he wanted to defeat and destroy McClellan right where he was.

Any future plans for Jackson and his small army depended on their being able to escape the trap presently closing on them. When Boteler left Jackson on May 31, Jackson was retreating southward, up the Valley. Fremont was on Stonewall's right front, Shields' division was on Jackson's left front, and Banks was in his rear, reinforced and ready for revenge.

It appeared that the three converging Federal forces had a fair likelihood of trapping Jackson and mauling him. Stonewall, however, seemed unworried. He quietly asked for reinforcements, and Lee sent him Lawton's Georgia brigade, en route to Richmond from Savannah.

Jackson told Lee that he planned to attack and defeat Shields first. Lee had every confidence that Stonewall would accomplish what he intended.

Stonewall, in fact, slipped between Fremont and Shields and retreated up the Valley. The Federals could not overhaul him. On June 8, he turned and dealt them a blow at Cross Keys. The next day he did the same at Port Republic. Both Fremont and Shields were battered, and turned and fled down the Valley. On June 10, Jackson sent a telegram to General Cooper that read, "Through God's blessing, the enemy at Port Republic was this day routed with the loss of six pieces of his artillery."[8] Now Lee was comfortable that the Valley was not immediately threatened, and Jackson and his men were available to do Lee's bidding.

Jackson's amazingly successful campaign in the Shenandoah Valley motivated Lee to devise a clever strategy to deceive the Federals. It would be a carefully designed double game that would give Lee several options. He would reinforce Jackson enough to allow him to strike the Federals hard there, while also making him powerful enough to leave the Valley and join Lee against McClellan before Richmond.

Lee knew that it was almost impossible to reinforce Jackson in secrecy. Federal spies were plentiful in Richmond. Therefore, Lee set about making the reinforcement of the Army of the Valley obvious. He had already ordered Lawton's brigade of 3,600 to Jackson's aid, and their route was by rail from Petersburg to Lynchburg, then northward to the Valley. Lee also sent two brigades (Whiting's and Hood's) of the Army of Northern

Virginia under Whiting. These 4,500 men marched through Richmond by daylight to the railroad station for the trip to Lynchburg. Lee knew this news would reach McClellan and Lincoln. Not wanting his deception to be excessively obvious, Lee asked the editors of the Richmond newspapers not to comment on the troop movements. Examples can be cited where refugees and deserters were employed to help spread the word. McClellan bought the ruse, hook, line and sinker. On June 18, he told Lincoln "If ten or fifteen thousand men have left Richmond to reinforce Jackson, it illustrates their strength and confidence."[9]

Simultaneously, Lee was working on his overall plan of attack. By June 5, he had given a general outline to President Davis. Lee stated that "I am preparing a line that I can hold with part of our forces in front, while with the rest I will endeavor to make a diversion to bring McClellan out." In stark contrast to the style of Johnston, Lee put significant effort toward explaining and discussing his plan with the President. Davis responded by promptly approving personnel changes Lee had submitted and pledging to give Lee what he needed.

Unlike Lincoln, Davis had excellent military credentials. He took his commander-in-chief responsibilities seriously, and expected to be seen in that light. Johnston never acknowledged Davis' credentials, and did not enjoy the President's confidence. Even Johnston came to realize that the new relationship between commanding general and President was an important benefit for the Confederacy.

The aforementioned relationship between Lee and Davis was well founded in personal trust and philosophical orientation. These underpinnings would assure that the general felt no need to withhold information from the President, and that the President gave the general adequate authority to meet his responsibilities. The relationship gave the Confederates a large advantage over their counterparts on the Federal side, where the dysfunctional relationship between Lincoln and McClellan caused constant problems.

Jefferson Davis was a student of the Swiss strategist Henri Jomini, who was an interpreter of the thinking of Napoleon Bonaparte. Davis believed that a good offense was the best defense. Lee was an audacious general, who believed that battles were to be won by maneuver rather than costly frontal assaults. Their thinking was sufficiently similar to foster a hand-in-glove approach to military planning.[10]

In making good on his promise to Davis, Lee had his engineers lay out new, improved defensive works east of Richmond. Combat units were set to work on their construction. Despite initial complaints that it was more properly the work of slaves, not white men, the work went forward. Lee, amused by their complaints, expressed to Davis that manual labor was a soldierly virtue, even in Roman times. Soon, almost all came to understand that the new works made Richmond defensible by fewer men, thus freeing up troops for maneuver.[11]

Now that he had a conceptual plan for getting at McClellan, and had found a way to incorporate Jackson's Army of the Valley, Lee could devote more time to the other major part of his mission, the reorganization and beefing up of the army. First on his list was surely G. W. Smith. After assuming command of the army due to Johnston's wounding, Smith experienced what we would consider a nervous breakdown. The general's doctors prescribed complete rest. Lee had seen Smith's performance at Seven Pines, and decided to remove Smith from the command of troops.

G. W. Smith was commander of the Left Wing of the army, so Lee discontinued the wing concept. Smith was also a division commander, so Lee also disbanded Smith's division. Two brigades, those of Whiting and Hood, were sent to reinforce Jackson, the regiments of another brigade were reassigned to other of Jackson's brigades. The other two brigades were given to A. P. Hill, forming a large division of six brigades. Smith spent the remainder of his military career in behind-the-lines duties, eventually resigning his commission. Lee decided Smith didn't pass muster as a combat commander, and there was no recovery from that verdict.[12]

By breaking up Smith's division, Lee made other changes necessary. A. P. Hill went from a brigade commander to a major general commanding a division of six brigades, the largest in the army. Magruder's command was reorganized from two divisions into three. About thirty regiments moved from one command to another. When the reorganization was complete, ten new infantry regiments had been formed and put into existing brigades. The artillery branch was finally organized to be more responsive to the army commander, and nine new batteries were added.

New commands joined the army. Lawton's brigade, as previously mentioned, was sent to reinforce Jackson. Ripley's brigade came up from Charleston, and was assigned to D. H. Hill's division. Ransom's brigade from North Carolina went to Huger's division. North Carolina sent Theophilus Holmes with three brigades. With Jackson's Valley Army, Lee would have 92,400 men at his disposal.

Even McClellan had predicted that the Confederates would scrape up every possible man to defend Richmond. They did, but did not achieve anywhere near the numbers McClellan had envisioned. This was, however, the largest army Lee had in the entire war, and was the closest he came to matching his opponent in number of troops.[13]

On the Federal side of the lines, McClellan was taking his own actions to ready his army for an advance on Richmond. He was cheerfully receiving reinforcements from Lincoln. A further bit of good news was that the elderly (78 years old) and difficult commander of Fort Monroe, General Wool, was replaced by General John Dix. Fort Monroe's garrison was also placed under McClellan's direct control.

McClellan wasted no time in making use of some of Dix's garrison. Nine infantry regiments were moved up to fill vacancies caused by the battle of Seven Pines. Washington also sent another infantry regiment, and a battery from Baltimore joined McClellan's army. Altogether, this swelled the rolls of the Army of the Potomac by 10,300 men. McClellan also convinced Washington to finally release McCall's I Corps division to him. McCall's men began arriving on June 10. With these reinforcements, McClellan could match the reinforcements Lee had brought up from the Carolinas and Georgia, man for man. McClellan would now have 105,900 men present-for-duty. There were still another 9,300 men in the garrison at Fort Monroe and 7,000 men in North Carolina under Burnside that McClellan could summon.[14]

Despite the receipt of all this help, McClellan wanted more. Looking at what he knew about recent events in the Western theater, he asserted that General Beauregard and a large part of his army were coming quickly to aide Lee in defending Richmond, so McClellan requested that Halleck send part of his command to reinforce the Federals before Richmond. This he did with no proof that Beauregard was on the move.

When made aware of McClellan's request, Halleck made the point that he had no intelligence reports of a planned move east by Beauregard. Halleck went further, claiming that any weakening of his army would motivate Beauregard to go back on the offensive in the West. McClellan, from this point in time forward, concluded that he was friendless in Washington, and gave up on getting help from Halleck. He claimed that Lincoln "has again fallen into the arms of my enemies, and is no longer a friend of mine."[15]

McClellan's opinion of Lincoln's views was far from accurate. Lincoln stood by McClellan far longer than perhaps he should have. The President was sincere in attempting to reinforce his general. To Stanton, Lincoln echoed McClellan's contention that Richmond was paramount. Letting his actions speak for him, Lincoln on June 8 ordered Stanton to deploy the remainder of McDowell's I Corps to move on Richmond. In the end, however, McDowell was never allowed to join McClellan's army. He was recalled yet a third time. I Corps was a very large corps, composed of five divisions. By mid-June, the divisions of Franklin and McCall had been sent to McClellan, that of Shields was too beat up to deploy, and those of King and Ricketts were retained to defend Washington. These last two were kept off the Peninsula by Lee's deception plan in the Valley.

It wasn't that Lincoln didn't understand what Jackson was doing in the Valley, he just didn't know what to do to stop it. To Lincoln's distress, he had no competent general in the Valley that could outthink and outmaneuver Stonewall. Most days, they could not even tell their President where the elusive Jackson was. So, Jackson continued to tie up Federal troops away from McClellan's army. Paranoia remained in Washington that Jackson was loose somewhere in the Federal rear, ready to fall on them without warning.[16]

McClellan continued to work hard on readying his army for the forthcoming campaign. One of his first projects was the repair of the Grapevine Bridge, followed by construction of eight more bridges across the Chickahominy upstream from the Grapevine span. To go with all the bridging, miles of roads were corduroyed. More roads were cut through the forest at appropriate places. McClellan was determined to be able to maneuver, even if it rained. He also had three miles of defensive works built facing Richmond. These works he supported with six earthen redoubts fitted with 40 guns. He wanted to prevent a repeat of the rout inflicted on Casey's division.

McClellan brought the II and VI Corps south of the river and had them dig in. Only Porter's V Corps was still north of the Chickahominy. Now McClellan moved his headquarters south of the river, to the Trent house on the Grapevine Bridge road. West Pointers would call this an "active defense," but some officers thought it looked more appropriate for an army preparing for a prolonged defense, rather than an assault. McClellan saw his preparations as a counter to what he thought was a numerically superior opponent.

McClellan was a frequent letter writer and detailed his plans in a letter to his wife, accompanied by a suitable map. He told her the next battle would be contested near Old Tavern, about a mile and a half south of the river. He planned to use his powerful artillery arm to gain Old Tavern, driving the defenders into their works around the city. He would then move up his heavy guns, shell the city and take it by assault.[17]

McClellan continued to tweak his organizational structure. He reorganized the artillery batteries in the II, III and IV Corps to provide each corps commander with a corps artillery reserve. This would give flexibility to the employment of their artillery. As with Lee and several of his generals, was intent on removing Casey, as he blamed Casey for the defeat at Seven Pines. McClellan assigned Peck to command Casey's division, and put

Casey in charge of the supply base at White House Landing. McClellan lacked confidence in Keyes, as well. Thus, he positioned Keyes' corps where he thought they had minimum chance of fighting. McClellan's plan for dealing with Sumner was to simply supervise him closely. McClellan also decided to make sure of his own personal safety, as Sumner would assume command if McClellan were wounded bad enough to leave the field. Porter, on the other end of McClellan's confidence scale, was put north of the river, responsible for the safety of the army's right flank. Porter's V Corps now had three divisions, McCall's I Corps division having arrived, and was the largest corps in the Army of the Potomac.[18]

During this short period between the battle of Seven Pines and the Seven Days, both Lee and McClellan accomplished a great deal. It was a day and night effort just to do the most essential of tasks to prepare their armies for what promised to be a fight that would certainly determine the course of the war. Nevertheless, during the period between Seven Pines and the Seven Days, some odd tasks were undertaken by these two military leaders.

McClellan found time to fix the blame for his failure to take Richmond on his superiors in Washington, even though the fight had not yet begun. He used the print media and the visits of foreign dignitaries to accomplish this task.[19]

McClellan even managed to stick his nose into the search for a peaceful resolution of the conflict. He communicated with Richmond regarding exchange of prisoners. When he assigned Colonel Thomas M. Key, a Kentuckian, to a flag-of-truce meeting with the Confederates, McClellan took the amazing step of suggesting to Key that he try to broaden the meeting to discuss possible steps toward ending the war. Key met with Brigadier General Howell Cobb.

Cobb, likely astute enough to know that Lincoln would not sanction such negotiations to be conducted between military, rather than civilian parties, declined and reminded Key of the narrow purpose of the meeting. Subsequently, McClellan offered to forward to President Lincoln some thoughts on "the present state of military affairs throughout the whole country."[20]

Another strange happening, which involved the leaders of both armies, was the matter of passing Mrs. Robert E. Lee through the Federal army to within Confederate lines. Mrs. Lee had moved from White House in May to Marlbourne, the home of Edmund Ruffin, a widely-known Virginia secessionist, on the Pamunkey River. McClellan's army occupied the plantation and placed guards around the home. Mrs. Lee voiced her objection, and McClellan was a bit embarrassed about the situation. On

June 10, she was transported in a carriage to McClellan, who greeted her with appropriate civility, and had her and a Confederate major, W. Roy Mason, sent by Lee, escorted by cavalry to Meadow Bridge, where she crossed to the Confederate side and was greeted by General Lee and his cheering troops.[21]

McClellan's planning for the capture of Richmond continued, still resting on the underlying assumption that Lee had a larger army. This assumption was based, in part, on reports from his chief spy, Allan Pinkerton. Pinkerton, who sometimes used the alias Major E. J. Allen, reported on June 15 that the Confederate army near Richmond numbered between 150,000 and 200,000 men. The estimate was refined to 180,000, and that, said Pinkerton, was likely an undercount.

McClellan thought the estimate was low. He gave no weight to Halleck's opinion, and believed that Beauregard was approaching Richmond. He had confidence, however, that his siege guns and well-constructed entrenchments would allow him to prevail. Still, he continued to stall Lincoln. On June 18, he wrote the President that "After tomorrow we shall fight the rebel army as soon as Providence will permit.. We shall await only a favorable condition of the earth and sky & the completion of some necessary preliminaries."

McClellan's delays were driving Lincoln a little crazy, but even worse was the effect of the general's delusion about the size of Lee's army. That delusion was causing McClellan to forgo opportunities to attack. The weather had been good for over a week, and the ground was dry. Jackson was not there yet; Lee didn't send for him until June 16, and his two divisions didn't begin their march until two days later. Beauregard was not coming. General McClellan, at this point, had 50% more men than Lee. This was the time to attack, and McClellan's delusion prevented him from doing so.

McClellan continued to want more assets before he attacked. He wanted Burnside's force from North Carolina, more heavy guns, his fortifications completely finished, supplies prepositioned near Drewry's Bluff, and the U.S. Navy to destroy a bridge between Richmond and Petersburg. On June 23, McClellan wrote to his friend Samuel Barlow, "We are making slow progress here—but I dare not rush this Army on which I feel the fate of the nation depends." He continued to delay during this time of golden opportunity. The result was that he had to fight Lee a week later, after Lee's army was up to full strength.[22]

While Lee and McClellan planned and prepared for the upcoming battles, the troops in the lines simply endured. The weather turned from warm to hot, and their collective health declined apace. On June 20, the Federal army had 11,000 men unfit for duty due to sickness. Those numbers should not have been surprising, as the men sometimes had no shelter, mediocre food, and were working hard to build McClellan's desired fortifications. The most common maladies were dysentery, chronic diarrhea, and a syndrome called "Chickahominy Fever" by the troops. It was likely malaria, typhoid or typhus. The men's diet, consisting primarily of salted meats and hardtack, allowed scurvy to make itself felt. Senior officers were not any luckier than the private soldiers. McClellan suffered malaria and acute neuralgia. A total of ten Federal generals became seriously ill, and one, William H. Keim died. On the Confederate side, five generals fell ill.[23]

Contributing factors to the high incidence of disease among the troops were the steamy atmosphere, called "miasma," and the poor drinking water. The engineers picked locations for their fortifications that maximized their effectiveness. The locations were not necessarily convenient to sources of springs for clean drinking water. The soldiers were reduced to drinking surface water. The longer a unit was camped at a given location, the greater the effect of poor sanitation on drinking water. The situation could only get worse with time.[24]

The soldiers, as do soldiers everywhere and in all wars, did their best to overcome their environment. They wrote home to have food items sent to them, bought items from nearby sutlers, stole eggs, foraged for berries, and even milked nearby farmers' cows in the night.[25]

South of the Chickahominy, the two armies faced each other at a distance of about a mile in heavy woods. The only contacts were small clashes between pickets. Occasionally, there were even friendly encounters, where privates exchanged items such as newspapers, coffee and tobacco, and agreements to not fire for a specified period of time were reached.

The soldiers even engaged in discussions of when and where the battle would be fought. Some were of the opinion that the works were a bad idea. They favored meeting in the open, fighting it out, and getting it over with. Others favored McClellan's pace, slow and sure.[26]

CHAPTER 14

Stuart's Ride Around McClellan

(June 12–15)

The Army of Northern Virginia in June of 1862 had a cavalry arm consisting of one brigade under Brigadier General James Ewell Brown "Jeb" Stuart. Stuart was a 29 year-old Virginian, West Point graduate and experienced with the 1st U.S. Cavalry on the Kansas frontier. He was well known to Robert E. Lee, having been Lee's aide at the capture of the abolitionist John Brown at Harper's Ferry. Stuart also served under Joseph E. Johnston, and fought bravely at First Manassas as commander of the 1st Virginia Cavalry.[1]

Stuart was famous throughout the Confederate Army for his appearance. He wore a gold-braided jacket, a yellow sash and cavalry cape. Add to those items gauntlets, shiny jackboots, then top it off with a plumed hat, and you have the last of the cavaliers. Fortunately for Stuart, he had the talent to go with the appearance.

Stuart was the master of reconnaissance and the gathering of intelligence. He was unmatched in his ability to examine an area and quickly evaluate its importance. Both Johnston and Lee shared this opinion.[2]

Lee called Stuart in on June 10, and ordered him to conduct an armed cavalry reconnaissance of McClellan's right. He wanted Stuart to determine exactly where McClellan's right flank was, how it was supported, and what was behind it. He directed Stuart to pay close attention to a ridgeline between the Chickahominy River and Totopotomoy Creek. Lee badly needed this information for a plan he was developing to attack Porter's V Corps north of the Chickahominy. The concept involved Jackson's Army of the Valley marching around Porter's right flank, thereby forcing him to abandon his entrenchments. Lee had to determine if the Federals were shifting their positions more to the right. He also needed to know how the Federals were protecting their supply line to White House Landing on the Pamunkey. Lee further cautioned Stuart to take full advantage of secrecy and surprise.

This mission was not a total surprise to Stuart, and Stuart and his scout John Singleton Mosby had already gathered some of the data Lee needed. Mosby and Stuart had engaged in a previous conversation on the area along the Pamunkey, and Mosby had remarked to Stuart that his cavalry was idle and he, Mosby, could find work for them.

Stuart went to Lee and described his scheme. He would develop McClellan's right flank, then circle the entire Federal army, returning along the shore of the James River. He attempted to sell the plan on the merits of a greater degree of surprise, and a better disguise of the purpose of the sortie. Lee did not forbid it to Stuart, but we have no record of his exact response. He again urged vigilance and caution. He also gave Stuart the latitude to manage the affair. It is highly likely that Stuart intended to circle McClellan's army if at all possible.[3]

Lee's order to Stuart advised him to take only hand-picked troopers and mounts, and to husband the mounts carefully. Stuart picked 1,200 men, and decided to take two guns of his horse artillery. At about 2:00 A.M. on June 12, Stuart roused his staff from their slumber. He made a terse announcement, "Gentlemen, in ten minutes every man must be in his saddle." The column was well gone from Richmond by dawn, heading north on the turnpike. The men had no idea what the mission was. Since they were riding north, some likely believed that they were going to the Shenandoah Valley to join Jackson's army there.

Stuart's 1,200 men came from the 1st and 9th Virginia Cavalry, part of the 4th Virginia Cavalry, two squadrons of the Jeff Davis (Mississippi) Legion Cavalry and the two-gun section of the Stuart horse artillery. The 1st Virginia Cavalry was commanded by Colonel Fitz Lee, the 9th Virginia Cavalry by Colonel "Rooney" Lee (Robert E. Lee's son), the six companies from the 4th Virginia Cavalry by Colonel William C. Wickham, the two squadrons of the Jeff Davis (Mississippi) Legion Cavalry by Major William T. Martin, and the Stuart horse artillery by Captain John Pelham. The column was accompanied by scouts, chosen because they came from the places that Stuart intended to examine. They had a good day's travel, due to their early start, riding about 22 miles. Camp was made three miles past Ashland.

The following morning, they turned east, passed Hanover Court House, then took the road southeast toward Old Church. Now all the men knew they were not going to the Shenandoah. They encountered mostly friendly civilians, glad to see the first Confederate troops since Branch had been driven from the vicinity of Hanover Court House by Fitz John Porter on May 27. The only Federals encountered were a few cavalry outposts, which were scattered or taken prisoner. This was part of the intel that Lee wanted badly. Stuart now knew that Porter had not extended his lines that far north. Concerned about Totopotomoy Creek being an impediment to Lee's plans, Stuart noted that the bridge was in good shape and unguarded.

Not more than a mile past the bridge, the column came across a Federal picket post that would not run without a fight. The two commanders of the units engaged met in individual mounted combat. Captain William Latane of the 9th Virginia Cavalry was killed by two revolver shots from Captain William Royall of the 5th U.S. Cavalry, after sustaining a saber wound from Latane. That was the only bright spot for the Federals. Reaching Old Church about 3:00 P.M., Stuart captured and destroyed the camp of the 5th U. S. Cavalry.

This point in the sortie was later described by Stuart as the turning point. He pretty much had all the information that Lee had wanted, and now had to decide whether to turn around and retrace his route back to Richmond, or execute his "favorite scheme" and circle McClellan's army. The facts relevant to the decision were clear to Stuart. The opposition had been weak, it was only about an eight mile ride to the York River Railroad and another eleven past that to the Chickahominy at Forge Bridge. After crossing the river, it should be an easy westward ride along the James. He gathered his commanders around him and broke the news. Some were startled. One officer, John Esten Cooke, suggested haste. Stuart then ordered the column to move out at a trot.[4]

By the time that Porter was informed of Stuart's sortie, the column was an hour's ride beyond Old Church. The reserve cavalry, under General Philip St. G. Cooke, was tasked to intercept Stuart's column and drive them from V Corps' rear.

It was going to be a bad day for Cooke, and on his birthday at that. Well, it was Friday the thirteenth. Beyond the date, there were other factors complicating General Cooke's assignment. First of all, the quarry, Jeb Stuart, was Cooke's son-in-law. Of perhaps more importance, Cooke's cavalry was not near as organized as Stuart's, and was scattered around the countryside. He eventually managed to assemble almost 500 troopers. To make matters seem even more impossible, Cooke received wildly exaggerated reports of the strength of Stuart's force. Lieutenant Richard Barnes of the 5th U.S. Cavalry was adamant that the Confederate force contained "five or six" regiments of infantry.

Understandably, Cooke was momentarily immobilized by the report. Five hundred horsemen, accompanied by the one infantry brigade at his disposal, could do little against such a force. By that evening, Cooke had picked up Stuart's trail at Old Church, but limited the speed of his pursuit to the rate of march of the infantry brigade, which was commanded by Brigadier General Gouverneur K. Warren of Sykes' division.

Warren urged Cooke to ride ahead, as the only indication of the presence of Confederate infantry was Byrnes' report. Cooke refused, evidently fearful of putting unsupported cavalry up against infantry accompanied by cavalry. Warren, disgusted with General Cooke, called the pursuit "a weary tramp, and an unsuccessful one foolishly managed."[5]

With the distance between Stuart's column and his pursuers steadily opening, Stuart reached Tunstall's station on the Richmond & York River Railroad. The Confederate cavalry was now only five miles from the massive Federal logistics base at White House Landing. Attempts to deceive the picket post were unsuccessful, and the Federals there made ready to defend the station. Stuart's men quickly took the station, then heard a train approaching from the west. There was insufficient time to barricade the tracks, and the engineer wisely added more steam and pushed his way through the few obstructions already on the track. A trooper managed to get alongside the locomotive and shoot the engineer, but the fireman took over and took the train safely into White House Landing.[6]

At this point, Stuart faced his second critical decision. The daylight was running out fast, and the Federals were surely all alerted by now. Unaware of the location and strength of his pursuers, he had to decide whether he should strike a blow at the White House base, or continue to make good his escape. Not knowing how much time he had before significant pursuers arrived to confront him, Stuart wisely chose to forego the opportunity before him. He did take the time to send a party of troopers to Garlick's Landing, upstream from White House. There they managed only to burn two schooners filled with forage, as well as a supply train of 75 wagons. Although this was but slight damage to McClellan's supply system, Stuart made the proper decision by not attacking White House. The defenses at White House consisted of 600 infantry, an artillery battery, and whatever support could be offered by the gunboats in the river. Stuart had also taken 165 prisoners and collected 260 horses and mules.[7] All taken together, this would be a very difficult fight for 1,200 tired cavalrymen. In retrospect, a brigade from V Corps reached Tunstall's by midnight. Stuart wisely didn't start a fight he probably wouldn't have been able to hang around and finish.

Stuart's men rode sleepily all night toward Forge Bridge. There was abundant moonlight, and the troopers and their prisoners, who were mounted upon mules to quicken the pace of the column, caught sight of the Chickahominy by daylight. Forge Bridge was unusable, having been burned by Johnston's retreat in May. Stuart had hoped to cross at a ford nearby, but the pesky little river was running swiftly due to recent storms. Several hours later, only a few dozen men were across. Stuart gambled the fate of his command on building a makeshift bridge on the remains of

Forge Bridge. A nearby barn supplied the timbers, and a skiff found nearby was pressed into service to set the timbers onto the remaining abutments. They were just barely long enough. The timbers were quickly planked by siding from the barn, and the bridge was soon operational. By 1:00 P.M., the troopers, prisoners and guns were across, and the recently built bridge was hastily fired by the withdrawing cavalrymen.

At the same time, a small scouting party of Federal cavalry appeared on the north bank, firing a few shots at the rear guard. Cooke's main body was still twelve miles away. Given the state of the Chickahominy, and the lack of a viable method of crossing, Stuart gave no more thought to the pursuit. He put Fitz Lee in command and rode ahead to Richmond, still some thirty-five miles away, to personally give his initial report to Robert E. Lee. It was late in the day on June 15 when the column arrived in Richmond to heroes' welcome.[8]

Many have written about Stuart's ride around McClellan. Most seem to have started out with an opinion as to whether it had a good result for the Confederates or an unintended bad result. From there, their research inevitably leads them to facts supporting their initial bias. I believe that this sortie, as with most events in human endeavor, had a mixed outcome. Certainly, Stuart provided Lee with the information he was sent to find. Stuart determined where McClellan's right flank was, that it was in the air, that Totopotomoy Creek could be easily crossed, that the Chickahominy was still a formidable barrier to the movement of troops, and that the Federal cavalry was scattered and ineffective. Unfortunately for the Confederates, it had the undesirable effect of a wakeup call to McClellan. It humiliated him, whether he was willing to admit it or not. It might have been the genesis of a slow effort to make the Federal cavalry equal to that of Lee, which eventually it was. It also gave McClellan pause to think about the security of his logistics base at White HouseLanding.[9]

The reaction in Richmond to Stuart's sortie was jubilant. Of late, only Jackson's victories in the Shenandoah provided any comfort to the South. Here was yet another new hero for the Confederacy, and they loved it. The newspapers printed articles about it *ad nauseum*. Some of the men who were on the sortie chuckled at the hyperbole of the periodicals.

There was more reaction than just runaway journalism. The sole Confederate casualty of the raid, Captain William Latane, was buried at a nearby plantation. The poet John R. Thompson composed a poem which was printed in the next issue of *Southern Literary Messenger*. The historical painter William D. Washington painted a scene of the funeral. Prints of that oil painting were found in Southern homes for many years thereafter. Latane became a true martyr, Stuart a hero, and the Ride Around McClellan a legend of the Confederacy.[10]

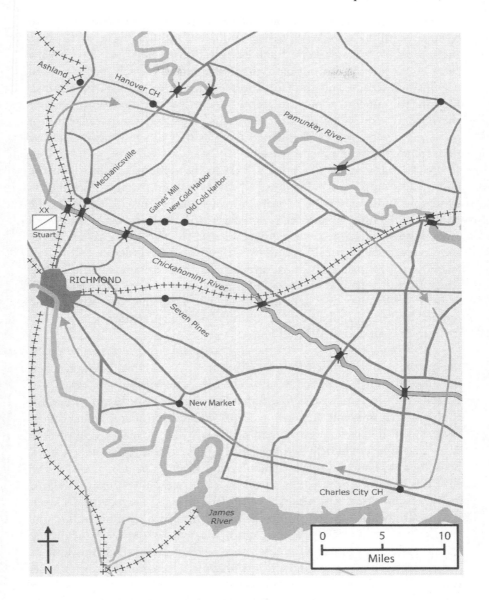

Map 14.1—Stuart's Ride Around McClellan, June 12–15

Stuart's ride evoked a variety of reactions, from surprise to fear to basic concern. One Federal soldier, William Y. Ripley, wrote to his wife that the rebels "gave us a start" and expressed that there must have been a "leak in our lines." We went on to detail the Federal casualties, the burned wagons and forage, and the Confederate attempt to destroy the railroad. Despite the concern about the ability of Confederate cavalry to get into the Federal rear, Ripley, in the same letter, expressed the popular rumor the Confederates would "skedaddle" again as they did at Yorktown, rather than stand and fight a major battle.

McClellan's public reaction, at least to his staff, was to proclaim the raid of little importance. On June 14, he attempted to calm Washington by stating "The stampede of last night has passed away." He made the point that the railroad and the supply base at White House Landing were undamaged. He claimed a lack of vigilance on the part of his cavalry as the spot to place the blame. He did, however, on June 18, order several vessels loaded with rations and forage around Fort Monroe and up the James River. In reality, he was preparing to support an attack on Drewry's Bluff. A better indication of where he intended to keep his base was that he ordered his big guns placed on barges at Yorktown, preparatory to sending them to the railroad at White House.[11]

All of the speculation about the psychological effect of Stuart's raid on the morale of both armies, the real effect was that Lee had been provided the information he needed to finalize the planning for his attack on Porter's V Corps. Stuart had found that Porter's lines would not extend far enough north to block the roads Jackson would use to flank Porter out of his excellent defensive position behind Beaver Dam Creek. Lee also now knew that if he could dislodge Porter, he could cut the Richmond & York River Railroad and sever McClellan's main supply line. On June 16, the day after receiving Stuart's report on his raid, Lee sent orders to Jackson to join Lee's army and attack Porter. Lee stressed secrecy to Jackson. Stonewall, always a master of secrecy, had no problem with his orders.

Early morning of June 18, Jackson started his Army of the Valley toward Ashland. He left a cavalry screen behind to cover his movement, and ordered the newly arrived Chase Whiting to immediately turn around and ride 20 miles back to the railroad where he'd left his troops. Jackson never told Whiting why. Although Jackson's unit commanders were accustomed to Old Jack's penchant for secrecy, Whiting was incensed.

Unfortunately for Jackson, the Virginia Central Railroad he wanted to use was much damaged by Porter's bridge-burning efforts over the last few weeks. The troops were ordered to board a hodge-podge of rolling stock and the Army of the Valley worked its way toward Beaver Dam Station.

The manner in which Jackson's army moved was called by some "riding and tiring." There weren't enough cars to haul the entire army at once, so the cars were filled, part of the army was hauled a number of miles down the railway, unloaded and left to walk for a while. Then the train went back and pick up those who had been walking, loaded them up, and leapfrogged them out in front, where they began walking.

No one but Jackson knew where they were headed or why. Speculation went from Washington to Fredericksburg. Not many guessed they were going to the defense of Richmond, mainly because Lee had just sent Whiting and two brigades to them from Richmond.

Jackson boarded the train and told his staff good bye. Now all were more confused. Where was Old Jack going? No one knew. He left the train at Fredericks Hall Station, mounted his horse and disappeared.[12]

On Monday afternoon about 3:00 P.M., some fourteen hours after leaving the train, Jackson rode up to Dabbs House on the Nine Mile road, where Lee had his headquarters. Lee could not see him immediately, so Jackson leaned on a fence in the yard and waited. D. H. Hill rode up, surprised to see his brother-in-law there. They were soon joined by Longstreet and A. P. Hill and Lee brought them inside the house. By the time this meeting occurred on June 23, Lee already had his plans virtually complete. The purpose of the meeting was to bring his four major generals up to speed.

Lee began by stating that his intent was to go on the offensive and avoid a siege of Richmond. He described his actions to reinforce Jackson, then bring him down to join in the attack. He then described the specific objective of the attack, Fitz John Porter's V Corps on McClellan's right flank, north of the Chickahominy River. Porter's corps was key, as it guarded McClellan's supply line to White House Landing.

Jackson would march to a start point north of Mechanicsville and move to Porters right rear. A. P. Hill would cross the Chickahominy west of Porter and move downstream on the north bank. As soon as the Mechanicsville Bridge was uncovered, D. H. Hill and Longstreet would cross and join the effort to push Porter downstream. South of the river, Magruder, Huger and Theophilus Holmes would defend against a Federal attack there.

Lee left the meeting for a while, allowing the four major generals to work out last minute details. There is some disagreement as to who said what regarding the start date for the attack. Longstreet, in a letter to D. H. Hill many years later, believed that he had suggested to Jackson that an extra day would be necessary for Jackson's troops to get into position. The final agreement was for 3:00 A.M. on June 26. The meeting went on

Seven Days Before Richmond

for four hours in total. There is no surviving record of the details of the meeting. Lee promised to issue written orders by the following day, and dismissed his generals before nightfall. Jackson mounted up and rode off to the north in the rain.[13]

PART V

THE SEVEN DAYS

"No man is fit to command in the camp or in the field who does not constantly recognize the great principles of humanity."

Rev. James J. Marks [1]

CHAPTER 15

Oak Grove

(June 25)

The battle of Oak Grove, sometimes referred to as King's Schoolhouse, French's Field or The Orchard, was the first of the Seven Days' battles. Some historians do not consider Oak Grove as part of the Seven Days because it did not result from General Lee's General Orders No. 75, but rather from McClellan's initiative. This author believes that the engagement must be considered as part of the Seven Days, in that its outcome influenced the thinking of both commanding generals. Other historians refer to Oak Grove as a skirmish, but the size of the forces involved, some 25,000 troops, and the ferocity at certain times during the day demand that it be considered a battle. McClellan had II, III, IV and VI corps, under Generals Sumner, Heintzelman, Keyes and Franklin, all south of the Chickahominy River. Lee had only the divisions of Magruder and Huger there.

Oak Grove took place on June 25, while Jackson's command was still in the process of joining Lee's army from their very successful campaign in the Shenandoah Valley. This battle, precipitated by the Army of the Potomac, had the potential of disrupting Lee's complex plan to turn McClellan's right flank and throw the Army of the Potomac back from the outskirts of Richmond. Timing would turn out to be the key to the overall result.[1]

Lee's plan, as detailed in General Orders No. 75, called for moving the preponderance of his army to the north bank of the Chickahominy River and augmenting it with Stonewall Jackson's Valley Army. Lee would then have Jackson flank McClellan's forces north of the river out of their works, and Lee would drive them to the east. Essentially, he wanted to fight McClellan outside of his works, where maneuver could compensate for Confederate inferiority in artillery and size of forces. Lee would begin his attack early on June 26.

McClellan had a plan of his own. He wanted to take a position near Old Tavern as a starting point of his advance to Richmond. Believing Lee had him outnumbered, he planned to use his heavy siege guns to force the Confederates back into their works around Richmond, then use those guns to weaken Lee's forces for a final assault. McClellan had not, as yet, chosen the sites for his big guns.

One of his VI Corps division commanders, Brigadier General William F. "Baldy" Smith was also pondering the situation, and on June 24 asked McClellan to visit VI Corps headquarters near Golding's farm, just south of the Chickahominy. McClellan agreed to the meeting, and Smith laid out his thoughts.

Smith took McClellan up to his picket line, pointing out to the commanding general the position called Old Tavern, at the intersection of Nine Mile road and the road that went to New Bridge. McClellan immediately saw Old Tavern as the key position to his plan for capturing Richmond. It would not only give him a suitable location for his siege guns, but taking it would allow him to make use of New Bridge. This bridge, farther west than Grapevine Bridge, would shorten his lines of communication with Porter's V Corps across the Chickahominy. With a little good fortune, he might even force that part of Lee's line back far enough to put his guns a little west of Old Tavern.

Baldy Smith told McClellan he could take Old Tavern in two days if was is given adequate support on his left flank. McClellan approved the operation, but ordered gun emplacements for his reserve artillery dug on Garnett's Hill. He wanted them completed before Smith's division attacked. They were done very quietly and completed by daylight of the 25th very near to the Confederate lines, but the ever cautious McClellan then second-guessed himself, and revised his plan to a more cautious two-stage event. First, the troops around Seven Pines would push straight to the west, directly toward Confederate lines. Next, Smith's division, with support from the troops to his right, would attack Old Tavern. Once the Richmond and York River Railroad was secured, the siege guns could be moved up into position. This would not occur until the evening of the 25th.[2]

At least McClellan had made a rare decision to attack. The troops selected were those of Heintzelman's III Corps. His division commanders were Hooker and Kearny. The brigadiers were aggressive officers, and ready for the fight, both having combat experience in Mexico and on the Peninsula.

About 6:30 P.M. on June 24, McClellan issued the attack order. Heintzelman's headquarters passed it along to the two division commanders. It was to begin the next morning. He advised Heintzelman to push his pickets out to look for a weak spot in the Confederate line, and promised artillery support in the morning. His stated objectives were to take Garnett Field by evening of June 25 and Old Tavern or more by the following evening. After that, he expected the fighting to be "chiefly an artillery and engineer affair." Kearny immediately notified his brigade commanders, Robinson, Birney and Berry, but Hooker chose to wait until morning to notify Grover, Sickles and Carr.

Just to the north of Heintzelman's III Corps was Sumner's II Corps. His 1st division, under Richardson, was available to support Heintzelman, if needed.

The action on the Federal right, the north end of the battle, began about 8:00 A.M., with Hooker's division leading the attack. Kearny's men were on the left. Richardson' division was standing by in the right rear.

Hooker had a low opinion of the ground they were fighting for. It didn't seem to him to be worth much blood. It was difficult to move through—heavy woods and swamp, then an open field a half mile across. The Confederates were waiting in the trees on the other side.

The division was arrayed in a classical fashion, with two brigades in line, and the third in reserve. Grover 's men were on the left and advanced between the Williamsburg and Charles City roads. Sickles' men (the Excelsior Brigade) were on the right and moved up along the Williamsburg road. Carr's brigade was the division reserve.[3]

Grover's brigade had five regiments, the 1st, 11th and 16th Massachusetts, the 2nd New Hampshire, and the 26th Pennsylvania. The lead regiments, the 1st and 11th Massachusetts, moved forward toward the Confederates and experienced stiffening resistance. Grover reacted by adding six companies of the 2nd New Hampshire to shore up the center of his advance, the remainder of that regiment to help out on his right. Grover then dispatched half of the 16th Massachusetts to support the left end of his line. At this point, Grover had committed three and a half of his five regiments, and his difficulties were increasing.

The reinforcements to his two lead regiments were required principally because Sickles' Excelsior brigade was having a tough time. Between penetrating the abatis, crossing the swamp, and moving through a heavily wooded area, the New Yorkers were advancing much more slowly than Grover's brigade. Grover was forced to move seven companies from the 26th Pennsylvania to his right, in an attempt to keep the line intact. Hooker, from division resources, sent the 8th New Jersey of Carr's five-regiment reserve brigade to lend further support to Grover.[4]

Hooker was supported on the left by Kearny's division, composed of the brigades of Robinson, Birney, and Berry. Hooker's attack was received by the troops of Huger's division, augmented by Ransom's brigade of Holmes' division. The four brigades were commanded by Generals Mahone, Wright, Armistead, and Ransom. These four brigades numbered about 9,000 men.

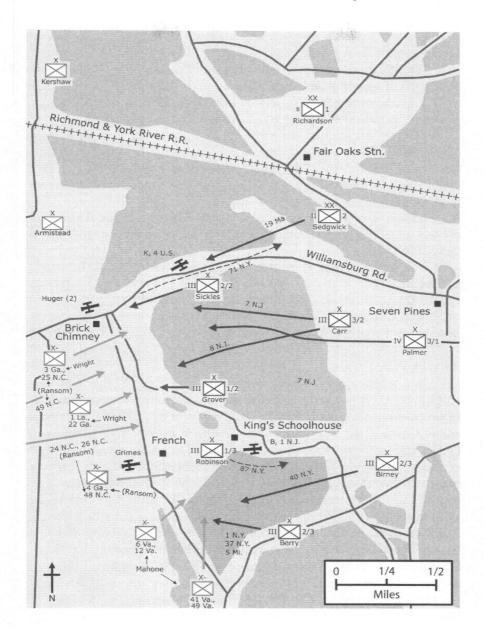

Map 15.1—Oak Grove, June 25}

Wright's brigade held the north end of Huger's line in the area of the Williamsburg road. The brigade was made up of the 3rd, 4th and 22nd Georgia, and the 1st Louisiana.

Mahone's men covered the Charles City road. His brigade was comprised of the 6th, 12th, 16th, 41st and 49th Virginia.

Armistead's brigade was the 9th, 14th, 38th, 53rd and 57th Virginia, as well as the 5th Virginia Battalion. It supported Wright's left.

Ransom's brigade had just arrived in the area from the Department of North Carolina and was temporarily attached to Huger's division. Composed of the 24th, 25th, 26th, 35th, 48th and 49th North Carolina, it was deployed in Wright's rear. There was also support available from Garland's brigade of D. H. Hill's division.

The 4th Georgia, assigned by Wright as pickets, was the first to feel the weight of the Federal attack. The 4th was commanded by Colonel George P. Doles.

Doles sent a courier to inform Wright of the character of the attack, but the message was never delivered. When Wright observed his pickets fleeing from the woods, he instantly brought forward the 22nd Georgia and the 1st Louisiana. These two regiments managed to push back the Federals and stabilize Wright's lines. The Federal troops were probably from Grover's brigade, but Grover never admitted to being pushed back several hundred yards.[5]

The intensity along Grover's front began to diminish a bit, and Sickles, on Grover's right, took the initiative. By this time, he had negotiated the majority of the obstacles in his front, and was trying to clear the remainder of the Confederate pickets from the woods. Suddenly, he observed two Confederate regiments moving toward him. They were the 3rd Georgia of Wright's brigade and 25th North Carolina, sent by Ransom after a request by Wright. The 25th took the lead in the spirited fight, as the two regiments struck the right flank of the Excelsior Brigade, just north of the Williamsburg road. The regiment that bore the brunt of the attack was the 71st New York, on the very right end of Sickles' line. Thinking they had been truly flanked, they began to withdraw, and the rest of the Excelsiors did also. Sickles, with the assistance of a staff officer, reformed the men and set about retaking the ground they had just given up.

Help for Sickles was already on the way. Carr sent Sickles the 7th New Jersey. Also on the way was the 19th Massachusetts from Dana's brigade of Sedgwick's II Corps division.

Despite a rather soggy route to the front, the 7th New Jersey had some success in pushing back the Confederates, although Wright's account of the action somewhat disputes the fact.[6]

About the same time, Heintzelman had sent Birney's brigade of Kearny's division to Hooker. Birney reported to Hooker at approximately 11:00 A.M., and almost immediately thereafter, Hooker received an order from McClellan's Chief of Staff, Brigadier General Marcy, to withdraw. Birney left and took his brigade back to their camps. Sickles', after sending a protest that he was taking Confederate ground, retreated as ordered. One of the Excelsior regiments, the 73rd New York, had advanced as far as the Brick Chimney, before being ordered to fall back. For an unknown reason, Grover never retreated. It's possible he never received the order, or felt he was in too hot a contact to risk a fighting retreat.

The author of the order to retreat was none other than Heintzelman. From the reports he was getting from the front lines, specifically Hooker's need for reinforcements, Heintzelman concluded he was vastly outnumbered, and ordered a prudent withdrawal. He also telegraphed the situation as he perceived it to McClellan.

McClellan was rethinking the entire attack. He telegraphed an order not to retreat any farther, and informed Heintzelman that the Commanding General was on his way to the front. Heintzelman stood his ground and the fighting became less intense.

McClellan arrived about 1:00 P.M., during a lull in the fighting. He climbed a tree, under fire, and, the rain having stopped, surveyed the Confederate line and even made notes. He concluded that the Federals, in fact, had the tactical advantage, and ordered the attack to recommence.

Sickles initiated an advance to retake the ground he'd been ordered, under protest, to give up. He was immediately hit by the 49th North Carolina, another of Robert Ransom's regiments. They had come up to support Wright's brigade. Sickles' men found their progress was slow and hard. The terrain and the enemy were a powerful combination. Once again, the 73rd New York reached the Brick Chimney, and found it occupied by Confederates. Again, they managed to evict the defenders.

More Federal help was committed to the fight. Couch's IV Corps division was then sent to support the attack. The brigades of Howe and Abercrombie were ordered to support Hooker's attack, and Palmer's brigade went to the aid of Sickles.

Simultaneously, Heintzelman ordered his Chief of Artillery to support Hooker with a section of artillery. Captain De Russy selected a section from Battery K, 4th U. S. Artillery. Under command of Lieutenant Tome Henderson, the section was sited on the Williamsburg road and commenced firing effectively.

Wright responded with Captain Frank Huger's Company D, Virginia Light Artillery. Huger moved within 800 yards of Henderson's Federal section before commencing fire. Henderson had already run out of ammunition once and been resupplied when Huger opened on him, and was forced to withdraw by the Confederate fire. Huger then concentrated on the Federal infantry, causing significant casualties in the 2nd Rhode Island. The Virginia artillerists finally ceased fire around sundown.[7]

A little to the south, Kearny's division was in line to support Hooker's left. The brigade on the right was that of Robinson. The brigade was made up of the 20th Indiana, 87th New York, the 57th, 63rd and 105th Pennsylvania. Robinson's regiments had moved forward apace with those of Hooker.

On Robinson's immediate left was the brigade of Berry. Composed of the 2nd, 3rd and 5th Michigan, and the 1st and 37th New York, their mission was to cover any potential Confederate attack from the Charles City road. The brigade of Birney, comprised of the 3rd and 4th Maine and the 38th, 40th and 101st New York, was in reserve just to Robinson's rear.[8]

The advances of Robinson and Grover were observed by Mahone, and he prepared to move north to support Wright. Mahone never made it there in time to help in the morning's fight, but was able to move into a wooded area to support Wright's right flank after the Federal advance had been stopped. He brought along a two-gun section of Captain Grimes' Virginia battery.

The heavy fighting on the south end of the line began with an artillery contest. Robinson had advanced with difficulty, having to commit his reserve, the 87th New York. The brigade had gone by King's Schoolhouse, chasing Confederate troops from several buildings. Another regiment, the 63rd Pennsylvania, pressed on and found itself the closest by far of Kearny's men to Richmond. It was able to hold its position for an hour before being withdrawn.

Mahone ordered Grimes' guns to fire. Confederate sharpshooters were also plying their trade from a two-story house. Robinson, therefore, asked Kearny for artillery help. Kearny sent up a two-gun section of Battery B, 1st New Jersey, commanded by Lieutenant A. Judson Clark. He also sent the 37th New York of Birney's brigade. The house was soon neutralized, but Grimes' effective fire caused Clark's section to withdraw.[9]

The 4th Georgia of Wright's brigade had been repositioned in the line since the morning's fighting, and now found itself on Wright's extreme right. The 48th North Carolina was again ordered to support the 4th. At approximately 6:00 P.M., Wright's brigade attacked the regiment in their front, the 87th New York.

On the Federal side, Robinson brought up the 20th Indiana to support the right flank of the 87th, and the fight was on. The 48th North Carolina showed signs of strain, so Mahone sent the 12th Virginia and some of the 6th Virginia in support. He then attempted to flank the Federals with the 41st and 49th Virginia. The effort of the 41st was ineffective; the regiment snagged in the dense woods. The 49th, however, successfully hit the New Yorkers in the flank, and broke them.

The collapse of the 87th New York meant that the 20th Indiana had no choice but to retreat. Fortunately for the Federals, a portion of Birney's brigade came to the rescue. Earlier in the day, Kearny had sent Birney on a mission to relieve Grover. Birney had taken the 40th New York, part of the 101st New York, and the 4th Maine to do the job. Arriving at Hooker's position, he was sent after a Confederate force that wasn't really there, then, after some confusion, ended up behind Robinson's position. He found his left flank up against the 1st New York of Berry's brigade.

Probably mindful that he had just beat a court-martial on the charge of disobeying an order, Birney asked for clarification of his orders at this point. Kearny instructed Birney to stay put until receiving further orders. Kearny then took the 40th New York and personally went to Robinson's rescue.

The 40th New York and the 20th Indiana counterattacked, stopping the Confederate advance. Two of Berry's regiments, the 5th Michigan and the 1st New York, helped seal the rupture in the Federal line. The 12th Virginia found itself flanked and wisely fell back.[10]

Just a little to the north, Wright ordered the 22nd Georgia and the 1st Louisiana to try and get back the ground in the center of his front lost earlier. The 24th North Carolina joined them, entering combat for the very first time.

Grover's reserve was gone, the major part of the 16th Massachusetts taken from him to support Robinson. The 8th New Jersey, previously supporting Grover's right, now moved to his left. Grover took on the fierce Confederate attack, and then withdrew. General Lee himself ordered the 26th North Carolina to relieve the 24th North Carolina. It is unclear whether Grover weathered the attack and then decided to withdraw, or Wright's attack forced the withdrawal. As with much Civil War history, there are reports to support either contention. It was approaching nightfall, and Birney's brigade, without the 40th New York, at last relieved Grover's men. Birney was withdrawn by dawn of the 26th.[11]

Although the firing had subsided, the night was restless. The jittery pickets of both armies caused "several picket stampedes", incidents in which troops of both sides behaved nervously, retreated from unsubstantiated threats, fired into friendly troops, and generally maneuvered in a less than purposeful manner.[12]

At the end of the day's fighting, the Federal pickets were some 600 yards advanced from that morning. The cost to McClellan was 68 killed, 503 wounded, and 55 missing. Lee suffered 66 killed, 362 wounded, and 13 missing.[13]

Heintzelman believed that the 600 yards of ground he had taken equated to a successful mission. McClellan left no record to dispute that contention, and after observing the afternoon's fighting, wired Stanton that his troops had "behaved splendidly."[14]

The battle of Oak Grove was a relatively small engagement in the Seven Days battles. Federal casualty estimates ranged between 626–700, and Confederate losses were 400–441. Of these total casualty figures, less than 100 men were killed in each army. With about 24,000 troops available, these were not heavy casualties.[15]

The significance of Oak Grove varies widely with the particular historian consulted. To some, it was only a skirmish, hardly worth serious consideration. To others, it was a small battle, with relative few casualties, but the result was a major consideration for the two commanding generals.

Had the Federal attack been totally successful, Lee might have opted to cancel the attack of the morning of the June 26. McClellan might have pressed on with his plan to take Old Tavern, and move up his siege guns. Thus, the battle of Mechanicsville might never have taken place, and the initiative might have remained with the Army of the Potomac. The end result of the Peninsula Campaign could well have been the siege of Richmond in the summer of 1862, rather than the summer of 1864. A shorter, less deadly war could have been the overall result. Since the result of Oak Grove was a mixed one, those two commanding generals steered a middle course, and merely prepared for the next day's fighting.

Lee continued with his plan based on General Orders No. 75. McClellan moved two brigades of McCall's division of Porter's V Corps to forward positions behind Beaver Dam Creek to defend against the anticipated Confederate attack.

McClellan ended his day by inspecting Porter's preparations and telegraphing Secretary of War Stanton with an upbeat message. He ordered more ammunition up to the front, then retired for a few hours sleep.

It is useful here to describe other activities which were taking place about this time, although not part of the action at Oak Grove. One of those activities was the movement of Jackson's army from the Shenandoah Valley to join the Army of Northern Virginia. The other was the situation of the Army of Northern Virginia in preparing for the upcoming battle north of the Chickahominy. More specifically, the state of mind of Lee and the movements of subordinate units of Lee's army to get into position for the attack planned for the morning of June 26 are significant.

A report reached Lee that Huger had not been with his troops during the morning's fighting. Already displeased at Huger's prior performance, and aware of Huger's role in the upcoming battle, Lee sent him a sharp note telling him to get with them and stay there.[16]

D. H. Hill moved his division to Mechanicsville Bridge. A. P. Hill marched his division to the Meadow Bridges. Longstreet made his men ready to take to the Mechanicsville Turnpike early the next morning. Because General Orders No. 75 called for Longstreet to follow A. P. Hill over the Meadow Bridges, he had the luxury of more preparation time. All of these generals prepared for battle with confidence in their men and the Commanding General. The only real unknown was the progress of Jackson, who had the longest distance to travel.

General Orders No. 75 called for Jackson's command to be at Ashland on the early morning of June 25. Leaving there, they were to "proceed ... from Ashland toward the Slash Church and encamp at some convenient point west of the Central Railroad. ... At 3 o'clock Thursday morning, 26th instant, General Jackson will advance on the road leading to Pole Green Church, communicating his march to General Branch..."[17]

Jackson's progress toward his jump-off point for the battle of Mechanicsville was marginal at best. While Jackson was away at the Dabbs House conference, his Chief of Staff, the Reverend Robert L. Dabney, was placed in charge of moving the troops toward Ashland. Apparently, he wasn't the right man for the job. A complicating factor was that Dabney was ill, suffering from an intestinal ailment. He criticized the young and inexperienced staff. Muddy roads added to the slowdown, stretching out the columns. The troops were also very tired. The march's progress on the 23rd was poor overall.

A tired Jackson rejoined his men at Beaver Dam Station early on the morning of June 24. By that evening, the head of his column was still some five miles from Ashland, and the trailing units were miles farther away from their goal. The railroad had been used to ferry trailing units to the head of the column several times, thus speeding up the march. However, the guide, Lincoln Sydnor, had gotten disoriented at one point, and a couple of storms had added to the slowdown and hurt morale. Again, the day's progress had been mediocre.[18]

Jackson needed to make Ashland in time to rest and prepare his troops for a 3:00 A.M. movement on the 26th. To do this, he had to have a good day on the 25th. It did not turn out to be that kind of day for Stonewall.

The 25th started out with good fortune for Jackson. Major Jasper Whiting joined Reverend Dabney's brother, C. W. Dabney, and they were now both providing guide service to Jackson. Both were knowledgeable about the area, and should have given Jackson all the help he needed.

Some time during the night, Jackson had received his written copy of General Orders No. 75. Comparing the document with his notes from the Dabbs House conference, he saw some discrepancies. The differences revolved around the roads to be used in moving from Ashcake road to the Mechanicsville Turnpike. The written order was specific in directing use of the road to Pole Green Church, but was ambiguous as to Old Cold Harbor versus New Cold Harbor. This was to turn out as a significant factor in the next day's movements. The written order did not pinpoint Jackson's bivouac area on the evening of the 25th. Obviously, the closer he was to Ashland, the better. The written order simply required "some convenient point west of the Virginia Central Railroad." Stonewall's notes from the Dabbs House conference leaned toward a bivouac near the Slash Church.[19]

It is interesting to note that neither the written copy of General Orders No. 75, nor Jackson's memo from the Dabbs House conference talks to Jackson fighting at Mechanicsville. He was to bear well to the left and pursue the enemy down the Richmond & York River Railroad, pushing him down the Chickahominy and away from Richmond.

Once Jackson's men started moving on the morning of June 25, events didn't go so well. It was raining, and some units were very slow in leaving their camps. Bridges were also a problem, due to the effects of the recent rain or Federal cavalry activity. The 8th Illinois Cavalry was operating in the area, and was driven away by the Jeff Davis (Mississippi) Legion Cavalry and the 4th Virginia Cavalry. Casualties on both sides were extremely light. By afternoon, lead elements of Stonewall's command reached Ashland. The Stonewall brigade arrived sometime later and Jackson's army was at Ashland for the night. He appeared to make no effort in pressing further east.

There is evidence that Jackson knew he needed to be on the march at 3:00 A.M. Jackson turned to one of his brigade commanders, Charles S. Winder, and told him that his men needed to have cooked rations and water in their possession by then.

Winder pointed out to Jackson that it was impossible to do, based on the position of the wagon trains. Jackson dismissed Winder's complaints, ordering him to make it happen. Jackson actually ordered that the men be ready to move at 2:00 A.M., an hour earlier than that specified in Lee's order.

Mindful that Jackson's army was five miles west of the Virginia Central Railroad, the extra hour would not be enough to make up the extra distance to be marched. Jackson messaged Lee that he would not be in position in time, and explained why. Lee sent a message to Jackson that two roads would be available for the march to Mechanicsville. Ewell and Winder suggested to Jackson that they use both available roads. Those advancing on the more westerly road, were expected to rendezvous with Branch's brigade, and the others would go to Pole Green Church. Some time could be recouped that way. Jackson put them off until morning. He was later observed on his knees in his tent praying.[20]

It is probable that Jackson had little or no sleep that night. The Confederate cause would pay a high price for the accumulated fatigue of one of its key generals. No officer, no matter how talented and motivated, can continue to perform at his best with acute sleep deprivation.

Lee's actions on the late evening of June 25 were affected by his concern for what happened at Oak Grove. He had to at least consider the possibility that McClellan had divined his basic concept as outlined in General Orders No. 75. That could explain the attack south of the Chickahominy. The fact that Porter, north of the Chickahominy River, had used his heavy guns to shell positions that McClellan planned to attack the next day added to Lee's worry. Was McClellan planning a major offensive toward Richmond south of the river? Lee shared his concerns over Oak Grove with Jefferson Davis, but also told his President that he had decided to go forward with the planned attack the next day. A less audacious general might well have put his immediate plans on hold, but Lee was not that sort of leader.

CHAPTER 16

Mechanicsville

(June 26)

Mechanicsville was the second battle of the Seven Days, in which Lee opened his offensive against McClellan's right flank, north of the Chickahominy River. Although it was not a very large battle, it served to set the tone for the remainder of the campaign. It was also the point in the campaign when both commanding generals had to make serious decisions about their grand strategies.

McClellan had all the necessary items in place to conduct a major advance toward Richmond, but was losing confidence rapidly. His plan to move on Richmond called for a major attack toward Old Tavern on the morning of June 26. Although all arrangements for the attack had been made by the previous evening, he let the morning go by without issuing the attack order. The only Federal activity was Porter's heavy artillery shelling Confederate artillery batteries near New Bridge.

The dispositions of major Federal and Confederate forces on the morning of June 26 reflected the plans of McClellan and Lee. Incredibly, both commanding generals had plans that were to be placed into motion on that same day. The relative timing of the actions of both generals and their armies on this day essentially determined the probable course of events for the remainder of the campaign.

Porter's V Corps of 15,000 men was dug in on the east bank of Beaver Dam Creek. These troops were the right flank of the Army of the Potomac, and had the mission of holding their ground, while the several corps to the south of the Chickahominy executed McClellan's planned attack at Old Tavern. Although not totally sure if Porter could hold his lines against the mounting Confederate pressure in the north, McClellan failed to reinforce Porter in a timely fashion.[1]

Lee knew that the Army of Northern Virginia could not again afford the sorts of problems caused at Seven Pines by the lack of a clear written battle plan. As mentioned previously, he had held a meeting of his four principal generals: D. H. Hill, Stonewall Jackson, A. P. Hill and

Longstreet. The meeting took place on June 23 at the Dabbs House, Lee's headquarters in the field. At this meeting, to which Jackson had to travel over 50 miles to attend, the details of the plan were agreed to, and Lee subsequently drew up General Orders No. 75. (*see* Appendix D). Although Jackson stated that his command could be in position to attack early on the morning of the 25th, the agreed upon date was the 26th. After the meeting, Jackson immediately left to return to his command, which was slowly approaching from the Shenandoah Valley.[2]

The Confederate plan was infinitely more complicated. As laid out in Lee's General Orders No. 75, the Confederate battle plan had too many moving parts. Not only was it complicated, but Lee's major subordinate commanders had little experience working together. A further factor, adverse to the likelihood of Confederate success, was the lack of intelligence on McClellan's army, especially on the intentions of its commanding general.

Jackson's command was to begin the day at 3:00 A.M., departing from a point west of the Virginia Central Railroad. He was to communicate his advance to Branch, who would then cross the Chickahominy. Jackson was to turn the flank of the Federals along Beaver Dam Creek. The major objective was to drive the enemy down the north side of the Chickahominy, uncovering New Bridge, thus regaining communication with the Confederate forces south of the river, and cutting McClellan's communications with his base on the York River.

Branch would begin the day near Half Sink. An easy crossing of the Chickahominy there would allow him to move parallel to the river, uncovering the Meadow Bridges for A. P. Hill, then the Mechanicsville Bridge for D. H. Hill. He was to time his advance so as to place himself on Jackson's right flank. Branch had to reposition his brigade into the forest near Half Sink to reduce his exposure to Federal pickets. Branch received a note from Jackson, written at 9:00 A.M., advising that Jackson's command was just crossing the Virginia Central Railroad. Branch failed to pass Jackson's note to A. P. Hill. This meant that Jackson was six hours behind plan, and no commander but Branch knew it. Instead, Branch crossed Chickahominy at 10:00 A.M.[3]

A. P. Hill was by Meadow Bridges. The plan was for his division to cross the Chickahominy by Meadow Bridges after discovering that Branch was in motion and Hill would clear the Federals from the north side of the bridges. Hill was then to move east, driving the Federals from the village of Mechanicsville and advancing toward New Cold Harbor. He would pin Fitz John Porter's front while Jackson swung around the Federal rear.

Seven Days Before Richmond

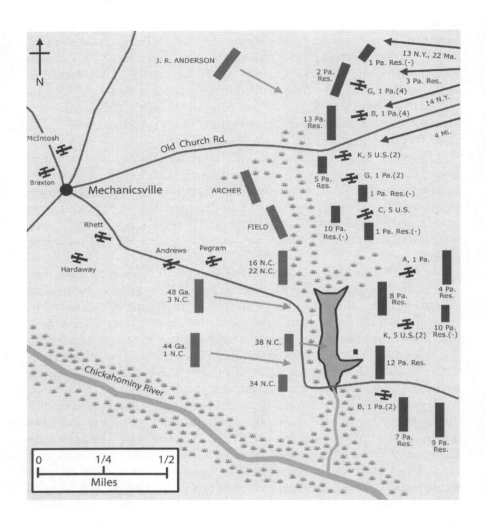

Map 16.1—Mechanicsville, June 26

D. H. Hill was by Mechanicsville Bridge as planned, with Longstreet behind him. Both were on the Mechanicsville Turnpike by 8:00 A.M.

When the Mechanicsville Bridge was uncovered by A. P. Hill, the division of D. H. Hill, then Longstreet's division would cross and commence the pursuit of the Federal forces. McClellan's men would be compelled to abandon their positions when flanked by Jackson.

Once all Confederate forces were across the river, their four divisions would advance *en echelon*, driving the Federals before them. As is so often true in combat, almost nothing went according to plan.

Jackson's day began with a delayed start. He delayed the march of his command by four hours in order to procure and distribute rations and water. He was never able to regain those four hours.

After crossing the Virginia Central Railroad, Jackson split his force. Jackson's route was through Taliaferro's Mill to Hundley's Corner, near Pole Green Church. He ran into obstructions and cavalry harassment, which further delayed him.[4]

At Totopotomoy Creek, a company of the 8th Illinois Cavalry had damaged the bridge and dropped trees across road. Hood's Texas brigade easily drove them off, but the result was added delay.

Ewell went south toward Shady Grove Church. He had the option, upon reaching the church, to join Branch & A. P. Hill's division or go east to join Jackson.

Branch's command also had to deal with frequent, almost continual skirmishes with Federal cavalry. As his brigade approached Atlee's Station, some five miles north of Mechanicsville, he encountered 200 troopers of the 8th Illinois Cavalry. They were blocking the road, and he was forced to deploy the 7th North Carolina to drive them off the road. After the Federals were fired upon by guns from Marmaduke Johnson's Virginia battery, they fled the field. Federal efforts to slow Branch's advance continued, however.

By noon, McClellan felt the pressure on his cavalry pickets. He assumed, correctly, that the unknown force approaching his right was Jackson. He telegraphed Washington such, and warned his superiors that he could suffer a possible cut of his communications. He also urged them to maintain their confidence in him.

Advancing slowly, Branch met Ewell a little north of Shady Grove Church about 3:00 P.M. At that point, the two commands were marching on parallel roads, only several hundred yards apart. After determining that Branch could provide no useful intelligence, and had no recent orders to offer, Ewell decided to proceed east to Hundley's Corner, where he hoped to join with Jackson's command.

McClellan was not without options to respond to the Confederate pressure on his right front and flank. His offensive options were two. He could attack south of the Chickahominy while attempting to hold his ground with Porter's Corps on the north end of his lines. A bolder strategy would be to reinforce Porter, and to mount a fierce attack north of the Chickahominy. When questioned on troops available to reinforce

Porter, the corps commanders south of the river offered McClellan only five brigades.

McClellan had at least two available defensive strategies. He could further reinforce his forces north of that river, and defend against the apparent developing Confederate attack. Alternatively, he could withdraw Porter's Corps to the south of the river, and change his base from White House Landing to somewhere on the James River. Such a "change of base" would be a necessity if communications to White House Landing were indeed cut.

McClellan had already taken some precautionary steps to facilitate a change of base to the James River. On the 23rd, he had directed General Van Vliet, his quartermaster, to advise Goldsborough of the possible requirement to escort transports from White House Landing to the James in the very near future. Although Goldsborough initially balked at the request, not pleased with the perceived manner of the discourse, McClellan communicated with him directly, and the Navy agreed to provide the needed support.

If McClellan did decide to change his base to the James, the Richmond & York River Railroad would be lost to the Army of the Potomac, and no ability to move and employ siege guns would exist from that point forward. The campaign would be one emphasizing assault and maneuver, rather than artillery and engineering, as McClellan had previously envisioned.[5]

Although, on the morning of June 26, McClellan probably hadn't made a firm decision on the change of base, he did message his corps commanders to take the appropriate measures to allow the flexibility of a change of base. Porter began to move artillery and logistic assets to the south side of the Chickahominy. White House Landing began to move supplies to the front, and the corps south of the river made ready to move in an as yet undetermined direction.[6]

Lee's plan for his troops south of the Chickahominy River was part of a large gamble. They were to make demonstrations, hoping to convince McClellan that a Confederate attack there was imminent. If McClellan believed the ruse, he could not afford to move more troops north of the Chickahominy to reinforce Porter's V Corps.[7]

To Lee's good fortune, Magruder was a principal commander there, and once again showed his talent for confusing McClellan and fixing him in place. With demonstrations similar to those used at Yorktown, Magruder and Huger were successful in convincing many Federals that Lee had a powerful force south of the river. McClellan truly believed that Jackson was approaching his right flank as well. He believed he could neither reinforce Porter to a very great extent, nor launch a major attack on the south side of the river. He could not bring himself to issue the orders for the planned attack in the area of Old Tavern, and he essentially decided to await further developments. Lee had gotten away with his risky deception plan.[8]

Despite the success of Magruder and Huger in fixing McClellan in place south of the Chickahominy River, events north of the river quickly diverged from the plan. The combination of an overly complicated battle plan, sloppy work by Jackson and his staff, and the natural difficulties of moving through the rain-soaked terrain began to take a toll.

Just southwest of Meadow Bridges, A. P. Hill and his newly formed division waited. They were to wait for Branch's troops to clear the north bank of the river. A. P. Hill's division would then cross at the Meadow Bridges and attempt to drive the Federals to Mechanicsville. This action would facilitate the attacks of D. H. Hill and Longstreet across the Mechanicsville Bridge.

The rub was that Branch's orders required him to maintain a position on Jackson's right flank, and Jackson was running considerably behind schedule. By 3:00 P.M., A. P. Hill still had no word from Branch or Jackson. He then reached the decision that to attack without waiting for Branch was less undesirable than continuing to wait. He decided to cross the river, but failed to inform Lee, nor is there record of any attempt by Hill to inform Branch or Jackson.

There has been considerable conjecture over the years as to whether Lee would have supported A. P. Hill's decision to attack without contact with Branch. We only know that there is no record of Lee criticizing Hill's decision.[9]

Perhaps Lee decided not to find fault with A. P. Hill because his own actions during the day of the 26th were somewhat less than perfect. In point of fact, Jackson, Hill, Branch and Lee can all be criticized for communicating in an insufficient manner. Branch was in between Jackson and Hill and could have facilitated communications between the two larger forces. Lee had a staff and couriers available to seek information. It must be remembered that this was Lee's first battle in command of a multi-division force. Additionally, a number of the units and their commanders were enjoying their first real combat experience.[10]

The division of A. P. Hill easily crossed the Chickahominy at Meadow Bridges, contested by only three companies of infantry from the 13th Pennsylvania Reserves of McCall's Division. This was the last easy event of the day for Powell Hill.

Seven Days Before Richmond

Library of Congress

Chickahominy Bridge on Mechanicsville Road

Not much more than a mile east of the village of Mechanicsville, Beaver Dam Creek ran south toward the Chickahominy River. A half mile from the mouth of the creek, a small dam created a mill pond. Ellerson's Mill sat on the east side of the pond. On the steep 70 foot high east bank of the creek, McCall's division of Porter's V Corps was dug in, waiting for a Confederate attack.

Porter, a favorite of McClellan's, had just assumed command of the newly created V Corps on May 18. His corps was composed of the divisions of George W. Morell, George Sykes and George A. McCall. V Corps strength was approximately 15,500 effectives. Porter also had the benefit of seven batteries of artillery supporting the line.

McCall's right flank was protected by John Martindale's brigade of Morell's division. The brigade of Daniel Butterfield, also of Morell's division, was assigned to protect the V Corps rear. After a number of contradictory orders, the brigade was finally positioned in Sykes' rear.

McCall had prepared his positions well. The only two bridges across Beaver Dam Creek had been destroyed, there were felled trees on the banks, and McCall enjoyed some open fields on the west side, providing fields of fire for his artillery.

A.P. Hill advanced eastward through Mechanicsville, driving small numbers of Federal troops before him. The Federals, according to plan, quickly retreated across Beaver Dam Creek to their prepared positions. This facilitated the lead brigade (Ripley's) of D. H. Hill's division to cross the Chickahominy via the Mechanicsville Bridge. Together, this Confederate force numbered about 16,000 men. Ripley's crossing commenced about 4:00 P.M., and was slowed by the poor condition of the bridge, damaged by retreating Federal troops.[11]

For some hard to fathom reason, A. P. Hill's division had brought only one artillery battery per brigade with them across the Chickahominy. Even these few pieces of artillery could not cross the marshy, steep-sided Beaver Dam Creek.

As A. P. Hill's troops approached Beaver Dam Creek, Porter observed them and decided to reinforce his front line with two brigades under John Reynolds and Truman Seymour. Porter added the brigade of Charles Griffin of Morell's division and Hiram Berdan's 1st U. S Sharpshooters. He then moved up artillery support and repositioned Sykes' Division closer to the front line.[12]

Field's brigade of A. P. Hill's division, moving east from Mechanicsville, came under fire from the artillery supporting Porter's lines across Beaver Dam Creek. The brigade consisted of the 40th, 47th, 55th and 60th Virginia regiments. Field, in his report, called it "the most destructive cannonading I have yet known." The meager number of guns brought across the Chickahominy by Powell Hill could not hope to match the Federal cannon fire. Attempts at counter-battery fire resulted in the loss of several Confederate guns.[13]

The position of Field's and Archer's brigades could not be maintained. They had no real cover, and were in the field of fire of Porter's batteries.

They needed to withdraw or close the distance. They chose to close with the enemy, in the hope that the artillery would decline to fire at targets so close to Federal troops. This they did by advancing almost a mile over open ground. Archer's brigade advanced under fire to the western edge of Beaver Dam Creek, where there was at least some modest cover from the trees.

Brigadier General Joseph Anderson, on the north end of the Confederate line, was able to get one of his batteries, under Captain David G. McIntosh, to open on the Federal batteries. He then took his brigade around the Federal right flank in an attempt to capture the Federal guns. McIntosh was able to maintain his fire for the duration of the day's action and well into the evening.

Throughout the Seven Days, the Army of Northern Virginia suffered from poor staff work, and was especially hampered by the lack of adequate maps. Although operating only a few short miles from the capital of the fledgling nation, the maps available to Lee's staff and subordinate units were woefully inaccurate.

Joseph Anderson's brigade felt the sting of working with poor maps when their navigation through the thickly wooded area west of Beaver Dam Creek resulted in their reaching the creek north of the planned point, but in sight of guns and sharpshooters.[14]

Anderson's 35th Georgia crossed the creek and pushed back the 1st Pennsylvania Reserves of Reynolds' division. The 14th Georgia & 3rd Louisiana Battalion crossed in support of the 35th Georgia.

The 22nd Massachusetts & 13th New York of Martindale's brigade came up on the right and the 2nd and 3rd Pennsylvania Reserves, along with four guns of Battery G, 1st Pennsylvania Light Artillery, came up on the left.[15]

After the initial Confederate advance faltered, a serious firefight developed. The Confederates brought up the battery of Captain Carter M. Braxton, but the force available to Anderson wasn't sufficient to push the Federals back across a ravine. After dusk, the Confederates fell back.[16]

Field and Archer were sure of their positions, but knew they could not successfully advance across Beaver Dam Creek. Their brigades fought four regiments of Pennsylvania Reserves (1st, 5th, 10th and 13th) from 4:00 until 9:00 P.M., when darkness forced a halt to the engagement. At some point, two regiments from Griffin's Brigade (4th Michigan & 14th New York) joined the fight. Additionally, artillery comprised of parts of Battery B, 1st Pennsylvania Light, Battery K, 5th U. S. Artillery and Battery G, 1st Pennsylvania Light came up in support.

Archer's brigade suffered many disadvantages in the day's fighting. The millpond made it virtually impossible to cross Beaver Dam Creek, and the Federals had felled a number of trees, which served to hamper Confederate maneuver. The Federal superiority in artillery assured the successful defense of their lines.

Ripley's brigade crossed the Chickahominy about 4:00 P.M. Robert E. Lee, Secretary of War George W. Randolph, and President Jefferson Davis crossed close behind Ripley, and Lee was compelled to order Davis and his entourage to move back to a somewhat safer vantage point.[17]

Lee's concern at this time had to be that he had a major engagement in progress at a location not as envisioned in his General Order No. 75. The three brigades thus far engaged were unable to force Porter back. He had intended for Porter to withdraw from his formidable position along Beaver Dam Creek without a major fight. Jackson's appearance threatening Porter's flank and rear would make that a certainty.

The fact that Porter was still holding his ground must have convinced Lee that Jackson was not where he was supposed to be. Without the appearance of Jackson, Porter had the option to stay and fight. His orders from McClellan compelled him to do so. Indeed, his V Corps fought well, and Lee's problem was how to improvise a new battle plan suitable to the reality on the ground.

If Lee's attempt to force Porter to withdraw at least as far as New Bridge failed, his army could not be reunited. The meager forces of Huger and Magruder would be hard pressed to resist an attack south of the Chickahominy. Disaster was a distinct possibility. Lee also had to consider McClellan's option to greatly reinforce Porter north of the river, and becoming more than a match for Confederate forces there.

The river crossings of D. H. Hill and Longstreet were slowed by damaged bridges, and Lee was forced to find a viable plan for the moment. He seized on Porter's nearby left flank.

Pender's brigade moved up on Field's right, but two regiments (16th & 22nd North Carolina) suffered from poor maps and navigated too far to the left, bumping up against Field's right flank. The other two regiments (34th & 38th North Carolina) moved east and approached the mill pond across from Ellerson's Mill. Pender ordered these two regiments to attempt to destroy a section of Battery K, 5th U.S. Artillery and a section of Battery B, 1st Pennsylvania. Only the 38th North Carolina, under Colonel William J. Hoke, came close to the objectives, and was then repulsed by Federal reinforcements from the 7th and 12th Pennsylvania Reserves of Truman Seymour's Brigade. Hoke was wounded and the regiment scattered during the retreat.[18]

Ripley's brigade was then ordered by Lee to attempt to flank the southern end of the Federal line, crossing Beaver Dam Creek south of the small dam that formed the mill pond, and avoiding the steep eastern slopes around Ellerson's Mill. Command and control on the field was muddled, as Lee, D. H. Hill, A. P. Hill, and even President Davis attempted to exert influence over Ripley's brigade.

Pender encountered D. H. Hill at this point, and offered to try to turn the Federal flank if Hill would task two of Ripley's regiments to join the attack, while the rest of Ripley's brigade attacked the Federal front. Hill approved the plan. Again, there was confusion as to exactly who ordered this movement – Davis, Lee or D. H. Hill. This appears to be yet more evidence of the poor generalship on the Confederate side.[19]

Lee had envisioned a turning of the Federal flank, but Hill and Pender included an element of frontal attack, albeit supported by artillery. The 44th Georgia and 1st North Carolina of Ripley's brigade advanced under Federal artillery fire. The 44th Georgia waded into the creek. From this incredibly disadvantaged position, they fought Porter's Federals dug in on the far bank, took heavy casualties, and withdrew when their ammunition ran low. The 1st North Carolina made it halfway down the western slope of the creek, and stubbornly stayed to fight. They lost most of their officers.

The 3rd North Carolina and 48th Georgia, also of Ripley's brigade, attempted to force a crossing of the creek north of Ellerson's Mill, but were unsuccessful, but took less casualties. Finally, five Confederate artillery batteries arrived on the scene, and the effect of their fire was to ease the hazard to their infantry brethren.[20]

The Confederates suffered about 1,400 total casualties out of about 10,000 troops engaged. The Federals lost 361 men out of approximately 14,000 in the fight. These men died in a battle neither army's commanding general had planned to fight.

Longstreet's division crossed the river last and completed its move by nightfall. By 9:00 P.M., the only firing was sporadic artillery. Lee held a meeting of the division commanders, but no one had been in communication with Jackson. Branch had at least seen Ewell briefly. The Army of Northern Virginia had not even come close to uncovering New Bridge. Huger and Magruder would be in a grave situation if McClellan attacked south of the Chickahominy. Lee directed those commands to hold at all hazards.

The expected post-battle actions were taken by Lee. The brigades that had seen hot action during the day were replaced in the line by fresh brigades of D. H. Hill and Longstreet. Preparations were begun for the next day's action. Still, no contact with Jackson had been effected.

Jackson had gone through a frustrating day. His departure delay for rations and water was just the first of several adverse events. Federal pickets spent the entire day attempting to slow Jackson's progress, with some success.

By 5:00 P.M., the head of Jackson's column had reached Hundley's Corner. Ewell arrived shortly on his right. He could hear firing to the south, but decided to put his troops into bivouac. His decision can be argued, but he had no recent intelligence of the enemy's disposition and strength, his troops were tired and strung out, and only a few hours of daylight remained. By the time he could have moved his men to the battlefield and deployed them into line, there would have been little daylight remaining. He had accomplished exactly what General Orders No. 75 had required, although he had done it much later than planned. He had no way of knowing whether the Federal cavalry pickets he'd encountered along the march had reported his presence to McClellan. It is certainly reasonable to assume so. Perhaps Jackson's movement had in fact served to force the withdrawal of Porter's V Corps from their Beaver Dam Creek lines.

It is unexplainable why Jackson had not asked Stuart, who was covering his left flank, to scout the ground ahead. Such a mission would have helped his understanding of the overall situation considerably.[21]

Stonewall's weary command settled into a restless night. Jackson ordered his pickets to shoot anything that moved. Federal skirmishers and unruly animals contributed to the unrest.

Many have criticized the late arrival of Jackson to the Mechanicsville battle. A case can be made that it would have been difficult for his troops to move much more rapidly, given the circumstances. He can, however, be roundly condemned for his lack of communication with Lee, Ewell and Branch. Lee, himself, can be deemed guilty of a similar lack of communication. Lee had too small a staff, but failed to use well what he did have.

On the Federal side of the lines, Porter was feeling good about the performance of his V Corps. They had held the line of Beaver Dam Creek through a five hour battle and had inflicted many more casualties than they had suffered. McCall's division had borne the brunt of the Confederate attack, and had used the advantage of their high ground along the east bank of the creek. The brigade commanders had acquitted themselves well, especially Reynolds and Truman Seymour, and the artillery had been effective.[22] Porter had little to complain about and much to be proud of.

McClellan had been with Porter for the entire battle, and, as the firing dwindled, McClellan telegraphed Marcy that they had held their ground, and praised Morell and McCall for their splendid performance. He then messaged Stanton that the battle was at a virtual end for the day and that he had moved V Corps's "impediments" across the Chickahominy and hoped to be ready for the coming day. He also claimed to have been victorious against great odds, which was patently incorrect, but McClellan always seemed to think he faced such odds. The Federals had not exactly been victorious, but had fought well and held their position.[23]

The immediate effect of the battle was to boost Federal troop morale. Oddly, most Richmonders had a lack of current information on the outcome of the day's fighting, and many thought that Jackson had arrived and had defeated McClellan. Even some New York City newspapers reported that McClellan had been defeated. In Washington, more reinforcements for McClellan were being readied.[24]

McClellan remained at Porter's V Corps headquarters until the wee hours of the 27th. Among the reports reaching McClellan were those verifying the arrival of Jackson's troops on the field. It was obvious to McClellan that Porter's Corps could not remain where it was without being isolated and destroyed. The next likely event would be the loss of communication with the Army's logistical base at White House Landing.

Porter made two suggestions to McClellan. He wanted McClellan to bring the whole army north of the Chickahominy and fight it out with Lee. This was not a viable option for logistical reasons. Porter's other suggestion was to bring across enough reinforcements for him to hold Lee at bay, while Federal forces south of the river attacked westward toward Richmond. Perhaps Porter had come to grasp Lee's desperate strategy. Curiously, McClellan chose not to implement Porter's latter suggestion. Smith and Franklin made an even more innovative suggestion. They urged the withdrawal of Porter's corps to the south of the river, destroying the bridges behind them and isolating Lee's four divisions on the north bank, while the Army of the Potomac attacked Richmond. The down side of this strategy was to force the abandonment of the White House base.

McClellan took neither of these suggestions. He believed that there was a huge Confederate force facing him, capable of attacking his lines of communication, while simultaneously defending Richmond from attack south of the Chickahominy. McClellan essentially ruled out any offensive strategy at this point.

The defensive choices left open to the Army of the Potomac were either to retreat down the peninsula or to change base to the James. He chose the latter option. McClellan did not immediately decide exactly what he wanted V Corps to do next. Porter would have to be reinforced, if V Corps was to remain north of the river. McClellan elected to return to his own headquarters and make the decision.[25]

The early morning of June 26 was a critical time for George McClellan. Had he made a firm decision to attack in force toward Old Tavern as planned, he likely would have been victorious. An attack anywhere on the south side of the Chickahominy would have been successful in cracking the relatively thin Confederate lines. Lee would have been forced to redeploy his forces to protect Richmond, and McClellan could have completed his change of base during that time. Now, some twenty-four hours later, his decision was even more difficult.

Whether an attack south of the river would have penetrated the Richmond defenses is not an appropriate criterion for deciding on an attack in force. Even without penetration of Richmond, at the end of the day, the Army of the Potomac would have been closer to their objective, would have attained a better appreciation of the true strength of their Confederate adversaries, and could have then laid siege to the city. The siege of 1864–1865 would have taken place two years sooner.

McClellan, however, was overwhelmed by his cautious side, and failed to act. This failure assured the bloody, inconclusive battles to follow, the eventual demise of his own military career, and a significant prolongation of the war. George B. McClellan could no longer win, because he was too afraid to lose.

CHAPTER 17

Gaines's Mill

(June 27)

The night of June 26–27 was a busy one for both armies. On the Confederate side, Lee ordered a rearrangement of his brigades to assure that fresh troops would be in the line for an early morning attack. He desired to attack at first light, and was extremely concerned that the day's fighting had failed to uncover New Bridge. Without control of that vital position, he could not reunite his army, and Huger's and Magruder's forces south of the Chickahominy would be wholly inadequate to hold their positions against the superior Federal forces in their front. Although Huger had received reinforcement in the form of most of John Walker's brigade from Drewry's Bluff, the situation was still critical. Huger came to believe that the Federals were planning to attack his garrison at Drewry's Bluff. Should McClellan attack there, the city of Richmond would be in grave danger.[1]

On the Federal side, a conference was just ending. At 1:00 A.M., McClellan told Porter to hold his ground, and returned to Army headquarters at the Trent house. He had made the decision to change his base to the James, and set about issuing orders to execute that strategy. With the help of McClellan's Chief Engineer, General John Barnard, Porter selected a new line of defense behind Boatswain's Swamp. This was a very defensible position near Gaines's Mill. It allowed Porter to protect Woodbury's, Alexander's and Grapevine Bridges. The remaining bridges would need to be preserved to allow Porter's corps to cross and follow the rest of the Army to the James. Barnard reported back to McClellan, and reminded him about reinforcing Porter's Corps.

About 3:00 A.M., Porter received his orders to withdraw to the line behind Boatswain's Swamp. He energetically set events in motion. Ammunition was distributed, weapons cleaned, and heavy artillery evacuated to the south of the Chickahominy. Trains were still crossing at 4:00 A.M. and the infantry brigades followed.

The battle of Gaines' Mill can be viewed as McClellan's use of Porter's already bloodied V Corps to buy time for the Army of the Potomac's change of base. McClellan, having made his decision to abandon White House Landing on the Pamunkey and establish a base on the James River, ordered V Corps, reinforced late in the afternoon by Slocum's division of Franklin's VI Corps, to serve as rear guard for the Army.

The "change of base" was viewed as a hazardous undertaking for any army engaged with the enemy, but McClellan had made some advance arrangements, and had a competent logistics structure. Unavoidably, some minor panic ensued at White House Landing as bountiful rumors overwhelmed scarce facts. McClellan directed General Casey not to abandon the base prematurely.[2]

At this point in the Peninsula Campaign, Lee was working under a set of erroneous assumptions. Despite his frequent ability to anticipate McClellan's thinking, Lee had misinterpreted the scant intelligence available to him. He believed that McClellan had a much larger portion of his army north of the Chickahominy River. The lethargy of Federal forces south of the river reinforced that belief. Lee concluded that McClellan would surely mount a strong defense of his communications with White House Landing.[3]

Lee felt an intense need to promptly advance eastward and cut off Federal communications with White House Landing. Based on the erroneous assumptions set forth above, Lee's plan of attack was ambitious and involved both the Hills, Longstreet and Jackson.

Longstreet, on the Confederate right, would conduct a feint to the Federal left. A. P. Hill, in the line to the immediate left of Longstreet would attack the Federal center. Jackson, would appear on A. P. Hill's immediate left, causing McClellan to shift troops to meet the threat from Jackson, lest the Federals be cut off from White House Landing. Upon this shift of troops, which would weaken the Federal left, Longstreet would conduct a full assault, driving the weakened Federal left eastward into Jackson's command, and that of D. H. Hill, whose troops would appear on Jackson's left.[4]

Battle plans seldom live past the opening shots of a battle, for a variety of reasons. In the case of this battle, the underlying assumptions upon which Lee based his battle plan were erroneous, and the plan inevitably didn't survive the day.

Fitz John Porter

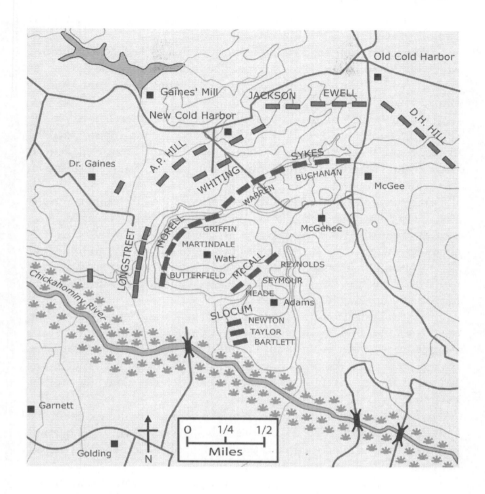

Map 17.1—Advance to Gaines's Mill, June 27}

A. P. Hill's rest was cut short by Federal artillery fire on his troops, one round passing through his very sleeping quarters. He immediately placed his division under arms. Federal muskets joined the cannon fire, which endured for about an hour. In response to the Federal shelling, Confederate infantry and artillery returned fire and D. H. Hill sent G. B. Anderson's and Garland's brigades to attempt to turn the Federal right. Brigadier General W. Dorsey Pender prepared his brigade, including his artillery, to attack, but discovered there were no Federal troops in his front.

Despite an effective hour-long delaying action by the 9th, 12th and 13th Pennsylvania Reserves, by 9:00 A.M., the Confederates were in pursuit of Porter's corps over recently repaired bridges. A significant number of the Federal rear guard were captured.

Jackson's division began to move early, roused by Federal cannon fire, which began somewhat before sunrise. The Stonewall Brigade moved out at 5:00 A.M., followed by the 2nd Brigade under Lieutenant Colonel Cunningham.[5]

Jackson moved to the Walnut Grove Church intersection. At the church, he encountered A. P. Hill, whose men were moving in a parallel direction, south of the Bethesda Church road. Shortly thereafter, General Lee arrived. Hill soon departed and Lee and Jackson had a conversation, overheard by no one.[6]

One can speculate, however, that the discussion likely centered on the plan for the day, and Jackson's part in it. Jackson's mission would be to turn the Federal right flank, thought by Lee to be on Powhite Creek. A circuitous march of some eight miles by way of Richardson to Old Cold Harbor would be necessary. If successful, Jackson would arrive in Porter's rear with a crushing force. Their conference concluded, Jackson excused himself and rejoined his command.[7]

A. P. Hill's division had the objective of reaching New Cold Harbor. He was to offensively engage the enemy wherever he found them. Maxcy Gregg's brigade was in the lead. Passing Lee's field headquarters at the Hogan house, Hill discussed Gregg's pending attack with Lee. One can assume that Lee expected a potent Federal defense along the line of Powhite Creek.

A. P. Hill's division, as well as Longstreet's advanced through the chaos of hastily abandoned Federal positions. A bonanza of Federal supplies and personal effects greeted them, and the undersupplied Confederates helped themselves to that which had not been burned.[8]

The lead elements of Gregg's brigade made contact with Federal forces about noon. These two lead regiments, the 1st and 12th South Carolina, encountered the 9th Massachusetts of Griffin's brigade of Morell's division, positioned at Gaines' Mill. With the support of Andrews' battery, the Federals were pushed back from the mill. The South Carolinians were forced to repair a bridge prior to crossing Powhite Creek.

It was becoming obvious that the creek was not, in fact, Porter's primary line of defense. Were it so, no two regiments could have forced a Federal retreat. Gregg continued to advance to the southeast. Pursuing retreating Federal skirmishers across a wheat field, Gregg's men came under significant musket and artillery fire. They appeared to have come upon the main body of Porter's V Corps.

Porter was well deployed on the far side of Boatswain's Swamp, with abundant artillery support. The position was extremely defensible. Hill's men had to cross an open field, advance over a rise, drop down about fifty feet to the swamp. From there, the Confederates would have to make their way through a tangle of underbrush, cross the swamp and attack the Federals on the high ground. Gregg wasn't able to determine how far north the Federal line extended. Whether or not Jackson could turn Porter's right in part depended in part on how far north the Federal line went.

The situation was strikingly similar to that of the previous day at Beaver Dam Creek. Once again, Lee's plan to use maneuver to force Porter out of a strong defensive position was turned by events into a pitched battle. Once more, poor Confederate staff work was a contributing factor. Although this battle was fought only a few miles from the Confederate capital, Boatswain's Swamp was not on the maps available to Lee's staff. Why hadn't that staff recognized the map shortfall, sought better ones, and/or procured one or more local guides?[9]

Porter had not wasted the time Lee had given him before attacking. With the help of his engineer officer, Colonel Barnard, Porter had selected the correct positions for his command. With Morell's division on the left and Sykes' division on the right, Porter made his headquarters in the Watt house. He placed William Chapman's brigade of Sykes' division in reserve, and spread his artillery along the line.

The ground, as mentioned previously, was favorable to the defense. Morell had Boatswain's Swamp to his front, and Sykes defended along a ridge covering the road which led to Grapevine Bridge from Old Cold Harbor.[10]

Although short on tools such as axes, Porter's men improved their positions as best they could in the time available to them. Tools borrowed from artillery units allowed the construction of adequate field fortifications. There was even a little time for the men to read their mail and scrounge some cigars from a sutler's store. By the middle of the morning, Porter's command was ready for Lee.[11]

McClellan awakened and sent a message to Stanton around noon, in which he reported Porter in contact with Confederate forces. As was common for him, he exaggerated the Confederate forces involved to three divisions. He even managed to report Jackson's command as involved. A few hours later, he sent another message, in which he painted an even darker picture. In defense of McClellan's grim outlook, Magruder was once again performing his previously successful charade. His activities included harassing Federal pickets, sporadic artillery fire and generally making a racket simulating a large force preparing to do something aggressive. This resulted in bringing McClellan to the conclusion that the Army of Northern Virginia was present in great strength south of the Chickahominy. McClellan was assisted toward this erroneous conclusion by a report from Professor Lowe, that his balloon reconnaissance detected that the Confederates south of the Chickahominy were ready to launch an attack.[12]

McClellan remained at the Trent house, south of the Chickahominy. Why he didn't remain with Porter on the north side of the river is somewhat puzzling. Perhaps Magruder's charade was a factor. Perhaps, lacking certainty of Lee's intentions, he chose to stay at his headquarters, so that his generals could find him straight away.

More than likely, McClellan chose to stay closer to those subordinates in which he had less confidence than he had in his favorite, Fitz John Porter. Although the hottest fighting would likely be in Porter's front, McClellan could well have been more concerned about his weaker corps commanders south of the river. Additionally, the Trent house was a central location.[13]

McClellan ordered a halt to Slocum's movement to reinforce Porter, as no fighting was occurring in Porter's part of the line. This, despite the fact that McClellan had to know that Porter would soon be attacked by superior Confederate forces. This order was later reversed when Porter again asked for help. McClellan immediately sent Slocum's division of Franklin's VI Corps at that point. By late afternoon, Porter wired that he was being pressed and might not be capable of holding his position. McClellan tasked Sumner to send two brigades to reinforce Porter.

By now, McClellan had tasked Franklin for an entire division and Sumner's II Corps for two brigades of Richardson's division. Keyes was also asked for a brigade, but that was too late in the day to make a difference. Heintzelman was then asked to ready a reserve, but his III Corps was well away from Porter. In McClellan's mind, moving any more strength north of the Chickahominy might be unwise, as he believed Lee had considerable troops south of the river.[14]

It is not clear why McClellan was so slow in reinforcing Porter. There is an established theory that an "aural anomaly" made the sounds of the fierce contact in which Porter was involved less audible to McClellan and others.[15]

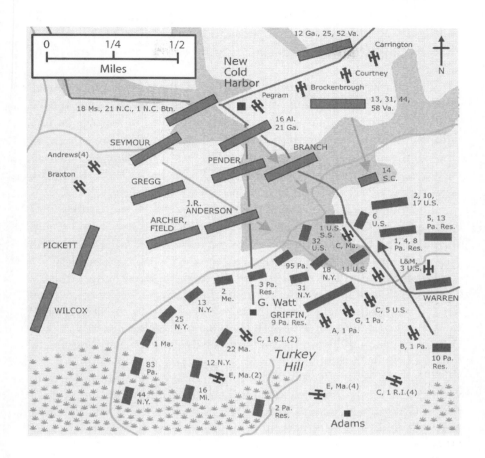

Map 17.2—Gaines' Mill, Initial Positions, June 27

On the Confederate side, Lee had much work to do. As he approached Boatswain's Swamp, he assessed the battlefield and struggled to devise a tactical plan to deal with the realities of the moment. He was sure that A. P. Hill and James Longstreet had their forces in place behind Powhite Creek. He assumed that D. H. Hill and Jackson were also in position. Once again, as at Mechanicsville, the plan was for Jackson's troops to flank the Federals on their right, forcing Porter to extend his right or retreat. Unfortunately for Lee, Porter had already extended his lines sufficiently to meet Jackson's advance.

One of A. P. Hill's brigade commanders, Maxcy Gregg, sought permission to initiate an attack, but Hill held him back. He preferred to give Longstreet more time to get into position. Sometime between 2:30 and 4:00 P.M., Hill ordered the attack on Porter's line. Hill recalled it as about 2:30 P.M., but others remember it being somewhat later in the afternoon.[16]

The attack began with artillery fire. The batteries employed by Gregg were those of Crenshaw and Johnson. Then began an assault by the 1st and 12th South Carolina. These regiments attempted to advance on line, with the 12th on the left. They suffered alignment problems advancing through the woods, and encountered the 5th New York (Duryea Zouaves), supported by the artillery of Edwards' 3rd U.S., Batteries L & M. The 5th New York was part of Warren's brigade of Sykes' division.

The Confederate assault was diminished by the Federal artillery fire, causing Gregg to order the 1st South Carolina Rifles (Orr's Rifles) to take the guns. The Federal artillery was moved rearward by Sykes, as the 5th New York was withdrawn slightly to escape the Confederate artillery.[17]

Upon arrival at the original position of the Federal battery, the 1st South Carolina found no Federal cannon, but came under heavy fire from five different regiments from all three brigades of Sykes' division. Despite the tactical situation, the 1st South Carolina pushed the Federals back to their reserve lines. A Federal counterattack led by the 5th New York finally forced a Confederate retreat.

The 1st South Carolina had been mauled, and was ordered to withdraw by Gregg. They retreated in a less than orderly manner. At least part of Company H, under Captain W. J. Haskell, failed to hear the order to retreat, and part of the company found its way back by way of several other regiments.[18]

The 13th South Carolina covered the left flank of the 12th, and the 14th South Carolina was just returning from picket duty. Gouverneur K. Warren, commanding the 3rd brigade of Sykes' division, then went on the attack. Buchanan, commanding the 1st brigade under Sykes, advanced the 12th and 14th U.S. Infantry regiments. Also poured into the mix were the 2nd, 10th and 17th U.S. from Lovell's 2nd brigade, supported by the 3rd U.S. Infantry from Buchanan.

Gregg responded by putting his reserve regiment, the 14th South Carolina into the center of his line, diluting the effect of the Federal attack. Both sides settled into a contact that substituted volume of fire for maneuver.[19]

Branch came up on Gregg's right, ordered the 7th and 28th North Carolina forward, where the 7th North Carolina made contact with the 10th New York, 6th U.S. and Berdan's Sharpshooters. Having outpaced its support, the 28th North Carolina, the 7th was forced to fall back. There were two friendly fire incidents between Federal units at this point, which served to delay effective fire on Branch's regiments.

Eventually, the Federals settled down and the combined fire of the Sharpshooters and the 9th Massachusetts, aided by a bayonet charge, halted the 7th North Carolina. The 37th North Carolina became the object of Federal attention, and the 37th, already hampered by the terrain, was forced back also. The 7th North Carolina and part of the 28th made another attempt to advance, but were repulsed. There the 7th lost its commander, Colonel Reuben P. Campbell, in the attempt.[20]

At that point, Branch attacked with three regiments, the 18th, 33rd and 37th North Carolina, contacting the Federal defenses just west of the original attacks. There they met three of Griffin's regiments, the 9th Massachusetts, 14th New York and 62nd Pennsylvania of Griffin's brigade. Branch was reinforced by Pender, with artillery from Andrews' battery as well as infantry from the 16th and 22nd North Carolina. These troops enjoyed some initial success, reaching the hill top, then being forced back by fire from the flanks. The 22nd's commander, Col. James Conner, was wounded in this contact.[21]

A. P. Hill then committed Joseph Anderson's brigade on Branch's right. Anderson attacked with all five of his regiments in line, but without artillery support. The brigade thrice charged the Federals, consisting of the 4th Michigan, part of the 14th New York from Griffin's brigade, and the 2nd Maine from Martindale's brigade. These Federal regiments made good use of improvised cover. Anderson's attack had little effect. After three unsuccessful charges, he dressed his lines and ordered his men to lie down north of Boatswain's Swamp.[22]

Archer's brigade (5th Bde.) came up on the right of Anderson, leaving one regiment, the 19th Georgia, in reserve. Archer was supported by the battery of Braxton. Charging across open terrain against the well dug in troops of Martindale, Archer's men had little chance for success. Although the 5th Alabama Btn. closed to within a few yards of the 5th Maine, they were forced to retreat.[23]

Only Field's brigade remained to be committed, and was ordered to support Anderson. In their first charge, accompanying Anderson's attack, they were repulsed at the 100 yard point. Supported by Pegram's battery, the second charge had a very similar outcome.[24]

To this point in the battle of Gaines' Mill, the entire effort on the Confederate side was conducted by A. P. Hill's division. He had performed well, committing all six of the Light Division's brigades, and a modest amount of artillery. However, Hill's attack can only be viewed as a complete failure. Once again, instead of pursuing an enemy retreating from a flanked position, he was forced to assault Federal troops in prepared defensive positions, with available artillery support.

The Light Division had lost about 2,000 of the 13,200 men available at the start of the day. The commander of the 47th Virginia reported that his regiment suffered 34 casualties, some of them from friendly fire. Some brigades, such as those of Gregg and Archer suffered crippling losses. The Army of Northern Virginia still hadn't won a battlefield victory.[25]

The tactical situation for the Confederates was not improving. Lee did not believe that time was on his side. It was now getting late on the afternoon of June 27, and once again a plan to force Federal forces out of their works by a flanking movement and attack them in retreat had failed to materialize. As at Mechanicsville the previous day, Lee was facing a competent corps commander in an excellent defensive position. The day, thus far, had cost 2,000 casualties, and his army hadn't gained an inch of the battlefield.

There was some good news, however. New Bridge had been uncovered, and therefore Lee had communications with Magruder and Huger on the south side of the Chickahominy. There was always the possibility that McClellan would realize how weak the Confederates were south of the river, mount a major attack on Magruder and Huger, and again split Lee's forces in two. Lee had no choice but to keep pushing ahead north of the Chickahominy.

The strategic situation differed from the tactical one. Although Porter's V Corps had been reinforced by McClellan, and was prepared to defend an excellent position, Porter was more or less isolated on the north side of the Chickahominy. Should a Confederate attack break his lines, there were few bridges available for advancing additional reinforcements or to conduct a retreat across the river.

Lee's best choice to continue the pressure on Porter was Longstreet's division. It was in reserve, intact and nearby. Longstreet's six brigades, commanded by brigadiers James L. Kemper, Richard H. Anderson, George E. Pickett, Cadmus M. Wilcox, Roger A. Pryor and Winfield S. Featherston were just on the west side of Powhite Creek. Longstreet received the order from Lee about 5:00 P.M. to "create a diversion on the Union left."[26]

Longstreet was cognizant of the superiority of Porter's position, but had no choice but to attack as ordered. Attempts to use Confederate artillery to silence Federal guns firing from both sides of the river had already proven unsuccessful. The cannon of Maurin's and Benjamin Smith's batteries simply didn't have the necessary range to get the job done.

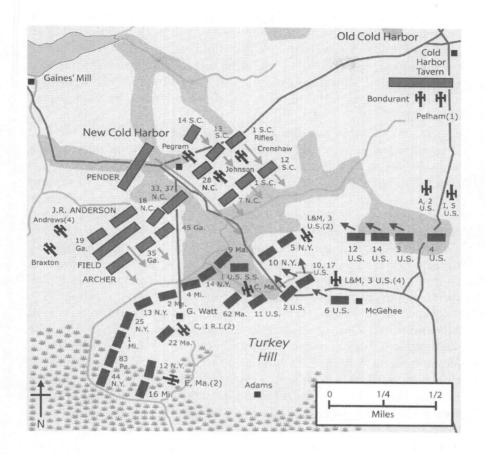

Map 17.3—Gaines's Mill, A. P. Hill's Attacks, June 27

Longstreet's three leading brigades, those of Wilcox, Pryor and Featherston, under the command of Wilcox, were sent against Porter's left flank. Their orders were to harass the Federals from a tree line, without exposing themselves unnecessarily. The Confederates began to rebuild a bridge across Powhite Creek, using debris found nearby. Both Wilcox and Pickett on his left were in contact by the time the improvised bridge was complete.

The Confederates were unable to gain the crest of a hill where Federal troops under Butterfield were dug in, and started taking significant losses. The defenders, specifically the 44th New York, comfortably held the attackers at bay.[27]

Longstreet's orders from Lee were to create a diversion on the extreme Federal left. This attack would be followed by another just to the left by A. P. Hill's division. A perceived imminent third attack, caused by the arrival of Jackson's troops, even farther to the Confederate left, would motivate Porter to move troops there from his left. A weakened Federal left would become the target of a vigorous Confederate attack by Longstreet's command.

At some point in the diversion, Longstreet reached the opinion that a diversion was of no value, and decided to make the transition to a full and vigorous attack. He selected the brigade of Richard Anderson to give him the momentum needed. Splitting up Anderson's brigade to support Pickett and Wilcox, Longstreet fed Kemper's brigade into the movement. At about this time, Whiting's division of Jackson's command emerged from the woods to Longstreet's left.[28]

Jackson's command had been joined by D. H. Hill's division, both trying to flank Porter's position and force his withdrawal. D. H. Hill moved his men along the Mechanicsville Turnpike and advanced to Bethesda Church. At the church, he planned to turn right toward the Federal position.

In contrast to Harvey Hill's efficient movement into position, Stonewall encountered an unexpected setback. Although provided a guide from the 4th Virginia Cavalry, moving roughly east on the Old Cold Harbor Road, Jackson managed to turn south one road too soon. After marching about a mile and a half along this wrong road, Jackson learned from the guide, a Private John H. Timberlake, that the road actually led to Gaines' Mill and New Cold Harbor. Jackson clarified with Timberlake that he wanted to go to Old Cold Harbor and reverse marched back to the Old Cold Harbor road. The unfortunate result of this poor communication between private and general was the loss of a precious hour. Other small obstructions along the line of march added slightly to the delay.[29]

D. H. Hill reached Old Cold Harbor well ahead of Jackson. His first action was to take possession of wagons, Confederate prisoners and ambulances abandoned by the retreating Federals. He then continued his advance to the south with two brigades, making contact with the Federal division of George Sykes in prepared positions behind Boatswain's Swamp. Taking intense musket fire, Hill ordered Bondurant's Jeff Davis Battery to engage the Federal infantry. However, Bondurant soon was outgunned by the rifled artillery batteries of Captains Weed and Tidball. Hill augmented Bondurant's fire with the batteries of Clark and Fry. This artillery duel began just after noon.[30]

Although not very far away at his headquarters at Selwyn, Lee, probably as a result of an acoustic shadow, did not become immediately aware of the artillery battle. Jeb Stuart arrived, skirmished with the 6th Pennsylvania Cavalry, then added Pelham's 2-gun Horse Artillery to the fracas.

D. H. Hill had two problems. First, he had contacted the Federal front rather than its right flank, as directed by General Orders No. 75. Second, he could not understand what body of water he was facing. Incredibly, Boatswain's Swamp wasn't on any of the Confederate maps. Hill decided to hold his position and wait for Jackson's three divisions to come up.[31]

Jackson, by about 2:00 P.M., had come up and began to assess the situation. Once again, he had found Porter's front, and faced the probability of trying to dislodge that stubborn V Corps, now reinforced with Slocum's Division, from another excellent defensive position. Jackson's first order was to have D. H. Hill pull his division back to the cover of a nearby wooded area. Next, he sent a message to Lee, carried by his engineer, Captain Boswell.[32]

The note written by Jackson, expressed to Lee that Jackson wasn't knowledgeable about the area and had concerns about a friendly fire incident. He suggested that Longstreet and A. P. Hill could possibly pressure Porter into retreating into D. H. Hill's division. It is doubtful that Lee would have been impressed by this tactical suggestion. After all, Porter didn't necessarily have to retreat northeastward toward D. H. Hill. Porter had the option of a retreat to the south toward the Chickahominy or southeast toward Bottoms Bridge. Additionally, a lack of pressure on the Federal right would only facilitate Porter's defense against Longstreet and A. P. Hill.[33]

Jackson, while seemingly uninspired, wasn't totally indolent. As D. H. Hill's division moved into the new positions assigned by Stonewall, the rest of Jackson's command, used a different road from Beulah Church, in an apparent effort to form a line of battle.

Apparently receiving an attack order from Lee, Ewell's division was ordered to attack on D. H. Hill's right. Ewell, cautioned by Jackson that the woods ahead were likely full of Federal troops, moved Elzey's brigade forward and found none of the enemy. At that point, Ewell elected to ask Jackson for further guidance. Before the courier, Major Campbell Brown, returned, orders arrived from Lee. Ewell was ordered to commit his two remaining brigades, those of Richard Taylor and Isaac R. Trimble. They were to be put in west of the New Cold Harbor road.

Major Brown soon returned. Stonewall had admitted that he had been misinformed as to the Federal positions. He confirmed that Lee's orders were correct. Major Brown, on Lee's orders, then left to bring up Winder's and Whiting's divisions.

Elzey advanced four of his seven infantry regiments to contact. The 13th, 31st, 44th and 58th Virginia moved through the woods, cleared them and struck the lines of Sykes' V Corps division. An intense fight ensued. Elzey suffered an ugly head wound, taking him out of combat for a significant period. The 13th Virginia suffered heavy casualties.[34]

Gregg's brigade of A. P. Hill's Light Division had internal command and control problems, which resulted in the fragmentation of the 13th South Carolina. However, the separated companies, under Major T. S. Farrow, joined up with remnants of the 1st South Carolina and were put in as support for Anderson's and Field's brigades by A. P. Hill.

Trimble's brigade, on Elzey's right, moved to the south, instead of the southeast, as Lee had intended. Major Campbell Brown rushed to their location, hoping to square them away before any harm was done. Sadly, they came under intense fire and moved even farther off line in an attempt to find cover. At that point, Elzey sent an officer to request help from Trimble. The request met with little sympathy.

Two of Trimble's regiments, the 15th Alabama and the 21st Georgia continued to advance, but two others, the 16th Mississippi and the 21st North Carolina became separated from the brigade. This was caused by retreating Confederate troops passing between them. The retreating troops were likely from either Pender's or Branch's brigades.

Trimble's regiments continued the advance, moving through a swamp and making contact with Warren's brigade, four regiments from Lovell's brigade (2nd, 6th, 10th and 17th U.S.) and Berdan's 1st U. S. Sharpshooters. These Federal troops greeted the advancing Confederates with a murderous volume of musket fire. Although reinforced by a Virginia regiment, Trimble's brigade could not pierce the Federal line, and was forced to simply hold their ground.[35]

Trimble had difficulty just holding his position. His situation was exacerbated by the problems of Richard Taylor's brigade, fighting on Trimble's right. Taylor had become ill on the evening of June 25, and did not arrive on the battlefield with his brigade. Command fell to Isaac Seymour, commander of the 6th Louisiana.[36]

Taylor's Brigade, composed of the 6th, 7th, 8th and 9th Louisiana Regiments, and the 1st Louisiana Special Btn., was arguably the most colorful in the Army of Northern Virginia. The 1st Louisiana Special Battalion was indeed special. Dubbed the "Louisiana Tigers" and commanded by Major. C. Roberdeau Wheat, they were reputed to have been raised by recruiting from the Parish Prison in downtown New Orleans.

While Taylor's brigade, under Isaac Seymour, moved toward contact, Porter elected to bring in more troops. He chose the brigade of George Meade. This was the 2nd Brigade of McCall's V Corps Division, composed of the 3rd, 4th, 7th and 11th Pennsylvania Reserves. Porter didn't commit the brigade all at one point of the line. Instead, he sent the 4th Reserves to support Warren, the 3rd Reserves to relieve the 4th Michigan of Griffin's brigade, and the 7th Reserves to aid Butterfield on the left end of the Federal line.

Porter had designated Truman Seymour's brigade, composed of the 9th, 10th and 12th Pennsylvania Reserves, as a general reserve, and now dispatched it to the right of Sykes, but the 9th and 10th Pennsylvania Reserves later were moved to Warren's rear, where the 9th Pennsylvania Reserves supported the 9th Massachusetts and the 62nd Pennsylvania of Griffin's brigade. The 62nd's commander, Colonel Samuel W. Black, was killed during one of several counterattacks mounted by Griffin's men.[37]

Elements of Reynolds' brigade of McCall's division filled the crease between Morell's and Sykes' divisions. Specifically, the 1st and 8th Pennsylvania Reserves aided Warren and the 2nd Reserves supported Martindale's brigade.[38]

By now, the VI Corps division of Slocum had come onto the scene. They had been just south of the Chickahominy, between Woodbury's and Alexander's Bridges, a little less than two miles to the rear of the center of Porter's lines. Slocum's brigades were commanded by George W. Taylor, Joseph J. Bartlett and John Newton.

Newton's brigade was the first ordered across the Chickahominy, receiving their orders about 2:00 P.M. He likely crossed the river via Alexander's Bridge and arrived at the Watt House by 4:00 P.M. His arrival was most timely, in that Porter had by then committed the last of his reserves on hand.[39]

When the van of Newton's brigade, composed of the 18th, 31st and 32nd New York, as well as the 95th Pennsylvania, appeared, they were required to wait some thirty minutes for orders to enter the battle. Porter's orders broke up the brigade and sent it in two directions. The 31st New York and 95th Pennsylvania went off to the northwest under Newton. The 18th and 32nd New York moved more to the north to support Warren's brigade. These two regiments were under the command of Roderick Matheson of the 32nd New York.

Matheson's arrival relieved Griffin, and his brigade was pulled back out of the line. The artillery battery of Lieutenant Emory Upton, which had arrived with Newton's brigade, was placed farther right.[40]

As Isaac Seymour's (Taylor's) brigade, made contact with the 95th Pennsylvania, which itself was still moving into line, Seymour was shot and killed. Command passed to Leroy Stafford, commander of the 9th Louisiana. Major Rob Wheat, commander of the Louisiana Tigers, was also hit and died in a short period. The first fifteen minutes of the engagement were very lethal. Newton's men produced a fire under which no force could stand. This fire was coming from prepared positions on high ground.[41]

As Seymour's brigade fell back, the 21st Georgia and 15th Alabama felt more pressure. Newton continued to push the 31st New York forward. In the momentary absence of the brigade commander, Isaac Trimble, General Ewell personally rallied the Georgians and Alabamians. He also took steps to get more artillery support to the Confederate line. Despite the addition of James B. Brockenbrough's and Courtney's batteries, little additional fire support was rendered. The chaotic situation made it difficult for artillerists to fire without hitting their own infantry.[42]

Most of Ewell's division had seen action by late afternoon. Some elements were holding on by their fingertips. One brigade had been hurt badly, losing too many officers. The hoped for salvation was the expected arrival of Whiting's division.

Jackson decided to order his divisions to advance *en echelon*, left to right and attack the enemy where he found them. The order of attack would be Ewell, Whiting, then Charles Winder. Just as Jackson's courier, the Reverend Dabney, was about to deliver Jackson's orders, Stonewall decided to send Major John Harman instead. This Jackson did due to Dabney's recent illness. Harman, a quartermaster, reached Whiting first, but was unable to adequately communicate Jackson's orders, owing to his lack of knowledge of tactical terms. Whiting understood to await orders, thus none of the brigades were able to advance.

No one can say why Jackson didn't take the time to put his orders in writing. Dabney, though ill, decided to follow up on Harman's task. Although Whiting put up a bit of an argument, Dabney was able to satisfy Whiting that Jackson wanted an attack, and Whiting moved out. Whiting was approached on his advance by the aides of several generals. All were seeking support for their hard pressed commanders. Whiting decided to stay focused on his assigned mission and continued on.[43]

Whiting arrived behind A. P. Hill's division, noting Hill's men to be tired, somewhat disorganized and a bit demoralized. Searching for the exact best point at which to enter the line, Whiting located Lee and was directed to the right. Arriving there, Whiting encountered Longstreet on the verge of initiating his own attack.[44]

Late in the afternoon, the intensity of the battle diminished. Porter had earlier reported to Army headquarters his success in beating back the vigorous Confederate assaults. Surprisingly, McClellan had suggested that Porter pursue the enemy, if he so desired. But by 5:00 P.M., Porter telegraphed a request for reinforcements, stating that his men were being pressed hard. The response from McClellan was to send Meagher's and French's brigades of Richardson's division (II Corps). These two brigades moved by way of Alexander's and Grapevine Bridges. McClellan reassured Porter that he would move the entire army north of the Chickahominy if necessary to beat the enemy. This would have been impossible to accomplish that day, if McClellan had been sincere, which is unlikely. In point of fact, he had no such intention.

The two brigades mentioned above made a great difference in the final outcome of the day's fighting. They were commanded by competent officers and arrived at a critical point.

Porter had already received all of Slocum's division, and would not receive more reinforcements until the arrival of Meagher's and French's brigades. Porter had already committed virtually all of the Pennsylvania Reserves of McCall's division. These Pennsylvania troops had fought doggedly all day. They were dealing with overheated and fouled muskets, and ammo was becoming a consideration. Some companies were running short of officers.[45]

As each of Slocum's brigades arrived, Porter had personally placed them where he needed them most. He likely felt that Slocum's troops would determine whether or not the Federal position could be held.

Newton's brigade came up first, moved into the seam between Morell's and Sykes' divisions. It consisted of the 18th, 31st and 32nd New York, the 95th Pennsylvania, and Upton's 2nd U. S. Artillery, Battery D.

Taylor's brigade arrived next and was placed in the hard pressed center of the line. It was composed of the 1st, 2nd, 3rd and 4th New Jersey, and Hexamer's Battery A, New Jersey Light Artillery.

The last of Slocum's brigades to arrive, that of Bartlett. It was made up of the 5th Maine, the 16th and 27th New York, the 96th Pennsylvania, and Josiah Porter's 1st Battery, Massachusetts Light Artillery. They were sent to the left of the line, in support of Butterfield's brigade.[46]

Arriving with his brigade on the left of the Federal line, Bartlett observed a unit under great pressure and in danger of breaking, and decided to insert his 16th New York. However, a staff officer from Porter arrived and sent Bartlett's brigade to the very right of Porter's line. It was then redirected to the left in support of Robert Buchanan's brigade near the McGehee house. While the infantry was committed, Porter's battery was put in reserve.[47]

D. H. Hill was having a memorable afternoon. He had suffered a shrapnel wound while riding along his lines. Now, as Bartlett was reinforcing Buchanan, D. H. Hill was preparing to move against Buchanan's position.

In response to Jackson's orders, by 5:00 P.M., D. H. Hill was just about ready to attack. His five brigades were arrayed from left to right, commanded by Garland, George B. Anderson, Rodes, Colquitt and Ripley. Hill also placed his entire artillery complement of seven batteries in support.

The terrain to be crossed in the assault was not favorable to the Confederates. In Hill's front, there was still some swamp to be crossed, followed by some 400 yards of open ground

Buchanan's position was a little north of the road between New Cold Harbor and the McGehee house. The brigade was composed of the 3rd, 4th, 12th and 14th U. S. Infantry regiments. They had the support of Weed's battery.

The brigade was deployed just north of the McGehee house, arrayed by regiments in line, facing north. From left to right were the 12th, 14th, 3rd and 4th U. S., with the 4th just east of the road from Old Cold Harbor to Grapevine Bridge.[48]

At least some of Buchanan's men had been under fire since noon that day. Confederate artillery fire began about then, with no significant effect. Other factors weighed on the morale of the men. They had lost most of their supplies the previous night, when they were forced to burn their camp prior to their retreat from Mechanicsville. On top of that sad experience, Major Delozier Davidson, commanding the 4th U. S., deserted the field on foot, leaving Captain Joseph B. Collins in command. Davidson was captured the following day by Confederate cavalry.[49]

D. H. Hill's troops were not having an easy time of advancing to contact. The remaining swampy terrain caused uneven progress of the regiments, causing serious misalignment. One regiment found itself behind another Confederate force, and at least one friendly fire incident occurred.

D. H. Hill observed the brigades of Winder (Stonewall Brigade) and Lawton from Jackson's old division coming up on Hill's right flank. Winder wasn't where he'd been ordered to go. He'd been ordered to take Jackson's brigades into the line just right of Whiting's men. Having lost contact with the unit ahead of him, he moved to the sound of the loudest gunfire. He encountered A. P. Hill, asked for orders, and was told to stay put. He was later told to send the 2nd and 5th Virginia to support the artillery battery of Pegram. Still later (30 min.), he was ordered to advance, picking up several units on the way.

Rudolph J. Schroeder, III

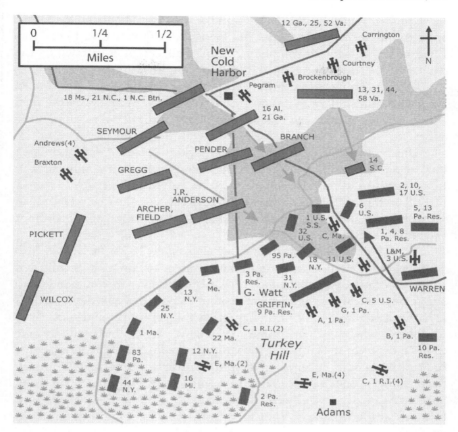

Map 17.4—Gaines's Mill, Ewell's Attacks, June 27

Lawton's brigade followed Winder, but angled a little to the right, and urged them to hurry. He came across Ewell, who was impressed and cheered the brigade on. Lawton's arrival in line solidified the Confederate left. There were two other of Jackson's brigades north of the river, and they were part of the planned assault. J. R. Jones' brigade, under Lieutenant Colonel Cunningham, strayed well to the right, and eventually supported Wilcox. The other brigade, that of Samuel V. Fulkerson, supported Whiting.[50] These brigade commanders were well qualified to fight this battle. They had fought for Stonewall in the Valley.

Behind Buchanan's front, Bartlett formed a second line. The intensity of fire indicated the critical point of the day's battle was imminent.

Lee finally encountered Jackson on the road from Beulah Church. He greeted him with the sentence, "Ah, General, I am very glad to see you. I had hoped to be with you before." Stonewall, certainly irritated by the day's events, nodded and replied in a mumble.

Told some time later that the Federals were not withdrawing as hoped for, Jackson ordered a pair of couriers to pass the word to "sweep the field with the bayonet." He then ordered all his artillery batteries to support the effort.

After his meeting with Lee had ended, Jackson located A. P. Hill, ordered him forward, and told him to pass the order to all other commanders.[51] Longstreet was already moving forward on Powell Hill's right, as was D. H. Hill on the left. The result was a huge, loosely coordinated attack on an exhausted, but entrenched Federal force. This was the moment of truth for two armies and their commanders.[52]

Although the final Confederate assaults at the battle of Gaines' Mill occurred at about the same time, there was not really one coordinated attack. Lee had ordered the word passed to all division commanders to attack, but there was little coordination between them. Sears describes it as a "hardly a picture-book charge, but rather a matter of fits and starts."

There was, however, some cooperative effort between brigade commanders. On the far left of the Confederate line, Garland and George B. Anderson were engaged in a spirited discussion of how to attack Buchanan's Federal brigade in the flank when D. H. Hill came upon them. Specifically, the two brigadiers were discussing the impact of a section of Edwards' artillery battery. When asked by D. H. Hill if said section would affect their movement, Garland stated that he was "willing to risk it." Anderson concurred, and D. H. Hill ordered the entire division forward. He also assigned some five regiments to capture the guns. Three regiments (1st, 3rd and 20th North Carolina) were to attack the Federal guns in a frontal attack, while the other two (25th and 52nd Virginia) were to work their way around to their rear and attack.[53]

Due to miscommunication, only the 20th North Carolina attacked, but successfully took the guns. The effort was costly, in that their commander, Colonel Alfred Iverson, and others were wounded.

Harvey Hill credited their charge with changing the balance of the battle to the Confederates' favor. The remainder of G. B. Anderson's brigade then attacked and carried the Federal position.

Also in D. H. Hill's division, Rodes was having his own problems with communication and troop handling. For some unknown reason, two of his regiments did not understand they were to advance, and didn't. This uneven advance prompted Rodes to believe that the division as a whole had major difficulties. Rodes went looking for more support. He found his two lagging regiments and Colquitt's brigade on his left. Rodes enlisted Colquitt's assistance there, then restarted the advance of his own brigade.

Colquitt was not immune from the confusion of the day. Only two of his regiments actually went into the battle. These two, the 5th and 26th Alabama were successful in capturing enemy guns. It was a costly action for the 5th. It lost its commander, Colonel Christopher C. Pegues.

Amazingly, the brigade of Roswell Ripley, on the right end of Harvey Hill's line was in an even greater state of disarray. Ripley was short two regiments. Part of the 1st North Carolina and the 44th Georgia were detailed to guard the Mechanicsville Turnpike Bridge, probably because they had suffered such high casualties the previous day. The 48th Georgia moved to its right to assist another regiment, but failed to get into the necessary position to do so. The rest of the 1st and the 3rd North Carolina were tasked to attack Federal guns with the 20th North Carolina, but believed they were in reserve and just watched the 20th's successful movement.[54]

Outside of D. H. Hill's division, other brigades were beginning to move to the attack. After a brief conversation, Jackson personally ordered Bradley T. Johnson to charge the enemy. Johnson moved his 1st Maryland Infantry forward through a chaotic mass of retreating Alabama and North Carolina troops. He assisted their officers in rallying them as best he could. Encountering still more shaken troops, Johnson steadied them and continued the advance. Colliding with the Federal line, they carried the position, but too late to bag Kingsbury's Federal battery, which had withdrawn.[55]

Winder, meanwhile, continued his advance. Jackson, desiring the Stonewall Brigade to find glory in this action, ordered Winder to move Jackson's old brigade to the fore. Winder complied and the Stonewall Brigade moved out with enthusiasm, passing and taunting Bradley T. Johnson's 1st Maryland Infantry in the process. Through dense wooded terrain, passing numbers of dead soldiers, the Stonewall Brigade advanced, aware of the heavy roar of cannon fire.

Leading the Stonewall Brigade, the 2nd and 5th Virginia regiments encountered heavy Federal fire and were stopped. The 2nd's commander, Colonel James W. Allen, was killed and their major mortally wounded.

The 33rd Virginia, contending with swampy terrain and a unit from Georgia in its way, was late entering the fray. William S. H. Baylor, commander of the 5th Virginia, was concerned about a gap between his regiment and the 2nd Virginia.

Seven Days Before Richmond

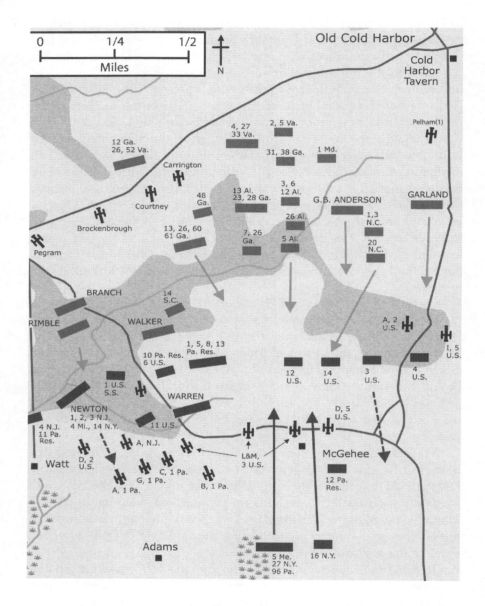

Map 17.5—Gaines's Mill, D. H. Hill's Attacks on Sykes, June 27

In that gap, but to the rear, Baylor spied another regiment. He determined that it was the 38th Georgia, commanded by Captain Edward P. Lawton. Although short on officers and ammo, they agreed to fill the gap between the Alabamians and press forward. The attack was successful, as the Federal infantry withdrew and abandoned their artillery. The remainder of the brigade advanced, pushing the Federals hundreds of yards south of the McGehee house.[56]

Buchanan and his brigade, on the far right of the Federal line, felt the pressure of the Confederate attack. At the same time, he heard a great deal of fire, as well as loud cheering, coming from his left. He wrongly concluded that the Federal left was collapsing, and began a retreat of his own.

The 3rd U. S. Infantry, fighting just west of the road from Old Cold Harbor to the Grapevine Bridge, had their commander, Major Nathan Rossell, mortally wounded. In the wake of that event, the 3rd fell back, causing the 14th U. S., immediately to the left of the 3rd, to fall back also. The 14th's commander, Captain John D. O'Connell, ordered a slow withdrawal. To the left of the 14th, the commander of the 12th U. S., Major Henry B. Clitz, took the same decision. During the withdrawal, he was twice wounded, then captured at the McGehee house. Clitz, an old friend of D. H. Hill, was taken that night to the General, who ordered Clitz cared for by a surgeon.[57]

The next victim of the Confederate assault was Bartlett's brigade of Slocum's VI Corps division. Bartlett began his resistance to the rebel onslaught with the 96th Pennsylvania and the 16th New York. Unhappy with the lack of celerity of the 96th, he soon added the 5th Maine, then the 27th New York. At last the 96th Pennsylvania was truly ready for the fight and advanced to contact, holding a position behind a fence.[58]

The 16th New York attacked the 20th North Carolina, also from the cover of a fence. The New Yorkers successfully retook the guns of Lieutenant Horace Hayden, this despite the severe wounding of the 16th's commander, Colonel Joseph Howland. The desperate fight resulted in the death or wounding of over 450 men in the two regiments combined. Lieutenant Colonel Faison assumed command of the 20th after Colonel Alfred Iverson was wounded, and Faison was mortally wounded himself.

The 27th New York with two companies of the 5th Maine attempted to assist the 16th New York. However, Bartlett was forced to retreat due to a shortage of ammunition and Lawton's brigade attacking on his left flank.[59]

Bartlett's men were not the only ones running short of ammunition. The 31st Georgia, 2nd, 10th and 17th U. S., as well as the 1st, 5th, 8th and 13th Pennsylvania Reserves also had ammunition shortage or exhaustion. Problems in sorting out enemy versus friendly units increased in the dusky conditions. This problem grew so bad for Lawton that he withdrew a few hundred yards to sort out the situation. Hearing an order to attack and knowing his support was needed, Bartlett led his men back into the fight.

As the daylight failed, the fighting on the extreme Federal right more or less stopped, and the Confederates made ready for the possibility of a counterattack.

The Federal brigade just to the left of Bartlett's was Lovell's brigade of Sykes' V Corps division, and was composed of the 2nd, 6th, 10th, 11th and 17th U. S. Just to Lovell's left was Warren's brigade, made up of only two regiments, the 5th and 10th New York.

Warren's brigade, as well as the 10th U. S. of Lovell's brigade, had not seen the heaviest of the Confederate assault. The most intense fighting had been off both their flanks. One regiment of Truman Seymour's brigade in McCall's division had run out of ammunition.

Warren's men and some of Reynolds' brigade of Seymour's division, who had been inserted in the line between Sykes' and Morell's divisions, had fought hard and held their ground all day. Their only withdrawals to this point were for support of artillery or lack of ammunition. With artillery support from Augustus Martin's Battery C, Massachusetts Light Artillery, as well as covering fire from the 11th U. S., an orderly Federal retreat occurred on this part of the battlefield.[60]

Left of Lovell's 11th U. S. was Newton's brigade. It was composed of the 18th, 31st and 32nd New York and the 95th Pennsylvania, and was augmented by the 1st and 3rd New Jersey of Taylor's brigade. Newton's command had held their lines for over two hours. The 1st New Jersey, commanded by Lieutenant Colonel Robert McAllister, as Colonel Torbert was ill, attempted to advance to contact through a swamp. Upon reaching their attack position, the undergrowth was found to be too thick to permit an infantry charge. The regiment hunkered down and tolerated the enemy fire of Elzey's brigade under Colonel James A. Walker, as well as the 16th Mississippi, 21st North Carolina and 1st North Carolina of Trimble's brigade.[61]

Advancing uphill, Trimble and his brigade moved through two retreating regiments, who, along with one of their colonels, tried to dissuade Trimble and his men from attempting to drive off the Federals. Trimble responded "Forward, boys, and give them the bayonet!" Small groups of the retreating regiments joined Trimble's brigade, and they moved up the slope, holding their musket fire until the last possible moment.

Two of Newton's regiments, the 95th Pennsylvania and the 31st New York, were in a desperate situation. They believed they were in danger of being cut off, and had to pull back. Colonel John M. Gosline and Major William B. Hubbs of the 95th Pennsylvania were both mortally wounded as they withdrew.

Rudolph J. Schroeder, III

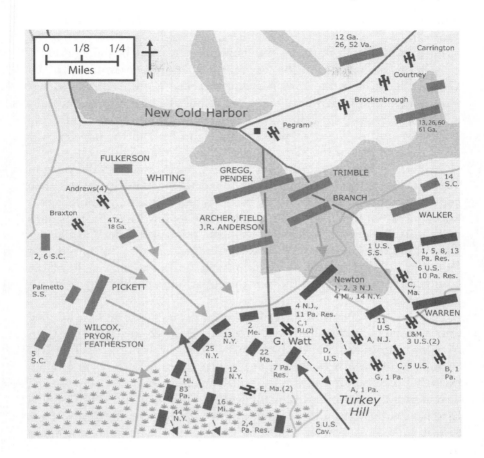

Map 17.6—Gaines' Mill, Whiting's Attack on Morell, June 27

The withdrawal of these two regiments created jeopardy for Newton's other two regiments, the 18th and 32nd New York. They fled as fast as they could, just barely avoiding capture by the advancing Confederates.

These retreats exposed McAllister's 1st New Jersey to a crossfire, and he feared they would be taken prisoner. His hastily ordered retreat was just in the nick of time. McAllister's artillery support, Hexamer's Battery A, New Jersey Light Artillery courageously held their position long enough to allow the regiment to clear their line of fire, then delivered case shot and canister before retreating. This gallantry cost Hexamer one gun captured, and earned him the respect of the Prince de Joinville.[62]

The Federal retreats began to resemble a string of dominoes falling. Now two regiments of Griffin's brigade, the 14th New York and the 4th

Michigan were forced to retreat when the unit on their left did. This in turn caused Upton's 2nd U. S. Artillery, Battery D to retire. Upton did manage to discharge a barrage of double canister before he pulled back.[63]

Upton was not the only battery commander under pressure. The 21st Georgia and part of the 15th Alabama attacked Easton's Battery A, 1st Pennsylvania Light Artillery. After repulsing the first charge, Easton's supporting infantry unit, the 2nd Pennsylvania Reserves, collapsed and Easton was killed. The attacking Georgians and Alabamians, joined by the 5th Texas and part of the 18th Georgia took all his guns.

DeHart's Battery C, 5th U. S. Artillery lined up just to the right of Easton's ill-fated guns. DeHart was wounded, and the battery was then commanded by Lt. Eben G. Scott. It was in time flanked by Confederates attacking out of the battlefield's smoke. They took three of Easton's guns and inflicted a number of casualties on the retreating Federal artillerists. The attacking Confederates next targeted Cooper's Battery B, 1st Pennsylvania Light. Despite the use of spherical case, the weight of the Confederate attack caused Cooper to retreat immediately, saving all his guns and people.

To the left of Newton's brigade, were those of Meade and Taylor. The only regiments holding fast were the 11th Pennsylvania Reserves from Meade's brigade and the 4th New Jersey from Taylor's brigade. This was to no avail, as the 5th Texas surrounded them. Reaching the high ground, the 5th Texas took fire from the 4th New Jersey, which was now in the Texans' rear. At that moment, many Federal officers saw the hopelessness of their situation, and urged surrender, rather than spend the lives of their men in a needless manner. The situation for the Federals was worsening by the minute. The 4th New Jersey, all save for 83 men, was captured.

More than Federal soldiers were taken. Seven coffee-mill guns, precursors to the Gatling guns, were deployed in Taylor's brigade. All seven of them were captured by the Confederates.[64]

On the far end of the line, the Confederate right was commanded by James Longstreet. They faced the V Corps division of Morell, whose brigades were led by Martindale, Griffin and Butterfield.

Longstreet then had the good fortune of the arrival of Whiting's division, consisting of the brigades of Law and Hood. Longstreet had some concern about a Federal counterattack, and Whiting's arrival obviated the need to use his reserve brigade, that of Kemper. Longstreet put Whiting's men in on Pickett's left, with Hood's brigade to the left of Law's. As Hood positioned his regiments, Lee came up, and related to Hood that no one had been able to break the Federal line. Lee then inquired of Hood, "Can you break this line?" Hood, naturally, replied that he would try to do so.

Whiting then pointed out a Federal battery that he felt needed to be taken, and that it had been attacked three times unsuccessfully. Hood stated that "I have a regiment that can take it," and went back to his duties.

As the assault began, Hood seized the opportunity to put his men in a gap he noticed between the troops of Longstreet and Law. He found the ground more favorable for the attack, being relatively open. The down side was that his men moving across the open ground attracted more Federal fire. Hood, personally leading the 4th Texas and part of the 18th Georgia, ordered the men to hold their fire until ordered otherwise. This was the crisis point of the entire day's battle. The 4th Texas moved through the debris of the day's battle—human, animal and mechanical. They also encountered severe enfilading fire and broken soldiers who volunteered the opinion that the Texans could not accomplish their mission. More determined than ever, the 4th Texas came across a line of Confederates hunkered down and refusing to obey a lieutenant's orders to move out.[65]

It mattered little that Colonel John Marshall, the official commander of the 4th Texas, was hit early in the fight, as Hood had assumed personal direction of the attack. Marshall's successor, Bradfute Warwick at one time ordered the 4th Texas to halt and fire a volley. Hood immediately countermanded the order and instead ordered the men to fix bayonets and charge at the double-quick. Advancing to and through Boatswain's Swamp and colliding with the defending Federals, Hood's men became an irresistible force. The Army of Northern Virginia had finally broken Porter's defenses.[66]

Hood's brigade wasn't attacking alone on the Confederate left. Whiting's other brigade, under Law, joined by the remainder of Hood's brigade and accompanied by Whiting himself, joined in the attack. The brigade, composed of the 4th Alabama, 2nd Mississippi, 11th Mississippi and the 6th North Carolina, moved forward. Whiting informed them that there would be no retreat order, and professed his confidence in their success. Whiting assured that they, as did Hood's brigade, charged with fixed bayonets and without firing their muskets. Law's brigade had similar success to Hood's, bursting through the Federal works, scattering the men of Morell's division and taking prisoners.[67]

To Whiting's right, Pickett's brigade of Longstreet's division, also joined the charge. Part of Richard H. Anderson's brigade then pitched in. The weight of over three brigades and the speed and ferocity of the assault assured that all three Federal lines were broken. Morell's men were sent reeling. Momentarily, the 16th Michigan of Butterfield's brigade attempted to stem the Confederate flood. After a spirited resistance, they were forced back, losing their regimental flag in the affair. The 16th's commander, Colonel Thomas B. W. Stockton and fifty-two of his men were captured.

This critical Confederate success was not without a price. Pickett received a shoulder wound, and thought it might be mortal. Hunton assumed Pickett's role afterwards.[68]

The Federal unit that bore the brunt of the three-brigade Confederate assault was the brigade of Martindale. This brigade, comprised of the 13th New York, 25th New York and the 1st Michigan, had fought off several charges behind works they had built. After fighting hard all afternoon, they were extremely tired and the sudden Confederate attack drove them back. The 22nd Massachusetts, in reserve, attempted to blunt the charge, but was soon flanked and forced to retreat. In this contact, their commander, Jesse A. Gove, was killed. A number of Federal prisoners were taken.[69]

The far right of Martindale's position was held by the 2nd Maine, and was not attacked directly. They were obliged to retreat with the other regiments. The 7th Pennsylvania Reserves of Meade's brigade were in the seam between Martindale's brigade and that of Butterfield to the left. The 7th was routed and their artillery support, a 2-gun section of Weeden's Battery, commanded by Lieutenant Buckley, lost its guns to the attackers. Buckley bravely fired his section to the last instant, having only three men per gun left, and no horses with which to remove them.[70]

Now three more of Longstreet's brigades, those of Wilcox, Pryor and Featherston, attacked *en masse*. Featherston was on the left, Pryor in the center, and Wilcox on the right. Running through Boatswain's Swamp, they fell upon Butterfield's brigade. The pressure was too much for the weary Federals. The 1st Michigan was in retreat, causing part of the 12th New York to break. Colonel Stryker and a portion of 44th New York also retreated. Colonel John W. McLane, commander of the 83rd Pennsylvania, was felled by troops of the 5th South Carolina. The 16th Michigan, attacked by the Palmetto Sharpshooters, held for a while, then gave way.[71]

All along the line, Federal units were in retreat. They were being pushed back towards the Chickahominy. Some even crossed the river without the luxury of a bridge to avoid capture. They found sanctuary among the troops of William F. Smith's VI Corps division in the vicinity of Golding's farm. A number of guns were taken by the swarming Confederates, despite some heroics by Federal gunners. Some of these guns were of necessity abandoned by the Federals because no horses were left alive to haul them to the rear.[72]

Upon reaching the precious high ground previously defended by Porter's men, Whiting called on Longstreet for reinforcements. Longstreet sent him Richard Anderson's brigade. Fulkerson's brigade was sent to reinforce Hood. Unfortunately, Fulkerson was mortally wounded while assessing the situation. Federal artillery fire was still a great hazard to Whiting's men. The 4th Texas, attempting to get at the Federal guns, were required to charge across 400 yards of open ground. As the charge began, the 4th lost its second commander of the day. Lieutenant Colonel Warwick was hit by shrapnel and mortally wounded. Hood called off the attack, added the 18th Georgia to the assignment, and reissued the order to attack the guns.[73]

The most controversial action of the day occurred at this point. The cavalry of Philip St. George Cooke was present on the Federal left. Their orders had been to shield the Federal left flank and attack the Confederates on the open plain between Powhite Creek and Boatswain's Swamp. Cooke understood that he had no tasking on the high ground where the main Federal position was.

The controversy resulted from the varying perceptions of the results of a cavalry charge that Cooke ordered on his own initiative. Cooke observed the collapse of the Federal infantry on the left of their line, and also the three batteries still firing at the enemy. He directed the 1st and 5th U. S. Cavalry to charge the attacking Confederates whenever they felt the safety of the batteries required it.

Cooke's report is straight-forward, and paints the cavalry in a positive light. Cooke also repositioned the 6th Pennsylvania Cavalry to support the presently unsupported Batteries B & L, 2nd U. S. Artillery. The 6th found their line of retreat in jeopardy, and withdrew about 400 yards., finding themselves in the company of part the 9th Massachusetts. Cooke then ordered the 1st U. S. Cavalry from their position in the rear to one on the left of the Federal infantry. The 4th Pennsylvania Cavalry arrived and positioned itself just left of the Regulars.

At this point, with Confederates advancing, a Federal battery fired from a position behind the cavalry, hitting friendly troopers. General Cooke reacted by ordering a retreat. Simultaneously, the 5th U. S. Cavalry began an almost suicidal charge. The Confederates responded with heavy musket fire and a bayonet charge. Horses, as well as troopers, were bayoneted. Most of the 5th U. S. Cavalry saddles were emptied. Their commander, Captain Charles J. Whiting, was captured. The artillery batteries did manage to escape during the melee.

Other officers had different recollections of the entire event. Two of General Cooke's captains, Wesley Merritt and James P. Martin, exaggerated the importance of the cavalry action as "saving Porter from destruction." The Comte de Paris was also sympathetic to Cooke's view.

Porter had a very different perception. His official report stated: "To this alone (the cavalry charge) is to be attributed our failure to hold the battle-field and to bring off all our guns and wounded." He reiterated same in a later article for *Battles and Leaders of the Civil War*.

Morell took a middle-of-the-road, somewhat diplomatic view. He agreed that the cavalry charge did sweep away some men and horses, but noted that it steadied nearby infantry.

James M. Robertson, who commanded two of the batteries in jeopardy, credited the cavalry charge for covering his withdrawal. Conversely, William Weeden, Morell's artillery chief, felt the confusion created by the cavalry charge had cost him one gun.

A few Confederate reports mention the Federal cavalry charge. Some thought it mostly unimportant. Others credit it with giving the Federal artillerists a little more time to save some of their guns.[74]

A common sense look with the help of hindsight leads to the conclusion that the battle was lost for Porter's men, and no regimental-sized attack could affect the overall outcome. The cavalry charge probably did save a gun or two, but probably wasn't worth the cost in lost lives and horses.

Federal artillery probably was partially responsible for blunting Confederate momentum. Some Federal artillerists, among them Robertson and Weeden, fired well after their infantry supports had broken. Nineteen of ninety-two guns assigned to Fitz John Porter were captured. Federal batteries south of the Chickahominy also played a significant role. Several Confederate officers commented that Federal fire from across the river prevented a more devastating defeat of Porter's command.

A little while after the controversial cavalry charge, there was cheering emanating from the Federal rear. Specifically, the brigades of Meagher and French were arriving. These last reinforcements sent by McClellan arrived too late to prevent Porter's defeat, but they were able to stop a full-scale rout.

The arriving brigades witnessed a depressing sight. Masses of men and horses were making for the nearest Chickahominy bridges with all haste. The 8th Illinois Cavalry was sent to stem the tide of stragglers, but enjoyed little success. French was the senior brigadier of the two, and called the shots. He directed Meagher to send troops up and attempt to stop the panic. A company of the 69th New York had some success.[75]

Porter ordered French and Meagher to a position on a crest near the Watt house and instructed them to hold that position. They did that for a time, then Confederate fire intensified from the right and Porter moved Meagher right to relieve Sykes. The light casualties (16) suffered by the two II Corps brigades indicates no intense fighting occurred from that point in time. Some other Federal brigades, such as Taylor's of Slocum's division, were beginning to rally with the stabilizing effect of the two fresh brigades that had recently arrived. Darkness soon fell and gunfire in the center of the battlefield ceased.[76]

The essence of the battle of Gaines' Mill is that Porter's V Corps, reinforced by Slocum's division from VI Corps and the brigades of French and Meagher of Richardson's II Corps division, totaling about 34,000 men, held an excellent defensive position behind Boatswain's Swamp for almost five hours against approximately 57,000 attacking Confederate troops.

Near sunset, the Confederates finally managed to mount a loosely coordinated attack across most of the front and overwhelmed Porter's position, forcing the Federals to retreat toward the Chickahominy River. It was an exceptionally bloody battle. Principals such as Jackson, Longstreet and Armistead Long agreed that it was the most intense, stubbornly fought battle of the war to date. Historian Stephen W. Sears summed the battle up most eloquently when he wrote that "Gaines's Mill was a battle fought entirely without subtlety; the tightly contained Federal position appeared to offer no opportunity for maneuver. The result was a straight-ahead slugging match in which the defenders held all the advantage of position."[77]

Total casualties were estimated to be about 8,700 for the Army of Northern Virginia and 6,837 for the Army of the Potomac. On the Federal side, units with extremely high casualty rates were the 9th Massachusetts and the 16th New York. On the Confederate side, the regiments hardest hit were the 1st South Carolina Rifles, the 4th Texas, the 20th North Carolina, and the 31st and 38th Georgia. Not only were the numbers of killed and wounded high, but the Federals suffered many troops captured by the advancing Confederates. Gaines' Mill was the bloodiest battle of the Seven Days and one of the deadliest of the entire war.[78]

The battle of Gaines's Mill was *the* decisive Confederate victory of the Peninsula Campaign. Although the Army of Northern Virginia paid a heavy price in casualties, the result was arguably worth it. The Army of the Potomac suffered a certain loss of confidence, especially on the part of their Commanding General. McClellan had lost the initiative and would be unable to regain it.

At this point, McClellan's ability to exert pressure on the city of Richmond was at an effective end. Lee had gotten what he wanted. McClellan's mighty army was in retreat, and the Army of Northern Virginia had the initiative. McClellan had little choice but to order a withdrawal across the Chickahominy, abandon his White House base, and retreat to the James River.

Seven Days Before Richmond

It was clear to General Lee that McClellan had now decided to change his base. What was unclear was whether Lee could devise a tactical plan that would allow him to trap and decimate or possibly even destroy the Army of the Potomac. Such an accomplishment could have major implications for potential European diplomatic recognition of the Confederate States of America, and perhaps the final outcome of the war.

CHAPTER 18

Garnett's and Golding's Farms

(June 27–28)

Robert E. Lee, in his General Orders No. 75, issued on June 24, 1862, penned a paragraph which detailed the tasking for those forces of the Army of Northern Virginia positioned south of the Chickahominy River. It stated:

> The divisions under Generals Huger and Magruder will hold their positions in front of the enemy against attack, and make such demonstrations Thursday as to discover his operations. Should opportunity offer, the feint will be converted into a real attack, and should an abandonment of his intrenchments by the enemy be discovered, he will be closely pursued.[1]

On June 27, while the battle of Gaines' Mill was being fought north of the Chickahominy River, Major General Magruder conducted the feint required by Lee's order. Late in the day, Federal units near Fair Oaks Station took under fire the 53rd Virginia of Armistead's brigade, Huger's division. The Federals used muskets and artillery to push back the Virginians. Despite the initial retreat of several companies on the right side of the 53rd, the remainder of the regiment counterattacked, then the regiment reformed, and the Federals were pushed back.[2]

This was not the sole nor the largest contact south of the Chickahominy that day. The farm of James Garnett was just north of Seven Pines, site of the battle fought May 31–June 1. It was on the high bluffs which ran along the south bank of the Chickahominy River. The Federal lines ran more or less north to south, about three-eighths of a mile east of Garnett's farm. The Confederate lines were parallel, and just east of Garnett's.

The terrain between the opposing forces was challenging, consisting of a ravine, a creek and a hill named for Mr. Garnett. The hill had already been fortified the previous night by William T. H. Brooks' brigade of Baldy

Smith's VI Corps division. When the artillery emplacements had been completed, Brooks was withdrawn, replaced by Hancock's brigade, and reinforced by a half dozen batteries from the artillery reserve. Hancock's men continued to improve the defenses, within sight of Confederate troops gathering near the Garnett house.

The troops near the Garnett house were those of David R. Jones' division, of Magruder's command. Jones served the Confederacy well until his untimely death of heart disease in January, 1863.[3]

The ravine mentioned above lay between the opposing troops. On the west or Confederate side of the ravine were the troops of Robert A. Toombs. His brigade was composed of the 2nd, 15th, 17th and 20th Georgia regiments. To Toombs' northwest was deployed the brigade of George T. Anderson, near the Price house. Anderson commanded the 1st Georgia Regulars and the 7th, 8th, 9th and 11th Georgia. The two brigades were little more than a half mile apart.

When D. R. Jones noticed the rifle pits the Federals had constructed overnight on the east side of the ravine, he reported that fact to Magruder, who responded by moving up a two-gun section of Captain James Brown's Wise (Virginia) Battery. The guns were placed east of Mrs. Price's house. A regiment from G. T. Anderson's brigade supported the guns. Another section of artillery was brought up from Stephen Lee's artillery, a part of Magruder's division, also close to Mrs. Price's house. Their orders were general in nature, to fire anytime they could see the Federals.[4]

On the Federal side of the ravine, Baldy Smith made ready to defend against an expected Confederate attack. He received an order to avoid a general engagement. Accordingly, he pulled Hancock back several hundred yards, and left a strong picket force in the recently dug rifle pits. Considerable artillery was then sent to cover the left flank of Hancock's brigade. The artillery consisted of Battery A, 5th U. S., most of the 1st Connecticut, and Battery E, 2nd U. S.

On the Confederate side of the ravine, they observed the repositioning of Hancock's men and the arrival of the bountiful artillery support. As chance would have it, McClellan rode by, precipitating cheers from the men, and Toombs' men took it as an indicator of the beginning of an attack. Confederate artillery commenced firing, and the Federal guns responded in kind. This reinforced the opinion that there was still considerable Confederate strength south of the Chickahominy.

Rudolph J. Schroeder, III

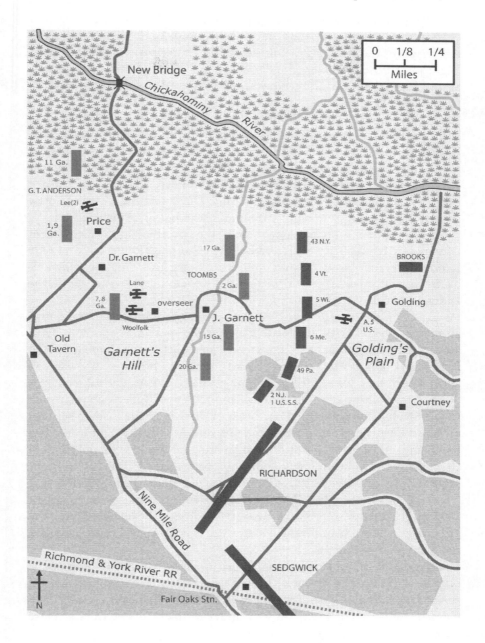

Map 18.1—Garnett's Farm, June 27

The Confederates then augmented their artillery with the remainder of the Wise (Virginia) Battery and Lane's Company E, Sumter (Georgia) Artillery. On the Federal side of the ravine, Battery A, 1st Rhode Island Light joined the brawl. Eventually, Stephen Lee was forced to withdraw all the Confederate artillery. He was outnumbered twenty-three tubes to ten, and the Federals were dug in.[5]

Neither Federal nor Confederate forces south of the river were oblivious to the fierce battle being fought to the northeast at Gaines' Mill. Both sides redirected some of their artillery fire across the river, hoping to aid their brethren there. At least some of the Federal artillery fire was effective. President Davis observed the battle from a house, was warned by Lee that the area was hazardous, and Davis left the house. Shortly thereafter, the house was hit by cannon fire and heavily damaged.

Both opponents on the south side of the river were at once confident and anxiety for their respective causes. Their vantage point allowed only intermittent and partial observation of the battlefield. The Confederates were especially hopeful of a victory, most believing that Jackson was on the Federal right flank.[6]

As the Confederates north of the river prepared to make their final assaults at Gaines' Mill, the relative lull on the south side was coming to an end. John Magruder, in an effort to secure a little more intelligence on his Federal opponents, directed Jones to send the brigades of Anderson and Toombs forward to feel the enemy positions. Magruder subsequently decided to be more specific. He desired another of Anderson's regiments to join the two already posted northeast of the Nine Mile road, in support of the artillery there. The cannon and muskets on Toombs' right would feel the enemy as a strong picket force. The remainder of the infantry would stand ready to follow up if an opportunity presented itself. When Toombs saw the units on his right move forward, he was to do the same.[7]

At approximately 4:00 P.M., one of Magruder's division commanders, Lafayette McLaws, moved up two of Joseph Kershaw's regiments, the 7th and 8th South Carolina. Their advance was short-lived and they gave ground due to intense fire.

About the same time, Richard Griffith also advanced some of his brigade. Additionally, by 6:30 P.M. or a little later, two batteries, the Ashland (Virginia) Artillery under Lieutenant James Woolfolk and Captain John Lane's Company E, Sumter Artillery, opened fire at close range on the Federal lines.

On the Federal side of the line, Hancock personally directed two companies of Berdan's 1st U. S. Sharpshooters from a meal break back to their rifle pits. As they arrived there, Woolfolk's Ashland (Virginia) battery commenced fire. Berdan's Sharpshooters, joined by Ames' battery, reacted to Woolfolk's fire. The artillery duel was brief, and the Confederates withdrew after ten minutes.

As the artillery duel wound down, Toombs became aware of firing on his right. The demonstration had begun. Upon hearing the "signal", he put forward the majority of the 2nd Georgia to the ravine in the immediate rear of his pickets.[8]

Hancock's withdrawal earlier in the day had put a wheat field between his position and that of Toombs. As Hancock observed Toombs and his men advance into the wheat field, he ordered them taken under fire. There was but scant cover in the wheat field, but the 2nd Georgia used it as best they could, and fought Hancock's brigade for about thirty minutes. At one point late in the day, the solo regiment advanced to within forty yards of Hancock's men.

Brooks commanded the Vermont Brigade in Smith's VI Corps division. The brigade was composed of the 2nd, 3rd, 4th, 5th and 6th Vermont.

Brooks first advanced the 4th Vermont from their supporting position and added the battered 2nd New Jersey of Taylor's brigade. He then reinforced the 2nd with Berdan's Sharpshooters. Brooks put these units into line with Hancock's brigade, the 2nd New Jersey extending Hancock's line a bit more to the south.

The 15th Massachusetts from Sedgwick's II Corps division moved up to rifle pits on Hancock's right, and Edwin Sumner, the II Corps commander, dispatched another of Sedgwick's regiments, the 7th Michigan, to make haste to Hancock's line. Neither regiment was necessary. Toombs, noticing Hancock being reinforced, responded instantly. He sent the 15th Georgia to reinforce the 2nd Georgia in the ravine, the 20th Georgia to the right flank, and the 17th Georgia to the left flank. Toombs likely wanted to tie down the Federal troops in his front, so that none could be sent across the river to assist Porter's V Corps. Fortunately for Toombs, it was late in the day, and darkness put a halt to the intense fighting in ninety minutes. It was a difficult day's fighting for both sides. The 2nd Georgia fired long enough to overheat their muskets, and the men of the 5th Wisconsin were hungry enough to eat while they fought.[9]

Although the fight was relatively brief, it was violent. Colonel William M. McIntosh, commander of the 15th Georgia, was mortally wounded. The 2nd Georgia, bearing the brunt of Hancock's fire, appeared to be under extreme pressure. Toombs took steps to reinforce his line with the 7th Georgia and reshuffle the regiments. Darkness made this unnecessary. In the night, Hancock was ordered back to his original position.

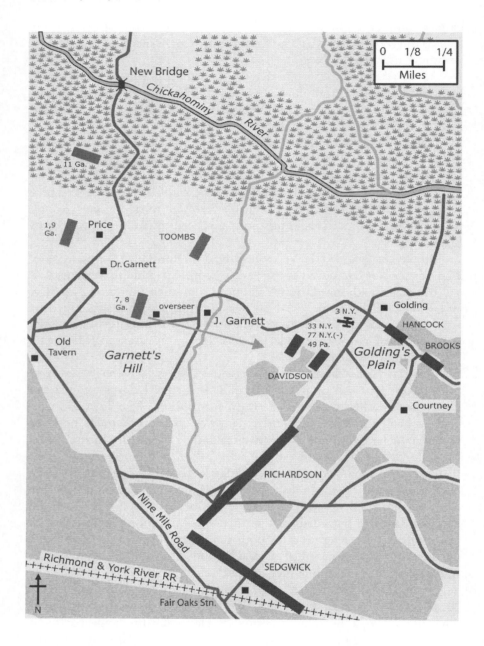

Map 18.2—Garnett's and Golding's Farms, June 28

The short, sharp firefight was of little significance. As was often the case, the Confederates started too late in the day with too little force to push the Federal forces away from the Chickahominy crossings. McClellan was able to reinforce Porter anyway, sending French and Meagher's brigades from Richardson's II Corps division. The only notable result was the casualties incurred. The Federals lost 105 killed or wounded, as well as 13 missing. The Confederates lost almost 200 men. These are considerable losses for a brief fight between two small opposing forces, and caused Franklin, the VI Corps commander, to believe the Confederate force was more than a single brigade. It may have had the effect of reinforcing McClellan's belief that Lee had a powerful force south of the river, as he was being attacked on both banks.[10]

Nightfall stopped the fighting on both sides of the river. June 27 had been a highly successful day for Robert E. Lee, albeit a very costly one. By pushing Porter out of Gaines' Mill, Lee had uncovered New Bridge, thereby connecting the two parts of his army. Erroneously, Lee believed that McClellan would retreat eastward, toward White House Landing. Taking the position at Gaines' Mill would make it more difficult for McClellan to cover that retreat. Lee dispatched a message to President Davis, informing him of the victory and thanking God for it. He also stated that he planned to attack again the following day. He would be disappointed the next morning to find Porter's V Corps gone.[11]

South of the Chickahominy, June 28 would also bring more fighting. On Garnett's farm, David R. Jones, one of Magruder's division commanders, was concerned that the Federal forces in his front might be withdrawing. He tasked Toombs to conduct a reconnaissance in force to verify or refute Jones' hunch.

Toombs was known to have a reputation as a hothead, disdainful of professional officers and disrespectful of his superior, John Magruder. Toombs ordered the brigade of G. T. Anderson to join him on the mission. By this unauthorized action, Toombs changed the requested reconnaissance in force to an outright assault. Baldy Smith's division repulsed the attack handily, inflicting serious casualties on two of Anderson's regiments, the 7th and 8th Georgia. These two regiments suffered the loss of 156 men between them. The further Anderson's men moved forward, the more fire they took. A factor in Smith's victory was the firepower of one or more coffee-mill guns, employed by the 49th Pennsylvania. (*see* Glossary)[12]

These two relatively small engagements on the 27th and the 28th, had little tactical significance. They could be classified as "fixing actions", having only the result of tying down a portion of the opponent's troops. The opposing forces remained essentially where they were positioned before their initial contact. While both sides suffered some casualties, the balance of combat power between them wasn't very much altered.

The real significance of Garnett's and Golding's Farms was strategic. It was but another piece of information that fed McClellan's erroneous thinking about the relative strength of Lee's army versus his own. He just knew that Lee had 200,000 men, and he felt a great need for caution. The fact that Lee's army had attacked him south of the river, while simultaneously mounting an overwhelming assault north of the river had to help convince him of the inferior strength of his army.

CHAPTER 19

Savage Station

(June 29)

John Magruder was a miserable man on the morning of June 28. Physically, he had several annoying problems. He was still suffering from indigestion, the effects of a medication given to him by his staff physician, and a distinct lack of sleep. He'd, in fact, slept not at all during the night.

Psychologically, he was an extremely worried man. Although he was aware of the Confederate victory at Gaines' Mill, he now had more Federal troops coming south of the river, with the potential to overwhelm his command at will. Counting the troops of General Huger, Magruder had less than 24,000 men in his command, and his concern was that the entire Army of the Potomac would pounce upon him, and Lee would not be able to get an appreciable number of troops across the river in time to save him.

Exacerbating his worried condition was the note he'd received from Lee the night before. Lee had stressed the need for vigilance, and had ordered Magruder to have his men sleep on their arms. At 3:30 A.M., the Federals had still been in their works in Magruder's front.

At dawn, Magruder's outlook took a turn for the better. He received notice that the Federal entrenchments were in fact now being vacated. In fact, two of Longstreet's engineers, Major Meade and Lieutenant Johnston, had completed their reconnaissance, reported back their findings, and Lee now knew the Federals were truly retreating.

Colonel Chilton arrived from Lee's staff, sent by the Commanding General to bring Magruder to army headquarters. By the time Prince John arrived there, Lee would have devised an appropriate plan to chase McClellan down. After all, Lee's strategic thinking from the time he assumed command was to get McClellan out of his works and attack him in the open, using mobility to counter the greater size of the Federal army.[1]

Almost immediately thereafter, a staff officer of Magruder's arrived, confirming the Federal retreat. Magruder, riding along with Chilton to meet Lee, became emboldened, and felt he had to take some offensive action. Magruder ordered an immediate advance. Griffith moved his brigade down the road toward Fair Oaks Station.

On Griffith's left was the division of David R. Jones. His brigadiers were Toombs and George T. Anderson. They moved across the ground over which they'd fought the previous two days.[2]

Contemporaneously, McLaws gave orders to Joseph Kershaw, to feel the Federal positions. Kershaw, in turn, sent the 2nd South Carolina, under John D. Kennedy, supported by the 8th South Carolina, under John W. Henagan, through the fog toward their opponents. As the fog cleared and the sun shone brightly, it was apparent that the Federals had gone. At that point, McLaws directed Kershaw to press on to Fair Oaks Station with his entire brigade.

Magruder sent word ahead to Lee, explaining what he meant to do. Magruder's courier found Lee and Longstreet at Dr. Gaines' house. Lee, cheered by the fact that he was now certain McClellan was retreating, and having no word from Ewell or Stuart that they were going to recross the Chickahominy, stuck with his belief that the Federals were retreating toward the James River. Lee thought he now had adequate concentration of forces and roads to move on McClellan and deliver a heavy blow. The blow must be struck before the retreating Federals reached the James and the fire support of their gunboats.

Lee was just finishing his plan to run down McClellan's army when Magruder's courier arrived. He immediately sent the courier back to Magruder with a light-hearted reply of approval.[3]

To all appearances, McClellan's situation was not very good. Lee had four roads he could use in the pursuit. They were: the Williamsburg road, the Charles City road, the Darbytown road, and the New Market road. (*see* Area Map on p. xvi) This is not to say that the movement would experience no difficulty. The Confederates, despite fighting very near to their capital, suffered from maps of terrible quality. Some had important terrain features, such as Boatswain's Swamp, missing. Others had roads missing or mislabeled. This problem cannot be overemphasized. Poor maps blind a commander in the field and can cause him to make poor decisions.

Roads were important to McClellan, as well. They were: the White Oak road, the Carter's Mill road, and the Willis Church road (Quaker road). Since these three were important to McClellan's retreat to the James, they became equally important to Lee.

McClellan's advantage at this point in time was that he knew exactly where he was going, and Lee only believed McClellan was going to some point on the James. One factor that probably was obvious to both generals was that the Army of the Potomac had to cross White Oak Swamp. There were only two bridges and a few fords that might be suitable for the river crossing. What had to be apparent to McClellan was that he had to keep the White Oak road open. Equally obvious to Lee was that he needed to slow the pace of the Federal retreat, thus allowing him sufficient time to get adequate forces south of White Oak Swamp to cut off the Army of the Potomac.

From McClellan's perspective, the only first step that mattered was getting his retreating army across White Oak Swamp. If the Confederates could catch a relatively small part of McClellan's force north of the river, they would likely destroy them.[4]

Any retreating general has to look in at least two directions. He must constantly look behind him to reassess the character of the pursuit. Pursuit can be conducted along a spectrum of types.

A loose pursuit employs a small but highly mobile force, whose only objective is to keep the retreating army aware they are being pursued, and provides constant intelligence to the pursuing commander of the character of the retreat. The pursuing commander needs to know where the retreat is going, how fast it is moving, and the state of morale of the retreating troops. Indicators of morale can be the amount of arms and equipment found abandoned along the line of retreat, the numbers of stragglers found sitting alongside the road, just waiting to be taken prisoner, etc. Prisoners can be interrogated to provide more detailed information of the state of affairs within the retreating regiments. This type of pursuit entails little risk to the pursuers, but inflicts little damage to the pursued.

On the other end of the spectrum, an aggressive pursuit has the objective of causing significant damage to the retreating forces. It is characterized by the commitment of enhanced combat power, likely provided by fresh infantry, as well as mobility. Perhaps it uses horse artillery to inflict damage deep into the retreating column. It attempts to take advantage of the inherent difficulty of a fighting retreat. This type of pursuit holds a bit more risk to the pursuers, in that the level of fighting is raised, and more casualties can be anticipated. Ambush is always a possibility.

The retreating general also must be looking ahead. He must assess the terrain to see if there is a strong point, a suitable defensive position where he might make a stand. Looking ahead, in this context, also entails watching the flanks for potential threats. The wise general uses his cavalry to accomplish this mission.

On June 29, 1862, there was a strong defensive position between McClellan's army and the James River. It was Malvern Hill, about seven miles south of Savage Station, as the crow flies, but quite a bit farther by road march. He would first have to march the northernmost elements of his army southeast to pick up the White Oak road, cross the White Oak Swamp, then proceed southwest through Glendale to Malvern Hill. And, he had to get there before Lee could put a blocking force in place.

Lee had in fact completed his plan for the pursuit and destruction of the Army of the Potomac. The plan, on which he was working when Magruder's courier found him, was complex, but achievable, if all of his generals played their parts well.

The essence of Lee's plan revolved around two objectives. First, he needed to slow down the Federal retreat to buy time. This time would be used to facilitate the second objective, which was to hurry a substantial blocking force to the areas of Glendale and Malvern Hill. If that force could arrive quickly enough and establish a commanding position there before McClellan could get his trains south of Malvern Hill, McClellan could be attacked from several directions while somewhat strung out along his route of retreat, wagon trains and all. The result could be disastrous for the Army of the Potomac, and for the Federal cause in general.

The nearest Confederate forces to the James, Huger's division, were farther away than the nearest Federal troops, Keyes' IV Corps. Lee still had to cross most of his army from the north bank of the Chickahominy. The whole situation boiled down to time. If Lee was to trap McClellan's army, his generals needed to move swiftly and simultaneously slow down the Federal retreat.[5]

An essential part of any operations plan is carefully choosing which subordinate units to assign each of the mission's tasks. In this particular case, Lee's options were limited by which divisions were close enough to reach their objectives in time. The forces of Longstreet, D. H. Hill and A. P. Hill were all north of the Chickahominy. If they crossed the river at New Bridge and used the Darbytown road, they would have some seventeen miles to march. They would arrive too late, and their regiments would be too spent to fight a major battle.

The closest troops to Glendale were those of Magruder and Huger. They were only about eight miles from the objective, but they were also the only force between McClellan and Richmond. They absolutely could not be assigned the task of racing the Federals to Glendale. Lee therefore tasked them to attempt to fix the Federal rear guard in place, hoping to slow down the retreat by forcing a fight. This would allow time for the rest of Lee's army to move south and get adequate rest and preparation for a battle on June 30.

Rudolph J. Schroeder, III

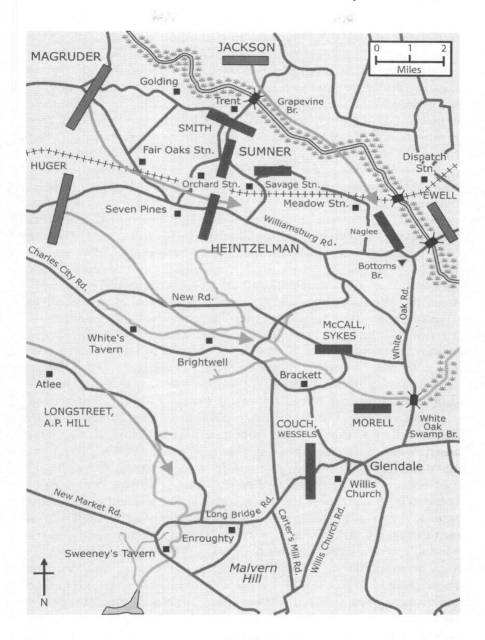

Map 19.1—Lee's Plan of Pursuit, June 29

Lee knew the realities of the situation precluded the big battle from occurring on the 29th. Jackson's command was still north of the Chickahominy, and would have to repair the Grapevine Bridge before he could join the battle. Lee had tasked Ewell to remain north of the river at Bottoms Bridge, in order to prevent McClellan from recrossing the river and making for White House Landing. Ewell would have to remain there until Lee was absolutely positive that McClellan was totally committed to retreating to the James. There was still some very slight possibility that McClellan would retreat down the peninsula. Lee depended on Stuart's cavalry to cover the bridges further downstream. He was most certainly aware that Stuart would need serious reinforcement if McClellan elected to force a crossing.

Huger, starting from a position on the railroad to the Charles City road, was tasked to move down the Charles City road, clear it of retreating Federal troops, and attack the flank of any troops retreating on the Williamsburg road. Magruder would start from a point north of Huger, specifically, between the railroad and the Chickahominy. He would move down the Williamsburg road, pursuing Federal units there. Hopefully, Magruder's men would close on Federal units that had turned south.[6]

Lee was not in a bad tactical position whether or not McClellan decided to recross the river. The forces of D. H. Hill and Stonewall Jackson would be able to react effectively to either contingency. If McClellan continued south to the James River, Jackson could repair the Grapevine Bridge and attack the right flank of any Federal troops making a stand at Savage Station. Otherwise, Jackson could move southeast to Meadow Station, following existing roads from there to the White Oak road. This all depended on repairing the Grapevine Bridge in a timely manner.

If McClellan decided to move east down the peninsula, Jackson could cut them off from the bridges farther downstream. He would only have to hustle to the Long Bridge and Jones' Bridge, as Ewell would easily be able to get to Bottoms Bridge in time. If Jackson could prevent McClellan from recrossing the Chickahominy, the full weight of the Army of Northern Virginia could be thrown against the retreating Federals.

The possibility that McClellan might change his plans was not communicated to Jackson. He was told simply to repair the Grapevine Bridge, move to Savage Station, then march east, keeping close to the river. He must not leave the Meadow road until he'd flanked any remaining Federal troops in the vicinity. Lee, despite his likely misgivings about the leadership of Magruder and Huger, had to depend on their success in tying up at least a part of McClellan's rear guard. Absent that assumption, there was little likelihood that Jackson could turn anyone's flank.

Powell Hill's and Longstreet's divisions had little danger, but much hard work in their task. They were to cross the Chickahominy at New Bridge, move to the Darbytown road, then head to the Long Bridge road to cut off any Federals still north of Glendale on the morning of June 30. Although these troops had rested on the 28th, this was a march in excess of fifteen miles. Lee put Longstreet in overall command, and his troops led the march.[7]

With the information Lee had in his possession at that point in time, his revised plan was about as good as could be expected. Although it required definite actions by each of Lee's generals, it was a simpler plan than that of General Orders No. 75. A major difference was that it did not pin down the timetable for each action. Communication should not be difficult, in that the subordinate units were relatively close together. Lee had been down some of these roads in the past, so the battle area should have been more familiar to him.

With the advantage of hindsight, some have criticized Lee's plan, suggesting that his subordinate units could have been tasked in a different manner that would have better assured success. At the time Lee made the revised plan, he probably couldn't have done any better. After all, Lee was still not entirely sure that McClellan would not turn to the east.[8]

Longstreet and A. P. Hill, the two generals with the greatest distance to march, set about getting their commands on the road. Lee, meanwhile, searched out Magruder on the Nine Mile road, and went over the plan with him as they rode forward. Magruder failed to completely understand Lee. Magruder thought that Lee's plan required Huger to move forward on the Williamsburg road, rather than the Charles City road. The two generals spoke again when they reached Fair Oaks Station, and Lee again briefed Magruder. Once again, Magruder apparently misunderstood. Lee then departed to visit Huger.

Kershaw's brigade of McLaws' division was at Fair Oaks Station, moving cautiously forward. Magruder had ordered more troops up earlier. They found empty fortifications, and captured a handful of stragglers. Magruder began the placement of the other brigades as they arrived. He put Kershaw's brigade south of the railroad, placed Semmes' troops around Fair Oaks Station, and when Griffith's men arrived, he put two regiments in Kershaw's rear, and the other two moved up the north side of the tracks in parallel with Kershaw. The next brigade was Cobb's of Magruder's division, and went into the line just north of the two regiments of Griffith north of the tracks.[9]

Magruder sent skirmishers forward as the arriving brigades were placed in line. They were sent from Kershaw's, Cobb's and Griffith's brigades. About two miles ahead was the road from Grapevine Bridge. Magruder likely warned Kershaw to advise his skirmishers to use caution not to suffer a friendly fire incident with Jackson's column as it moved toward Savage Station.

After advancing about halfway from Fair Oaks Station to the road Stonewall was to use, Kershaw began taking fire from his left front. He advanced a set of regimental colors to determine the identity of the firing troops, who turned out to be the Federal rear guard. They were probably from Baldy Smith's VI Corps division.[10]

Baldy Smith's division was composed of the brigades of Hancock, Brooks and Davidson. Smith's tasking was straight forward, if difficult. He was to cover the last of the trains to withdraw, as well as stop any Confederate advance across the Chickahominy in the area of Grapevine Bridge.

Starting from the area of Golding's Farm, he moved east to Trent house. Elder's was the last battery of J. Howard Carlisle's reserve artillery brigade departed Savage Station around 9:00 A.M. The artillery had been retreating since midnight. After all the trains had left the area of the Trent house, Smith sent Hancock's brigade to protect Savage Station from attack across Sumner's Lower Bridge. This was a bridge built by the Federals, and was almost two miles downstream from Grapevine Bridge. Davidson's brigade went into line a little more to the west, near the Dudley farm, and Smith left Brooks' brigade at the Trent house. With Naglee's brigade of Peck's IV Corps division protecting Bottoms Bridge and the railroad bridge, and Meagher's brigade of Richardson's II Corps division near Meadow Station, Smith had to believe Savage Station was well defended from the north.[11]

Heintzelman's III Corps also had a role in the rear guard. Hooker's division was given the task of defending the Williamsburg road. He had only a mile to march to get into position. Grover's brigade faced west, with their right flank on the railroad. Sickles, on Grover's left, their left on the Williamsburg road. Carr's brigade was the division reserve, and positioned themselves a little to the east of the other brigades.

Kearny's division moved south of the Williamsburg road, brigades arrayed with Berry left, Robinson center, and Birney on the right, closest to the Williamsburg road. Kearny directed his men to carry 150 rounds of ammunition, much more than the usual.[12]

The Federals believed they now had the north and west-southwest covered. Between the forces that covered those two avenues of approach, there was a gap. Sumner's II Corps was given the task of filling that gap. Richardson's division, sans the brigade of Meagher, pulled back to the vicinity of Allen's Farm. French's brigade formed a line of battle, with Caldwell's brigade behind them. Thus, Richardson had the Meadow road protected from Confederate attack.[13]

French's brigade was composed of the 52nd, 57th, 64th and 66th New York, the 53rd Pennsylvania and the 2nd Delaware. French decided that he wanted to occupy several structures in his front to deny them to the Confederates when they arrived. Richardson and Sumner blessed the idea, and French sent the 53rd Pennsylvania forward to occupy them. He sited four of Hazzard's guns from the two batteries (Batteries A & C, 4th U. S. Artillery) under his command on high ground in the 53rd's immediate rear.[14]

Richardson passed up the opportunity to deploy the other four guns assigned to Hazzard. He relocated them to Savage Station, along with Pettit's battery (Battery B, 1st New York Artillery).

Caldwell's brigade was made up of the 5th New Hampshire, the 57th and 61st New York, and the 81st Pennsylvania. On Richardson's orders, Caldwell put the 5th New Hampshire forward as pickets.

Sumner placed Sedgwick's division south of that of Richardson. Sedgwick's division was made up of the brigades of Sully, Burns, and Dana.

Burns went into line on French's left with his four Pennsylvania regiments, the 69th, 71st, 72nd and 106th. As directed by Sedgwick, Burns put out the 71st Pennsylvania as pickets. Sedgwick also brought his two artillery batteries into position. They were Battery A, 1st Rhode Island Light. under John A. Tompkins and Battery I, 1st U. S. Artillery under Edmund Kirby.

Dana's brigade was comprised of the 19th and 20th Massachusetts, the 7th Michigan, and the 42nd New York. Dana went into line on the left of Burns. He moved up the 20th Massachusetts about 600 yards to his front to take advantage of a tree line.

Sully's brigade was the 15th Massachusetts, the 1st Minnesota, and the 34th and 82nd New York. His brigade was placed behind the brigades of Burns and Dana.[15]

The placements of Heintzelman's III Corps and Sumner's II Corps created a Federal line that extended from just east of Allen's Farm north of the Richmond & York River Railroad on the right almost to Anderson's sawmill on the left end of the line. To the north of French, there was still a gap of three-quarters of a mile to Brooks' brigade. The terrain in this gap was passable for a sizeable enemy force. This was a significant vulnerability of McClellan's rear guard.[16]

Kershaw continued his advance to the east, failing to discover the gap in the Federal lines. With the mid-morning sun in their eyes, Kershaw's men were at a disadvantage. The two regiments sent forward by French and Caldwell, the 5th New Hampshire and the 53rd Pennsylvania, had the sun at their backs. Nearing Fair Oaks Station, the 5th New Hampshire observed some of Kershaw's men now occupying the old Federal works there. Samuel G. Langley, commanding the 5th, seeing himself outgunned, sent word to Richardson as to his situation. Richardson ordered him to hold his current position, but Langley pulled the main part of his regiment back into a tree line. A little over a quarter-mile to the south, the 71st Pennsylvania of Burns' brigade was also advancing toward the west, nearing to their brigade's old camps. Their commander, William G. Jones also became aware of the major Confederate presence. Kershaw's troops kept on moving forward, so Jones withdrew his men to the cover of some trees near the Allen house.

The Federal regiments received some fire support from Kirby's and Tompkins' batteries, firing from the vicinity of Allen's farm. The Federal batteries fired effectively, and targeted an advancing Confederate battery, that of Del Kemper, moving up with Kershaw's brigade. After a while, the Federal division chief of artillery shut down the fire, fearing for Federal troops in the line of fire. Some of the Federal artillery was allowed to keep firing, and received counter-fire from Henry Carlton's Troup (Georgia) Artillery. The Federal artillery presence helped to convince the Confederate brigade commanders that there was significant Federal force in the area. McLaws passed the information back to Magruder, while Kershaw pulled back a bit.[17]

While Kershaw was fighting the Federal picket force, Brigadier General David R. Jones and his division came out of the Labor-in-Vain Swamp. Had Jones advanced southeast, he would have discovered the gap in the Federals' defensive line. However, Magruder had asked Jones to move in the direction of Fair Oaks Station, to assure no accidental contact with Jackson's command. In so doing, Jones approached Fair Oaks Station and veered to the east, with G. T. Anderson's brigade in the lead. Moving through Federal works, Anderson's Georgians helped themselves to food and drink left by withdrawing Federals. The 1st Georgia Regulars were out front under William J. Magill, and made first contact, most likely with the 53rd Pennsylvania in the Allen's Farm buildings. This regiment on regiment contact grew in size, as several Federal batteries pitched in to help.

Pushing into a clearing, Magill observed at least two other regiments besides the 53rd Pennsylvania, and decided to pull back into the tree line.

The Federals continued the artillery fire, but Hazzard's batteries exhausted all the ammunition on hand, and had to send for more. Richardson ordered Pettit's battery to assist Hazzard. Sumner had been following the fight, and ordered four of Tompkins' guns to the relief of Hazzard.

Tompkins' battery arrived and set up to fire. Shortly thereafter, Pettit arrived, then two caissons of ammunition summoned by Hazzard. Pettit opened fire and Hazzard's men retired to Savage Station. Several other Federal regiments joined the fight. They were the 1st Minnesota, the 63rd New York, the 20th Massachusetts, the 71st Pennsylvania and the 5th New Hampshire. The lively fight, primarily an artillery contest, lasted about two hours, then both opposing forces withdrew, ending the fight at Allen's Farm.[18]

Kershaw inflicted relatively high casualties on the 5th New Hampshire and the 71st Pennsylvania. Magill's 1st Georgia Regulars hurt the 53rd Pennsylvania and the other two regiments to a lesser extent. Total casualties of both sides combined were probably around 300 men, with the notable mortal wounding of General Griffith, who was hit in the thigh by shrapnel while sitting his horse awaiting orders from Magruder. Griffith died the next day in Richmond.[19]

Magruder was working on a different approach to the Federal defenses of Savage Station at this point. The Confederates had designed and constructed a railroad gun, which consisted of a 32-pound rifled gun on a railway car. It was partially protected by sheets of steel. They called it "the Land Merrimac." It had been used in the artillery contest at Allen's Farm, and now Magruder planned to take it along with his command as he pursued the retreating Federals.

Magruder was concerned about Jackson's progress, and sent a courier, Major Henry Bryan, to determine Jackson's position. He likely assumed that Jackson was already across the Chickahominy. As he waited for Bryan to return, McLaws sent him a message describing the Federal forces in his front. Very soon thereafter, his other division commander, David Jones, sent a similar message. Magruder quickly concluded that McClellan had left a sizeable force behind, not just a reasonable rear guard. He believed his three weakened divisions would be unable to dislodge that Federal force, and any attempt to do so unassisted would result in needless casualties. He was also worried that the enemy might just attack him anyway.

Magruder also knew that there was still a chance of trapping a good part of McClellan's army, which was still north of the White Oak Swamp. Critical to achieving that objective was Huger moving rapidly down the Charles City road to Glendale, as Lee had planned.

The flaw in Magruder's thinking was that he had misunderstood Lee's instructions to him earlier, and thought Huger was behind him on the Williamsburg road. Magruder, therefore, sent a courier, Major Joseph L. Brent to ask Lee for Huger's support in attacking the Federals and fixing them in place.[20]

Brent had no difficulty finding Lee, who was at Huger's headquarters near the Williamsburg road, where Huger's command had already reached the abandoned Federal works. When Huger's advance unit, the 4th Georgia, found the only Federals there to be several medical personnel, a surgeon and some sick soldiers. Huger, in a touch of gallantry, allowed the surgeon to stay with the sick, and did not make him a prisoner.

Wright to this point had no information from his pickets, so he sent a staff officer, Captain Girardy, to fire up the pickets. By 8:00 A.M., Girardy was back reporting the Federals were gone from Wright's front. He issued an order for the brigade to pursue in force, but was overridden by Huger, who ordered him to pull back his men and feed them breakfast. After the men were fed, they were to go over to the Charles City road and advance down it with caution. As Wright's brigade became ready to cross over to the Charles City road, new orders arrived to move down the Williamsburg road. Puzzled, Wright rode over to Huger, and was shortly ordered to go over to the Charles City road. The confusion among the Confederate generals seemed to be spreading.

Armistead's and Ransom's pickets also found the enemy in their front had gone. They moved up and entered the abandoned Federal works, then returned to their camps to prepare for the day's operations. Huger finally got his command on the road. Mahone's brigade led the march, followed by Armistead, Wright and Ransom. After a brief conversation with Lee, Huger rejoined his troops. Lee decided to remain at Huger's headquarters to monitor the events of the unfolding day.[21]

When Brent gave Lee Magruder's message, Lee was most interested in Brent's assessment of the Federal strength in Magruder's front. When pressed for his personal opinion, Brent simply repeated Magruder's message. Lee decided to take some of the pressure off of Magruder, and ordered Huger to send Magruder two brigades to the Williamsburg road. The brigades were to be sent back to the Charles City road if not in contact by 2:00 P.M. Brent tarried in conversation with Lee's staff for a while, then headed back to Magruder with Lee's response.[22]

Apparently, Lee did not believe the message brought by Major Brent. If he had, there was still an opportunity to trap a sizeable part of McClellan's army. He had only to put Magruder in a defensive mode and expedite Huger's command down the Charles City road. This would have resulted in the Federals being boxed in by Magruder, Huger, Jackson and the Chickahominy. Once again, McClellan's luck held and he was able to continue his retreat.[23]

The Army of the Potomac continued its retreat to the James River, skillfully using a large rear guard force to cover the retreat of their wagon train and some of their artillery. Erasmus Keyes' IV Corps was covering the Glendale crossroads.

Just south of White Oak Swamp, Federal troops were making their morning coffee, when they were set upon by Confederate cavalry. Much of Lee's cavalry, under Jeb Stuart, was on an extended reconnaissance in force north of the Chickahominy. The cavalry not with Stuart was under the command of Colonel Laurence S. Baker.

Baker had arrived on June 28 from North Carolina along with five companies of his 1st North Carolina Cavalry. That very evening, Lee sent Baker to scout south of the river. Baker took the 3rd Virginia Cavalry along with his North Carolina horsemen and moved down the Charles City road to the Long Bridge road. Baker had information that Federal troops were at the Willis Church. He soon collided with pickets from Averell's 3rd Pennsylvania Cavalry, screening for Keyes' corps.

It didn't take the Federal troopers long to decide to pull back to the safety of the nearest infantry unit, Innis Palmer's brigade of Couch's division. There was more Federal support waiting there. Two sections of artillery, supported by 2nd Rhode Island and the 7th Massachusetts, as well as more Federal cavalry, were nearby.

Baker and his troopers made the lethal mistake of pursuing the federal pickets right into a barrage of case shot and canister. Turning to retreat, the Confederates were pursued by two companies of the 3rd Pennsylvania Cavalry. Baker had fulfilled his mission of feeling the enemy, but at a great cost. Baker's force suffered over sixty casualties, the majority of them missing and presumed killed, wounded or captured. Major Thomas N. Crumpler of the 1st North Carolina Cavalry was mortally wounded. Federal losses were one killed and five wounded.

Although it was a bizarre sort of engagement, Keyes took it seriously. He feared this probe was the harbinger of a large-scale Confederate attack, and he ordered Morell's V Corps division from the Britton farm to support IV Corps if needed. Even some troops coming from Brackett's Ford went into line as a precaution.[24]

Seven Days Before Richmond

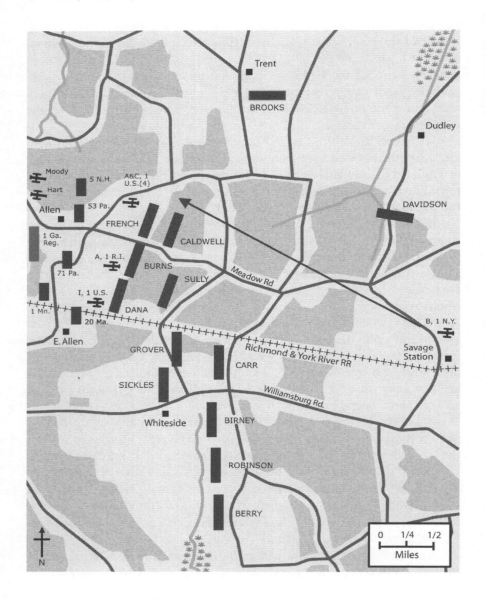

Map 19.2—Allen's Farm, June 29

McClellan had moved his headquarters to the Britton farm. He came up to the position of the 3rd Pennsylvania Cavalry to see the situation for himself. Averell had earlier ridden back to McClellan's headquarters and reported on Baker's charge. Averell's report summed up by stating that he thought the path to Richmond was "fairly clear," and he felt the Army of the Potomac could attack the city. McClellan's reply was slanted toward preserving his army, not taking Richmond. Little Mac, accompanied by the Prince de Joinville, surveyed the area and appeared pleased with Averell's performance and his troop placement.

After Averell's action, Keyes was ready to move his troops to the river, but some one else would need to take their place. Porter placed Morell's division in a loose line of battle slightly west of Glendale for the day. The logistics situation for the Federals obviously was impacted by the retreat, and Morell's 1st Brigade under Martindale had little to eat on June 29. Morale was reported to be good, as the latter part of the day's march had been westward, and the private soldiers, kept in the dark by their officers, hoped the westward movement was an indicator of some McClellan plan for them to resume the offensive.

Sykes was able to rest at least part of his division from 2:00 A.M. until dawn, when they resumed the march southward. They crossed White Oak Swamp at Brackett's Ford and went into position on the Charles City road to the right of Couch.

McCall's division had been retreating with little rest, and reached White Oak Swamp around midday. McClellan then ordered them to prepare to defend their position against a Confederate attack from the west. This they did, and didn't continue their movement south until 5:00 P.M. Some of McCall's troops marched virtually all day long.

McClellan had to move all his army, not just the infantry. Each type of unit presented different problems in a massive retreat of this sort. The reserve artillery was making faster progress than the infantry. As they finished the day's march, some batteries were attached to infantry or cavalry units.

At least one artillery brigade, the 1st Brigade of William Hays, had moved all night and reached the Glendale area in the morning. Benson's Battery M, 2nd U. S. Artillery went to the 3rd Pennsylvania Cavalry and the 8th Pennsylvania Reserves. George W. Getty's 2nd Brigade reached Glendale later in the morning. Elder's battery was sent to Keyes, and Randol's Battery E, 1st U. S. Artillery went to McCall. Ames' 3rd Brigade didn't cross White Oak Swamp until about 4:00 P.M. They stopped at Glendale. Around 5:00 P.M, Otto Diederich's Battery A and John Knieriem's Battery C of the 1st Battalion, New York Light were attached to McCall's division. Edward R. Petherbridge's 4th Brigade arrived at White Oak Swamp around noon and made camp. Howard Carlisle's 5th Brigade, starting at 3:00 A.M., moved to White Oak Swamp by midday. At 3:00 P.M., Carlisle's artillery was ordered by General Marcy to cover the approaches to the White Oak Swamp Bridge. The end result of the long and tiresome day was that the Federal artillery reserve was gathered in the area between White Oak Swamp and Glendale by mid-afternoon, except for those batteries attached to infantry or cavalry units.[25]

Slocum's VI Corps division arrived at Savage Station around 5:00 A.M. on June 29. They had only marched three miles, but it had taken them six hours to do so. Understandably, the roads between the Trent house and Savage Station were severely overtaxed. They were very tired, but were ordered to the vital White Oak Swamp Bridge. This was a longer march, and took several more hours, again due to congested roads. Slocum eventually arrived at about 2:00 P.M. Three hours later, Slocum received orders to relieve IV Corps covering the Long Bridge road approach to Glendale. Slocum closed his new position at around 7:00 P.M. Although his men were exhausted from two days of marching, about half of them were immediately put on picket duty. No real rest was in their immediate future.[26]

After IV Corps was relieved that afternoon, McClellan ordered Keyes to move his corps to the James River, establish liaison with the gunboats, and protect the bridge across Turkey Island Creek on the River road, south of Malvern Hill. This task was vital to the Federals, as the entire Army of the Potomac would need this bridge to get to their new base on the James. McClellan allowed Keyes to pick his own route to the James. This decision was a good one, as Keyes probably knew the roads in the area as well as any other member of the army.

The shortest and preferable route from Glendale to the James was the Willis Church road. It intersected the River road very near the Turkey Island Creek Bridge. Keyes was, however, made aware of a long-unused road which paralleled the Willis Church road, and lay just a little to the east. Learning from a local resident that the old road would lead east of Malvern Hill to the bridge, Keyes decided that he could get to the bridge more quickly using both roads. Sending his trains on the Willis Church road guarded by the 8th Illinois Cavalry, and his infantry, artillery and cavalry on the old road, he set his command in motion.

As the day wore on, and more and more of Keyes' corps used it, it was naturally widened. By the end of the movement, hundreds of carriages, ambulances, guns and cattle used it.[27]

The important fact about Keyes' movement was that in clearing and using the long-unused road, it was now suitable for trains, not just for infantry. Additionally, it was at least a mile farther east and a greater distance from potential Confederate attack. Despite the good fortune of finding and improving the newly discovered road, there is no evidence that

Keyes urged McClellan to exploit its use. Why didn't Captain Keenan of the 8th Pennsylvania Cavalry urge his discovery to be publicized up to Army level? Why didn't Keyes pass the word to McClellan and the other corps commanders? Why wasn't this road used from the start of the retreat? It could have allowed completion of the move in one less day.[28]

McClellan had problems other than the adequacy of roads from Glendale to the James. He still had to get the rest of his army across the White Oak Swamp. Two bridges were supposedly constructed on the previous day, but it is unclear exactly when they were completed. A couple of hours past sunrise on June 29, both bridges were suitable for use by trains, but traffic was still moving slowly. There was a lack of discipline amongst the teamsters, and in their zeal to get to their destinations, fights broke out and some wagons were overturned. Bliss even had to resort to using the 6th Pennsylvania Cavalry to restore order and enforce discipline. Although it took until late afternoon, all the wagons eventually crossed the White Oak Swamp.[29]

McClellan's first priority for the day was the safe withdrawal of his trains. This meant keeping them moving, positioning infantry units to protect them, and choosing the final destination for his army. McClellan moved his headquarters to the Britton farm, caught a two-hour nap and rested a while at a private house. He was suffering from an acute lack of sleep over the last several days, but still put forth a pleasant demeanor.

Why McClellan didn't delegate some of his activities has always been a mystery. A number of the tasks he undertook could have been well performed by his engineers and others on his staff. In fairness to McClellan, he did delegate some important work. He had given the job of finding a suitable base on the James to Brigadier General Barnard, who, in turn, tasked Chief Engineer Colonel Barton S. Alexander, accompanied by Lieutenants Cyrus B. Comstock and Francis U. Farquhar, to do the scouting. Alexander and Comstock departed Savage Station near midnight, stopped by to confer with General Woodbury near the White Oak Swamp Bridge, then went to Keyes' headquarters. There they obtained a cavalry escort from the 2nd U. S. Dragoons, led by Major Alfred Pleasonton.

Alexander soon heard the sounds of a skirmish on the James River road. This prompted him to try to get more roads cut through the woods to facilitate better troop movement, but he was unsuccessful.

Alexander then rode back to see McClellan, drew a crude sketch of the road structure for the general, then rode south again about midday. Alexander arrived at Shirley Plantation on the James about 5:00 P.M. At Carter's Landing there, he acquired a boat and went to confer with the U. S. Navy. After returning about 7:00 P.M., he reported in writing to

McClellan. Subsequently, Alexander was able to get Commodore Rodgers, captain of the *Galena*, to agree to send transports for the wounded and supplies to Harrison's Landing.

Rodgers preferred that the new base be located at the mouth of the Chickahominy River, as it would be difficult to provide security for supply boats so far up the river as Harrison's Landing. Rodgers' choice of base was some fifteen miles downstream from Harrison's Landing. Alexander remained overnight at Shirley Plantation, hoping to find a better solution the next day.

McClellan also failed to leave tactical command of the rear guard to a specific general officer. He ordered Sumner, Heintzelman and Smith to retreat to preplanned positions, hold them until nightfall, then cross White Oak Swamp. Sumner was the senior officer, and McClellan seemed to have little faith in Sumner's ability to lead great numbers of troops. Sumner was a career officer with combat experience in the Mexican War. His reputation was for fearless service, but had limited judgment. This fact leads one to believe that McClellan purposely left each of the three subordinate commanders to manage independently. Whether this assumption is correct or not, McClellan created a potential train wreck for his army.[30]

The ambiguous command and control situation created by McClellan was not the only ticking time bomb faced by the Army of the Potomac on June 29. There was still the gap in the Federal lines between Brooks' brigade and Sumner's II Corps, which could be easily used to great advantage by any Confederate commander lucky enough to stumble upon it.

Even knowledge of the existence of the gap was a scarce commodity. Smith knew it was there and believed Sumner was responsible for filling it. Smith also thought that Slocum was on his right flank, but in fact had been ordered south of White Oak Swamp by McClellan. No one had informed Smith, nor his corps commander, William Franklin, of Slocum's move south. Sumner didn't know the gap was there. He was focused on resuming the fight and pushing Magruder back to the west.

Franklin arrived in the area and had the cavalry do a quick reconnaissance. The problem was finally revealed. The cavalry even found a few Confederates in the gap. Smith and Franklin rode to Savage Station seeking out Slocum. They only came across Meagher's brigade from II Corps nearby and the 15th Massachusetts at the station.

The Federal tactical situation was a mess. As previously mentioned, any Confederate commander south of the Chickahominy could happen across the "gap" and cause serious problems. Also, there was the possibility that Jackson's command (or another force) could cross White Oak Swamp at Grapevine Bridge and easily flank Baldy Smith's division. Fortunately for the Federals, Franklin quickly comprehended the situation, saw the danger, and took action. He did the only thing he could to rectify the problem. He ordered Smith to withdraw to Savage Station, then worked on getting Sumner to fall back also. Franklin knew that they could not defend the extended line that their present positions had forced upon them. He sent a note to Sumner, stating that Smith's division was in extreme peril in their present placement, and requested that Sumner pull back so they could provide mutual support. Sumner responded in a reasonable fashion. He was, at present, engaged with the enemy and couldn't pull back, but would do so as soon as practicable.

Shortly thereafter, Sumner's II Corps began moving east toward Savage Station. It was a hot day, and some of Sedgwick's men, moving fast, discarded anything they didn't feel they needed. The heat created some casualties; men dropped to the ground along the roads. Some were taken prisoner later that day by advancing Confederate troops.

Richardson's division stopped just east of Savage Station. Sedgwick's division found a good location on high ground just south of the station. Dana's brigade pushed the 42nd New York about a thousand yards to the west to try and determine Confederate movements.[31]

The lack of a single officer in charge of the rear guard began to create serious problems. Apparently Sumner thought he was in command, but Heintzelman had no such conviction. Sumner sent an order to Heintzelman to cover the Williamsburg road. Heintzelman sought out Sumner to discover what Sumner thought their course of action was to be, then returned to his corps and decided on his own course of action.

Heintzelman first directed that all excess supplies should be burned. This included miscellaneous supplies, ammunition and even some nearby railroad cars. One of Heintzelman's staff officers and some cavalry troopers carried out the task. Heintzelman next decided that the immediate area around Savage Station was occupied by too many troops. He felt that they could not maneuver and fight effectively in their present placements. He recalled a road to Brackett's Ford that had earlier been traveled by Kearny's division, and ordered his entire corps to retire down that convenient road. He did reluctantly leave Osborn's and Nairn's batteries behind to support Smith's division. Smith had already sent his own division artillery to White Oak Swamp.

Kearny's division withdrew first, leaving the 20th Indiana as a rear guard. He positioned them in the fortifications west of the road to White Oak Swamp, and left Thompson's battery in support.

Heintzelman was perhaps hasty in retiring due to troop congestion around Savage Station. Even if Sumner didn't need Heintzelman's corps to help him defend Savage Station, it would have been a great asset if the opportunity to turn Magruder's flank had presented itself. Heintzelman did later state that he felt that the roads out of Savage Station would not suffice if he had stayed and the entire Federal host had been forced to retreat. The result would have been increased casualties.[32]

By 2:00 P.M., Sumner's corps had arrived at their positions east of Savage Station. This withdrawal left Savage Station unprotected, and the destruction of stores was speeded up. Items the advancing Confederates could only dream of were being burned, such as coffee, salt, sugar, dried fruit and whiskey. Much could not be burned in time, and was simply abandoned. Magruder's men found equipment such as tents, bedding, furniture, trunks and chests at Fair Oaks Station. To the east, at Savage Station, the Federals had located their main supply depot. There the guns and ammunition were stored. The primary Federal field hospital was also there.

The 15th Massachusetts had arrived the previous night, and had labored hard all day in the heat, attempting to destroy as much as possible. There were huge piles of burning rations and explosions from burning ammunition. A possible million rounds were destroyed. Other ammunition was thrown into wells and standing pools of water to ruin it. Smashed rifles were in evidence, and whiskey, coffee and sugar were poured out on the ground. Not all of the whiskey made it to the ground.

Many useful stores could not be destroyed in time, and found good service with Confederate troops and local citizens. Some items ended up for sale in Richmond and thereabouts. Perhaps the most costly monetary loss for the Federals was a train of about twenty-five cars and a locomotive which was burned.[33]

One of the more flamboyant acts of destruction was that of a trainload of ammunition set on fire, accelerated to top speed and run into the Chickahominy over the recently burned railroad bridge near Bottoms Bridge. All this was viewed through field glasses by Generals Ewell and Trimble from their side of the river. The event was truly spectacular, with flames, explosions, screeching and hissing sounds, the gigantic cloud which resulted, and the panic of those troops who just knew they were too close to the action to survive.

Ewell immediately recognized that the deliberate destruction of an ordnance train could only mean one thing. The Federals were in full retreat. Ewell knew his division was no longer needed to block a Federal crossing of the Chickahominy. Instead, he would soon be able to cross to the Federal side.[34]

Across the area, Federal camps were being abandoned and stores either abandoned or destroyed. Many Confederate troops were treated to a windfall of items they normally couldn't obtain, but some obtained little benefit from the situation. They were either too engaged or were in the wrong part of the battlefield. Even those who didn't personally benefit from the Federal retreat probably enjoyed the fact that their opponents were losing many of their creature comforts, and that the soldiers of the Army of the Potomac were probably a little demoralized.[35]

Another demoralizing factor besides the loss of so much of their stores was the abandonment of the Federal field hospital near Savage Station. The hospital at that point in time was filled with approximately 3,000 sick and wounded soldiers. There had been even more there the previous day. Even if there had been time and sufficient transport to move all of them away from the advancing Confederates, a portion of them were too ill to move. It was a difficult decision for the Federal leadership to make. Some doctors and nurses chose to remain behind with their charges, a decision frequently taken during the course of the war.

A Federal chaplain, Reverend J. J. Marks, who later wrote a book on the campaign, personally made Heintzelman aware of the hospital crisis at Savage Station. Marks had been advised to leave, but elected to stay with the hospital, believing his duty to the wounded required it. Others took the same course of action. Even some local inhabitants helped out, some simply for personal gain.

Marks advised all the ambulatory patients to start walking, taking their weapons if they were strong enough to carry them. A sizeable number of the men took his advice. The prospect of being captured was sufficient to motivate them to travel in their weakened condition. Some of the partings between those leaving and those forced to stay behind were sad indeed. They were between friends and even between family members. It was a war in which regiments were raised in individual towns or counties, and it was not uncommon for a regiment to contain fathers and their sons or two or three brothers. In the backs of their minds, there had to be the fear that this parting would be final. Perhaps forty percent of the wounded left before the Confederates arrived.[36]

The wounded making their tortured escape were unwittingly aided by Magruder, whose next attack was waiting for staffers to return with the latest information on Jackson and Huger. Magruder had already asked Lee for reinforcements and Huger for two brigades. Huger promised Wright's and Ransom's men. Both brigadiers responded, and Wright moved to the French house near Oak Grove and Ransom to Seven Pines.

Huger accompanied Ransom's brigade and met Magruder on the march. Magruder insisted that the enemy was preparing to attack him, and asked Huger to put him men into line. Magruder specifically asked Huger to make his right at Seven Pines and his left on the railroad. Huger obliged him and ordered Ransom into line.

Magruder had just received news of Jackson. At noon, Major Bryan and Jackson's chief engineer, Captain J. K. Boswell, brought word that Jackson would have the repairs to Grapevine Bridge completed by 2:00 P.M. The crossing of Jackson's corps had just begun, and Magruder would have to delay if he desired a coordinated attack at Savage Station.[37]

Jackson, in fact, was planning on repairing and using two bridges to cross the Chickahominy. The Grapevine Bridge had been more or less destroyed by high water about the end of May, and subsequently had been repaired. The second bridge, Alexander's Bridge, was located some 400 yards upstream.

When Porter's V Corps retreated south after their defeat at Gaines' Mill, they destroyed both Grapevine and Alexander's Bridges, as well as others, behind them. Jackson had 20,000 infantry as well as artillery and trains to cross, and would need both bridges. Evidence indicates that Alexander's Bridge had originally been the superior of the two, as judged by Federal engineers.

Grapevine Bridge was probably repaired in the morning by a work party of a couple of dozen men. The work then concentrated on Alexander's Bridge, directed by Reverend Dabney in the absence of an engineer at the scene. His effort was a failure and wasted precious time. Jackson next tapped Captain C. R. Mason, a quartermaster, who was at Ashland, some fifteen miles away. After a long move, Mason jumped into action. Refusing the offer of a set of plans, Mason made immediate progress.

Jackson was likely encouraged, as he positioned Winder's division to cross immediately upon completion of the repairs to the bridge. Jackson's optimism was shared by Magruder, and he seemed to quit worrying about an imminent Federal attack. However, Stephen Lee's scouts reported Federals moving forward, so Magruder cautiously moved Howell Cobb's brigade forward several hundred yards to an advantageous position, along a likely Federal axis of attack. The left end of Barksdale's brigade, formerly that of Griffith, was to move forward in support. Unfortunately, Huger picked that moment to send Magruder notification that Wright's and Ransom's brigades were being returned to their divisions for other duties.[38]

Huger wasn't acting on impulse or hunch, but was following orders from Lee. The order came in a note received from Lee as he was positioning his two brigades behind McLaws' division as Magruder had requested. The note simply restated Lee's previous guidance that if Huger wasn't needed with Magruder, he should proceed down the Charles City road. It took Huger no time at all to arrive at that conclusion, and passed Lee's note on to Magruder. Wright was at the French house, waiting for further orders, and Huger ordered his brigade to the Charles City road. This was the third, and fortunately the last, time that day that Wright had received that order. Ransom was already moving from Seven Pines down the same road after a wait of some three hours.

Huger should not have been faulted on his actions. Magruder had no real need for Huger's two brigades on the Williamsburg road, and Lee's orders were clear. The delay in getting the two brigades to where they could be effectively used was not Huger's fault. Unfortunately, Magruder was still laboring under the wrong interpretation of Lee's plan for the day's movement. He still believed that Huger was supposed to be on the Williamsburg road. Another setback hit Magruder about then. He received a message from David Jones informing Magruder that Jones was in front of Cobb's brigade and that Federal troops were in abundance on his right front. Jones thought an attack would not be successful unless it was a coordinated effort by all of the army. Jones also passed to Magruder that he had sent a message asking Jackson for his cooperation, but had received a disconcerting reply that he could not cooperate, "as he has other important duties to perform."[39]

Jackson's alleged statement that he had "other important duties to perform" has been the subject of much speculation. One can either conclude that Jackson's interpretation of Lee's plan required him to remain close to the river to contain the Federals or one can conclude that he merely made a cryptic remark to Jones, as he was reticent to share his frustration at not being able to repair the bridges and cooperate with Magruder as Lee had intended. No evidence exists that Jackson had any other "important duties" to perform that day.

No less a critical thinker than E. Porter Alexander attributed Jackson's lethargy to the fact that June 29 was a Sunday, and Jackson hated to fight on the Sabbath. Porter's theory must be tempered with the knowledge that he was no fan of Jackson. Also countering Porter's theory is the fact that Jackson had tasked Reverend Dabney to oversee some of the bridge repair.

Basically, Jackson needed two decent bridges to cross the Chickahominy with all his infantry, artillery and trains. With the lack of skilled labor, it took him almost all day to get them in shape. As to alternate bridges and fords, the river was too swollen from recent rains to use nearby fords, and New Bridge was being used by Longstreet and A. P. Hill.

At least one post-war writer, Armistead L. Long, stated his understanding that the commands of Jackson, Ewell and Stuart were to "remain in observation lest the Federals might change their line of retreat." By this statement, it seems that Lee still felt the need to protect against the possibility that McClellan would force a crossing of the Chickahominy at Bottoms Bridge and attempt to retreat toward White House Landing, thus retaining his base on the Pamunkey. Other bits of evidence contradict this theory.

The recollections of the Reverend Dabney of Jackson's staff were that Jackson's orders called for him to cross the Chickahominy. Even more telling is an order from Lee issued through Colonel Chilton of Lee's staff to Stuart that directed him to observe all crossings as far downstream as Jones' Bridge to determine if McClellan's troops were moving in that direction. Should Stuart determine that they were, he was to inform Jackson, that Jackson might defend the appropriate crossings. Stuart was to pass the order on to Jackson.

Lee's order caught up with Stuart at White House Landing, where Stuart employed a howitzer from Pelham's horse artillery to chase the Federal gunboat *Marblehead* away from the landing. With the gunboat removed from the scene, Stuart was more free to assess the situation at McClellan's recently abandoned base.[40]

Despite Casey's best attempt to haul away or destroy all of value at White House Landing, Stuart rode into a virtual horn of plenty. Many Federal government stores and even sutlers' stores remained undamaged. Fruits and sugars, cured fish, bacon, eggs, liquors, weapons and ammunition were there for the taking. Some heavy equipment was in evidence and untouched, and probably included a pontoon train, a locomotive and a number of railroad cars. Perhaps the most interesting description of the treasures left behind was written by Captain W. W. Blackford, who said,

> It was a curious thing to see the evidences of the luxury in which the Federal army indulged at that period of the war. Their sutler's shops were on the most elaborate scale—quantities of barrels of sugar, lemons by the millions, cases of wine, beer and other liquors of every description confectionery, canned meats, and fruits and vegetables, and great quantities of ice, all still in excellent condition. The eggs were packed in barrels of salt, and

where they had been exposed to fire, the salt was fused into a solid cake with the eggs, deliciously roasted, distributed throughout the mass; it was only necessary to split off a block and then pick out the eggs, like the meat of a nut.[41]

Stuarts's men were virtually out of rations, and began to help themselves. They soon lost discipline and a few became drunk on the found liquor. Rooney Lee solved the problem by starting a rumor that the liquor left behind had been poisoned by its previous owners. This immediately resulted in much broken glass.

Stuart spent most of the remaining day provisioning his men and completing the destruction of the base. Before noon, he received a note from Lee, then later in the day the order from Chilton. He sent Fitzhugh Lee and the 1st Virginia Cavalry to watch the river crossings. As directed by Chilton's note, he forwarded same to Jackson, who received it about 3:00 P.M. Stonewall endorsed it with the comment, "General Ewell will remain near Dispatch Station & myself near my present position." It is probable that he sent the note back to Stuart by the courier who delivered it.

This note of Chilton's, and more importantly, the manner in which Jackson responded to it, are compelling evidence that Jackson's "other important duties" meant staying north of the river where he could effectively react to news from Stuart. What we cannot know is exactly what General Lee really intended for Jackson to do.

We know that Chilton's note to Stuart, then to Jackson in turn, was written later than Jackson's original orders for the day. Was it a change of thinking on the part of Lee, or simply an adjustment prompted by the fact that Lee believed the bridge repairs would likely take all day? We will never know the answer.

On the evening of June 29, Lee reacted as though some mistake had been made, but offered no clarifying evidence as to when and by whom. It appears that either Lee, Chilton or a combination of the two caused the confusion.[42]

In all likelihood, it really didn't matter how the confusion was created. The important facts were the condition and time of repair of Grapevine and Alexander's Bridges. Grapevine Bridge had taken over a week to build. Repairing it would take some time. Alexander's Bridge was not totally repaired until nightfall, but was fully capable at that time of supporting artillery and trains. Grapevine Bridge, on the other hand, was crossed by Jackson and staff sometime in the afternoon, but was only sturdy enough for infantry and a little cavalry. The conclusion can easily be reached that Jackson could not have crossed the Chickahominy with his whole command early enough on the 29th to have made a difference in the fighting on the south side.

After crossing the river, Jackson rode to the Trent house for a better observation point and a look at the recently abandoned telegraph station. Depending on whose account is referenced, Jackson spoke with Toombs, Magruder and Lee. Winder's command went back to its previous bivouac. Jackson returned to his command and opted for some much needed sleep.[43]

As Jackson was crossing the Chickahominy with his staff, Magruder's command was again on the attack. Magruder for a time waited for the arrival of Jackson. Eventually, he received word that Jackson wasn't coming that day at all. Magruder should then have known that he couldn't be too aggressive in attacking McClellan's rear guard without Jackson's help. However, Magruder seemed to act in an opposite manner.

Whether from a desire to follow Lee's original order to press the Federals vigorously, or perhaps out of extreme frustration with how things were going for him, Magruder suddenly got aggressive. He issued orders to all his subordinate commanders to attack any Federals they could locate, whether in the open or in their works.

Such an order was potentially foolhardy, as Magruder had only 14,500 troops, and the potential was for five Federal divisions to be waiting in his front. Sumner's II Corps, Heintzelman's III Corps, and Smith's VI Corps division were all at Savage Station early in the day, a total of about 40,000 men. Fortunately for Magruder, Heintzelman had decided to leave, marching his corps to the south, and Baldy Smith was en route to the White Oak Swamp, following in the wake of Slocum's VI Corps division. The result of these Federal decisions was a boon to Magruder, as his attack was resisted only by Sumner's II Corps, a command of about 16,000.

Kershaw's brigade led the attack, moving forward about 3:00 P.M. The brigade had advanced a little past Orchard Station. Their right flank made contact with Federal troops, and moving into open ground, they observed the 20th Indiana and an artillery battery. The battery was James Thompson's, and had been left there by Kearny to ease Heintzelman's retreat. It was behind field fortifications, so Kershaw called a halt and brought up Del Kemper's battery. At the same time, he began a flanking movement to the south with the 2nd and 3rd South Carolina.

Thompson's battery opened fire on Kershaw's men, but the 20th Indiana held their fire, probably because of trees that were in the way. Del Kemper's guns began firing, quickly finding the range. The two Carolina regiments worked their way, with difficulty, to a position from which to charge the fortifications, but the Federals had disappeared. Kearny had ordered his troops to hold their position for only forty-five minutes, and they followed their orders exactly. On a side note, Thompson got separated from the 20th Indiana and went the wrong direction for quite a while, before discovering his error in navigation and reversing course.

Once Kershaw received, via Major Brent, Magruder's order to attack any and all Federals, he was on the move again. Before Brent left, Kershaw expressed his concern about his right flank, which extended no farther south than the Williamsburg road. Kershaw asked Brent to find him some help. The response was rapid. Semmes repositioned two of his regiments, the 32nd Virginia and the 10th Georgia to Kershaw's right flank.[44]

The general Confederate attack was discovered by Generals Sedgwick and Franklin while riding to Heintzelman's headquarters. Not exactly sure of Heintzelman's location, they were crossing a field when they spied troops emerging from a patch of woods. On discovering what was probably Cobb's brigade, the two senior officers made their escape, with a brace of Confederate cannon attempting to fire on them. This was essentially the first of the battle of Savage Station.

At almost the same moment, the Confederate movement to the east was being reported by Federal signal officers. Confederate artillery consisting of Kemper's battery and the unique railroad gun began firing. Some Federal units were taken by surprise. Osborn's Federal battery, along with Nairn's, were on the way to rejoin Hooker's division, but couldn't get past Confederate troops in their path. Osborn was ordered by Sumner to set up to fire. Sumner wasn't aware of the Confederate infantry accompanying their artillery. Osborn gladly made the general aware of the real character of the threat facing them. As to Sumner's frantic question concerning the whereabouts of Heintzelman, Osborn had no answer.[45]

Sumner had no time to get answers to his questions. It was critical for him to marshal troops to confront the Confederate attack from the west. Sumner didn't have a lot of assets to work with. Heintzelman's III Corps was on its way to White Oak Swamp and Baldy Smith's VI Corps division was also gone from the immediate area. Sumner had Burns' brigade facing Bottoms Bridge, and Meagher's brigade at Meadow Bridge. There was also the IV Corps brigade of Naglee right at Bottoms Bridge. Burns was the closest asset, so Sumner ordered Burns to have two regiments, the 72nd and 106th Pennsylvania, move into the woods west of Savage Station, between the Williamsburg road and the Richmond and York River Railroad.

Burns set about putting his regiments into position, and was soon informed by scouts that there were considerable Confederates on the

Williamsburg road. These were Semmes' troops. Burns could even hear Confederate officers shouting orders in the woods to his front. There were also Confederates to be seen to the north of the railroad. Burns feared he would be attacked from several directions at once. He sought immediate help from Sumner, who responded by ordering Sedgwick to send the 1st Minnesota of Sully's brigade into line on Burns' left flank. The Minnesotans managed to get into position before Semmes attacked.

Smith's division had departed the immediate area of Savage Station earlier in the day, and was now some two miles away. He was contacted and told to return to help face the approaching Confederate threat. Smith immediately moved toward the west, with Hancock's brigade in the lead, moving right of the road. Brooks' brigade advanced on the left. Davidson was ill with sunstroke, and his brigade, led by Colonel Robert F. Taylor, was the reserve. The 81st Pennsylvania from Caldwell's brigade supported Smith's left flank and the 7th New York of the same brigade went to Smith's right flank. French's brigade was along the railroad, bringing up the rear.[46]

Meagher's brigade was under command of Colonel Robert Nugent. The brigade had rejoined Richardson's division, having received the order to move to Savage Station around 4:00 P.M. Meagher was placed under arrest earlier in the day for failing to obey an order from Richardson to rejoin the division. This despite the fact that McClellan had told Sumner to leave the brigade where it was. Nugent ordered the 88th New York toward Burns. Richardson looked for French, desiring French to move forward, but could not locate him.

Artillery was being quickly moved to the support of the infantry. Pettit's and Hazzard's batteries were placed close to the Williamsburg road. When Smith's division had departed earlier

in the day, Kirby's and Tompkins' batteries of Sedgwick's division had gone with Smith, and so returned with him. Tompkins' rifled guns were placed on Hancock's left. Kirby's battery and Tompkins' howitzers went to Hancock's right. The batteries of Pettit, Nairn and Hazzard were set up right and left of Osborn.[47]

The Federal concentration of artillery was impressive, and the Confederate response was less so. A series of Confederate batteries, those of Del Kemper, Brown and Hart, moved into position and opened fire, but were silenced one at a time. McCarthy and Lane were receiving fire, but couldn't effectively return it, due to their poor position near the railroad. McCarthy tried moving to several other positions, and was run out of each by very heavy Federal fire. He finally moved south of the Williamsburg road to a position of relative safety without having fired a single round. The

Confederates tried out their railroad gun on the Federal reserve troops, however several rounds impacted near the Federal field hospital, and a flag of truce appeared from the Federal lines. They sent a note reminding the Confederates that the hospital contained some wounded Confederate troops. Overall, only Kemper's battery provided good support, firing from the Confederate right.[48]

When Kemper moved his battery south of the Williamsburg road, Kershaw moved the 8th South Carolina south of the road to support the battery and protect the brigade's right flank. Kershaw then moved the entire brigade forward. This precipitated the infantry battle. The attack was led by the 2nd and 3rd South Carolina. The left flank of the 2nd South Carolina was on the railroad, and Kershaw's line extended south from there with the 3rd and 7th South Carolina to the right of the 2nd. The right flank of the 7th South Carolina was on the Williamsburg road.

The Confederates were moving through a couple of hundred yards of heavy timber, then through very heavy undergrowth. When they broke out of the heavy cover they were right on the Federal lines, at some points within twenty-five yards. Some Federals were so surprised that they surrendered immediately. Despite heavy Federal artillery fire, the 106th Pennsylvania was driven back and their commander, General Burns, was wounded. The attackers broke the Federal line and prepared to press farther to the east.[49]

Kershaw called a halt at that point. He had several reasons for doing so. Semmes' brigade attacked south of the Williamsburg road, and encountered the 3rd Vermont in the thick vegetation there. The Vermonters were from Brooks' brigade of Baldy Smith's division. They were positioned there in support of Burns' left flank.

Brooks moved his men forward into the thick woods. He had the 5th Vermont just to the south of the Williamsburg road, the 6th Vermont to their left. The 2nd Vermont and 3rd Vermont were their supports. The 1st Minnesota was in the woods, having held fast when the Pennsylvania troops of II Corps had earlier fallen back. When Brooks gave the command for the Vermonters to move forward, the Minnesotans, believing the command came from their commander, advanced also. Semmes, opposite the left flank of the Federal line, was in good position but badly outnumbered.

The fight took place in those woods. It was intense, and at close quarters. At times, it was hand-to-hand. Soon the two supporting regiments from Brooks' brigade, the 2nd and 3rd Vermont, entered the fight. Semmes had to restrain at least one regimental commander from attacking into woods so thick that men could not see well enough to fight effectively. Friendly fire was a problem in the thick vegetation. As the firefight continued, muskets overheated and soldiers ran short or completely out of ammunition. Brooks suffered a leg wound, but remained in command of his brigade.[50]

Seeing Semmes's attack come to a halt, Magruder sent Major Brent with the 17th and 21st Mississippi from Barksdale's brigade to Semmes' aid. Brent directed the regiments to the position desired, then rode back north of the railroad to rejoin Magruder. At that point, Magruder ordered the railroad gun to move forward. Unfortunately, advancing the large gun stripped it of the protection of the railroad cut and exposed it to fire from Burns' brigade. Since the gun was not designed with much protection when fired upon from the sides, it had to retreat in a hurry.

The brutal clash between Brooks and Semmes took place southwest of Kershaw's position, essentially in his rear. The 7th South Carolina, on the right end of Kershaw's brigade, was hit in the right flank by the right regiment of Brooks' brigade.

Colonel D. Wyatt Aiken had insufficient visibility in the woods to see his entire regiment at the same time. He'd put his lieutenant colonel in charge on the right. That officer was wounded and two companies were cut off from the regiment. When informed of this setback by his sergeant major, Aiken immediately ordered a regimental withdrawal. Unfortunately, only two companies heard the order. Aiken was eventually able to marshal all of the regiment, even the two companies that had been cut off, at a crossroads. After carefully listening in all directions to the sounds of battle, he was able to exit the woods, find the 2nd and 3rd South Carolina, and reform his regiment on the right of the line.[51]

Other regiments had their difficulties in such an intense fight in thick cover. The men of the 3rd South Carolina heeded a shouted order to hold position and to cease firing. Their commander, James D. Nance, had not given the order, and immediately moved to the right end of his line to determine the origin of the confusion. There he found an officer and asked the source of the order. The answer Nance received was that the order came from his right, and that the company was firing on fellow Southerners. Other soldiers thought they had heard southern voices in their front. Unsure of the 7th South Carolina's exact position on the right, Nance issued the order for the entire regiment and the 3rd fell back. The 2nd followed suit.

The 8th South Carolina under John Henagan was also having difficulties. It had repositioned to its right to allow room for Del Kemper's battery to set up. The battery attracted Federal artillery fire and was withdrawn.

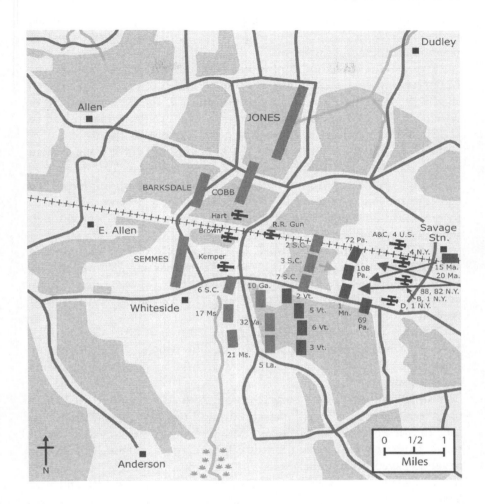

Map 19.3—Savage Station, June 29

Henagan then moved the regiment a bit farther right to get out from under the continuing Federal artillery shells and resumed the advance. Soon thereafter, the 8th was required to move back to its left, as the 10th Georgia was in front, advancing to contact with the brigade of Brooks. The next trouble came very soon. The 8th came under fire from the Federals in its front and Confederate troops in its rear. This friendly fire was likely from some of the three regiments of Semmes' brigade that had not moved forward when Kershaw did. After settling down the regiments behind them, the 8th prepared to resume the advance. Once again, the

10th Georgia was a problem. Henagan had had enough. He pulled the regiment back to the new site of Del Kemper's battery and held that position until the fight was over.[52]

After all the chaos and confusion of the firefight in the woods, Burns' troops had regrouped and mounted a counterattack. They had also received significant reinforcements. First on the scene was the 88th New York of Meagher's Irish Brigade, sent by Sumner. The 5th New Hampshire of Caldwell's brigade was also sent, but never made it to the fight. Burns was able to put the 88th in along the Williamsburg road, placing them between the 69th and 106th Pennsylvania, on the Federal left.

Sully's brigade contributed the 82nd New York, which reinforced the center of the line. These two reinforcing New York regiments managed to force the 3rd South Carolina, the last of Kershaw's brigade, back through the thick woods and into a ravine.

The earlier Confederate attack had left the 106th Pennsylvania in a state of slight disarray. The 15th Massachusetts, commanded by John W. Kimball, had spent most of the day destroying stores near Savage Station, before entering the fight in support of the 1st Minnesota and the 82nd New York.

South of the Williamsburg road, the 20th and 49th New York of Davidson's brigade moved to aid Brooks. The two New York regiments were personally led by Baldy Smith. Darkness spared these regiments from entering the fight.

North of the Williamsburg road, the 20th Massachusetts of Dana's brigade replaced the 72nd Pennsylvania, and the 71st Pennsylvania and the 7th Michigan moved to the fore. Although the 7th Michigan hastened to the front, it wasn't really needed. Likewise, the 71st Pennsylvania was never damaged in the fight.

Barksdale's brigade had two regiments in the fight, the 17th and 21st Mississippi, and they weren't as lucky as the late arriving Federal reserves. They arrived around sundown, and were ordered to cease fire after a short while, as their fire was too close to Semmes' men. Subsequently, the Mississippians were invited to resume fire, then again told they were firing into friendly troops. During this chaos, Barksdale's men took heavy fire and a number of casualties. This might have come from a Georgia regiment. Soon, nightfall made the fire die out, and the battle of Savage Station had come to an end.[53]

For the number of troops engaged, the Savage Station had been relatively bloody, and had accomplished little. The Confederates, through gross mismanagement of their forces, had engaged only nine of their infantry regiments. Once again, the battle had been decided by darkness, and the Federal army had retreated in the night.

Kershaw committed his entire brigade, consisting of the 2nd, 3rd, 7th and 8th South Carolina, as well as Kemper's battery, some 1,496 officers and men. Kershaw suffered 48 killed, 236 wounded and 9 missing. The 3rd South Carolina took the heaviest losses.

Semmes fought three of his regiments, the 10th Georgia, 32nd Virginia and the 5th Louisiana, about 755 men. Semmes incurred 11 killed, 53 wounded; the 10th Georgia suffered the most.

Barksdale's brigade contributed to the fight with the 17th and 21st Mississippi, about 850 men. They joined the fight late in the day, and thus probably suffered lighter losses, though they were not reported separately.

Counting reinforcements, some 3,950 Confederate troops were involved at Savage Station. Total Confederate casualties are estimated at 375.

On the Federal side, Burns committed four regiments, the 69th, 71st, 72nd and 106th Pennsylvania, about 2,400 men. Brigade losses were 100 killed and 152 wounded. The 72nd Pennsylvania also suffered considerable losses, with 14 killed, 10 mortally wounded and 75 wounded. The 71st Pennsylvania only entered the fight at the very end of the day, and suffered very little, having only 2 men killed.

Brooks fought four of his regiments, the 2nd, 3rd, 5th and 6th Vermont. Heaviest losses were in the 5th Vermont, which bore the brunt of the brigade's fight. The regiment had 45 killed, 27 mortally wounded, 116 wounded and 26 men missing. The other three regiments were reported to have had 37 men killed. Total casualties for the brigade were 455.

When the participation of reinforcements, the 20th and 49th New York of Davidson's brigade, the 82nd New York and 15th Massachusetts of Sully's brigade, the 88th New York of Meagher's brigade, the 5th New Hampshire of Caldwell's brigade, and the 20th Massachusetts and 7th Michigan of Dana's brigade is considered, some 7,300 Federal troops were involved at Savage Station. Some of the reinforcements scarcely fired a shot. Total Federal casualties are estimated at 600.

Not counted in the Federal casualties estimate above were the 2,500–3,000 Federal sick and wounded taken by the advancing Confederates when the field hospital at Savage Station was abandoned.[54]

It is difficult to imagine why the battle of Savage Station took place in the manner that it did. It should have been a much larger fight, with the potential for a significant result on the campaign. The Confederates used only nine of twenty-eight available regiments, and the Federals were denied the services of an entire corps because Heintzelman decided on his own to go south and left the battle area, rather than engage the approaching Confederates.

Magruder's orders from Lee were to press the enemy vigorously, yet Magruder was only able to engage nine of his regiments, some 3,100 men. David Jones' division, made up of the brigades of Toombs and G. T. Anderson, located to Magruder's left, never fired a shot. Jones was in a perfect position to strike the Federal right flank or even the rear, yet Magruder failed to see this fact or failed to act on it. Magruder, subsequent to the battle, claimed he couldn't find Jones to give him orders. Likewise, Jones claimed he couldn't find Magruder. Toombs made no report of the fighting of June 29, and Anderson's report complained of being marched in line of battle most of the day through woods and fields without entering the fight. Cobb's brigade never came in sight of the battle and Barksdale's two uncommitted regiments supported Cobb.[55]

Although history might rightfully blame Magruder for botching the tactical management of the battle of Savage Station, there is no scarcity of blame to be distributed among the Confederate generals for the day's activities overall. Had Jackson moved down from the north as ordered, the Federal position at Savage Station would have been untenable. Had Huger been more forthcoming as to his understanding of his orders, Magruder would have been better served. Had Lee exercised more personal control over events, Magruder would have had less opportunity to mismanage the fight.

Magruder made a lot of mistakes on June 29 before the battle even began. He yelled for reinforcements before personally assessing what was going on in his front. He failed to communicate clearly with either Lee or Jackson, thus going into the fight with serious misconceptions of the situation. Magruder still believed that Huger was going to be on the Williamsburg road rather than on the Charles City road. He also believed that pressure from Jackson would come into play very soon. These errors and misconceptions materially affected his decisions during the day.

Once Magruder commenced the fight with Sumner, he really had little opportunity to accomplish more than he did. The thick vegetation made coordinated infantry maneuver difficult and degraded the effect of artillery support. Sumner was a tough opponent, who could have hurt Magruder badly, had the Confederate attack been pressed more energetically.

Unfortunately for Magruder, Lee had a different perception of Magruder's performance and was not happy. That evening, Lee sent Magruder a note: "I regret much that you have made so little progress today in the pursuit of the enemy. In order to reap the fruits of our victory the pursuit should be most vigorous. I must urge you, then, again to press on his rear rapidly and steadily. We must lose no more time or he will escape us entirely." It can be argued, however, that Sumner might well have welcomed a more vigorous pursuit by Magruder.

June 29 can be considered, among other things, a day of lost opportunities. The foremost of these was the failure of Jackson to cross the Chickahominy. Had he managed to do so, he would have been in an excellent position, with great combat power at his disposal, to inflict great damage on McClellan's rear guard. Another was the failure of Lee or any other Confederate leader to become aware of the gap in the Federal troop placement between Brooks' brigade near the Trent house and Sumner's II Corps straddling the Meadow road. Lastly, Lee missed an opportunity by not pushing Huger rapidly down the Charles City road. That was where Confederate troops needed to be to disrupt the retreat. By sending Huger with two brigades to Magruder, then bringing them back, Lee wasted much of Huger's day. Magruder shouldn't have sought help quite so soon, but Lee had a responsibility to determine if it was really needed before delaying Huger's movement. The case can also be made that the Federals really missed an opportunity at Savage Station.[56]

Arguably, the leadership on the Federal side was equally poor, and likely saved Lee from a really bad drubbing. Subsequent to Heintzelman's unilateral withdrawal from the Savage Station area, there were still 40 regiments available to Sumner. He failed to give orders to more than 14, and two of those, the 20th and 49th New York, arrived in the line after the fighting had stopped for the day. Sumner, in his frantic effort to rescue Burns, micromanaged his regiments instead of using his division and brigade commanders. Sumner was heavy on reserves and light on combat power in the line. At least one Federal general, John Sedgwick, believed their performance at Savage Station should not be a source of pride. While other officers complained about the order to retreat, Sedgwick maintained his silence on the matter.[57]

Both sides had a bit of luck which probably saved them from more severe losses. The Federals were fortunate that Franklin and Sedgwick accidentally observed Confederate troops emerging from the woods north of the railroad. Had this not occurred, the Federals might has been caught unprepared for battle. The Confederates had their own great fortune in that Heintzelman decided to pull out of Savage Station earlier in the day. If Heintzelman had stayed in position, his corps would have been a perfect flanking force to attack Semmes, and could have done great damage to Magruder's command.[58]

Although tactically a draw, the battle of Savage Station has to be considered a failure for the Army of Northern Virginia, in that only

Magruder was engaged, and his men failed to break through the Federal lines. This failure meant that there was no significant disruption of the retreat of the Army of the Potomac to the James. Another chance to cut off Federal trains or part of the rear guard was squandered.

On a positive note for the Confederates, their continued pressure on McClellan's army forced the destruction of huge amounts of military stores, and the abandonment of the Federal field hospital at Savage Station, with some 2,500 or more wounded soldiers in residence.

The general retreat of the Army of the Potomac had been ongoing all day on June 29. With Heintzelman pulling out of Savage Station, the rear guard now consisted of three divisions—the II Corps divisions of Richardson and Sedgwick, and the VI Corps division of Smith.

Heintzelman's plan upon leaving Savage Station was to march III Corps, with Kearny's division in the lead, to the area of Glendale. The route chosen took the corps across White Oak Swamp at Jordon's Ford, some three miles upstream from White Oak Swamp Bridge. He chose that particular crossing to avoid the expected congestion at White Oak Swamp Bridge and at Brackett's Ford. From Jordon's Ford, there was a road that lead to the Charles City road that would take the corps to Glendale. The route had been scouted in the morning, and no enemy activity was observed.

During the afternoon, Kearny had his 3rd brigade commander, Hiram Berry, assess the fords ahead. Berry decided that Jordon's and Fisher's Fords needed improvement, and assigned the 4th Maine to do it. As Berry returned to the corps, the 4th was already underway.

It was a hot, exhausting march, made more difficult because the men were packing the weight of extra ammunition. Kearny's decision to order extra ammunition was a major factor in the outcome of the day's fighting. Some cases of heat exhaustion occurred, and there was some lack of discipline along the route of march, as regiments tried to pass others, and artillery vied with infantry for the road.

The lead brigade, that of Birney, crossed both forks of the White Oak Swamp via Jordon's Ford and soon came under fire from Mahone's brigade of Huger's division, tasked by Lee to move down the Charles City road. Mahone had been on the lookout for Federals crossing at Jordon's or Fisher's Fords, and was alerted by the discovery of a Federal cavalry patrol where the road form Jordon's Ford ran into the Charles City road. Pushing forth scouts, they reported to Mahone that Federal forces were indeed crossing the swamp. Mahone put the brigade into line of battle and sent skirmishers forward to harass the Federals.

Kearny put out skirmishers from the 3rd Maine, who returned fire. Kearny looked over the situation. Mahone then put forward two infantry regiments. Certain he was facing a significant Confederate force, Kearny ordered Birney to pull his brigade back, and go for Brackett's Ford by way of New road.

Except for Berry's brigade, Kearny's division crossed the swamp at Brackett's Ford. Berry crossed at Fisher's Ford. Experiencing no further difficulties, Kearny moved his men through Porter's V Corps and encamped astride the Charles City road by 10:00 P.M.

Huger made an erroneous assumption as to Kearny's actions. He assumed that Kearny was still north of the swamp near Jordon's Ford, and feared to push farther down the Charles City road, lest he leave Kearny a chance to use New road to get in the Confederate rear. The 44th Alabama of Wright's brigade, accompanied by an artillery battery, was dispatched to cover the intersection of the Charles City and New roads. The Confederates would have to clear the New Road the next morning. They were taking no chances. Both Mahone's brigade and Lewis Armistead's brigade behind him were ordered to sleep on their arms. The division rear was brought up by Ransom's large brigade.[59]

The net effect of the afternoon's events resulted in Huger's troops being stretched out over several miles. Other parts of Lee's army were not too far away. Magruder was between Orchard and Savage Stations. Jackson had repaired Alexander's Bridge by evening, and had crossed D. H. Hill's attached division, with the rest of Jackson's command making ready to follow. Ewell left Bradley Johnson's Maryland Line to watch Bottoms Bridge and moved about 6:00 P.M. to rejoin Jackson on the north side of the Chickahominy.

The remaining Confederate divisions, those of A. P. Hill and James Longstreet, had a long way to go. They marched all day, and suffered from the very hot and dusty conditions. President Davis, as was his nature, joined the column and traveled with them for part of the march. By the end of the long day's march along the Darbytown road, they had passed the Atlee house, and were about seven miles from Glendale. The 3rd Virginia Cavalry had rejoined them. Straggling was common in the heat.[60]

Another night of thunderstorms made sleeping difficult for the Confederates, while Federal troops were marching south. Hooker's division had crossed at Brackett's Ford, following Kearny's, and encamped on the Charles City road. Some soldiers were told that Federal troops had been passing down the road since late the previous evening. Hooker's men suffered from the heat and humidity, and were covered with dust stirred up from the long columns on the road.[61]

Keyes' IV Corps was also on the march. By morning, it had reached Haxall's Landing, below Turkey Island Creek Bridge on the James River, after an extremely tiresome march. Naglee's men, who had been posted across the Chickahominy from Ewell's division at Bottoms Bridge, had started from there about 5:00 P.M. and reached White Oak Swamp Bridge the next morning. Slocum's VI Corps division relieved Keyes and held their position all night. Slocum did provide the 1st New Jersey of Taylor's brigade to protect the White Oak Swamp Bridge.

Both soldiers and officers were happy to pause in their retreat long enough to eat and sleep. Even General Slocum hadn't eaten for thirty-six hours, until brought some soup by one of his regimental commanders, Colonel Pratt of the 31st New York.[62]

McCall set his division in motion about 5:00 P.M. from near White Oak Swamp to guard the Glendale crossroads. This movement was covered by Averell's 3rd Pennsylvania Cavalry, Benson's battery and the 8th Pennsylvania Reserves from Seneca Simmons' brigade. Conditions were very unfavorable for moving a large body of infantry. It was a rainy night, and the muddy roads were clogged with wounded, stragglers, wagons and even livestock. The division passed the intersection of the Darbytown and Long Bridge roads, and continued down the Long Bridge road. About midnight, McCall's men encountered Confederate cavalry, likely the 5th Virginia Cavalry.[63]

Before that encounter, however, several V Corps subordinate commanders realized that something was wrong with their movement. George Meade, commander of McCall's 2nd brigade, was moving with the front of the V Corps column. He had already come to the conclusion that he was on the wrong road. In point of fact, the whole V Corps had gone astray. All three divisions were to move by the Quaker road. In actuality, the correct road was the nearby Willis Church road. McCall was supposed to stop on the New Market road. The other two division commanders, Sykes and Morell, who had begun their march at about sundown, were to continue on to Turkey Island Creek Bridge.

The crux of the problem was that the column was marching on the wrong Quaker road, one which departed the Long Bridge road approximately two miles west of Glendale. Meade was sure enough that he was off the march to halt his brigade and examine this "other" Quaker road. It proved to be an unused, overgrown, seemingly unusable road, complete with crossing fences and ditches. Meade passed this word to McCall, who passed it to Fitz John Porter.

Porter's problem was that his guide had convinced him that the "other" Quaker road was in fact the correct one. According to some accounts of the movement, Porter sent Morell and Sykes down the "other" Quaker road, but they were forced to countermarch. The veracity of that account cannot be determined, as Meade ran into Confederate pickets at that point. It can't be accurately determined exactly when the Confederates were encountered. Further confusion on Porter's part was likely due to the fact that McClellan had given orders directly to McCall to provide guard to the army's trains, as well as Glendale. Porter probably believed that he shouldn't be issuing orders to McCall at that point.

Regardless of the command relationships at that point in time, McCall had no choice but to stay put for the night. Randol's battery came up and parked in a nearby field, leaving their horses hitched. The morning light revealed that some of the men from the 7th Pennsylvania Reserves had spent the wee hours inside the Confederate lines.[64]

Even after reaching their bivouacs, some units had a miserable night. Simmons' brigade of McCall's division attempted unsuccessfully to sleep in line of battle. This was only three nights after their first combat, and sleep was mostly prevented by spurious firing, unruly horses, barking dogs and a number of nightmares. Little sleep was possible.

Longstreet ended up fairly close to the Federals. He was prevented from executing a night attack by the rainy weather and the sheer exhaustion of his troops after the long, hot march.[65]

Morell and Sykes finally found the correct Quaker road and arrived at Malvern Hill around 9:00 A.M. That still left the rear guard around Savage Station, consisting of Sumner's II Corps and Baldy Smith's VI Corps division. They had both received McClellan's order to cross White Oak Swamp that night, and Franklin, the VI Corps commander, intended to get Smith's division out of there promptly. When Franklin informed Sumner he was leaving, Sumner became emotional, forbade Franklin to leave, and proclaimed that he never left the field of a victory. Franklin tried showing Sumner the written order from McClellan, but Sumner maintained his stance to hold his position. Sumner's position was that McClellan had issued the order in ignorance of the results of the battle of Savage Station.

Smith anticipated a problem getting Sumner to withdraw, so Smith had requested that his aide, Major Caspar Berry, go with Franklin back to Sumner and explain to him that McClellan had in fact been fully aware of the battle of Savage Station, and yet still wanted the rear guard to withdraw. Shortly, Colonel Sacket, McClellan's inspector general, appeared with two orders.

The first was written, and was enough to get Sumner to agree to the withdrawal. The other private order was to arrest Sumner if he didn't obey the first one. Franklin then started Smith's division on the withdrawal, and Sumner allowed Sedgwick and Richardson's divisions to follow.[66]

It cannot be overemphasized how difficult the period from the 26th through the 30th of June was for all of the troops involved. For the Federals, they marched all night, often in thunderstorms, organized themselves in the mornings, and defended themselves against fierce Confederate attacks in the afternoons. Many, almost all, failed to understand why they were retreating day after day, sometimes after successful days on the battlefield. They had to wonder why they had to leave their dead and wounded on the battlefield. These soldiers had the additional emotional burden of watching their rations, tents, medicines and other items dear to them burn or gathered in by the Confederates as the Army of the Potomac retreated.

For the Confederates, they marched in the same rain, following their quarry on roads more the muddy for the Federals having used them, and rebuilt a number of bridges destroyed in their path. Each time they formed into columns to march after the retreating foe, they became aware that their companies were diminished. Daily they experienced the frustration of not quite being able to trap McClellan's army, which was always just out of reach. Each time they walked through an abandoned Federal camp, they found more evidence of how much better the Federal soldier lived than the Confederate one. Lee's men had to be extremely thankful that the Federals weren't more efficient in destroying their supplies and equipment as they retreated.

At this point in the campaign, both armies suffered from a lack of rations and decent drinking water. Fatigue was an adequate one word summary for the last few days of near constant fighting and marching.[67]

CHAPTER 20

Glendale

(June 30)

The battle of Glendale had many aliases. It was also known as Frayser's Farm, Nelson's Farm, Charles City Crossroads, White Oak Swamp, New Market Road or Riddell's Shop. It was a long and complicated day, with fighting taking place in four different areas. Therefore, Glendale is considerably more difficult to understand and describe in print.

Richardson's II Corps division was the last division of the Federal rear guard to leave the Savage Station area. They finally were all on the march at 1:00 A.M. on June 30. Confusion reigned at Savage Station. Some units, such as the pickets of the 20th Massachusetts, were not properly notified to withdraw, and were nearly captured by the advancing Confederate pickets.[1]

Being the last to leave meant using the roads in their worst condition. They moved in virtual silence in the rain and the mud, the cavalry attempting to awaken those who fell out and slept along the roadside. Those who were missed were likely taken prisoner by the advancing Confederates. Once across White Oak Swamp, the men fell fast asleep. They had a dire need to keep going, as the pursuing Confederates somehow did.

Hazzard's batteries A & C, 4th United States Artillery, never left until first light. In their fatigued state, they slept in the rain and were awakened to the sounds of Confederate bugles and drums from a nearby camp. Hazzard moved out smartly, and was able to get across White Oak Swamp just before William French's men, the Federal rear guard, set fire to the bridge. The battery was completely across by 10:00 A.M.

With Hazzard's batteries safely across, the whole of the Army of the Potomac was on the south side of White Oak Swamp. They were not the only troops making a crossing at that time. Jackson's first division to cross the Chickahominy was that of D. H. Hill, which started across at 3:00 A.M. on June 30. Harvey Hill's men were followed by those of Whiting, Jackson's own division, then Ewell's.

Magruder was on the Williamsburg road, preparing to start the day's movement, when he encountered Jackson riding south on the road from Grapevine Bridge. One of the men of McCarthy's battery, close to Magruder, described Jackson as "worn down." Jackson was said to be covered with dust, his uniform shabby.[2]

Soon, Lee arrived, quite the contrast in appearance and demeanor. He was dressed immaculately and was alert. After a brief greeting, the two generals dismounted and had a conversation, while one of them drew a diagram in the dirt with the toe of his boot. The diagram seemed to be in the shape of a "V". Then one of the generals drew a third line, closing the triangle. He then stamped the drawing with his foot and uttered the phrase, "We've got him!" The conversation was overheard by Lieutenant Robert Stiles. Their horses were called for, and the two generals rode off.

No records exist of the conversation, and most of what we know comes from the observation of Stiles, an artillerist of the Richmond Howitzers. Stiles stated that he was watching closely, and that it was Jackson who drew the triangle in the dirt, and that Stonewall was talking in a "jerky, impetuous way." It is not possible to determine with any certainty the meaning of the triangle in the dirt described above. One side could have been the line of the Darbytown road or the New Market/River road. The second line could have represented the White Oak/Willis Church road. There doesn't seem to be a meaning for the third side in this case. If the assumption is made that the two lines drawn energetically in the dirt were White Oak/Willis Church road and the Charles City or Williamsburg road, then the third side could have represented the Darbytown or River road. The third side would be where the Confederates would attack to cut off McClellan's retreat. Some researchers have theorized that the lines were not roads at all, but positions of major Confederate units. The answer is just not knowable.[3]

Lee's plan for the day was little more than a slight revision of his plan for the previous day. A. P. Hill and James Longstreet, from their bivouacs near Atlee's farm, were to continue down the Darbytown road until reaching the Long Bridge road, proceed east, and attack the enemy wherever he was found.

Huger was to continue down the Charles City road and do the same. There was one modification to the previous day's plan relating to Huger's tasking. Due to his contact with Kearny's men on the 29th, Rans Wright's brigade was sent down the New road to assure that it was clear of Federals, thus protecting Huger's left flank.

Rudolph J. Schroeder, III

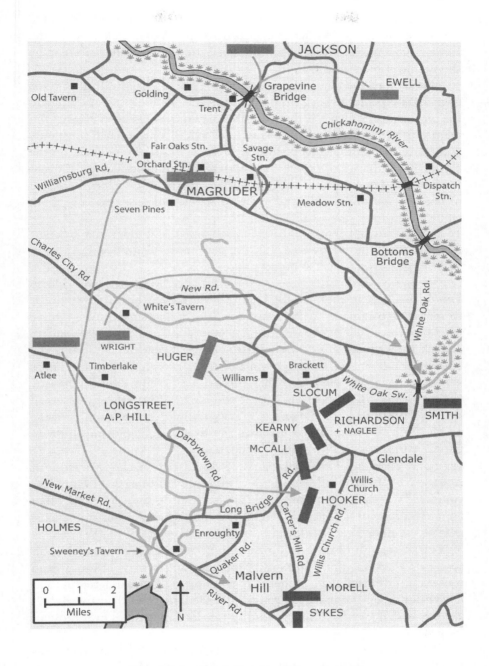

Map 20.1—Lee's Revised Plan, June 30

Stonewall was to remain on the road closest to the river. His route would be down the Williamsburg road to the White Oak road to the Long Bridge road, so leading to the intersection near Glendale. There he should find Longstreet.

The key to the plan was that the three forces would attack at once, triggered by Huger firing guns on his approach. The sole major change to the previous day's plan was the part to be played by Magruder. Prince John seemed to be sure he faced several divisions in his front, and had constantly asked Lee for reinforcements, in case Jackson was sent elsewhere on the battlefield. Perhaps Prince John had been unnerved by Jackson's actions of the previous day. Magruder's actions, such as giving orders all night instead of sleeping, must have indicated to Lee that Magruder was insecure about being supported by Jackson.

Jackson arrived about 3:30 A.M. and assured Magruder that Jackson's divisions would arrive by daybreak. At that news, Magruder was able to sleep. The sleep was much needed.[4]

Probably a little later, Lee personally visited Magruder and briefed him on his part in the plan for June 30. Magruder's new role would be to move his command to the Darbytown road, and serve as the reserve for Longstreet and A. P. Hill. Lee apparently felt that the key point to contest the Federal retreat was a little south of Glendale. By adding the combat power of Magruder's command to that of A. P. Hill and James Longstreet, he was confident that those forces could prevail over any enemy encountered, and thus cut off the retreat. This strategy assumed that the commands of Huger and Jackson could put enough pressure on the Federal rear guard to prevent any troops from moving south to reinforce those Federals south of Glendale.

Some historians have analyzed Lee's decision to be simply a result of his lack of confidence in Magruder. The evidence indicates that Magruder's command was the correct one for Lee to send south as a reserve, as the other apparent choice was Huger's men, and Wright's brigade was unavailable as it was in the process of clearing the New road, north of the White Oak Swamp. Although Huger's command might have reached Glendale a bit sooner, it was a simpler plan to use Magruder, and Magruder's command was more powerful than Huger's by a couple of thousand troops, and power down south was what Lee really needed, more so than speed. It is also likely that Lee preferred Magruder's leadership abilities over those of Huger.[5]

The collective result of all Lee's orders was that the entire army was moving toward Glendale. He obviously intended that the forces of Huger, Longstreet and A.P. Hill converge near Glendale. It is reasonable to assume

Rudolph J. Schroeder, III

that Lee knew that three Federal divisions had fought at Savage Station on the evening of June 29. This strong rear guard fighting north of White Oak Swamp meant that McClellan would be compelled to stop and fight one more battle, most likely near Glendale, before all of his army could reach the safety of the James and the protection of the Federal gunboats. Lee hoped that his planned troop movements would put pressure on the Glendale intersection from several directions, perhaps trapping those three Federal rear guard divisions. Success depended on A. P. Hill and Longstreet closing the Willis Church road before those divisions could escape to the south.

Lee had one more source of combat power, not previously part of the Army of Northern Virginia. On June 26, Theophilus Holmes, commander of the Department of North Carolina, was ordered to leave Petersburg and move north of the James River. Holmes' command had already been diminished by previous orders. On the 25th, Ransom's brigade was attached to Huger's command for combat at Oak Grove. On the 27th, Walker's brigade had been taken from Holmes. That left him only the brigade of Junius Daniels.

After noon on June 29, Holmes crossed the James River with Daniels' brigade. It consisted of the 43rd, 45th and 50th North Carolina, along with three cavalry companies and two artillery batteries. Later that night, Walker's men, along with two more artillery batteries, were returned to Holmes, from north of the Chickahominy River. On the morning of the 30th, Holmes moved his men to the intersection of the New Market and Long Bridge roads. Holmes was joined there by Henry A. Wise, commanding the 26th and 46th Virginia and two more artillery batteries.

Upon Holmes' request, Wise brought almost all of his men from Chaffin's Bluff on the north side of the James River. Holmes now had about 6,300 infantry, 130 cavalry and six batteries.

Holmes was in a good location to help Lee's cause. From his position on the New Market road, which was called the River road east of the intersection with the Long Bridge road, Holmes could move quickly towards Malvern Hill and mount a flank attack on the retreating Federals. Having no orders to initiate such an attack, he went into a defensive posture at his present position and waited for orders from Lee. Once again, President Davis appeared on the field, and approved of Holmes' actions and the annexation of Wise's command.[6]

Library of Congress

White Oak Swamp

In actuality, McClellan had much more than a rear guard under threat by Lee's plan for June 30. Out of eleven divisions in the Army of the Potomac, there were seven plus a brigade still between White Oak Swamp and Willis Church. They were in a fairly compact disposition and covered the approaches to Glendale. All but Baldy Smith's division were close to the White Oak Swamp Bridge. Smith's men were protecting the southward movement of the trains. After their retreat from Bottoms Bridge, Naglee's brigade of Peck's IV Corps division was placed under Smith's command. Richardson's II Corps division, the last major unit to leave Savage Station, joined them as well. Richardson had to motivate a group of stragglers to clear the White Oak Swamp Bridge. He managed to get everyone across before the Confederates reached the swamp. Once across, Richardson went into line on Smith's left, just to the west of the White Oak road. The men from the different divisions shared one common problem. All were exhausted from several days of digging, retreating and fighting. They attempted to get a little sleep.

Artillery from Smith's division protected the bridge against the pursuing Confederates. All or parts of the batteries of Mott, Ayres, Cowan, Wheeler and Hazzard were arrayed to prevent Jackson from forcing a crossing of White Oak Swamp.[7]

The Federal divisions near the White Oak Swamp Bridge weren't in isolation. McClellan ordered Franklin, the VI Corps commander, to reposition Slocum's division to the Charles City road, about halfway between Brackett's Ford and Glendale. The artillery batteries of Hexamer, Upton and Porter were positioned near a road that connected the Charles City and White Oak roads. The artillerists had infantry support with them.

Kearny's division was eventually positioned on the Charles City road. Starting the day from a bivouac near Brackett's Ford, Kearny marched his men to Deep Run, which fed into White Oak Swamp. It was determined that the Deep Run position was very strong, but was not optimal, so Kearny was then sent to the left of Slocum, between the Charles City and Long Bridge roads. Heintzelman further refined the troop dispositions, resulting in another short move for Kearny, who was irritated that his final placements had his division stretched too thin. Kearny ended up with Robinson's brigade on the left with Thompson's battery, Birney's brigade and Randolph's Battery E, 1st Rhode Island Light, were on the right. The reserve force was Berry's brigade.

Heintzelman was still not done refining the III Corps dispositions. He sent one of Robinson's regiments, the 87th New York, as well as a single gun from Hexamer's battery to Brackett's Ford to watch the destroyed bridge there. Once in position, the men used a little quiet time to eat breakfast and rest while they could.[8]

When McClellan, in a meeting with Sumner, Heintzelman and Franklin, had worked out the troop dispositions in the morning, he had intended for Hooker to be adjacent to Kearny, on Kearny's left. Hooker would take responsibility for the area between the Long Bridge and Willis Church roads. Incredibly, McClellan seems to have failed to assign McCall's division to a place in the line of battle or the reserve. McCall had fallen back from a vulnerable position southwest of Bottoms Bridge to the area near Glendale, pausing near Willis Church road to let some retreating trains pass. The stop was used to treat some of the wounded. The men anticipated being ordered to continue on to the south to rejoin the rest of V Corps. Surprisingly, they were put in line between Kearny and Hooker's divisions, while the other two V Corps divisions, those of Morell and Sykes, were setting up at Malvern Hill. McCall had the artillery support of Kerns, Cooper, Randol, Diederich and Knieriem.[9]

Hooker was unaware of McCall's position, even though McCall was just to Hooker's right front. However, at least some of Hooker's men were likely aware of the presence of McCall's division. Around 9:00 A.M., Hooker placed his division in a line parallel to the Willis Church road and approximately a half mile west of it. Sickles was on the left, Carr in the center and Grover on the right. The right end of Grover's line was just west of Willis Church. Hooker didn't believe he'd need his division artillery on the 30th, and his batteries went toward Malvern Hill.

Around 11:00 A.M., Hooker observed several wagons belonging to McCall's division. He rode over and examined McCall's troop dispositions, noted the 600 yard gap between his right and McCall's left, but didn't make any changes.[10]

The Federal defenses around Glendale were shaping up well. The line from right to left was Smith, Richardson plus Naglee's brigade, Slocum, Kearny, McCall and Hooker.

Sedgwick's division was in reserve at Glendale. The approach to Glendale via the Long Bridge road was well guarded by McCall and Hooker, with Sedgwick in close reserve. Sedgwick had marched from the White Oak Swamp with a number of short stops, welcome in the heat and humidity. Another benefit was that the slow pace was conducive to stragglers rejoining the division.[11]

With about 55,000 Federal troops in the defensive line and about 70,000 Confederates converging from three directions, June 30 had the potential to be an even more furious battle than Gaines' Mill. The rest of the Army of the Potomac lay south of Glendale.

Couch's division, augmented by Wessell's brigade from Peck's division, was at Haxall's Landing on the James River, some four miles to the south of Glendale. These troops were exhausted from a night march and badly wanted to stay at Haxall's. On the River road, the bridge across Turkey Island Creek was essentially the last critical point in McClellan's retreat to Harrison's Landing, and was at present guarded by the 7th Massachusetts and 2nd Rhode Island of Palmer's brigade. Morell's division was sent by Porter south of the bridge and went into camp. Sykes' division, along with the artillery reserve, stayed on Malvern Hill. Porter took immediate steps to defend the hill, pointing his artillery to the north and west. His line consisted of Buchanan on the right, Lovell to Buchanan's left, and Warren's small brigade covering the River road from a valley just west of Malvern Hill.[12]

McClellan was as busy as any of his generals throughout the morning. He'd already briefed three of his corps commanders regarding his desired troop disposition for the expected Confederate attack at Glendale, and rode along their lines to assure that his wishes had been carried out. He observed the still numerous trains inching their way southward to the James. There were literally thousands of wagons rushing along at a snail's pace on the pathetic roads. At points along the road, officer leadership was not present or was present but ineffective, and discipline broke down. The result was individual teamsters or units vying for right of way. Fights broke out and stores were destroyed or abandoned.

As McClellan became aware of the problem with the retreat, he gave orders that would buy some more time for his trains. This was accomplished by Heintzelman, who had trees dropped across roads leading into Glendale, specifically the Charles City road and the road leading from Brackett's Ford to the Charles City road.

McClellan's problem was significant, but not quite as critical as he then believed. Erasmus Keyes had already discovered and was using an alternate road from the area of Glendale to Haxall's Landing area, but hadn't quite gotten around to telling the Commanding General. McClellan was laboring under the false assumption that all of his trains had to travel down the Willis Church road. To add to McClellan 's worries, he still hadn't heard from his engineers, Alexander, Comstock and Farquhar, who were to help him make the final decision on a final site for the army's new base on the James. Since McClellan was unaware of Keyes' discovery of the secondary road, he could not rationally divide the wagon traffic to make the optimal use of the roads available. For the present, most of his wagons would use the Willis Church road, unless individual unit commanders became aware of the secondary road and decided on their own initiative to use it. With some good fortune, and after an exciting and frustrating day, all of the trains reached their destination by the evening of June 30. They spent the night either at the Malvern Hill/Haxall's Landing area or at the Berkeley Plantation at Harrison's Landing.[13]

McClellan's crisis concerning the trains was almost irrelevant to the need to defend Glendale for another day. Losing the Glendale intersection to the Confederates on June 30 would have left the Federal divisions defending at White Oak Swamp Bridge with no easy way to retreat to the James.

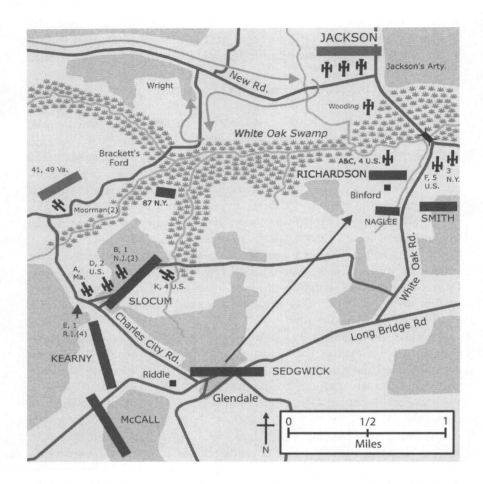

Map 20.2—White Oak Swamp and Brackett's Ford, June 30

At this point in time, it was necessary for McClellan to plan for fighting on both the June 30 and July 1. He knew that he couldn't establish his army in a new base on the James any sooner than late on the 1st or early on July 2. He also knew that his army, as large as it was, couldn't defend from the White Oak Swamp to the James. He had to hold Glendale for another day, while simultaneously defending White Oak Swamp Bridge against a crossing by Jackson. This would allow time for his engineers to report back on the best site for the new base, make his decision on the location for that base, and set the trains in motion for the last leg of their retreat. He would also have to protect against a Confederate attack from the west or southwest. If the enemy attacked along the Carter's Mill road, then turned up the Willis Church road and hit Hooker's left flank, there could be horrific results, perhaps even the decimation of several of his divisions.

McClellan also couldn't weaken his forces around Malvern Hill, as they were necessary to protecting the trains that had already made it that far south. The infantry on Malvern Hill, thin though it was, had bountiful artillery support, and should be able to hold against a Confederate attack from the River road until reinforced.

McClellan settled on a plan that would allow him a good chance to hold Glendale through June 30, then retreat south to reinforce Malvern Hill on July 1. Malvern Hill was an outstanding defensive position, and could easily withstand assault once he moved the rest of his infantry there. The fight on July 1 would be less difficult than holding Glendale on June 30.

McClellan's plan was overall very adequate, but did have some worrisome aspects. The plan provided for a defense against a forced crossing of White Oak Swamp, a strong defense of the key roads around Glendale, an impressive artillery presence on Malvern Hill, accompanied by barely adequate infantry, and a defense of the key Turkey Island Creek Bridge. Additionally, if these defenses held through the 30th, there would be a retreat to and consolidation at Malvern Hill for one last fight on the 1st. By July 2, the Army of the Potomac would be together on their new base on the James and under the protection of the U. S. Navy's gunboats.[14]

The troubling aspects of McClellan's plan revolved around the condition of two of his divisions and their assigned taskings. Whether accidentally or intentionally, both McCall's and Slocum's divisions, though battered and exhausted, were given challenging roles by McClellan.

McCall's V Corps division had lost just short of 2,000 men in two days at the battles of Mechanicsville and Gaines' Mill. Since then, they had been retreating for two days and had been afforded no time to regroup. Despite this recent battle history, McCall's battered division was posted on the Long Bridge road, defending Glendale against attack from the west. They could expect to come up against a major Confederate force including the troops of James Longstreet and A. P. Hill. Slocum's VI Corps division had also lost about 2,000 men, all at Gaines' Mill. They had also been on the retreat since the 27th, and were posted on the Charles City road, also in defense of Glendale. They could expect to be attacked by Huger's command.

Perhaps just as troubling, McClellan decided not to remain on the field for the battle of June 30, yet named no overall commander for the expected battle. Instead of personally directing the battle, the general spent the day dealing with the issues of the final selection of the base on the James and the logistics of establishing the new base.

To add to the problem of no one general designated in command, previous orders had scrambled the corps structure. Franklin had been given overall command at White Oak Swamp Bridge, but only two of the five brigades there were from his corps. Franklin's other division, that of Slocum, was on the Charles City road, over a mile to the west. Heintzelman's III corps had the impediment of McCall's V Corps division posted smack in the middle of his corps. Sumner, commander of II Corps, had only Sedgwick's division to direct, as Richardson's division had been placed under Franklin up at White Oak Swamp Bridge. In any case, the corps commanders were on their own to attempt to coordinate the battle.[15]

Much speculation has been made over the decades as to the reason for McClellan's failure to provide a crystal clear command structure for the battle of Glendale. McClellan later stated that he wanted to scout the route all the way to Haxall's Landing. Some have suggested that he deliberately left no one in charge at Glendale. McClellan perhaps wanted to give Sumner reduced responsibility, because he had no confidence in him.

McClellan's specific actions on June 30 are a puzzlement to many. After reaching Haxall's Landing, he probably had a conversation with Keyes and was told of the discovery of the secondary road. McClellan then returned to Malvern Hill to tweak his troop dispositions and refine the wagon train movement. Using couriers and aides, he informed his generals at Glendale of the steps he was taking, and inquired as to their final troop placements. McClellan next returned to Haxall's Landing and boarded the gunboat *Galena* to meet with Commodore Rodgers to discuss locating the new army base.

Rodgers suggested the base be located some miles down the James, at the confluence of the Chickahominy. This would not be appreciated by McClellan, as it would have put his army twenty miles farther from Richmond. Barton S. Alexander, McClellan's engineer had met with Rodgers, but had left before McClellan's arrival. It is not known if Barton Alexander had given McClellan a written report on his scouting expedition.

Rodgers' problem with a base near Haxall's was that the river's channel there would take the transports too close to the Confederate batteries at City Point on the south bank of the James. Rodgers couldn't assure their safety in that area, and much preferred the downstream site. The two men compromised on Harrison's Landing, only a few miles downstream from Haxall's.[16]

McClellan dined aboard the *Galena* with Rodgers, then went ashore, where he immediately messaged his chief of staff, Randolph Marcy, to relocate the Army's headquarters temporarily to Haxall's Landing. He also told Marcy that the army would not hold Malvern Hill on a long-term basis. McClellan asked several questions. He inquired about the progress of his retreating trains, as well as the roads between the Chickahominy crossings of Long Bridge and Jones' Bridge and Glendale. He then headed for Malvern Hill for the night.

En route to Malvern Hill, McClellan stopped at his newly established headquarters at Haxall's Landing, where he sent a message to Secretary of War Stanton, demanding significant reinforcements be sent to him immediately. He also asked for more gunboats.

This message was the first Lincoln had received from McClellan in 48 hours. To make matters worse, messages sent in the previous two days from McClellan's headquarters had given an erroneous, positive outlook for the results of the fighting. The messages from McClellan's paymaster made the defeat at Gaines' Mill look like an ordered retrograde, rather than a rout. They also indicated that McClellan would be concentrating the army near Richmond. Only on the 30th, did Lincoln hear that White House Landing had been abandoned, and the army was moving to the James River. The lack of feedback was worrisome to Lincoln.

Rumors abounded in Washington and other cities of the Northeast. Lincoln sent his Secretary of State, William Seward to visit several governors, secretly calling for more volunteers. Some critics, including George Templeton Strong, saw the situation for what it was, "disaster and ruin."[17]

Also sending a message to his wife, McClellan's tone was less dismal. He wrote "I am well but worn out—no sleep for many days....I still hope to save the army." He had decided to spend the 30th tending to the logistics of establishing the new base at Harrison's landing, rather than leading his army in battle. What made this decision most bizarre, was that, as opposed to the 29th, his army was in a somewhat critical situation on the 30th. With a little bad fortune, disaster could result. Additionally, Alexander was a very competent officer and an engineer. Why did McClellan feel the need to do Alexander's job for him? The critical location would be Glendale, and McClellan chose not to be there.

A number of reasons or explanations have been put forth over the years. A lack of personal courage is not a reasonable supposition. McClellan had put himself in harm's way too many times before. Fatigue was a more reasonable explanation. He did mention his lack of sleep in the telegraph message to his wife. At least one of McClellan's staff officers had informed the general's wife that McClellan was "cut down" by the lack of sleep.

The third potential explanation was that McClellan had lost "the will to command." He seemed to be able to function as a staff officer, such as he was doing in working the logistics issues of the new base. However, he seemed to avoid taking personal command of the troops of the army in battle. In writings and testimony after the war, McClellan's generals could not seem to agree on the most probable explanation for their commanding general's behavior.[18]

As mentioned, McClellan spent most of June 30 away from the battlefield, worrying over the establishment of his new base on the James. His Confederate counterparts, meanwhile, were moving toward the imminent fight, hoping to trap part of the Federal rear guard.

Jackson was marching his command toward White Oak Swamp. Having gotten an early start, he was still concerned that he was behind schedule. Stonewall arrived at a crossroads where he was to meet Colonel Thomas Munford and his 2nd Virginia Cavalry at daybreak. Munford and his troopers were running late due to the miserable weather, and his command was the better part of a mile away.

When Munford arrived and explained to Jackson why he was late and had only a few dozen men with him, Jackson refused to accept the cavalry commander's explanation. Instead, he ordered Munford to press on with those men he did have, and drive in the Federal pickets when he found them. The annoyed Stonewall did offer artillery support from Crutchfield's guns.

Jackson kept observing Munford's men riding past him, trying to catch up to their leader. Still annoyed, he sent riders to Munford to complain about the stragglers. Munford responded by again trying to explain his problems, including the lack of food for his cavalrymen. Stonewall expressed no sympathy. Munford then ordered his adjutant to form up the stragglers where they were, rather than have them ride past Jackson in ones and twos. The exasperated Munford pressed on with about fifty men, ran into the Federal pickets and drove them back across White Oak Swamp.[19]

D. H. Hill had his division ready at dawn, but was unhappy with the plan Lee had devised. He foresaw disaster. Only a kind Providence could allow a more favorable result.

Harvey Hill was traveling with the head of his division column, and saw men in blue uniforms as he neared Savage Station. At first they appeared to him to be a Federal unit in line of battle, but turned out to be captured Federals from the field hospital. Continuing on, Hill's men passed the site where Semmes' and Brooks' brigades had fought on the 29th. Dead soldiers from the 5th Vermont lay everywhere, and all the nearby houses were filled with the wounded. Passing Savage Station proper, Hill's men started gathering up Federal stragglers. Tasking the 4th North Carolina of G. B. Anderson's brigade and the 5th North Carolina of Samuel Garland's brigade to handle the stragglers, the division eventually took in about 1,000 men.

As Hill's division advanced through ground that had been behind Federal lines when the fighting began on the 29th, they began to encounter all manner of supplies McClellan's army was forced to leave behind. After hauling away all they could and destroying all that time permitted, much of value was left behind. They came across a bounty of mules, pontoon trains, food, tools, cooking gear, clothing and medical supplies. Even some of the items the Federals had set on fire were still usable. The road ahead was littered with items from the knapsacks of the Federal troops.[20]

Huger's command, starting the day's movement from the vicinity of the Brightwell House and consisting of the brigades of Mahone, Armistead and Robert Ransom, was moving east on the Charles City road. They were having a similar experience as Hill's men in regard to stragglers.

Mahone's brigade was in the lead. Not being fully sure that all Federal troops had left the area, he prudently covered the road to Fisher's Ford. His men found a set of orders on a dead enemy soldier that directed Kearny's division to retreat, while keeping a strong artillery battery with the division. The order was no more specific than that, so wasn't all that useful to the Confederates. It did, however, reinforce Huger's concern for his left flank. False alarms caused several pauses to form a line of battle, then resumption of the march eastward. A conversation with a local near Fisher's Ford revealed that no significant enemy forces were nearby. Continuing the march down the Charles City road, Huger soon encountered Federal pickets and impediments such as felled trees in the road. The obstructions slowed the march for about a mile, up to the Brackett field. This put Huger's command about a mile from Slocum's VI Corps division, still some two miles from Glendale.[21]

At this point, Mahone had several options in dealing with the obstructions in the road. He could have his men climb over them, or he could have them leave the road and move through the trees around them. Both choices meant leaving his artillery behind. The rest of Huger's artillery, which was behind Mahone, would also have to be left behind. Another option was to cut up the trees in the road and manually remove the pieces. This would likely have to be done under fire from Federal pickets. The final option was to cut a bypass road through the trees, a relatively safe option. Mahone had a background as a railroad construction engineer, and should have fully understood the important factors in making the decision.

Mahone chose to cut up trees, but the Federals up ahead were felling more trees in the road, and were better equipped or more experienced woodmen. For a reason impossible to determine for sure, Mahone elected not to attempt to drive off the Federal axe men ahead. The obstruction problem and the concern for his left flank assured that Huger would fall behind schedule. Later in the morning, he notified General Lee that he was making slow progress.[22]

Wright's brigade, the fourth of Huger's command, was still north of White Oak Swamp. They had bivouacked near the intersection of the Charles City and New roads. At daybreak, the brigade moved east down the New road, leaving at the intersection the Georgia Sumter Artillery of Captain H. M. Ross. Wright had been told that Kearny's division had left, and the Confederates reached the north side of Jordan's Ford by 8:00 A.M. The ford was unusable, due to fallen trees, a broken down bridge and the presence of Federal pickets just west of the ford.

Wright wasted no time in dealing with the situation. He pushed forward skirmishers to drive off the Federal pickets, and sent an officer from the 3rd Georgia, Lieutenant Lorenzo F. Luckie, to find an alternate crossing site, a ford rumored by Wright's guide to be about a half mile to the west. Luckie crossed the swamp to determine the enemy position. Wright ordered Colonel Doles of the 4th Georgia to send men to look for another crossing. Fortunately for Wright, his skirmishers took two Federal prisoners who told the Confederates that the main Federal body was moving to the White Oak Swamp Bridge. Soon thereafter, Lieutenant Luckie returned and confirmed that information. Wright then ordered the brigade to continue its march. They scattered the pickets in their front as well as a rear guard and crossed the swamp. Moving into a deserted Federal camp and finding a substantial amount of abandoned stores and equipment, Wright continued eastward along the New road well into the afternoon. The brigade occupied more Federal camps, took some prisoners, and found still more abandoned stores, including a large quantity of small arms, tents, camp equipage, commissary and quartermaster's stores, a large number of entrenching tools and a very considerable quantity of medical stores.[23]

A. P. Hill and Longstreet were having a different kind of day. Starting their marches from Atlee's farm, they moved southeast along the Darbytown road. After a while, Lee joined the column, which was assigned the vital mission of interdicting the Willis Church road. The column reached the intersection with the Long Bridge road, and took it to the east. By 11:00 A.M., they were only a mile west of Glendale, and there awaited the sound of Huger's and Jackson's guns, their signal to attack. The wait was welcome in one respect. Powell Hill needed to secure water for some of his troops and arrange his brigades. He also chose to set up field hospitals.[24]

Magruder's day was probably off to the worst start of all the Confederate generals. He had been ill for two days with a digestive problem, had been up until 3:30 A.M. on the 30th, and had only about an hour's real sleep. One of Magruder's staff officers, Major Brent, described Magruder as nervously excited and involving himself in all manner of details of the command. After getting a somewhat delayed start to the day's march, Brent brought up the subject of the general's condition. Magruder admitted his digestion problem and complained that the medicine the surgeon had given him probably contained some morphine, which he knew normally irritated him. Magruder also complained about his lack of sleep.

Once the march began, few problems developed. Lee had sent Magruder a guide, but McLaws, further back in the column, grumbled about the lack of same. The column reached the Darbytown road and marched down it, following the troops of Longstreet and A. P. Hill.[25]

Thus, all of Lee's forces but those of Holmes were in motion toward Glendale. Holmes waited on the River road. As Lee's plan for June 30 started to gel, only the question of whether the trap could be closed in time remained to be answered.

While all this Confederate advance was taking place, Federal units were preparing for the expected attack. At Glendale, destined to be the focal point of the fighting on June 30, one Federal unit stood out as the most vulnerable to successful attack. McCall had the misfortune to command a V Corps division before Glendale. The division had been wracked by casualties, from the previous days' fighting and the long weeks of exposure to disease. A number of men in the line should have been in a field hospital. Psychologically, many of the men were more than ready to retreat down the Willis Church road to the protection of the gunboats of the U. S. Navy.

McCall's division had the disadvantage of being positioned a bit in front of the divisions on both flanks and was astride the Long Bridge road. Although the sound of artillery fire to the north was reported before midday, he most feared an attack from the west. His reaction was to send an infantry regiment to augment the 4th Pennsylvania Cavalry on picket duty.

Two of McCall's brigade commanders, Meade and Truman Seymour, made a personal reconnaissance of the line, did not observe the 4th Pennsylvania Cavalry, and reported back to McCall. He responded by ordering the 1st and 3rd Pennsylvania Reserves forward as pickets and set the rest of the division in line.[26]

McCall made his troop dispositions after examining the ground between the Long Bridge road and Willis Church. He placed Meade's brigade north of the Long Bridge road, along with Randol's battery. Seymour's brigade was positioned on Meade's left, responsible for the area between the Long Bridge road and the Whitlock farm. Two other batteries, those of Cooper and Kerns, were placed close to the Long Bridge road. On the left end of Truman Seymour's line were the batteries of Diederich and Knieriem. The division reserve was Seneca Simmons' brigade.

The terrain in front of McCall's division was friendly to his defense. The area was mostly farmland, open with a few trees. One small stream flowed through a large clearing. The fields of fire would be good for McCall's men. There was more open ground than McCall could defend without support on his flanks. The problem was that there were gaps on both flanks. McCall hoped the Confederates attacked down the Long Bridge road, not to either side of it.

The 3rd Pennsylvania Reserves moved smoothly into position south of the Long Bridge road by 11:00 A.M. The 1st Pennsylvania Reserves weren't so fortunate. Their commander was Colonel R. Biddle Roberts. He was provided with a Negro guide, who supposedly knew the local area. Roberts was assigning positions to individual companies as the regiment moved forward. As he placed the final company, Roberts realized that the guide had taken him right into the Confederate picket line. The Federal colonel beat a hasty retreat, marshaled the regiment, moved back to the road and set up his pickets in a less dangerous area. The guide was shot to death for his assumed treachery.[27]

The 3rd Virginia Cavalry was commanded by Thomas F. Goode. Colonel Goode was leading Longstreet's column up the Long Bridge road, and was likely the unit observed by Roberts. Longstreet was told at noon that Federal skirmishers were seen ahead. With Longstreet in command of the entire force, Richard Anderson was commanding Longstreet's division. Jenkins was acting as commander of the lead brigade, that of Anderson, and found the 1st and 3rd Pennsylvania Reserves in his front. A small firefight resulted. Meade, upon hearing the musket fire, went to the position of the 1st Reserves. He found Roberts riding up and down, trying to draw the Confederates out of their cover. Meade ordered Roberts back to his men. Roberts reported the contact to McCall, who was unsure of the situation and directed Roberts to fire on the Confederates to draw their return fire so as to determine their strength.[28]

Horatio G. Sickel, commander of the 3rd Pennsylvania Reserves, had caught sight of the Confederates, as the Virginians attempted to flank Sickel's men. Sickel wisely counterattacked and the Confederates pulled back. Sickel then withdrew his regiment toward the main Federal lines. This completed McCall's troop dispositions.

Longstreet's men were also completing their troops placements. Longstreet was personally away from the head of the column at this time, and A. P. Hill had been temporarily placed in tactical command by either Longstreet or Lee. A. P. Hill and Richard Anderson together made the troop placements, suitable for attack or defense.

Jenkins' brigade stayed astride the Long Bridge road, with three regiments north of it. James L. Kemper's brigade formed on Jenkins' right. Wilcox and Pryor were placed north of the road, backed up by Featherston. Hunton, commanding Pickett's brigade, was positioned in the center of the line. Branch's brigade went to support Kemper. The remainder of A. P. Hill's division did not leave the road.

Lee, who was still traveling with Longstreet's column, sent an order to Magruder to halt wherever he was and rest his troops. Magruder was to be ready to move again on a moment's notice. Longstreet returned at that point (between 2:30 and 3:00 P.M.) and heard cannon fire to the north. Assuming it was Huger's signal, he ordered it answered.[29]

In reality, the guns Longstreet heard were Jackson's, firing at Smith's VI Corps division near the White Oak Swamp Bridge. Jackson's chief of artillery, Stapleton Crutchfield, arrived at the north end of the bridge shortly after retreating Federal troops had set it afire. Looking around, he saw Federal artillery on the high ground south of the swamp, and sharpshooters very near the bridge. Crutchfield grabbed the artillery of the first arriving Confederate division, that of D. H. Hill, and had it hauled to high ground northwest of the bridge.

There is conflicting information about the extent and composition of Crutchfield's effort. Somewhere between 23 and 31 guns were placed on the high ground. Some came from Whiting's division as it arrived. Some of the batteries that were involved were Carter's, George W. Nelson's, Hardaway's and Rhett's, all from D. H. Hill's division. Balthis' and Reilly's batteries from Whiting's division were also there. Between 1:45 and 2:00 P.M. the batteries were set up and ready.[30]

The Confederate barrage literally caught some Federal troops with their pants down. Baldy Smith had just finished his bath, and wasn't yet dressed. A peek out the door allowed him to see the character of Jackson's artillery barrage. It was some minutes before the general was ready to provide leadership to his division.

General Smith wasn't the only Federal to be caught by surprise. Napping soldiers were confused and startled. Artillery horses and mules were motivated to stampede, causing great embarrassment for their teamsters, as well as causing injuries in Meagher's brigade. The men of a hospital panicked and fled, only to be rallied by the oaths of one of their surgeons.[31]

The 7th Maine had crossed the White Oak Swamp during the morning of June 30, and the men were trying to get some much needed sleep before the expected battle. When awakened, 200 men were sent to the right end of the Federal line as pickets. No sooner had they settled into their picket positions then the Confederate artillery barrage commenced. The Federal artillerists promptly attempted to respond, specifically the batteries of Ayres and Thaddeus P. Mott. Ayres prudently sent two guns a bit to the rear to set up their firing positions, likely because they would have a greater chance of success there. The problem for the Federals was twofold. They could not clearly see the Confederate guns at the outset of the barrage, and they were under a severe disadvantage in numbers of guns.

The Confederate fire was fairly effective. Numerous casualties in men and horses were inflicted, an ammunition chest was exploded, and great confusion occurred. Mott's battery left the field, leaving one gun behind. Ayres was able to maintain his position, but Baldy Smith ordered Ayres to withdraw.[32]

Federal artillery was only one target of the Confederate gunners. Baldy Smith's division was very vulnerable. It was well within range of the Southern gunners, on relatively flat ground. Smith's men began to retreat out of range. At least one civilian casualty occurred. The owner of the Britton house was mortally wounded when a ball struck his house.

Smith ordered the infantry of his division to withdraw about a half mile, and take cover in the woods where he'd already sent his artillery. The withdrawal was mostly orderly, with the exception of the 20th New York. In places, the ground was littered with their hats. It took two days to marshal the regiment.

Once in the woods, Smith's infantry sought such cover as they could find, mindful that they needed to support their artillery batteries. The Confederate artillery continued to pound Smith and his men.[33]

Jackson, from his vantage point north of the White Oak Swamp, could readily observe part of the Federal retreat in progress. However, his view to the west was limited, especially west of the White Oak road, where

Richardson's division and Naglee's brigade were positioned. Stonewall ordered Munford's cavalry regiment to cross to the south side of the swamp and recover a cannon abandoned by Mott's 3rd New York Light. Jackson, as well as D. H. Hill and a few staff officers decided to ride along for a closer look at the area. While crossing the swamp, the party received heavy fire from Federal troops on the south side of the swamp. Surprisingly, a Federal battery came up and added to the danger. Jackson and Hill quickly retired to the north side of the swamp.

Munford also realized that he needed to get his troopers out of harm's way. Rather than recross the swamp, which was getting deeper and wider from the recent rain, he led them downstream to a cattle path which led to a usable ford. Munford's regiment crossed there uneventfully. En route, Munford moved through several of Baldy Smith's recently abandoned camps. They recovered knapsacks and blankets, and Munford sent some Washington newspapers to Jackson, along with a note detailing his route back to the north side of the swamp. The Confederates did leave a few skirmishers on the south bank until the next day. Jackson had also ordered artillery support for Munford's sortie by having Wooding's Danville (Virginia) Artillery to suppress the Federal sharpshooters. When Munford returned to the north bank, Wooding's battery was withdrawn.[34]

The Federal artillery fire that had been aimed at Munford's cavalry and Wooding's battery was from Hazzard's battery placed west of White Oak road. The Confederates could approximate the location of Hazzard's guns, although none of the artillerists could see their opponents through the foliage. Richardson moved Hazzard's guns around for a while, attempting to find an advantage. Eventually, Hazzard was positioned back where he started and the duel continued. Ayres came up to support Hazzard and found Hazzard in his line of fire. Ayres solved the conflict by moving a short ways to the east. Setting up in his new position, he spied the gun that Mott had abandoned earlier. This was puzzling to Ayres, as he had given orders for its removal earlier in the day.[35]

The casualties of the artillery duel were thus far very light. One exception was the result of the rather precise fire of Confederate artillery against Hazzard's batteries. Although Hazzard's men were positioned on the back side of a hill from the Confederates, and suffered little from solid shot, bursting ammunition was another case. While exhibiting a bit of hands-on leadership, Captain Hazzard was struck by a bursting shell fragment, breaking his leg. Several months later, he died from complications of the wound.

Although the Federal batteries were outnumbered all afternoon, they were reinforced by Pettit's battery, sent up from Glendale by Richardson.

With Hazzard out of the fight, Lieutenant Rufus King, Jr. assumed command of the battery. King was able to scatter some Confederates he observed near the White Oak Swamp Bridge. A barrage of canister sent them back into the woods.

Ammunition became a problem to King at one point. His supply reached exhaustion, and he withdrew into a nearby hollow. As soon as he was resupplied, he ordered three guns back to their former position. Just then, Lieutenant Pettit came up and positioned his guns just to the right of King's. Once King showed Pettit the target areas he'd been firing at, Pettit engaged them with case shot. King withdrew one of his three guns back to the hollow to join the rest of his battery, leaving two up forward next to Pettit's. Pettit went to work, to the tune of some 1,600 rounds.

On the Confederate side of the swamp, Crutchfield was having similar difficulties. The most similar problem was the inability to see specific targets through the trees. Although the artillery exchange lasted until dusk, no guns were destroyed, but both sides claimed one caisson.[36]

On the Federal side, there exists no accurate casualty count of the fight at White Oak Swamp Bridge. Since the fight was predominantly an artillery affair, with indirect fire the mode of engagement, total Federal losses were likely less than 100. On the Confederate side, the exposure was even less, with only three batteries reporting casualties of only 4 killed and 19 wounded. Wise fixes the Confederate losses as 2 killed, 29 wounded and 6 missing. Perhaps the casualties would have been heavier had Jackson involved more of his artillery.[37]

After Jackson's excursion to the south bank of the swamp, he sent Hill's and Whiting's divisions to take shelter in an area thickly covered in pine. He also ordered the White Oak Swamp Bridge to be repaired, but the officers could not get the pioneers to work while exposed to the Federal artillery fire. Jackson considered the casualties the repair would likely cost and stopped the work. The ford that Munford's cavalry had found and used was available, and not under fire. For some inexplicable reason, Jackson chose not to cross his infantry there. In fact, he did not even explore that option.

Wright and his brigade had spent the day assuring that the New road was clear of Federals. By afternoon, he had come so far east that he approached the White Oak road about the time that the artillery contest was getting well started. Wright's orders from Huger didn't call for anything more, so he asked Jackson for further orders. Stonewall directed Wright to find a crossing upstream from the White Oak Swamp Bridge, as the Federals were there in force.

Wright's brigade moved back to the west, and, with the help of a guide, found a road to Brackett's Ford. He put out skirmishers from the 3rd Georgia and the 1st Louisiana on the west and east side of the road, respectively, and moved down to assess the feasibility of a crossing at Brackett's. The bridge there was destroyed and the road on the far bank of the swamp was obstructed by felled trees. Next, they made contact with pickets of the 87th New York from John C. Robinson's brigade of II Corps, who gave ground. This allowed Wright's men to assess the defenses on the south bank. To their dismay, they could see Slocum's VI Corps division with artillery support. Although Slocum's men seemed to be arrayed so as to cover the Charles City road, they could easily maintain observation of Brackett's and react if the Confederates tried to force a crossing there. Wright's men brought in two Federals captured from the pickets and they confirmed his assessment. Having no artillery with him, Wright knew he could not force a crossing against a whole division with artillery, so he backed off and continued to the west. The next crossing was Fisher's Ford, and Wright's brigade crossed there and bivouacked near the Fisher house. Wright informed Huger of Jackson's difficult situation at White Oak Swamp Bridge, but there is no record that Wright ever told Stonewall of his findings at Brackett's.

At least one Federal general (Franklin) was surprised the Confederates didn't attempt a crossing at Brackett's Ford. Franklin wrote years later that a simultaneous attack by the Confederates at White Oak Swamp Bridge and Brackett's would have caused great difficulty for the defending Federals. Jackson and Wright must share the blame for not communicating Wright's assessment of a potential at Brackett's. The end result of the day's Confederate activity was that Jackson's command did not cross the swamp and join in the battle.[38]

Franklin was wasting no time in moving up reinforcements. There was a gap of well over a mile between Richardson's and Slocum's divisions, and Richardson became aware of it right after Jackson began his artillery barrage. Franklin had been returning from a meeting with McClellan at Army headquarters, and was greeted by the sound of artillery. Understandably not pleased with the tactical situation, he promptly requested Sumner's help. Sumner gave Franklin two brigades of Sedgwick's division, which was the designated reserve at Glendale. Dana was in command of his and Sully's brigades, while Colonel William R. Lee moved up to command Dana's brigade.

Sully took ill and passed command of his brigade to Colonel James A. Suiter. These troops were fairly rested and marched smartly to the fight. Franklin asked Dana to place one brigade on Richardson's left flank, and Dana chose Suiter's men. Lee's brigade was placed in reserve. This probably improved Franklin's view of the situation.[39]

The Confederates weren't finished with looking for a suitable crossing of White Oak Swamp. Brigadier General Wade Hampton was looking in the area around Franklin's right flank. Hampton's brigade of Winder's division was in line of battle east of White Oak Swamp Bridge, but west of Munford's crossing spot. His men were in a pine forest extending from the road to the swamp. Thereabouts, Hampton discovered another suitable crossing. He cautiously crossed the swamp with a staffer and an aide (his son Wade) and discovered that the stream there was narrow and shallow, with a sand bottom. He soon observed a line of Federals facing the bridge site, in the cover of a ravine. Hampton noticed that the Federals had an exposed flank that could be exploited.[40]

Hampton returned to the north bank and sought out Whiting, then Jackson. Stonewall showed some interest in Hampton's report, asking if Hampton could build a bridge at the crossing site. Hampton agreed to build an infantry bridge, but felt the construction of a more substantial bridge would entail too much noise. Jackson ordered Hampton to proceed. Hampton formed a detail to begin the project by cutting poles well away from the swamp, thus minimizing the noise. Finishing the bridge rapidly, Hampton again crossed to the south side, and found the Federals unaware of any changes in their surroundings. Hampton returned to Stonewall to report.

What happened next was one of the more bizarre events of the war. Hampton found Stonewall sitting on a fallen tree next to White Oak road. Hampton sat down next to his superior and told him the bridge was ready for use and that the Federals were vulnerable to the right attack. Jackson listened wordlessly, hat brim pulled down and eyes closed. After Hampton finished his report, Jackson sat motionless for a while, then got up and walked away.

Jackson accomplished next to nothing the remainder of the afternoon. A staffer from Longstreet, Major J. W. Fairfax, came from Glendale, looking for reinforcements. Jackson related to Fairfax that he was stymied by the situation. Jackson passed some time by writing a letter to his wife, complaining that he was tired. Next he fell soundly asleep, so soundly asleep that nothing would awaken him. He awoke in time for the evening meal, but fell asleep while eating. After the meal, he looked around and said, "Now, gentlemen, let us at once to bed and rise with the dawn, and see if to-morrow we cannot *do something*."[41]

Later, Jackson blamed the delay in crossing the swamp on a combination of the destroyed bridge, marshy ground, and the Federals on the south bank. Other than Jackson, and possibly Lee, no one seems to have been satisfied with Jackson's thinking on the matter. Jackson did admit in a letter to his wife shortly after the Seven Days battles, that he'd suffered from "sickness and debility." Those who were there could not agree on the real reason or reasons for Jackson's poor performance on the Peninsula. Many thousands of words have been written in trying to explain Jackson's mediocre performance during the Seven Days battles, but it will likely always remain a mystery. Most writers believed physical exhaustion was a major factor, some thought sickness was in fact the prime cause, and others believed he simply was trying to protect his troops from shouldering too heavy a share of the fighting.[42]

The cause or causes of Jackson's poor performance on the Peninsula is not the only area of disagreement surrounding Stonewall. Although Jackson's contemporaries largely agree that he was guilty of "failure" at Mechanicsville, Gaines' Mill, Grapevine Bridge and White Oak Swamp, serious researchers disagree as to the quality of his performance. It has been argued that Jackson probably wouldn't have been successful in forcing a crossing at White Oak Swamp Bridge, given the forces Franklin had on hand and available nearby.[43]

Jackson did in fact affect the fighting at Glendale by his action or lack of it at White Oak Swamp Bridge. By the very presence of Jackson's command across the swamp, Franklin was compelled to keep his men in place, and even called for and received two of the three Federal reserve brigades for a time. Jackson can fairly be criticized for not ordering an infantry demonstration somewhere along the swamp, so as to further worry Franklin. We know there were three other crossings nearby: Brackett's, Hampton's and Munford's. At least Hampton's appeared to have promise. Jackson failed to properly exploit the information brought to him concerning available crossings, and let the day slip away. Jackson's best course of action would have been to stage feints at several crossings to confuse Franklin, then cross in force at Hampton's discovered site.

Some researchers claim that Jackson's orders restricted his options as to where he could cross the swamp. Surely a crossing at Hampton's site would be within Stonewall's discretion. Why else would he have asked Hampton to construct an infantry bridge there? Additionally, Jackson always had the option of sending a courier to Lee, who was with Longstreet, and asking for an amendment to his orders. The path to Longstreet was clear, as demonstrated by the ability of Major Fairfax to get through to Jackson earlier in the day. Even Jackson's Chief of Staff, Reverend Dabney wondered why this communication wasn't attempted.[44]

The discussion of the degree of Jackson's "failure" on the Peninsula and the causes for it is a fascinating one, but what is more important is the effect on the fighting of June 30. The reality is that Jackson failed to fully occupy Franklin for the day. Although Franklin initially was in a bit of a panic, and was given two of Sedgwick's reserve brigades as reinforcements, later in the day Franklin was able to send them back to Glendale. Even later in the day, Franklin sent two of Richardson's brigades to Glendale. Therefore, about 10,000 infantry went to Glendale that could have been tied down by a more aggressive Stonewall Jackson.

It is hard to argue with the criticism of Jackson's failure to communicate with Lee. However, General Lee may fairly share the blame for poor communication that day. Lee failed to check on Jackson's progress, even though Jackson had performed poorly on three previous occasions that week. Poor communication and poor maps were common problems all week in the Army of Northern Virginia.[45]

Although the criticisms of Jackson's performance at White Oak Swamp on June 30 vary considerably, the contention by some that Stonewall Jackson was trying to keep his men out of the fight at Glendale, or that he was deliberately disobeying Robert E. Lee's orders is unsupportable. Of all the officers in Lee's army, Jackson would be the least likely to be guilty of such behavior. A deeply religious and highly principled gentleman, his service to country always took first priority in his actions.

The answer to the mystery likely lies in a combination of causes. They can be summed up, however, in two words—total exhaustion. Jackson was suffering from sleep deprivation, physical exhaustion, poor nutrition, stress and frustration. It was perhaps just happenstance that this combination of factors caused him to break down on the afternoon of the 30th, at one of the key moments of the campaign. The signs of an impending inability to function were there all along, but were not noticed by Jackson, his staff or his surgeon.[46]

Huger had a fairly straight-forward assignment for June 30. He was to march his command eastward on the Charles City road until he made contact with the Federal lines northwest of Glendale. His progress had been slow and frustrating. The Federal pickets had felled trees in the road for some two miles. William Mahone's brigade, in the lead, finally reached the Brackett field, in the vicinity of the Williams house. This was likely in mid-afternoon, after Wright had determined that Brackett's Ford was unsuitable for a crossing of White Oak Swamp.

From the Brackett field, numerous Federal troops were observed less than a mile in front, on a ridge. This was Henry Slocum's VI Corps division. Unable to maneuver freely due to the obstructions in the road,

Huger decided to use his artillery. He moved up a section of Moorman's battery, which opened fire.

Slocum decided to respond in kind. Two full batteries, under Porter and Upton, as well as a section of Hexamer's battery, engaged Moorman's guns. The distance between the opposing forces were short. Some Federal pickets were only a hundred yards from Moorman's guns. Mahone moved his brigade around trying to confuse the Federal gunners, but they always seemed to know his position.

De Russy's battery pitched in for a while. Some of Porter's guns overheated during the engagement, and two sections of Randolph's battery were sent forward to relieve Porter, but were never ordered to commence firing. On the Confederate side, Lieutenant Colonel Allen S. Cutts, commander of the Sumter (Georgia) Battalion of the Reserve Artillery, advanced three batteries, but also failed to get the order to fire. Amazingly, Moorman's section forced the Federals to lie down to dodge the grape and canister.[47]

This contact has been called the Action at Brackett's. Though seemingly an unequal contest in terms of guns, it lasted for several hours and consumed a large quantity of ammunition. Slocum was running very low at one point. The result of the fight was negligible. Casualties were less than a hundred on the Confederate side, and less than fifty for the Federals.

During the artillery fight, both opponents examined ways to employ their infantry effectively. Huger and Mahone looked at several tactics to employ, but could not come up with a plan before the daylight remaining was in short supply. Huger did order the brigades of Armistead and Wright, who had just rejoined the command, to move south at first light the next morning. The Confederates spent the night on the soggy ground. Huger retired to the Fisher house.

On the Federal side, it took Slocum's plan a little longer to materialize. When he became aware that the Federals at Glendale were under pressure, and the fight in his front had ceased, he ordered Bartlett's brigade to take position near the Brackett field. Bartlett started his men toward the new position, but Confederate troops appeared across Hass Creek. Upton's battery took them under fire with canister and the Confederates withdrew in a hurry. Before Slocum could take another action, Heintzelman arrived and asked for a brigade to reinforce Kearny. Slocum gave up Taylor's brigade, then decided to retain Bartlett's men.[48]

Huger's advance was weak at best. Jackson had advanced not at all. Lee's plan, once again, was falling apart. Both subordinate generals had failed General Lee, dooming his plan for the day. Lee's subsequent report seems to be more critical of Huger than of Jackson.[49]

By not creating any significant pressure on the defenders at White Oak Swamp Bridge, Jackson had allowed about 10,000 additional Federal troops to fight at Glendale. By his ineffective advance down the Charles City road, Huger had allowed Slocum the option of sending Taylor's brigade to Glendale to fight. Neither Jackson nor Huger had a surplus of combat power relative to the defenders they faced. Neither had a great probability of successfully performing their assigned tasks, but neither performed satisfactorily. Jackson didn't even seem to try. Their poor performances meant that Glendale would be well defended, and Longstreet and A. P. Hill would have a rough day there.

Lee's generals were poor communicators during most of the Seven Days, especially on June 30. Huger was, relatively speaking, better than average on that day. He at least notified Lee that he was encountering obstructions, even if his message was ambiguous. Lee, as guilty as his subordinates, failed to request clarification or amplification of the message. While Jackson had a choice of several crossings at which to feint, demonstrate or actually try to cross, Huger had few options, and some would bring him no advantage. He could go south to the Long Bridge road, but that was contrary to his orders and would simply serve to put him with Longstreet and A. P. Hill. Huger would be in the way, so to speak. Had Huger asked Lee to send him south to Malvern Hill via the Carter's Mill road, he would have arrived after dark, accomplishing nothing. His mission was to put pressure on the defenders at Glendale. He failed to do this.[50]

As mentioned above, Lee's report seemed to treat Huger's failure in a harsher manner than those of Jackson. While Huger failed to put sufficient pressure on Slocum on the Charles City road, Jackson let 25,000 Confederate troops sit essentially idle while their commanding general was in a dysfunctional physical/mental state.

Lee, as he often chose to do, was traveling with Longstreet. None other than President Davis rode up to Lee, just as Longstreet ordered his batteries to fire, in response to what he thought was Huger's arranged signal. In an obvious attempt to turn the tables on Lee for a conversation the two had at Mechanicsville a few days prior, Davis remarked to Lee that Lee was in too dangerous a position for a commanding general. Lee brushed off the jab by claiming to be gathering information about enemy movements and plans, and told Davis that he, as President of the Confederacy, was not in a proper place. Davis replied that he was on the same mission.

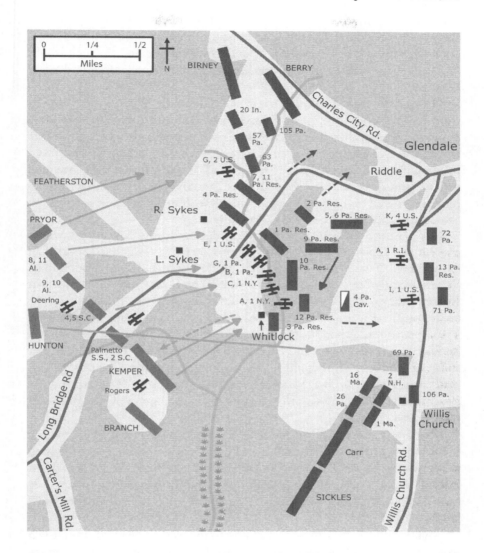

Map 20.3—Glendale, Longstreet's Attacks, June 30

The verbal fencing complete, the two leaders turned the conversation to the plans for the day. Longstreet joined the conversation and later remembered it as a "pleasant conversation, anticipations of the result of a combination supposed to be complete and prepared for concentration."[51]

The pleasant conversation was interrupted by Federal artillery fire in reply to Longstreet's ordered fire, and A. P. Hill took charge of the situation, ordering both Lee and Davis off the field, reminding them of the potential disaster for the Confederacy should one fateful shell take both their lives. They moved again, and Hill was satisfied. As luck would have it, Federal fire soon swept the area, wounding one courier and a few horses.[52]

Longstreet set about engaging the offending Federal guns, which were from Cooper's battery, firing from near the Long Bridge road. Jenkins, commanding Richard Anderson's brigade, was closest to the target, and Longstreet tasked Jenkins to silence Cooper's guns. The was a misunderstanding between Longstreet and Jenkins. Longstreet intended to have the guns silenced, but Jenkins thought he was to attack them. Jenkins ordered his entire brigade to advance, minus four companies of the 6th South Carolina out on the skirmish line.

At his time, General Lee was moving over to the River road, where pickets had reported enemy presence. Rosser's 5th Virginia Cavalry had encountered Federal skirmishers that morning on the Long Bridge road. When Longstreet came up, Rosser withdrew. Longstreet then had sent Rosser over to the River road to assess the situation there. Upon his arrival on the River road, Rosser had an unpleasant surprise. He observed V Corps troops, either Morrell's or Sykes' division, marching toward the James River across Malvern Hill. Rosser knew that any Federals that got south of Malvern Hill would not be captured or killed. Rosser sent this information about 1:00 P.M. to Holmes and Longstreet. They apparently never received the message. Rosser then decided to go see General Lee at Jeb Stuart's request.

Lee went to personally observe the Federal retreat across Malvern Hill. He told Longstreet that Holmes had Federals in his front, then rode with Rosser to the River road. Lee sent Longstreet's engineer, Major Meade, to inform Holmes of what Rosser had observed. Although it is unsure, Lee probably saw Federal troops organizing and digging in or their trains still crossing Malvern Hill.[53]

Sykes' division was, in fact upon and to the west of Malvern Hill. Even worse for the Confederates, McClellan was sending him many batteries with which to defend the eminence. The eight batteries of Carlisle, Edwards, Weed, Robertson, Nairn, Beam, Smead, and Voegelee were there. Warren's brigade was in the valley to the west of Malvern Hill. The rest of the troops were on the hill itself, which was a superb defensive position. The plateau was about 75 feet above the River road, adding extra range to the Federal guns. The field of fire was excellent in all directions. Morell's V Corps division was also there, as well as most of Couch's IV Corps division.[54]

Not only did the Federals have a perfect position from which to fight one more day to complete their retreat to the James, but they were fortunate to have Porter there, organizing the defense. By 4:00 P.M., Porter watched the last of the trains and retreating artillery pass his position. At this point, Lee could only hope to cut off the Federal rear guard at Glendale. Most of McClellan's army had already escaped. Lee did have the possibility of inflicting some damage on McClellan's trains as they completed the last leg of their long retreat. The instrument of Lee's intention would have to be Holmes' command.

Based on a suggestion by one of his staffers, Holmes ordered James Deshler, his artillery chief, to post a battery of rifled guns about a half mile from the Federal positions. Deshler took one section each from Branch's, Brem's and French's batteries. To site the guns, Deshler had to move them through heavy foliage, and was only able to set up five of them. The 30th Virginia was tasked to support the guns, but Holmes, eager to better assess the tactical situation, moved forward with most of his command.

Holmes found Lee already there. Lee approved Holmes' actions and directed that the attack begin only when Holmes had all his men in position. Lee departed and Holmes continued his preparations for his attack. The dust clouds kicked up by Holmes' movements revealed their positions, and the Federals signaled their gunboats in the nearby James River. As soon as Deshler's artillery commenced firing (around 4:00–5:00 P.M.) the Federal response was immediate and overwhelming. Fire came from the aforementioned eight batteries on Malvern Hill, Osborn's battery north of the plateau, and Martin's battery moving to support Warren's brigade in the valley west of Malvern Hill. The lopsided artillery duel was 44 guns to five. There were even a few rounds fired by the Federal gunboats.

The effect of the Federal artillery fire was immediate and startling. Cavalry horses stampeded, knocking down objects in their path. Even some reserve artillery batteries could not take the pounding and withdrew. Fleeing guns became hung up in the thick Virginia underbrush, motivating drivers to cut traces and abandon them. A number of guns and caissons were left in the wood. Some were taken by Warren's brigade.

President Davis showed up at the scene of the chaos and succeeded in personally rallying many of the fleeing infantry and artillerists. Shortly thereafter, another shell impacted near the top of a tree, and the rout resumed.[55]

Holmes requested an infantry regiment from Junius Daniel just after the cavalry and artillery rout began. Daniel sent the 45th North Carolina under Lieutenant Colonel John H. Morehead, and told them to lie down in the road. The 45th was under a double hazard. Federal artillery was firing in their direction, and Confederate gunners were coming down the road toward the infantrymen. The regiment soon broke and its officers were unable to quickly reorganize them. In due time, the 45th was rallied and moved toward Holmes' position. Holmes was in a house and was extremely hard of hearing. Upon exiting from the house, he remarked, "I thought I heard firing."

Deshler maintained the losing side of the artillery duel for about an hour. A hour was long enough to prove its futility for the Confederates. Many gunners and horses had become casualties, and caissons were left behind, as there were insufficient horses to bring off all the guns. Some caissons were blown up by one side or the other. The withdrawal of the Confederate guns did not totally stop the Federal artillery. The gunboats *Aroostook* and *Galena* maintained a fire for several hours, and at least one Federal army battery continued to fire canister. No battery commander would claim responsibility, however, as at least one officer and two corporals from Buchanan's brigade were apparently killed by errant rounds. Weed blamed the battery of Joseph Nairn, which Weed claimed fired numerous rounds of canister at a target some 1,500–1,800 yards away. This allegation was supported by the report of Captain Thomas W. Walker of the 3rd U. S. Infantry.

This engagement was called Malvern Cliff or Turkey Bridge. Casualties on the Federal side were almost negligible, with two artillerists in Weed's battery killed. On the Confederate side, seventeen artillerists were wounded. In the infantry, there were three killed and 42 wounded by enemy fire, and several men were hurt by fleeing horses.[56]

A number of authors have roundly criticized Holmes, claiming that he could have done more on June 30. He is characterized as insufficiently aggressive and too quick to call for reinforcements. Some even believe that Holmes could have captured Malvern Hill.

Although Holmes might be rightly criticized for his handling of his troops on June 30, it is not realistic to assert that Malvern Hill could have been taken by Holmes with his 6,300 infantry and supporting artillery. Porter had a tremendous advantage of position, and many additional troops to call upon if needed. Holmes had a mission that had little probability of success. He did the only thing he could reasonably do, use some of his artillery to annoy the retreating trains. It is interesting to note that Porter reportedly slept through the entire artillery duel. Perhaps this is the best indicator that Holmes was not a serious threat to Malvern Hill.[57]

Around 9:00 P.M., Holmes gave up the idea of mounting any attack on Porter. He prudently withdrew his command back towards the intersection of the Long Bridge and River roads, and went into bivouac. There were similarities between his performance and those of Huger and Jackson. Essentially, all three generals fought only with their artillery. There was a difference between them, however. Holmes did all he was capable of doing. That cannot be said of the others.[58]

This leaves Magruder's activities on June 30 to examine. Magruder, with 14,000 men, began his day just west of Savage Station. Prince John's mission for the day was to move his men to the Darbytown road and function as the reserve for the commands of Longstreet and A. P. Hill. Lee likely did this to be sure that Longstreet had enough combat power to break the Federal lines at Glendale. Magruder had a long day's march, so he had to begin his day rather early.

The reinforcements that Holmes had requested earlier in the day were supplied from Magruder's force. Magruder had been making uneven progress on his march. He had suffered a delay when he came up on the rear of A. P. Hill's division, and was in the vicinity of Timberlake's store, about a mile southeast of Atlee's when Lee's message caught up with him. Lee's instructions were for Magruder to hold his position. After two and a half hours of doing nothing, he was ordered to go to Holmes' assistance.

There is still some uncertainty of how the request for Magruder to assist Holmes came about, and exactly the routing of the order, but Magruder said the order came through Longstreet. Whatever the case, the order had far-reaching negative consequences for the Confederate cause. A second communication from Longstreet advised Magruder to move more quickly by leaving behind his artillery. It promised that Longstreet would provide artillery if Magruder later needed it.

Next, Colonel Chilton sent word that he wanted to show Magruder his positions. Magruder sent one of his staff officers, Major Brent, to Holmes to coordinate Magruder's positions. Since Chilton was going to give Magruder his positions, this action seemed likely to cause more uncertainty. If nothing else, at least Magruder had opened communication with Holmes.

Magruder went to see Chilton, and Magruder's men began to move. Semmes' brigade, responsible for protecting the artillery, used the Darbytown road, but the rest of the command took a short cut suggested by a local farmer. Major Brent used the shortcut also, found General Holmes, and asked for the advice on positions that Magruder desired. Holmes was short with him, asserted that he had no advice to offer, and said he couldn't tell Brent where the Federals were. Brent decided to return to Magruder, and Holmes had no message whatsoever for the major to take with him. Brent did take a few minutes to talk with some of the men around Holmes, and came away thinking Holmes unfit for command. This meeting took place after the cannon fire and the rout of Holmes' men.[59]

Chilton and Magruder met at the intersection of the Long Bridge and Darbytown roads. Magruder briefed Chilton on the current position of his command. Chilton then instructed Magruder as to their assigned position in the line. The two men rode to the intersection of the Long Bridge and River roads. This intersection was where Lee wanted Magruder's right flank to be. From there, Magruder was to march to Malvern Hill to aid Holmes.

Magruder was animated. He sent a staffer to bring back Semmes' brigade, and another to try and hurry up the rest of his command. A third staff officer was to stay at the intersection and place the troops as they arrived. Magruder rode at a gallop to find Holmes, looking for an hour unsuccessfully. Near sunset, Magruder gave up the search, assigned the task to a staffer and returned to Semmes' position.

The rest of Magruder's men, other than Semmes' brigade, reached the Long Bridge/River road intersection around 6:00 P.M. Shortly thereafter, they received an order from Magruder's inspector general, Lieutenant Colonel Cary, to move to the point specified by Chilton. On the River road, McLaws came upon Henry A. Wise, and told him where they were all headed. Wise was aghast that they would be in range of the dreaded Federal gunboats. Another messenger from Magruder rerouted McLaws down the Long Bridge road.

After turning onto the Long Bridge road, McLaws had gotten only about a mile when he met Magruder. Magruder had already found Semmes in position, and ordered him to move his men into the woods. Semmes didn't want to do that, as it was getting dark and it would be hard to stay organized in the woods. Magruder was adamant, inferring that the order came from Lee. Semmes complied.

Magruder continued toward the River road, now receiving an order from Longstreet instructing Magruder to march with half his force to Glendale. Magruder rode to the west until he found McLaws, ordering him to rest his men in position. Magruder then decided to stay put and rest while his staff rounded up Jones' and Magruder's own division for the move to Glendale. While Magruder was speaking with McLaws, Semmes rode up. As Semmes had feared, the move into the dark woods had caused the brigade to become separated.

Magruder rode back to the intersection of the Long Bridge and River roads. There he received yet another change of orders, his seventh message of the day. It was from Chilton, and directed that Magruder come to Glendale with his entire command. Magruder remained at the intersection and sent staff officers to relay the newest orders to his units. Eventually, he went to meet Longstreet and Lee. Lee wanted Magruder to relieve Longstreet's men, which took Prince John until 3:00 A.M. on July 1. Magruder finally sought some desperately needed sleep.

The march was about seventeen miles for some of Magruder's men, and they were on the road for some eighteen hours, a combination of marching and waiting. It was a hot June Virginia day, and most of the men remembered it as "most fatiguing."[60]

Lee returned to Longstreet's position near Glendale after reviewing Holmes' situation west of Malvern Hill. By the time Lee returned, the battle was ongoing. At 4:00 P.M., Jenkins' brigade moved forward to silence Cooper's battery. Jenkins, with the 4th and 5th South Carolina as his left, the Palmetto Sharpshooters and 2nd South Carolina as his right, moved toward McCall's line, somewhat right of center.

Cooper's battery was supported by the 9th Pennsylvania Reserves of Truman Seymour's brigade. The 9th went into line of battle just behind the battery. The 10th Pennsylvania Reserves went into line perpendicular to the 9th, with the 10th's right adjacent to the 9th's left. The 12th Pennsylvania Reserves were on the left of the 10th. Six companies of the 12th were moved forward to some improvised fortifications near the Whitlock farmhouse. Their position put them on the left end and some 200 yards out in front of the rest of the brigade. The 10th and 12th Pennsylvania Reserves were supporting the batteries of Diederich and Knieriem. Truman Seymour also found a small hill slightly behind the right four companies of the 12th Reserves, put two guns on it and pulled the four companies behind the guns.

To the right of McCall, Randol positioned his battery. He placed two sections on the northwest side of the Long Bridge road, decided there wasn't room enough for Olcott's section, and kept them limbered up. James Thompson's battery of Kearny's division was placed to Randol's right. Both Meade and Truman Seymour requested Thompson to aid them in fending off a Confederate attack down Long Bridge road. This task would have required Thompson to change his front, so he reminded the two brigade commanders that his primary duty was to support his own troops first. General Kearny ordered Thompson to reposition so that his guns would be pointed west. Once Kearny left, Thompson put his guns in echelon, and tried to cover as large an area as possible. Randol then put one of Olcott's guns to his own left, on the Long Bridge road.

The 4th Pennsylvania Reserves was put in Randol's immediate rear, and the last available troops of the 11th Pennsylvania Reserves formed up behind the 4th Reserves. In the center, most of Seneca Simmons' brigade, consisting of the 2nd, 5th, 8th and 13th Pennsylvania Reserves, were in reserve. The 4th Pennsylvania Cavalry was positioned behind Truman Seymour on the left.[61]

Jenkins advanced toward McCall's lines, causing the 1st and 3rd Pennsylvania Reserves to continue falling back. The 1st Reserves moved close to Cooper's battery, motivating Jenkins to have Cooper's artillery horses shot. When Jenkins' men fired a volley at the horses, the 9th Pennsylvania Volunteers changed front to repel a Confederate attack from its left. Once in their new alignment, they could no longer support Cooper's guns. However, the 1st Pennsylvania Reserves replaced them in their original position.

The 3rd Pennsylvania Reserves had the discipline to allow the Confederates of Jenkins' brigade to come within about fifty yards of their lines before delivering a volley of musket fire. A second volley stopped the attack briefly. Jenkins resumed the attack under musket and artillery fire, and the 3rd Pennsylvania Reserves looked for a way to escape the charge. About this time, the 3rd also took some friendly fire and broke. They fled the field to the rear, and were not able to fight as a unit for the remainder of the day. Some of the better soldiers fought with other regiments, however.

Jenkins had a problem. He was advancing without support, as his orders had been no more than to silence a battery. Longstreet was still waiting for the signal from Huger to initiate the main battle. As the sole attacking Confederate brigade, Jenkins drew everyone's attention on the Federal side of the line. Of the nearby Federal batteries, a gun from Olcott's section of Randol's battery, as well as the batteries of Amsden and Cooper took particular notice of Jenkins. Jenkins knew he needed artillery support, and attempted to bring up Edmund G. Chapman's battery. Chapman's three guns were forced to withdraw by the thirteen Federal guns arrayed against them.[62]

Despite the fact that charging artillery in the open without artillery support of your own is desperate work, Jenkins continued his attack. A mounted officer is always a desirable target for enemy infantry as well as artillery. Jenkins was extremely fortunate not to have shed his blood during the charge on Cooper's battery. He lost his sword, had tack damaged, his overcoat ruined, was hit twice by spent fragments, and lost two horses during the day, all this from musket balls and shrapnel.

Once again, President Davis appeared on the field and tried to involve himself in affairs at the brigade level. He intended to gather troops in the rear and personally lead them back into the battle, but was fortunately convinced that a staff officer should do it instead.[63]

Trying to overcome the guilt of suffering so many casualties in his brigade, Jenkins determined to continue his effort to capture Cooper's battery. Three more times Jenkins charged, and each time his brigade was repulsed by the Federal batteries and six companies of the 1st Pennsylvania Reserves. Muskets overheated, bayonets were ordered, and fighting became hand-to-hand at times.[64]

The Pennsylvanians had been holding on all afternoon primarily due to their artillery superiority. Unfortunately, at the start of the artillery fight, Seymour had ordered the caissons of Amsden's battery to the rear. When it became time to bring them up to replenish their ammunition, Amsden's men could not locate them. Inevitably, Amsden exhausted his ammunition supply, and McCall ordered the battery to withdraw. Amsden tearfully complied.

With the use of Amsden's battery denied to him, Seymour had a whole different situation on his hands. The Confederates saw Amsden leave, their spirits buoyed by the fact, and stepped up their efforts, concentrating on the left flank of the 1st Reserves. Despite Cooper's continuing fire of canister, Jenkins' men forced the Federal artillerists to abandon their guns and retire back toward the Willis Church road.

Almost immediately, the Federals bounced back. The 1st Reserves took cover in some trees, firing from some protection there. The 9th Reserves was moving back to its original position. Its commander, Colonel C. F. Jackson, met Cooper, who told of losing his guns. Jackson's men, aided by Randol's battery, drove the Confederates back. Fighting was again hand-to-hand over the contested guns. Cooper was able to carry off his dead and wounded.

Jenkins was joined by the 9th and 10th Alabama from Wilcox's brigade. Again the Federals were forced from their guns, since no horses were there to remove them. The 2nd Reserves then charged, but was repulsed and went back to its original position. The 9th Reserves also decided to retire. The 10th Alabama lost its colors in the close quarters fighting.[65]

It had been a very sanguinary contest for Cooper's guns. The Pennsylvania Reserves paid dearly. The 1st Reserves lost 14 killed, 83 wounded and 10 missing. The 9th Reserves lost 17 killed, 84 wounded and 36 missing. Cooper lost 4 killed and 10 wounded. The Confederates, as attackers, paid even more dearly. The Palmetto Sharpshooters lost 39 killed and 215 wounded. The 9th Alabama lost 31 killed, 95 wounded and 4 missing. Overall, Jenkins, according to Porter Alexander, lost 562 killed or wounded and 27 missing. This was from a brigade that entered the fight with only 1200 men. Wilcox's brigade, to include the 10th Alabama, lost 213 men.[66] Sadly for the Confederates, this great sacrifice failed to break the Federal line at Glendale. The Army of the Potomac still had a viable line of retreat. The fight of June 30 would go on.

It quickly became obvious to Longstreet that Jenkins had greatly exceeded his orders to simply silence a battery, and had become totally engaged with the center of McCall's line. At around 5:00 P.M., Longstreet ordered James L. Kemper, who was on Jenkins' right, to attack. Kemper's brigade, with the 24th, 7th, 1st, 11th and 17th Virginia aligned from left to right, had been previously cautioned by Longstreet to watch the right flank. Kemper aligned the 17th to face to the right, advanced some skirmishers farther out front, and placed Rogers' battery on a small hill near the 17th. As soon as Kemper got Longstreet's order to attack, he realigned the 17th Virginia and passed the word down the line to attack. Due to the dense foliage, Kemper soon discovered it was almost impossible to move a brigade in good order. A Federal artillery barrage provided by the batteries of Knieriem and Diederich made the maneuver that much more difficult. As the Virginians drove in the enemy pickets, they seemed to gain motivation, and advanced at too rapid a pace.

Kemper's brigade moved rapidly through two bands of woods and into the Whitlock field. Kemper's men had hit a critical part of the Federal line. The two batteries were supported by six companies of the 12th Pennsylvania Reserves. A break in the Federal lines here could allow Kemper to reach the Willis Church road. If he could advance that far, and be reinforced there, Lee's objective of cutting off Federal retreat could be reached.[67]

The two Federal batteries maintained their fire as Kemper advanced. A few rounds from Cooper's battery also fell on the Confederates. After the first three volleys from the 12th Pennsylvania Reserves had little noticeable effect on the advancing Virginians, the Confederate attack continued unimpeded. Other than some difficulty by part of the 17th Virginia in crossing McDowell Creek, the Confederate advance was orderly and steady. After a brief hand-to-hand combat, the Federals were driven back, and Kemper's men captured Knieriem and Diederich's guns. Knieriem had only two guns there and Diederich was already out of canister and explosive shells. This resulted in the 12th Reserves abandoning the Whitlock house. Behind the Whitlock house, the men of the 4th Pennsylvania Cavalry had to retreat on foot, as they were dismounted when Confederate pressure reached them. There was not sufficient time for the troopers to reach their mounts.

The flight of infantry, artillerists and dismounted troopers to the rear was noticed with alarm by the regiments on both flanks of the 12th Reserves, including Hooker to the south of the Whitlock farm, and

Edwin Sumner, who only had a single brigade left in the Glendale area. Sumner put Burns' brigade in line and personally placed the regiments. He positioned the 72nd Pennsylvania on the right, the 69th Pennsylvania in the center, the 106th Pennsylvania on the left, and the 71st Pennsylvania behind Kirby's battery, which was on a slight eminence close to the R. H. Nelson house. This put Kirby about a half mile east of the Whitlock house. Before long, however, Sumner pulled the 69th out of line and sent it to Hooker. Sumner further tweaked his dispositions by moving the 106th Pennsylvania to where it could better support Grover's brigade.

Grover's brigade was on the right end of Hooker's line and, therefore, the closest to the embattled brigade of Truman Seymour. Grover had the 26th Pennsylvania and the 16th Massachusetts in front, with the 1st Massachusetts and 2nd New Hampshire behind them. Grover's fifth regiment, the 11th Massachusetts, was positioned far away on the division left, protecting that flank.[68]

McCall was moving the 13th Pennsylvania Reserves to the left of his line as he saw the rout of the 12th Reserves. McCall ordered Simmons to commit his regiments to bolster the line. Simmons picked the 5th and 8th Reserves, and added three companies of the 1st Reserves. The 10th Reserves were also moving from their position in the right rear of the 12th Reserves to attack the Confederates' left flank.

Unfortunately for James L. Kemper, his attack had gone too far, too fast. The Confederate units on his flanks had not kept pace. Branch's brigade, on Kemper's right, received the order to attack while preparing supper, and essentially fell in behind Kemper. Branch also lacked a local guide. Jenkins had been on Kemper's left, but was well into his advance, and had moved in a slightly different direction. Kemper and his men knew their right flank was vulnerable. Some of the men were urging retreat. Kemper ordered a withdrawal.

Before Kemper's ordered withdrawal could go very far, Seneca Simmons and the 10th Pennsylvania Reserves attacked. Kemper's men broke, and many were captured. Kemper made every effort to reform his brigade along the Long Bridge road. Of the 1,443 men he took into battle that day, he lost 414. Some were captured simply due to bad luck, such as getting away from the fighting and wandering into Federal troops that had not been involved in the fighting. Some were captured while simply trying not to get trampled by attacking Federals.[69]

The retreat of Kemper's brigade did not equal salvation for McCall. While Kemper was retreating, Branch was coming up. Kemper indicated to Branch's men where he had just retreated from, and Branch pressed on. Eppa Hunton, sick but in command of Pickett's brigade, joined the advance. They had begun moving to Jenkins' left, west of the Long Bridge road. In front of them, Dearing's battery had set up and commenced fire. This drew an artillery response from the Federals. Hunton's men suffered some casualties. About 5:00 P.M., Hunton's brigade began moving east, crossed Long Bridge road, aligned their ranks and continued on. Crossing McDowell Creek, they had to pass through retreating troops from Kemper's brigade, which made keeping their formation just a bit more difficult.

Meanwhile, the 10th Reserves had rallied around the Whitlock house. McCall was fortunate to get Knieriem's and Diederich's gunners back to their guns. Casualties to officers were significant. Capt. Henry Biddle was mortally wounded while trying to get orders to the artillerists. Colonel George Hays, commander of the 8th Pennsylvania Reserves, was injured when his horse was killed and fell on him. This left the 8th Reserves without their colonel for the next Confederate attack.

Hunton's brigade continued their advance, but without Hunton. Suffering from physical exhaustion, he passed command to Colonel John B. Strange, commander of the 19th Virginia. Strange noticed they were taking fire from the right, and ordered the brigade slightly to the left, where there was a woods in which they could adjust and reform. This put them onto Branch's right.

There was a surplus of confusion on the part of both sides. Identifying friend from foe became difficult for Federals and Confederates alike. The Confederates began to kill or capture that part of the 10th Pennsylvania Reserves that were fighting from the breastworks. When this happened, the remainder of the 10th Reserves, as well as the 5th and 8th Reserves, rose up to charge. Immediately, they received a volley of musket fire that happened to cause numerous casualties in their officer ranks. Seneca Simmons was mortally wounded. Truman Seymour's horse was hit, and threw his master.

After some intense fighting, the Federals broke. Infantry, artillerists and horses fled the battlefield. The Confederates captured two of Knieriem's guns, but Diederich's battery limbered up and left early. The German batteries had again wasted no time in fleeing, getting a head start just as Strange began his charge.

Just as the rout began, the 13th Reserves (Bucktails) had just made it to the Nelson house. Major Stone had his men in line, and ordered them to lie down. Fleeing troops ran past them, and Stone urged the officers of the retreating troops to reform behind his regiment. As soon as the field of fire was clear, Stone's men fired a volley at the pursuing Confederates. Stone knew he couldn't hold his position with the small force at his command.

It was apparent that Branch's and Strange's men were now a real threat to the Willis Church road.[70]

As soon as unfolding events appeared to be negative, Sedgwick sent for the brigades of Sully and Dana. These two brigades had earlier been sent to the White Oak Swamp area to reinforce the Federal troops there. They had marched up there as rapidly as they could, and now were called back, also in a hurry. The heat and dust made rapid marching even more difficult. Some men fell out from exhaustion, and were left by the roadside. General Sumner sent several messages urging Dana and Sully to hurry. Sedgwick also sent a similar message. He was concerned that the brigades would either arrive too late or would be shocked by the sight of the embattled Pennsylvania Reserves.

Sully arrived and, though he was sick, tried to gather up and reform some of the Pennsylvania Reserves. The best he could manage was a line some 400 yards behind the front lines. There Stone organized the 13th Reserves. Seymour was missing from the battlefield. Between his horse falling on him, and the rout of his brigade, Seymour was in a daze. He was discovered around 6:00 P.M. walking on the road to White Oak Swamp Bridge, in a bedraggled condition, with a bullet hole in his hat. He said that his brigade was "entirely dispersed." He was searching for Franklin, to get help. Finding him, Franklin gave his dazed comrade a brandy to settle him down. Thus, the Pennsylvanians had the double liability of Seneca Simmons dead and Seymour temporarily unfit to command.[71]

The Federal resistance was desperate. Kirby's battery maintained a steady fire on the Confederates, who reacted by preparing to attack the battery. Burns moved one of his regiments, the 72nd Pennsylvania, into the woods in front of the battery to support the artillerists. Some help was received from Tompkins' battery, positioned to the north of Kirby. Then Seeley's battery added its fire to the defense. The Confederates continued their advance.

The 19th Massachusetts, from Dana's brigade, arrived and moved into the trees. They were shortly joined by the 20th Massachusetts of the same brigade. The 7th Michigan came into line south of the Massachusetts regiments, and the 42nd New York formed on the left of the 7th Michigan. This completed the deployment of Dana's brigade at Glendale.

Sully's brigade began to arrive, led by the 1st Minnesota. Dana personally placed them in the woods south of the 72nd Pennsylvania. As the three remaining regiments of Sully's brigade arrived, they were placed to extend the line to the north of the 1st Minnesota. From north to south, they were the 82nd New York, the 34th New York and the 15th Massachusetts.[72]

Hooker's division was positioned south of McCall's, and he witnessed the shattered units retreating past his right flank and even through his lines. He had concern about the effect on his men from seeing their broken comrades go by. Soon the Confederates appeared, and Grover's brigade was closest to the approaching attackers. The 16th Massachusetts was the right end of Grover's line, and opened fire. The 69th Pennsylvania of Burns' brigade and a company of the 26th Pennsylvania joined in the musket fire as the Confederates came into their view. The attacking Confederates were Strange's small brigade, down to only 723 muskets, and the heavy Federal fire caused them to break. They retreated so fast that they were forced to abandon prisoners they had taken. Grover took advantage of this Confederate break and pursued with the 1st Massachusetts. Strange was forced back into the woods. The 69th Pennsylvania had advanced uphill to the previous site of Diederich's and Knieriem's batteries and joined in the pursuit of Strange. The 26th Pennsylvania also advanced slightly. In the relative safety of the woods, Strange struggled to rally his men.

A little to the north, Branch was in an intense fight with John Sedgwick's division. Branch's brigade had a strength of about 2,000 men, but had been able to hold in the face of a divisional attack. The Federals were having trouble with muskets overheating and fouling, and the firefight went on. Eventually, the 7th Michigan broke after their left flank did. The 42nd New York broke next. Burns called up the 71st Pennsylvania and the 19th Massachusetts to shore up his lines. The 19th had been told to find the 7th Michigan in their front. It was surprised to find two Confederate regiments there instead. The 19th lost about a third of their men, broke and retreated to a fence line at the edge of a woods.

The 20th Massachusetts had been fortunate enough to advance farther than the rest of Dana's regiments, passing some abandoned guns, likely those of Cooper. Their commander, Colonel Lee, was hit by a wounded artillery horse, and had to leave the field. The 20th, now without the leadership of their colonel, and in a crossfire from Wilcox and Jenkins, fell back in good order to the Willis Church road.

Burns and Sedgwick desperately and heroically tried to rally their men. Burns had blood all over his face and Sedgwick had suffered two wounds, neither of them serious. The Confederate attack from their right had failed, as had their attack from the center, to drive the Federals across the Willis Church road. All four of McCall's regiments in this area of the battlefield had broken, and had suffered about 300 total casualties. Fortunately for the Federals, Sedgwick's two brigades had arrived just in time to prevent a disaster. Grover's steady fight had also been a big factor in the outcome to this point.[73]

On the left of the Confederate line, Wilcox's brigade, consisting of the 9th, 10th, and 11th Alabama, observed artillery rounds passing overhead from both opponents. The Alabamians had been in position and waiting for about two hours, when Eppa Hunton moved forward on Wilcox's right. After some conflicting orders, Richard Anderson finally gave Wilcox clear orders to attack. Wilcox sent forward the 9th and 10th Alabama to the east of the Long Bridge road. They played a part in the fight over Cooper's battery. The 8th and 11th Alabama, augmented by four companies of the 6th South Carolina left behind by Jenkins, moved forward on the west side of the road. The North Carolinians were led by Major James L. Coker, who conferred with Wilcox from the hill occupied by Coker's men. Wilcox wanted to establish whether the enemy could be seen from the hill. The impact nearby of a Federal solid shot emphatically answered Wilcox's question. With the question answered, Wilcox ordered the attack, the target of which was the battery of Alanson Randol, including the section of Olcott. Lieutenant Olcott had been out of the fight at one point, but had come back to help defend Cooper's Federal battery. Randol's battery had to change front to face Wilcox's attack. The change of front was complicated by the fact that the 4th, 7th, and 11th Pennsylvania Reserves were intermingled with Randol's limbers and caissons. James Thompson's battery was also available to defend against the next Confederate attack.

First contact was made by the 8th Alabama, on the left of Wilcox's brigade. The attack got off to an uncertain start for the regiment. Just before the order to attack was given, the 8th's position was adjusted a bit to the left. In the process of carrying out this minor move, the 8th missed the order for the brigade attack. However, their commander, Lieutenant Colonel Young L. Royston, observed the brigade moving forward and gave the order for his regiment to attack. The 8th Alabama made a gallant charge at the Federal guns, and advanced to within fifty yards of Randol's battery. Nevertheless, the total firepower of two batteries and two regiments of supporting Federal infantry were too much to withstand, and the Alabamians were repulsed and fell back. A second charge produced a similar result. On the 8th's right, the 11th Alabama attempted a similar charge with a like result. A few Confederates were captured, and some Federal infantry unwisely gave pursuit. Receiving a solid Confederate volley, the pursuing Federal infantry broke for safety, but found themselves between the Confederates and Randol's battery.

Randol had a major problem. His infantry supports were in front of his guns, so he could not fire at the now attacking Confederates, and he'd lost so many horses that he couldn't limber up at withdraw his guns. Randol could only wait to see what happened. Some surviving horses bolted and ran through the 7th Pennsylvania Reserves, injuring Colonel Elisha B. Harvey. Randol finally had a clear field of fire when the attackers were only thirty yards away. It was too late to prevent the battery from being overrun. The swarming Confederates ran down the gunners, bayoneting and shooting them at will. Some were taken prisoner. Less than a hundred escaped. General Meade, the brigade commander at that point on the Federal line, was severely wounded and left the field.

Randol did not give up his guns easily. He gathered up some infantrymen and mounted an impromptu charge at Wilcox's brigade. The fighting was hand-to-hand, with muskets, bayonets, revolvers, swords and clubbed muskets used as appropriate. Randol and his men were able to drive the 11th Alabama away from his guns and capture their colors. The 11th fled to the woods on the east side of the road, which they then shared with the 9th and 10th Alabama, who had retreated there earlier, after their attempt to take Cooper's guns. The remaining regiment of Wilcox's brigade, the 8th Alabama, held their ground and maintained their fire. Randol saw more Confederate troops advancing, and made a prudent decision to withdraw his rag-tag infantry. The opponents were mutually exhausted.[74]

The casualties from this fight were significant. On the Confederate side, Wilcox's two regiments lost 65 killed, 178 wounded and 12 missing. For the Federals, the 4th, 7th and the portion of the 11th Pennsylvania Reserves engaged lost a combined total of 21 killed, 113 wounded and 139 missing. The combat power of McCall's division was pretty well dissipated at this point in the day. Every regiment had been broken one or more times. Leadership was becoming a problem, as well. The three brigades had all lost the services of their commanders. Simmons was dead, Meade was severely wounded, and Truman Seymour temporarily unfit to command. On the center and right of McCall's line, it appeared that any substantial number of Confederate reinforcements would insure a Federal disaster.[75]

The next Confederate attack spared the Pennsylvania Reserves of McCall's division. The lead Confederate brigade was Pryor's of Longstreet's division. Pryor's starting position was to the left of Wilcox's, and was ordered to attack at the same time as Wilcox, but Pryor was delayed by more difficult ground. His objective was James Thompson's battery and John C. Robinson's brigade of Kearny's III Corps division. There was also another section of Federal artillery in the area, that of Lieutenant Pardon S. Jastram. This section belonged to Randolph's battery, but was left behind when Randolph was sent to help Slocum's division. Jastram was sent from Kearny's headquarters to a field south of the Charles City road, with no instructions other than to "fire toward the sun." Needless to say, the lieutenant had been put in an uncomfortable position, and was nervous about it. Jastram had Federal infantry retreating through and to the left of his position, and he fired slowly and carefully, concerned with hitting friendly troops. After less than a half dozen rounds, the nervous lieutenant decided to withdraw. To his relief, an officer came up and ordered the section to withdraw. Due to a wounded horse, Jastram had to spike one gun and withdraw with the other.

Kearny, for some reason, was incensed about Jastram's performance, and recommended a court of inquiry. The court met later in the year, after General Kearny had been killed, and recommended no further action.

Thompson's battery was sited west of the Long Bridge road, on Robinson's left. Their supports were the 63rd Pennsylvania, just behind the battery, the 57th Pennsylvania next on the right, and the 20th Indiana to the right of them. The brigade reserve was the 105th Pennsylvania.

Because of the terrain, Pryor could not advance his regiments line abreast, but had to move them in column. This meant he had to attack one regiment at a time. The first regiment to attack was the 14th Alabama. Although confident they could take the battery, they were repulsed by double canister fired over the heads of the 63rd Pennsylvania, then volley fire from the 63rd fired from the prone position. The results were devastating to the Alabamians. Their commander, Lieutenant Colonel Baine, was killed and most of his officers wounded.

The 14th Louisiana was making ready to attack next as Pryor rode along the lines. Thompson's battery took a shot at him and hit his horse. The Louisianans attacked and were unsuccessful, sustaining numerous casualties. Pryor ordered his men to take what cover they could find and exchanged fire with the Federals.[76]

Longstreet's reserve brigade, the small brigade of Winfield Featherston, was still uncommitted. After Wilcox and Pryor had attacked, Featherston was moved up, and arrived next to Pryor without difficulty. Pryor said he needed help, and Featherston agreed. Featherston's problem was that he was the left end of the Confederate line, and was overlapped by the Federals. He sent a staff officer to request reinforcements, and decided it was more prudent to defend his present position than to attack. The regiment traded shots with the men of John Robinson in their front, likely the 57th Pennsylvania, part of the 20th Indiana, and the recently arrived 105th Pennsylvania, and waited for help. Shortly, thereafter, Featherston was wounded and had to leave the field.

Longstreet had no reinforcements to send to Featherston's brigade. He had used all of his brigades, broken McCall's line in three places, but could not sustain their gains. Four brigades were spent and had fallen back. The other two, Pryor's and Featherston's were holding, but in danger of being flanked. Longstreet had two basic choices, break off the contact and withdraw, or commit the rest of A. P. Hill's division. Thus far, only Branch's brigade had been committed.

The original plan for the day was for Powell Hill's men to finish off the victory, but the failure of Jackson and Huger to accomplish their missions had resulted in a failure for the Confederates. Now Longstreet had to use A. P. Hill's men to relieve pressure on the Confederate line.[77]

The next brigade into the fight was that of Brigadier General Maxcy Gregg, comprised of the 1st South Carolina, the 1st South Carolina Rifles, and the 12th, 13th and 14th South Carolina. After a long day's march, they quickly moved to bolster the Confederate left. In the lead was the 14th South Carolina, commanded by Colonel McGowan.

McGowan's skirmishers, under Captain A. P. West, came across the wounded Featherston, who urged McGowan to advance immediately. McGowan sent the 14th forward through the woods to the edge of the trees, where they came upon the 20th Indiana in their works. The two groups settled in for a lengthy firefight.

The 13th South Carolina moved into position on the left of the 14th. Concerned about firing into friendly troops in their front, they had to wait for an hour, before being ordered to fix bayonets. Approaching darkness forced the cancellation of the attack. Gregg's other three regiments were never heavily engaged, though they moved into line on the left of the 13th South Carolina, or to supporting positions.

The extended firefight between the 20th Indiana and the 14th South Carolina continued on, with a lull just after sunset. In the reduced visibility of smoke and twilight, confusion reigned and men became prisoners by wandering into enemy positions. These captures helped restart the firefight.

On Pryor's front, the 57th Pennsylvania fired an extremely high number of rounds, and John C. Robinson asked for the help of Berry's brigade. The 1st and 37th New York were sent to support James Thompson's battery, and the 63rd Pennsylvania and 2nd Michigan went to support the 20th Indiana. The 3rd Michigan was sent to reinforce Birney's brigade. This left only the 5th Michigan as Berry's reserve.

Thompson had run out of canister and case shot, and so informed Colonel Alexander Hays, commander of the 63rd Pennsylvania, the infantry support for the battery. Thompson said he would have to leave the battlefield. Hays ordered a charge, which resulted in hand-to-hand combat. Both sides then fell back, and Thompson attempted to remove his guns, but due to harness failure and lack of horses, had to spike and leave one gun. Again Kearny was furious and later ordered a court of inquiry.

Help for Robinson soon came in the form of Caldwell's brigade. Caldwell's brigade and Meagher's brigade, still under Colonel Nugent, had been summoned from the defenses at White Oak Swamp to help out at Glendale.

Nugent's brigade halted at Glendale, but Caldwell continued to the front. Kearny was eager for his help. Confusion was such that Federals were accidentally firing on their own men. The 61st New York became separated from the rest of Caldwell's brigade, but encountered John Robinson, who wasted no time using them to relieve the 63rd Pennsylvania.

The 61st's commander, Colonel Francis C. Barlow, placed his regiment behind a fence, waited for a lull in friendly fire, then crossed the fence to initiate a charge. There were no Confederates in his front to charge. Moving forward, they finally encountered Confederates and Barlow requested help. His sister regiment, the 81st Pennsylvania, was sent and went to work. Fearing he was about to be flanked on his left, Barlow withdrew both regiments to the fence he had previously used for cover. With the assistance of the 5th New Hampshire, also of Caldwell's brigade, they held their position until the battle ended.

On the Confederate side, it is likely that it was the 40th Virginia of Field's brigade that received Barlow's attack. Field had come into line on Gregg's right. The 55th and 60th Virginia were on the east of the Long Bridge road, and 47th Virginia and the 2nd Virginia Battalion on the west side of the road. The 40th Virginia became separated from the left of the brigade by terrain, but Field sent orders to Colonel John M. Brockenbrough for the 40th to press forward and attack the Federal right. Shortly thereafter, the Federals in front of Brockenbrough charged, closing to twenty feet before being driven back.[78]

The remainder of Field's brigade continued to advance toward the batteries of Cooper and Randol. After the counterattack of Randol's rag-tag infantry, McCall scoured the battlefield for any available troops to seal the breach. He found two of Berry's regiments and asked for their help. The regimental commanders asked for orders from Kearny, who rode up just then. Kearny was optimistic that the Confederates could be stopped, gave orders to the two regiments, and left. The 47th Virginia and 2nd Virginia Battalion then charged Randol's battery. Randol managed to get off a shot or two of canister, but caused no damage. The onrushing Confederates of Colonel Robert M. Mayo drove the artillerists into the woods, despite a flanking fire from their left.

Seven Days Before Richmond

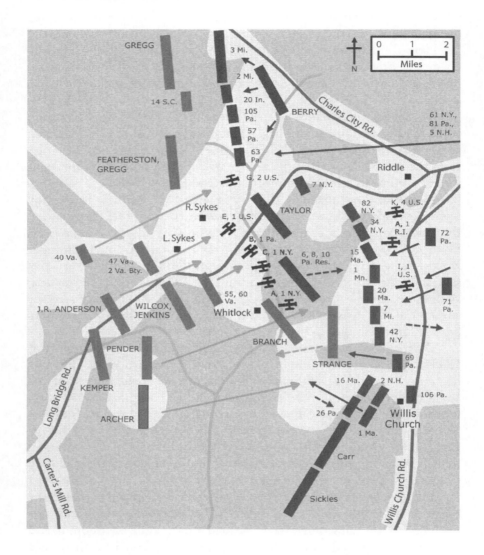

Map 20.4—Glendale, A. P. Hill's Attacks, June 30

One of Randol's guns was turned to fire into the woods. Mayo better positioned his regiment to protect the guns, but his brigade commander, Brigadier General Charles Field rode up and told him to cease the cannon fire, as he was not sure whose troops were in the woods. Horses were heard to the east on the Long Bridge road. Major Stone of the 13th Pennsylvania Reserves had gathered about 500 men from several regiments and was bringing them to the critical point in the Federal line. McCall took over the column and led it to the contested batteries. Halting the column close to the batteries, McCall, Stone and two other men rode forward. They soon encountered some soldiers. Neither group immediately recognized the other as enemy. When McCall inquired as to the command of the strangers, he was told they were from Field's command, McCall claimed not to know a General Field. The Confederate officer, Lieutenant W. Roy Mason, of Field's staff took McCall prisoner. Stone escaped with a minor wound, in the midst of a couple of volleys.

Meanwhile, Field's other two regiments captured Cooper's battery. The 60th Virginia of Colonel William E. Starke, with fixed bayonets, promptly drove the Federals back about a mile from their guns. Starke's men were receiving flanking fire, likely from Slocum's division.

Heintzelman had earlier ridden over to Sumner's position, shortly after McCall was attacked. Unconcerned with the situation there, he rode back to Glendale. Kearny requested help from Heintzelman, who rode over to Slocum's division, saw they were not under pressure, and got Taylor's brigade started toward Kearny's position.

Although Kearny did not choose to admit in his report that he had asked for help, it appears the Confederates had found a gap in his line. In point of fact, he found Confederates where he expected McCall to be found. Kearny was almost captured, but he managed to bluff his way out in the gathering dusk. Kearny briefed Taylor on the situation, and Taylor positioned his men behind the two recently abandoned Federal batteries. Confederate batteries sent shot over their heads, but the Confederates soon pulled back and the fighting died away for the night on the Federal right.[79]

On the Confederate right, Archer took his brigade to the aid of Strange and Branch. Moving forward, Archer's troops encountered the men of the 56th Virginia, who were retreating. Archer's confident troops moved up and ran into the 1st Massachusetts, who mistook them for fellow Federals. The Virginians loosed a volley, and the 1st withdrew to a position behind the 15th Massachusetts of Sully's brigade, which had relieved the 69th Pennsylvania, due to their ammo exhaustion. The 26th Pennsylvania had cleared the Confederates from their front about then. Strange was still firing the two guns captured from Knieriem, and continued to do so until after dark. For the most part, activity on Hooker's front was done for the day.

To the north of Hooker, Pender was moving his brigade forward. He met retreating men who told him the troops in the line were in need of help. Pender then came upon a party of Federals who seemed unaware of the threat near them. Firing from fairly close range, they dispersed the Federals and moved on to skirmish with other Federals, until they moved into the woods and encountered the 1st Minnesota and the 72nd Pennsylvania.

These two regiments were the right end of Sedgwick's line, such as it was. Pender left a small force to protect his right flank from a possible attack from Hooker's division, and continued the advance. Unfortunately for Pender, he ran out of ammunition, and was faced by heavy Federal fire. He pulled his brigade back, unaware that Field was somewhere out in front of him.[80]

A. P. Hill was concerned about the pressure still being put on by the Federals, and committed his last remaining brigade, that of Joseph R. Anderson. The brigade consisted of the 14th, 35th, 45th and 49th Georgia, and the 3rd Louisiana Battalion.

President Davis made one of his numerous appearances on the battlefield as the brigade was preparing to move forward. He was roundly cheered by the troops he encountered. The brigade went forward, the 14th Georgia and the 3rd Louisiana Battalion on the west side on the Long Bridge road, and the 35th, 45th and 49th Georgia to the east of the road. The Louisianans led off, followed shortly by the remainder of the brigade. Anderson cautioned the brigade that there were other Confederates somewhere in their front. The brigade was crossing a fence when Anderson spied a mass of troops marching toward the brigade. Anderson was sure they were Federals, but some of his men weren't. The strangers muddied the issue by asking Anderson's men to hold their fire, as they were friends. Anderson commanded a bayonet charge, but some of his men were still uncomfortable with the situation. When an intense volley of musket fire came from the ranks of the strangers, Anderson's men became believers. The 45th Georgia was hardest hit. Anderson was struck in the head by a spent ball and knocked down. Powell Hill, still worried, rallied some of Wilcox's men and led them forward, urging them to cheer "long and loudly." The men did as the general urged, and followed him forward. Soon thereafter, all firing ceased.

In the Confederate rear, the captured McCall was brought to Longstreet. They had known each other in the regular army prior to the war. McCall had outranked Longstreet in the 4th U. S. Infantry. As McCall was brought in and dismounted, Longstreet went to greet him, attempting to shake hands. McCall reacted in a rude manner, and desired no pleasantries. Longstreet had him escorted into Richmond. The following day, McCall was reported to be emotional, crying over the deaths of his staff officers.[81]

The battle of Glendale was relatively brief. Fighting began about 4:00 P.M., and most units weren't in contact until an hour or more later. Almost all firing ceased within a few minutes after dark. It was supposed to be a large battle. Lee's plan called for the involvement of about 125,000 men. As it turned out, only about 23,500 Federals and 19,500 Confederates entered the fight.

Casualties, as usual, are hard to nail down, but best estimates are around total Federal losses of 2,853 and total Confederate losses of 3,615. Some divisions, such as those of George McCall, A. P. Hill and James Longstreet were especially hard hit.

Another characteristic of the battle of Glendale was its ferocity. Volleys of musket fire at very close ranges and hand-to-hand combat seemed to be almost common. Artillery fire was often restricted by the close quarters infantry fighting.[82]

A look at what was accomplished by the battle of Glendale must first examine whether ground was gained or lost by the belligerents. At the end of the day's fighting, the lines were approximately where they had been in the morning. The reality was that McClellan's line of retreat down the Willis Church road had not been interdicted. Many more wagon trains had rolled south to the protection of the Federal gunboats on the James River.

It is questionable whether Lee had sufficient combat power to carry out the plan he devised for the battle. Given the superiority in numbers and quality of artillery pieces enjoyed by the Army of the Potomac, as well as the defensive positions they enjoyed, Lee would have needed to execute his battle plan flawlessly. This was not the case, as the battle was initiated by an unplanned attack by the brigade of Jenkins, rather than in a controlled manner by Lee. Over the years, there has been ample criticism between the Confederate generals involved. Some of this criticism has merit, and some is just not supported by the records. The common problem faced by all the Confederate commanders was that they lacked sufficient tactical intelligence to make flawless decisions as to where and how to apply the forces at hand.[83]

Some have criticized Lee's plan. The plan should not be blamed for the Confederate failure. It was simpler than the plan for Mechanicsville, in that the timing was not as critical. It failed because two key individuals, Jackson and Huger failed to carry out their parts of the overall plan. Their task was simple. Just keep pressure on the enemy's rear. Had they done so, there was a real chance of Confederate success. They did very little with the assets at their command, and Lee's plan failed. They also failed to keep General Lee informed of their delays and difficulties. With more information, Lee would have at least been given the opportunity to adjust the plan. In fairness, Lee did not actively seek progress reports on Jackson and Huger. Instead, Lee went personally to examine Holmes' perceived crisis.[84]

Lee is certainly not blameless for the failure of his army at Glendale. He knew from previous fighting that he had some weak generals in his army. Perhaps he should have been at Huger's side for the commencement of the battle, rather than with Longstreet. Surely, he could have been more forceful in his communications with several of his key generals.

All this said, the basic fact is that Jackson failed miserably to carry out his assignment. Therefore, a major portion of Lee's army essentially did nothing for an entire day. Because of the failure of Jackson to cross the White Oak Swamp and attack McClellan's rear, some 10,000 Federal troops were freed up to move to Glendale and make it impossible for Longstreet and A. P. Hill to cut off the Federal retreat. Jackson not only failed to do his duty, he failed to try.

About a fifth of Lee's army had spent the day marching and countermarching, and had scarcely fired a shot. It was primarily Magruder's command that did the marching, having received seven sets of orders during the day. One must ask if all that marching was really dictated by events. Was it logical to have that much of an army's combat power denied to it for a day? If those men hadn't been marching, where would they have been most effectively used and what would they have accomplished? To answer these two questions, we can look at each venue across the battle area and theorize how the addition of a Confederate command to the mix might have affected the outcome of fighting in that venue.

The area of Malvern Hill is a simple venue to examine. The Federal forces near there numbered 23,500. There were also at least eight batteries of artillery, as McClellan had sent much of Hunt's artillery reserve there. There were also several Federal gunboats in the James that could and did support Porter. The opposing Confederate force was that of Holmes, who had 6,300 infantry and some eight batteries. At one point in the day, Magruder's command marched to Holmes' aid, then was ordered away. Had Magruder been allowed to stay and join Holmes in an attack on Malvern Hill, what outcome could we have expected?

Magruder's command consisted of about 13,000 infantry and eight batteries. Together, they would not have been able to knock Porter and his friends off of Malvern Hill, given the natural defensive superiority of that eminence and the late hour of the day. All things considered, the Confederates would have been unsuccessful, and would have incurred a higher number of casualties.

Glendale is a different story. Magruder's command would have been better used there, going in behind A. P. Hill's division. He could have been used there at the outset, but as a follow-on force. The extra infantry could have been used to exploit the break in the Federal lines created by James Longstreet and A. P. Hill. This could have resulted in a very successful day for Lee's army.

It is hard to understand why Lee, after a look at Holmes' situation, would have elected to commit any of Magruder's command to aid Holmes. Holmes had no real possibility of success, and wasn't in any real danger where he was. Holmes simply needed to do earlier in the day what he did at nightfall, withdraw out of range of the Federal artillery on Malvern Hill and the Federal gunboats on the James. He still would have been able to tie down the Federal troops atop Malvern Hill. They had to stay there to protect the trains in any case.

All this theorizing must be placed in the context of the weak performances of Huger and Jackson. If either or both of them had accomplished their assigned mission for the day, General Lee would likely have let Magruder support Longstreet and A. P. Hill at Glendale, and had Theophilus Holmes maintain a simply defensive role. It is somewhat less possible that Lee would have opted to use Magruder elsewhere, such as supporting Holmes by attacking Malvern Hill from another direction, such as the north.

There has been much written about the supposed "mistaken guide" directing Magruder down the wrong road. Whether or not it really happened, and what effect it actually had is arguable. The critical facts of the day are that Huger and Jackson failed to carry out their missions, Holmes was assigned an impossible task, and communication between the Confederate generals remained pathetic. Perhaps the most critical mistake of the day was Lee wasting the combat power of Magruder's command by unnecessarily marching them to the aid of Holmes, then back to Glendale too late to exploit a Confederate breakthrough.[85]

William Franklin was a worried man late in the afternoon of June 30. His assignment was to keep Jackson's command from crossing the White Oak Swamp Bridge until nightfall. Franklin was concerned that the Confederates might cut the Willis Church road at Glendale, leaving his VI Corps caught between two powerful arms of Lee's army. When nightfall came, Franklin was more than ready to move his men rapidly south and away from Lee's trap.

During the day, a road was discovered by a member of the VI Corps staff, Captain C. F. West, that had the potential of being an alternate route south out of a potential trap. This was an important find, as the

Willis Church road would probably have been inadequate to withdraw all the Federal troops north of Malvern Hill. Right after nightfall, Franklin informed Heintzelman that he was pulling out, and ordered Richardson to have French's brigade and Ayres' battery cover the crossing until the rest of the VI Corps was away. Franklin had Smith's division on the march, followed by Naglee's brigade around 10:00 P.M. Smith, like so many combat leaders, was fatigued after six days of combat. After he had organized the march, he decided to get a much needed hour's sleep. He told his staff to wake him in time to move out, but they also slept, and the general and his staff hurriedly rode down the dark road to catch up with the division. Other units, such as two regiments of Naglee's brigade, were briefly left. It was a scary night march for the retreating Federals. French and Ayres, the designated rear guard, could hear the Confederates repairing the White Oak Swamp Bridge as they left, and fired a few rounds at them before leaving. At this point, Jackson could now easily cross the White Oak Swamp.[86]

Franklin's very successful withdrawal created another worried Federal general, Samuel Heintzelman. With Franklin gone, Heintzelman's right flank was wide open to attack by Jackson's command streaming across White Oak Swamp, and he knew there were Confederates between him and Malvern Hill. He felt that he was in real danger of being cut off. Heintzelman had a related problem, in that he had no orders from McClellan to withdraw. Heintzelman messaged McClellan that he believed it was time to leave Glendale.

Although McClellan might have liked to keep a formidable presence at Glendale, Franklin's withdrawal changed McClellan's mind. McClellan had no fresh troops to commit at Glendale, and now that Magruder's command was back at Glendale from their excursion, it could have been a bad outcome for the Federals if McClellan chose to keep his men there. The alternative of concentrating the Army of the Potomac at Malvern Hill and fighting one more defensive battle was much more attractive to McClellan. Heintzelman was incredulous when informed that Franklin had left, but Truman Seymour had returned from Franklin's headquarters and convinced him it was really so. Heintzelman even tried to get Franklin to stay in place until they could hear from McClellan, but it was now too late for that to happen.

Slocum was in a tight spot and his men in a bad way. His division was close to running out of both rations and ammunition. He also messaged army headquarters, then joined Heintzelman. Slocum decided on his own to withdraw to the south, and moved out instantly and quietly. Kearny's division followed Slocum's, which left about 2:00 A.M. on July

1. Lieutenant Jastram's bad luck continued, as no one informed him about the withdrawal.[87]

Once Heintzelman completed arrangements for the retreat, he met with Edwin Sumner. One can safely assume that Bull Sumner was irked by the order to retreat after another good day on the battlefield. He had, however no other viable option, so the brigades of John Caldwell, Robert Nugent, John Sedgwick and Truman Seymour followed Kearny's division south. The artillerists weren't even allowed to attempt to retrieve the guns left between the armies.

Hooker was left to hold the road while the others retired. He maintained his position until daylight on the July 1, then quietly had the division's pickets called in and took his division south along the Willis Church road. By the time Hooker left, they could see Confederates searching for their wounded by torchlight, as well as hear the wounded crying out for help. Some Confederates came very close to the pickets of several Federal regiments, but were not engaged.[88]

A Federal field hospital had been established at the Willis Church by the 10th Pennsylvania Reserves. The surgeons labored until 2:00 A.M. on July 1, when the hospital was taken down and most of the medical personnel moved on with the retreating column. One surgeon was left behind with those wounded considered too critical to move.

All the time used by the Federals to withdraw from Glendale was used by Lee to reorganize his army and reposition his divisions. Magruder's command, after a day of marching to and fro, took over the front line. Despite their fatigue, they labored to succor the wounded from both armies in their front. Whiting's men repaired the bridge across White Oak Swamp, while Jackson slept. Huger stayed in position. Johnson's Maryland Line was still north of the Chickahominy, and was finally ordered out of the Bottoms Bridge area. Holmes was bivouacked on the River road. Lee was likely taking stock of the results of the 30th, and wondering how his plan went to pieces.[89]

Farther south, McClellan probably had an improved view of the world at that point in time. For the first time in a number of days, his army was concentrating. He was holding an excellent defensive position, and he knew if his men could fight well just one more day, he would have his tired and battered army intact at its new base on the James River.

CHAPTER 21

Malvern Hill

(July 1)

The Army of the Potomac was essentially concentrated on or about Malvern Hill on July 1, 1862. Porter and a substantial number of artillery pieces had been there since the previous morning. Porter had first set up defenses against an attack from the River road. A major portion of that defense was the guns of Hunt's artillery reserve, which Porter lined up on the western side of the plateau, overlooking the River road, and supported with the infantry of Sykes' regulars.[1]

Heintzelman's III Corps reached Malvern Hill at about 1:30 A.M. As McClellan had instructed him, upon arrival, he sought to consult the army's chief engineer, John Barnard, and V Corps commander Fitz John Porter to determine where Heintzelman's men would be positioned in the defense of Malvern Hill. They decided to wait until daybreak to take action. After dawn, McClellan arrived and rode the lines with Heintzelman. This time, McClellan left the placing of units to two staff officers.

Kearny's division arrived next and was placed on the eastern crest. Hooker and his division, arriving last, were positioned just south of Kearny. Sumner's II Corps marched through the lines and stopped near the southern edge of Malvern Hill, near the Malvern house.

McCall's division was the most battered in the entire army, and was now commanded by Truman Seymour, as McCall was now in a Confederate prison in Richmond. It also came to rest near the Malvern house, within sight of the James River.

Near Haxall's Landing, Peck's IV Corps division was consolidated as Naglee's fatigued men joined Wessell's large brigade. Slocum's VI Corps division positioned itself on Peck's left, and the other VI Corps division, that of Smith, went to the left of Slocum.[2]

The morning of July 1 found the Federals at Malvern Hill in an excellent defensive formation on very favorable ground. Their lines were U-shaped, with the open end to the south, the direction in which they planned to move after the fight. The units were positioned, from the left to right along the Federal lines as follows:

Sykes' V Corps division had responsibility for the west side of the plateau, and were the left of the Federal line. Warren's brigade, augmented by the 11th U. S. of Lovell's brigade, covered the River road. The remaining four regiments of Lovell were on the hill, close enough for rapid reinforcement of Warren. The remaining small brigade, that of Colonel Robert Buchanan, was located a bit north of Lovell.

Protecting the northwest section of the plateau was Morell's V Corps division. The brigade of General Charles Griffin was placed out in front, a little north of the Mellert (Crew) house. They faced toward the Long Bridge road. The brigade of Martindale was in the left rear of Griffin, and Butterfield's brigade was to Griffin's right rear. Berdan's Sharpshooters were out front as skirmishers. All of the division was west of the Long Bridge road.

The northeastern section of the plateau was held by Couch's IV Corps division. Innis Palmer's brigade was short two regiments. The 7th Massachusetts and 2nd Rhode Island had been detached to cover Turkey Island Creek Bridge on the River road. This put them in Warren's rear. The remaining two regiments were placed north of the West house and east of the Willis Church road. On Palmer's right, on the very northeast corner of the plateau, was Brigadier General Albion Howe's brigade, facing north and northeast. Howe's men also supported artillery in Palmer's left rear. The brigade of Brigadier General John J. Abercrombie was to the rear of Howe.

The east side of the plateau was protected by Heintzelman's III Corps and, to their south, Sumner's II Corps. Sumner was the right of the Federal Line. Two of Sumner's brigades, those of Meagher and Caldwell of Richardson's division, were positioned in the very center of the plateau, as reserves behind Morell's and Couch's divisions. Heintzelman's troops looked out on the valley of Western Run, and Sumner's men on that of Turkey Island Creek. Though these were small streams, they would be an additional obstacle to potential attacking Confederates, as they would serve to slow down attacking infantry. The Federal line was extended even father south by Franklin's VI Corps and Peck's II Corps division.[3]

As fortune would have it, the Federal artillery would decide the battle of Malvern Hill. July 1 marked the first occasion in the Seven Days battles that the Army of the Potomac was all in one place, infantry, artillery and cavalry. The combat power of 53 batteries, some 268 guns, plus the siege artillery, was at McClellan's disposal. Six batteries were still on the west side of the line from the shelling of Holmes the previous day. One battery was with Warren's brigade. Griffin had control of seven batteries, some 31 guns. On the east side of the line, in the II and III Corps area, there were ten batteries, some 60 guns, available to thwart an attack from the northeast. Besides the numerous batteries embedded with infantry units all along the edge of the plateau, there were a number of batteries, including heavy siege guns just north of the Malvern House. The heavy pieces had been laboriously hauled up the south slope of the plateau with the aid of mule teams and a lot of manpower. This artillery reserve, parked near the Malvern House, comprised some ten batteries, about 52 guns.[4]

This superb defensive setup was the result of the skilled labors of several key Federal officers. McClellan gave the broad guidance concerning the position. The engineers, Barnard and Humphreys, placed II and III Corps. Porter chose the original line for Morell's and Sykes' divisions, and likely Couch's. Hunt, of course, positioned the reserve artillery, as well as the other pieces.

The result of all this frantic effort in the middle of the fighting of the 30th, was a superb defensive position. On the Federal left, Sykes still had total command over the River road. On the right end of the line, Porter and Heintzelman had the advantage of the creeks in their fronts, much like at Mechanicsville and Gaines' Mill. Last minute efforts at cutting trees to block roads enhanced their situations. On the north end of the plateau, in the Federal center, there was a lesser advantage of elevation, but the fields of fire for the Federals were excellent. There was little cover for attacking Confederate infantry. Batteries were positioned to be mutually supporting.

Whether through stroke of military genius or plain blind luck, the divisions most likely to shoulder the impending Confederate attack were the best rested. The attack was expected from the west or north. Sykes and Morell had an easy time of it since the 27th at Gaines' Mill, and Couch hadn't really fought yet.

The Confederates also knew the strength of the Federal position. Lee had made personal visits to Shirley plantation and knew that it had "great natural strength." To make matters worse for the Confederates, McClellan had 53,000 men on the plateau and another 1,000 under Warren in the low area to the west. Lee would only be able to attack with a total of 55,000, including the 7,000 of Holmes on the River road.[5]

While the ground and the troop placements were superb for the defense of Malvern Hill, the command structure was unorthodox and probably nowhere near ideal. McClellan had put Porter in command of the troops at the northern end of the plateau, including Couch's division. This was the part of the line most likely to receive the Confederate attack.

Porter had also been the commander at the battles of Mechanicsville and Gaines' Mill. Sumner still commanded II Corps and Heintzelman his III Corps. Sumner, however, seemed put out by the command arrangement, and complained that he was not any longer in command. Although Sumner did not elaborate, perhaps he referred to the fact that two of his brigades were distant from the remainder of his corps. Once again, McClellan did the most unlikely thing. After riding the lines early in the morning and delegating the troop placements to a pair of staff officers, he disappeared from the battlefield.

McClellan obviously had things to do that he considered more important than leading his army in battle. He first went to Haxall's Landing, where he sent several telegraph messages. One of these was addressed to his wife, in which he complained of fatigue, and also made the melodramatic statement that the men "cheer me as of old as they march to certain death & I feel prouder of them than ever." He sent a telegram to the adjutant general of the U. S. Army, Brigadier General Lorenzo Thomas, that the Confederates might not attack on the 1st, and that he hoped to retreat to Harrison's Landing after nightfall. He also admitted to Thomas that his troops were too tired to stay at Malvern Hill or attack Richmond, owing to the "superior numbers" he faced. McClellan requested that Major General John Dix, commander at Fort Monroe, send any available reinforcements to Harrison's Landing.[6]

By 9:15 A.M., McClellan was at Haxall's Landing onboard the gunboat *Galena*, and by 10:00 A.M., they were underway down the James. McClellan intended to confer with Commodore Rodgers, so they could finalize the plans for the army's new base. McClellan had brought Franklin along with him. After two hours, McClellan and Franklin went ashore at Harrison's Landing. The pair walked the ground to determine if the site was truly suitable as a base for the Army of the Potomac, then reboarded the *Galena*. After noon, McClellan returned to Malvern Hill and spent less than an hour with Porter. Then he rode the lines for a second time that day, deciding that the right flank concerned him most. Porter urged McClellan to look after the areas to the right of his, those controlled by the other corps commanders and Peck. McClellan obliged Fitz John, went forward and stayed until the battle was joined, likely watching through a glass.

After the fight, McClellan stopped by Keyes' headquarters, described the battle and assured Keyes that his position was not under threat. He then left, telling Keyes that he was returning to the *Galena* to direct gunfire. When McClellan arrived at the gunboat, the battle was over and the general stayed on board overnight as it steamed down the James River.

McClellan's failure to stay on the battlefield at the critical point of attack at Malvern Hill is puzzling. Some might say he lacked courage, others that he lacked military competence. Still others point out that he was away the entire day of the 30th, a battle which had even more potential to truly damage his army. It is truly a puzzle, much like that of Jackson's bizarre behavior at White Oak Swamp. Like Jackson, McClellan was suffering from acute fatigue, but that cannot be the total explanation for his actions. Whatever the real reason for McClellan's behavior, it was the height of poor judgment. By the time an officer arrives at the point in his career where he commands over a hundred thousand men, he should have learned to delegate significant tasks to competent staff officers and concentrate his personal efforts on the key decisions that affect victory and defeat. There were a number of engineer officers that could have conferred with the U. S. Navy to pin down the details of the new base on the James. If McClellan truly felt he was outnumbered, and was really worried about the right flank, that's where he needed to be.

Another facet of his poor judgment was his failure to establish a clear and effective command structure in his absence from the battlefield at Malvern Hill. He managed to make this same mistake twice in one week. Should the Confederates have mounted two strong attacks at widespread points along the line, Porter might have had a hard time getting the major generals to give up any of their troops to quickly realign the defense. Porter and the other corps commanders would have to hope Lee concentrated his attack on one front. Otherwise, they would have to try running the army by committee, a bad plan on any given day.[7]

Lee wasn't enjoying the first day of July. He was exhausted, as well as disappointed and frustrated. Lee's condition was obvious to his immediate subordinates. Jubal Early had come back to the Army after recovering from a wound suffered in May at the battle of Williamsburg. He had come to Lee on the evening of the 30th to seek a brigade command. Returning on the morning of the 1st to receive Lee's official decision giving him a command, Jubal Early made mention of his concern that McClellan might escape, Lee replied "Yes, he will get away because I cannot have my orders carried out!" Once again Lee was forced to improvise a revised plan to salvage something from a campaign gone awry.[8]

This battle would be unique in the Peninsula Campaign, in that it would be the only time either army was concentrated. The White Oak Swamp Bridge had been repaired in the night by Whiting's men. His division crossed before daybreak. The other three divisions in Jackson's command followed, first D. H. Hill's, then Winder's, and lastly, Ewell's. Near Glendale, the head of Whiting's column encountered Magruder's skirmishers. After dawn, the skirmishers had experienced the sights kept from them in the night. They suffered the abandoned guns, the dead of the Pennsylvania Reserves, and the human debris near the Whitlock house, where a temporary field hospital had been for a short time. They shared the macabre scene with Mrs. Whitlock, who had just returned home that morning. The Confederates stepped over the Federal dead, trying not to show any feeling.

There was some contact with the enemy. Hooker's rear guard was caught up by Magruder and driven. The 21st Mississippi of Barksdale's brigade took prisoners who had simply slept too well and too long. Magruder ordered his command to advance in line, rather than in column, as he could not be sure of how many Federals were in his front. Lee joined Magruder and they sent Brent to ride ahead to the front and report back what he observed. Brent encountered Confederate troops, which he correctly identified as Whiting's division of Jackson's command. Brent was directed to Jackson, found him just leaving a nearby house, and Jackson immediately asked Brent about Lee's position. Stonewall and Brent rode to meet Lee and Magruder. The troops continued their march, with Jackson's command on the east side of the Willis Church road and Magruder's troops on the opposite side. In the midst of much cheering from the troops, the three generals discussed the coming battle. Lee used his map to show Stonewall and Prince John where they were and what he wanted them to do. Lee wanted Jackson on the left of the Quaker road and Magruder on the right. Jackson would lead the attack with his rested troops, and Magruder would follow.[9]

General Lee desired Huger's command on the front line. Huger had sent the brigades of Wright and Armistead south at 3:00 A.M. that day. Since Huger didn't know at that time the Federals had fled, it was most likely a flanking maneuver. The brigades were moving through the woods south of the Charles City road. Longstreet later informed Huger that the Charles City road was devoid of enemy activity as far as Glendale. Huger then sent the brigades of Mahone and Robert Ransom down the road. These brigades observed the evidence of the fierce fighting at Glendale, which was a surprise to some. Some desirable items were recovered from the knapsacks of dead Federals.

Huger continued slowly southward along the crowded road, but was unsure of where he was supposed to go until Colonel Taylor of Lee's staff came along and directed him to the front. Armistead, who had started out through the woods, was now progressing south along a rural road to Long Bridge road a bit west of Glendale. Lee came across him there and ordered him down the Carter's Mill road. A mile or so later, Armistead saw Major Thomas M. R. Talcott, another of Lee's staff officers, who told Armistead that the Federals could be found not far away. Armistead reacted by putting out skirmishers and placing the remainder of his brigade in a ravine less than a mile north of the Mellert (Crew) house. Wright stopped his brigade behind Armistead. These brigades were the Confederate right at this point in time. Longstreet and A. P. Hill, both of whom had been through heavy fighting in the previous several days, became the army's reserve. Holmes moved up part of his command from the crossroads of the Long Bridge and River roads.[10]

Lee's choice of troops was a good one. He now had his freshest troops in the front of his army, and hoped they would compel the Federals to stand and fight. This would buy Lee some time to improvise once again a plan to try and cut them off from the protection of their gunboats on the James. He still had to decide whether to attack Malvern Hill or devise some other stratagem to secure an advantage. There was a diversity of opinions among Lee's generals on the issue of whether or not to attack Malvern Hill. Harvey Hill advised Lee against an attack. Hill had received a good description of the Federal position from Reverend L. W. Allen. Hill passed it on to Lee and Longstreet. Hill added the comment, "If General McClellan is there in force, we had better let him alone." Longstreet laughed at Hill's comment and responded, "Don't get so scared, now that we have got him whipped." This seems a bizarre comment, coming from Longstreet, considering the casualties McClellan's army inflicted on Longstreet's command the previous day at Glendale. The only plausible explanation is that Longstreet observed the amount of muskets, knapsacks and other equipment abandoned by the Federals in their retreat all the way from Beaver Dam Creek and reached the conclusion that they were thoroughly demoralized and had little fight left in them.

Lee decided to move up his army, but to hold off on launching a frontal attack on Malvern Hill until alternative courses of action could be examined. Perhaps because he was fully aware of his fatigue, or perhaps because he just wanted another opinion on such a serious matter, Lee decided to take another senior officer with him. Since Longstreet's division was in reserve, Longstreet was available to accompany Lee on a reconnaissance of the battlefield. They split up after a while, Longstreet rode to the Confederate right, and Lee went to the army's left, investigating the area along the Willis Church road, where Whiting's men were near the Willis Church parsonage.[11]

Longstreet thought he had found several good possibilities. He went to Armistead's position, and found a plateau nearby that had about the same elevation as the Federal artillery. Armistead was conferring with the commander of the 38th Virginia, Col. Edward C. Edmonds, appraising their part of the potential battlefield. The visibility from the small plateau allowed Longstreet to see all the way across Malvern Hill to Whiting's division, placed east of the Willis Church road. Longstreet believed that the plateau was large enough to set up forty to sixty guns, a "grand battery," that would permit a flanking fire on the Federals in Jackson's front. Longstreet thought that Jackson could mass almost a hundred guns if he could find that many, and that second "grand battery" could support his infantry as it advanced. The artillery cross fire would have a devastating and demoralizing effect on the federals. An intense assault like the final one at Gaines' Mill could be conducted by Jackson's men. Longstreet knew the plan was risky, stating that "the tremendous game at issue called for adventure." If successful, a portion of the Army of the Potomac could be destroyed.[12]

While still considering his proposed plan, Longstreet observed Magruder, his column marching southwest on the Long Bridge road, also analyzing the situation. The two generals had a discussion, and Magruder agreed with Longstreet's plan for employment of the Confederate artillery. Longstreet mentioned to Magruder that he thought Prince John was moving his troops away from the position he had been assigned. Magruder had three local guides with him, and they assured Magruder that he was going in the right direction, and that they would soon turn on to the Quaker road. The road ran from near the Enroughty farmhouse to near Sweeny's Tavern on the River road. It was not the only road that connected the Long Bridge and River roads. The one they were going to was, however, used very little in the recent past. It was the only one nearby that was called the Quaker road.

This turned out to be a minor setback for the Confederates. General Lee had not intended for Magruder to use the road toward which he was now marching. Lee was using a map that depicted the Willis Church road as the Quaker road. The Willis Church road would have been the best choice for Magruder to reach his designated place in the line, a bit better than the Carter's Mill road. The "Quaker road" Magruder was marching to would take him to the River road about a mile southeast of its intersection with the Long Bridge road. This would put Prince John nearly two miles west of where Lee wanted him to go. Magruder would come closer to Holmes than to Malvern Hill. It is unclear whether Magruder had failed to pay attention when Lee was briefing him on the march, or whether Lee had used a faulty map. Both possibilities were fairly likely. The Confederates suffered from poor cartography throughout the Peninsula Campaign.[13]

When Longstreet informed Magruder that he was going down the wrong road, Prince John offered to reverse course if Longstreet ordered him to do so, but Longstreet declined, as to do so could be construed as ordering Magruder to ignore an order from Lee. Therefore, Magruder turned down the "Quaker road." Longstreet reported back to Lee regarding the proposed plan for using the artillery, as well as Magruder's errant march. Lee accepted Longstreet's plan for the artillery, and sent a pioneer party to clear trees along the Carter's Mill road for batteries to get to the correct spot, while protected from Federal observation.

Longstreet began to locate batteries to create the "grand battery" and was having misgivings about not ordering Magruder to go to the proper road. Longstreet rode back to find Magruder about a mile and a half down the "Quaker road." Simultaneously, Colonel Chilton, Lee's chief of staff, arrived. Lee had agreed with Longstreet about Magruder's mistaken navigation, and Chilton instructed Magruder to go to the correct road. Magruder complied immediately. He turned his divisions around, thus reversing the order of march. Now McLaws' division was in the lead, followed by Magruder's, then Jones'.[14]

Magruder's roundabout march to his assigned position in the Confederate lines had a price, paid in two ways. First, it delayed the final placement of the army. Second, it took coherence from the deployment. Lee had a concept for the battle, and it became distorted because of Magruder. Lee wanted Jackson on the left, Magruder on the right, and Huger to be committed wherever his troops were most needed. With Magruder not there at the expected time, Lee had to once again improvise. This had the possibility of muddling the command structure. Lee had not seen Huger as yet, and might have the necessity of letting each command decide its own movements, or he could designate an overall tactical commander. Given the personalities involved, there was always the possibility that the tactical commander's authority might be challenged at some critical juncture. Lee hoped to overcome these possible problems, follow Longstreet's plan, and not lose too much to confusion.

No final plan could be put in place until Lee saw Malvern Hill himself and fully understood the tactical situation. Lee needed to know if McClellan was really "there in force" and where McClellan's flanks, especially the right one, rested. When D. H. Hill made his comment about the danger of attacking McClellan at Malvern Hill, Jackson suggested turning the Federal right, but Lee overruled him. When Lee finally saw the Federal position at Malvern Hill, he easily reached the conclusion that Longstreet's plan for employing the artillery could be implemented at little cost. He would have the luxury of waiting to see if the two "grand batteries" would have the desired effect. If they did, he could attack. If they did not, he could conduct further reconnaissance and improvise a different plan. He still considered turning McClellan's right flank and cutting him off from his new base on the James.[15]

On the Confederate left, Whiting started receiving Federal artillery fire as he approached the Willis Church Parsonage. Whiting was about three-quarters of a mile from the Federal batteries sited near the West house, just after 11:00 A.M. Stonewall received an order from Lee to begin massing guns for the second "grand battery." He began gathering up guns, beginning with Reilly's Rowan Artillery and Balthis' Staunton Artillery. Then came Poague's Rockbridge Artillery from the Stonewall Brigade. Whiting ordered Balthis to cut down trees to site more guns. Whiting wisely decided to prepare a clearing for fifty guns before any moved on to the field. Unfortunately, Jackson rode up and ordered the few batteries already in the vicinity to move into the clearing. Whiting advised Jackson that the few batteries would not be able to survive the federal fire that their appearance would precipitate, but Jackson curtly repeated his order. Whiting replied, "I always obey orders promptly but do not obey these willingly."

Reilly's battery went first, and immediately drew a Federal artillery crossfire. Kingsbury, Osborn and Bramhall opened on Reilly, and were joined by the III Corps batteries of Beam, James Thompson and John M. Randolph, as well as the II Corps battery of Wolcott. Even the heavy siege guns joined in.[16] There cannot be certainty as to which batteries fired at which targets throughout the day, but this is a reasonable estimate.

The Federal artillery barrage seemed to be impacting everywhere. One round killed an aide of Colonel James A. Walker, commander of the 13th Virginia, while the three men were lounging on the ground eating. Jackson, Ewell and Whiting were just riding into the Poindexter field when several solid shot impacted close to them. Jackson had just dismounted when a round spooked his horse, which bolted and pulled Stonewall to the ground before he could release the reins. Stonewall took cover, and both calmed down and went about the business of battle. D. H. Hill had his coat torn by a fragment of a shell bursting nearby. Infantry units, such as those from Whiting's division, endured two hours of artillery fire as they moved to support Confederate batteries.

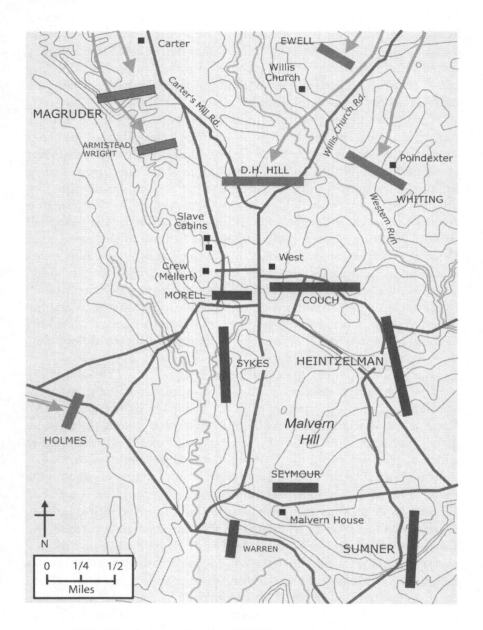

Map 21.1—Lee's Advance to Malvern Hill, July 1, 1862

The inevitable result of the horrendous Federal barrage was much as Whiting told Jackson it would be. Reilly was literally shot out of his position. Jackson had personally posted Poague's battery, and it, along with that of Baltis, were able to keep firing to an extent. A couple of other Confederate batteries came up, one of which was Cutshaw's Jackson Artillery. The arriving artillery dispersed some of Whiting's infantry, who were trying to use the road. From an unknown source came an order for the batteries to leave the field. Most refused to do so, but at least one obeyed and departed. As the one battery withdrew to the north, it met the arriving battery of Lieutenant Carpenter and a two-gun section of the Alleghany (Virginia) Artillery moving south. Carpenter began looking for a place to set up, but his guns departed with the withdrawing battery. Carpenter caught up with them. Whiting rode up and sent Carpenter forward, where he set up his section on the right of Poague. Balthis, wounded seven times that day, soon exhausted his ammunition and left the field. Poague then withdrew one gun because he no longer had enough men to run all his guns. A two-gun section from Wooding's Danville Artillery came up, the others of the battery out of ammunition at the time.[17]

Although they were hopelessly outgunned, the Confederate artillery did manage to have some deadly effect on the enemy. Captain Beam was killed by a bursting shell. Other Federal batteries, such as those of Kirby and Tompkins, were forced to change positions to avoid the worst of the fire. Wolcott reported that the shelling near the Malvern house was "galling." Pettit's battery was not permitted to return fire, but absorbed considerable fire. Confederate shells were reported to be bursting over a hundred feet above the ground, scattering their shrapnel over a wide radius. The only battery sent from Hunt's Artillery Reserve was Snow's Battery B, Maryland Light Artillery. He was sent to Howe's right and was able to fire on Confederates in an open field.

As the artillery began to fire, Sumner moved his troops into line of battle from their camp positions to support the Federal guns. Likewise, Hooker moved into position. One brigade, Birney's of Kearny's division, was motivated to entrench themselves. Even Bull Sumner, known for his fearlessness, vacated the crest to afford his men some measure of protection from the Confederate barrage. Sedgwick's division took some casualties. A field hospital was moved out of range of the Confederate guns. The infantry stayed put, and seemed not to be demoralized by the shelling. The men of the Army of the Potomac were not the battered and discouraged soldiers that Longstreet wanted to believe they were. Federal commanders did everything they could to keep spirits high, including lemonade, water and music. Some of the troops likely preferred that the Confederates attack, rather than to sit and endure the artillery fire.[18]

Despite the best efforts and bravery of the artillerists, the Confederate "grand batteries" were a dramatic failure. Longstreet had wanted 80 to 100 guns massed in the Poindexter field. In reality, only 20 were fired from there, and no more than 14 at any one time. Four guns didn't stay very long and four others exhausted their ammunition. The "grand battery" was opposed by 32 Federal guns and the range was fairly short. The Confederates had an impossible task.

The right of the Confederate line had similar problems. Armistead and Wright suffered a lack of artillery support because the four batteries attached to their brigades had not marched with the infantry. When the brigadiers finally decided they needed their guns, they had to summon them from the rear. The wait deprived them of guns that would have helped mass the 40 to 60 that Longstreet's plan called for. There were in fact other batteries that could be put to work. Mahone, who was marching down the Charles City road, met either Longstreet or one of his staff officers, who told Mahone that Armistead was in need of guns. Moorman and Carey F. Grimes immediately took their batteries forward. Pegram's battery of A. P. Hill's division, roughed up at both Mechanicsville and Gaines' Mill, also went forward. Moorman arrived at Armistead's position first, but was concerned about the situation. Armistead, a career U. S. Army Regular, had no need for the captain's concern, and drove him from the field. While that was taking place, Grimes arrived, having been told to report to Wright. Before he could unlimber, there was a meeting between Armistead, Wright and Grimes, in which Armistead stated his need for an artillery battery that would fight, and Wright gave him Grime's battery. Armistead asked Carey F. Grimes to set up on a hill south of the ravine in which the brigade was deployed. Armistead used the 14th Virginia to drive back the Federal skirmishers, thus clearing a way for Grimes and his men. Grimes and his battery moved to the north end of the Mellert field.

Grimes had a major problem, in that the south end of the Mellert field was held by Federal artillery. As soon as the Confederates moved into the field, the Federal batteries of Livingston, Ames, Kingsbury and Hyde, and perhaps others opened fire. With 18 guns at short range, the two Confederate guns that had the range to engage the Federals had no chance to survive very long. It is possible that long range siege guns and the heavy guns of Voegelee and Carlisle from Sykes' line pitched in. Grimes claimed to fire for two hours, but it was likely a shorter fight than that. The end result was two men killed and many wounded among the Confederate artillerists. Numerous artillery horses were also killed.

Although a number of Federals had respect for the Confederate artillery effort, it was inevitably unsuccessful. Armistead again and again requested more artillery. Longstreet personally promised to provide more guns, but none arrived northwest of Malvern Hill until the wayward Magruder arrived.[19]

Sadly for the Confederates, there were plenty of guns available, they just weren't put efficiently to use. Discounting the batteries of Holmes and Stuart, Lee's army had about 63 batteries. The majority of them, 46 to be more exact, were assigned to brigades or divisions on a permanent basis. The other 17 batteries were in Brigadier General William N. Pendleton's artillery reserve. William Pendleton had sent 11 of the 17 to serve with infantry units on a temporary basis. Jackson and Longstreet managed to gather up portions of nine of these batteries. Some 28 guns were gathered up, and 13 of those were forced out of the fight.

On Longstreet's front, Magruder had promised to gather 30 rifled guns from his command. Magruder had some 13 total batteries assigned. However, Magruder didn't return from his wayward march until Longstreet had departed from Armistead's position. This was probably too late to be a salvation to Longstreet. Magruder would have experienced the problem of guns being embedded in infantry units and strung out all along the line of march. It would not have been simple to rush them to the front. The narrow lanes available for moving the artillery were, in some places, vulnerable to Federal artillery fire. Sadly, only parts of two of Magruder's batteries, McCarthy's battery and a section of Hart's, actually fired on the Federals in the artillery duel. McCarthy had a scary time moving into his firing position. Huger's artillery never got into the fight, but they were in the very rear of the column.

On Jackson's end of the line, Crutchfield was ill, and not available to repeat the excellent work he did at White Oak Swamp. Chase Whiting had only two batteries assigned, Reilly's and Balthis'. The next division in the column was that of D. H. Hill, who had 5 permanently assigned and 2 attached batteries. Unfortunately, all were out of ammunition and had been sent back to Seven Pines. Jackson's division had 5 batteries assigned and Ewell's division had 3, but they were mixed in the infantry and hard to bring up.

There were two remaining groups of artillery available to put into the two "grand batteries" First were the batteries of A. P. Hill and Longstreet. Powell Hill had eleven batteries and Longstreet had seven. These were in reserve at Glendale. Some of these artillerists were in good shape and wanted to get into the fight. When they finally received orders and arrived at the front, the day and the battle were over. Longstreet had promised to get his guns to the front, and he sent a staff officer to Glendale to get them moving. When the officer returned and told his general that one battery would be delayed while the commander saw that his horses were watered, an angry Longstreet had the battery commander relieved and another captain assigned to bring the battery up. Hill reported Pegram's and Davidson's batteries engaged. Crenshaw reported that his battery had been ordered back for refit prior to Malvern Hill, and missed the fight. This still leaves some 16 batteries for which there is no record of participation in the battle. They were likely at Glendale in reserve, less than two miles from the location Longstreet picked for his "grand battery." Why weren't they brought forward? It is almost impossible to fix blame for this gross blunder, however, Longstreet must take responsibility for not using the guns assigned to him.[20]

The second group was William Pendleton's artillery reserve. Pendleton only had six batteries under his immediate command, the others being sent out to infantry commanders. After a day off the battlefield due to illness on the 29th, William Pendleton spent the 30th trying to reposition his batteries to make them as useful as possible. He had a few large bore rifled guns, and they were sent down the Darbytown road to the crossroads with the Long Bridge road. Some of Pendleton's batteries, under Colonel J. Thompson Brown, had passed that way the previous day. Pendleton, as the officer in charge of the artillery reserve, was responsible for employing his batteries on July 1. He truly tried, but was unsuccessful. He lost touch with the tactical situation, and attempted to understand the needs of the army and respond. He started out trying to find General Lee and could not. Failing that, he then attempted to find a firing location that would allow him to support the infantry without endangering them. Finally, he gave up, stayed put, and waited for orders.

It is difficult to understand how a brigadier general could fail to find someone to assist, or someone to give him orders. Bearing in mind that he only had six batteries; he could be no more than a minor factor in concentrating artillery. Also, we must consider the fact that none of the key generals seemed to try to find Pendleton. It almost appears that all of them forgot that the army had an artillery reserve and an experienced officer to employ it for them.

It is apparent that the Confederate artillery was poorly utilized at Malvern Hill. Most of the problem wasn't the poor decision-making on July 1, but the awful organization and management. Rather than have all the artillery under Pendleton's direct command, as was the Federal artillery under Henry Hunt, most of the Confederate guns were assigned or attached to brigades or divisions. Pendleton wanted a unified command,

and Lee had approved its creation. It just didn't happen in time for the battle of Malvern Hill. Only such an arrangement would have allowed Pendleton to be a significant factor on July 1.

There was an additional problem for the Confederates regarding Malvern Hill. Their task in moving guns into position was formidable. The guns had to move down narrow roads, jammed with infantry and wagons, often under enemy observation and fire. Once arriving in the area of the battlefield, there were only a few decent firing positions available. These factors were acknowledged by several Confederate generals in their post-war writings. It is a pity that these factors had not been explored and analyzed before Longstreet devised his artillery plan and Lee approved it. It was a reasonable idea, but it just could not be executed. The infantry attacks later that day never should have been allowed to take place.[21]

While the generals were having their problems conducting the artillery duel, the Confederate infantry continued to press forward. Harvey Hill's division, which had been following that of Whiting, turned off the Willis Church road a bit north of the junction with the Carter's Mill road. Hill's division turned right into the woods, and were at the base of Malvern Hill. They received artillery fire as they crossed open ground and Western Run to reach the cover of the trees. They advanced toward the Federal batteries of Kingsbury, Ames, Livingston, Bramhall and Osborn. The Confederates also had to endure the musketry of two of Palmer's regiments. One Confederate regiment, the 14th North Carolina of George B. Anderson's brigade, advanced to within a hundred yards of the Federal guns, but was forced to retire by the intense fire. Some of Palmer's men pursued the retiring Confederates. The regiment lost their colors and General Anderson was wounded. The 14th held some of the ground it had gained, remaining south of Western Run.[22]

Farther right on the Confederate line, Armistead observed a skirmish line in his front. They were Berdan's Sharpshooters, serving as a picket line for Morell's division. Armistead opted to send the 14th, 38th and 53rd Virginia to oppose them. A part of Wright's men followed the Virginians. Wright initially ordered his men to halt their advance, but ordered his whole brigade forward when he learned that Armistead had ordered his regiments forward.

There was some confusion at the regimental level as to what Armistead's purpose and object were. Colonel Edmonds of the 38th Virginia saw no other possibility than that Armistead was assaulting the main Federal line, so he joined in the attack. The other regiments had to make due without orders, but some of the troops followed Colonel Edmonds, as the Federal skirmishers were pushed out of a swale about 400 yards in front of the

Federal lines. Displacing the Federal skirmishers, the Confederates were happy to enjoy the relative protection of the depression in the battlefield. Wright saw an overall disadvantage to the position and ordered his brigade to pull back. Armistead had a dilemma. He could not work out a method of advancing on the Federal guns or withdrawing his regiments from the depression. He decided to hold position until some artillery came up.[23] Again, it is impossible to know exactly which Federal batteries fired at which targets.

The ground that Armistead had gained and held made a difference to Lee. Hoping that the concentrated artillery barrage would have the desired effect, Lee needed to decide how to coordinate the attack by his infantry. When Armistead observed a Federal retreat, he would be able to pass a signal to the rest of the army to move forward together. Lee directed Colonel Chilton to write an order to make that happen. Chilton wrote an order that read: "Batteries have been established to rake the enemy's lines. If it is broken, as is probable, Armistead, who can witness the effect of the fire, has been ordered to charge with a yell. Do the same."

It is hard to see how this order could have served to launch a coordinated attack of an army the size of the Army of Northern Virginia at Malvern Hill. The primary weakness of the order is the use of the shouting troops of an attacking brigade to initiate the attacks of all the other brigades. Given the noise level on a battlefield such as Malvern Hill, the reliability of shouting as a signal is very dubious. Shouting coming from Armistead's location could very well originate from a charge by the Federals in his front. Even though Longstreet later testified that it was Lee's plan, it is hard to believe that Lee desired the order to be written in the fashion that it was. Armistead was a new brigade commander, and should not have be burdened with the responsibility of triggering the general attack of a huge army. Lee himself or one of his trusted staff officers should have been positioned within sight of Armistead's brigade, along with the necessary couriers to spread the word for a general attack. The longest distance to any of Lee's troops was only a mile and a half. Lee could not have found a more important place to be at that point in the fighting. It was his responsibility to make the crucial decision, and he didn't do it.

It is interesting to note that the order had a date, but no time. Perhaps of no consequence, but also possibly a source of confusion to some. This is but another example of the inadequate staff work produced by Lee's headquarters. Such carelessness can and often does lead an army to great disaster.[24]

No simple explanation for the order has ever been expressed. The obvious fatigue of General Lee could certainly have been a factor. The

President even prevented McLaws from waking Lee at one point. Davis was evidently concerned for Lee's physical condition. In some instances, Lee was apparently functioning normally, despite his fatigue.

Armistead's report fails to mention Lee's order or the criticality of Armistead's part in executing it. It is possible that the order wasn't distributed down to the brigade level. That would make Huger responsible for passing the order down to Armistead. The order didn't affect Armistead much early in the day. Harvey Hill was afforded adequate time to deploy his brigades, analyze the Federal lines, wait a while before he received the order. Magruder received his copy after returning to the field from his wanderings. Hill even had time to message Stonewall that, since the artillery barrage was failing, perhaps the attack should be scrubbed. Stonewall affirmed that the order was still in effect.[25]

Lee, although fatigued, must have become aware that Longstreet's plan was a failure, as he began to seek another way to go. Lee and Longstreet rode together and discussed turning the Federal right. They identified a road with some fairly level ground and some cover for moving troops. Lee directed Longstreet to move his and A. P. Hill's divisions in the direction of the newly found road. Branch, commanding one of A. P. Hill's brigades, was ordered down the Long Bridge road.

The topology of Malvern Hill deserves some description. The crest of Malvern Hill runs southeast for a mile and a half from the intersection of the Carter's Mill and Willis Church roads, then it drops quickly down to a plain west of Turkey Island Creek. The ground rises and is wooded east of the creek. That higher ground reaches to the River road, south of Malvern Hill and the Turkey Island Creek Bridge. An easy march of about six miles via Keyes' road would deliver the Confederates to the River road, south of Turkey Island Creek. It would also be a relatively safe march, out of Federal artillery range. It is possible that Lee or Longstreet might have observed Franklin's VI Corps already occupying the area desired by the Confederates. Other nearby areas, such as near the millpond northeast of Haxall's, would also serve the Confederates nearly as well. Hood and Hampton suggested to Whiting that an advance down a small valley that ran from just north of the Poindexter field would have been successful earlier in the day. They based their suggestion on a reconnaissance made by some of Hood's men. Whiting declined the suggestion.

As with so many Confederate operations, time was the main opponent. Powell Hill and James Longstreet could possibly have made it into position that day, but an attack before dark was unlikely. Lee likely knew at that point that a victory would again elude him. There was the possibility that he could reinforce his left after dark and try the Federal right on the morning of July 2. Knowing that his troops at Malvern Hill could keep the Federals busy, while he attacked their right flank, Lee still held out hope for cutting the Army of the Potomac into two more digestible parts.[26]

At that time, Magruder returned to the battlefield, this time with his command. Lee had ordered Magruder to move to Huger's right, and Longstreet had then directed Magruder to support Armistead. Barksdale's brigade, the first of Magruder's units to come up, was already positioned at Armistead's right rear. Therefore, Magruder sent forward the three uncommitted regiments of Cobb's brigade, the 24th Georgia, 2nd Louisiana and 15th North Carolina. As Cobb moved his regiments forward, Prince John went to determine the precise situation. Lee also sent Brent to discover how Magruder's command would connect with that of Huger.

Brent had previously examined that area of the battlefield from the branches of a tree, observed the Federal artillery in abundance there, and concluded the Malvern Hill was a strong position. Brent encountered Ransom's brigade and inquired as to Huger's whereabouts. Ransom wasn't sure, but a staff officer pointed the way. It was a mile ride to the rear for Brent to find Huger. General Huger's attitude was strange. He was unsure of the ends of his lines and the location of his brigades. He complained that someone other than he had positioned them, that he was no longer in command of his division, and that he was staying out of the situation.

Huger had a valid complaint. Lee had positioned the brigades of Armistead and Wright that morning. That afternoon Lee had met Huger, as he was leading his remaining two brigades onto the battlefield. Lee ordered Huger to send Mahone to aid Cobb. Lee had clearly put his right wing under John Magruder.[27]

Despite the surprising nature of Huger's reaction, his men were on the battlefield. Brent rode east along the alleged line and met D. H. Hill, whose troops were positioned between the Willis Church and Carter's Mill roads. Hill made it clear to Brent that Hill had the problem of his right flank in the air, and Brent went to report back to Magruder. It is unclear whether Hill expected Magruder to remedy Hill's uncovered right flank.

Magruder didn't know quite what to think about Huger's attitude. He was also puzzled by the Federal position. The Federals were working hard while the Confederates were figuring out their improvised plan for the remainder of the day. Sedgwick and Smith had coordinated their defense of Turkey Island Creek Bridge, planning to defend it from a turning movement, much like Lee was preparing to try. Dana's brigade was on the south end of the line. On Dana's right was the 106th Pennsylvania of

Burns' brigade, filling the gap with Smith's brigade. Sully's brigade was positioned on Dana's left. Two batteries, those of Charles M. Morgan and Samuel S. Elder, were placed in Smith's front. This reinforcement of the army's right might have been ordered by McClellan after he returned, as it weakened the reserves set aside for the left and center, and McClellan hadn't left any one general in charge during his absence.

Closer to the front, Abercrombie moved his brigade to align with the remainder of Couch's division. Abercrombie sent the 61st Pennsylvania and 65th New York to support Kingsbury's battery and the 67th New York and the 23rd and 31st Pennsylvania were positioned behind Palmer and Howe's other regiments. Howe then moved his men up to a more desirable position, and the regiments refined their positions. The 31st Pennsylvania and the 65th New York supported Palmer's two regiments near the ravine just north of the West house, as the 61st Pennsylvania and the 67th New York filled the gap between Howe and Palmer. The 23rd Pennsylvania now supported Howe's right. These refinements now made Couch's line lie in an arc from Willis Church road to the northeast ridge of Malvern Hill.

The Federals were also refining the deployment of their artillery. Kingsbury, already getting low on ammunition and having suffered some damage to several of his guns, left the line. The remaining guns of Weeden's battery, under Lieutenant Richard Waterman, as well as Hyde's two guns, came from the left of the Griffin's line to replace Kingsbury. Edwards' battery came from the south end of Sykes' line to take Livingston's place. Livingston was also out of ammunition. Bramhall was sent to Heintzelman, and Osborn was sent to Couch, and shortly thereafter, to Hooker.

The Confederates were aware of the Federal movements, but didn't understand them. One Confederate observer, Porter Alexander, felt they were almost perfect as a deception. Whiting, had made his way, supported by Hampton and Trimble, into the Poindexter field. He was working his way along the edge of a wooded area that separated the field from the base of the hill. Whiting made the mistake of believing that the Federals were retreating instead of refining their defensive positions.[28]

During that time period, David Jones' division was also moving into their assigned position. Longstreet had placed G. T. Anderson's brigade behind Cobb's men, which were in Armistead's rear. Toombs' brigade was on the right rear of G. T. Anderson. Magruder ordered Cobb and Anderson to move forward at the same time. When this occurred, Toombs assumed Anderson's previous position. This had the effect of a column of four brigades on the west side of Carter's Mill road, and added up to a great deal of offensive combat power. G. T. Anderson was inadvertently and anonymously ordered to move to the right of the Confederate line, but Magruder soon put them back where he wanted them.

McLaws was positioned at the Carter house, on the Carter's Mill road. Longstreet had ordered McLaws down the Carter's Mill road, and McLaws immediately rode to familiarize himself with the area. He came across Wright and Armistead in the position that Longstreet had assigned him. He reported the fact back to Longstreet, and was told to hold his present position. When Magruder returned from his journey to the Quaker road, McLaws' division became the rear of the line, with Semmes west of the Carter's Mill road and Kershaw to the east.

Magruder studied the Federal position while his men were settling into position. He had probably stopped taking the medicine that had bothered him earlier in the week, but suffered from a lack of nourishment and sleep. Brent stated that Magruder had been awake almost all the night before, but had eaten nothing. Brent remembered having a full haversack, and Magruder and the rest of the staff now ate. Magruder probably didn't eat again once the battle began. He appeared to have abundant physical energy, but it is impossible to gauge his mental energy and judgment. Magruder messaged Lee that Magruder's command was in position, and that Armistead had already made contact with the Federals and driven them. This report likely reached Lee about the time as Whiting's report that the Federals were retreating.[29]

These two reports, arriving almost simultaneously, though they contradicted earlier indicators, might have led Lee to conclude that the Confederate artillery barrage had induced McClellan to order a withdrawal from Malvern Hill. If Lee applied more pressure on McClellan, in the form of an infantry assault, would the Federals collapse? Could this possibly lead to a Confederate victory?

Unfortunately for Lee, McClellan was simply rotating his batteries and reinforcing his lines. Unlike the Confederates, the Army of the Potomac had the resources to rest units periodically. There was no real success by Armistead's brigade. They were only able to pin down several Federal regiments. Lee had earlier decided that an assault was not feasible. Although nothing of significance had changed, Lee now believed that a change had occurred. He had Captain Andrew G. Dickinson take a message to Magruder that said: "General Lee expects you to advance rapidly. He says it is reported that the enemy is getting off. Press forward your whole line and follow up Armistead's success." Lee also promised to move Mahone's brigade into Anderson's position., and that Ransom's brigade was moving to support Howell Cobb. Lee had never canceled the previous order, and failed to issue new orders to his other subordinate commanders. Therefore, when they heard shouting on the right, they would attack per the old order.

While Dickinson rode to Lee and back, Magruder received Lee's earlier orders. Under either orders, Magruder was required to attack in support of Armistead. He was gathering up all the men he could. He believed the entire Army of the Potomac was in his front. Brent came upon Ransom, whose brigade was in the woods near the Carter's Mill road. Mahone was likely just across the road on Ransom's right. When Brent returned, Prince John ordered him back on his horse to go back to Ransom, with orders for Ransom to hasten to the front. Ransom had been ordered by Huger not to leave his current position until Huger ordered him elsewhere. He explained to Brent that he could not move, even though he personally would like to do so. Mahone, also encountered by Brent, had received the same orders from Huger, but was a little more flexible in his thinking.

Brent gave Magruder the bad news that neither of Huger's brigadiers were willing to come up. He ordered Brent to go back to them and stay until at least one of them would come up as requested. Brent was to then march that brigade to the aid of Wright. Brent chose to revisit Billy Mahone first. Billy had just received word that Lee had ordered his brigade put under Magruder's command, so Mahone moved up as requested. He was made to leave behind one regiment, the 49th Virginia, to guard a battery. Ransom, rechecking with Holmes, was still under orders to stay put until Huger released him. Huger met with Ransom and again ordered him to hold his position.

About this time, Magruder received Lee's order. Prince John had no doubt about Marse Robert's intent. Magruder's command had to attack and exploit any success enjoyed by Lewis Armistead. Magruder also was certain that the brigades of Mahone and Ransom were under his command. He felt he must attack immediately, with a strength of 15,000 men, 23,000 if he counted Mahone and Ransom. The latter number would include two artillery batteries, those of McCarthy and Davidson from A. P. Hill.[30]

Magruder, Wright and Armistead surveyed the area around them. Wright now had most of his brigade concentrated. They had become separated on the advance to Malvern Hill, and the 22nd Louisiana, whom Wright knew had been slightly battered earlier, still had not rejoined the brigade. Magruder gave final instructions for a coordinated advance, then saw Mahone's men and spoke to them briefly. Prince John personally ordered Armistead to start his advance. When Armistead complained that three of his regiments were green, Magruder gave him three of Cobb's regiments for the middle of the attack.

The Confederate artillery fire resumed on Jackson's end of the line, reinforced by the batteries of Carrington and Courtney from Ewell's division. Jackson gave personal attention to the setup of one of the batteries. These additions allowed a crossfire to be poured onto Martindale's and Butterfield's brigades of Morell's division. The Confederate good fortune was short-lived, as the Federal artillery quickly zeroed in on the new gunners. Carrington's position was somewhat protected, but Jackson ordered the battery to retire after only a quarter of an hour. Carrington suffered numerous horses lost in the encounter. Carpenter's guns, firing from the start of the artillery duel, finally ran out of ammunition and retired.

On Magruder's end of the Confederate line, his infantry was on the attack, and probably drew some of the Federal artillery fire from the Confederate guns. Things weren't getting better, however. McCarthy soon exhausted his ammunition. Greenlee Davidson was stunned that he was assigned a position just west of the Carter's Mill road. He didn't expect his battery to survive very long there. Fortunately for Davidson, he suffered no casualties while he was setting up the battery, and by loading his guns on the back side of a minor hill and running them forward to fire each shot, he was able to stay in the fight. A section of Hart's battery joined in the fray, but soon ceased firing for fear of hitting friendly troops. The battle eventually boiled down to Confederate infantry attacking Federal artillery and infantry in an excellent defensive situation.[31]

The Federal artillery situation was superb. Both the gunners on the front line and those positioned near the Malvern house could fire effectively at any Confederates moving down the Carter's Mill road, which ran through mostly open ground. On the Confederate right, the situation was a little different. Several small ridges and ravines gave some protection from the Federal guns. On the River road, Martin's battery had several guns positioned so they had more of the Confederates in sight. Wright and Mahone moved through the rougher terrain toward the Federal left. Wright was in front, with the 3rd Georgia on the left, the 4th Georgia on the right, and the 1st Louisiana and part of the 22nd Georgia in between. The entire brigade was estimated by Wright to be less than 1,000 men, the others being sick or shirkers. Mahone's brigade followed behind.

Near the Mellert (Crew) house was the northwest corner of the Federal position. There the east/west line turned into a north/south line along the bluff. It was a potential weak point in the Federal defense, and Wright and Mahone were heading directly for it. The regiment on the corner was the 14th New York of Griffin's brigade. They were overlooking a ravine that ran downhill to the northwest. To the north and west of Griffin's brigade was a newly cut wheat field. The shocks of cut wheat offered cover for Berdan's sharpshooters, who were first to observe the

Confederate brigades approaching. Berdan sent his lieutenant colonel to the division commander with the news. Morell reacted immediately, notifying Colonel James McQuade, the commander of the 14th New York, and also Martindale, Butterfield and Porter.

Butterfield and Martindale had earlier been given discretion by Morell to support each other and even Griffin without asking for further orders. With only a little shelter from the Confederate artillery, Martindale's and Butterfield's brigades had been hurt by the artillery fire. This, despite intense return fire from the Federal artillery. Martindale walked along his lines, encouraging his men. He made it clear to them that the position must be held. When he received the word that the Confederates were coming toward the 14th New York, he directed the 13th New York to support them, and personally led them.

On the Confederate side of the line, Wright noticed the 13th New York's movement to aid the 14th, and committed the 3rd Georgia to oppose it. Wright's other two regiments advanced to about 300 yards of the Federals, then ducked into the shelter of a hollow. Braving Berdan's fire from the wheat field, Mahone's brigade quickly caught up with Wright's men, and all sheltered in the hollow. There, they were immune from musket fire from the bluff, but subject to the artillery of the batteries of Carlisle, Voegelee, Weed and Nairn. Berdan's Sharpshooters also continued to fire at the Confederates.[32]

The forward elements of Armistead's brigade could see the advance of Wright's and Mahone's brigades. Armistead's Virginians joined in the charge, closing to seventy-five yards of the Federals, then firing their muskets. After their volley, they tried to overrun the guns. The Federals there were of Griffin's brigade. The guns were the batteries of Edwards, Ames, Weeden, Hyde and perhaps others. The infantry supports were, from left to right, the 4th Michigan, 9th Massachusetts and 62nd Pennsylvania. Griffin had instructed them to hold their fire until the Confederates were very close. The three regiments were joined by Berdan's men, back from their skirmishing assignment. Most of the men heeded Griffin's orders, and when they fired, the Confederates were repulsed.

Although the Confederate attack had been thrown back, it gave a boost to the spirits of Wright's and Mahone's men. Mahone waved a battle flag and led his brigade forward. They closed to about 150–200 yards before being driven back by intense Federal fire. There was no more Confederate progress at this point in the line for the remainder of the day.[33]

The three regiments from Cobb's brigade, the 2nd Louisiana, the 24th Georgia, and the 15th North Carolina followed three of Armistead's regiments. Armistead's remaining regiments, the 9th and 57th Virginia, followed behind Cobb's men. The 16th Georgia of Cobb's brigade later followed the attack. The robust Confederate attack caused Griffin's men to return to their original lines. About 25 men of the 9th Massachusetts were captured when they failed to retreat to their lines with other Federals. There were also friendly fire casualties among Massachusetts troops, caused by the 4th Michigan. To further complicate matters for the Federals, Colonel Woodbury, commander of the 4th, was killed at that point. Other than Edwards' battery, which had limbered up after the first charge, all the Federal batteries continued to pour canister into the attacking Confederates. The 57th Virginia had a bad first combat experience. Two captains were hit and the confused regiment "stampeded in all directions upon being ordered to fall back. A minority part of the regiment was rallied and participated in two subsequent attacks. Most did not fight any more that day.

It was a terribly lethal day for color bearers on both sides. From privates to at least one colonel, the colors were picked up when the bearer was hit. Anywhere near regimental colors was a dangerous place to be. In the fog of battle, there was also a friendly fire event between two Confederate units, causing the victimized regiment, the 16th Georgia, to break for the rear. On balance, most of the troops performed well. The first of the half dozen Confederate attacks was the most effective, and came closest to breaching the Federal lines.[34]

The Confederate attacks had run both Griffin's brigade and Berdan's sharpshooters out of ammunition, and they were replaced by the brigade of Butterfield. He and Couch had decided earlier in the day that the seam between Morell's and Couch's divisions was a potential weak point. Butterfield promised his support to Couch, and sent the 16th Michigan and 83rd Pennsylvania to the spot. The 16th moved from there to support artillery recently positioned a little west of the Willis Church road. The 83rd advanced straight ahead, and replaced the 9th Massachusetts. Butterfield was very ill that day, but self-medicated and remained on the field. He urged the Pennsylvanians to seek revenge for their fallen commander, Colonel McLane, who had been killed several days earlier at Gaines' Mill. The 83rd moved to their left, passing through the right of Martindale. They ran up against the Confederate attack and stopped it, some 150 yards from the Federal lines. On the 83rd's left, the 44th New York had replaced the 62nd Pennsylvania, and used the bayonet to stop other Confederates. The attackers lost their colors, which were brought to Butterfield. Meanwhile, the 16th Michigan held its position under repeated Confederate pressure, until its artillery support retired.

Butterfield ordered the 12th New York to the left of the line. Their commander, Lieutenant Colonel Robert M. Richardson, failed to find Confederates on the left, so he took the unit to the front instead. Finding other Federal troops there in support of artillery, Richardson turned left again in search of the enemy. He advanced to the ravine in front of the Mellert (Crew) house, where he happened upon the 4th Michigan in a bad way. The Michiganders were under attack from a flank by Wright's and Mahone's troops, and short of ammunition. The Confederate attack had inflicted much damage on the 4th.

Richardson and the 12th New York attacked right through the battered 4th Michigan and drove the Confederates back. The New Yorkers' major, Henry Barnum, appeared to be mortally wounded, and was taken to the Malvern house to die. Surprisingly, he survived.[35]

Magruder's first attacks at Malvern Hill achieved very little for the Confederate cause. Magruder would better have been sent further along the Quaker road. Casualties were significant. Wright's brigade, which began the fight with less than 1,000 men, suffered a total of 393 casualties. Mahone, starting the day with 1,226 men, sustained a total of 329. An individual private in the 1st Louisiana was promoted to captain after all of the officers in his company were taken out of action.

Armistead's casualties totaled 388 of about 1,000 men. As with the casualties in Wright's and Mahone's brigades, some of Armistead's regiments suffered inordinately high casualties, while others got off relatively lightly. Cobb's brigade sustained even higher casualties than Armistead, 413 of about 1,500.

On the Federal side of the line, Griffin's brigade lost 494 killed or wounded. The casualties included two regimental commanders. Colonel Thomas Cass of the 9th Massachusetts was mortally wounded and Colonel Dwight Woodbury of the 4th Michigan was killed. General Porter stated that the 4th Michigan saved the Army of the Potomac that day.[36]

As Magruder began his first assaults, D. H. Hill and his five brigade commanders were meeting north of Malvern Hill, trying to analyze Chilton's order. Rodes was ill, and had been replaced by John B. Gordon of the 6th Alabama. George B. Anderson had been wounded, and he had been replaced by Colonel Charles C. Tew of the 2nd North Carolina. The six meeting participants had observed the artillery duel and saw no effect. Samuel Garland assumed there would be no infantry fight, since the Confederate artillery had failed to damage the Federal guns. As the conference was ending, a couple of Confederate brigades emerged from the woods, charging toward the Federal lines while yelling. Harvey Hill decided that this was the general advance alluded to in Chilton's order, and told his colleagues to bring up their brigades and pitch in.

Seven Days Before Richmond

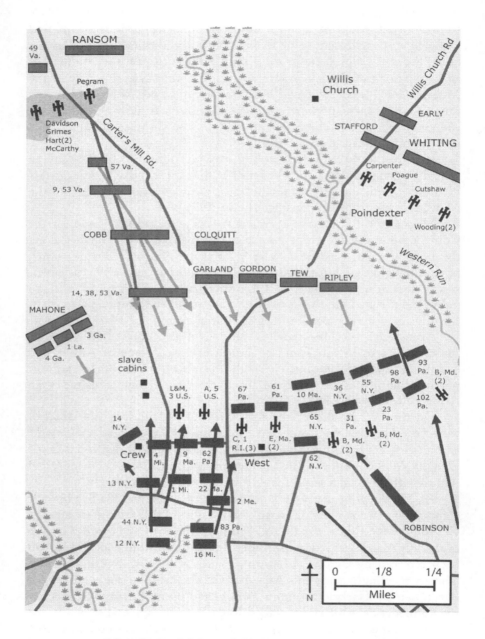

Map 21.2—Malvern Hill, First Attacks, July 1

Hill's brigades were not where they were originally positioned when they came up. Garland was now on the Confederate right, with his left on the Willis Church road. Ripley had moved to assume the Confederate left. Gordon was the middle of the line, and Colquitt's brigade was in Garland's rear on the right. Tew was between Ripley and Gordon. As quickly as their commanders returned, the brigades began to move forward. As Chilton's order specified a coordinated attack, they'd gotten off to a good start.

Harvey Hill's division was advancing uphill. Their opponents numbered more than a division, supported by artillery. After the meeting between Butterfield and Couch, Butterfield advised Porter of the imminent Confederate attack. Caldwell's brigade, in the process of eating their suppers, was moved from the vicinity of the Malvern house to Couch's rear. When Gordon, Tew and Ripley hit this section of the Federal position, the Confederates suffered a huge reversal. They held for a bit, then the 102nd Pennsylvania of Howe's brigade attacked the flank of the 1st North Carolina, a regiment previously cut up at Mechanicsville. Part of the 3rd North Carolina went to the aid of the 1st, but the 3rd's commander, Colonel Gaston Meares, was killed then, and Ripley pulled his brigade back down the hill.

On the Federal side, Howe's brigade was then reinforced by the 4th Maine and four companies of the 3rd Maine from Birney's brigade, the 23rd Pennsylvania from Abercrombie's brigade, as well as two guns of Snow's battery.[37]

Gordon was on Ripley's right, and struggling through dense woods, meadows and hills to get in position. One of Tew's regiments, after becoming disoriented, joined Gordon. He moved the 5th and 26th Alabama to the left to get them out of sight of the Federal artillery. He then stood on a stump and told the Alabamians that they had to take a battery just over the hill and personally led them toward the Federals of Abercrombie and Palmer. Gordon was without the services of the 12th Alabama, which had been detailed to take prisoners to Richmond.

Tew's brigade attacked on Gordon's immediate left. As soon as the attack began, the Federal artillery and infantry began to cut up Tew's and Gordon's brigades, and their progress was only 200 yards. Despite their heavy losses, they reformed and tried again. Once again, it was a costly attack for color bearers. The 30th North Carolina at one point was out in front of the other Confederate infantry, and came up against the four Federal regiments which drove the Tarheels back down the hill. The Federals suffered a number of casualties, including Major Ozro Miller of the 10th Massachusetts, as they ran the enemy back down the slope. John B. Gordon had a rough time going up and then down the hill. His revolver was damaged, his coat torn, his canteen ruptured, and a shell showered him with dirt.[38]

Garland's brigade was attacking on Hill's right. The brigade had been taking Federal artillery fire even before they began their charge up the hill. The 23rd North Carolina advanced up the west side of the Willis Church road, and suffered from a lack of cover. They were falling behind the rest of the brigades under the heavy fire. At about 400 yards from the Federal lines, the men of the 23rd, without orders, lay down and fired. Garland quickly concluded that he could progress no farther, and sent word to D. H. Hill that he needed reinforcements just to maintain his current position. Hill responded by sending the 6th Georgia from Colquitt's brigade and searching for more available troops.

By this time, Hill's troops had reached a point where they wanted no more of trying to fight their way up Malvern Hill. Members of General Ewell's staff attempted to rally some of Hill's men, but had little success. The division went to the back of the line. The attack was costly in casualties and morale. It was dark before all the brigades were reformed. They had suffered casualties totaling almost 1,750 men, almost 20% of those who started up the hill. Gordon was hit hard, losing 425 of about a thousand. The 3rd Alabama alone lost 200 men, over half of the regiment. The 44th Georgia, badly mauled at Mechanicsville, also lost half its men. Garland and Tew lost 850 between them, and the reserve brigade of Colquitt still lost 200 men. After the war, D.H. Hill wrote that "It was not war—it was murder." It seems an appropriate comment for what happened to his division at Malvern Hill.[39]

Even as D. H. Hill's division was being repulsed, Couch's IV Corps division was being reinforced. After the Confederate attackers had retreated down the hill, Couch was stronger than before. His division had lost only 600 men. Robinson's brigade of Kearny's III Corps division furnished three regiments, the 57th and 63rd Pennsylvania, and the 87th New York. They were assigned to support artillery. The 5th New Hampshire of Caldwell's brigade in Richardson's II Corps division also gave support to a pair of batteries in Howe's part of the line. Three fresh batteries, those of Frank, De Russy (under Francis Seeley), and Benson rushed up to replace Weeden and Hyde. Frank and Seeley arrived before Benson, and Frank had to split his battery to find room for his guns. He put four on each flank of Ames' battery.

The Confederates had more troops coming up, too. Toombs' brigade of David Jones' division struggled through thick woods filled with obstructions to reach the battlefield. They could only rely on the sounds of battle to guide them, and thus came out in the center of the Confederate line, instead of behind Cobb and G. T. Anderson, where they were assigned. Coming out into the open, Toombs organized his formations while under enemy artillery fire. Resuming his advance, Toombs came upon the advance units, halted, and had his troops lie down. Presently, an order, likely from David Jones, Toombs' division commander, directed the regimental officers to move to the left. As it turns out, this was merely a suggestion, and the suggestion came from a mere captain on David Jones' staff. Toombs was unhappy about the "order," but was unable to do anything about it. Most of the brigade had veered left, crossed the Carter's Mill road, and gone into the same woods that D. H. Hill's division had tread on its way to the fight.

Some of the regiments had more difficulty than others in executing the movement. Toombs observed that the brigade had become divided, and ordered the 17th Georgia to follow the other regiments. Unfortunately, the 17th became split into two parts while changing front. Toombs was personally lagging behind his men, and couldn't manage to control the confusion.

D. H. Hill encountered the brigade in this state of confusion, their commander not in evidence. He ordered them to the support of Garland's brigade, but they couldn't take the fire upon reaching the brow of Malvern Hill, and they retreated in haste. When Hill finally found Toombs, Hill screamed, "Where were you when I was riding in front on my horse trying to rally your brigade?" Hill definitely had little respect for Toombs. In a subsequent letter, which stated, "My remarks were personal to yourself and not to your brigade. I did not in the slightest degree reflect on your men." Toombs was mad enough to challenge Hill to a duel, which Hill refused. Some speculated that Toombs had been drinking, and thus couldn't keep up with his men. Whether Toombs was drunk or not, his brigade contributed little to support the efforts of D. H. Hill's division on July 1. They did suffer casualties, however.

George T. Anderson's brigade advanced on Toombs' right, just west of the Carter's Mill road. As the left end of the brigade (9th and 11th Georgia) emerged from the woods, they moved ahead of the remainder of the brigade (1st Georgia Regulars, 7th and 8th Georgia). The two halves of the brigade were diverging, with the right end drawing up near the brigades of Wright and Mahone. Before Anderson could correct the situation, Magruder rode up and ordered the 1st, 7th and 8th regiments to attack. Anderson was not with those regiments, but with the 9th and 11th Georgia. A part of the 11th broke, and Anderson appealed to them to rally. No part of the brigade progressed very far. The right end of the brigade advanced to the foot of Malvern Hill, but could go no farther.

Anderson finally drew them back. The retreat back through canister and shot was almost as dangerous as the attack, and the 8th Georgia fell back in less than an orderly fashion.[40]

To the right of G. T. Anderson, Magruder personally placed Barksdale's brigade. Prince John ordered them to support Wright and Mahone. The Mississippians had been subjected to Federal artillery fire for some time. Barksdale had told the brigade that the offending battery had to be taken. On the advance, they found and took advantage of a sheltering ravine. They enjoyed clear fields of fire, and had Armistead and Cobb on their left and Wright and Mahone on their right. They lost a little order in reaching the ravine, and probably stopped a firefight on the way there. Volunteers from Berdan's Sharpshooters were attempting to draw fire away from the Federal guns by engaging a party of Confederates left over from earlier charges.

Barksdale's men headed for the 12th and 44th New York, but couldn't advance past the brow of Malvern Hill. They never closed inside of a couple of hundred yards of the Federal lines. At that time, no Federal batteries were directly in Barksdale's front, but batteries on Couch's left and Morell's right engaged the Mississippians. At least three batteries, those of Frank, Ames and Snow, poured their fire into Barksdale's men, and about a third of the brigade were casualties, some 400 in all. The leaders of every regiment were wounded.

Barksdale's attack did put pressure on Butterfield's brigade. The 44th New York and the 83rd Pennsylvania fought continuously. Ammunition was virtually gone in the 83rd Pennsylvania, while the 12th New York continued fighting for in excess of an hour. As this occurred, Martindale was putting his troops into the fray. He pulled the 2nd Maine back to reinforce the 22nd Massachusetts and the 1st Michigan. Martindale then sent all three regiments to support Butterfield and Griffin. The 1st Michigan went to the aid of the 83rd Pennsylvania, which was out of ammunition, and the 1st ran out itself. The 22nd Massachusetts then replaced the 1st Michigan, and the 22nd likewise exhausted its ammunition.

Porter, observing the line with Martindale, saw the stragglers and the wounded moving to the rear from the pressured part of the line. Using that remainder of the 25th New York available to him, he set them about redirecting the stragglers back to their regiments and the wounded to medical assistance. Farther behind the line, the 3rd Pennsylvania Cavalry had this responsibility for the entire army.[41]

Porter decided to request reinforcements, motivated by the pressure the Confederates were putting on his lines. He first had Hunt send the batteries of Tidball and Robertson, as well as the 32 pound howitzers of

Battery D, 1st New York Light Artillery. Tyler's siege guns had ceased fire and were being pulled down the southern slope of Malvern Hill. This might have been because Porter wasn't sure he could hold his position, and siege guns take a long time to move. The fire of the gunboats in the James could also be a factor. There are widely differing accounts of the role played by the gunboats. Confederate survivors all describe the large projectiles and loud reports of the guns firing, but in fact they didn't join in the fight until fairly late in the day. Porter complained that they hit as many Federals as Confederates. Although the Federal signal corps tried valiantly to communicate with the gunboats to direct their fire, smoke on the battlefield made that very difficult. Porter finally told the boats, "For God's sake, stop firing, you are killing and wounding our men." Two gunboat rounds landed among the siege guns, another in Weeden's battery. Several Federals were killed and wounded by gunboat fire.

Porter needed infantry and told Sykes. General Sykes sent Buchanan and Lovell north towards the left end of Morell's line. Porter scrutinized Couch's part of the line, and decided that the fight would go on for a long time. He then asked Sumner for two brigades. Sumner and Samuel Heintzelman were together on the right when they received Porter's note. Sumner's reaction was to study the note and think about the request, but Heintzelman was quick to offer help to Porter. Meagher's and Sickles' brigades were sent. As Meagher had earlier been released from arrest, he commanded the brigade as it went to Porter's aid.[42]

On the Confederate side of the lines north of Malvern Hill, Robert Ransom entered the fray. Earlier, he had sent the 24th North Carolina to help Magruder, after an urgent request from Prince John. He simultaneously dispatched a staff officer to Huger for instructions. Huger's response was indicative of what his behavior was to be the remainder of the day. He told Ransom that he could go to Magruder's assistance if he so desired, but that he (Huger) would not put himself under Magruder's orders. At that point, Huger was done making decisions and taking action that would affect anything. He became inactive the rest of the day, much as he had been the previous five. The difference this day was that his behavior seemed intentional or purposeful.

Huger appeared irate that Lee had taken troops from him to assign to other missions. He was slow, indolent, lacking in initiative, somewhat hindering others from entering the fray. On top of all those criticisms, we can also accuse him of being non-communicative. He failed to keep the commanding general apprised of his early moves, and he also failed to seek information that could have helped him. Had his behaviors been the opposite of what they actually were, Lee would have been able to get all of the Army of Northern Virginia formed up and ready to do battle earlier in the day. It may not, however, have significantly altered the outcome of the fight. For that to happen, the battle had to be initiated in a more satisfactory manner, and fought much differently. Huger could not have made that happen.[43] Most authors rate Huger's performance as poor. Only Sears believed better performance by Huger could have made a real difference.

Magruder had sent Major Brent back to Ransom. Once Ransom moved out, Brent returned to Magruder. Brent remembered that the noise level of the artillery fire at that moment was about the loudest he experienced in the war.

Ransom's men advanced, not as a brigade, but as individual regiments. The first to stray was the 24th North Carolina. Magruder then ordered the 25th and 35th North Carolina to charge. Both of these two regiments suffered significant casualties. The 25th's commander, Colonel Henry M. Rutledge, was dazed by an exploding artillery round, and the regiment's major was severely wounded. The 35th's commander, Colonel Matt W. Ransom, brother of the brigade commander, was twice wounded and taken to the rear. Command fell to Lieutenant Colonel Oliver C. Petway, who was then mortally wounded. The three regiments withdrew, and Robert Ransom took them to the right and reformed them. The other two regiments of the brigade had already gone to the right. The 26th North Carolina had navigational and straggler troubles.

By now, Magruder was concerned that he might be driven back from his position, and asked Lee for help. General Lee, riding with McLaws, only had one unused unit, and immediately sent it to Magruder. He then asked A. P. Hill for the brigades of Branch and Colonel Edward Thomas (Joseph Anderson's brigade). Neither brigade got into action due to nightfall. Magruder was helped by Longstreet, who moved his division to the right and back to bolster that flank.

Magruder received a note from Lee that instructed Prince John to press more to the right, rather than shift to the left as he had thus far. Magruder interpreted the note as an order to attack again, and sent Major Hyllested to speed up McLaws and locate two more artillery batteries. Hyllested failed to find McLaws, but found both of his brigadiers and passed Magruder's message to them.[44]

On the east side of the Willis Church road, D. H. Hill was also in need of reinforcements. He doubted he could hold his position on Malvern Hill in the face of a serious Federal attack. Jackson ordered his division and Richard Ewell's to the front.

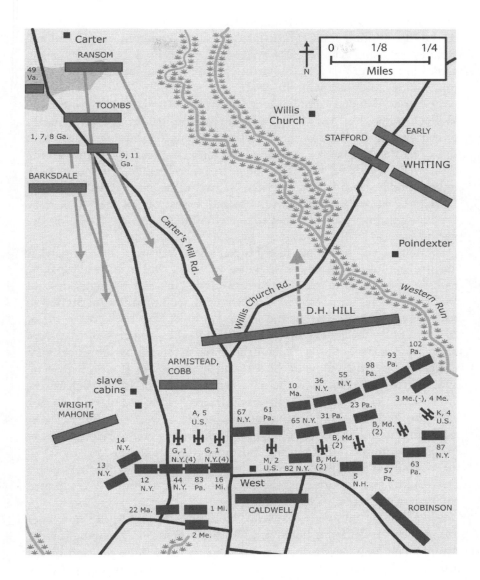

Map 21.3—Malvern Hill, Second Attacks, July 1

Ewell began his movement to the front from behind Whiting's division. Ewell's brigades were now commanded by Trimble, Leroy Stafford and Jubal Early. Only Trimble had been in command since the campaign began. Trimble was on Whiting's extreme left, Leroy Stafford on Whiting's right in a ravine, and Early was behind Stafford, close to the Willis Church road. The Maryland Line, commanded by Colonel Bradley Johnson, had recently arrived, and was on Jubal Early's right, somewhat behind D. H. Hill's starting position. Trimble and Early moved immediately after receiving the order.

Charles Winder, commanding Jackson's division, had been near the Willis Church, but had moved a little to the north, to get out of range of the Federal artillery. When the battle began, the division moved into line of battle. Alexander Lawton was on the east side of the road with the Stonewall Brigade on the west side. J. R. Jones' brigade, with Jones back in command, was in the rear of the Stonewall Brigade. Jackson ordered Winder to move his and Lawton's brigades west of the road, and make contact with Harvey Hill. Jones followed Winder, but had to stop on the narrow road to let some traffic get by.

Though not anything like Huger, Stonewall was also somewhat inactive on July 1. After his response to D. H. Hill's request for help, Jackson added little to the Confederate effort. He made no suggestions to Lee, and took no initiative. It is fair to note that, no matter what Stonewall had done, it is unlikely that the Federals would have been forced off of Malvern Hill. The Federal defenses seemed to get stronger as the day wore on. By late afternoon, the Federal right was defended by John Peck's IV Corps division, the whole of the VI Corps, Sedgwick's II Corps division, and French's brigade from the II Corps division of Israel Richardson. This force, occupying the high ground, along with seventeen batteries, gave the Federals more than enough combat power to resist Jackson's 27,000 men and inferior artillery. It would not do for Jackson to move his entire command in a turning movement against the Federal right. To do so would allow a flank attack against the Confederate divisions to his immediate right. In summary, there was no way that Stonewall could turn the Federal right.

Jackson, in tune with his lack of initiative on July 1, did not order all his men forward, but held back Whiting's division. It may be that he wanted Whiting there to protect his artillery. One more division in the attack would not have changed the outcome. There were too many Federal infantryman, too good a hill to defend, and too efficient an artillery operation for Jackson to succeed. Additionally, the Federal defense was relatively compact. Any weak point could be rapidly reinforced by troops nearby.[45]

Late in the afternoon, Holmes moved his command down the River road, soon reaching the approximate positions it had held the previous day. Henry A. Wise's command advanced on the left of the road and reached the intersection with the Willis Church road. They were inside a mile from the Federal lines on Malvern Hill, and could hear cheering coming from there. Wise's men were ready to make up for their poor showing of the previous day. Holmes, however, had no such intention, and ordered no attack. Instead, he pulled some of them back to find adequate campgrounds for the night. Despite the criticisms of Magruder and D. H. Hill in their reports, Holmes had too small a force to have any effect on the outcome of the battle. The only possible effect of an attack by Holmes along the River road would be more useless Confederate casualties caused by the numerous Federal guns on the hill.[46]

Robert Ransom formed his line on Magruder's far right, under the western brow of Malvern Hill. He ordered them to advance, and they went forward, apparently unnoticed by the enemy. He even observed some Federal troops moving away. It was rapidly growing dark, and Ransom's men closed to a hundred yards of the batteries from the flank. Ransom was out front, mounted, and exhorting his men forward to take the batteries.

Sykes and his division were waiting for Ransom. As Ransom's men climbed the slope through a ravine, the 12th and 14th U. S. of Buchanan's brigade moved part way down the slope to improve their fields of fire. Because of wheat growing on the slope, the Federals waited until the attackers were within a scant twenty yards of the artillery before opening fire. The two Regular regiments fired two volleys into the attackers, then the 14th New York fired a volley. The flashes of hundreds of muskets in the twilight were "beyond description" to Ransom. This was the third repulse of a major assault on the 14th New York on the day. Ransom's men broke and hastened down the hill. They sustained 69 killed, 354 wounded, and a total of 499 casualties. The 25th and 35th North Carolina also suffered heavily.[47]

Semmes and his brigade finally appeared on Ransom's left. Although on paper, Semmes' brigade had six regiments, only 557 men came up with their commander. Federal artillery had concentrated on the brigade as they moved to the front, and severely reduced their numbers. The commander of the 15th Virginia, Colonel T. P. August, was wounded. Colonel Alfred Cumming of the 10th Georgia was incapacitated by a shell exploding nearby, and Semmes had his coat ripped by shrapnel.

The Federal artillery and straggling, which was common in Magruder's command that day, had combined to take a toll on Semmes' brigade. Kershaw's brigade lost about 250 to straggling. G. T. Anderson couldn't give a number, but used the term "many." Cobb started the day with 2,700, but late in the day claimed to have only 1,500. Despite efforts by Magruder to get the stragglers back with their units, it didn't happen in time for the fight at Malvern Hill. They remained scattered all over the area.

At last, Semmes moved the right side of his line, the 15th and 32nd Virginia and the 5th Louisiana farther left to some cover. This move put them behind the 10th and 53rd Georgia. Semmes, out in front, ordered the 10th and 53rd Georgia to move forward. The 10th Louisiana joined them. A smattering of men from the 1st Georgia Regulars of G. T. Anderson's brigade and a few men from Robert Ransom's and Barksdale's brigades also went forward, putting themselves between the 10th Louisiana and the two Georgia regiments. None of the other Confederate troops nearby dared to try the hill again. The Federal line they were charging had adequate reserves. The remainder of Buchanan's brigade, the 3rd and 4th U. S., was waiting behind the line. Up front, the V Corps had been relieved by Meagher's Irish Brigade, comprised of the 29th Massachusetts and the 63rd, 69th and 88th New York. The 69th lead the way. Fitz John Porter lead the reinforcements to the front. Porter was worried enough that he destroyed his dispatch book and diary.

Meagher arrived at the same time as Semmes. Unfortunately for Semmes, his attack on the guns was at an angle to the lines, and his right flank was exposed to muskets of the 69th and 88th New York. The 69th was able to fire first, slowing the Confederate advance. When the 88th was able to fire, it took the Confederates almost in the right rear, breaking their charge. The only cover they found were some out buildings near the Mellert (Crew) house, only sixty yards from the Federal lines.

One regiment, the 10th Louisiana, reached the Federal lines, and hand-to-hand combat ensued. The result was that the commander of the 10th, Lieutenant Colonel Eugene Waggaman and thirty-seven other Louisianians were captured. The rest of the regiment retreated.

On the Federal side of the front, the batteries of Robertson and Tidball came up, and were supported by the 29th Massachusetts and then the 63rd New York. Tidball was only able to site two guns because there was so much infantry around him. When Tidball and Robertson commenced firing, it was already dark. Semmes lost about 135 men, 63 of them captured. The 69th New York bore the brunt of the Confederate attack, losing 127 men killed or wounded.

With Semmes' retreat, the fighting west of the Willis Church road was over. Some Confederates remained in their advanced positions, to include Armistead, Wright and Mahone. The 49th North Carolina of Ransom's brigade was with Wright. The other brigade commanders involved, Toombs, Anderson, Barksdale and Cobb, withdrew their men. All were exhausted. Semmes needed help to get back to his camp.[48]

The last of Magruder's brigades to fight was Kershaw's. The brigade began its march from east of the Carter's Mill road, and traveled through the woods east of the road. This took them toward Couch's lines. They passed through three lines of Confederates while enduring a variety of artillery fire, shell, canister and grape. They closed to within 200–300 yards of Couch's men. The brigade had the complication of finding other Confederates between them and their objective. The men were probably remnants of the attacks of Toombs or of D. H. Hill. The left end of Kershaw's line broke into the open and opened fire, but the rest had to endure the artillery barrage without a chance to return fire.

Kershaw's men were taking fire from fresh Federal troops. Caldwell had ordered the 61st New York and 81st Pennsylvania, consolidated under Colonel Francis Barlow, as well as the 7th New York, to reinforce Howe. Albion Howe, to his credit, determined that the greatest pressure on the lines was to his left, so he sent Barlow's combined regiment and the 23rd Pennsylvania from Abercrombie's brigade there. They relieved the 67th New York and 61st Pennsylvania of Abercrombie's brigade and the 36th New York of Palmer's brigade. These three regiments had exhausted their ammunition supply. The 7th New York formed on Barlow's left. Some of the troops of Caldwell's brigade tried to stand up and fire their muskets, but thought better of it due to the artillery firing canister from behind them.[49]

Sickles and his brigade arrived from III Corps. Sickles, never at a loss for words, gave his men a quick pep talk as they moved toward the front. Sickles intended to move to the left of the line and report to Porter for assignment, but encountered Kearny, who told him he was not needed there. Kearny then received word that Couch was being pressured on the right, and Kearny suggested to Sickles that he would have to decide where to go. Sickles continued on and found Porter, who sent Sickles to support some batteries in Couch's front. Sickles had just set up in his assigned position, when a staff officer came along and made Sickles' orders more general, namely "support Couch in any way necessary." Requests for help soon came from Couch's units, who were running out of ammunition. Sickles ordered the 72nd New York to relieve the 31st Pennsylvania of Abercrombie's brigade. Sickles then sent the 71st New York to relieve the 65th New York. The 74th New York came up to support the 72nd New York. The 70th and 73rd New York remained in reserve.

On the Confederate side of the line, Kershaw's brigade, augmented by the 2nd Georgia and a part of the 20th Georgia of Toombs' brigade, were unable to advance any further into the Federal fire. There was also a friendly fire problem for Kershaw's men at this point.

Seven Days Before Richmond

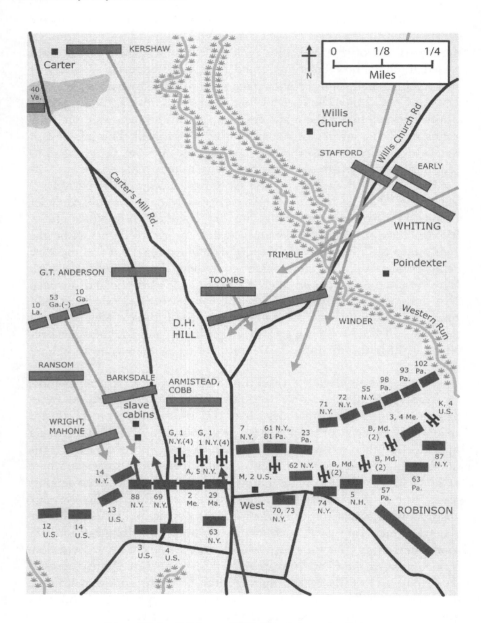

Map 21.4—Malvern Hill, Final Attacks, July 1

It was obvious to Kershaw that he could not advance further, and that even withdrawal would have a price. Knowing that to maintain his position part way up the hill would mean the total demoralization of his brigade, Kershaw ordered a withdrawal to a specified rendezvous point. The retreat was conducted a bit differently by each regiment. Some went in good order, others did not. Only the 2nd and 20th Georgia went to the rendezvous point, where they took cover until sunset. The other regiments fell back to their original starting positions.[50]

The friendly fire situation that Kershaw suffered was essentially fire from the 26th Georgia of Lawton's brigade. Lawton was part of the movement of Ewell's and Winder's divisions, responding to D. H. Hill's request for help. Ewell reached the front ahead of Winder, the result of a shorter required march. Jubal Early's brigade went to a woods between the Willis Church and Carter's Mill road, where D. H. Hill had started his advance earlier. The brigade tried to move through the brush. The movement quickly developed problems. The brush slowed everything down, and Ewell led Early's brigade across an old dam, rather than going though a nearby ravine. Inevitably, the generals lost contact with their men. Another factor was that the woods were full of troops sheltering there from earlier repulses, and the confusion kept increasing. Ewell gave orders directly to four of Early's regiments, and the result was a badly scattered brigade.

Jubal Early, Baldy Ewell and their staffs attempted to rally some of the Confederates taking refuge in the woods. They enjoyed little success. Ewell then requested Kershaw to assist Early by loaning him the 2nd South Carolina, which Kershaw unhappily did. Early personally persuaded but a few of Toombs' men to join him. Then Early saw the 12th Georgia come into view, followed by the 25th and 31st Virginia. Early took command of this put-together brigade, but was ordered to simply maintain his position just west of the Willis Church road, and not to attack. It was dark by then, the Federal artillery was still firing, and just holding position was the most that could be expected of Early.

Winder was unable to find D. H. Hill, the man he was sent to help, so Winder sent Lieutenant McHenry Howard in search of Hill. Because he could hear heavy firing on his left, Winder took his men in that direction. The extremely heavy fire made it impossible to keep his command together in the dark. Winder and 100 men of the 4th and 33rd Virginia managed to move through a ravine on the left end of the Confederate line and came upon a small group of the 1st and 3rd North Carolina of Ripley's brigade. They couldn't see the strength of the Federals, but were still feeling the effects of the artillery fire from Seeley's guns. Several dozen men of the

33rd Virginia were hit. Colonel John F. Neff, commander of the 33rd, was slightly hurt by two spent minie balls. The rattled troops fired in the dark without clear targets, and friendly fire casualties were likely.

The 2nd and 5th Virginia had moved into an open field west of the Willis Church road. They observed numerous troops moving downhill, and quickly concluded that the entire Confederate army was retreating. The commander of the 2nd, Lieutenant Colonel Lawson Botts, was uncomfortable with his situation, and he and the 5th's commander, Colonel William S. H. Baylor, pulled their men back to the Willis Church road.

Winder was in search of the rest of his men, but instead found Lawton. Alexander Lawton had experienced the same problem with troops getting separated in the brush and darkness. Lawton and the 13th Georgia were using the sound of the Federal guns as an aid to navigation. This put Lawton on Winder's path, so when Winder returned, Lawton was there. Winder convinced Lawton to join with him. Lawton permitted Colonel Marcellus Douglas and part of the 13th Georgia to move straight ahead, while the rest of the regiment followed Winder and his men. Marcellus Douglas even became separated from his group of a hundred or less. Despite all the problems, they were still intending to mount an attack.

Next, the Georgians came upon Stafford's brigade, which had come under Whiting's orders. An unknown officer ordered the brigade forward. The 6th, 7th and 8th Louisiana went forward, but the 9th Louisiana did not. It is unclear whether or not the 9th ever got the order. The Louisiana Tigers were not ordered to go in. As with all the other Confederate attacks of the day, this one on Couch's left failed. The Louisianans were said to have "fought like wildcats," only stopped by the troops of Sickles and Barlow within twenty yards of the Federal lines.

The 7th New York expended all their ammunition, as well as that found on the nearby dead and wounded, and were told to use their bayonets. The 8th Pennsylvania Reserves stayed on the field until the fight ended, despite being totally devoid of ammunition. Barlow's troops also resorted to the bayonet. The only regiment with ammunition was the 72nd New York, which made trips to the rear to replenish its supply. Even Seeley's Battery K, 4th U. S. Artillery expended all their ammunition and was withdrawn by Couch.

The Georgians and Louisianans tried to withdraw cleanly, but their retreat was not orderly. Some fell back to Winder's line. The 27th Virginia under Colonel Grigsby and the remainder of the 4th and 33rd Virginia now came forward.

During the advance, Colonel Grigsby was wounded and left the battlefield. Winder knew he had an insufficient number of troops, and went back for the rest of Lawton's men, Jones' men, and the Maryland Line. J. R. Jones' brigade was once again commanded by Lieutenant Colonel Cunningham, as General Jones was wounded earlier by shrapnel. Winder put all these men into the right of his line. Johnson was on the extreme right. Winder's men were close enough to the Federal lines to hear their officers give commands. They were the last and only Confederates on Malvern Hill east of Willis Church road after dark. Their casualties were moderate.[51]

In reaction to D. H. Hill's cry for help, Whiting sent Isaac Trimble forward. Trimble and his men, not in serious fighting since Gaines' Mill, were ready for a fight. Trimble had to go around the troops of Hood and Law to put his brigade into position. Once there, Trimble and D. H. Hill rode as close as a hundred yards of the Federal lines, looking for an opportunity. Trimble believed he saw a way to attack one of Couch's batteries in the flank. Hill was not keen on a night attack with the batteries still in operation. Trimble was not willing to be shut down by Hill. Jackson found him preparing to launch an attack, and gave him advice, "I guess you had better not try it." Jackson elaborated, "General Hill just tried it with his whole division and has been repulsed. I guess you had better not try it, sir." Trimble had been convinced, and his men had to stay where they were, enduring the fire of three Federal batteries.

Although the infantry was done for the day, the artillery was relentless. Henry Hunt was there with a pair of 32 pound howitzers by nightfall, and they began firing. Lieutenants Randol and Olcott, having lost their guns at Glendale, assisted the gunners. Other guns fired into the night. At last, they all were silent. The bloody battle of Malvern Hill was finally over.[52]

The battle can be easily summarized. The Confederates had about 30,000 men engaged and suffered slightly more than 5,600 casualties without gaining an inch of ground. D. H. Hill noted that over half of the Confederate casualties were due to artillery fire. This fact can be easily explained. Firstly, almost all of the Confederate troop movements to the foot of Malvern Hill could be targeted by Federal artillery. Thus, Confederate infantry were subjected to Federal fire more hours than usual for a one-day battle. Secondly, the deployment of the Federal guns was extremely well done.

Malvern Hill would be expected to be a battle causing high casualties to the attacking army. The Federals occupied an excellent defensive position, had their army well concentrated, and had an abundance of artillery support. Any infantry force attacking uphill against dug in infantry with superior artillery support will suffer heavy casualties, especially if the attacking regiments persist even after fully aware of the "majestic murder" being committed upon them by the Federal guns.

The numbers prove the case. The Confederates sustained 869 killed, 4,241 wounded, and 540 missing/captured. Very few were captured, and most of the missing were probably dead. Thus, the total casualties were 5,650. The Confederate casualty rate was thus about 19%. More than half of the casualties were caused by the extremely effective Federal artillery. Only Gaines' Mill cost a higher price, but it was a victory. Malvern Hill was a Confederate tragedy, and probably should not have been fought. Harvey Hill, in a cynical but accurate statement, said the Confederates "did not move together, and were beaten in detail.... It was not war—it was murder."

Total Federal casualties were 3,214, not much more than half of Lee's. They suffered 397 dead, 2,092 wounded, and 725 missing. About 27,000 Federal troops were engaged. This made the casualty rate about 12%. The casualties were mostly in the commands of Griffin, Couch, Butterfield and Martindale. Other than these commands, few Federals were hit by Confederate artillery fire.[53]

Despite what can only be considered a Federal victory, McClellan continued his withdrawal to his new base at Harrison's Landing on the James River. There, under the protection of the gunboats of the U. S. Navy, he believed that he was safe from a major assault by the Army of Northern Virginia.

The battle of Malvern Hill ended the major fighting of the Peninsula Campaign. Subsequent contacts between the opposing armies consisted mostly of skirmishes and occasional artillery fire. Reconnaissance was conducted by both sides, but no major fighting occurred.

There is little argument that the battle of Malvern Hill was a costly defeat for Lee's army. An analysis of why this engagement occurred and why it became such a resounding loss for the Confederates leads us to several fairly evident facts.

Lee's decision to give battle at Malvern Hill was based on unwarranted optimism. He simply didn't realize how well Porter had deployed the Federal army on the eminence. The second, related factor was that Stuart's cavalry was not present soon enough to provide proper reconnaissance of the battle area. Hindsight reveals that a better strategy would have been to attempt to turn the Federal right, but no proper cavalry probe of that end of the Federal line was possible prior to the engagement.

Once the battle was joined, the Federals enjoyed a number of tactical advantages. They had the high ground. They had the advantage of shorter distances to move to concentrate forces at the point of Lee's attack, and they had a relatively short distance to retreat to their chosen new base at Harrison's Landing. Their objective was simple. Fight well one more day, then retreat to the covering firepower of their gunboats in the James. There, they would be able to rest and be resupplied. They didn't have to win the fight, but just maintain their lines until dark, then retreat one more time.

One factor which did not assist the Federal army at Malvern Hill was the strange behavior of its commanding general. One would expect that officer to plant his flag squarely atop the eminence and personally provide guidance to his corps commanders as the battle developed. Secondary tasks, such as arranging logistics at Harrison's Landing or conferring with his U.S. Navy counterpart would be handled by a senior staff officer. His decision to absent himself from the battlefield for much of the day and not officially designate a general to overall tactical command, was certainly not in alignment with commonly accepted military behavior. McClellan was indeed fortunate that Fitz John Porter, although junior among the corps commanders on Malvern Hill, took the initiative and coordinated with his peers. What could have been a more costly day for the Federals, turned out as a successful defense of their position.

An analysis of the Confederate leadership reveals poorly contrived strategy, weak communication, and apathetic behavior on the part of Huger. Despite the bravery of many men, the leadership was insufficient to even provide a possibility of victory. Lee's acceptance of Longstreet's idea of a "grand battery" was a poor decision, and assured a Federal victory. The poor performance of Huger and Longstreet, had it not occurred, would not have changed the result of the fight. The only two possibilities for July 1 were a Federal victory or a lack of battle.

CHAPTER 22

Journey's End

(July 1–3)

Jeb Stuart and his men arrived at Rock Church around sunset on July 1, back from the mission given to him by Lee on June 29. Stuart had ridden to White House Landing, taken all the undamaged provisions they could transport, then burned as much of the rest as possible. Stuart left White House on the morning of the 30th, leaving behind Cobb's Legion Cavalry Squadron. Stuart rode toward the Chickahominy bridges, following Fitz Lee. Lee, leading the 1st Virginia Cavalry, encountered Federal pickets and two sections of artillery at Long Bridge.

Stuart and the rest of his command rode to Jones' Bridge, where they were confronted by a squadron of the 3rd Pennsylvania Cavalry under Captain J. Claude White. White also had 200 infantrymen and two guns of Battery M, 5th U. S. Artillery under Lieutenant Valentine H. Stone. This blocking force had been sent by Averell the previous morning. As Stuart reached the crossing early in the afternoon of June 30, Major John Pelham employed his two remaining howitzers. The Federals instantly disappeared, and Will T. Martin and part of the command crossed the river to determine where they had gone. Pelham moved his guns down to the bridge to better support Martin, but Stone opened up on him from only 400 yards away. After a short artillery duel, the Federals departed to rejoin their army.

Stuart and his troopers camped near the crossing. About 3:30 A.M. on July 1, Stuart received a message that General Lee wanted his cavalry to rejoin the army, suggesting a crossing of the Chickahominy at Grapevine Bridge. Stuart asked and was told that Lee had written the message some six and a half hours ago, just after the battle of Glendale concluded. Stuart's analysis of the tactical situation led him to conclude that Bottoms Bridge would be clear of Federals, and roused his men. They started very soon thereafter for Bottoms Bridge. Riding ahead of the column, he crossed the Chickahominy to scout the area around White Oak Swamp. He observed columns of Confederate infantry moving south, and knew his cavalry wasn't needed there, so he decided to cross at Jones' bridge. He sent a message to Jackson to that effect. Turning back, he reached his men just as they were nearing Bottoms Bridge, and had them turn around. They had to ford the river at Jones' Bridge and rode west. They arrived at Rock Church just after nightfall. Although Stuart's men were able to disperse a number of Federal pickets, Stuart knew he could not advance farther, as he could see the campfires of a large Federal command, probably Peck's division. He could not make it to Haxall's Landing that night. They had ridden 42 miles that day, so he camped for the night and sent Eugene Blackford to tell Stonewall, who was gleeful at the news.

As with other Stuart missions before and after this one, there has been speculation whether it had a net positive or negative effect on Lee's army. Although Lee had a few cavalry assets to do reconnaissance in Stuart's absence, there is little argument that Stuart was the best cavalry commander in the Army of Northern Virginia. Critics say Stuart should have been more available to Lee to scout east of Jackson's command to determine the feasibility of turning the Federal right. Alternatively, Stuart might have been able to operate in McClellan's rear and help to demoralize the Army of the Potomac. It must be remembered that Stuart went on his mission to White House in obedience to Lee's orders.[1]

McClellan's army was readying itself to leave Malvern Hill as Stuart's command was approaching. Some of McClellan's officers and soldiers did not agree with his decision to once again retreat from a battlefield on which they had just been successful. Porter messaged McClellan that he felt they needed little more than rations and ammunition to hold their present position. Porter even thought a counterattack might be in order. At the same time Porter's message was being taken to McClellan, McClellan was sending a message to his generals on Malvern Hill to withdraw their commands to Harrison's Landing on the James. The order of withdrawal was: Morell, Couch, Sykes, Kearny, Hooker, Sumner, Franklin and Keyes.

Porter and Kearny were the two officers most opposed to the retreat. Porter spent a good part of the night trying to get the commanding general to reverse his decision. Kearny was incautious in his criticism of McClellan, going so far as to state that the decision to retreat had to result from "cowardice or treason."[2] Even some Confederates in Richmond, including General Joseph E. Johnston, were concerned that McClellan could still strike to the west, overwhelm Lee's battered army, and capture Richmond.

McClellan himself, went aboard the gunboat *Galena*, and had a much different perception of his army's situation. He was observing masses of Confederate troops moving around the right flank of his army, threatening to cut it off from Harrison's Landing and the protection of the gunboats. Commodore Rodgers had already told McClellan that the Navy could not assure the safety of Federal transports anywhere upstream of Harrison's Landing. His mindset was to save the army, not use it to attack the enemy. He'd been leaning toward that view ever since late in the evening on June 25, after the minor battle at Oak Grove. To save the army, he had to put it where he could resupply it, and that had to be where the gunboats could protect the unarmed naval transports required to carry the huge amount of stores such a large army required. If he could move the army intact to Harrison's, it could regroup there.[3]

There were logical factors that favored the Army of the Potomac remaining at Malvern Hill. The Confederates were battered, tired and demoralized. They knew they had suffered a defeat on the slopes of Malvern Hill. Despite having their entire army concentrated for the first time in the campaign, Lee's men could not shove the Federals off of even a small part of the hill. The Federals had more fresh troops available at the end of the battle. Although Lee had used every regiment at one point or another in the last two days, McClellan had left untouched about half of II Corps, almost the entire III Corps, a division of IV Corps, and all of VI Corps.

The factors favoring remaining at Malvern Hill were of no interest to McClellan. He supposedly was of the belief that Lee had about 180,000 men, based mainly on Pinkerton's flawed analysis. He had already made up his mind that the only safe course of action was to move to Harrison's Landing. The outcome at Malvern Hill was irrelevant. In fact, he didn't stick around until the end of the day's fighting.

From McClellan's perception of the situation, the move to Harrison's Landing was the only sound choice available to him. The soundest reason for another retreat was the lack of supplies. A number of Federal regiments had suffered from ammunition exhaustion during the fighting at Malvern Hill. Many of them had exhausted their rations. Now McClellan was leading them to the land of plenty, a base that had all his remaining wagons, with a port protected by gunboats, and transports that could bring them shiploads of wonderful things.[4]

So, the Army of the Potomac retreated again. The headquarters at Malvern Hill was struck, and they moved out for Harrison's Landing. Except for a section of Benson's battery, Hunt's artillerists moved out shortly after firing ended. The engineers left next. Truman Seymour's V Corps division, the Pennsylvania Reserves, left a little before midnight. Another V Corps division, that of Morell, started out about 11:00 P.M. Martindale's brigade was in the lead, but the road was narrow and jammed with men and artillery, and parts of the division became mixed with other troops. There was sufficient confusion during the night retreat to enable the 29th Massachusetts to be unnotified and remain until the following morning.

Couch's IV Corps division was also on the march before midnight. Again, there was confusion in the dark, and part of the 36th New York became lost, and almost stumbled into the Confederate lines. The brigades of Sickles and Caldwell followed Couch, Sickles without any orders. The 5th New Hampshire of Caldwell's brigade was another regiment that was overlooked. They waited near the front for a battery that never showed up. The regiment was commanded by Captain Edward E. Sturtevant, who decided about 5:00 A.M. not to remain there almost alone. Likewise, the 63rd Pennsylvania of John C. Robinson's brigade was never notified to leave. The 71st New York of Sickles' brigade was ordered to stay behind on rear guard duty.

After midnight, Sykes started Lovell's brigade south. They took along with them a group of about twenty-five Confederate prisoners. Buchanan's brigade, the 3rd Pennsylvania Cavalry, the 71st New York, and likely the section of Benson's battery were placed under Averell, and remained in place as a sort of delaying force. Warren's small brigade and Martin's battery finally departed about 1:00 A.M.

Heintzelman had his orders by 11:00 P.M., but his report stated that the road was so jammed that only a part of III Corps left shortly thereafter. Some III Corps units, such as those of Kearny, Grover and Carr didn't move until 3:40 A.M. Most of Sumner's II Corps moved about midnight, but the 1st Minnesota remained until dawn. William French never received orders to retreat, but left anyway at dawn.

Slocum's division left about 11:00 P.M., but Baldy Smith and his men remained to cover the bridges across Turkey Island Creek. The road east of the bridge was assigned to Peck. He had only two brigades, under Wessells and Naglee. Wessells formed up his brigade on high ground east of Haxall's just after midnight. Naglee positioned his brigade a mile to Wessell's rear.[5] Most of McClellan's army was off Malvern Hill by dawn of July 2.

Lee's army, for the most part, remained where they were until the morning of July 2. Some were on the slopes of Malvern Hill, others were in more comfortable camps. Wright's and Mahone's brigades, along with the 49th North Carolina of Robert Ransom's brigade, were on the actual slopes of the hill. Wright sent a plea to Magruder to be relieved. He wanted to collect his brigade. There was no relief on the way, but they could hear the sounds of the Federal troops retreating. All the Confederates could do was get water to the troops and try to assist the wounded. They could see lanterns in the night, as the Federals tried to do the same. Lewis Armistead's brigade, which was part of the earliest attack, was also sleeping on the battlefield that night.

Jubal Early's troops were to Armistead's left. They could also hear the Federals moving out and the cries of the wounded, and saw the lanterns to their front. Winder had reformed his line and reported his position, very close to the Federal lines, to Jackson and Harvey Hill. Jackson's men could hear the noise of wagons and artillery moving.

The concerns of Confederate division commanders farther back from the line were much different. They were too far away from the top of Malvern Hill to hear the wagons and artillery pieces forming up and leaving, so they still feared a Federal attack. Some took precautionary actions. Ewell ordered Major Campbell Brown to take 30 to 40 captured ammunition wagons all the way to the north of White Oak Swamp to insure their safety from a counterattack. Several staff officers decided to wake Stonewall. After some effort, they were successful. Expressing their fears and concerns to Jackson, he replied, "Please let me sleep. There will be no enemy there in the morning."

G. T. Anderson, Toombs, Semmes, Kershaw, Cobb, Barksdale and Robert Ransom camped close around the Carter house on Carter's Mill road. Whiting's troops and Hampton's brigade stayed where they were. At midnight, Trimble withdrew his brigade into the woods. Leroy Stafford withdrew those of his command that were still with him to a gate by the Willis Church road. The men were able to fetch water from the church and return to the gate. Harvey Hill's brigade commanders spent the night trying to get their men organized, and most set up camp near Willis Church. Powell Hill's division went back to the Long Bridge road, and Longstreet remained on the right rear of the army.[6]

Both armies were subjected to the sounds of the wounded piercing the summer night. Along most of the lines, informal truces were commonplace. Although there were a few non-participants, most soldiers cooperated to the advantage of the wounded. Some of the men on or near the top of the hill actually were able to sleep through the agonizing cries of the dying.

Some Federal wounded, resting near the Malvern House, were ordered to get to their feet and retreat, lest they be captured by the Confederates. Some arose and left without waiting for first aid.[7]

As it seemed to occur just after many Civil War battles, it started to rain at Malvern Hill. The prospects for the two armies were decidedly different. The Confederates simply hunkered down where they were, but the Federals had a seven mile march to crown their exhausting day. It was not a cool, light summer shower, but a hard, driving rain that made the heavily used roads worse by the hour. The Federal officers made their best efforts to maintain an orderly march, with infantry and artillery on one side of the road, and wagons on the other. This sensible method of using the sad road did not last. By and large, the infantrymen were the losers. Wagons and artillery forced many of the foot soldiers onto the shoulders. After a while, the roads were no better than the shoulders. Animals and wagons got stuck and men dropped from exhaustion. The progress of some elements of the army was incredibly slow. Engineers built fires to light the way, but the men were in misery.[8]

Keyes prudently used every road of which he was aware to move his trains from Haxall's to Harrison's Landing. He even went to the extent of opening a new road, which ran from Haxall's to the River road, intersecting that road about four miles southeast of Turkey Island Creek Bridge, which had been obstructed by Naglee's brigade. Keyes later estimated that about 1,000 wagons made use of the new road.

Peck used the fields when he could to move his wagons more quickly, taking some of the damage away from the roads. It is likely that every Federal corps commander expected to lose some wagons along the line of retreat. Although Heintzelman claimed that his wagons all made it to Harrison's Landing, it probably wasn't the case. Mishaps were numerous. Axles broke, horses drowned in a stream, roads were temporarily blocked, and an unlucky drummer boy was crushed under the wheels of a wagon.

The march to Harrison's Landing was described by various individuals in a number of ways. It was said to be done in "a perfect rush." The army was described as "a disorganized mob." Manners suffered numerous lapses, as regiments barged right through the middle of other regiments. Just waiting for the privilege of entering the road and suffering along took a long time for some. The psychological strain was as miserable and the physical discomfort of the mud and bedlam. This was a retreat, and the possibility of being attacked while strung out along a road was in the backs of many minds. Baldy Smith's division had to wait for everyone else to pass before they could withdraw along the River road. This took until daylight on July 2. When Smith's men finally passed Wessell's brigade and Miller's battery covering the Turkey Island Creek Bridge. Smith advised Wessell that Smith's division would return to support Wessell if they were needed. This occurred about 10:00 A.M. on the 2nd. Peck only needed Averell's command to pass before withdrawing.[9]

Averell decided to wait until dawn to withdraw. Daybreak brought dense fog, with less than fifty yards visibility. He first moved his cavalry to the front, finding Buchanan, who reported that the Confederates were trying to flank his line. Averell put his three Regular regiments into line with the 71st New York. Next he had the 3rd Pennsylvania Cavalry cover the flanks. He also sent for an artillery battery. He then rode to the spot where the Federal lines had been during the battle. From there he could overlook the slopes upon which the Army of Northern Virginia had struggled the previous day.

Averell witnessed the enormity of the tragedy that was a Civil War battle. Over 5,000 dead and wounded were before him. Two-thirds of them were still moving, giving the impression of the ground "crawling." He could see the history of the three Confederate charges by the lines of the dead. Small parties of men, some on horseback, meandered around the field.

The requested battery still had not come up, so Averell tasked small groups of his troopers to pretend they were gun crews. The 14th U.S. Infantry spread out its skirmishers to try to appear a larger force. John D. Frank arrived with four guns, but it was a wasted ride for the artillerists. The Confederates had ceased any attempt to advance. Instead, they contented themselves to care for their wounded and gather up their dead. By 10:00 A.M., Averell was informed that the army's rear was already two miles south of him, and he set about his own withdrawal. He first pulled back his reserve infantry and guns, then his main line, then the skirmishers, and finally his cavalry. As soon as the infantrymen had retrieved their knapsacks, they started down the road. The 3rd Pennsylvania Cavalry was forced to burn twelve wagons, having no mules to pull them. Finally, the last of the Federals were off of Malvern Hill. Once all his men were across the Turkey Island Creek Bridge, Averell had some of his men cut the bridge away and felled trees over it. The Army of the Potomac was now behind a water barrier.[10]

Back at Malvern Hill, the Confederates had no intention of attacking Averell's rear guard. They labored on in the chilling rain, and were too few in number to mount another attack up the slope, even had they the intent. Jubal Early awoke on the 2nd and began to look around. He saw a small party off to his right and went over there. They were a group of a dozen, and Armistead was one of them. Early inquired of Armistead where his brigade was, and Armistead answered that the dozen around them were his, and the only others he knew about were lying out there on the slope. Armistead saw another group of men off to the right, which turned out to be survivors of Wright's and Mahone's brigades. They were prepared to defend the details out walking through the dead and wounded. They were not, however, able or willing to attack the Federal rear guard before it departed. As quickly as the details finished their unpleasant work, all of them made it down the slope to try and recover and regroup.

There were a few shots fired in anger that morning, but only a few. The Maryland Line took a couple of shots at a Federal cavalry officer, and when this was related to Stonewall, he was pleased. Stonewall seemed back to normal, recovered from his lethargic demeanor of the previous day. He requested that the dead be removed from his front, as he planned to attack as soon as the fog lifted, and did not care to have his men step over their fallen comrades in their advance. Other officers, such as Charles Winder, were more concerned about being able to defend against a Federal attack down the hill. They were delighted that no such threat materialized.

Stonewall met Munford and asked the cavalryman if he thought some buttermilk could be procured. Munford took Stonewall to a farmhouse and asked the lady if she could prepare breakfast for General Jackson. The woman had to be convinced that she had the real Stonewall Jackson under her roof, them gladly provided the general breakfast with buttermilk.

The battlefield was a ghastly sight, with thousands of dead and wounded still there when the fog lifted. The sight had a decided effect on some of the Confederate leaders. Ewell was probably affected most. He was so distressed that he was for a while doubled up on the floor of a nearby shack. Moxley Sorrel found Ewell there, and he lamented aloud to Sorrel about the loss of so many men. Toombs was also gloomy, spoke of the large losses, and could only gather a handful of men from his brigade. He was concerned about the Federals attacking all the way into Richmond. Major Brent had looked over the battlefield and seen rows of dead Confederates all along the slopes, all across the Mellert fields to the Confederate right. Many were victims of the efficient Federal artillery. Far to the north, the trees had been damaged by shells and grapeshot. Pegram's battery was covered with dead artillery horses. Various observers of the scene had difficulty finding words to describe its horror, and many had difficulty ever forgetting it.[11]

General Lee had set up his temporary headquarters at the Poindexter house. It was raining again. Lee began to receive reports that the Federals were demoralized. Returning from a scouting sortie, Stuart had reported this, as he had captured scores of enemy troops and noticed a great deal of equipment abandoned along the line of retreat. Lee was dictating orders to his staff, and Jackson was there with him. Longstreet came in, wet from the rain. Lee asked Longstreet if he had examined the battlefield, and what he thought. Longstreet, in a manner of sparing Lee's feelings, said that he had, and that, "I think you hurt them about as much as they hurt you." Lee replied with, "then I am glad we punished them well, at any rate." It is unlikely that either man was stating what he truly felt.

Lee probably started issuing orders to his generals at that point, as A. P. Hill and Longstreet began to move their commands. Lee continued to discuss various strategies for pursuit of McClellan. Once again, Jefferson Davis appeared, unexpected by General Lee. Jackson was still there, and he and Davis had never met, but Jackson was already no fan of the President. This was because of a perceived slight in the past. Lee introduced the two strong-willed men, and Jackson managed only a military salute and President Davis a bow.

Despite the awkwardness of the situation, business had to be conducted, so Davis and Lee continued to mull over the possibilities for pursuit. Jackson remained there, but said little. After a while, Lee and Davis agreed that a massive pursuit of the Federal army was a poor idea in the rain. At that point, Jackson spoke up, saying, "They have not all got away if we go immediately after them." In fact, some of McClellan's units could have been caught up, if Lee had immediately ordered the nearest command after them. The problem was that much more than a single division would be needed when the pursuers caught up with their prey. With the condition of the roads, sending a large enough force after the tail of the Federal army could well put Richmond at risk.

All that occurred before consideration of the condition of Lee's army. Most of the divisions were in no shape to embark upon a fast, lengthy march which culminated in a battle. The bottom line was that Lee and Davis were right and Jackson was wrong. Jackson, without D. H. Hill, could be ready to move right away. His command would total about 16,000 men. Longstreet and A. P. Hill, with about 16,000 men did move about two miles, and went into camp near the Poindexter house. If Stonewall's men marched that far, they would still be short of the Turkey Island Creek Bridge. This could not be construed as a pursuit with any chance of success. Peck's and Baldy Smith's divisions would have to be defeated before the trains could be attacked. The only benefit for Lee would be to position his army closer to the enemy. Lee had made the wise decision. Stop and regroup, think the matter through, reorganize, then act.[12]

D. H. Hill's division spent about a week taking away the wounded, burying the dead, and gathering up what could be salvaged from the battlefield. On the other end of the battlefield, Huger and Magruder were doing the same thing. Jackson's command camped near Willis Church, and Holmes turned around when he received General Lee's order and marched back to Drewry's Bluff, after leaving Henry A. Wise's men at Chaffin's Bluff. By the afternoon, Lee had become aware of reports that McClellan might even be trying to cross his army to the south side of the James. If true, this would be a dangerous development for the Confederates. If

McClellan were able to cross a major portion of his men to the south bank of the river, he could easily overwhelm the defenders at Drewry's Bluff and be free to run Federal gunboats up the river all the way to Richmond. Because this was even a possibility, Lee kept Magruder, Huger with Robert Ransom's brigade, and D. H. Hill near Malvern Hill.[13]

While the Confederates were thus occupied, McClellan's army continued to move into their new base at Harrison's Landing. The headquarters staff arrived between 2:00 and 3:00 A.M. on July 2. Instead of marching in the rain, they endured the dust at their new home. The reserve artillery started arriving about 6:00 A.M. Morell and most likely Couch arrived around sunrise. Artillery batteries rolled in from 4:00 A.M. until 9:00 A.M. Slocum's division had only a short march, and arrived early.

A part of Sumner's II Corps arrived at 8:00 A.M. At least one regiment, the 5th New Hampshire of Richardson's division, was left behind at Malvern Hill, and didn't leave there until 5:00 A.M. on the 2nd., arriving at Harrison's Landing about 11:00 A.M. Sedgwick's division, also part of Sumner's II Corps, started late, marched fast, and arrived from 10:00 A.M. until 2:00 P.M. Heintzelman's III Corps arrived from 8:00 A.M. until afternoon. Baldy Smith's VI Corps division, which had some rear guard responsibilities, arrived a little after noon. Gouverneur Warren's brigade of Sykes' V Corps division, was the tail end of the main body of troops, and arrived in camp at 5:00 P.M. Averell's command, the rear guard of the army, made it there late in the day and his cavalry, the 3rd Pennsylvania Cavalry, didn't make camp until after dark.[14]

Although Harrison's Landing was to be the salvation of McClellan's army, as moving there gave them the protection of the Federal gunboats, the camp was far from a paradise on the James. In reality, it was a sea of mud. A field of full-grown wheat had been turned into a bog by the many boots, wagon wheels and hooves of the Army of the Potomac. There were staff officers attempting to direct each arriving unit to their proper place, according to a master plan of some sort. The men looked for any available shelter from the elements, and some just sat there in the rain for up to six hours. The mud was as much as three feet deep in some places. The wheat did serve the men both as straw for bedding and another source of food.

Baldy Smith tells of his indelicate arrival at Harrison's:

> On reaching Harrison's Landing, I came to a steep path down to a valley. The soil was of clay and the heavy rain had made it very slippery. The descent was so steep that I dismounted to lead my horse down. I had no

sooner touched the crest then my feet went out from under me,—the bridle was pulled out of my hand and I ploughed a hollow track clear to the bottom, an excess of mud falling over my legs in cataracts. On reaching the bottom I looked up and saw my dejected horse with head down and a picture of woe. I could not get back to him and was in a quandary, when fortunately a soldier, probably a straggler, appeared and led my horse to me,—when I mounted I had pounds of extra mud for him to carry. I finally reached Harrison's Landing and found that stakes and flags had been stuck up for the camping ground of each brigade in the army.[15]

Many officers and soldiers slept for an extended period after arrival, due most likely from the fatigue of the last several days and the relief of feeling they were now rescued from the relentless pursuit of Lee. Even relief from fear and much needed sleep could not take away the misery and demoralization most felt at this point in their lives.

Porter sent messages to McClellan in which he stated that he hoped the retreating was at an end, and that the army would hold its ground, and prepare to renew the offensive against Richmond. There is no record of a response from McClellan.

McClellan had spent the night of July 1 in relative comfort aboard the gunboat *Galena*. Arriving at Harrison's on the 2nd, he likely received Lincoln's message which read, "If you think you are not strong enough to take Richmond right now, I do not ask you to try just now." Lincoln promised some reinforcements, but not the 50,000 McClellan desired. The fatigued McClellan sent a return message reporting the army's arrival, and blamed his change of base on being cut off from White House Landing.[16]

McClellan was already receiving troops and supplies. The previous day the 18th Massachusetts of Martindale's brigade and boatloads of supplies had sailed in from White House Landing. On the second, the 17th New York of Butterfield's brigade came ashore. Of greater importance was the arrival of Brigadier General Orris A. Ferry with his brigade from Shields' division from the Shenandoah. The rest of the division was supposed to follow. McClellan sent a telegram of thanks to Lincoln. These arrivals tended to help morale. Shields generously shared his men's rations with the hungry others. By nightfall on July 2, Peck's two brigades and a small part of the wagon trains were all that kept the army from being intact.

After Averell had passed Peck's position, Peck moved Wessell's men to Naglee's immediate rear. The 85th New York was given the rear guard duty for the trains, and was forced to destroy some disabled wagons. Wessells then moved back into position and Naglee crossed his brigade over Kimage's Creek, several miles southeast of Haxall's. Naglee's march went past the abandoned wagons, dead mules and teams mired in the mud. These depressing sights were seen all along the route.

All the roads concerned were ruined by heavy use by this point. Wagons could only cross Kimage's Creek one at a time. This caused a backup of about 1,000 wagons just west of the creek. Peck finally decided about 5:00 P.M. that it was impossible for all the wagons to cross that evening. He took decisive action, putting Wessell's brigade on the west side of the creek, and supporting it with Miller's battery and part of the 8th Pennsylvania Cavalry.

It must be remembered that all along, Stuart and his troopers were busily gathering up stragglers and Federal equipment along the retreat route. He was able to spare Will Martin, commanding the Jeff Davis (Mississippi) Legion Cavalry and 4th Virginia Cavalry. Martin, also accompanied by Pelham's howitzers, went about bothering the rear guard. Martin went down near the James and captured both men and mules within range of the *Monitor*. He then dispersed more Federals near Shirley, and chased them toward Harrison's. When he ran into Wessell's brigade, there was some skirmishing before Martin prudently withdrew.[17]

Seven Days Before Richmond

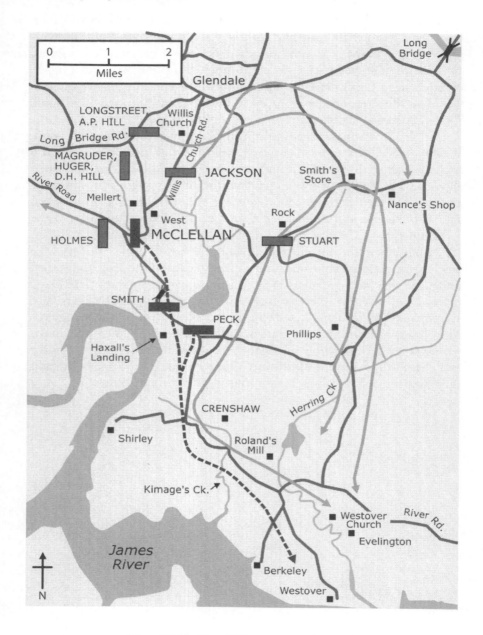

Map 22.1—Final Movements, July 2–3

CHAPTER 23

Evelington Heights

(July 3)

July 2 began with a meeting in the Poindexter house, east of the Quaker road. Lee and his generals were discussing what to make of McClellan's army retreating from Malvern Hill. They had little hard evidence. All they really knew for sure was that the Federals had retreated to the east, north of the James River. They didn't know exactly why he would pull his army from a victorious battlefield, or where he was going. Lee badly needed to know what McClellan was up to. There were even rumors that a part of the Army of the Potomac had crossed to the south bank of the James. After being summoned by Lee, Stuart and his men had arrived from their reconnaissance of White House Landing. Lee ordered him to find the Federals and determine what their plans might be.[1]

Stuart and his cavalry spent July 2 running down stragglers and gathering up abandoned equipment. As the morning of July 3 matured, Stuart had already scouted in the direction of the Charles City Court House, hoping to bother McClellan's flank if the Federals were planning to move further down the peninsula than Harrison's Landing. There had been no traffic of Federals there, and Stuart was hoping to cause them some problems if they came down the River road. He ordered Captain John Pelham, with one 12-pound howitzer and a squadron of the 1st Virginia Cavalry, to move to the River road between Shirley and Charles City Court House. They were to assess the situation there.

Pelham found much more than he could have hoped for. From the vantage point of an eminence called Evelington Heights, he had a panoramic view of the Army of the Potomac in their new base at Harrison's Landing. Pelham notified Stuart and prudently refrained from making the Federals aware of his presence or their blunder in not occupying the eminence.[2]

Stuart received Pelham's findings during the morning of the 3rd, and they were relayed on to Jackson, then to Lee. Stuart also set his men in motion. He sent the 9th Virginia Cavalry to Evelington Heights by way of

Nance's Shop. They were to be on the lookout for Federals arriving from down the peninsula. The rest of the command rode down the River road.

Lee had already ordered Jackson's and Longstreet's commands down the River road. Lee gave Longstreet the lead. When Lee considered Stuart's report, which mentioned obstructions on the River road, he decided to change his plan slightly. He halted the column and let Longstreet lead the force back and move by the Long Bridge road, through Nance's Shop, to the south and Evelington Heights.[3]

Stuart arrived at Evelington Heights about this time. This was the location of the plantation of Edmund Ruffin, an outspoken secessionist, one of the "fire breathers." Stuart instantly recognized the possibilities of artillery fire from the heights, which rose about sixty feet above Herring Creek, a meandering stream which formed the northern and eastern boundary of the plain at Harrison's Landing. The creek banks were swampy for the whole distance from Roland's Mill to the James, a straight-line distance of about four miles. This was an impassable natural barrier for McClellan's army. The only road out of Harrison's Landing was the River road. Evelington Heights commanded both Harrison's Landing and the only escape route. It was probably a better defensive position than Malvern Hill, in that the tidal stream and swampy ground would make infantry assault more or less unrealistic. It was at least possible that if Lee could get the majority of his army onto Evelington Heights, with artillery, he could bottle up McClellan and destroy a major portion of his army. Only the Federal gunboats would be able to help McClellan in that situation.

By 9:00 A.M., Stuart had sent Will Martin down the north bank of Herring Creek to the James. Despite a suggestion by a staff officer to the contrary, Stuart directed John Pelham to open fire on the camp. The lonely howitzer couldn't cause too much damage, but did cause widespread panic in the camp. The Federals were trying to rapidly form up their regiments, but no orders were immediately forthcoming, and some of the men reached the conclusion that McClellan was going to let the Navy deal with the offending artillery. McClellan was erroneously informed that a large Confederate force was approaching. He was at that time engaged in saying goodbye to Randolph Marcy, his chief of staff, who was heading back to Washington to deliver McClellan's initial report on the week's battles. McClellan seemed to be surprised at being under attack, although he could not have yet known the tiny size of the attacking force. The previous day, John Barnard, McClellan's chief engineer, had sent McClellan a note advising the occupation of Evelington Heights, stating, "we must push our forces further forward, or we are bagged." McClellan was upset on receiving the note, because he had previously ordered this done, and his orders were not executed. He immediately calmed his panicky troops by riding along their front, then ordered Baldy Smith to lead his VI Corps division and a battery to clear Evelington Heights of Confederates and occupy it.

On the heights, Stuart was getting intelligence from recently captured Federals and local residents. They led him to believe that the Federal army was demoralized. He knew they were not in a great defensive position, with his men occupying the high ground. He had also been informed by General Lee that reinforcements were en route to the heights. Stuart determined to hold Evelington Heights as long as he could, hopefully until help arrived. Pelham, with one small-caliber mountain howitzer and a limited supply of ammunition, could not long deter a Federal infantry assault. Soon, Baldy Smith's division arrived. The lead brigade was that of Brigadier General Nathan Kimball, attached to Smith's division, and recently arrived from the Shenandoah Valley. Stuart deployed his sharpshooters in cover along the road, but when Tidball's battery came up, Jeb Stuart knew he had to have immediate reinforcement or flee. Just then, he received word that Longstreet was still six miles away, at Nance's Shop, allegedly delayed by an incompetent guide. Pelham fired his last ammunition at 2:00 P.M. and Stuart evacuated Evelington Heights, with the satisfaction that he had put a good scare into McClellan's army. He was said to be "chuckling over the confusion he had produced in the camps of the enemy."[4]

Stuart had committed a major tactical error. By his token artillery attack with a single light gun on an army of almost 100,000 men, he had caused Lee to lose the advantage of the high ground of Evelington Heights, and denied the Confederates one last chance to inflict major damage to the Army of the Potomac.

What possible justification could Jeb Stuart offer for his poor decision to order Pelham to open fire? Even if he thought that help was almost there and it wouldn't hurt to give away his position, he would not be on solid ground. He ordered Pelham to open fire at 9:00 A.M., and Longstreet's division, the first reinforcements to arrive, got there at sunset. He could say that it really didn't matter, because McClellan was going to put troops on Evelington Heights anyway, he would be guilty of gross speculation. The army down below him had been fighting every day and marching every night for the better part of a week. McClellan had, in fact, ordered the heights manned. It probably hadn't been done because both officers and men were exhausted and somewhat disorganized, and there was no perceived immediate threat.[5]

Seven Days Before Richmond

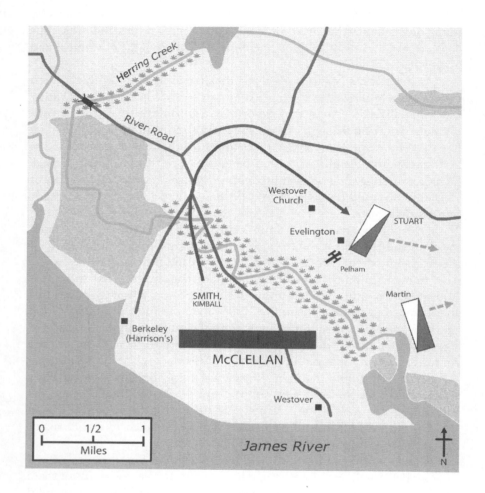

Map 23.1—Affair at Evelington Heights, July 3

One can only speculate whether or not the Confederates could have really damaged McClellan's army from Evelington Heights. It may be that the gunboats would have been able to chase them from the heights. The gunboats, while not very accurate in their fire, had the advantage of rather large projectiles. The question is academic. No infantry and only one gun were there. Stuart stated that guides had caused Longstreet to be delayed in reaching him, but, based on Lee's concern about the River road being obstructed, the alternate route from Malvern Hill to Evelington Heights goes by Nance's Shop. There was no way for Longstreet to reach Stuart before sunset. Jackson had a shorter distance to travel, and his men were strung out along the road between Nance's Shop and Willis Church.[6]

Regardless of what we may speculate, Stuart must take responsibility for opening fire on McClellan's army with a single gun, alerting them to a serious deficiency in their defense, and motivating them to almost instantly rectifying that deficiency. What he did was grossly imprudent, but he did it. It can not be said with certainty that there was an opportunity there for Lee. McClellan, now alerted that his order to occupy Evelington Heights had not been carried out, had the opportunity to see that it was before the threat to his army intensified. He took more than adequate action. He sent Slocum to back up Smith's reinforced brigade, moved Heintzelman to the left of VI Corps and put Keyes on Heintzelman's left. By late afternoon, McClellan had more than solved his problem.

By than, the very last of the trains were about to cross Kimage's Creek. Wessells had been reinforced by two of Naglee's regiments, the 56th New York and the 104th Pennsylvania. Despite Herculean efforts, it was 7:00 P.M. to get the last of the wagons across the creek. Once the wagons were safe, Wessells silently withdrew his men in phases. The last of them, the 85th New York, crossed by 11:00 P.M. Every member of the Army of the Potomac was now in its new base.

Keyes was highly praised by McClellan for his efforts in getting almost all of the wagons home safely. Keyes' work here and his location of an alternate road from Glendale to the James made him a key figure in the successful retreat of the Army of the Potomac.

Robert E. Lee remained at the Poindexter house. He maintained the rest of his army at Malvern Hill, because he had insufficient information to cause him to move it elsewhere. After reading Stuart's reports, his concern for the safety of Drewry's Bluff was diminished. On the morning of July 4, he sent David Jones' division to Longstreet and Jackson and followed them down the River road.

Jackson had been upset by the slow progress of July 3. Although Longstreet had been very near to Evelington Heights by sunset of the 3rd, Jackson had some distance to go, so he moved his command at dawn. Longstreet went forward to see for himself where the enemy was, then set about positioning Confederate units as they arrived. Jackson was in the center of the front line, A. P. Hill to the right. When they arrived, Jones' division went to the left.

The heights were well peopled by Federals by this point in time. Three corps were either on the heights or ready to support those who were there. Stuart's imprudent decision to shell the huge encampment with a single howitzer had seen to that.

Ewell's division skirmished with the Federals. They had the occasion to again fight Nathan Kimball's brigade, their old adversaries from the Shenandoah.[7] Longstreet was ready to order an attack, using Jackson's and A. P. Hill's divisions, and holding his own division in reserve. Jackson protested Longstreet's plan, claiming that his men were not ready to do battle. He wanted Longstreet to wait for Lee, and let the commanding general decide the matter. Longstreet agreed to wait.[8]

Lee, arriving just behind Jones' division, was asked by Longstreet for approval to attack. After observing the Federal infantry and artillery on the heights, and considering the gunboats on the James, Lee wisely decide not to attack, saying to Jefferson Davis, "As far as I can see, there is no way to attack him to advantage, nor do I wish to expose the men to the destructive power of his gunboats."[9]

General Lee set up headquarters at the Phillips house, just in case a weak point in the Federal defenses could be discovered. No such good fortune occurred for the Confederates. The fighting of the Peninsula Campaign was now truly over.

On the 4th of July, an informal truce occurred. Men of both armies spent time blackberrying and trading tobacco for newspapers. For many Federal soldiers, the 4th of July, an important day in their nation's history, was a day of quiet thankfulness for their survival. McClellan did his best to lift up their spirits, ordering salutes fired and bands to play. He even made an address, probably not credible, to his men that congratulated them on their performance during the campaign. McClellan then finished his day in his usual fashion, that is, he wrote an upbeat letter to his wife, in which he whined about how Lincoln regarded him. He then again asked Washington for more reinforcements.[10]

There was another incident on the morning of July 4, the end of the Confederate balloon operation. Porter Alexander had once more inflated his colorful balloon, and using the armed tugboat *Teaser*, had navigated down the James to the area of Malvern Hill. He intended to better understand the position of McClellan's army. Later in the day, due to high winds, the balloon was reeled in and stored aboard the *Teaser*. Unfortunately, the little tug went aground on a mudflat and was set upon by the Federal gunboat *Maratanza*. The *Teaser's* captain and crew abandoned the tug and waded ashore. Their attempt to use her own boiler to destroy her failed, and the *Maratanza* carried away the tug and balloon. Alexander was much distressed by the loss of his balloon, which had been constructed of colorful silks donated by the ladies of Richmond.[11]

The affair at Evelington Heights was important because it marked the real end of the Peninsula Campaign. Even though Malvern Hill was the last great battle, until Lee made the decision not to attack McClellan on Evelington Heights to get at the Federal army at Harrison's Landing, there was the possibility of more significant fighting, and the campaign was not truly over. Evelington Heights was another example of poor generalship, as Jeb Stuart should have lain low until sufficient Confederate troops came up to take the undefended heights. There was at least a chance that McClellan's weary staff would not promptly follow up on his order to occupy the heights. For the Confederates, it was yet another opportunity squandered.

PART VI

AFTERMATH

"Hardly a week earlier, McClellan's grand army was in sight of Richmond's spires and listening to the city's clock bells chime the hours. Now it was thirty-five miles distant by way of the James and twenty miles as the crow flies. The Confederacy's capital had truly been spared."

Stephen W. Sears [1]

CHAPTER 24

Stasis at Harrison's Landing

Harrison's Landing was an area of flat land, shaped like an ox bow, and fronting on the James River. The River was on the open end of the ox bow, and the other sides fronted a plateau. For better or worse, there was only one road out of the area. Relatively few troops could defend the area, due to the favorable geography. Conversely, few troops were required to keep an army bottled up at Harrison's. Unfortunately for the Federal soldiers, it was not a favorable place for a large camp. It was low ground, drained poorly, and was a difficult place to maintain sanitary conditions for a large army.[1]

One of McClellan's first actions at Harrison's Landing was to send a telegram to Secretary of War Edwin Stanton. On the morning of July 2, McClellan stated to Stanton:

> I have succeeded in getting the army to this base on the banks of the James River. I have lost but one gun, which had to be abandoned because it broke down. An hour and a half ago the rear of the wagon train was within a mile of the camp, and only one wagon abandoned... I have not yielded an inch of ground unnecessarily, but have retired to prevent the superior force of the enemy from cutting me off... and to take a different base of operations.[2]

On July 3, McClellan telegraphed Washington that he needed a hundred thousand or more additional men to capture Richmond and put an end to the rebellion. Two days prior, he asked for 50,000 men if sent promptly.[3]

By July 4, McClellan was acting like a general that had just overrun the enemy's capital, rather than one who had been driven back twenty miles by an inferior force, and was now cowering in a swampy camp protected by Navy gunboats. Despite the millions of dollars of materiel that was lost during the Federal retreat, McClellan managed to save his portable printing press, and used it to produce a July 4th address to the army. It was an eloquent piece of distorted truth, in which he praised the army, telling them they had been "attacked by vastly superior forces," had "changed your base" by a flank movement, had "saved all your materiel, all your guns...., and in every conflict beaten back your foes with enormous slaughter." His army certainly did deserve great praise. They had fought well every day, and retreated almost every night, often while their commanding general was steaming up and down the James on an ironclad gunboat, doing a job which could easily been handled by a lieutenant colonel of engineers. How he expected to sell his version of events to brave men, some of which had run for their lives at Gaines' Mill, seen a locomotive deliberately run into a river, left their wounded comrades to the mercy of the enemy as an entire field hospital was abandoned at Savage Station, is difficult to imagine. Nevertheless, McClellan's message to his men was that they had done a wonderful job of handling the adversity they had faced. Nowhere in his address did he accept any responsibility for what had happened to them. As was McClellan's habit, he blamed the shortcomings of the campaign on others. He also had a well-defined idea of where he desired to place responsibility for the poor outcome of the overall endeavor. McClellan's belief was that there was an intention by Stanton and his friends to have McClellan fail and be removed from command. McClellan believed he was a major political force in the government and was convinced that Stanton had a strong desire to see McClellan out of power as a political advantage to Stanton and his cronies. They would more easily have their way in governing the North if McClellan were removed from the scene. McClellan, in a letter to his mentor, Samuel Barlow, even described Stanton et al as "heartless villains."

Few armies in the history of warfare have ceased to exist after a failed campaign. The Army of the Potomac, though suffering many casualties at the hands of Lee's Army of Northern Virginia, was left essentially intact. Though McClellan's overarching goal of capturing Richmond was not attained, the spirit of the Federal troops was not broken. The men were resting and unwinding under the protection of U. S. Navy gunboats, enjoying their new circumstances. They were no longer fighting every day and retreating every night, as they had been for almost a week. Lost equipment and supplies were in the process of being replaced, and personnel replacements were already being supplied.

As soon as he was convinced that the Army of the Potomac was in fact redeploying to the Washington area, Lee began to plan for the future and act to facilitate those plans. Lee moved quickly to redeploy his troops. On July 7, he sent Robert Ransom's brigade back to Holmes' command and Huger's division to the south side of the James. The following day, he ordered the withdrawal of Jackson's, Longstreet's (including D. R. Jones' division) and A. P. Hill's commands to positions nearer to Richmond. Parts of Lee's army built temporary camps along the roads to Richmond for the purpose of getting some rest, receiving packages from loved ones back home, and being refitted by the Confederate government. The men had fought hard against a superior force, and were badly in need of nutritious meals and new uniforms, as well as many other items.

Stuart and his cavalry were given the responsibility for watching McClellan's army, and Stuart kept pickets fairly near to Harrison's Landing. When, on July 9, Lee established his headquarters at the Dabbs house, he was already looking forward to his next opportunity to engage "those people."

Lee spent some time at this point considering what the Federals would do next. He'd had a similar situation after Gaines' Mill. He had the initiative, but didn't want to move until the Federals revealed their strategy. The complicating factor was that there were several Federal armies to consider, not just that of McClellan.

McClellan, of course, was in command of the largest Federal force and the closest to Richmond. Stuart was watching him closely at Harrison's Landing. Burnside had a force at Newport News, recently arrived by water from coastal North Carolina. The other two Federal commands were at Fredericksburg and in the Shenandoah Valley. These were the opponents of Jackson earlier in the year, and still posed a threat from the north. Newspapers in the North printed stories indicating that the two Federal forces in the Shenandoah and at Fredericksburg were now part of Pope's Army of Virginia. Since McClellan's army was closest and largest, it deserved more of Lee's attention. Lee had to consider a variety of possible Federal strategies. Burnside, just a couple of days' march away, could be there as support for McClellan, with both armies combining to push their way back up the Peninsula. Another possibility would be to have Burnside's command land on the south side of the James and attack Petersburg while McClellan attacked north of the river. Alternatively, McDowell could attack from the north, while Lee would have much of his army held in place by McClellan's presence at Harrison's Landing. Another possibility would be for Pope to cut the Virginia Central Railroad around Gordonsville. That event would deprive the Confederacy of the products of the Shenandoah. The latter two strategies could be facilitated by moving Burnside's command north by water. Lee, however, had the advantage of central position.

Pope was the fist to tip his hand. Lee received reports that Pope was advancing southward, in the direction of the Virginia Central Railroad. Lee's reaction was to order Jackson, commanding Ewell's and Winder's divisions, to the north to meet Pope's advance. Jackson told Lee that he had insufficient force to attack Pope, so Lee sent A. P. Hill's division as reinforcements. Fortunately for Lee, Burnside and McClellan showed no sign of movement.[4]

Lee also used this time period to make personnel moves to improve the leadership of the Army of Northern Virginia. Magruder was sent away to Texas, and Huger, as well as Holmes, also disappeared to undertake less critical endeavors. Lee had Richard Anderson promoted to assume command of Huger's division, and McLaws inherited most of Magruder's division. Holmes' command was broken up, and part (2 brigades) was returned to its home in the Department of North Carolina. Longstreet's power and influence seemed to be enhanced, and he became Lee's right-hand man for the remainder of the war. Jackson's poor performance seemed to be a non-issue for General Lee, and Stonewall continued on as a commander.[5]

While McClellan was retreating across the Virginia peninsula, Lincoln had gathered up troops from a number of commands and, on June 26, formed them into the Army of Virginia. This command he entrusted to Major General John Pope, who was brought in from the West.

The evening of July 8 brought McClellan a visitor in the form of Abraham Lincoln. The President steamed down to Harrison's Landing aboard the *Ariel* to personally appraise the condition of his army and its leadership. McClellan came on board, and the greetings were mutually warm. Although the two men had not met in over three months, Lincoln's visit was to last less than twenty-four hours, and he wasted no time. He and McClellan got down to business, with Lincoln asking pointed questions about the size of the Army of the Potomac, their health, and the whereabouts of Lee's army. He then asked the most pointed question of McClellan. If the general desired to do so, could the army be safely removed from the Virginia Peninsula. According to Lincoln's record of the conference, McClellan replied that "it would be a delicate & very difficult matter."[6] Lincoln performed the obligatory review of the troops, and found them in better shape than he had expected.

The next morning, the President took the unusual step of meeting with the five corps commanders without their commanding general present. He also concluded that the troops were ready to fight, but their commanding general was not. Lincoln was also of the belief that McClellan as yet had no comprehensive plan for resuming the fight for Richmond, and probably would not be keen on cooperation with Pope's newly formed army. Lincoln then sat down with McClellan to ask a number of pointed questions. Lincoln had to be concerned about the trend of recent events. After all,

Jackson had made asses of four Federal generals in the Shenandoah, McClellan had deceived him about the adequacy of the defensive force left behind near Washington at the start of the Peninsula Campaign, and that campaign had been bloody, costly and unsuccessful. Lincoln's largest and most powerful army was now sitting idle, being slowly weakened by disease, while Lee maneuvered his forces almost at will.

Lincoln discussed with McClellan the general's thoughts on how the two armies could cooperate to best advantage. Lincoln considered that a good approach might be to extract McClellan's army from Harrison's Landing, combine it with Pope's command, and mount a large overland offensive.

As Lincoln already knew, McClellan had the firm opinion that his army should remain near the James and attack Richmond from there. McClellan then asked that "reinforcements should be sent to me rather much over than much less than 100,000 men." He had already sent letters to Lincoln and Stanton citing Lee's superior strength and his own army's high rate of sickness.

Lincoln asked the same question of Little Mac's five corps commanders. Keyes and Franklin favored withdrawal of the army, but Heintzelman, Sumner and Porter favored remaining in place, lest the men become demoralized. Heintzelman went so far as to say that he believed that pulling the army out could ruin the country.[7]

Before Lincoln departed for Washington, McClellan gave him a document which later came to be known as the "Harrison's Landing letter." It read:

> "Mr. President,
> You have been fully informed that the rebel army is in our front, with the purpose of overwhelming us by attacking our positions or reducing us by blocking our river communications. I can not but regard our condition as critical, and I earnestly desire, in view of possible contingencies, to lay before your Excellency, for your private consideration, my general views concerning the existing state of the rebellion, although they do not strictly relate to the situation of this army, or strictly come within the scope of my official duties. These views amount to convictions, and are deeply impressed upon my mind and heart. Our cause must never be abandoned: it is the cause of free institutions and self government. The Constitution and the Union must be preserved, whatever

may be the cost in time, treasure and blood. If secession is successful other dissolutions are clearly to be seen in the future. Let neither military disaster, political faction, nor foreign war, shake your settle purpose to enforce the equal operation of the laws of the United States upon the people of every State."

The time has come when the government must determine upon a civil and military policy covering the whole ground of our national trouble. The responsibility of determining, declaring and supporting such civil and military policy, and of directing the whole course of national affairs in regard to the rebellion must now be assumed and exercised by you, or our cause will be lost. The constitution gives you power sufficient even for the present terrible exigency.

This rebellion has assumed the character of war; as such it should be regarded; and it should be conducted upon the highest principles known to Christian civilization. It should not be a war looking to the subjugation of the people of any state in any event. It should not be at all a war upon population, but against armed forces and political organizations. Neither confiscations of property, political executions of persons, territorial organizations of the states, or forcible abolition of slavery should be contemplated for a moment. In prosecuting the war, all private property and unarmed persons should be strictly protected, subject only to the necessity of military operations. All private property taken for military use should be paid or receipted for: pillage and waste should be treated as high crimes: all unnecessary trespass sternly prohibited, and offensive demeanor by the military toward citizens promptly rebuked. Military arrests should not be tolerated, except in places where active hostilities exist, and oaths not required by enactments constitutionally made, should be neither demanded nor received. Military government should be confined to the preservation of public order and the protection of political rights. Military power should not be allowed to interfere with the relations of servitude, either by supporting or impairing the authority of the master, except for repressing disorder, as in other cases. Slaves deemed contraband under the act of Congress, seeking military protection, should receive it. The right of the government to appropriate permanently to its own service, claims to slave labor, should be asserted, and the right of the owner to compensation therefore should be recognized.

This principle might be extended, upon grounds of military necessity and security, to all slaves within a particular State, thus making manumission in such State; and in Missouri, perhaps in West Virginia also, and possibly even in Maryland, the expediency of such a measure is only a question of time.

A system of policy thus constitutional and conservative, and pervaded by the influences of Christianity and freedom, would receive the support of almost all truly loyal men, would deeply impress the rebel masses and all foreign nations, and it might be humbly hoped that it would commend itself to the favor of the Almighty.

Unless the principles governing the future conduct of our struggle should be made known and approved, the effort to obtain requisite forces will be almost hopeless. A declaration of radical views, especially upon slavery, will rapidly disintegrate our present armies.

The policy of the government must be supported by concentrations of military power. The national forces should not be dispersed in expeditions, posts of occupation, and numerous armies, but should be mainly collected into masses, and brought to bear upon the armies of the confederate states. Those armies thoroughly defeated, the political structure which they support would soon cease to exist.

In carrying out any system of policy which you may form, you will require a commander-in-chief of the army; one who possesses your confidence, understands your views, and who is competent to execute your orders by directing the military forces of the nation to the accomplishment of the objects by you proposed. I do not ask that place for myself. I am willing to serve you in such a position as you may assign me, and I will do so as faithfully as ever subordinate served superior.

> I may be on the brink of eternity, and as I hope for forgiveness from my Maker, I have written this letter with sincerity towards you, and from love for my country.
> Very respectfully, your ob't servant,
> G. B. McClellan,
> Major-General, Comd'g.[8]

The letter was the result of several weeks of thought, and McClellan had amazingly come to the conclusion that the nation needed the fruits of his thinking to guide its war strategy. An insight to McClellan's thinking at that time is the fact that he wrote his wife that his conscience dictated that "he try to shape war policy in his own image." The letter, as much a political manifesto as a military blueprint, related to Lincoln that confiscation of Southerners' property and freeing their slaves were "radical views." To make abolitionism government policy would result in the disintegration of the Federal armies. This audacious act on McClellan's part, was likely an attempt by the egocentric general to demonstrate how deep a thinker he was, and to reclaim the general-in-chief position. Lincoln was probably stunned to receive political strategy advice from a general who seemed to be having trouble doing his own job. Lincoln took the letter, read it, then reboarded the *Ariel* without commenting on it.[9]

Abraham Lincoln returned to Washington, then of the opinion that the counsel he was receiving from McClellan was inadequate. He next summoned Major General Henry W. Halleck from the West to be general-in-chief of the Federal armies, effective July 11. McClellan was not informed in advance. He became aware of his demotion by reading a newspaper. McClellan was likely very surprised at the turn of events, in that he had recently been assured by both Lincoln and Stanton that they remained totally supportive of him. McClellan, taking them at their word, had begun planning an attack from south of the James to threaten Richmond. Although he was at last working on a plan for offensive tactical operations, he seemed to have lost his understanding of the strategic situation.

On July 19, Fitz John Porter reported the Confederates working their way to the north, possibly in the direction of Washington. Porter also believed that Lee was keeping his divisions where he could easily withdraw them to the vicinity of Richmond if the need arose. McClellan's belief in the great size of Lee's army was reinforced by Lee's seeming ability to threaten in several directions at once. It was a clever and dangerous game Lee was playing, and only McClellan's persistent delusion concerning the size of the Army of Northern Virginia kept the game viable for Lee.[10]

As July wore on, transports continued to land at Harrison's, significantly improving the lot of McClellan's army. By July 20, "Quartermaster General of the Army Rufus Ingalls reported that the army had on hand 3,100 wagons, 350 ambulances, 7,000 cavalry horses, 5,000 artillery horses, and 5,000 team horses, in addition to 8,000 mules." The transports still standing off the river bank contained an abundance of supplies. The army was ready to resume offensive action.

On July 25, Halleck went to Harrison's Landing to assess the situation and try to develop a strategy to get the war effort going again. The new general-in-chief was immediately disappointed, as McClellan could show him no concrete plan for renewing the offensive. McClellan did speak in general terms of attacking Petersburg or having Pope and his army join him on the peninsula. General McClellan wanted the outrageous force of 300,000 men to attack Richmond. Halleck gave McClellan a clear set of choices. He could attack with minimal reinforcements or he could withdraw to Northern Virginia. McClellan couldn't seem to make the choice. On July 30, Halleck ordered McClellan to begin evacuating the sick. On August 2, McClellan began an advance, but Halleck had already made his decision to withdraw the Army of the Potomac from the Peninsula.

Halleck had been authorized by Lincoln to remove McClellan if he saw fit. Lincoln had clearly decided to do so, as evidenced by the fact that he had already offered the command to Major General Ambrose Burnside, who had declined, citing his lack of qualifications for the position. Halleck endeavored to make the point with McClellan that the Federal army in the East was divided, as McClellan was down on the James with three-quarters of it, and Pope was further north defending Washington with the remainder. Halleck wanted the Army reunited, but waited until August 3 to issue the order.[11]

Although Lee seemed to no longer regard McClellan and his army as an immediate threat to Richmond, he was not yet finished tormenting Little Mac. Lee's Chief of Artillery, William N. Pendleton, gathered 47 rifled guns on the south side of the James. Pendleton carefully chose the firing positions and determined the ranges so that the barrage could be conducted at night. On August 1, about a half hour past midnight, the Confederates commenced their barrage. Firing from the opposite bank of the James from locations described by McClellan as Coggins Point and the Coles House, the fire was sustained for half an hour, and directed at shipping and the camp in general. The firing was random and their ammunition supply was somewhat limited. Of course, the Federals returned fire from gunboats and the camp. With all the chaos in the camp, and the inherent inaccuracy of random firing at night, little damage was done to either side. The Federals suffered some 40 casualties, and the Confederate gunners lost two or three men. McClellan reported 10 killed, 15 wounded. No damage was reported to the vessels moored nearby, although several were hit.[12]

The Federals responded the following day by crossing the river, destroying the Coles House and cutting down the adjacent timber. McClellan occupied Coggins Point on August 3 as a security measure. He planned to entrench there using contraband labor. He also sent Averell and a party of 300 cavalry from the 5th U.S. and the 3rd Pennsylvania Cavalry to scout south of the James. They ran across a Confederate cavalry force of 550 troopers at Sycamore Creek, and reported that they drove the Confederates off and burned their camp. Averell also reported taking two prisoners and suffering only two wounded.[13]

As to be expected, the newspapers in Richmond had nothing but high praise for Robert E. Lee and his army. They believed the Seven Days battles to be one big running battle that had turned the campaign around. Richmond had been spared from capture, and the citizens felt a great sense of relief.[14]

General Lee was not quite so sanguine about the results of the campaign. He had to be feeling a sense of disappointment that McClellan's army was still on the peninsula and essentially intact, if a bit battered and weary. Although Richmond was no longer facing an imminent threat, McClellan's army was still only a few days' march away. Lee's disappointment sprang from the fact that he had been confident that his strategy should have allowed him to destroy the Army of the Potomac. In his official report on the campaign, he wrote the oft quoted statement, "Under ordinary circumstances, the Federal army should have been destroyed."[15]

The reality of the common soldiers of McClellan's army was that they were now huddled in a swampy camp on the banks of the James River, albeit protected by the gunboats of the U. S. Navy, yet suffering through 103 degree heat, Virginia humidity, mosquitoes, flies, bad drinking water and poor sanitary facilities. Sickness was rampant in the camp. The men renamed Chickahominy fever to James River fever. During July alone, some 42,911 cases of illness were reported. McClellan's Medical Director, Doctor Jonathan Letterman, reported 18,000 sick at one point in July. Numerous Federal soldiers died at Harrison's Landing. It was the most costly month of the campaign in terms of casualties from disease. George McClellan did what he could to recuperate the army from their campaign. He issued them replacement uniforms and other equipment, brought in replacements for the men lost, and kept them busy. Despite all this, the sickness resulted in an army which grew slightly less potent each day. In this sad environment, Private Oliver Norton composed a new "lights out" bugle call. Assisted by Brigadier General Daniel Butterfield, *Taps* was born.[16]

At first, McClellan's political friends tried to support his perennial claim that he had faced a superior Confederate army. Northern newspapers even took up the lie for a while, probably because much of the available information on the Army of the Potomac came from McClellan's headquarters. This support largely evaporated rather quickly. Salmon P. Chase and Edward Bate, both members of Lincoln's Cabinet, turned on Little Mac. The Radical Republicans cried out for the general's dismissal. They saw no reason to have a Democrat as the head of their most powerful army. The discourse degenerated into a verbal feud between Democrat and Republican politicians and newspapers. The Democrats shrewdly tried to lay the blame on Secretary of War Stanton.[17]

On the Confederate side of the border, McClellan's "change of base" became a term of derision. High ranking officers such as Major General D. H. Hill referred to McClellan as "the great Mover of his Base." Even at the level of the privates, "change of base" was a term used as a taunt by Confederate cavalry pickets to shout across the space between them and Federal pickets at Harrison's Landing.[18]

The Confederate victory over the Army of the Potomac, limited and costly though it was, served to dissipate the immediate threat to Richmond. Lee now felt he had more flexibility in how he deployed his troops, and sent Stonewall Jackson's command to operate against the army of John Pope, in the area along the Rapidan River. It was desirable to Lee to move the center of fighting away from Richmond, and after reorganizing his army and securing such replacements as were available, plans were made to move northward. This shift of Confederate troops was the prelude to the battles of Cedar Mountain and Second Manassas, the Confederate victories there, and the subsequent Confederate invasion of Maryland.[19]

CHAPTER 25

The Cost of Gallantry

As the Peninsula Campaign ended, the capitals of the two warring nations had one sad property in common. Both cities were grim, chaotic and looked more like rudimentary hospital complexes than anything else. The Confederate capital was in worse shape than Washington. It was already overcrowded due to the relocation of the Confederate government there from Montgomery, Alabama. Additionally, Richmond was the *de facto* logistics base for the Army of Northern Virginia. These two factors created an atmosphere of chaos and a shortage of almost anything imaginable. As the war progressed to its predictable conclusion, the suffering of Richmond increased measurably.

As the wounded came in from the Peninsula, volunteers began arriving from all parts of the fledgling nation to nurse them. Almost anything with wheels was turned into an ambulance or a "dead wagon" and used to move the dead and wounded back to the city. Gravediggers couldn't work fast enough to keep up with the demand for their services. It is trite to state that the number of hospitals and doctors were grossly insufficient to meet the deluge of wounded from the battlefields.

In the Washington area, steamers continued to arrive with the wounded from the Peninsula. Medical personnel and relief workers met them to move the wounded to hospitals. Family members also came down to the docks, looking to find their wounded loved ones or claim their bodies. The newspapers published lists of the killed and wounded as accurately as possible. As McClellan's army retreated after most of the battles, many Federal dead were buried by the Confederates. As the pursuing army, they had limited time and resources to devote to the burial of their foes. The fallen Federals were sometimes interred hastily, in poorly marked graves. Some families struggled for years to find their loved ones' remains and rebury them in the north. Some Federal soldiers were never returned to their families.[1]

Armies in wartime lose men to three main causes—enemy action, accidents and sickness. A very few are lost to suicide, homicide and desertion. In the Civil War, sickness was the greatest taker of lives, followed closely by enemy action. For most historians, losses to enemy action are of greatest interest, but some authors have attempted to describe the extent and nature of the effect of sickness on the participating armies. By and large, accidents weren't reported diligently or accurately.

It is difficult for modern society to totally comprehend the lethality of the American Civil War. The lethality of any war is largely a result of the weaponry employed, the tactics used, and the ability of the medical establishment to save the wounded from death. In the American Civil War, all three of these factors contributed to high lethality. The battles of the Peninsula Campaign were no exception.

The significant increase in accuracy and effective range which ensued from the fielding of the rifled musket cannot be overstated. Where smooth-bore muskets weren't very accurate beyond a hundred yards, the rifled muskets that replaced them could often hit a man several hundred yards out. Improvements to the size and quality of artillery pieces, and improvements to projectiles and fuses also added to the death rate.

As to the tactics employed, they lagged sadly behind the developments in weapons. The American Civil War is often referred to as the first modern war, based largely on the use of telegraph, railroads, aerial observation from balloons, etc. It can more accurately be described as a transitional war, in which hardware (weapons) had become modern, but tactics were still Napoleonic. That is to say, the officers still shouted voice commands which resulted in regiments attacking in dense formations which were hard to miss with rifled musket or artillery piece. Where there were persistent assaults on prepared positions, such as at Mechanicsville, Gaines' Mill and Malvern Hill, heavy casualties were sustained. Any large offensive movement was almost assured of sustaining extensive casualties. Almost incredibly, generals on both sides were willing to sacrifice many hundreds of their men to achieve objectives they perceived to be vital.

The medical infrastructure also contributed to the high death rate. Insufficient attention and assets were committed to retrieving the wounded from the battlefield and getting them to a field hospital where they could be given a fair chance at survival. In some cases, such as at Malvern Hill, many hundreds of wounded were left on the battlefield for an extended period before a temporary truce allowed them to be retrieved. Soldiers wounded in the Civil War often suffered amputation. The particular projectile fired from the muskets of the day tended to shatter the bones of the extremities, and the medicine of the day quite often had only amputation as a lifesaving procedure.

We mustn't forget that there were a number of battles in the Peninsula Campaign before the Seven Days. The first shots were exchanged during a Federal reconnaissance, even before the month-long siege of Yorktown.

Despite the volume of artillery fire exchanged between the two armies, as well as one significant firefight on the 16th of April at Dam # 1, overall casualties at Yorktown were light. The Federals suffered 183 total casualties, and the Confederates sustained a total of 295.

At the battle of Williamsburg, fought on May 5, total Federal losses were 2,239. The 70th New York of Hooker's III Corps division had 330 total casualties and the 72nd New York sustained 195. The Confederates lost a total of 1,560. The 24th Virginia of Jubal Early's brigade, D. H. Hill's division, sustained 189 casualties. Brigadier General Jubal Early was wounded in the shoulder. The reader must keep in mind that this engagement was fought by only a minor part of each army.

The fight at Eltham's Landing, fought on May 7, judged by some as a heavy skirmish, by others as a battle, involved only a small part of each army, and was of short duration. Total Federal casualties were 186, and the Confederates lost 48.[2]

The engagement at Hanover Court House, fought on May 27, was a ferocious fight. Although it was an uneven battle, with essentially a Confederate brigade under Brigadier General Lawrence O'B. Branch opposing a Federal corps commanded by Brigadier General Fitz John Porter, casualties were not that lopsided. Federal casualties were 355 killed or wounded, with 70 men captured. Two Federal regiments were hit pretty hard. The 25th New York sustained 158 total casualties, and the 44th New York suffered 86. Confederate casualties were about 275–300 killed and wounded and 731 captured. Most of the Confederates taken prisoner were stragglers gathered up by Federal cavalry after the battle ended.[3]

The most significant of these battles was at Seven Pines (Fair Oaks), fought on May 31–June 1. Federal total casualties were 5,061. Several Federal regiments were badly hurt. The 61st Pennsylvania sustained 263 casualties, the 104th Pennsylvania had 206, and the 5th New Hampshire suffered 180. On the Confederate side, total losses were 6,134. D. H. Hill's division had substantial casualties, with thirteen regiments sustaining over a hundred casualties each. The worst suffering was in the 6th Alabama (373), the 4th North Carolina (369), and the 6th South Carolina (269). General Joseph E. Johnston was severely wounded and Brigadier General Robert Hatton was killed at Seven Pines, both on the first day of the battle.

As the attacking army during most of the Seven Days, the Army of Northern Virginia suffered a higher casualty rate than its opponent. At Mechanicsville, Gaines' Mill and Malvern Hill, where the Federals fought from excellent defensive positions, the Confederate casualties were especially high. The Federal advantage in number and quality of artillery pieces also had a marked effect on casualty rates. From Oak Grove on June 25 through Malvern Hill on July 1, Lee's army lost 3,494 killed, 15,758 wounded, and 952 missing/captured. This totaled 20,204 men, some 22% of the Confederates who went there to fight.[4]

As mentioned above, an obvious factor in determining casualties is whether an army is primarily on offense or defense. As the defending army in every fight after Oak Grove, the Army of the Potomac suffered relatively less casualties in the Seven Days. The Federals suffered 1,434 killed, 8,066 wounded, and 6,055 missing/captured, for a total of 15,855.[5]

The Federal casualties were not reasonably shared among the five corps of the Army of the Potomac. Primarily due to the negligent manner in which McClellan exercised command during the week of fighting, there were great imbalances in the amount of fighting required of individual corps. The heaviest burden, and therefore, the most casualties fell upon Fitz John Porter's V Corps. They bore the brunt of the fighting at Mechanicsville, Gaines' Mill and Malvern Hill. One of Porter's three divisions, that of George McCall, was also out front at Glendale. The V Corps suffered 7,575 total casualties, about 28% of Porter's corps. The Pennsylvania Reserve Corps, which comprised 100% of the infantry of George McCall's V Corps division, suffered almost 20% of the total Federal casualties. The 11th Pennsylvania Reserves suffered 684 casualties and the 4th New Jersey of Slocum's VI Corps division took 585 at Gaines' Mill alone. The 1st New York of Kearny's III Corps division sustained 230 total casualties at Glendale.

At the other end of the spectrum was Keyes' IV Corps, which only fought at Malvern Hill, and there with only one of its two divisions. IV Corps losses totaled only about 800 men for the week. The VI Corps got off relatively light, except for Slocum's division at Gaines' Mill. The III Corps divisions of Joe Hooker and Phil Kearny were asked to fight only at Oak Grove and Glendale.

Casualties in the Seven Days weren't evenly distributed across the Confederate divisions, either. A. P. Hill's division suffered high casualties in the earlier battles of the Seven Days. At Mechanicsville, they suffered 764, and at Gaines' Mill 2,688 killed and wounded. In the course of the Seven Days, Longstreet's division also paid a heavy price, sustaining 4,438 killed and wounded in the Seven Days battles. Four of the division's brigades lost 49% or more of their strength. Specifically, Anderson lost 62.9%: Pryor, 61.5%; Wilcox, 57.0% and Featherston, 49.3%. These heavy losses were sustained mainly at Gaines' Mill and Glendale. D. H. Hill's division suffered a 41% loss at Malvern Hill on July 1. Jackson's division, on the other hand, only lost 208 men killed and wounded in the entire Seven Days.

A number of general officers were killed, wounded or captured during the Seven Days. On the Federal side, Brigadier General George McCall was captured and Brigadier General George Meade was severely wounded at Glendale. On the Confederate side, Brigadier General Richard Griffith was mortally wounded at Savage Station.

Even more tragic was the distribution of casualties across individual regiments. Keeping in mind that this was a war fought almost completely by volunteer regiments, often raised from single towns or rural counties, it was not uncommon for several members of a family to fight in the same company or regiment. Fathers saw their sons die, brothers witnessed their siblings fall, and small towns were made to suffer terribly when a regiment of their community was cut up in a particular bloody engagement. Examples of regiments who were decimated aren't difficult to find. Perhaps the most tragic example of the decimation of a particular family occurred at the battle of Hanover Court House. Three of the four Robinett brothers were dead on the battlefield, all from Company G, 37th North Carolina.[6]

On the Confederate side, the prime example is the Palmetto Sharpshooters of South Carolina, which lost 67.7% of its complement on June 30 at Glendale. Regiments losing at least fifty percent of their men in a single day were the 44th Georgia at Mechanicsville (65.1%), the 1st South Carolina Rifles at Gaines' Mill (56.9%), the 11th Alabama at Glendale (50.7%), and the 3rd Alabama at Malvern Hill (56.4%).

Sometimes a regiment was battered by bad generalship. The decimation of the 44th Georgia at Mechanicsville was to be expected. They were tasked to do the impossible. As part of Ripley's brigade of D. H. Hill's division, they paid the price for a battle plan gone wrong. Robert E. Lee never intended a frontal attack across Beaver Dam Creek, but rather Stonewall Jackson flanking Porter's V Corps out of their works. Jackson was delayed in reaching the battlefield and impatience ruled over prudence among the Confederate leaders. Ordered to attack the dug in Federals supported by artillery across Beaver Dam Creek up the steep bank, the 44th Georgia, followed by the 1st North Carolina, gallantly attempted to fulfill their assignment. The result was totally predictable. Porter Alexander commented, "A more hopeless charge was never entered upon." The 44th lost 335 men killed and wounded, to include its colonel, lieutenant colonel, two captains and ten lieutenants. They had reached the creek, and foolishly stood in the water exchanging fire with Federals in prepared positions on the far bank. Some were killed at close range by canister from the dug in Federal artillery. When their ammo ran out, the

44th retreated. The supporting regiment, the 1st North Carolina, which had advanced about half way down the near bank, stayed there and fought, though thrice ordered to fall back. They were also hit hard, losing their colonel, lieutenant colonel, major, six captains and lieutenants Total killed and wounded were 133 men.

It is interesting to note that the 44th Georgia, after being mauled at Mechanicsville, suffered a 45.7% loss at Malvern Hill only five days later. Of the 514 men of the 44th Georgia who started the day at Mechanicsville, only 77 were available for duty after Malvern Hill.[7]

As the Federals retreated after Mechanicsville and every subsequent battle, they understandably had about six times as many men captured as did the Confederates. Advancing units of Lee's army snatched up many hundreds of exhausted stragglers along the muddy roads. Some were demoralized, all were hungry and exhausted. Many had discarded their muskets and other equipment and were found simply sitting on the ground all along the line of retreat, waiting for someone to end their misery by taking them prisoner. At least two Confederate regiments were pulled out of the advance and detailed to escort prisoners to Richmond. The Federals were also forced to leave many of their dead and wounded on the battlefield as they stole away in the night.

Accidents claim lives in any army, whether or not it is in combat. Men are thrown from horses, run over by wagons, accidentally shot by friendly troops and drown while crossing rivers. Although the losses from accidents are far exceeded by those from sickness or enemy action, they cannot be ignored.

The impact of disease in the Peninsula Campaign cannot be overstated. Sickness was a great killer in the American Civil War in general. The state of medicine in that time period made it most difficult to cope with many ailments, especially the variety of fevers common to troops operating in warm weather and swampy terrain. Additionally, camps such as the Federal army occupied at Harrison's Landing during July and early August of 1862 soon became unsanitary. As mentioned in a previous chapter, July of 1862 was the month in which the Army of the Potomac had the greatest number of men sick, with over 18,000 sick at one point. Wounded were evacuated by steamer down the James and up the Chesapeake Bay and Potomac River to Washington. While they are a number of sources of data available to try and comprehend the extent of the impact of disease on the two armies, the data are truly imperfect and sometimes contradictory. Steiner's *Disease in the Civil War* is probably the best source for a quick understanding of the issue.[8]

The situation for the Confederates was a bit different. While not nearly as well supplied as the Federals in the field, they were fighting on their home soil, and had the important advantage of being able to remove their sick by ambulance to hospitals in the nearby capital of Richmond.

In summary, sickness was a major killer of soldiers in the Civil War, and the Peninsula Campaign was no exception. The most deadly disease was camp fever. It swept through both armies at one time or another, and was dubbed "Chickahominy Fever" for the swampy little river that wound its way through the battle area. It took its deadly toll day after day. After the Army of the Potomac came to rest at Harrison's Landing, the increasingly poor sanitary conditions provided a perfect incubator for camp fever. This was an army that had been forced to fight every day and retreat overnight for a week, an army that was wet and hungry upon arrival. The fever added to their demoralization. Throughout the conflict, childhood diseases such as measles also debilitated armies in crowded camps. To their credit, many of the soldiers still wanted their leader to put them back on the offensive.

The Federals lost more in the Peninsula Campaign than just men. Their losses in materiel were huge, mostly because their initial supply of assets was huge. McClellan, the consummate organizer and logistician, had seen to that. They were arguably the best supplied expeditionary force in the history of warfare. Although they made a desperate attempt to destroy what they couldn't carry away with them, they largely failed to deny significant assets to the Confederates. What George McClellan's army failed to destroy prior to the several retreats was eagerly gathered up by advancing Confederate troops and put to immediate good use.

Lee's men were amazed at the relative luxury enjoyed by Federal soldiers on the Peninsula. Items recovered from abandoned Federal camps included whiskey, wine, beer, sugar, tobacco, fruit such as lemons, oysters, pickled eggs, even ice and other delicacies unknown in Confederate army camps. There was almost no category of supplies or equipment that wasn't enthusiastically gathered up by Lee's men at some point. This windfall was a great morale booster for Lee's men.

Jeb Stuart's cavalry rode into the Federal base at White House Landing just as the last Federal gunboat was making its exit from the area. The horsemen used their mountain howitzer to expedite the Federal Navy's departure. It took them some time to load up all their plunder and destroy what they couldn't take away. Reports vary, but virtually all describe the loss of at least 40 artillery pieces, a minimum of 31,000 small arms, hundreds of wagons and ambulances, many horses and mules, tons of ammunition, many thousands of rations, extensive medical supplies, a complete field hospital with many of its patients at Savage Station, a number of railroad cars and even at least one locomotive.[9]

See Appendix B for a tabular presentation of casualty numbers.

CHAPTER 26

Redeployment

Finally, Washington could stand it no more. An army of 90,000 men, camped for a month on the banks of the James, essentially contributing nothing to the Federal war effort, could not be tolerated. Additionally, Washington had concern about the toll on the army from sickness if it was required to remain encamped along the James for much longer. There was also concern about Lee attacking Pope up north. On August 3, the order was received via telegraph from General-in-Chief Henry W. Halleck in Washington directing the Army of the Potomac to march to Fort Monroe. They were to redeploy by water to the Washington area and ordered to land at Aquia Creek, on the west bank of the Potomac River south of Washington.[1]

McClellan obviously did not desire to carry out Halleck's order, and immediately requested that the order be rescinded. McClellan made a spirited and somewhat logical defense of his thinking and policies to date. He stated that the Army of the Potomac was in good condition and that discipline was also good. It was secure in its present location, being well protected by U. S. Navy gunboats on the James River. He made the excellent point that it was where the action should be. "Here, directly in front of this army, is the heart of the rebellion. All points of secondary importance elsewhere should be abandoned and every available man brought here; a decided victory and the military strength of the rebellion is crushed. It matters not what partial reverses we may meet with elsewhere. Here is the true defense of Washington."[2]

Halleck could not accommodate McClellan. He had his orders from Lincoln, and meant to carry them out. Halleck's answer to McClellan was not gentle or tactful. "The order will not be rescinded and you will be expected to execute it with all necessary promptness." Halleck had been tired of McClellan's stalling for some time. On July 30, Halleck had ordered McClellan to begin evacuating his sick troops, ostensibly to make the army less encumbered and more able to move in any direction.

On that same day, McClellan received another dispatch from Halleck that related the fact that Pope had intelligence to suggest that the Confederates were moving south of the James, and that the defenders of

Richmond were few in number. Halleck suggested that McClellan press in that direction to determine the accuracy of Pope's report. As McClellan had no other information to rely on but Halleck's latest telegrams, he took them at face value and believed that Washington had plans for him to go back on the offensive, possibly south of the James. Not all the telegrams that came from Pope to Halleck to McClellan were that credible. On July 31, one of them even claimed that the Confederates were abandoning Richmond and falling back on Lynchburg and Danville.[3]

McClellan, besides making an excellent verbal case for rescinding the order to withdraw up the bay, took some concrete action to support his contention that the Army of the Potomac was where it needed to be. He had previously been asked by Halleck to feel out the Federals. Now, under threat of being forced to withdraw his army to the defense of Washington, McClellan attacked the Confederates at Malvern Hill, forcing them to beat a hasty retreat. This was not so easily accomplished as it might seem. The initial attempt, conducted by Hooker's division and Pleasonton's cavalry on the night of August 2, was unsuccessful. McClellan told Washington that incompetent guides were to blame. On August 4, Sedgwick's division was added to Hooker's, and Malvern Hill was taken. McClellan claimed 100 prisoners, while Federal losses were only three killed and eleven wounded.[4] McClellan then showed even more initiative, ordering Averell's cavalry to make a reconnaissance as far as Savage Station. In typical McClellan boastful phraseology, he reported, "Our troops have advanced twelve miles in one direction and seventeen in another toward Richmond today."[5]

McClellan's token show of initiative was too little, too late to affect the course of events. Doubtless, Halleck, Stanton and President Lincoln had reached the conclusion that if they left McClellan and his army in place on the James, he would simply continue to inflate his estimate of the size of Lee's army, ask for more reinforcements, and do almost nothing to further the war effort. There also had to be concern that the wily Lee might elect to hold the timid McClellan in place with a minor portion of his army, move the remainder north to destroy Pope's smaller force of about 30,000 men, then return to attack McClellan. In other terms, destruction in detail.[6]

In fact, as soon as Lee was sure that McClellan's army was leaving Harrison's Landing, he took positive steps to attack the numerically inferior army of John Pope. The engagement was the battle of Second Manassas, fought on August 29–30. This resounding victory was in part made possible because not all of the Army of the Potomac had been able to travel up the Chesapeake Bay and join Pope in time. Also, those troops which had arrived from the Peninsula did not operate in harmony with the rest of Pope's army.[7] Pope's defeat caused Lincoln to retain McClellan as a key figure in rebuilding the again demoralized and defeated Federal army in the East.[8]

On August 14, the Army of the Potomac began its evacuation of Harrison's Landing. Not all of the corps took the same route home. The remaining sick, as well as the V Corps division of George McCall, now commanded by Truman Seymour since McCall's capture on June 30, boarded naval transports at Harrison's Landing and sailed to support Burnside. This used up the available transports off Harrison's Landing. The remainder of V Corps were the first to march out of Harrison's Landing. They moved rapidly, and arrived at Williamsburg on August 16. McClellan had ordered Porter to remain there until the entire army was safely across the Chickahominy. Heintzelman's III Corps marched out of Harrison's Landing, covered by William Averell's cavalry, crossed the Chickahominy River at Forge Bridge, and marched on to Williamsburg. The remainder of McClellan's army marched eastward through Charles City Courthouse, crossing the Chickahominy where it met the James at Barrett's Ferry. McClellan had Major Duane's engineers build a 2,000 foot long pontoon bridge across the Chickahominy there. From there, the army traveled through Williamsburg to Fort Monroe. It was, of course, an extremely long column, the head of which was crossing the Chickahominy while units in the rear were still within sight of Berkeley Plantation.[9]

An army is seldom more vulnerable to attack than when it is strung out along a road in a lengthy movement. The accompanying wagon train makes rapid maneuver all but impossible, and it is difficult to concentrate combat power at any given point along the train. Fully aware of this vulnerability, McClellan made extensive preparations for the movement. Quaker cannon were left behind, along with scarecrow sentries, clad in Federal blue uniforms. A rear guard comprised of Pleasonton's cavalry, the "Irish Brigade," and several batteries of artillery was assembled. The rear guard remained at Haxall's Landing behind Turkey Creek. On August 16, when informed that the last of the army had departed Harrison's Landing, the rear guard felled trees across the road and moved to a new position just west of Berkeley Plantation. McClellan wrote his wife that he took a "savage satisfaction" in being the last man to leave.

By and large the retreat went unmolested. Only a few Confederate troopers came to skirmish. By 10:00 A.M. on August 18, the last of McClellan's men crossed the pontoon bridge over the Chickahominy at Barrett's Ferry, and Federal engineers immediately disassembled it. Now the huge invading army traveled back largely along the same route on which they had advanced earlier in their quest to capture Richmond.[10]

The process of redeploying to the Washington area took several weeks, from receipt of the order on August 3 to the last of the army sailing on August 28, except for IV Corps, which remained at Fort Monroe. The pace of redeployment was limited by the availability of vessels. Porter's V Corps sailed from Newport News on August 19 and 20; Heintzelman's III Corps sailed from Yorktown on August 21; Franklin's VI Corps on the 23rd and 24th, and Sumner's II Corps on the 26th.

Halleck had directed McClellan to leave garrisons in Fort Monroe, Yorktown, etc. as McClellan deemed appropriate. The garrison troops were to be replaced by fresh troops as soon as possible. McClellan tasked Keyes to set up the defenses at Yorktown. McClellan, ever the micromanager, involved himself in the tasks at Yorktown and Gloucester across the York River, right down to requesting two good ordnance sergeants from Halleck. The major part of Keyes' IV Corps embarked on the 29th, but John Peck's division was left at Yorktown to cover the overland approaches to Fort Monroe.[11]

As the redeployment progressed, a voluminous stream of telegraph messages passed between Halleck and McClellan. General McClellan, with his sharp sense of logistics and eye for detail, asked Halleck about the latter's desires as to ammunition, forage, etc. He also pressed Halleck for a better sense of what was going on west of Washington, and what his role might be. Halleck seemed to answer all the logistics questions, but revealed little about Washington's plans for McClellan.

Much of the message traffic between the two generals revolved around two themes: (1) the number of days between the order to redeploy and the actual movement of units out of Harrison's Landing, and (2) what steps Washington was taking to help McClellan accelerate the redeployment.

Messages originating on Halleck's end seemed to indicate that he and others in Washington felt McClellan had taken too many days to get the army moving, that he still was not moving fast enough, and that he was not keeping them properly informed. In point of fact, McClellan had done a pretty fair job of reporting every troop movement. Halleck sent messages to McClellan which explained that the Government was also in the process of moving Ambrose Burnside's command from Fort Monroe to Aquia Landing en route to reinforcement of Pope. Also, the point was again made that there were no reinforcements to spare. The point Halleck sought to make was that there were only so many steam and sailing vessels, and he had engaged almost all of them and was wisely using them.[12]

Messages from McClellan generally denied the above allegation, instead pointing to a lack of water transportation, as well as citing the complexity of moving such a large army, and the need to retreat wisely to avoid being attacked on the way to the embarkation points. McClellan insisted that he had faithfully and energetically carried out Halleck's order, and that Halleck had been misinformed as to the number of sick to be evacuated, as well as the amount of transport available. In numerous messages to Halleck, McClellan repeated his contention that he was moving his army as swiftly as possible, that there weren't enough ships, that the landing facilities at Aquia were inadequate, and that no one could make it go any faster. He repeated the theme that Halleck's staff was misinforming him of the true situation. In response to a Halleck comparison of Burnside's move from Fort Monroe to the ongoing movement of McClellan's troops, the general reminded his superior that Burnside wasn't slowed down by sick, wounded, cavalry, artillery, wagons or teams, and most of the command's baggage remained stowed aboard the ships.[13]

More light can be shed on the dynamic between Halleck and McClellan by looking at some specific exchanges of telegrams. They will serve to give some perspective to the real problems McClellan had, and the urgent, near panicky approach of Halleck, in his haste to get reinforcements to Pope.

One of Halleck's complaints about McClellan was that he failed to keep Washington well informed. Yet, it appears at times it was Halleck who resorted to one-line responses to comprehensive messages. For example, on August 5 at 1:00 P.M., McClellan messaged Halleck from Malvern Hill, reporting that Hooker's division had attacked "a very considerable force of infantry and artillery..." Hooker, supported by Sedgwick, had allegedly driven the enemy in the direction of New Market and taken about 100 prisoners, suffering only three killed and eleven wounded. McClellan then opined that Malvern Hill was a good place from which to begin another assault on Richmond, and that he could advance there in five days if reinforced. Halleck's reply, sent at 3:00 A.M. the following day, was, "I have no reinforcements to send you."[14] One must keep in mind that before these two messages were exchanged, McClellan had already received Halleck's order to redeploy his army to Aquia Landing. In fact, McClellan acknowledged receiving the order on August 4. At 10:00 P.M. on August 6, McClellan sent a letter to Hooker, ordering him to withdraw his men back to Harrison's Landing.[15] Perhaps Halleck saw Hooker's operation as evidence of McClellan foot-dragging.

Evacuation of the wounded from Harrison's Landing was the topic of numerous messages and often contentious. As early as July 30 at 8:00 P.M., Halleck had ordered McClellan to begin the evacuation of his sick. He also required the evacuation to be conducted as quickly as possible, and to be advised of their departure. On August 2 at 3:45 P.M., Halleck follow up his previous message. He was direct, and said, "you have not answered my telegram about the removal of your sick. Remove them as rapidly as possible, and telegraph me when they will be out of your way. The President wishes an answer as soon as possible." McClellan's reply to Halleck's latest message was sent at on August 3 at 11:00 P.M. He began by acknowledging receipt of Halleck's second message. He then reported that he had at that point 12,500 sick. He believed that approximately 4,000 were capable of making "light marches." He plainly stated that he had available transport for only 1,200, and planned to send that number out the following day, the worst cases, of course. He then related that his medical staff thought it would take 7–12 days to move the remainder. At this point, McClellan again asked what the plan was for his army. He eloquently made the case that the longer he was kept in the dark, the less able he was to fulfill Halleck's wishes. He again closed diplomatically, pledging to do his best to satisfy Halleck.[16] Once again, McClellan seemed not to be able or perhaps not willing to follow the orders given him by Halleck. Again, Halleck's tone was direct and lacking in respect for an officer, while his subordinate in the pecking order, was still a fellow major general.

Another example of the character of the communication between the two generals is their exchange of messages regarding Halleck's order regarding cavalry. On August 6, Halleck sent the following message to McClellan. "You will immediately send a regiment of cavalry and several batteries of artillery to Burnside's command at Aquia (or Acquia) Creek. It is reported that Jackson is moving north with a very large force." McClellan's response was ambiguous, and certainly lacking in deference to the General-in-Chief. He responded by stating that he had but 4,000 cavalry remaining, and could spare no more. He really needed more cavalry to safely comply with Halleck's order to redeploy the army to Acquia Landing. He justified his non-compliance by stating that the Confederates were advancing on Malvern Hill. This also justified not sending any artillery to Burnside either. McClellan did promise to comply with Halleck's order as soon as circumstances would allow. He closed by complaining about the lack of transportation for his wounded. He vowed to incur no avoidable delays.[17]

McClellan, in several messages, hammered home the point that he lacked sufficient transportation for his sick, and asked what Washington wanted him to do with those he couldn't move for lack of steamers. Halleck, likewise, continued to press McClellan for concrete numbers relative to the evacuation of the sick. On August 7 at 10:00 A.M., Halleck bluntly ordered McClellan to specifically report the number of sick already evacuated, the remainder to be sent, and the number of sick that could be transported on the ships McClellan had available.[18]

It seems that in the matter of available water transport for McClellan to redeploy his army, Halleck simply counted the size and number of the ships that were known to be with McClellan's army. Halleck and his staff seemed to have been oblivious to the fact that these ships, mostly anchored off Harrison's landing, were really floating warehouses, containing the supplies that the army was consuming daily. They were not really usable for redeploying troops, animals and artillery batteries. There was an inability of Washington and McClellan's harbor to communicate accurately and facilitate the prompt redeployment of the Army of the Potomac. As a result, Pope was disadvantaged. Afterwards, much effort was expended in placing blame for Pope's defeat, a loss that might have been avoidable.[19]

McClellan replied almost immediately to Halleck's message on August 7 at 10:40 A.M. The report stated the number of sick already transported at 3,740. The remaining sick numbered at 5,700. He made the point that shipping five batteries, as previously ordered, consumed all water transport except ferry boats. McClellan had summoned all the transports capable of making their way up to Harrison's Landing to come up by the next day. McClellan then stated that the cavalry ordered by Halleck could not be moved for a couple or three days, owing to lack of transport. McClellan promised to send the 1st New York Cavalry as soon as a ship was available. He went on to describe how the movement would gain momentum as soon as the sick were taken care of.[20]

The two men seemed to be repeatedly making their same points, while each largely ignored the responses of the other. This poor communication between the key Federal generals likely hindered the timely reinforcement of Pope and contributed to his resounding defeat at the battle of 2nd Manassas.

Robert E. Lee should have been thrilled to see George McClellan and his army depart the Virginia Peninsula, as it freed Lee to pursue offensive opportunities elsewhere in the East. Lee and his army allowed the Federals to embark and sail northward virtually unmolested.[21]

Despite the prolonged bickering, whining and posturing of Halleck and McClellan, the Army of the Potomac continued to redeploy. As armies always seem to do, they got the job done despite their generals. As McClellan's army, corps by corps, arrived at Aquia Creek, they were quickly sent to join Major General John Pope's Army of Virginia. On July 22, as another method of reinforcing John Pope, the IX Corps was created from the Department of North Carolina and the Department of the South. Its three divisions were placed under command of Major General

Ambrose E. Burnside, an old friend of McClellan's, and the newly created corps was sent immediately to the support of General Pope, arriving at Aquia Landing during the first week of August. The intent of the powers in Washington was to concentrate the Federal army in the East behind the Rappahannock River.[22] McClellan himself reached Aquia Creek on August 24, and reported for orders at Alexandria on August 27.[23]

PART VII

CONSEQUENCES

"The history of the campaign, in short, is the history of a lamentable failure—nothing less…"

Alexander S. Webb[1]

CHAPTER 27

The Armies Go On

It seems useful to examine the events that befell the two armies in the period of months just after the Peninsula Campaign in order to put the campaign in context, contrast the commanding officers of the two armies, which will allow better definition of the significance of the campaign. Therefore, we will examine the events transpiring within and between the two armies up to that point in the autumn of 1862 when McClellan was permanently relieved of command. These events were all in some way shaped by what happened on the Peninsula, and by the two men who led the opposing armies there. This look at the battle of Second Manassas and Lee's Maryland Campaign, while in no way comprehensive, will amply demonstrate that the performances of Lee and McClellan on the Peninsula were not atypical, but rather were normal manifestations of their personalities, talents and weaknesses as military leaders.

As soon as he took command of the Army of Virginia, Major General John Pope concentrated what was a scattered array of troops and put them in front of Washington, along the line of the Orange and Alexandria Railroad . This army numbered about 50,000 men and had a threefold mission: to safeguard Washington, to protect the Shenandoah Valley, and to operate against Confederate communications in the direction of Charlottesville and Gordonsville. The last mission would hopefully have the effect of drawing Confederate troops from the Peninsula, thus aiding McClellan. When Pope's movements threatened to cut Lee's communications with Southwestern Virginia, Lee was forced to act promptly.[1]

Lee responded by pushing forward Stonewall Jackson with his and Richard Ewell's divisions. Jackson advanced toward Gordonsville, reaching there on July 19. He wisely hesitated to take on Pope's whole army and called for reinforcements. Lee sent A. P. Hill's division, which was in place by August 2.

Jackson crossed the Rapidan on August 7 and 8, and moved toward Culpepper. Jackson fought Banks' Corps at Cedar Mountain on August 9. Stonewall had difficulty holding the field. The fight was stalemated until the 11th, when Jackson withdrew to Gordonsville. This was at least a partial success by Pope.[2]

Lee discovered McClellan's entire army on the move from Harrison's Landing to Fort Monroe. Lee felt comfortable in moving the rest of his army northward to attack Pope and acted almost immediately. When Longstreet moved to reinforce Jackson, Stonewall promptly moved up to the Rapidan, and waited for Longstreet to arrive, which occurred on August 20. This caused Pope to wisely withdraw to the north bank of the Rappahannock, which allowed Lee to advance his army to that river. Lee, always audacious, left Longstreet to watch the fords, which were well guarded by Pope, and dispatched Jackson on a turning movement through Warrenton. Jackson crossed the Rappahannock on August 22, but Ewell was forced to recross the river due to a storm-caused high water. About the same time, Stuart reached Catlett's Station, burned the camp there, took several hundred prisoners, as well as Pope's official papers and personal baggage.[3]

Federal strategy was to quickly redeploy McClellan's four corps from the Virginia Peninsula to Aquia Landing, then immediately send them to reinforce Pope west of the Capital. This would have been a sound strategy, had the redeployment been conducted with appropriate urgency and efficiency. It was not.

Porter's V Corps disembarked at Aquia Landing on August 22, and Heintzelman's III Corps at Alexandria the same day. Franklin's VI Corps landed at Alexandria on the 24th, with Sumner's II Corps also arriving at Alexandria on the 28th. The remaining corps, Keyes' IV Corps, would remain temporarily at Yorktown.

Although McClellan's infantry was arriving smoothly, the artillery was strung out from the loading docks at Fort Monroe to Alexandria. Various other difficulties presented themselves. Porter's V Corps reached Aquia Landing on August 21 with six batteries, but the corps' reserve ammunition was not with them. Numerous divisional and reserve batteries arrived later than the infantry. A further complication was the apparent lack of discipline and organization of Pope's army. Artillerists coming ashore at Aquia and Alexandria attempted to draw supplies from Pope's quartermasters and found that those attempts were futile. Disorder reigned everywhere. Not all of the blame for this Federal logistical nightmare can be laid upon General Pope and his staff. Had McClellan's quartermasters "combat loaded" the transports at Fort Monroe, the army would have come ashore in units composed of infantry, artillery and the requisite supplies they needed to move out smartly to Pope's assistance.[4]

On August 24, McClellan returned from the Virginia Peninsula and stepped ashore at Aquia Landing. He expected to now be in command of the Army of the Potomac, as well as the Army of Virginia. Instead, he was shocked to learn that he would have no control over the Army of Virginia. That army would be commanded by General Pope. As to the Army of the Potomac, McClellan saw his divisions immediately sent to join Pope west of Washington. Very soon, the "Young Napoleon" was left to command only a handful of staff officers and orderlies. Unfortunately for the Federals, not all of the Army of the Potomac had joined Pope's army before the battle of Second Manassas began. Those divisions that went with Pope into the battle were soundly defeated. Lee once again outgeneraled his Federal counterpart.[5]

In the simplest possible terms, Jackson occupied the old Manassas battlefield on August 28. Pope attacked him on the 29th, anticipating a reasonably easy victory, but Jackson stubbornly fought throughout the day. Pope squandered his opportunity to fight his entire army against Jackson's corps by the useless marches and counter-marches created by contradictory orders. Had Pope effectively employed his brigades, Jackson would likely have been routed.[6]

Lee united the remainder of his army and counterattacked on the afternoon of August 29. Pope's forces were driven from the battlefield. Lee unsuccessfully attempted to turn the flank of the retreating Federals, and the fighting ended near Chantilly. Despite Halleck's strident telegraphic exhortations for celerity, McClellan had waited for the artillery of Sumner's II Corps and Franklin's VI corps to arrive at Alexandria before releasing the two corps to go to Pope's aid. These reinforcements arrived too late to affect the outcome of the fight, but in time to cover the retreat of Pope's defeated army. McClellan's actions created the appearance that he had intentionally dragged his feet, desiring Pope's defeat. McClellan made the situation worse for himself by his poor choice of words in a dispatch to Lincoln, in which the general urged the President to "Leave Pope to get out of his scrape & at once use all our means to make the Capital perfectly safe."[7] This was a battle that didn't necessarily have to result in a clear Federal defeat, but Pope was seriously overmatched by Lee, and not well supported by McClellan.

In essence, McClellan played no active part in the battle of Second Manassas. His sole role was to forward forces from their ports of arrival to General Pope. In fact, he was all but ignored by his superiors. This would have been a permanent arrangement, had Pope prevailed at Second Manassas. General-in-Chief Henry Halleck seemed to be in favor of McClellan's removal, and needed only Pope to be successful in the very near term. Unfortunately for the Federals, Lee had other plans for Pope and his army.[8]

It is not uncommon after a campaign for generals who performed well to be promoted or given greater responsibilities. Likewise, those who fared poorly, through weak performance or just ill luck, are often shuffled off to less critical jobs or even pushed into retirement. So it was after the Peninsula Campaign. Lee also desired to make some changes in the roles of his subordinate generals.

Although Lee never publicly distributed blame for the imperfect result of his campaign on the Peninsula, he had definite ideas regarding where the weak points in the army were, and set about eliminating them. He wasted little time reorganizing his army and getting rid of those generals he no longer wanted to command his troops in the field. By and large, he was supported by President Davis in his actions.

Benjamin Huger, after some speculation of a posting to South Carolina, was transferred by Lee to a staff position as Inspector of Artillery and Ordnance. His pre-war experience in the old army was in artillery. The transfer was made with no public notice. Lee's complaint with Huger was likely that he made no real contributions to the campaign. Huger never was able to make the transition from peacetime staff work to combat commander. There seems to be no record of a protest by General Huger against the transfer.[9]

If Huger got a raw deal, William Pendleton received a free pass from Lee. His performance at Malvern Hill was negligent and cost needless Confederate casualties. Part of the problem with Confederate artillery performance during the Peninsula Campaign was that Pendleton failed to carry out a reorganization of the army's artillery, as approved by Lee some time earlier in the year. Pendleton's own account of his actions during the period June 29–July 1 are proof enough of his negligence. He admits that he spent the day of the battle of Malvern Hill looking unsuccessfully for General Lee. Not finding him, Pendleton took no initiative, and his reserve artillery was idle all day. Nevertheless, he was not sanctioned by Lee after the campaign.[10]

Holmes was seen by many as negligent as Huger or Magruder throughout the Peninsula Campaign. Holmes, in General Lee's opinion, had likewise contributed very little to the Peninsula Campaign. His performance on the River road west of Malvern Hill on June 30 left much to be desired. A case can be made that his command was weak and that Lee sent him against very strong Federal positions. Holmes was soon sent to Magruder's old command in the Trans-Mississippi District.[11]

Magruder was also sent to the Trans-Mississippi District, Department No. 2. His personality and temperament, from Savage Station on, seemed inappropriate to a field commander. Perhaps Magruder's greatest contribution to the campaign was his deception of McClellan at Yorktown, and again south of the Chickahominy, where he paraded his men back and forth, making lots of noise and creating the image of a much larger force. Other than those two more or less non-combat activities, Magruder contributed little to Lee's army. Magruder was eager for the transfer; he had been for some time. Sadly for him, the transfer didn't occur until October 10.[12]

Oddly, Lee seemed not to care about the puzzling, apathetic performance of Stonewall Jackson on several occasions during the campaign. Rather, Lee seemed to have learned that complex battle plans that require almost perfect timing between subordinate commanders would have to be avoided. He would have to provide closer direction to his generals, and make fewer assumptions about his orders being carried out. The Peninsula Campaign served to baptize the Confederate generals, making them much stronger for the future.[13]

On September 1, Lincoln met with Halleck and McClellan. The President ordered McClellan to take command of the Washington defenses and garrison troops. He also informed McClellan that he had been told that some officers of the Army of the Potomac weren't cooperating with their commanding general, John Pope.[14]

Lincoln had received a message dated that same day from Pope that alleged "unsoldierly and dangerous conduct" of "many" officers of his army. Pope would not name names, but resorted to name calling to describe them, and recommended that the Government "draw back this army to the intrenchments in front of Washington, and set to work in that secure place to reorganize and secure it. You may avoid great disaster by doing so."[15]

The appearance was that McClellan acted out of conviction, and held back Sumner and Franklin, a force of some 25,000 men until their arrival in the battle area was of little significance. Other dispatches McClellan sent to Halleck helped reinforce Lincoln's opinion of what McClellan had done. Yet Lincoln did not do immediate harm to McClellan's career.

Lincoln was uncertain about Pope's ability to retain command of the army, and thought the infighting within it a curse. At the same time, the President distrusted McClellan. He described McClellan as a "chief alarmist and grand marplot of the Army." Lincoln also referred to McClellan's messages as "weak, whiney, vague, and incorrect dispatches." President Lincoln also confided to John Hay that McClellan appeared to want Pope to fail. He said, "That is unpardonable."[16]

McClellan most certainly had his detractors in Lincoln's cabinet. On September 1, the Secretaries of War, Treasury, Interior and the Attorney

General signed a paper intended for Lincoln that urged the removal of McClellan from command of any Federal army. The paper was never presented to the President, however.[17] Lincoln was fully cognizant of the fact that McClellan had enemies in the Cabinet, in the Congress, and among the President's more powerful political supporters.

Weighed down by yet another battlefield defeat at Manassas, Lincoln was becoming cynical about the great struggle. Despite this, he knew he had an immediate, important decision to make. He must decide which general to give the task of again rebuilding the army and preparing it to assume the offensive. His cynicism became pragmatism. He had to choose from those generals he had. He told his friend Hay, "I must have McClellan to reorganize the army and bring it out of chaos. McClellan has the army with him." This was a very critical decision for Lincoln.[18]

Lincoln, in his characteristic firm and courageous manner, made the decision to give McClellan responsibility for the defense of Washington, and then command of his and Pope's armies. The President's decision was likely based on two factors. First, Lincoln's belief that McClellan was a superb officer when it came to training, organizing and equipping an army. After all, he had done it after the Federal rout at First Manassas. Second, the army was now demoralized, and Lincoln knew they worshiped McClellan and would certainly fight for him. The situation now was strikingly similar to the one just after First Manassas, and Lincoln once again came to the conclusion that McClellan was still the right man for the job.[19]

Thus, the tenure of General Pope as commanding general of the Federal army in the East was quite brief. McClellan, now back in command, once again began the arduous task of rebuilding the army. It was what he did best, and he quickly produced results.

McClellan began by moving several corps back to their old positions near to Washington. Morale rapidly improved and the army began to regain their confidence. The men were happy to have their old commander back to watch over them. They now knew they could successfully defend their capital. McClellan next set about re-equipping the troops, assuring they had all they needed to meet Lee's army again. These successful steps vindicated Lincoln's decision to place McClellan back in command.[20]

When Lee sent a major part of the Army of Northern Virginia north to the vicinity of Manassas, he had no intention to do other than arrest the movements of Pope's Army of Virginia and inflict damage upon it before it could be reinforced by McClellan's army redeploying from the Peninsula by water. The resounding victory which resulted at Second Manassas changed Lee's planning. The center of the war in the east had shifted from the vicinity of the Confederate capital to that of the Federals. Lincoln's armies were now on the defensive, and there was dissention in the officer corps.

The harvest season was approaching in the Shenandoah Valley, and the Confederates were now to be the reapers there. Lee had to decide his next move, and audaciously decided to cross his army into Maryland and invade the North.[21]

Lee never had any doubt throughout the war that it was a fight to the death. He also appreciated that time was on the side of the Federals. Given enough time, their larger population and material resources would allow them to overwhelm the Confederacy. It, therefore, should not be too startling to see him take the war to the enemy. Lee had been advised by John Slidell, Confederate commissioner in Paris, that European leaders would be more impressed by military victories, and Lee moved into Maryland to seek them.

Special Orders No. 191 contained all the specifics of Lee's instructions to his generals. It detailed the movement to Harper's Ferry, to be taken by September 12, and the march of all the units of Lee's army. The Army of Northern Virginia was then to reconcentrate at Hagerstown or Boonsboro, and advance further into Pennsylvania.[22]

Unfortunately for Lee, a spare copy of Special Orders No. 191 fell into Federal hands, and was brought to McClellan. Some nameless staff officer under D. H. Hill had wrapped three cigars in the order, as it wasn't needed by Hill. This seemingly innocuous act had far-reaching consequences, and could have spelled disaster for Lee's army and the Confederacy.

The reader can only appreciate the critical nature of this order falling into McClellan's hands by viewing the order itself, reprinted below.

Rudolph J. Schroeder, III

Special Orders No. 191

Headquarters Army of Northern Virginia,
September 9, 1862

The army will resume its march to-morrow, taking the Hagerstown road. General Jackson's command will form the advance, and after passing Middletown, with such portion as he may select, take the route toward Sharpsburg, cross the Potomac at the most convenient point, and by Friday night take possession of the Baltimore and Ohio Railroad, and capture such of the enemy as may be at Martinsburg, and intercept such as may attempt to escape from Harper's Ferry.

General Longstreet's command will pursue the same road, as far as Boonsboro, where it will halt with the reserve, supply, and baggage trains of the army.

General McLaws, with his own division and that of General R. H. Anderson, will follow General Longstreet; on reaching Middletown, he will take the route to Harper's Ferry, and by Friday morning possess himself of the Maryland Heights, and endeavor to capture the enemy at Harper's Ferry and vicinity.

General Walker, with his division, after accomplishing the object in which he is now engaged, will cross the Potomac at Cheek's Ford, ascend the right bank to Lovettsville, take possession of Loudoun Heights, if practicable, by Friday morning, Key's Ford on his left and the road between the end of the mountain and the Potomac on his right. He will, as far as practicable, cooperate with General McLaws and General Jackson in intercepting the retreat of the enemy.

General D. H. Hill's division will form the rear-guard of the army, pursuing the road taken by the main body. The reserve artillery, ordnance, and supply trains, etc., will precede General Hill.

General Stuart will detach a squadron of cavalry to accompany the commands of Generals Longstreet, Jackson, and McLaws, and with the main body of the cavalry will cover the route of the army and bring up all stragglers that may have been left behind.

The commands of Generals Jackson, McLaws, and Walker, after accomplishing the objects for which they have been detached, will join the main body of the army at Boonsboro or Hagerstown.

Each regiment on the march will habitually carry its axes in the regimental ordnance wagons, for use of the men at their encampments, to procure wood, etc.

By command of General R. E. Lee.

R. H. Chilton
Assistant Adjutant-General[23]

Any other Federal commanding general, having total knowledge of his adversary's plans and commanding a larger, better equipped army, would have, without question, destroyed his opponent. Not George McClellan. Initially, he was jubilant, telegraphing Washington that he had in his possession Lee's plan of campaign, and would defeat him. McClellan ordered a rapid advance toward Harper's Ferry. Lee, unaware that Special Orders No. 191 had been compromised, was surprised that McClellan's army was advancing as rapidly as it seemed to be. Lee then began to receive more bad news. Jeb Stuart reported Federals nearing the passes of South Mountain. These passes, if they fell to the Federals, would allow McClellan to attack Lee's army before it could reunite. The outcome could be disastrous for Lee. McClellan was in a situation where, with bold action, great success was almost certain. Nevertheless, he acted more cautiously than boldly, thus giving up much of the advantage gained from the precious order falling into his hands.[24]

Specifically, on September 14, the battle of South Mountain was fought. The Federals, having a huge edge in numbers of troops available, fought their way through Crampton's, Turner's and Fox's Gaps and achieved access to Pleasant Valley. This was a bloody affair that cost the lives of Federal General Jesse Reno and Confederate General Samuel Garland, Jr. At this point in time, Robert E. Lee's army was still vulnerable to a bold thrust by McClellan. With Crampton's Gap in Federal hands, they could move directly into Lafayette McLaws' rear. Lee's army was scattered into five parts, and in definite peril.

For some reason, McClellan's army was lethargic on September 15, and the consequences were significant. Harper's Ferry finally fell to Jackson on the morning of September 15, and McLaws was given sufficient time to rejoin the main body of Lee's army near Sharpsburg. McClellan had squandered the advantage of possessing Special Orders No. 191.

Michie, in describing the performances of Generals Lee and McClellan at the Battle of South Mountain, stated:

> The military situation presented exceptional advantages to McClellan, and threatened the gravest of disasters to Lee. The generalship displayed by each of these commanders, whereby one failed to reap the legitimate fruit of the situation and the other extricated himself in a masterly manner from his critical position, is exceedingly characteristic of their abilities and capacity for command.[25]

After a period of some severe anxiety, Lee concentrated his army between Antietam Creek and Sharpsburg, Maryland. Jackson was the last to join, marching from Harper's Ferry. The danger of the Confederate position was that, in case of disaster, the only available route of retreat was the crossing of the Potomac at Shepherdstown. One of the bloodiest battles of the war was fought on September 16 and 17. The Confederates, although outnumbered, essentially held their ground. Lee masterfully directed the battle, without micromanaging his army.

On the evening of the 17th, Lee met with his generals and concluded that an offensive operation the following day was impossible, but the army could and would defend its present positions. He improved the positioning of his artillery to cover the key bridge across Antietam Creek and ordered rations to be cooked. The troops were cheered by the arrival of a number of stragglers, and abundant supplies of meat and bread were available, allowing the men to have a decent supper. The Army of Northern Virginia would be ready for McClellan's army on the morning of the 18th. Once again, Lee's audacity allowed him to stand before a much larger and more powerful force, with the Potomac in his rear.[26]

The morning of September 18 came, and McClellan failed to attack. An informal truce allowed the wounded and the mortally wounded to be removed from the battlefield.

After dark on September 18, Lee reconsidered his situation. His weary army, although improving in spirit, was too battered to take the offensive. Federal reinforcements were anticipated to arrive soon, and there was little to be gained by standing fast. About 2:00 A.M. on the 19th, Lee informed Longstreet that the army would cross into Virginia. They began marching for the crossing of the Potomac River at Shepherdstown, their only viable route of retreat. Longstreet's corps crossed first and formed in line of battle on the far bank to cover the remainder as they crossed.

On September 20, Lee withdrew his army to the vicinity of Martinsburg. He studied the possibility of crossing the Potomac farther upstream, for the purpose of again attempting a campaign of maneuver on the opponent's soil. Unfortunately for Lee, his army was too weak in infantry, with only 36,418 present for duty, and too ill-equipped to fight such a campaign. Specifically, many of his men lacked shoes and blankets, most of their uniforms were in tatters, and straggling was still a major problem. Although Lee urged Richmond to immediately correct this problem, he realized that his Maryland Campaign had come to an end.[27]

McClellan had taken his army into Maryland to defend against Lee's invasion there, and had succeeded in forcing Lee to retire back to Virginia. His next endeavor should have been to rest and reconstitute his army, then invade Virginia, pressing toward Richmond. McClellan commenced just such an endeavor, requiring over a month to prepare and get the army on the move. During that month, there was very little fighting in that part of the East. Only Stuart's Chambersburg raid broke the peace. Stuart moved north across Maryland, seized the town of Chambersburg, Pennsylvania, and burned significant quantities of Federal stores there. He then completed the circuit of the Federal army and recrossed the Potomac below the mouth of the Monocacy River.

McClellan at first wanted to attack Lee through the Shenandoah, but decided to move south on the east side of the Blue Ridge. Using the rising Potomac to cover him further west, he crossed the Potomac via pontoon bridge at Berlin, some five miles downstream of Harper's Ferry, on October 26. By November 2, the entire army was across the river.

Operating more shrewdly than ever before, McClellan forced Lee to leave Jackson's command in the Shenandoah by threatening to move through the mountain passes into the great valley. This was a boon to McClellan, as it kept Lee from concentrating his army.

By November 9, the Army of the Potomac had reached Warrenton, and General Lee found himself with an army divided. Half of it was at Culpepper, the other half west of the Blue Ridge. It was a two day march from one end of the army to the other. McClellan intended to strike southwestward and put his numerically superior force between the two halves of the Army of Northern Virginia. He did not accomplish this, because President Lincoln prevented it.[28]

Late on the evening of November 7, 1862, in a heavy snowstorm, Brigadier General Catharinus P. Buckingham arrived in a hurry at McClellan's tent near Rectortown. He carried from Washington the following dispatch, which he handed to McClellan:

General Orders No. 182

War Department, Adjutant General's Office
Washington, November 5, 1862

By direction of the President of the United States, it is ordered that Major-General McClellan be relieved from command of the Army of the Potomac, and that Major-General Burnside take the command of that army.
By order of the Secretary of War.
E. D. Townsend
Assistant Adjutant-General.

As fortune would have it, Burnside was at that moment there in McClellan's tent. McClellan opened the dispatch, read it, and handed it to Burnside. McClellan displayed no emotion, saying only, "Well, Burnside, you are to command the army."[29]

McClellan was likely not very surprised at the receipt of Special Orders No. 182. The quantity and nature of his correspondence with his superiors in Washington of late was one indicator. Another was his awareness of the impending arrival of a special train bearing Buckingham from Washington. Yet another was the fact that McClellan kept Burnside close to him on the movement down from the Potomac, keeping his second in command fully informed of the daily movements of the several corps.[30]

At about 2:00 P.M. on November 7, McClellan began, as he did most days, writing a letter to his wife, Mary Ellen. Apparently, various interruptions prevented him from completing it, and one paragraph is headed by the time of "11 ½ pm." In that paragraph, he tells his dear wife that Buckingham has brought the order relieving McClellan from command. He mentions that no reason for his relief was stated in the order. He relates that he read the order, and brags that he did so "without any expression of feeling on my face." He goes on to say that "They shall not have that triumph." Then, his great ego still intact, writes "They have made a great mistake – alas for my poor country – I know in my innermost heart she never had a truer servant."[31]

The following day, McClellan wrote and signed a broadside addressed to the "Officers & Soldiers of the Army of the Potomac," in which he informed them that Burnside was now in command, and lovingly praised and thanked them for their duty and loyalty. The broadside ended with the expression "Farewell!" The preserved documents have that last word stricken, and substitute the sentence, "We shall also ever be comrades in supporting the Constitution of our country & the nationality of our people."[32]

General Orders, No. 182 essentially ended the military career of George Brinton McClellan. This action by Lincoln was certainly best for the long-term interests of the United States, and was probably better for McClellan. He had never understood, nor accepted, the Constitutional requirement of subordination of military officers to civilian control. He would never have become the general that Lincoln needed to put down the Rebellion.

It is ironic to note that Lincoln's greatest problem with McClellan was his lack of speed in combat operations. The irony is that, at the moment McClellan was relieved, he had a very good plan, was executing it well so far, and had excellent prospects for inflicting a severe defeat upon Lee. Burnside, upon assuming command, literally parked the army for ten days and reorganized it. He formed the six corps into three Grand Divisions of two corps each, to be commanded by Sumner, Hooker and Franklin. The ten day delay gave Lee adequate time to reconsolidate his army. However, the point is moot, as Burnside intended to change his base to Fredericksburg on the Rappahannock River.

There is no apparent, nor even subtle, military logic to what Burnside did immediately upon assuming command. The prime objective for the Federal army in the East was the destruction of Lee's army, yet General Lee literally had to chase after Burnside to engage him. When the two armies finally did come to battle again, it was in mid-December at Fredericksburg, some five weeks later.[33]

McClellan was ordered to turn over the army to Burnside and report to Trenton, New Jersey for orders. McClellan remained with Burnside for just a few days, assisting his successor in becoming accustomed to his new position, without stepping on his old friend's toes. McClellan seemed to feel no animosity toward Burnside, and sincerely tried to be helpful to him. McClellan then went to Trenton, and shortly thereafter established his residence at Orange, New Jersey. As a Regular officer in the United States Army, he waited there for orders which never came.[34] He resigned his commission on November 8, 1864, the day of the U. S. Presidential election.[35]

CHAPTER 28

The Significance of the Campaign

The Peninsula Campaign of 1862 is important for several reasons. In terms of the number of troops involved, the casualties, the monetary cost, the precious war materials consumed, and the technology employed, it was a large and significant event. In terms of the effect it had on the course and nature of the conflict, it was very influential. The campaign marked a sea change in the course of the fighting in the East, and affected the war as a whole.

Before discussing the changes it brought about, we must first put the campaign in perspective. The military context in the spring of 1862 was one of optimism for the North, and the opposite for the South. Between February and June of that year, Federals forces in the East and West ran up a string of victories. The only good news for the leadership in Richmond was a number of modest successes by Major General Thomas J. Jackson in the Shenandoah Valley, where he outwitted a quartet of diverse and barely competent Federal generals. It appeared to many that the end result of the conflict was a given. There seemed to be no way in which the Confederacy could survive for an extended period. The Peninsula Campaign changed that perception for many on both sides of the conflict.[1]

Although we may state that there was optimism in the North that the war would soon end with the Union intact and relatively unchanged, there was a powerful faction in the North that sought to avoid that outcome. That faction was populated by the Radical Republicans, who saw the war as the perfect vehicle to abolish slavery in all the states and territories. Among them was Charles Sumner of Massachusetts, a staunch abolitionist, who desired no cessation of hostilities until emancipation could be made a precondition. Secretary of State William H. Seward believed in the Spring of 1862 that the military power of the rebellion would soon be broken, but pondered over what would occur then.[2]

The larger political context at that point in the war was one in which the Lincoln Administration's sole war aim was to preserve the Union. Had the Confederacy decided to negotiate a settlement in the spring of 1862, it is likely that it would have been allowed to go back to the status quo just prior to Fort Sumter. This is not to say that all political groups in the

North and South would have been well pleased by that sort of settlement, but it could have been done. Surely, there would have been considerable grumbling from the Radical Republicans in the North and the Fire Eaters in the South. Yet the benefits of an early cessation of hostilities, and the chance to work out differences, would likely have appealed to the majority of both belligerent nations.

The immediate and primary result of the campaign was that the Federal attempt to take Richmond and quickly end the war was totally thwarted. The campaign also produced a new Confederate military leader, General Robert E. Lee of Virginia, who reorganized the Confederate Army of the Potomac into the new Army of Northern Virginia, an effective fighting force that would give the larger Federal army all the fight it could handle for three long years. With the possibility of a quick Federal victory excluded, the war became one of protracted fighting, and the nature of that fighting became much less civilized. It soon became obvious to the Federal leadership that a harsher, more drastic strategy would be needed. The strategy eventually adopted by Lincoln even included the desperate step of promulgating his Emancipation Proclamation. This action by Lincoln assured a total war, as Southerners believed it sought to fundamentally change their fortunes for the worse. The Confederate success on the Peninsula increased optimism in the South that they could win their independence and continue to maintain their accustomed way of life.[3]

An additional result of the Peninsula Campaign was that it was the first major step in the destruction of Major General George B. McClellan's military career. Although he was granted a second opportunity to command the Federal army in the East later in the year, the die was essentially cast by early August. McClellan had disappointed many and annoyed even more important people. McClellan had to go.

Relieved of command by Lincoln in November of 1862 and sent to New Jersey to await orders which never came, McClellan turned to politics, running unsuccessfully for President in the November, 1864 election. From that point on, he concentrated his efforts on overseas travel and a series of civilian administrative positions in the Northeast.

The most immediate significance of the Peninsula Campaign was that the Confederate capital of Richmond was saved from capture by the invading Federal army. There was a resultant resurgence of optimism there. The focus shifted from concerns about having to flee the city and relocate the government, to efforts to aid the thousands of wounded placed in the city's hospitals and private homes.

There were several collateral results of the campaign. The most interesting was the enhancement of the stature of General Robert E. Lee. Prior to assuming command of the Army of Northern Virginia, Lee's combat record in the war had been lackluster, having never commanded in a major battle. Many Southerners did not expect great things of him. After General Joseph E. Johnston was severely wounded at the battle of Seven Pines, President Davis provided Lee with a golden opportunity to demonstrate his abilities. Despite being outnumbered and outgunned by McClellan, Lee's audacity and creativity allowed him to prevail on the Peninsula and force the withdrawal of McClellan's army from the near vicinity of Richmond. The rise to prominence of Lee gave the South an advantage in the East, where the Federal army struggled for another year to find a truly competent commanding general. Another important benefit was the almost instant and astronomical rise of Lee's popularity with his troops. In the span of only four weeks, he came to be totally trusted by the men, and considered the best general in the war by them. This devotion and respect endured all the way to the surrender at Appomattox.[4]

Despite the favorable immediate outcome of the Peninsula Campaign for the Confederacy, Robert E. Lee experienced a sense of failure. He was said to be "deeply, bitterly disappointed" and thought that he should have been able to destroy McClellan's army. What was lacking on the Confederate side was competent performance by some of his generals at certain key times during the fighting. Divisional leadership was most in need of improvement, with artillery effectiveness a close second. Objectively, the campaign was a Confederate military success, but costly in terms of casualties. Southern civilian opinion was mixed. Many Southerners were relieved and thankful that McClellan's army was gone, but others were sadly disappointed that it escaped almost intact.[5]

Douglas Southall Freeman believes the reasons for Lee's failure to destroy McClellan's army are clear. He states:

> The Federal army was not destroyed for four reasons: (1) The Confederate commander lacked adequate information for operating in a difficult country because his maps were worthless, his staff work inexperienced, and his cavalry absent at the crisis of the campaign; (2) the Confederate artillery was poorly employed; (3) Lee trusted too much to his subordinates, some of whom failed him almost completely; and (4) he displayed no tactical genius in combating a fine, well-led Federal army.[6]

One must assume that by "well-led," Freeman was referring to some of the corps and division commanders, not McClellan, who absented himself from much of the fighting. Had McClellan performed well, the goals of the campaign might well have been achieved.

Lee became well aware that the performance of his army during the Peninsula Campaign could have been considerably better. Only a generous portion of good luck allowed Lee's army to fare as well as it did. With any reasonably competent cooperation between Confederate divisions, much more damage could have been inflicted on the Federal army. McClellan's army might even have been decimated. Lee likely knew that part of the problem was his fault, in that he asked the division commanders to perform complicated maneuvers, with which they had little or no prior experience. Lee learned from his errors, and in future campaigns, he attempted to simplify operations whenever possible.

General Lee also saw the need for some changes in his army. We have already looked at his actions to remove several generals he considered lacking. He next needed to promote several officers and reorganize the army. He did this well, assisted by the firm support of President Davis. Lee gave Huger's division to Richard H. Anderson of South Carolina, who had been promoted to major general, and Major General D. H. Hill replaced Theophilus Holmes. Lee, though he never said as much, had to be disappointed by Jackson's performance. A sterling performance by Jackson might have resulted in a very different overall outcome of the campaign. Rather than sanction Jackson, Lee simply transferred a portion of Jackson's command to Longstreet. Jackson's infantry was thus reduced from fourteen to seven brigades. Longstreet thus became Lee's right-hand man, and controlled more troops than any other Confederate general under Lee.

How William Pendleton survived is a puzzlement, as his performance was nothing short of pathetic, especially at Malvern Hill, a battle clearly won by the Federal artillery. Pendleton went into the Seven Days with his batteries ill-apportioned between the divisions, even though Lee had earlier approved a better employment of the guns. By his own writings, Pendleton admitted spending the day looking for General Lee to give orders for the reserve artillery. Surely a brigadier general should be expected to do better than that.[7]

There is no record of Jackson ever discussing his poor performance during the Seven Days, nor did he complain about having a considerable part of his infantry taken from his command. Lee seems not to have lost faith in Stonewall, but objectively assessed and methodically reorganized the army for the maximum overall benefit of all.

Lee stopped short of attempting to reorganize his personal staff, the general staff or the artillery. This was perhaps a mistake, as poor staff work and ineffective artillery support had plagued him during the campaign. His reluctance to extend the reorganization to the staffs and artillery at that time was likely due to his desire to hasten north to engage Pope.[8]

Lee knew he must improve his command and control system, if the Army of Northern Virginia was to reach its true potential. He was painfully aware that he, his subordinate generals and his staff had performed in a dismal fashion at many times during the Peninsula Campaign. Perhaps the best asset Lee had on his staff was George McClellan, whose fear of long casualty lists, self-doubt and incredible caution made it possible for Lee to prevail.[9]

This reorganization was also a significant result of the campaign, in that the new structure and enhanced leadership of the Army of Northern Virginia allowed it to fight the much larger and better supplied and equipped Federal army for three more years. The feats of Lee and his army prolonged what could have and probably should have been a relatively short war.[10]

Lee also learned from some of his own mistakes made during the Seven Days. The frontal attacks he attempted at Beaver Dam Creek, Gaines' Mill and Malvern Hill cost a great many Confederate lives. Although Gaines' Mill was a victory, it might have been better to attack the Federal far right instead of the left. Beaver Dam Creek and Malvern Hill would have had a greater chance of success with turning maneuvers, rather than frontal attacks. Except for Pickett's charge at Gettysburg, Robert E. Lee used frontal attacks against fortified positions rather sparingly in the course of the war.[11]

The Federal commanding general had a very different experience from his Confederate counterpart. Despite having a clear superiority in every measurable military category except intelligence, McClellan managed to allow himself to be pushed twenty miles to the rear, resulting in a failed campaign. In the process, he squandered the summer fighting season of 1862, wasted many Federal lives and millions of Federal dollars, and angered his superior, President Lincoln. His failure on the Peninsula resulted in the destruction of his military career. Amazingly, in his official report on the campaign, McClellan seemed to view it as a success. He dwelled on the difficulty of his "change of base" and continued to spout the fantasy that the Confederate army was much larger than his own, as large as 200,000 men. It is probable that a majority of Federal soldiers supported McClellan, but civilian opinion, divided along political party lines, seemed to be split between adherents to Secretary of War Edwin Stanton's "hard-war" approach, and those believing in McClellan's opposing, more genteel position.[12] It must be remembered that, although no apologist for the institution of slavery, McClellan shared with Lincoln the belief that it would slowly disappear, nudged into extinction by compensated emancipation.[13]

As the war went on, it became considerably less civilized in the manner it was fought. Respect by both armies for private property, such respect previously being common, began to disappear. Officers of both armies no longer took pains to see that their soldiers stayed out of private homes, barns and stock pens. Later in the war, whole cities were put to the torch, primarily by the army of Federal Major General William T. Sherman.

Instead of paroles, captured prisoners were transported by both armies well to the rear and imprisoned in miserable conditions for the remainder of the war. Even prisoner exchanges became almost nonexistent. Temporary truces on the battlefield for the purpose of removing the dead and rescuing the wounded often weren't agreed to in time to save lives. Atrocities on the battlefield, which had previously been scarce, became a bit more common. The fighting in the West became especially savage. No one continued to harbor the illusion of a negotiated peace in their heart of hearts. It was now a long desperate struggle for survival. As Clifford Dowdey so well expressed it, "the period of the attempted settlement was over. Arbitration by arms had already drifted into a policy of subjugation by total war, soon to be followed by the expediency of the Emancipation Proclamation."[14]

Perhaps the most eloquent summary of the Peninsula Campaign is that of Frederick Edge, who placed the majority of the blame for the failure of the campaign on George McClellan.

> Whatever answers shall be given to these questions, it must at all events be conceded that the campaign on the Yorktown Peninsula was the first great effort of the North to deal seriously with the Rebellion. The preparations extended over many months; and when General McClellan led his divisions to the banks of the Chickahominy, he could pride himself upon being at the head of an army as numerous, and incomparably better armed and equipped than any of modern times.
>
> He failed lamentably in achieving aught but disaster, and by sheer chance alone was his army saved from annihilation. To what cause history will ascribe his failure—whether to incompetence, want of energy and courage or disbelief in his country's destiny—I say not;

but it never will be said that means were not placed at his disposal sufficient to command success, had he but possessed the ability and patriotism of other American commanders.

The world never believed in the possibility of the Southern States achieving their independence until it heard the news of the disastrous retreat from the lines of the Chickahominy; and Major General George Brinton McClellan will indubitably be held responsible by history for the result of that humiliating campaign, and the subsequent change in the sympathies of the world.[15]

It is interesting that Edge seems to have questioned the extent of McClellan's patriotism. Edge's position was not unreasonable, mainly because of the wild accusations of McClellan's political enemies in the Radical Republican camp and McClellan's injudicious use of the written word. Two prime examples of the latter are his infamous telegram to Lincoln on June 28, 1862, as well as the letter he gave to Lincoln when the President visited the army on July 8. Both of these communications could not have helped but cause doubt in Lincoln's mind about McClellan's agenda.[16]

Despite his doubters, it seems clear that McClellan, though no abolitionist, sincerely wished to defeat the rebellion, but thought it unnecessary to wage a total war that would destroy the Southern economy and culture. Even after his defeat in the November, 1864 Presidential election, he reaffirmed his devotion to the preservation of the Union.[17]

The Peninsula Campaign had several lasting effects that changed the stature of both commanders and the very nature and course of the American Civil War. Robert E. Lee rose to prominence, the Army of Northern Virginia was strengthened through reorganization, George McClellan was permanently damaged, and European powers took a wait and see position on possible intervention in the conflict. The war was thus prolonged and made more savage. It became a total war, one that could only result in one of two outcomes, the complete independence of the Confederate States of America or the economic and political destruction of the South.

EPILOGUE

A hard look back at McClellan's Peninsula Campaign of 1862 reveals an amazing panorama of courage, gallantry, talent, patriotism, ego, ineptitude, and tragedy. Seemingly small events helped to make great changes in the outcome of the campaign, and thus the overall course of the war. One is struck by the incredible enormity of the combat of two great armies, the smaller navies of both sides, and the unfortunate civilians caught in the middle of the desperate struggle.

As with many military campaigns, McClellan's Peninsula Campaign didn't take place in a manner similar to either commanding general's campaign plan. The strategic situation kept changing prior to the Federal army's deployment, and McClellan did his best to adapt to those changing conditions. Events beyond his control, such as Lincoln removing troops from the Army of the Potomac and Confederate military actions, forced McClellan to make significant changes in his deployment and plan of employment. Some of the choices he was forced to make considerably diminished his chances of successfully assaulting Richmond.

Perhaps the primary difficulty for McClellan was the exaggerated perception he maintained of the size and capability of the Confederate army opposed to him. Allan Pinkerton's intelligence was seriously flawed, and it fed McClellan's inherent cautious side. This fear of McClellan's that he was facing a superior force colored all his decisions. He was considering a "change of base" to the James River as early as the evening of June 25, immediately after the relatively small and inconclusive engagement of Oak Grove.

Each successive battle reinforced McClellan's belief that he had to move to the James, and the campaign quickly devolved into a fighting retreat lasting for six days. Much of the army's supplies and equipment were destroyed or abandoned to the Confederates. The previously well organized, fed, rested and equipped army arrived on the James on July 2, hungry, tired and bloody. There, under the protection of U. S. Navy gunboats, they attempted to reconstitute themselves. For six long weeks, they sweltered in the Virginia summer heat on that wretched sandbar called Harrison's Landing, slowly being diminished in number by disease.

McClellan often bickered with Lincoln and Stanton, and alleged to be soon ready to cross the James and assault Richmond by way of Petersburg. Despite all his messages to the leadership in Washington, McClellan never convinced Lincoln that he would ever lead the promised assault. Lee, certain that McClellan presented no imminent threat to the Confederate capital, had withdrawn most of his forces, redeployed them to Northern Virginia, and threatened Pope's army southwest of Washington.

Lincoln had seen enough of McClellan's inaction at this point, and ordered the Army of the Potomac withdrawn from the James back to the Washington area. As each division arrived, it was sent toward Manassas and placed under the command of General Pope. At this point in time, McClellan's power and influence was extremely limited. He was, however, accused by some of once again acting too slowly. Some believed that McClellan took too long to redeploy his army from the James and get them to Pope, thereby causing Pope's defeat.

It is difficult, virtually impossible, to assign a primary cause for the failure of McClellan's Peninsula Campaign. It seems more reasonable to blame a combination of Lincoln's actions, Pinkerton's exaggerations, McClellan's excessive caution and Lee's audacity. One thing is clear, however. There are many points in time during the campaign where we can easily ask why and what if?

LIST OF ILLUSTRATIONS

George Brinton McClellan

Joseph Hooker

Edwin Vose Sumner

James Longstreet

Thomas Jonathan Jackson

Joseph Eggleston Johnston

Robert Edward Lee

Chickahominy Bridge on Mechanicsville Road

Fitz John Porter

White Oak Swamp

APPENDIX A

Orders of Battle

This appendix attempts to detail the forces present at each engagement of the Peninsula campaign – from Yorktown through Evelington Heights. An effort has been made to identify commanders of units down to the regimental and battery level. Perhaps this is a fool's errand, but the brave men who led regiments and directed batteries in this deadly campaign deserve at least the effort. Even the partial information provided by this appendix should better serve the reader than what is normally found in many history books. Additionally, a substantial order of battle appendix can be a great help to researchers, in that it can provide another path to finding answers about particular units and the roles they might have played in a given battle.

A number in parenthesis found to the right of a unit name is a best available estimate of the strength of that unit entering the particular part of the campaign. If that number is a somewhat rough estimate, it is preceded by a symbol in parenthesis to signify approximately (~), less than (<), or greater than (>). Simple codes in parentheses are used to designate officers killed (k), mortally wounded (mw), wounded (w), sick (s), captured (c) or arrested (a).

The sources for this appendix are both primary and secondary, with much of the data coming from the *Official Records*. To be sure, the knowledgeable reader of Civil War works will be aware that an error-free Order of Battle appendix can never be constructed. A particularly difficult task is to sort out artillery batteries, which were sometimes referred to by two or three different names, and were frequently reassigned between commands, even during a day's fighting. On occasion, even two-gun sections were shifted to other commands for a period of only a few hours. The fact that this conflict took place almost a century and a half ago, and that there was much burning of public buildings in the defeated capital of Richmond in the last days of the war make it clear that this part of the book will never be totally complete or correct.

At Yorktown (April 5-May 3)

Federal -

        Army of the Potomac
        Maj. Gen. George B. McClellan

    I Corps
    (HQ not present)

    1st Division
    Brig. Gen. William B. Franklin

    1st Brigade (on transports)
    Brig. Gen. Philip Kearny

1st New Jersey (Col. Alfred T. A. Torbert)
2nd New Jersey (Col. Isaac M. Tucker)
3rd New Jersey (Col. George W. Taylor)
4th New Jersey (Col. James H. Simpson)

    2nd Brigade (on transports)
    Brig. Gen. Henry W. Slocum

16th New York (Col. Joseph Howland)
27th New York (Col. Joseph J. Bartlett)
5th Maine (Col. Nathaniel J. Jackson)
96th Pennsylvania (Col. Henry L. Cake)

    3rd Brigade (on transports)
    Brig. Gen. John Newton

18th New York (Col. William H. Young)
31st New York (Col. Calvin E. Pratt)
32nd New York (Col. C. Roderick Matheson)
95th Pennsylvania (Col. John M. Gosline)

    Artillery (on transports)
    Capt. Edward R. Platt

Massachusetts Light, Battery A (Capt. Josiah Porter)

1st New York Light, Battery F (Capt. William R. Wilson)
New Jersey Light, Battery A (Capt. William Hexamer)

Cavalry

1st New York Cavalry (Col. Andrew T. McReynolds)

II Corps
Brig. Gen. Edwin V. Sumner

1st Division
Brig. Gen. Israel B. Richardson

1st Brigade
Brig. Gen. Oliver O. Howard

5th New Hampshire (Col. Edward E. Cross)
61st New York (Col. Francis C. Barlow)
64th New York (Col. Thomas J. Parker)
81st Pennsylvania (Col. James Miller)

2nd Brigade (Irish Brigade)
Brig. Gen. Thomas F. Meagher

63rd New York (Col. John W. Burke)
69th New York (Col. Robert Nugent)
88th New York (Col. Henry M. Baker)

3rd Brigade
Brig. Gen. William H. French

52nd New York (Col. Paul Frank)
57th New York (Col. Samuel K. Zook)
66th New York (Col. Joseph C. Pinckney)
53rd Pennsylvania (Col. John R. Brooke)

Artillery
Capt. George W. Hazzard

1st New York Light, Battery B (Capt. Rufus D. Pettit)
1st New York Light, Battery G (Capt. John D. Frank)

2nd Btn., New York Light, Battery A (Capt. William H. Hogan)
4th U. S., Battery A (Capt. George W. Hazzard)
4th U. S., Battery C (Lt. Rufus King, Jr.)

Cavalry

6th New York Cavalry, Co. D (Capt. Raymond Wright)

2nd Division
Brig. Gen. John Sedgwick

1st Brigade
Brig. Gen. Willis A. Gorman

15th Massachusetts (Col. Charles Devens, Jr.)(Lt. Col. John W. Kimball)
(1st Co., Mass. (Andrew) Sharpshooters, attached) (Capt. John Saunders)
1st Minnesota (Lt. Col. Steven Miller)
34th New York (Col. James A. Suiter)
82nd New York (Lt. Col. Henry W. Hudson)

2nd Brigade
Brig. Gen. William W. Burns

69th Pennsylvania (Col. Joshua T. Owen)
71st Pennsylvania (Col. Isaac J. Wistar)
72nd Pennsylvania (Col. DeWitt C. Baxter)
106th Pennsylvania (Col. Turner G. Morehead)

3rd Brigade
Brig. Gen. Napoleon J. T. Dana

19th Massachusetts (Col. Edward W. Hinks)
20th Massachusetts (Col. William R. Lee)
7th Michigan (Col. Ira R. Grosvenor)
42nd New York (Col. Edmund C. Charles)

Artillery
Col. Charles H. Tompkins

1st Rhode Island Light, Battery A (Capt. John A.   Tompkins)
1st Rhode Island Light, Battery B (Capt. Walter O. Bartlett)

1st Rhode Island Light, Battery G (Capt. Charles D. Owen)
1st U. S., Battery I (Lt. Edmund Kirby)

Cavalry

6th New York Cavalry, Co. K (Capt. Riley Johnson)

Corps Cavalry
Col. John F. Farnsworth

8th Illinois Cavalry

III Corps
Brig. Gen. Samuel P. Heintzelman

1st Division
Brig. Gen. Fitz John Porter

1st Brigade
Brig. Gen. John H. Martindale

2nd Maine (Col. Charles W. Roberts)
18th Massachusetts (Col. James Barnes) 22nd Massachusetts (Col. Jesse A. Gove)
13th New York (Col. Elisha G. Marshall)
25th New York (Col. Charles A. Johnson)
2nd Co., Massachusetts Sharpshooters (Lt. Charles D. Stiles)

2nd Brigade
Brig. Gen. George W. Morell

14th New York (Col. James McQuade)
4th Michigan (Col. Dwight A. Woodbury)
9th Massachusetts (Col. Thomas Cass)
62nd Pennsylvania (Col. Samuel W. Black)

3rd Brigade
Brig. Gen. Daniel Butterfield

16th Michigan (Col. Thomas B. W. Stockton) (Brady's Co, Michigan Sharpshooters, attached) (Capt. Kiniston S. Dygert)

12th New York (Col. Henry A. Weeks)
17th New York (Col. Henry S. Lansing)
44th New York (Col. Stephen W. Stryker)
83rd Pennsylvania (Col. John W. McLane)

Artillery
Capt. Charles Griffin

Massachusetts Light, Battery C (Capt. Augustus P. Martin)
Massachusetts Light, Battery E (Capt. George D. Allen)
1st Rhode Island Light, Battery C (Capt. William B. Weeden)
5th U. S., Battery D (Lt. Henry W. Kingsbury)

Cavalry

8th Pennsylvania Cavalry, Co. A (Capt. Thomas J. Frow)

Sharpshooters
Col. Hiram Berdan

1st U. S. Sharpshooters

2nd Division
Brig. Gen. Joseph Hooker

1st Brigade
Brig. Gen. Cuvier Grover

2nd New Hampshire (Col. Gilman Marston)
1st Massachusetts (Col. Robert Cowdin)
11th Massachusetts (Col. William E. Blaisdell)
26th Pennsylvania (Col. William F. Small) (Maj. Casper M. Berry)

2nd Brigade
Col. Nelson Taylor

70th New York (Maj. Thomas Holt)
71st New York (Col. George B. Hall)
72nd New York (Col. Nelson Taylor)
73rd New York (Col. William R. Brewster)
74th New York (Col. Charles K. Graham)

3rd Brigade
Col. Samuel H. Starr

5th New Jersey (Col. Samuel H. Starr)
6th New Jersey (Col. James T. Hatfield)(Col. Gershom Mott)
7th New Jersey (Col. Joseph W. Revere)
8th New Jersey (889) (Col. Adolphus J. Johnson)

Artillery
Maj. Charles S. Wainwright

1st New York Light, Battery D (Capt. Thomas W. Osborn)
1st U. S., Battery H (Capt. Charles H. Webber)
4th New York Independent Light (Lt. Joseph E. Nairn)
6th New York Independent Light (Capt. Walter M. Bramhall)

3rd Division
Brig. Gen. Charles S. Hamilton
Brig. Gen. Philip Kearny

1st Brigade
Brig. Gen. Charles D. Jameson

57th Pennsylvania (Col. Charles T. Campbell)
63rd Pennsylvania (Col. Alexander Hays)
105th Pennsylvania (Col. Amor A. McKnight)
87th New York (Col. Stephen A. Dodge)

2nd Brigade
Brig. Gen. David B. Birney

38th New York (Col. John H. H. Ward)
40th New York (Col. Edward J. Riley)
3rd Maine (Lt. Col. Charles A. L. Sampson)
4th Maine (Col. Elijah Walker)

3rd Brigade
Brig. Gen. Hiram G. Berry

2nd Michigan (Col. Orlando M. Poe)
3rd Michigan (Lt. Col. Ambrose A. Stevens)

5th Michigan (Maj. John D. Fairbanks)
37th New York (Col. Samuel B. Hayman)

Artillery
Capt. James Thompson

1st New Jersey Light, Battery B (Capt. John E. Beam)
1st Rhode Island Light, Battery E (Capt. George E. Randolph)
2nd U. S., Battery G (Capt. James Thompson)

Corps Cavalry
Col. William W. Averell

3rd Pennsylvania Cavalry (Col. William W. Averell)
1st New Jersey Cavalry (Col. Percy Wyndham)

IV Corps
Brig. Gen. Erasmus D. Keyes

1st Division
Brig. Gen. Darius N. Couch

1st Brigade
Brig. Gen. John J. Peck

55th New York (Lt. Col. Louis Thourot)
62nd New York (Col. John L. Riker)
93rd Pennsylvania (Col. James M. McCarter)
98th Pennsylvania (Col. John F. Ballier)
102nd Pennsylvania (Col. Thomas A. Rowley)

2nd Brigade
Brig. Gen. L. P. Graham

65th New York (Lt. Col. Alexander Shaler)
67th New York (1st Long Island) (Lt. Col. Nelson Cross)
23rd Pennsylvania (Col. Thomas H. Neill)
31st Pennsylvania (Col. David H. Williams)
61st Pennsylvania (Col. Oliver H. Rippey)

3rd Brigade

Col. Henry S. Briggs

7th Massachusetts (Col. David A. Russell)
10th Massachusetts (Col. Henry S. Briggs)
2nd Rhode Island (Col. Frank Wheaton)
36th New York (Maj. James A. Raney)

Artillery
Maj. Robert M. West

1st Pennsylvania Light, Battery C (Capt. Jeremiah McCarthy)
1st Pennsylvania Light, Battery D (Capt. Edward H. Flood)
1st Pennsylvania Light, Battery E (Capt. Theodore Miller)
1st Pennsylvania Light, Battery H (Capt. James Brady)

Cavalry

6th New York Cavalry, Co. F (Capt. Dudley C. Hannahs)

2nd Division
Brig. Gen. William F. Smith

1st Brigade
Brig. Gen. Winfield S. Hancock

5th Wisconsin (Col. Amasa Cobb)
6th Maine (Col. Hiram Burnham)
43rd New York (Col. Francis L. Vinton)
49th Pennsylvania (Col. William H. Irvin)

2nd Brigade
Brig. Gen. W. T. H. Brooks

2nd Vermont (Col. Henry Whiting)
3rd Vermont (Col. Breed N. Hyde)
4th Vermont (Col. Edwin H. Stoughton)
5th Vermont (Col. Henry A. Smalley)
6th Vermont (Col. Nathan Lord, Jr.)

3rd Brigade
Brig. Gen. John W. Davidson

7th Maine (Col. Edwin C. Mason)
33rd New York (Col. Robert F. Taylor)
49th New York (Col. Daniel D. Bidwell)
77th New York (Col. James B. McKean)

Artillery
Capt. Romeyn B. Ayres

1st New York Light, Battery E (Capt. Charles C. Wheeler)(a on April 27)
1st New York Independent Light (Capt. Terrence J. Kennedy)
3rd New York Independent Light (Capt. Thaddeus P. Mott)
5th U. S., Battery F (Capt. Romeyn B. Ayres)

3rd Division
Brig. Gen. Silas Casey

1st Brigade
Brig. Gen. Henry M. Naglee

52nd Pennsylvania (Col. John D. Dodge)
104th Pennsylvania (Col. W. W. H. Davis)
56th New York (Col. Charles H. Van Wyck)
100th New York (Col. James H. Brown)
11th Maine (Col. John C. Caldwell)

2nd Brigade
Brig. Gen. William H. Keim

85th Pennsylvania (Col. Joshua B. Howell)
101st Pennsylvania (Col. Joseph H. Wilson)
103rd Pennsylvania (Col. Theodore F. Lehmann)
96th New York (Col. James Fairman)

3rd Brigade
Brig. Gen. Innis N. Palmer
Brig. Gen. Charles Devens, Jr.

81st New York (Col. Edwin Rose)
85th New York (Col. Jonathan S. Belknap)

92nd New York (Lt. Col. Hiram Anderson, Jr.)
93rd New York (Col. John S. Crocker)(c on Apr 23)
98th New York (Maj. Albon Mann)

Artillery
Col. Guilford D. Bailey

1st New York Light, Battery A (Capt. Thomas H. Bates)
1st New York Light, Battery H (Lt. Charles E. Mink)
7th New York Independent Light (Capt. Peter C. Regan)
8th New York Independent Light (Capt. Butler Fitch)

Cavalry

6th New York Cavalry, Co. H (Capt. William P. Hall)

Reserve

Infantry Reserve, Regular Brigade
Brig. Gen. George Sykes

2nd U. S. (Capt. Adolphus F. Bond)
3rd U. S. (Maj. Nathan B. Rossell)
4th U. S. (Maj. Delozier Davidson)
6th U. S. (Capt. Thomas Hendrickson)
10th U. S. (Maj. Charles S. Lovell)
11th U. S. (Maj. DeLancey Floyd-Jones)
12th U. S. (Maj. Henry B. Clitz)
14th U. S. (Capt. John D. O'Connell)
17th U. S. (Maj. George L. Andrews)
5th New York (Lt. Col. Hiram Duryea)

Artillery Reserve
Col. Henry J. Hunt

1st U. S., Battery E (Lt. Alanson M. Randol)
1st U. S., Battery G (Capt. James Thompson)
1st U. S., Battery K (Lt. Samuel S. Elder)
2nd U. S., Battery A (Capt. John C. Tidball)
2nd U. S., Battery B (Capt. James M. Robertson)
2nd U. S., Battery E (Lt. Samuel Benjamin)

2nd U. S., Battery M (Capt. Henry Benson)
3rd U. S., Battery C (Capt. Horatio G. Gibson)
3rd U. S., Battery F (Capt. LaRhett L. Livingston)
3rd U. S., Battery G (Capt. Horatio G. Gibson)
3rd U. S., Battery K (Capt. LaRhett L. Livingston)
3rd U. S., Battery L & M (Capt. John Edwards)
4th U. S., Battery G (Lt. Charles M. Morgan)
4th U. S., Battery K (Lt. Francis W. Seeley)
5th U. S., Battery A (Lt. Adelbert Ames)
5th U. S., Battery I (Capt. Stephen H. Weed)
5th U. S., Battery K (Capt. John R. Smead)
1st Battalion New York, Battery A (Capt. Otto Diederich)
1st Battalion New York, Battery B (Capt. Adolph Voegelee)
1st Battalion New York, Battery C (Capt. John Knieriem)
1st Battalion New York, Battery D (Capt. Edward D. Grimm)
5th New York Battery (Capt. Elijah D. Taft)

Cavalry

9th New York Cavalry (Col. John Beardsley)(Note: 150 men under Maj. William Sackett served as artillerists in the artillery reserve)

Cavalry Reserve
Brig. Gen. Philip St. George Cooke

1st Brigade
Brig. Gen. William H. Emory

5th U. S. Cavalry (Capt. Charles J. Whiting)
6th U. S. Cavalry (Maj. Lawrence Williams)
6th Pennsylvania Cavalry (Col. Richard H. Rush)

2nd Brigade
Col. George A. H. Blake

1st U. S. Cavalry (Col. George A. H. Blake)
8th Pennsylvania Cavalry (Col. David Mc M. Gregg)
McClellan Dragoons (Co. I, 12th Illinois) (Maj. Charles W. Barker)

Engineers

U. S. Engineer Battalion
Capt. James C. Duane

Companies A, B, C

Volunteer Engineer Brigade
Brig. Gen. Daniel P. Woodbury

15th New York (Col. J. McLeod Murphy)
50th New York (Col. Charles B. Stuart)

Siege Train
Col. Robert O. Tyler

1st Connecticut Heavy Artillery (Col. Robert O. Tyler)

General Headquarters

2nd U. S. Cavalry (Maj. Alfred Pleasonton)
4th U. S. Cavalry (Co.'s A & E) (Capt. James B. McIntyre)
Oneida (New York) Cavalry (1 Co.) (Capt. David P. Mann)
8th U. S. Infantry (Co.'s F & G) (Capt. Royal T. Frank)
17th U. S. Infantry (Co.'s B & D) (Capt. John P. Wales)
Sturges Rifles (Illinois) (Maj. Granville O. Haller)

Confederate

Army of Northern Virginia
Gen. Joseph E. Johnston

Left Wing
Maj. Gen. Daniel H. Hill

Rodes's Brigade (3,040)
Brig. Gen. Robert E. Rodes

5th Alabama (660) (Col. Christopher C. Pegues)
6th Alabama (1,100) (Col. John J. Seibels)
12th Alabama (550) (Col. Col. Robert T. Jones)
12th Mississippi (660) (Col. William H. Taylor)
Carter's King William (Virginia) Battery (80) (Thomas H. Carter)

Featherston's Brigade (2,224)
Brig. Gen. Winfield S. Featherston

27th Georgia (428) (Col. Levi B. Smith)
28th Georgia (518) (Col. Thomas J. Warthen, Sr.)
4th North Carolina (739) (Lt. Col. John A. Young)
49th Virginia (539) (Col. William Smith)

Early's Brigade
Brig. Gen. Jubal A. Early

5th North Carolina (460) (Col. Duncan K. MacRae)
23rd North Carolina (540) (Col. John F. Hoke)
24th Virginia (740) (Col. William R. Terry)
38th Virginia (Col. Powhatan B. Whittle)
Bondurant's Jeff Davis Alabama Battery (80) (Capt. James W. Bondurant)

Rains's Brigade (2,981)
Brig. Gen. Gabriel J. Rains

13th Alabama (474) (Col. Birkett D. Fry)
26th Alabama (283) (Col. Edward A. O'Neal)
6th Georgia (703) (Col. Alfred H. Colquitt)
23rd Georgia (370) (Col. Thomas Hutcherson)
Heavy Artillery: 19 batteries (1,151)

Ward's Command (attached) (890)
Col. George T. Ward

2nd Florida (530) (Col. George T. Ward)
2nd Mississippi Battalion (360) (Lt. Col. John G. Taylor)

Crump's Command (Gloucester Point) (1,119)
Col. Charles A. Crump

46th Virginia (356) (Col. James Lucius Davis)
9th Virginia Militia (29) (Lt. Col. Thomas R. Gresham)
21st Virginia Militia (39) (Col. Warner T. Jones)
61st Virginia Militia (201) (Col. John G. Bohannon)

Eastern Shore Co. (58) (Capt. John H. White)
3rd Virginia Cavalry (18) (1 Co.)
1st Maryland Battery (40) (Captain R. Snowden Andrews)
4th Battalion, Virginia Heavy Artillery (332) (Col. John T. Goode)
Armistead's Mathews (Virginia) Battery (46) (Capt. Andrew D. Armistead)

Center
Maj. Gen. James Longstreet

A. P. Hill's Brigade (2,512)
Brig. Gen. Ambrose P. Hill

1st Virginia (400) (Col. Lewis B. Williams, Jr.)
7th Virginia (700) (Col. James L. Kemper)
11th Virginia (750) (Col. Samuel Garland, Jr.)
17th Virginia (600) (Col. Montgomery D. Corse)
Rogers's Loudoun (Virginia) Battery (62) (Capt. Arthur L. Rogers)

R. H. Anderson's Brigade
Brig. Gen. Richard H. Anderson

5th South Carolina (650) (Col. Micah Jenkins)
6th South Carolina (550) (Col. John Bratton)
4th South Carolina Battalion (450)(Lt. Col. James H. Williams)
St. Paul's (Louisiana) Foot Rifles (Capt. McGavock Goodwyn)
Palmetto (South Carolina) Sharpshooters (1100) (Col. Micah Jenkins)
Stribling's Fauquier (Virginia) Battery (68) (Capt. Robert M. Stribling)

Pickett's Brigade (2,460)
Brig. Gen. George E. Pickett

8th Virginia (450) (Col. Eppa Hunton)
18th Virginia (700) (Col. Robert E. Withers)
19th Virginia (650) (Col. John B. Strange)
28th Virginia (600) (Col. Robert C. Allen)
Dearing's Lynchburg (Virginia) Battery (Capt. James G. Dearing, Jr.)

Wilcox's Brigade (2,616)
Brig. Gen. Cadmus M. Wilcox

9th Alabama (550) (Col. Samuel Henry)
10th Alabama (550) (Col. John J. Woodward)
11th Alabama (656) (Col. Sydenham Moore)
19th Mississippi (800) (Col. Christopher H. Mott)
Stanard's Richmond Howitzers (3rd Co.) (60) (Capt. Edgar F. Moseley)

Colston's Brigade (1,750)
Brig. Gen. Raleigh E. Colston

3rd Virginia (550) (Col. Joseph Mayo, Jr.)
13th North Carolina (575) (Col. Alfred M. Scales)
14th North Carolina (625) (Col. Junius Daniel)

Pryor's Brigade (2,310)
Brig. Gen. Roger A. Pryor

8th Alabama (800) (Col. John A. Winston)
14th Alabama (700) (Col. Thomas J. Judge)
14th Louisiana (750) (Col. Zebulon York)
Macon's Richmond Fayette (Virginia) Battery (60) (Capt. Miles C. Macon)(s on April 27) (Lt. William I. Clopton)

Right Wing
Maj. Gen. John B. Magruder

McLaws's Division (2nd Div.) (11,803)
Brig. Gen. Lafayette McLaws

Semmes's Brigade (2.981)
Brig. Gen. Paul J. Semmes

5th Louisiana (744) (Col. Theodore G. Hunt)
10th Louisiana (595) (Col. Mandeville de Marigny)
10th Georgia (582)(Col. Alfred Cumming)
15th Virginia (476) (Col. Thomas P. August)
Noland's Virginia Battalion (162) (Lt. Col. Callender St. George Noland)
1st Louisiana Btn. (315) (Lt. Col. Charles D. Dreux)
Garrett's Williamsburg (Virginia) Battery (50) (Capt. William R. Garrett)
Young's Norfolk (Virginia) Battery (57) (Capt. John J. Young)

Griffith's Brigade (2,774)
Brig. Gen. Richard Griffith

13th Mississippi (640) (Col. William Barksdale)
18th Mississippi (684) (Col. Erasmus Burt)
21st Mississippi (792) (Col. Benjamin G. Humphreys)
1st Louisiana Zouave Btn. (315) (Lt. Col. Georges A. G. Coppens)
McCarthy's Richmond Howitzers (1st Co.) (10) (Capt. Edward S. McCarthy)
Sands' Henrico (Virginia) Battery (80) (Capt. Johnson H. Sands)
Read's Pulaski (Georgia) Battery (72) (Capt. John P. W. Read)
Manly's North Carolina Battery (37) (Capt. Basil C. Manly)
Cosnahan's Peninsula (Virginia) Battery (51)(Capt. Joseph B. Cosnahan)

Kershaw's Brigade (2,567)
Brig. Gen. Joseph B. Kershaw

2nd South Carolina (616) (Col. Ervine P. Jones)
3rd South Carolina (550) (Col. James H. Williams)
7th South Carolina (581) (Col. Thomas Glasscock Bacon)
8th South Carolina (467) (Col. Ellerbe Boggan Crawford Cash)
Gracie's Alabama Battalion (276) (Maj. Archibald Gracie, Jr.)
Kemper's Alexandria (Virginia) Battery (77) (Capt. Delaware Kemper)

Cobb's Brigade (2nd Bde.) (3,796)
Brig. Gen. Howell Cobb

16th Georgia (488) (Col. Goode Bryan)
24th Georgia (660) (Col. Robert McMillan)
Cobb's Georgia Legion (594) (Col. Thomas R. R. Cobb)
2nd Louisiana (782) (Col. William M. Levy)
17th Mississippi (692) (Col. William D. Holder)
15th North Carolina (532) (Col. Robert M. McKinney)(k on Apr 16) (Col. Ross R. Ihrie)
Page's Morris Louisa (Virginia) Battery (48) (Capt. Richard C. M. Page)

Artillery
Col. Henry C. Cabell

D. R. Jones's Division (4,699)

Brig. Gen. David R. Jones

Toombs's Brigade (2,357)
Brig. Gen. Robert A. Toombs

1st Georgia Regulars (367) (Col. Charles J. Williams)
2nd Georgia (607) (Col. Edgar M. Butt)
15th Georgia (441) (Col. Thomas W. Thomas)
17th Georgia (398) (Col. Henry L. Benning)
20th Georgia (560) (Col. John B. Cumming)

G. T. Anderson's Brigade (2,342)
Col. George T. Anderson

7th Georgia (611) (Col. W. T. Wilson)
8th Georgia (251) (Col. L. M. Lamar)
9th Georgia (411) (Richard A. Turnipseed)
11th Georgia (573) (Col. George Thomas Anderson)
1st Kentucky (496) (Col. Thomas H. Taylor)

Reserve
Maj. Gen. Gustavus W. Smith

Infantry Reserve

Hood's Brigade (1,922)
Brig. Gen. John B. Hood

18th Georgia (634) (Col. William T. Wofford)
1st Texas (477) (Lt. Col. Alexis T. Rainey)
4th Texas (470) (Col. John Marshall)
5th Texas (341) (Col J. J. Archer)

Hampton's Brigade (2,225)
Col. Wade Hampton

14th Georgia (379) (Col. Felix L. Price)
19th Georgia (395) (Col. William W. Boyd)
16th North Carolina (721) (Col. Champion Thomas Neal Davis)
Hampton's South Carolina Legion (658) (Capt. James Reilly)
Moody's Madison (Louisiana) Battery (72) (Capt. George V. Moody)

Whiting's Brigade (2,398)
Brig. Gen. W. H. C. Whiting

4th Alabama (459) (Col. Evander McIvor Law)
2nd Mississippi (477) (Col. William C. Falkner) (Col. John M. Stone)
11th Mississippi (504) (Col. Philip F. Liddell)
6th North Carolina (715) (Col. W. Dorsey Pender)
Balthis' Staunton (Virginia) Battery (111) (Capt. William L. Balthis)
Reilly's Rowan (North Carolina) Battery (132) (Capt. James Reilly)

S. R. Anderson's Brigade (attached) (~2,030)
Brig. Gen. Samuel R. Anderson

1st Tennessee (Col. Peter Turney)
7th Tennessee (Col. Robert Hatton)
14th Tennessee (Col. William A. Forbes)
Braxton's Fredericksburg (Virginia) Battery (50) (Capt. Carter M. Braxton)

Pettigrew's Brigade (attached) (2,017)
Brig. Gen. James J. Pettigrew

2nd Arkansas Battalion (146) (Maj. William N. Bronaugh)
35th Georgia (545) (Col. Edward Lloyd Thomas)
22nd North Carolina (752) (Col. Charles E. Lightfoot)
47th Virginia (444) (Col. George W. Richardson)
Andrews's 1st Maryland Battery (130) (Capt. R. Snowden Andrews)

Ewell's Command (Williamsburg)
Col. Benjamin S. Ewell

17th Virginia (Co. I) (Capt. Stephen W. Pressman)
32nd Virginia (Co. F) (29) (Capt. Thomas Tinsley)
52nd Virginia Militia (30) (Col. Carter Hill)
68th Virginia Militia (20) (Lt. John W. Cloves)
115th Virginia Militia (40) (Col. Charles T. Mallory)

Carter's Command (Jamestown)
Col. Hill Carter

Allen's 10th Battalion Virginia Heavy Artillery (Maj. William H. Allen)
Rambaut's Independent Company, Virginia Heavy Artillery (Capt. Gilbert V. Rambaut)
Jordan's Bedford (Virginia) Battery (100) (Capt. Tyler C. Jordan)

Cavalry Reserve

Cavalry Brigade (1289)
Brig. Gen. J. E. B. Stuart

1st Virginia Cavalry (437) (Col. Fitzhugh Lee)
3rd Virginia Cavalry(Col. Thomas F. Goode)
4th Virginia Cavalry(540) (Lt. Col. William C. Wickham)
9th Virginia Cavalry(Col. William H. F. Lee) (absent)
Jeff Davis (Mississippi) Legion Cavalry (171) (Lt. Col. Will H. Martin)
Wise's (Virginia) Legion Cavalry (10th Virginia Cavalry) (Col. J. Lucius Davis)
Stuart Horse Artillery (141) (Capt. John Pelham)

Artillery Reserve
Brig. Gen. William N. Pendleton

Pendleton's Corps

Brown's Richmond Howitzers, 2nd Co. (Capt. Henry Hudnall)
Nelson's Hanover (Virginia) Battery (Capt. William Nelson)
Southall's Albemarle (Virginia) Battery (Capt. William H. Southall)
Carlton's Troup (Georgia) Battery (Capt. Marcellus Stanley)
Richardson's James City (Virginia) Battery (Capt. Lucien W. Richardson)
C. L. Smith's Hampton (Virginia) Battery (Capt. C. L. Smith)
Page's Magruder (Virginia) Battery (Capt. Thomas J. Page, Jr.)

Walton's Corps (1,050)
Col. James B. Walton

Washington (Louisiana) Artillery Btn., 1st, 2nd, 3rd, 4th Co.'s (Col. James B. Walton)

At Williamsburg (May 5)

Federal

Army of the Potomac (partial) (40,768)
Maj. Gen. Edwin V. Sumner

III Corps
Maj. Gen. Samuel P. Heintzelman

2nd Division
Brig. Gen. Joseph Hooker

1st Brigade (~2878)
Brig. Gen. Cuvier Grover

1st Massachusetts (Col. Robert Cowdin) (708)
11th Massachusetts (Col. William E. Blaisdell) (~700)
2nd New Hampshire (Col. Gilman Marston) (770)
26th Pennsylvania (~700) (Col. William F. Small) (w on May 5) (Maj. Casper M. Berry)

2nd Brigade (Excelsior Brigade)
Col. Nelson Taylor

70th New York (700) (Col. William Dwight, Jr.)(w, c on May 5) (Maj. Thomas Holt)
72nd New York (Lt. Col. Israel Moses)
73rd New York (Col. William R. Brewster)
74th New York (Lt. Col. Charles H. Burtis)

3rd Brigade
Brig. Gen. Francis E. Patterson

5th New Jersey (Col. Samuel H. Starr)
6th New Jersey (Lt. Col. John P. Van Leer)(k on May 5) (Maj. George C. Burling)
7th New Jersey (Lt. Col. Ezra A. Carman)(w on May 5) (Maj. Francis Price, Jr.)
8th New Jersey (Col. Adolphus J. Johnson)(w on May 5) (Maj. Peter H. Ryerson)(k on May 5)

Artillery
Maj. Charles S. Wainwright

1st New York Light, Battery D (Capt. Thomas W. Osborn)
4th New York (Capt. James E. Smith)
6th New York (Capt. Walter M. Bramhall)
1st U. S., Battery H (Capt. Charles H. Webber)

3rd Division
Brig. Gen. Philip Kearny

1st Brigade
Brig. Gen. Charles D. Jameson

87th New York (Col. Stephen A. Dodge)
57th Pennsylvania (Col. Charles T. Campbell)
63rd Pennsylvania (Col. Alexander Hays)
105th Pennsylvania (Col. Amor A. McKnight)

2nd Brigade (5,000–6,000)
Brig. Gen. David B. Birney

3rd Maine (Col. Henry G. Staples)
4th Maine (Col. Elijah Walker)
38th New York (Col. John H. H. Ward)
40th New York (Col. Edward J. Riley)

3rd Brigade
Brig. Gen. Hiram G. Berry

2nd Michigan (~300) (Col. Orlando M. Poe)
3rd Michigan (Col. Stephen G. Champlin)
5th Michigan (Col. Henry D. Terry)(w on May 5) (Lt. Col. Samuel E. Beach (w on May 5) (Maj. John D. Fairbanks)
37th New York (Col. Samuel B. Hayman)

Artillery
Capt. James Thompson

2nd U. S., Battery G (Capt. James Thompson)
1st New Jersey Light, Battery B (Capt. John E. Beam)

1st Rhode Island Light, Battery E (Capt. George E. Randolph)

IV Corps
Maj. Gen. Erasmus D. Keyes

1st Division
Brig. Gen. Darius N. Couch

1st Brigade (not engaged)
Col. Julius W. Adams

65th New York (1st U. S. Chasseurs) (Lt. Col. Alexander Shaler)
67th New York (1st Long Island) (Lt. Col. Nelson Cross)
23rd Pennsylvania (Col. Thomas H. Neill)
31st Pennsylvania (Col. David H. Williams)
61st Pennsylvania (Col. Oliver H. Rippey)

2nd Brigade
Brig. Gen. John J. Peck

55th New York (Col. Regis de Trobriand)
62nd New York (Col. John L. Riker)
93rd Pennsylvania (Col. James M. McCarter)
98th Pennsylvania (Col. John F. Ballier)
102nd Pennsylvania (Col. Thomas A. Rowley)

3rd Brigade (not engaged)
Brig. Gen. Charles Devens, Jr.

7th Massachusetts (Col. David A. Russell)
10th Massachusetts (Col. Henry S. Briggs)
2nd Rhode Island (Col. Frank Wheaton)

Artillery
Maj. Robert M. West

1st Pennsylvania Light, Battery C (Capt. Jeremiah McCarthy)
1st Pennsylvania Light, Battery D (Capt. Edward H. Flood)
1st Pennsylvania Light, Battery E (Capt. Theodore Miller)
1st Pennsylvania Light, Battery H (Capt. James Brady)

2nd Division
Brig. Gen. William F. Smith

1st Brigade(2,547)
Brig. Gen. Winfield S. Hancock (also temp. in command of 3rd brigade)

5th Wisconsin (Col. Amasa Cobb)
6th Maine (Col. Hiram Burnham)
43rd New York (Col. Francis L. Vinton) (not engaged)
67th New York (1st Long Island) (Lt. Col. Nelson Cross) (not engaged)
49th Pennsylvania Volunteers (Col. William H. Irwin)

2nd Brigade (not engaged)
Brig. Gen. William T. H. Brooks

2nd Vermont (Col. Henry Whiting)
3rd Vermont (Col. Breed N. Hyde)
4th Vermont (Col. Edwin H. Stoughton)
5th Vermont (Lt. Col. Lewis A. Grant)
6th Vermont (Col. Nathan Lord, Jr.)

3rd Brigade
Brig. Gen. Winfield S. Hancock (temp.)
Brig. Gen. John W. Davidson

33rd New York (Col. Robert F. Taylor)
49th New York (Col. Daniel D. Bidwell)
76th New York (Col. James B. McKean) (not engaged)
7th Maine (Col. Edwin C. Mason)

Artillery
Capt. Romeyn B. Ayres

1st New York Independent Light (Capt. Andrew Cowan)
3rd New York Independent Light (Capt. Thaddeus P. Mott)
1st New York Light, Battery E (Capt. Charles C. Wheeler)
5th U. S., Battery F (Capt. Romeyn B. Ayres)

Cavalry

5th U.S. Cavalry (4th Sqdn.) (Capt. William P. Chambliss)

3rd Division (not engaged)
Brig. Gen. Silas Casey

1st Brigade
Brig. Gen. Henry M. Naglee

11th Maine (Col. John C. Caldwell)
56th New York (Col. Charles H. Van Wyck)
100th New York (Col. James M. Brown)
52nd Pennsylvania (Col. John C. Dodge, Jr.)
104th Pennsylvania (Col. W. W. H. Davis)

2nd Brigade
Brig. Gen. William H. Keim

96th New York (Lt. Col. Charles O. Gray)
85th Pennsylvania (Col. Joshua B. Howell)
101st Pennsylvania (Col. Joseph H. Wilson)
103rd Pennsylvania (Maj. Audley W. Gazzam)

3rd Brigade
Brig. Gen. Innis N. Palmer

81st New York (Lt. Col. Jacob J. De Forest)
85th New York (Col. Jonathan S. Belknap)
92nd New York (Lt. Col. Hiram Anderson, Jr.)
93rd New York (Lt. Col. Benjamin C. Butler)
98th New York (Col. William Dutton)

Artillery
Maj. Guilford D. Bailey

7th New York (Capt. Peter C. Regan)
8th New York (Capt. Butler Fitch)
1st New York Light, Battery A (Capt. Thomas H. Bates)
1st New York Light, Battery H (Capt. Joseph Spratt)

Cavalry Advanced Guard
Brig. Gen. George Stoneman

Cavalry Division
Brig. Gen. Phillip St. George Cooke

1st U. S. Cavalry (Lt. Col. William N. Grier)
6th U. S. Cavalry (Maj. Lawrence Williams)

1st Brigade, Cavalry Reserve
Brig. Gen. William H. Emory

3rd Pennsylvania Cavalry (Col. William W. Averell)
8th Illinois Cavalry (Col. John F. Farnsworth)
McClellan (Ill.) Dragoons (Maj. Charles W. Barker)

Artillery Reserve
Col. Henry J. Hunt

Hays' Brigade (Horse Artillery)
Lt. Col. William Hays

2nd U. S., Battery B and L (Capt. James M. Robertson)
2nd U. S., Battery M (Capt. Henry Benson)
3rd U.S., Batteries C & G (Capt. Horatio G. Gibson)
3rd U. S., Battery K (Capt. John C. Tidball)

Confederate

Army of Northern Virginia (partial) (31,823)
Gen. Joseph E. Johnston (not present until late)

Longstreet's Division (2nd Div.)
Maj. Gen. James Longstreet

A. P. Hill's Brigade (1st Bde.)
Brig. Gen. Ambrose P. Hill

1st Virginia (Col. Lewis B. Williams, Jr.)(w, c on May 5) (Maj. William H. Palmer)(w on May 5)
7th Virginia (Col. James L. Kemper)
11th Virginia (Col. Samuel Garland, Jr.)(w on May 5)
17th Virginia (Col. Montgomery D. Corse)
Rogers's Loudon (Virginia) Battery

R. H. Anderson's Brigade (2nd Bde.) (2,000–3,000)
Brig. Gen. Richard H. Anderson
Col. Micah Jenkins

4th South Carolina Btn. (Maj. Charles S. Mattison)
5th South Carolina (460) (Col. John R. R. Giles) (Maj. William M. Foster)
6th South Carolina (Col. John Bratton) (Lt. Col. John M. Steedman)
Palmetto Sharpshooters (Col. Micah Jenkins) (Lt. Col. Joseph Walker) (Maj. William Anderson)
St. Paul's (Louisiana) Foot Rifles (Capt. McGavock Goodwyn)
Fauquier (Virginia) Battery (Capt. Robert M. Stribling)
Williamsburg (Virginia) Artillery (2 guns) (Capt. William R. Garrett)

Pickett's Brigade (3rd Bde.) (1529)
Brig. Gen. George E. Pickett

8th Virginia (Col. Norborne Berkeley)
18th Virginia (Lt. Col. Henry A. Carrington)
19th Virginia (Col. John B. Strange)
28th Virginia (Col. Robert C. Allen)

Lynchburg (Virginia) Battery (Capt. James G. Dearing, Jr.)

Wilcox's Brigade (4th Bde.)
Brig. Gen. Cadmus M. Wilcox

9th Alabama (Col. Samuel Henry)
10th Alabama (Col. John J. Woodward)
11th Alabama (absent)
19th Mississippi (501) (Col. Christopher H. Mott)(k on May 5) (Lt. Col. Lucius Q. C. Lamar)
Stanard's Richmond Howitzers, 3rd Co. (Capt. Edward F. Moseley)

Pryor's Brigade (5th Bde.) (~700)
Brig. Gen. Roger A. Pryor

8th Alabama (Lt. Col. Thomas E. Irby)(k on May 5) (Maj. Young L. Royston)
14th Alabama (Maj. Owen K. McLemore)
14th Louisiana (Lt. Col. Zebulon York)(w on May 5) (Maj. David Zable) (w on May 5) (Capt. Richard W. Jones)
32nd Virginia Btn. (det.) (Capt. John F. Seger)
Richmond Fayette (Virginia) Battery (Lt. William I. Clopton)

Colston's Brigade (6th Bde.)
Brig. Gen. Raleigh E. Colston

3rd Virginia (Col. Joseph Mayo, Jr.)
13th North Carolina (Col. Alfred M. Scales)
14th North Carolina (Col. Philetus W. Roberts)
Donaldsonville (La.) Battery (3 guns) (Lt. Lestang Fortier)

D. H. Hill's Division (4th Div.)
Maj. Gen. Daniel H. Hill

Early's Brigade (1st Bde.)
Brig. Gen. Jubal A. Early (w on May 5)
Col. Duncan K. McRae

24th Virginia (~500) (Col. William R. Terry)(w on May 5) (Lt. Col. Peter Hairston)(w on May 5) (Maj. Richard L. Maury)
38th Virginia (Lt. Col. Powhatan B. Whittle)(w on May 5)

5th North Carolina (Col. Duncan K. McRae) (Lt. Col. John C. Badham)
(k on May 5) (Maj. Peter J. Sinclair)
23rd North Carolina (Col. John F. Hoke)(s) (Maj. Daniel H. Christie)

Rodes's Brigade (2nd Bde.) (not engaged)
Brig. Gen. Robert E. Rodes

5th Alabama (Col. Christopher C. Pegues)
6th Alabama (Col. John B. Gordon)
12th Alabama (Col. R. T. Jones)
12th Mississippi (Col. William H. Taylor)
Carter's King William (Virginia) Battery

Featherston's Brigade (4th Bde.) (not engaged)
Brig. Gen. Winfield S. Featherston
Col. George B. Anderson

27th Georgia (Col. Levi B. Smith)
28th Georgia (Col. Thomas J. Warthen, Sr.)
4th North Carolina (Col. George B. Anderson) (Lt. Col. John A. Young)
(Maj. Bryan Grimes)
49th Virginia (Col. William Smith)

Rains's Brigade (3rd Bde.) (not engaged)
Brig. Gen. Gabriel J. Rains

13th Alabama (Col. Birkett D. Fry)
26th Alabama (Col. Edward A. O'Neal)
6th Georgia (Col. Alfred H. Colquitt)
23rd Georgia (Col. Thomas Hutcherson)
Virginia (Hanover Arty) Battery (Capt. George W. Nelson)

Unattached

2nd Florida (700–800) (Col. George T. Ward)(k on May 5) (Lt. Col. S. St. George Rogers)
2nd Mississippi Btn. (Lt. Col. John G. Taylor)

Cavalry Brigade
Brig. Gen. J. E. B. Stuart

1st Virginia Cavalry (Col. Fitzhugh Lee)
3rd Virginia Cavalry (Col. Thomas F. Goode)
4th Virginia Cavalry (Lt. Col. William C. Wickham) (w on May 4)
(Maj. William H. F. Payne)(w, c on May 5) (Capt. Robert E. Utterback)
Jeff Davis (Mississippi) Legion Cavalry (Lt. Col. Will T. Martin)
Wise's Virginia Legion Cavalry(10th Virginia Cavalry) (Col. James L. Davis)
Stuart Horse Artillery (Capt. John Pelham)

Artillery Reserve
Brig. Gen. William N. Pendleton

At Eltham's Landing (May 7)

Federal

I Corps (partial)

1st Division
Brig. Gen. William B. Franklin

1st Brigade
Brig. Gen. George W. Taylor

1st New Jersey (Lt. Col. Robert McAllister)
2nd New Jersey (Col. Isaac M. Tucker)
3rd New Jersey (Col. Henry W. Brown)
4th New Jersey (Col. James H. Simpson)

2nd Brigade
Brig. Gen. Henry W. Slocum

5th Maine (Col. Nathaniel J. Jackson)
16th New York (Col. Joseph Howland)
27th New York (Col. Joseph J. Bartlett)
96th Pennsylvania (Col. Henry L. Cake)
1st Massachusetts Battery (Capt. Josiah Porter)

3rd Brigade
Brig. Gen. John Newton

18th New York (Col. W. H. Young) (Col. Calvin E. Pratt)
32nd New York (Col. C. Roderick Matheson)
95th Pennsylvania (Col. John M. Gosline)
New Jersey Artillery, Battery A (Capt. William Hexamer)

Artillery
Capt. Richard Arnold

II Corps (partial)

2nd Division
Brig. Gen. John Sedgwick

Dana's Brigade

1st Massachusetts Battery (Capt. Josiah Porter)
1st Rhode Island Light, Battery A (Capt. John A. Tompkins)

Confederate

Smith's Division (1st Div.)
Brig. Gen. William H. C. Whiting

Hood's Brigade (1st Bde.) (Texas Bde.)
Brig. Gen. John B. Hood

1st Texas (Col. Alexis T. Rainey)(w on May 7)
4th Texas (Col. John Marshall)
5th Texas (Col. James J. Archer)
18th Georgia (Col. William T. Wofford) (Lt. Col. Solon Z. Ruff)
Staunton (Virginia) Battery (Capt. William L. Balthis)

Hampton's Brigade (2nd Bde.)
Col. Wade Hampton

19th Georgia (Lt. Col. Thomas C. Johnson)
Hampton Legion Infantry (450) (Lt. Col. James B. Griffin)

Anderson's Brigade (3rd Bde.)
Brig. Gen. Samuel R. Anderson

1st Tennessee (Col. Peter Turney)
7th Tennessee (Col. Robert Hatton)
14th Tennessee (Col. William A. Forbes)
6th North Carolina (Col. W. Dorsey Pender)

At Hanover Court House (May 27)

Federal

V Corps
Brig. Gen. Fitz John Porter

Cavalry Reserve

1st Brigade
Brig. Gen. William H. Emory

5th U.S. Cavalry (detachment) (Capt. Charles J. Whiting)
6th U. S. Cavalry (detachment) (Maj. Lawrence Williams)
Berdan's 1st U. S. Sharpshooters (attached) (Col. Hiram Berdan)
2nd U. S. Artillery, Battery M (Benson's Horse Battery) (Capt. Henry Benson)

1st Division (reinforced)
Brig. Gen. George W. Morell

1st Brigade
Brig. Gen. John H. Martindale

18th Massachusetts (Col. James Barnes) (absent)
22nd Massachusetts (800) (Col. Jesse A. Gove) (2nd Co., Massachusetts Sharpshooters, atch.)
2nd Maine (350) (Col. Charles W. Roberts)
25th New York (349) (Col. Charles A. Johnson)(w on May 27)
44th New York (Col. Stephen W. Stryker) (attached from 3rd bde.)
Massachusetts Light Artillery, Battery C (Capt. Augustus P. Martin)

2nd Brigade
Col. James McQuade

14th New York (Lt. Col. Charles H. Skillen)
4th Michigan (Col. Dwight A. Woodbury)
9th Massachusetts (Col. Thomas Cass)(s on May 27) (Lt. Col. Patrick R. Guiney) (Col. Thomas Cass)
62nd Pennsylvania (Col. Samuel W. Black)
Massachusetts Light Artillery, Battery E (Capt. George D. Allen)

3rd Brigade
Brig. Gen. Daniel Butterfield

16th Michigan (Col. Thomas B. W. Stockton) (Brady's Co. Michigan Sharpshooters, attached) (Capt. Kiniston S. Dygert)
12th New York (Col. Henry A. Weeks)
17th New York (Col. Henry S. Lansing)
83rd Pennsylvania (Col. John W. McLane)
5th U. S., Battery D (Capt. Charles Griffin) (Lt. Henry W. Kingsbury)

Sharpshooters
Col. Hiram Berdan

1st U.S. Sharpshooters

2nd Division
Brig. Gen. George Sykes

1st Brigade
Col. Robert C. Buchanan

3rd U. S. (Maj. Nathan B. Rossell)
4th U. S. (Maj. Delozier Davidson)
12th U. S. (Maj. Henry B. Clitz)
14th U. S. (Capt. John D. O'Connell)

2nd Brigade
Lt. Col. William Chapman

2nd U. S. (Capt. Adolphus F. Bond)
6th U. S. (Capt. Thomas Hendrickson)
10th U. S. (Maj. Charles S. Lovell)
11th U. S. (Maj. Delancy Floyd-Jones)
17th U. S. (Co.'s A, C & E) (Maj. George L. Andrews)

Provisional Brigade
Col. Gouverneur K. Warren

5th New York (detachment) (725) (Lt. Col. Hiram Duryea)
13th New York (attached) (475) (Col. Elisha G. Marshall)
1st Connecticut Heavy Artillery (as infantry) (785) (Col. Robert O. Tyler)
6th Pennsylvania Cavalry (2 Rgts.) (Col. Richard H. Rush) (630)
Rhode Island Battery (Capt. William B. Weeden)

Artillery
Capt. Stephen H. Weed

3rd U. S., Battery L & M (Capt. John Edwards)
5th U. S., Battery I (Capt. Stephen H. Weed)

Confederate

Hill's Light Division (partial)
Brig. Gen. A. P. Hill (not present)

Branch's Brigade
Brig. Gen. Lawrence O'B. Branch

7th North Carolina (Col. Reuben P. Campbell)
18th North Carolina (Col. Robert H. Cowan)
28th North Carolina (Col. James H. Lane) (890)
33rd North Carolina (Lt. Col. Robert F. Hoke)
37th North Carolina (Col. Charles C. Lee)

Attached

45th Georgia (Col. Thomas Hardeman)
12th North Carolina (Col. Benjamin O. Wade)
Latham's (NC) Battery (1 Sect.) (Lt. J. R. Potts)
4th Virginia Cavalry (partial) (Col. Beverly H. Robertson)
9th Virginia Cavalry, Co. H (Capt. Beverly B. Douglas) (atch.)

At Seven Pines (May 31–June 1)

Federal

        Army of the Potomac (126,089)(44,944 engaged)
        Maj. Gen. George B. McClellan

    II Corps (17,412)
    Brig. Gen. Edwin V. Sumner

  1st Division
  Brig. Gen. Israel B. Richardson

1st Brigade
Brig. Gen. Oliver O. Howard (w on June 1)
Col. Thomas J. Parker

5th New Hampshire (Col. Edward E. Cross)(w on May 31) (Lt. Col. Samuel G. Langley)
61st New York (432) (Col. Francis C. Barlow)
64th New York (Col. Thomas J. Parker) (Captain Rufus Washburn)
81st Pennsylvania (Col. James Miller)(k on June 1) (Lt. Col. Charles F. Johnson) (Capt. Nelson A. Miles)

  2nd Brigade (Irish Brigade)
  Brig. Gen. Thomas F. Meagher

63rd New York (Col. John W. Burke)
69th New York (Col. Robert Nugent)
88th New York (Lt. Col. Patrick Kelly)

  3rd Brigade
  Brig. Gen. William H. French

52nd New York (Col. Paul Frank)
57th New York (Col. Samuel K. Zook)
66th New York (Col. Joseph C. Pinckney)
53rd Pennsylvania (Col. John R. Brooke)

  Artillery
  Capt. George W. Hazzard

1st New York Light, Battery B (Capt. Rufus D. Pettit)
1st New York Light, Battery G (Capt. John D. Frank)
4th U. S., Batteries A & C (Capt. George W. Hazzard)

Cavalry

6th New York Cavalry, Co. D (Capt. Raymond Wright)

2nd Division
Brig. Gen. John Sedgwick

1st Brigade
Brig. Gen. Willis A. Gorman

15th Massachusetts (Lt. Col. John W. Kimball) (1st Co., Mass. Sharpshooters, attached) (Capt. John Saunders)
1st Minnesota (Col. Alfred Sully) (2nd Co., Minn. Sharpshooters, attached) (Capt. William F. Russell)
34th New York (Col. James A. Suiter)
82nd New York (Lt. Col. Henry W. Hudson)

2nd Brigade
Brig. Gen. William W. Burns

69th Pennsylvania (Col. Joshua T. Owen)
71st Pennsylvania (Maj. Charles W. Smith)
72nd Pennsylvania (Col. DeWitt C. Baxter)
106th Pennsylvania (Col. Turner G. Morehead)

3rd Brigade
Brig. Gen. N. J. T. Dana

19th Massachusetts (Col. Edward W. Hinks) (absent)
20th Massachusetts (Col. W. Raymond Lee)
7th Michigan (Col. Ira R. Grosvenor)(s) (Maj. John H. Richardson)
42nd New York (Col. Edmund C. Charles)

Artillery
Col. Charles H. Tompkins

1st Rhode Island Light, Battery A (Capt. John A. Tompkins)

1st Rhode Island Light, Battery B (Capt. Walter O. Bartlett)
1st Rhode Island Light, Battery G (Capt. Charles D. Owen)
1st U. S., Battery I (Lt. Edmund Kirby)

Cavalry

6th New York Cavalry, Co. K (Capt. Riley Johnson)

III Corps (16,999)
Brig. Gen. Samuel P. Heintzelman
(commanding III & IV Corps)

2nd Division
Brig. Gen. Joseph Hooker

1st Brigade
Brig. Gen. Cuvier Grover

2nd New Hampshire (Col. Gilman Marston)
1st Massachusetts (Col. Robert Cowdin)
11th Massachusetts (Col. Gilman Marston)
26th Pennsylvania (Col. George D. Wells)
8th Pennsylvania Cavalry, Co. M (Capt. Craven)

2nd Brigade
Brig. Gen. Daniel E. Sickles

70th New York (Maj. Thomas Holt)
71st New York (Col. George B. Hall) (s) (Lt. Col. Henry L. Potter)
72nd New York (Col. Nelson Taylor)
73rd New York (Major John D. Moriarty)(w on May 31) (Capt. Charles B. Elliot)
74th New York (Col. Charles K. Graham)

3rd Brigade
Brig. Gen. Francis E. Patterson (s on May 31)
Col. Samuel H. Starr

5th New Jersey (Col. Samuel H. Starr)(Maj. John Ramsey)
6th New Jersey (Col. Gershom Mott)
7th New Jersey (Maj. Francis Price. Jr.)

8th New Jersey (Lt. Col. Joseph Trawin)

Artillery
Maj. Charles S. Wainwright

1st New York Light, Battery D (Capt. Thomas W. Osborn)
1st U. S., Battery H (Capt. Charles H. Webber)
4th New York Independent Light (Capt. James E. Smith)
6th New York Independent Light (Capt. Walter M. Bramhall)

3rd Division
Brig. Gen. Philip Kearny

1st Brigade
Brig. Gen. Charles D. Jameson

57th Pennsylvania (Col. Charles T. Campbell)(w on May 31) (Lt. Col. Elhanon W. Woods)
63rd Pennsylvania (Col. Alexander Hays) (Lt. Col. A. S. M. Morgan)(w on May 31)
105th Pennsylvania (Col. Amor A. McKnight)(w on May 31)
87th New York (Col. Stephen A. Dodge)(w, c on May 31) (Lt. Col. Richard A. Bachia)

2nd Brigade (1,300)
Brig. Gen. David B. Birney (a on May 31)
Col. J. H. H. Ward

38th New York (Col. J. H. H. Ward) (Maj. William H. Baird)
40th New York (Lt. Col. Thomas W. Egan)
3rd Maine (Col. Henry G. Staples)
4th Maine (Col. Elijah Walker)

3rd Brigade
Brig. Gen. Hiram G. Berry

2nd Michigan (Col. Orlando M. Poe)
3rd Michigan (Col. Stephen G. Champlin)(w on May 31) (Lt. Col. Ambrose A. Stevens)
5th Michigan (Col. Henry D. Terry)

37th New York (Lt. Col. Gilbert Riordan)(temporarily) (Col. Samuel B. Hayman)

Artillery
Capt. James Thompson

New Jersey Light, Battery B (Capt. John E. Beam)
1st Rhode Island Light, Battery E (Capt. George E. Randolph)
2nd U. S., Battery G (Capt. James Thompson)

Corps Cavalry
Col. William W. Averell

3rd Pennsylvania Cavalry

IV Corps (17,132–17,546)
Brig. Gen. Erasmus D. Keyes

1st Division
Brig. Gen. Darius N. Couch

1st Brigade (>2,000)
Brig. Gen. John J. Peck

55th New York (Lt. Col. Louis Thourot)
62nd New York (Col. John L. Riker)(k on May 31) (Lt. Col. David J. Nevin)
93rd Pennsylvania (Col. James M. McCarter)(w on May 31) (Capt. John E. Arthur)
98th Pennsylvania (Col. John F. Ballier)
102nd Pennsylvania (Col. Thomas A. Rowley)(w on May 31) (Lt. Col. Joseph M. Kinkead)

2nd Brigade
Brig. Gen. John J. Abercrombie

65th New York (1st U.S. Chasseurs) (Col. John Cochrane)
67th New York (1st Long Island) (Col. Julius W. Adams)
23rd Pennsylvania (Col. Thomas H. Neill)
31st Pennsylvania (Col. David H. Williams)

61st Pennsylvania (Col. Oliver H. Rippey)(k on May 31) (Capt. Robert L. Orr)

3rd Brigade
Brig. Gen. Charles Devens, Jr. (w on May 31)
Col. Charles H. Innes

7th Massachusetts (Col. David A. Russell)
10th Massachusetts (500)(Col. Henry S. Briggs)(w on May 31) (Capt. Ozro Miller)
36th New York (Col. Charles H. Innes) (Lt. Col. Daniel E. Hungerford)

Artillery
Maj. Robert M. West

1st Pennsylvania Light, Battery C (Capt. Jeremiah McCarthy)
1st Pennsylvania Light, Battery D (Capt. Edward H. Flood)
1st Pennsylvania Light, Battery E (Capt. Theodore Miller)
1st Pennsylvania Light, Battery H (Capt. James Brady)

Cavalry

6th New York Cavalry, Co. F (Capt. Dudley C. Hannahs)

2nd Division (5,000)
Brig. Gen. Silas Casey

1st Brigade
Brig. Gen. Henry M. Naglee (w on May 31)

52nd Pennsylvania (Col. John C. Dodge, Jr.)
104th Pennsylvania (Col. William W. H. Davis)(w on May 31) (Capt. Edward L. Rogers)
56th New York (Lt. Col. James Jourdan)
100th New York (Col. James M. Brown)(k on May 31) (Col. George F. B. Dandy)
11th Maine (Col. Harris M. Plaistead)

2nd Brigade (1000)
Brig. Gen. Henry W. Wessells

85th Pennsylvania (Col. Joshua B. Howell)
101st Pennsylvania (Lt. Col. David B. Morris)(w on May 31) (Capt. Charles W. May)
103rd Pennsylvania (Maj. Audley W. Gazzam)
96th New York (Col. James Fairman)

3rd Brigade (1,200)
Brig. Gen. Innis N. Palmer

81st New York (Lt. Col. Jacob J. DeForest) (w on May 31) (Capt. William C. Raulston)
85th New York (Col. Jonathan S. Belknap)
92nd New York (Col. Lewis C. Hunt)(w on May 31) (Lt. Col. Hiram Anderson, Jr.)
98th New York (Col. William Dutton) (Lt. Col. Charles Durkee)

Artillery
Col. Guilford D. Bailey (k on May 31)
Maj. D. H. Van Valkenburgh (k on May 31)
Capt. Peter C. Regan

1st New York Light, Battery A (Lt. George P. Hart)
1st New York Light, Battery H (Capt. Joseph Spratt)(w on May 31) (Lt. Howell)(w on May 31) (Lt. Charles E. Mink)
7th New York Independent Light (Capt. Peter C. Regan)
8th New York Independent Light (Capt. Butler Fitch)(unattached)
1st U. S., Battery E (Lt. Alanson M. Randol)

Cavalry

6th New York Cavalry, Co. H (Capt. William P. Hall)

Corps Cavalry
Col. David McM. Gregg

8th Pennsylvania Cavalry

V Corps (17,546)(not engaged)
Brig. Gen. Fitz John Porter

1st Division
Brig. Gen. George W. Morell

1st Brigade
Brig. Gen. John H. Martindale

2nd Maine (Col. Charles W. Roberts)
18th Massachusetts (Col. James Barnes)
22nd Massachusetts (Col. Jesse A. Gove) (2nd Co., Mass. Sharpshooters, atch.) (Capt. Lewis E. Wentworth)
13th New York (Col. Elisha G. Marshall)
25th New York (Lt. Col. Henry F. Savage)

2nd Brigade
Col. James McQuade

14th New York (Lt. Col. Charles H. Skillen)
4th Michigan (Col. Dwight A. Woodbury)
9th Massachusetts (Col. Thomas Cass)
62nd Pennsylvania (Col. Samuel W. Black)

3rd Brigade
Brig. Gen. Daniel Butterfield

16th Michigan (Col. Thomas B.W. Stockton) (Brady's Co. Michigan Sharpshooters, atch.) (Capt. Kiniston S. Dygert)
12th New York (Col. Henry A. Weeks)
17th New York (Col. Henry S. Lansing)
44th New York (Col. Stephen W. Stryker) (Lt. Col. James C. Rice)
83rd Pennsylvania (Col. John W. McLane)

Artillery
Capt. Charles Griffin

Massachusetts Light, Battery C (Capt. Augustus P. Martin)
Massachusetts Light, Battery E (Lt. John B. Hyde)
1st Rhode Island Light, Battery C (Capt. William B. Weeden)
5th U. S., Battery D (Lt. Charles E. Hazlett)

Sharpshooters
Col. Hiram Berdan

1st U. S. Sharpshooters

2nd Division
Brig. Gen. George Sykes

1st Brigade
Col. Robert C. Buchanan

3rd U. S. (Maj. Nathan B. Rossell)
4th U. S. (Maj. Delozier Davidson)
12th U. S. (Maj. Henry B. Clitz)
14th U. S. (Capt. John D. O'Connell)

2nd Brigade
Lt. Col. William Chapman

2nd U. S. (Capt. Adolphus F. Bond)
6th U. S. (Capt. Thomas Hendrickson)
10th U. S. (Maj. Charles S. Lovell)
11th U. S. (Maj. Delancy Floyd-Jones)
17th U. S. (Co.'s A, C & E) (Maj. George L. Andrews)

3rd Brigade
Col. Gouverneur K. Warren

5th New York (Lt. Col. Hiram Duryea)
1st Connecticut Heavy Artillery (as infantry) (Col. Robert O. Tyler)

Artillery
Capt. Stephen H. Weed

3rd U. S., Battery L & M (Capt. John Edwards)
5th U. S., Battery I (Capt. Stephen H. Weed)

Artillery Reserve
Col. Henry J. Hunt

1st Brigade
Lt. Col. William Hays

2nd U. S., Battery M (Capt. Henry Benson)
3rd U. S., Battery C-G (Capt. Horatio G. Gibson)

2nd Brigade
Lt. Col. George W. Getty

1st U. S., Battery E (Lt. Alanson M. Randol))
1st U. S., Battery G & K (Lt. Samuel S. Elder)
4th U. S., Battery G (Lt. Charles H. Morgan)
5th U. S., Battery A (Lt. Adelbert Ames)
5th U. S., Battery K (Capt. John R. Smead)

3rd Brigade
Maj. Albert Arndt

1st Btn. New York, Battery A (Capt. Otto Diederich)
1st Btn. New York, Battery B (Capt. Adolph Voegelee)
1st Btn. New York, Battery C (Capt. John Knieriem)
1st Btn. New York, Battery D (Capt. Edward D. Grimm)

4th Brigade
Capt. J. Howard Carlisle

2nd U. S., Battery E (Capt. J. Howard Carlisle)
3rd U. S., Battery F-K (Capt. La Rhett L. Livingston)
4th U. S., Battery K (Lt. Francis W. Seeley)

VI Corps (19,580)(not engaged)
Brig. Gen. William B. Franklin

1st Division
Brig. Gen. Henry W. Slocum

1st Brigade
Brig. Gen. George Taylor

1st New Jersey (Lt. Col. Robert McAllister)
2nd New Jersey (Col. Isaac M. Tucker)
3rd New Jersey (Col. Henry W. Brown)
4th New Jersey (Col. James H. Simpson)

2nd Brigade
Col. Joseph J. Bartlett

16th New York (Col. Joseph Howland)
27th New York (Col. Joseph J. Bartlett)
5th Maine (Col. Nathaniel J. Jackson)
96th Pennsylvania (Col. Henry L. Cake)

3rd Brigade
Brig. Gen. John Newton

18th New York (Col. William H. Young)
31st New York (Col. Calvin E. Pratt)
32nd New York (Col. C. Roderick Matheson)
95th Pennsylvania (Col. John M. Gosline)

Artillery
Capt. Edward R. Platt

Massachusetts Light, Battery A (Capt. Josiah Porter)
New Jersey Light, Battery A (Capt. William Hexamer)
2nd U. S., Battery D (Lt. Emory Upton)

2nd Division
Brig. Gen. William F. Smith

1st Brigade
Brig. Gen. Winfield S. Hancock

5th Wisconsin (Col. Amasa Cobb)
6th Maine (Col. Hiram Burnham)
43rd New York (Col. Francis L. Vinton)
49th Pennsylvania (Col. William H. Irvin)

2nd Brigade
Brig. Gen. William T. H. Brooks

2nd Vermont (Col. Henry Whiting)
3rd Vermont (Col. Breed N. Hyde)
4th Vermont (Col. Edwin H. Stoughton)
5th Vermont (Col. Henry A. Smalley)
6th Vermont (Col. Nathan Lord, Jr.)

3rd Brigade
Brig. Gen. John W. Davidson

7th Maine (Col. James B. McKean)
33rd New York (Col. Robert F. Taylor)
49th New York (Col. Daniel D. Bidwell)
77th New York (Col. James B. McKean)

Artillery
Capt. Romeyn B. Ayres

1st New York Light, Battery E (Capt. Charles C. Wheeler)
1st New York Independent Light (Capt. Andrew Cowan)
3rd New York Independent Light (Capt. Thaddeus P. Mott)
5th U. S., Battery F (Capt. Romeyn B. Ayres)

Cavalry

5th Pennsylvania Cavalry (Co.'s I & K) (Capt. John O'Farrell)

Corps Cavalry

1st New York (Col. Andrew T. McReynolds)

Reserve

Cavalry Reserve
Brig. Gen. Philip St. George Cooke

1st Brigade
Brig. Gen. William H. Emory

5th U. S. Cavalry (Capt. Charles S. Whiting)
6th U. S. Cavalry (Maj. Lawrence Williams)
6th Pennsylvania Cavalry (Col. Richard H. Rush)

2nd Brigade
Col. George A. H. Blake

1st U. S. Cavalry (Lt. Col. William N. Grier)
8th Pennsylvania Cavalry (Col. David McM. Gregg)

Advance Guard
Brig. Gen. George Stoneman

2nd Rhode Island (Col. Frank Wheaton)
98th Pennsylvania (Col. John F. Ballier)
8th Illinois Cavalry (Col. John F. Farnsworth)
2nd U. S., Battery A (Capt. John C. Tidball)
2nd U. S., Battery B & L (Capt. James M. Robertson)

Engineers

U. S. Engineer Battalion
Capt. James C. Duane

Co.'s A, B, C

Volunteer Engineer Brigade
Brig. Gen. Daniel P. Woodbury

15th New York (Col. J. McLeod Murphy)
50th New York (Col. Charles B. Stuart)

White House Command
Lt. Col. Rufus Ingalls

93rd New York (Co.'s B, C, D, E, G & I) (Col. Thomas F. Morris) (Capt. John E. Arthur)
11th Pennsylvania Cavalry (5 Co.'s) (Col. Josiah Harlan)
1st New York Light, Battery F (Capt. William R. Wilson)

General Headquarters

2nd U. S. Cavalry (Maj. Alfred Pleasonton)
4th U. S. Cavalry (2 Co.'s) (Capt. Thomas B. McIntire)
Oneida (New York) Cavalry (Capt. David P. Mann)
McClellan Dragoons (Illinois) (Maj. Granville O. Haller)
8th U. S. Infantry (Co.'s F & G) (Capt. Royal T. Frank)
93rd New York (Co.'s A, F, H & K) (Maj. Granville O. Haller)
Sturgis Rifles (Illinois) (Maj. Granville O. Haller)

Confederate

Army of Northern Virginia (62,696–73,928)
(41,816 engaged)
Gen. Joseph E. Johnston (w on May 31)
Maj. Gen. Gustavus W. Smith (relieved on June 1)
Gen. Robert E. Lee

Left Wing:
Maj. Gen. Gustavus W. Smith

Smith's Division (10,592)
Brig. Gen. William H. C. Whiting (temporary)

Hood's Brigade
Brig. Gen. John B. Hood

18th Georgia (Col. William T. Wofford) (Lt. Col. Solon Z. Ruff)
1st Texas (Col. Alexis T. Rainey)
4th Texas (Col. John Marshall)
5th Texas (Col. James J. Archer)

Hampton's Brigade
Col. Wade Hampton (w on May 31)

14th Georgia (Col. Felix L. Price)
19th Georgia (Lt. Col. Thomas C. Johnson)
16th North Carolina (Col. Champion T. N. Davis)(k on May 31)
Hampton's South Carolina Legion (Lt. Col. Martin W. Gary)
Moody's Madison (Louisiana) Battery (Capt. George V. Moody)

Whiting's Brigade (10,592)
Col. Evander M. Law

4th Alabama (Col. Evander M. Law) (Lt. Col. Owen K. McLemore)
2nd Mississippi (Col. John M. Stone)
11th Mississippi (Col. Philip F. Liddell)
6th North Carolina State Troops (Col. W. Dorsey Pender) (Maj. Isaac E. Avery)
Staunton (Virginia) Battery (Capt. William L. Balthis)
Reilly's Rowan (North Carolina) Battery (Capt. James Reilly)

Pettigrew's Brigade
Brig. Gen. James J. Pettigrew (w, c on May 31)

2nd Arkansas Battalion (Maj. William N. Bronaugh)
35th Georgia (Col. Edward L. Thomas)
22nd North Carolina (Col. Charles E. Lightfoot)(c on May 31)
47th Virginia (Col. Robert M. Mayo)
Andrews's 1st Maryland Battery (Capt. R. Snowden Andrews)(w on May 31) (Lt. William F. Dement)

Hatton's Brigade
Brig. Gen. Robert Hatton (k on May 31)

1st Tennessee (Col. Peter Turney)
7th Tennessee (Col. John F. Goodner)
14th Tennessee (Col. William A. Forbes)
Braxton's Fredericksburg (Virginia) Battery (Capt. Carter M. Braxton)

A. P. Hill's Division (~4,000)
Maj. Gen. Ambrose P. Hill

Field's Brigade
Brig. Gen. Charles W. Field

5th Alabama Battalion (Col. Christopher C. Pegues)
40th Virginia (Col. John M. Brockenbrough)
47th Virginia (Col. Robert M. Mayo)
55th Virginia (Col. Francis Mallory)
2nd Virginia Heavy Artillery (becoming 22nd Virginia Btn.) (Capt. James C. Johnson)
Pegram's Purcell (Virginia) Battery (Capt. William J. Pegram)

Gregg's Brigade
Brig. Gen. Maxcy Gregg

1st South Carolina (Col. Daniel H. Hamilton)
1st South Carolina (Orr's) Rifles (Col. Jehu F. Marshall)
12th South Carolina (Col. Dixon Barnes)(w on June 27)
13th South Carolina (Col. Oliver E. Edwards)
14th South Carolina (Col. Samuel McGowan)

Davidson's Letcher (Virginia) Battery (Capt. Greenlee Davidson)

J. R. Anderson's Brigade
Brig. Gen. Joseph R. Anderson

34th North Carolina (Col. Richard H. Riddick)
38th North Carolina (Col. William J. Hoke)
45th Georgia (Col. Thomas Hardeman, Jr.)
49th Georgia (Col. Andrew J. Lane)(w on May 31)
3rd Louisiana Battalion (Lt. Col. Edmund Pendleton)
McIntosh's Pee Dee (South Carolina) Battery (Capt. David G. McIntosh)
Crenshaw's Virginia Battery (Capt. William G. Crenshaw)

Branch's Brigade
Brig. Gen. Lawrence O'B. Branch

7th North Carolina State Troops (Col. Reuben P. Campbell)
12th North Carolina (Lt. Col. Benjamin O. Wade)
18th North Carolina (Col. Robert H. Cowan)
28th North Carolina (Col. James H. Lane)
33rd North Carolina (Lt. Col. Robert F. Hoke)
37th North Carolina (Col. Charles C. Lee)
Branch's North Carolina Battery (Lt. Col. James R. Branch)
Johnson's Richmond (Virginia) Battery (Capt. Marmaduke Johnson)

Right Wing
Maj. Gen. James Longstreet

Longstreet's Division (13,816)
Brig. Gen. Richard H. Anderson (temporary)

Kemper's Brigade
Col. James L. Kemper

1st Virginia (Lt. Col. Frederick G. Skinner)
7th Virginia (Lt. Col. Walter E. Patton)
11th Virginia (Col. David Funsten)(w on May 31) (Lt. Col. Maurice S. Langhorne)(w on May 31)
17th Virginia (Col. Montgomery D. Corse)
Rogers' Loudoun (Virginia) Battery (Capt. Arthur L. Rogers)

R. H. Anderson's Brigade
Col. Micah Jenkins

5th South Carolina (Col. John R. R. Giles)(k on May 31) (Lt. Col. Andrew Jackson)
6th South Carolina (Col. John Bratton)(w, c on May 31) (Lt. Col. John M. Steedman)(w on May 31)
4th South Carolina Battalion (Maj. Charles S. Mattison)(w on May 31)
Palmetto (South Carolina) Sharpshooters (Lt. Col. Joseph Walker) (Maj. William Anderson)
1st Louisiana Zouave Btn. (Coppens) & St. Paul's Foot Rifles (Lt. Col. Georges A. G. Coppens)
Stribling's Fauquier (Virginia) Battery (Capt. Robert M. Stribling)

Pickett's Brigade (1,700)
Brig. Gen. George E. Pickett

8th Virginia (Lt. Col. Norborne Berkeley)
18th Virginia (Col. Robert E. Withers) (Lt. Col. Henry A. Carrington) (w on June 1)
19th Virginia (Col. John B. Strange)
28th Virginia (Col. William Watts)
Dearing's Lynchburg (Virginia) Battery (Capt. James G. Dearing, Jr.)

Wilcox's Brigade
Brig. Gen. Cadmus M. Wilcox

9th Alabama (Lt. Col. Stephen F. Hale)
10th Alabama (Col. John J. Woodward)
11th Alabama (Col. Sydenham Moore)(mw on May 31)
19th Mississippi (Maj. John Mullins)
Stanard's Richmond Howitzers, 3rd Co. (Capt. Robert C. Stanard)

Colston's Brigade
Brig. Gen. Raleigh E. Colston

3rd Virginia (Col. Joseph M. Mayo, Jr.)
13th North Carolina (Col. Alfred M. Scales)
14th North Carolina (Col. Philetus W. Roberts)

Pryor's Brigade
Brig. Gen. Roger A. Pryor

8th Alabama (Col. John A. Winston)
14th Alabama (Col. Thomas J. Judge)
14th Louisiana (Col. Zebulon York)
32nd Virginia (Lt. Col. William R. Willis)
Macon's Richmond Fayette (Virginia) Battery (Lt. William I. Clopton)

Artillery

Maurin's Donaldsonville (Louisiana) Battery (Capt. Victor Maurin)
Brown's Richmond Howitzers, 2nd Co. (Capt. David Watson)

D. H. Hill's Division (11,151)
Maj. Gen. Daniel H. Hill

Rodes's Brigade (3rd Bde.) (2,200)
Brig. Gen. Robert E. Rodes (w on May 31)
Col. John B. Gordon

5th Alabama (Col. Christopher C. Pegues)
6th Alabama (632) (Col. John B. Gordon)
12th Alabama (408) (Col. Robert T. Jones)(k on May 31) (Lt. Col. Bristor B. Gayle)
12th Mississippi (Col. William H. Taylor)
4th Virginia Heavy Artillery Btn. (as infantry) (Capt. Charles C. Otey)(k on May 31) (Capt. John R. Bagby)
Carter's King William (Virginia) Battery (Capt. Thomas H. Carter)

Featherston's Brigade (1,865)
Col. George B. Anderson

27th Georgia (Col. Levi B. Smith)(w on May 31) (Lt. Col. Charles T. Zachry)
28th Georgia (Lt. Col. James G. Cain)(w on July 1) (Capt. John N. Wilcox)
4th North Carolina (Maj. Bryan Grimes)
49th Virginia (Col. William Smith)(w on May 31)

Garland's (Early's) Brigade (2,065)
Brig. Gen. Samuel Garland, Jr.

5th North Carolina State Troops (Col. Duncan K. McRae)(s on May 31) (Lt. Col. Peter J. Sinclair)
23rd North Carolina (Col. Daniel H. Christie)(w on May 31) (Lt. Col. Robert D. Johnston)(w on May 31) (Maj. Edmund J. Christian)(mw on May 31)
24th Virginia (Maj. Richard L. Maury)(w on May 31) (Capt. William F. Gardner)
38th Virginia (Col. Edward C. Edmonds)(w on May 31) (Lt. Col. Powhatan B. Whittle)(Col. Edward C. Edwards)
2nd Florida (Col. Edward A. Perry)
2nd Mississippi Battalion (~300) (Lt. Col. John G. Taylor)
Bondurant's Jeff Davis (Alabama) Battery (Capt. James W. Bondurant)

Rains's Brigade (2,870)
Brig. Gen. Gabriel J. Rains

13th Alabama (Col. Birkett D. Fry)(w on May 31) (Lt. Col. Reginald H. Dawson)(w on May 31)
26th Alabama (Col. Edward A. O'Neal)(w on May 31)
6th Georgia (Col. Alfred H. Colquitt)
23rd Georgia (Lt. Col. William P. Barclay)
Nelson's Hanover (Virginia) Battery (Capt. George Washington Nelson)

Wise's Brigade (attached)
Brig. Gen. Henry A. Wise

4th Virginia (Col. Charles A. Ronald)
26th Virginia (Col. Powhatan R. Page)
46th Virginia (Col. Richard T. W. Duke)
Armistead's Mathews (Virginia) Battery (Capt. Andrew D. Armistead)
French's Giles (Virginia) Battery (Capt. David A. French)

Artillery

Hardaway's Alabama Battery (Capt. Robert A. Hardaway)
Rhett's Brooks (South Carolina) Battery (Capt. A. Burnet Rhett)

Huger's Division (5,008)
Maj. Gen. Benjamin Huger

Mahone's Brigade
Brig. Gen. William Mahone

3rd Alabama (Col. Tennant Lomax)(k on June 1) (Col. Cullen A. Battle)
12th Virginia (Lt. Col. Fielding L. Taylor)
41st Virginia (Col. John R. Chambliss, Jr.)
Grimes's Portsmouth (Virginia) Battery (Capt. Cary F. Grimes)

Blanchard's Brigade
Brig. Gen. Albert G. Blanchard

3rd Georgia (Col. Ambrose R. Wright)
4th Georgia (Col. George P. Doles)
22nd Georgia (Col. Robert H. Jones)
1st Louisiana (Lt. Col. William R. Shivers)
Huger's Norfolk (Virginia) Battery (Capt. Frank Huger)

Armistead's Brigade
Brig. Gen. Lewis A. Armistead

9th Virginia (Col. David J. Godwin)(w on May 31)
14th Virginia (Col. James G. Hodges)
53rd Virginia (Col. Harrison B. Tomlin)
5th Virginia Battalion (Lt. Col. Fletcher H. Archer)
Turner's Goochland (Virginia) Battery (Capt. William H. Turner)

Artillery

Maurin's Donaldsonville (Louisiana) Battery (Capt. Victor Maurin)
Watson's Virginia Battery (Capt. David Watson)

Reserve (15,920)
Maj. Gen. John B. Magruder

McLaws's Division
Brig. Gen. Lafayette McLaws

Semmes's Brigade (not engaged)
Brig. Gen. Paul J. Semmes

5th Louisiana (Col. Theodore G. Hunt)
10th Louisiana (Lt. Col. Eugene Waggaman)
10th Georgia (Col. Alfred Cumming)
15th Virginia (Col. Thomas P. August)
Noland's Virginia Battalion (Lt. Col. Callender St. George Noland)
Garrett's Williamsburg (Virginia) Battery (Capt. William R. Garrett)
Young's Halifax (Virginia) Battery (Capt. E. R. Young)

Griffith's Brigade (not engaged)
Brig. Gen. Richard Griffith

13th Mississippi (Col. William Barksdale)
18th Mississippi (Col. Thomas M. Griffin)
21st Mississippi (Col. Benjamin G. Humphreys)
McCarthy's Richmond Howitzers, 1st Co. (Capt. Edward S. McCarthy)

Kershaw's Brigade
Brig. Gen. Joseph B. Kershaw

2nd South Carolina (Col. John D. Kennedy)
3rd South Carolina (Col. James D. Nance)
7th South Carolina (Col. D. Wyatt Aiken)
8th South Carolina (Col. John W. Henagan)
Gracie's Alabama Battalion (Maj. Archibald Gracie, Jr.)
Kemper's Alexandria (Virginia) Battery (Capt. Del Kemper)

Cobb's Brigade
Brig. Gen. Howell Cobb

16th Georgia (Col. Goode Bryan)
24th Georgia (Col. Robert McMillan)
Cobb's Georgia Legion (Col. Thomas R. R. Cobb)
2nd Louisiana (Col. Isaiah T. Norwood)
17th Mississippi (Col. William D. Holder)
15th North Carolina (Col. Henry A. Dowd)
Page's Morris Louisa (Virginia) Battery (Capt. Richard C. M. Page)

D. R. Jones's Division
Brig. Gen. David R. Jones

Toombs's Brigade
Brig. Gen. Robert A. Toombs

1st Georgia Regulars (Col. William J. Magill)
2nd Georgia (271) (Col. Edgar M. Butt)
15th Georgia (441) (Col. William M. McIntosh)
17th Georgia (398) (Col. Henry L. Benning)
20th Georgia (560) (Col. John B. Cumming)
38th Georgia (Col. William H. Battey)

G. T. Anderson's Brigade
Col. George T. Anderson

7th Georgia (611) (Lt. Col. William H. White)
8th Georgia (Col. Lucius M. Lamar)
9th Georgia (411) (Col. Richard A. Turnipseed)
11th Georgia (573) (Lt. Col. William Luffman)
1st Kentucky (496) (Col. Thomas H. Taylor)

Artillery
Col. Henry C. Cabell

Cosnahan's Peninsula (Virginia) Battery (Capt. Joseph B. Cosnahan)
Manly's North Carolina Battery (Capt. Basil C. Manly)
Read's Pulaski (Georgia) Battery (Capt. John P. W. Read)
Sand's Henrico (Virginia) Battery (Capt. Johnson H. Sands)

Cavalry Brigade
Brig. Gen. J. E. B. Stuart

1st Virginia Cavalry (Col. Fitzhugh Lee)
3rd Virginia Cavalry(Col. Thomas F. Goode)
4th Virginia Cavalry(Col. Beverly H. Robertson) (Lt. Col. William T. Martin) (absent)
9th Virginia Cavalry (Col. W. H. F. Lee) (absent)
Cobb's (Georgia) Legion Cavalry (Col. Pierce M. B. Young)
Jeff Davis (Mississippi) Legion Cavalry (Lt. Col. William T. Martin)
Hampton's (South Carolina) Legion Cavalry (Maj. Matthew C. Butler)

Wise's (Virginia) Legion Cavalry (Col. J. Lucius Davies)
Stuart Horse Artillery (Capt. John Pelham)

Artillery Reserve
Brig. Gen. William N. Pendleton

Pendleton's Corps

Southall's Albemarle (Virginia) Battery (Capt. William H. Southall)
Carlton's Troup (Georgia) Battery (Capt. Henry H. Carlton)
Richardson's James City (Virginia) Battery (Capt. Lucien W. Richardson)
C. L. Smith's Hampton (Virginia) Battery (Capt. Charles L. Smith)
Page's Magruder (Virginia) Battery (Capt. Thomas J. Page, Jr.)
Jordan's Bedford (Virginia) Battery (Capt. Tyler C. Jordan)
Clark's Long Island (Virginia) Battery (Capt. Patrick H. Clark)
Peyton's Orange (Virginia) Battery (Capt. Thomas J. Peyton)
Kirkpatrick's Amherst (Virginia) Battery (Capt. Thomas J. Kirkpatrick)

Walton's Corps
Col. James B. Walton

Washington (Louisiana) Artillery, 1st Co. (Capt. Charles W. Squires)
Washington (Louisiana) Artillery, 2nd Co. (Capt. John B. Richardson)
Washington (Louisiana) Artillery,, 3rd Co. (Capt. M. B. Miller)
Washington (Louisiana) Artillery, 4th Co. (Capt. Joseph Norcom)
Chapman's Dixie (Virginia) Battery (Capt. Edmund G. Chapman)

At the Seven Days (June 25–July 1)

Federal

Army of the Potomac (105,300)
Maj. Gen. George B. McClellan

II Corps (17,300)
Brig. Gen. Edwin V. Sumner

1st Division (8,100)
Brig. Gen. Israel Richardson

1st Brigade
Brig. Gen. John C. Caldwell

5th New Hampshire (Lt. Col. Samuel G. Langley) (Capt. Edward E. Sturtevant)
7th New York (Col. George W. Von Schack)
61st New York (Col. Francis C. Barlow)
81st Pennsylvania (Col. Charles F. Johnson)(w on June 30) Lt. Col. Eli T. Connor)(k on July 1) (Maj. H. Boyd McKeen)

2nd Brigade (Irish Brigade)
Brig. Gen. Thomas F. Meagher
Col. Robert Nugent
Brig. Gen. Thomas F. Meagher

63rd New York (Col. John W. Burke)(w on July 1) (Lt. Col. Henry Fowler)(a on July 1) (Capt. Joseph O'Neill)
69th New York (Col. Robert Nugent)
88th New York (Col. Henry M. Baker) (Maj. James Quinlan)
29th Massachusetts (Col. Ebenezer W. Pierce)(w on June 30) Lt. Col. Joseph H. Barnes)

3rd Brigade
Brig. Gen. William H. French

52nd New York (Col. Paul Frank)
57th New York (Col. Samuel K. Zook)
64th New York (Col. Thomas J. Parker)
66th New York (Col. Joseph C. Pinckney)
53rd Pennsylvania (Col. John R. Brooke)
2nd Delaware (Lt. Col. William P. Bailey) (Capt. David L. Stricker)

Artillery
Capt. George W. Hazzard (mw on June 30)

1st New York Light, Battery B (Capt. Rufus D. Pettit)
4th U. S., Batteries A & C (Capt. George W. Hazzard) (Lt. Rufus King, Jr.)

2nd Division (8,700)
Brig. Gen. John Sedgwick

1st Brigade
Col. Alfred Sully
Col. James A. Suiter

15th Massachusetts (Col. John W. Kimball) plus 1st Co. Mass. Sharpshooters) (Capt. John Saunders)
1st Minnesota (Lt. Col. Stephen Miller) (plus 2nd Co. Minn. Sharpshooters) (Capt. William F. Russell)
34th New York (Col. James A. Suiter)
82nd New York (Col. Henry W. Hudson)

2nd Brigade
Brig. Gen. William W. Burns (w on June 29)

69th Pennsylvania (Col. Joshua T. Owen)
71st Pennsylvania (Lt. Col. William G. Jones)
72nd Pennsylvania (Col. DeWitt C. Baxter)
106th Pennsylvania (Col. Turner G. Morehead)

3rd Brigade
Brig. Gen. N. J. T. Dana (s)
Col. William R. Lee
Col. James A. Suiter

19th Massachusetts (Col. Edward W. Hinks)(w on June 30) (Capt. Edmund Rice) (Lt. Col. Arthur F. Devereux)
20th Massachusetts (Col. William R. Lee)
7th Michigan (Col. Ira R. Grosvenor)
42nd New York (Col. Edmund C. Charles)(mw, c on June 30) (Lt. Col. James J. Mooney)

Artillery
Col. Charles H. Tompkins

1st Rhode Island Light, Battery A (Capt John A. Tompkins)
1st U. S., Battery I (Lt. Edmund Kirby)

Corps Artillery Reserve (400)

1st New York Light, Battery G (Capt. John D. Frank)
1st Rhode Island Light, Battery B (Capt. Walter O. Bartlett)

1st Rhode Island Light, Battery G (Capt. Charles D. Owen)

Corps Cavalry

6th New York (Co.'s D, F, H & K) (Lt. Col. Duncan McVicar)

III Corps (18,900)
Brig. Gen. Samuel P. Heintzelman

2nd Division (9,400)
Brig. Gen. Joseph Hooker

1st Brigade
Brig. Gen. Cuvier Grover

1st Massachusetts (Col. Robert Cowdin)
2nd New Hampshire (Col. Gilman Marston)
11th Massachusetts (Col. William E. Blaisdell) (Lt. Col. George F. Tileston)
16th Massachusetts (Col. Powell T. Wyman)(k on June 30) (Lt. Col. George A. Meacham)(w on June 30) (Maj. Daniel S. Lamson)
26th Pennsylvania (Lt. Col. George D. Wells)

2nd Brigade
Brig. Gen. Daniel E. Sickles

70th New York (Maj. Thomas Holt)
71st New York (Col. George B. Hall)
72nd New York (Col. Nelson Taylor)
73rd New York (Capt. Alfred A. Donalds)
74th New York (Col. Charles K. Graham)

3rd Brigade
Col. Joseph B. Carr

5th New Jersey (Maj. John Ramsey)
6th New Jersey (Col. Gershom Mott)
7th New Jersey (Col. Joseph W. Revere) (Capt. Henry C. Bartlett)
8th New Jersey (Maj. William A. Henry) (Capt. William S. Tipson)
2nd New York (Lt. Col. William A. Olmsted)

Artillery
Lt. Col. Charles S. Wainwright

1st New York Light, Battery D (Capt. Thomas W. Osborn)
1st U. S., Battery H (Capt. Charles H. Webber)
4th New York Independent Light (Lt. Joseph E. Nairn)

3rd Division (8,300)
Brig. Gen. Philip Kearny

1st Brigade
Brig. Gen. John C. Robinson

20th Indiana (Col. William L. Brown)
87th New York (Lt. Col. Richard A. Bachia)
57th Pennsylvania (Lt. Col. Elhanon W. Woods)
63rd Pennsylvania (Col. Alexander Hays)
105th Pennsylvania (Col. Amor A. McKnight)(Lt. Col. William W. Corbet)(s on May 30) (Capt. Calvin A. Craig)

2nd Brigade
Brig. Gen. David B. Birney

3rd Maine (Lt. Col. Charles A. L. Sampson)(a on June 26) (Maj. Edwin Burt)
4th Maine (Col. Elijah Walker)
38th New York (Col. J. H. H. Ward)
40th New York (Lt. Col. Thomas W. Egan)
101st New York (Col. Enrico Fardella)

3rd Brigade
Brig. Gen. Hiram G. Berry

2nd Michigan (Maj. Louis Dillman)(s) (Capt. William Humphrey)
3rd Michigan (Lt. Col. Ambrose A. Stevens) (Maj. Byron R. Pierce)
5th Michigan (Maj. John D. Fairbanks)(mw on June 30) (Capt. Judson S. Farrar)
1st New York (Col. Garrett Dyckman)
37th New York (Col. Samuel B. Hayman)

Artillery
Captain James Thompson

1st Rhode Island Light, Battery E (Capt. George E. Randolph)
2nd U. S., Battery G (Capt. James Thompson)

Corps Cavalry
Col. William W. Averell

3rd Pennsylvania Cavalry (Col. William Averell)

Corps Artillery Reserve (400)
Capt. Gustavus A. De Russy

New Jersey Light, Battery B (Capt. John E. Beam)(k on July 1) (Lt. John B. Monroe)
6th New York Independent Light (Capt. Walter M. Bramhall)
4th U. S., Battery K (Lt. Francis W. Seeley)

IV Corps (14,700)
Brig. Gen. Erasmus Keyes

1st Division (8,300)
Brig. Gen. Darius N. Couch

1st Brigade
Brig. Gen. Albion P. Howe

55th New York (Lt. Col. Louis Thourot)
62nd New York (Col. David J. Nevin)
93rd Pennsylvania (Capt. John E. Arthur) (Capt. John S. Long)
98th Pennsylvania (Col. John F. Ballier)
102nd Pennsylvania (Lt. Col. Joseph M. Kinkead)

2nd Brigade
Brig. Gen. John J. Abercrombie

65th New York (1st New York Chasseurs) (Col. John Cochrane) (Lt. Col. Alexander Shaler)
67th New York (1st Long Island) (Lt. Col. Nelson Cross)
23rd Pennsylvania (Col. Thomas H. Neill)

31st Pennsylvania (Col. David H. Williams)
61st Pennsylvania (Capt. Robert L. Orr) (Lt. Col. Frank Vallee)

3rd Brigade
Brig. Gen. Innis N. Palmer

7th Massachusetts (Col. David A. Russell)
10th Massachusetts (Maj. Ozro Miller)(w, c on July 1) (Capt. Frederick Barton)
2nd Rhode Island (Col. Frank Wheaton)
36th New York (Maj. James A. Raney)

Artillery
Maj. Robert M. West

1st Pennsylvania Light, Battery C (Capt Jeremiah McCarthy) (Lt. William Munk)
1st Pennsylvania Light, Battery D (Capt. Edward H. Flood)

Cavalry

6th New York Cavalry, Co. F (Capt. Dudley C. Hannahs)

2nd Division (5,300)
Brig. Gen. John J. Peck

1st Brigade
Brig. Gen. Henry M. Naglee

11th Maine (Col. Harris M. Plaistead)
56th New York (Col. Charles H. Van Wyck)
100th New York (Lt. Col. Phineas Staunton)
52nd Pennsylvania (Lt. Col. Henry M. Hoyt)
104th Pennsylvania (Lt. Col. John W. Nields)

2nd Brigade
Brig. Gen. Henry W. Wessells

81st New York (Col. Edwin Rose)
85th New York (Col. Jonathan S. Belknap)
92nd New York (Lt. Col. Hiram Anderson, Jr.)

96th New York (Col. James Fairman)
98th New York (Lt. Col. Charles Durkee)
85th Pennsylvania (Col. Joshua B. Howell)
101st Pennsylvania (Capt. Charles W. May)
103rd Pennsylvania (Col. Theodore F. Lehmann)

Artillery

1st New York Light, Battery H (Lt. Charles E. Mink)
7th New York Independent Light (Capt. Peter C. Regan)

Cavalry

6th New York Cavalry, Co. H (Capt. William P. Hall)

Corps Cavalry
Col. David McM. Gregg

8th Pennsylvania Cavalry (Col. David McM. Gregg)

Corps Artillery Reserve (400)
Maj. Robert M. West

1st Pennsylvania Light, Battery E (Capt. Theodore Miller)
1st Pennsylvania Light, Battery H (Capt. James Brady)
8th New York Independent Light (Capt. Butler Fitch)
5th U. S., Battery M (Capt. James McKnight) (Lt. Valentine H. Stone)

V Corps (30,300)
Brig. Gen. Fitz John Porter

1st Division (12,000)
Brig. Gen. George W. Morell

1st Brigade
Brig. Gen. John H. Martindale

2nd Maine (Col. Charles W. Roberts)
1st Michigan (Col. Horace S. Roberts)
13th New York (Col. Elisha G. Marshall) (Maj. Francis A. Schoeffel)

25th New York (Maj. Edwin S. Gilbert) (c on June 27) (Capt. Shepard Gleason)
18th Massachusetts (detached) (Col. James Barnes)
22nd Massachusetts (Col. Jesse A. Gove)(k on June 27) (Maj. William S. Tilton)(w, c on June 27) (Capt. Walter S. Sampson) (Capt. David K. Wardwell) (plus 2nd Co., Mass. Sharpshooters) (Lt. Charles D. Stiles)

2nd Brigade
Brig. Gen. Charles Griffin

14th New York (Col. James McQuade)
4th Michigan (Col. Dwight A. Woodbury)(k on July 1) (Lt. Col. Jonathan W. Childs)(w on July 1) (Capt. John M. Randolph)
9th Massachusetts (Col. Thomas Cass)(mw on July 1) (Lt. Col. Patrick R. Guiney)
62nd Pennsylvania (Col. Samuel W. Black)(k on May 27) (Lt. Col. Jacob B. Sweitzer)(w, c on July 1) (Capt. James Hull)

3rd Brigade
Brig. Gen. Daniel Butterfield

16th Michigan (Col. Thomas B. W. Stockton)(c on July 1) (Lt. Col. John V. Ruehle) (Brady's Co. Michigan Sharpshooters, attached) (Capt. Kiniston S. Dygert)
12th New York (Lt. Col. Robert M. Richardson) (Lt. Col. James C. Rice)
17th New York (detached) (Col. Henry S. Lansing)
44th New York (Col. Stephen W. Stryker) (Lt. Col. James C. Rice)
83rd Pennsylvania (Col. John W. McLane)(k on June 27) (Lt. Col. Hugh S. Campbell)(w on July 1)

Artillery
Capt. William B. Weeden

Massachusetts Light, Battery C (Capt. Augustus P. Martin)
Massachusetts Light, Battery E (Lt. John B. Hyde)
1st Rhode Island Light, Battery C (Capt. William B. Weeden) (Lt. Richard Waterman)
5th U. S., Battery D (Lt. Henry W. Kingsbury)

Sharpshooters

1st U. S. Sharpshooters (Col. Hiram Berdan)
44th New York (Lt. Col. James C. Rice)
83rd Pennsylvania (Lt. Col. Hugh S. Campbell)

2nd Division (6,000)
Brig. Gen. George Sykes

1st Brigade
Col. Robert C. Buchanan

3rd U. S. (Maj. Nathan Rossell)(k on June 27) (Capt. Thomas W. Walker) (Capt. John D. Wilkins)(s on June 27) (Maj. Thomas Hendrickson) (assumed command on June 27)
4th U. S. (Maj. Delozier Davidson)(deserted on June 26)(c on June 27) (Capt. Joseph B. Collins)
12th U. S. (Maj. Henry B. Clitz)(w & c on June 27) (Capt. John G. Read) (Capt. Matthew M. Blunt)(w on June 27)
14th U. S. (Capt. John D. O'Connell)

2nd Brigade
Lt. Col. William Chapman (s on June 27)
Maj. Charles S. Lovell

2nd U. S. (Capt. Adolphus F. Bond) (Lt. John S. Poland)
6th U. S. (Capt. Thomas Hendrickson)(w on June 27)
10th U. S. (Co.'s B, E, G & I) (Maj. Charles S. Lovell) (Maj. George L. Andrews)
11th U. S. (Maj. De Lancey Floyd-Jones)
17th U. S. (Co.'s A, C & E) (Maj. George L. Andrews)

3rd Brigade
Col. Gouverneur K. Warren

5th New York (Duryea Zouaves) (Lt. Col Hiram Duryea)
10th New York (Col. John E. Bendix)

Artillery
Capt. Stephen H. Weed

3rd U. S., Batteries L & M (Capt. John Edwards)
5th U. S., Battery I (Capt. Stephen H. Weed)

3rd Division (Pennsylvania Reserves)(9,500)
Brig. Gen. George A. McCall (c on June 30)
Brig. Gen. Truman Seymour

1st Brigade
Brig. Gen. John F. Reynolds (c on June 28)
Col. Seneca G. Simmons (k on June 27)
Col. R. Biddle Roberts

1st Pennsylvania Reserves (Col. R. Biddle Roberts) (Maj. Lemuel Todd)
2nd Pennsylvania Reserves (Lt. Col. William McCandless)
5th Pennsylvania Reserves (Col. Seneca G. Simmons) (Col. John H. Taggart) (Lt. Col. Joseph W. Fisher)
8th Pennsylvania Reserves (Col. George S. Hays) (w on June 30)
13th Pennsylvania Reserves (1st Penn. Rifles) (Co.'s A, B, D, E, F and K) (Maj. Roy Stone)

2nd Brigade
Brig. Gen. George G. Meade (w on June 30)
Col. Albert L. Magilton

3rd Pennsylvania Reserves (Col. Horatio G. Sickel)
4th Pennsylvania Reserves (Col. Albert L. Magilton)
7th Pennsylvania Reserves (Col. Elisha B. Harvey)
11th Pennsylvania Reserves (Col. Thomas F. Gallagher)(c on June 27) (Capt. Daniel S. Porter)

3rd Brigade
Brig. Gen. Truman Seymour
Col. C. Feger Jackson

6th Pennsylvania Reserves (detached) (Col. William Sinclair)
9th Pennsylvania Reserves (Col. C. Feger Jackson) (Capt. John Cuthbertson)(w on June 30)
10th Pennsylvania Reserves (Col. James T. Kirk)
12th Pennsylvania Reserves (Col. John H. Taggart)

Artillery

1st Pennsylvania Light, Battery A (Capt. Hezekiah Easton)(k on June 27) (1/Lt. William Stitt)(w on June 27) (2/Lt. Jacob L. Detrich) (Lt. John G. Simpson)
1st Pennsylvania Light, Battery B (Capt. James H. Cooper)
1st Pennsylvania Light, Battery G (Capt. Mark Kerns)(w on June 27) (Lt. Frank P. Amsden)
5th U. S., Battery C (Capt. Henry V. DeHart)(mw on June 27) (Lt. Eben G. Scott)

Cavalry
Col. James H. Childs

4th Pennsylvania Cavalry (Col. James H. Childs)

Corps Cavalry Reserve
Col. John F. Farnsworth

8th Illinois Cavalry (Col. John F. Farnsworth)

Corps Artillery Reserve (2,100)
Col. Henry J. Hunt

1st Brigade (Horse Artillery)
Lt. Col. William Hays

2nd U. S., Battery A (Capt. John C. Tidball)
2nd U. S., Battery B & L (Capt. James M. Robertson)
2nd U. S., Battery M (Capt. Henry Benson)
3rd U. S., Batteries C & G (detached) (Capt. Horatio G. Gibson)

2nd Brigade
Lt. Col. George W. Getty

1st U. S., Battery E and G (Lt. Alanson M. Randol)
1st U. S., Battery K (Lt. Samuel S. Elder)
4th U. S., Battery G (Lt. Charles H. Morgan)
5th U. S., Battery A (Lt. Adelbert Ames)
5th U. S., Battery K (Capt. John R. Smead)

3rd Brigade
Maj. Albert Arndt

1st Btn. New York Light, Battery A (Capt. Otto Diederich)
1st Btn. New York Light, Battery B (Capt. Adolph Voegelee)
1st Btn. New York Light, Battery C (Capt. John Knieriem)
1st Btn. New York Light, Battery D (Capt. Edward D. Grimm)

4th Brigade
Maj. Edward R. Petherbridge

Maryland Light, Battery A (Capt. John W. Wolcott)
Maryland Light, Battery B (Capt. Alonzo Snow)

5th Brigade
Capt. J. Howard Carlisle

2nd U. S., Battery E (Capt. J. Howard Carlisle)
3rd U. S., Battery F & K (Capt. La Rhett L. Livingston)

Siege Train
Col. Robert O. Tyler

1st Connecticut Heavy Artillery (Col. Robert O. Tyler)

VI Corps (19,300)
Brig. Gen. William B. Franklin

1st Division (9,200)
Brig. Gen. Henry W. Slocum

1st Brigade
Brig. Gen. George W. Taylor

1st New Jersey (Col. Alfred T. A. Torbert)(s on June 27) (Lt. Col. Robert McAllister)
2nd New Jersey (Col. Isaac M. Tucker)(k on June 27)
Maj. Henry O. Ryerson) (k on June 27) (Lt. Col. Samuel L. Buck)
3rd New Jersey (Col. Henry W. Brown)
4th New Jersey (Col. James H. Simpson)(c on June 27)

2nd Brigade
Col. Joseph J. Bartlett

16th New York (Col. Joseph Howland)(w on June 27) (Lt. Col. Samuel Marsh) (mw on June 27) (Maj. Joel J. Seaver)
27th New York (Col. Joseph J. Bartlett) (Lt. Col. Alexander D. Adams)
5th Maine (Col. Nathaniel J. Jackson)(w on June 27) (Lt. Col. William S. Heath)(k on June 27) (Lt. Col. Jacob G. Frick) (Capt. Clark S. Edwards)
96th Pennsylvania (Col. Henry L. Cake) (Lt. Col. Jacob G. Frick)

3rd Brigade
Brig. Gen. John Newton

18th New York (Lt. Col. George R. Myers)(s on June 27, after the battle) (Major John C. Meginnis)
31st New York (Col. Calvin E. Pratt)(w on June 27) (Maj. Alexander Raszewski)
32nd New York (Col. C. Roderick Matheson)
95th Pennsylvania (Col. John M. Gosline)(mw on June 27) (Lt. Col. William B. Hubbs)(mw on June 27) (Lt. Col. Gustavus W. Town)

Artillery
Capt. Edward R. Platt

Massachusetts Light, Battery A (Capt. Josiah Porter)
2nd U. S., Battery D (Lt. Emory Upton)
1st New Jersey Light (Capt. William Hexamer)

2nd Division (9,300)
Brig. Gen. William F. Smith

1st Brigade
Brig. Gen. Winfield S. Hancock

5th Wisconsin (Col. Amasa Cobb)
6th Maine (Col. Hiram Burnham)
43rd New York (Col. Francis L. Vinton)
49th Pennsylvania (Col. William H. Irwin)(s) (Maj. Thomas M. Hulings)

2nd Brigade

Brig. Gen. William T. H. Brooks (w on June 29)

2nd Vermont (Col. Henry Whiting)
3rd Vermont (Lt. Col. Wheelock G. Veazey)
4th Vermont (Col. Edwin H. Stoughton)
5th Vermont (Lt. Col. Lewis A. Grant)
6th Vermont (Col. Nathan Lord, Jr.)

3rd Brigade
Brig. Gen. John W. Davidson (s on June 29)
Col. Robert F. Taylor

7th Maine (Col. Edwin C. Mason)
20th New York (Col. Francis Weiss)
33rd New York (Col. Robert F. Taylor)
49th New York (Col. Daniel D. Bidwell)
77th New York (Col. James B. McKean)

Artillery
Capt. Romeyn B. Ayres

1st New York Light, Battery E (Capt. Charles C. Wheeler)
1st New York Independent Light (Lt. Andrew Cowan)
3rd New York Independent Light (Capt. Thaddeus P. Mott)
5th U. S., Battery F (Capt. Romeyn B. Ayres)

Cavalry

5th Pennsylvania Cavalry (Co.'s I & K) (Capt. John O'Farrell)

Corps Cavalry

1st New York Cavalry (Col. Andrew T. McReynolds)

Army Reserve

Cavalry Reserve (2,100)
Brig. Gen. Philip St. George Cooke

1st Brigade
Brig. Gen. William H. Emory

5th U.S. (Co.'s A, D, F, H & I) (Capt. Charles J. Whiting) (c on June 27)
(Capt. Joseph H. McArthur)
6th Pennsylvania Cavalry (Col. Richard H. Rush)

2nd Brigade
Col. George A. H. Blake

1st U. S. Cavalry (Co.'s A, C, F & H) (Lt. Col. William N. Grier)
4th Pennsylvania Cavalry (2 Co.'s) (Col. James H. Childs)

Advance Guard
Brig. Gen. George Stoneman

17th New York (Col. Henry S. Lansing) (Lt. Col. Nelson Bartram)
18th Massachusetts (Col. James Barnes)
5th U. S. Cavalry (Co.'s B, C, F, G & J) (Capt. Joseph H. McArthur)
6th U. S. Cavalry (detail) (Lt. Stephen S. Balk)
3rd U. S. Artillery, Batteries C, D, E, F & G

Engineers (1,500)

U. S. Engineer Battalion
Capt. James C. Duane

Companies A, B, C

Volunteer Engineer Brigade
Brig. Gen. Daniel P. Woodbury

15th New York (Col. J. McLeod Murphy)
50th New York (Col. Charles B. Stuart)

White House Command
Brig. Gen. Silas Casey

6th Pennsylvania Reserves (5 Co.'s) (Lt. Col. Henry B. McKean)
93rd New York (Co.'s B, C, D, E, G & I) (Col. Thomas F. Morris)
4th Pennsylvania Cavalry (2 Co.'s) (Col. James H. Childs)
11th Pennsylvania Cavalry (Co.'s B, D, F, I & K)(Col. Josiah Harlan)
1st New York Light, Battery F (Capt. William R. Wilson)

General Headquarters (1,300)

2nd U. S. Cavalry (7 Co.'s) (Maj. Alfred Pleasonton)
4th U. S. Cavalry (Co.'s A & E) (Capt. James B. McIntire)
Oneida (New York) Cavalry (Capt. James B. McIntyre)
McClellan Dragoons (2 Co.'s) (Illinois) (Maj. Alfred Pleasonton)
8th U. S. Infantry (Co.'s F & G) (Capt. Royal T. Frank) (Lt. Eugene Carter)
93rd New York Infantry (Co.'s A, F, H & K) (Maj. Granville O. Haller)
Sturges Rifles (Illinois) (Maj. Granville O. Haller)

Confederate

Army of Northern Virginia (88,500)
Gen. Robert E. Lee

Jackson's Command (28,400)
Maj. Gen. Thomas J. Jackson

Jackson's Division (7,000)
Brig. Gen. Charles S. Winder

Winder's Brigade (Stonewall Brigade) (1,400)
Brig. Gen. Charles S. Winder

2nd Virginia (Col. James W. Allen)(k on June 27) (Lt. Col. Lawson Botts)
4th Virginia (Col. Charles A. Ronald)
5th Virginia (Col. William S. H. Baylor)
27th Virginia (Col. Andrew J. Grigsby)(w on July 1) (Capt. G. C. Smith)
33rd Virginia (Col. John F. Neff)(w on July 1)
Carpenter's Alleghany (Virginia) Battery (Lt. John C. Carpenter)
Poague's 1st Rockbridge (Virginia) Battery (Capt. William T. Poague)

J. R. Jones's Brigade (1,100)
Lt. Col. Richard H. Cunningham, Jr.
Brig. Gen. John R. Jones (s on June 27, w on July 1)
Lt. Col. Richard H. Cunningham, Jr.

21st Virginia (Capt. William P. Moseley) (Lt. Col. Richard H. Cunningham, Jr.) (Capt. William P. Moseley)
42nd Virginia (Lt. Col. William Martin) (Maj. Henry Lane)
48th Virginia (Capt. John M. Vermillion)
1st Virginia (Irish) Battalion (Capt. B. Watkins Leigh)
Caskie's Hampden (Virginia) Battery (Capt. William H. Caskie)
Cutshaw's Jackson (Virginia) Battery (Capt. Wilford E. Cutshaw)

Fulkerson's Brigade (1,000)
Col. Samuel V. Fulkerson (mw on June 27)
Col. Edward T. H. Warren
Brig. Gen. Wade Hampton

10th Virginia (Col. Edward T. H. Warren)
23rd Virginia (Col. Andrew V. Scott)
37th Virginia (Maj. Titus V. Williams)
Wooding's Danville (Virginia) Battery (Capt. George W. Wooding)

Lawton's Brigade (3,500)
Brig. Gen. Alexander R. Lawton

13th Georgia (Col. Marcellus Douglas)
26th Georgia (Col. Edmund N. Atkinson) (Maj. E. S. Griffin)
31st Georgia (Col. Clement A. Evans)(w on June 27) (Maj. J. H. Lowe)
38th Georgia (Lt. Col. Lewis J. Parr)(w on June 27) (Capt. Edward P. Lawton) (Capt. William H. Battey)
60th Georgia (or 4th Georgia Battalion)
(Lt. Col. William H. Stiles) (Maj. Thomas J. Berry)
61st Georgia (Col. John H. Lamar)

Cavalry (400)

2nd Virginia (Col. Thomas T. Munford)

Ewell's Division (6,800)
Maj. Gen. Richard S. Ewell

Elzey's Brigade (4th Bde.)(2,000)
Brig. Gen. Arnold Elzey (w on June 27)
Col. James A. Walker
Brig. Gen. Jubal A. Early

12th Georgia (Capt. James G. Rodgers)
13th Virginia (Col. James A. Walker) (Lt. Col. James B. Terrill) (Col. James A. Walker)
25th Virginia (Lt. Col. John C. Higginbotham)
31st Virginia (Col. John S. Hoffman)
44th Virginia (Lt. Col. Alexander C. Jones)(w on June 27) (Lt. Col. Norvell Cobb)
52nd Virginia (Lt. Col. James H. Skinner) (Col. William C. Scott)
58th Virginia (Col. Samuel H. Letcher) (Lt. Col. Francis H. Board)(w on June 27)

Trimble's Brigade (7th Bde.)(2,400)
Brig. Gen. Isaac R. Trimble

15th Alabama (Col. James Cantey)
21st North Carolina (Lt. Col. Saunders F. Fulton) (Lt. Col. William W. Kirkland)
1st North Carolina Btn. Sharpshooters (Maj. Rufus W. Wharton)
21st Georgia (Maj. Thomas W. Hooper)(w on June 27)
16th Mississippi (Col. Carnot Posey)
Courtney's Henrico (Virginia) Battery (Capt. Alfred R. Courtney)

Taylor's Brigade (8th Bde.)(2,000)
Brig. Gen. Richard Taylor
Col. Isaac G. Seymour (k on June 27)
Col. Leroy A. Stafford

6th Louisiana (Col. Isaac G. Seymour) (Lt. Col. Henry B. Strong)
7th Louisiana (Col. Harry T. Hays) (Maj. Davidson B. Penn)
8th Louisiana (Col. Henry B. Kelly)
9th Louisiana (Col. Leroy A. Stafford)
1st Louisiana Special Btn. (Maj. C. Roberdeau Wheat)(k on June 27) (Capt. Robert A. Harris)
Carrington's Charlottesville (Virginia) Battery (Capt. James McD. Carrington)

Maryland Line (400)
Col. Bradley T. Johnson

1st Maryland Infantry(Col. Bradley T. Johnson)

1st Maryland Cavalry, A Co. (Capt. Ridgely Brown)
Brockenbrough's Baltimore (Maryland) Battery (Capt. James B. Brockenbrough)

Whiting's Division (attached)(4,400)
Brig. Gen. W. H. C. Whiting

Hood's Brigade (Texas Brigade)(2,000)
Brig. Gen. John B. Hood

18th Georgia (Lt. Col. Solon Z. Ruff) (Maj. John C. Griffis)
1st Texas (Col. Alexis T. Rainey)(s, w on June 27) (Lt. Col. Phillip A. Work)
4th Texas (Col. John Marshall)(k on June 27) (Lt. Col. Bradfute Warwick)(mw on June 27) (Maj. John C. G. Key)(w on June 27) (Capt. William P. Townsend)
5th Texas (Col. Jerome B. Robertson)(w on June 27) (Lt. Col. John C. Upton)
Hampton's South Carolina Legion (Lt. Col. Martin W. Gary)

Law's Brigade (2,200)
Col. Evander M. Law

4th Alabama (Col. Owen K. McLemore)(w on June 27) (Capt. Lawrence H. Scruggs)(w on July 1)
2nd Mississippi (Col. John M. Stone)
11th Mississippi (Col. Philip F. Liddell)
6th North Carolina (Lt. Col. Isaac E. Avery)(w on June 27) (Maj. Robert F. Webb)

Artillery

Balthis' Staunton (Virginia) Battery (Capt. William L. Balthis)(w on July 1) (Lt. Asher W. Garber)
Reilly's Rowan (North Carolina) Battery (Capt. James Reilly)

D. H. Hill's Division (attached)(9,800)
Maj. Gen. Daniel Harvey Hill

Rodes's Brigade (1,600)
Brig. Gen. Robert E. Rodes (s)

Col. John B. Gordon

3rd Alabama (Lt. Col. Charles Forsyth)(s on June 28) (Maj. Robert M. Sands)
5th Alabama (Col. Christopher C. Pegues)(mw on June 27) (Capt. E. Lafayette Hobson)
6th Alabama (Col. John B. Gordon) (Capt. Briscoe G. Baldwin)
12th Alabama (Col. Bristor B. Gayle)
26th Alabama (Col. Edward A. O'Neal)
Carter's King William (Virginia) Battery (Capt. Thomas H. Carter)

G. B. Anderson's Brigade (2nd Bde.)(1,600–1865)
Brig. Gen. George B. Anderson (w on July 1)
Col. Charles C. Tew

2nd North Carolina (Col. Charles C. Tew)
4th North Carolina (Col. Bryan Grimes) (Col. Edwin A. Osborne)
14th North Carolina (Lt. Col. William A. Johnston)
30th North Carolina (Col. Francis M. Parker)
Hardaway's Alabama Battery (Capt. Robert A. Hardaway)

Garland's Brigade (1,800)
Brig. Gen. Samuel Garland, Jr.

5th North Carolina (Col. Duncan K. McRae)
12th North Carolina (Col. Benjamin O. Wade)
13th North Carolina (Col. Alfred M. Scales)
20th North Carolina (Col. Alfred Iverson)(w on June 27) (Lt. Col. Franklin J. Faison)(k on July 1) (Maj. William H. Toon)
23rd North Carolina (Col. Daniel H. Christie)(w on June 27) (Capt. Isaac J. Young)(w on July 1) (Lt. William P. Gill)(k on July 1)
Bondurant's Jeff Davis Alabama Battery (Capt. James W. Bondurant)

Colquitt's Brigade (4th Bde.) (1,800)
Col. Alfred H. Colquitt

13th Alabama (Col. Birkett D. Fry)
6th Georgia (Lt. Col. James M. Newton)(k on July 1)
23rd Georgia (Maj. Emory F. Best) (Capt. James H. Huggins)
27th Georgia (Col. Levi B. Smith)
28th Georgia (Col. Thomas J. Warthen, Sr.)(mw on July 1)

Nelson's Hanover (Virginia) Battery (Capt. George W. Nelson)

Ripley's Brigade (5th Bde.) (2,300)
Brig. Gen. Roswell S. Ripley

1st North Carolina (Col. Montford Stokes)(mw on July 1) (Lt. Col. John A. McDowell)(w on June 26) (Maj. T. L. Skinner)(k on June 26) (Capt. Hamilton A. Brown) (Lt. Col. William P. Bynum)
3rd North Carolina (Col. Gaston Meares)(k on July 1) (Lt. Col. William L. De Rosset)
44th Georgia (Col. Robert A. Smith)(mw on July 1) (Lt. Col. John B. Estes)(w on July 1) (Capt. James W. Beck)(w on July 1)
48th Georgia (Col. William Gibson)(w) (Lt. Col. Reuben P. Campbell)

Artillery (700)
Col. Stapleton Crutchfield

Jones's Artillery Btn. (attached)
Maj. Hilary P. Jones

Rhett's Brooks (South Carolina) Battery (Capt. A. Burnet Rhett)
Clark's Long Island (Virginia) Battery (Capt. Patrick H. Clark)
Peyton's Orange (Virginia) Battery (Capt. Thomas J. Peyton)(s) (Lt. C. W. Fry)

Hill's Light Division (14,000–14,800)(atch. to Longstreet, June 29–July 1)
Maj. Gen. Ambrose P. Hill

Field's Brigade (1st Bde.)(1,500)
Brig. Gen. Charles W. Field

40th Virginia (Col. John M. Brockenbrough)
47th Virginia (Col. Robert M. Mayo)(w on June 29)
55th Virginia (Col. Francis Mallory)
60th Virginia (Col. William E. Starke)(w on June 26) (Lt. Col. B. H. Jones)(s) (Col. William E. Starke) (Maj. John C. Summers)

Gregg's Brigade (2nd Bde.)(2,500)
Brig. Gen. Maxcy Gregg

1st South Carolina (Col. Daniel H. Hamilton)(s)
1st South Carolina Rifles (Orr's Rifles) (Col. Jehu F. Marshall)
12th South Carolina (Col. Dixon Barnes)(w on June 26)
13th South Carolina (Col. O. E. Edwards)
14th South Carolina (Col. Samuel McGowan)(w on June 27)

J. R. Anderson's Brigade (3rd Bde.)(2,000)
Brig. Gen. Joseph R. Anderson (w on June 30)
Col. Edward L. Thomas (w on June 26)

14th Georgia (Lt. Col. Robert W. Folsom)(w on June 26)
35th Georgia (Col. Edward L. Thomas)(w on June 26)
45th Georgia (Col. Thomas Hardeman)(w on June 30)
49th Georgia (Col. Andrew J. Lane)(w on June 26) (Lt. Col. Thomas J. Simmons)(w on June 26)
3rd Louisiana Battalion (Col. Edmund Pendleton)

Branch's Brigade (4th Bde.)(3,500)
Brig. Gen. Lawrence O'B. Branch

7th North Carolina (Col. Reuben P. Campbell)(k on June 27) (Col. Edward G. Haywood)(w on June 30) (Maj. J. L. Hill)
18th North Carolina (Col. Robert H. Cowan)
28th North Carolina (Col. James H. Lane)(w on June 27)
33rd North Carolina (Lt. Col. Robert F. Hoke)(w on June 26)
37th North Carolina (Col. Charles C. Lee)(k on June 30) (Lt. Col. William M. Barber)

Archer's Brigade (5th Bde.)(2,000)
Brig. Gen. James J. Archer

1st Tennessee (Lt. Col. John C. Shackelford)(k on June 27)
7th Tennessee (Col. John F. Goodner)
14th Tennessee (Col. William A. Forbes)
19th Georgia (Lt. Col. Thomas C. Johnson)(k on June 26)
5th Alabama Battalion (Capt. A. S. Van de Graaf)(w on June 27)

Pender's Brigade (6th Bde.)(2,500)
Brig. Gen. W. Dorsey Pender (w on July 1)

2nd Arkansas Battalion (Maj. William N. Bronaugh)(k on June 26)

16th North Carolina (Col. John S. McElroy)
22nd North Carolina (Col. James Conner)(w on June 26) (Lt. Col. R. H. Gray) (Maj. Christopher C. Cole)
34th North Carolina (Col. Richard H. Riddick)(w on June 26)
38th North Carolina (Col. William J. Hoke)(w on June 26) (Lt. Col. R. F. Armfield)
22nd Virginia Btn. (Lt. Col. Edward P. Taylor)(Capt. James C. Johnson)

Artillery (800)
Lt. Col. Reuben L. Walker
Lt. Col. Lewis M. Coleman

Pegram's Purcell (Virginia) Battery (Capt. William J. Pegram)
McIntosh's Pee Dee (South Carolina) Battery (Capt. David G. McIntosh)
Crenshaw's Virginia Battery (Capt. William G. Crenshaw)
Johnson's Richmond (Virginia) Battery (Capt. Marmaduke Johnson)
Braxton's Fredericksburg (Virginia) Battery (Capt. Carter M. Braxton)
Andrews's 1st Maryland Battery (Lt. William F. Dement)
Letcher (Virginia) Artillery Battery (Capt. Greenlee Davidson)
Masters' (Virginia) Battery (improvised siege) (Capt. L. Masters)
Charleston (South Carolina) German Battery (Capt. William K. Bachman)

Longstreet's Division (8,831–9,600)
Maj. Gen. James Longstreet
Brig. Gen. Richard H. Anderson

Kemper's Brigade (1st Bde.)(1,400)
Brig. Gen. James L. Kemper

1st Virginia (Capt. George F. Norton)
7th Virginia (Col. Walter T. Patton)
11th Virginia (Capt. Kirkwood Otey)
17th Virginia (Col. Montgomery D. Corse)
24th Virginia (Lt. Col. Peter Hairston, Jr.)
Rogers's Loudon (Virginia) Battery (Capt. Arthur L. Rogers)

R. H. Anderson's Brigade (2nd Bde.)(1,250–1,300)
Brig. Gen. Richard H. Anderson
Col. Micah Jenkins (w on June 30)

2nd South Carolina Rifles (Col. John V. Moore) (Maj. Thomas Thomson)
4th South Carolina Battalion (Maj. Charles S. Mattison) (Capt. D. L. Hall) 5th South Carolina (Lt. Col. Andrew Jackson)(w on June 27) (Capt. John D. Wylie)
6th South Carolina (Col. John Bratton)
Palmetto (South Carolina) Sharpshooters (Colonel Micah Jenkins) (Lt. Col. Joseph Walker) (Maj. William Anderson)(mw on June 27)

Pickett's Brigade (3rd Bde.) (1,500)
Brig. Gen. George E. Pickett (w on June 27)
Col. John B. Strange
Col. Eppa Hunton (s)
Col. John B. Strange

8th Virginia (Col. Eppa Hunton) (Lt. Col. Norborne Berkeley)
18th Virginia (Col. Robert E. Withers)(w on June 27) (Capt. Edwin G. Wall)(w on June 27)
19th Virginia (Col. John B. Strange)
28th Virginia (Col. Robert C. Allen)
56th Virginia (Lt. Col. Philip P. Slaughter)(w on June 27) (Col. William D. Stuart)

Wilcox's Brigade (4th Bde.)(1,850–1,900)
Brig. Gen. Cadmus M. Wilcox

8th Alabama (Lt. Col. Young L. Royston)(w on June 30)
9th Alabama (Maj. Jere H. J. Williams)(s on June 27) (Capt. J. H. King)(w on June 30)
10th Alabama (Col. John J. Woodward)(k on June 27) (Maj. J. H. J. Caldwell)(w on June 30)
11th Alabama (Lt. Col. Stephen F. Hale)(w) (Capt. George Field)(w on June 30)
Anderson's Thomas (Virginia) Battery (Capt. Edwin J. Anderson)

Pryor's Brigade (5th Bde.)(1,400)
Brig. Gen. Roger A. Pryor

14th Alabama (Lt. Col. David W. Baine)(k on June 30)

2nd Florida (Col. Edward A. Perry)(w on June 30) (Capt. Alexander Moseley)
14th Louisiana (Col. Zebulon York)
3rd Virginia (Lt. Col. Joseph V. Scott)(k on June 29)
1st Louisiana (Zouave) Btn. (Coppens) & St. Paul Foot Rifles (Lt. Col. Georges A. G. Coppens)(w on June 29)
Maurin's Donaldsonville (Louisiana) Battery (Capt. Victor Maurin)

Featherston's Brigade (6th Bde.)(1,300–1,350)
Brig. Gen. Winfield S. Featherston (w on June 30)

12th Mississippi (Maj. William H. Lilly)(w on June 27) (Capt. Samuel B. Thomas)
19th Mississippi (Maj. John Mullins)(w on June 27)
2nd Mississippi Battalion (Lt. Col. John G. Taylor)(k on June 30)
Stanard's Richmond Howitzers, 3rd. Co. (Capt. Benjamin H. Smith, Jr.)

Artillery (800)
Col. James B. Walton

Washington (Louisiana) Artillery, 1st Co. (Capt. Charles W. Squires)
Washington (Louisiana) Artillery, 2nd Co. (Capt. John B. Richardson)
Washington (Louisiana) Artillery, 3rd Co. (Capt. M. B. Miller)
Washington (Louisiana) Artillery, 4th Co. (Capt. Joseph Norcom)
Lynchburg (Virginia) Artillery (Capt. James G. Dearing, Jr.)
Chapman's Dixie (Virginia) Battery (Capt. William H. Chapman)

Magruder's Command (13,000–13,700)
Maj. Gen. John B. Magruder

McLaws's Division (4,200)
Maj. Gen. Lafayette McLaws

Semmes's Brigade (2,500)
Brig. Gen. Paul J. Semmes

5th Louisiana (Col. Theodore G. Hunt)
10th Louisiana (Lt. Col. Eugene Waggaman) (c on July 1)
10th Georgia (Col. Alfred Cumming)(w on July 1) (Capt. Willis C. Holt)
53rd Georgia (Col. Leonard T. Doyal)

15th Virginia (Col. Thomas P. August)(w on July 1) (Maj. John S. Walker)(k on July 1)
32nd Virginia (Lt. Col. William R. Willis) (Maj. Jefferson Sinclair)(w on July 1) (Capt. William J. Stores) (Capt. Henry St. G. Tucker)
Manly's (North Carolina) Battery (Capt. Basil C. Manly)

Kershaw's Brigade (1,700)
Brig, Gen. Joseph B. Kershaw

2nd South Carolina (Col. John D. Kennedy) (Maj. Franklin Gaillard)
3rd South Carolina (Col. James D. Nance)
7th South Carolina (Col. D. Wyatt Aiken)
8th South Carolina (Col. John W. Henagan)
Kemper's Alexandria (Virginia) Battery (Capt. Del Kemper)

D. R. Jones's Division (4,100)
Brig. Gen. David R. Jones

Toombs's Brigade (1,600)
Brig. Gen. Robert A. Toombs

2nd Georgia (Col. Edgar M. Butt)(mw on July 1) (Lt. Col. William R. Holmes)
15th Georgia (Col. William M. McIntosh)(mw on June 27) (Col. William T. Millican)(s) (Maj. Theophilus J. Smith)(s) (Capt. Stephen Z. Hearnsberger)
17th Georgia (Col. Henry L. Benning)
20th Georgia (Col. John B. Cumming)

G. T. Anderson's Brigade (2,100)
Col. George T. Anderson

1st Georgia (Regulars) (Col. William J. Magill)
7th Georgia (Lt. Col. William W. White)(w on June 28) (Maj. Eli W. Hoyle)(k on July 1) (Capt. George H. Carmical)
8th Georgia (Col. Lucius M. Lamar)(w, c on June 28) (Lt. Col. John R. Towers)(c on June 28) (Major E. J. Magruder)(w on June 28) (Capt. George O. Dawson)
9th Georgia (Col. Richard A. Turnipseed) (Maj. William M. Jones)
11th Georgia (Lt. Col. William Luffman)

Artillery (400)
Maj. John J. Garnett

Brown's Wise (Virginia) Battery (Capt. James S. Brown)
Hart's Washington (South Carolina) Battery (Capt. James F. Hart)
Moody's Madison (Louisiana) Battery (Capt. George V. Moody)
Dabney's Richmond (Virginia) Battery (Capt. William J. Dabney)
Lane's Sumter (Georgia) Btn., Battery E (Capt. John Lane) (attached)
Woolfolk's Ashland (Virginia) Battery (attached) (Lt. Pichegru Woolfolk, Jr.)

Magruder's Division (5,000)
Maj. Gen. John B. Magruder

Griffith's Brigade (3rd Bde.)(2,000)
Brig. Gen. Richard Griffith (mw on June 29)
Col. William Barksdale

13th Mississippi (Col. William Barksdale) (Lt. Col. James W. Carter)(w on July 1) (Maj. Kennon McElroy)
17th Mississippi (Col. William D. Holder)(w on July 1) (Lt. Col. John C. Fiser)
18th Mississippi (Col. Thomas M. Griffin)(w on July 1) (Lt. Col. William H. Luse)
21st Mississippi (Col. Benjamin G. Humphreys) (Lt. Col. William L. Brandon)(w on July 1) (Capt. William C. F. Brooks)
McCarthy's Richmond Howitzers, 1st Co. (Capt. Edward S. McCarthy)

Cobb's Brigade (2nd Bde.)(3,000)
Brig. Gen. Howell Cobb

16th Georgia (Col. Goode Bryan)
24th Georgia (Col. Robert McMillan)
2nd Louisiana (Col. Isaiah T. Norwood)(mw on July 1)
15th North Carolina (Col. Henry A. Dowd)(w on July 1) (Lt. Col. William McRae)
Cobb's (Georgia) Legion (Col. Thomas R. R. Cobb) (Lt. Col. Gazaway B. Knight)
Carlton's Troup (Georgia) Battery (Capt. Henry H. Carlton)

Artillery (400)
Lt. Col. Stephen D. Lee

Read's Pulaski (Georgia) Battery (Capt. John P. W. Read)
Richardson's James City (Virginia) Battery (Capt. Lucien W. Richardson)
Sands' Henrico (Virginia) Battery (Capt. Alfred R. Courtney)
Jordan's Bedford (Virginia) Battery (Capt. Tyler C. Jordan)
Page's Magruder (Virginia) Battery (Capt. Thomas J. Page, Jr.)
Kirkpatrick's Amherst (Virginia) (Capt. Thomas J. Kirkpatrick) (temp. attached)

Huger's Division (9,000)
Maj. Gen. Benjamin Huger

Mahone's Brigade (2nd Bde.)(2,700)
Brig. Gen. William Mahone

6th Virginia (Col. George T. Rogers) (Lt. Col. Henry W. Williamson)
12th Virginia (Col. David A. Weisiger)
16th Virginia (Lt. Col. Joseph H. Ham)
41st Virginia (John R. Chambliss, Jr.) (Lt. Col. William A. Parham)(w on July 1)
49th Virginia (Col. William Smith)
Grimes's Portsmouth (Virginia) Battery (Capt. Carey F. Grimes)
Moorman's Lynchburg (Virginia) Beauregard Battery (Capt. Marcellus N. Moorman)

Wright's Brigade (3rd Bde.)(2,200)
Brig. Gen. Ambrose R. Wright

44th Alabama (Col. James Kent)
3rd Georgia (Maj. John R. Sturges)(k on July 1) (Capt. Reuben B. Nisbet)
4th Georgia (Col. George P. Doles)
22nd Georgia (Col. Robert H. Jones) (Lt. Col. Joseph Wasden)
1st Louisiana (Lt. Col. William R. Shivers)(w on June 25) (Capt. Michael Nolan)
Huger's Norfolk (Virginia) Battery (Capt. Frank Huger)
Ross's Sumter (Georgia) Battalion, Battery A (Capt. H. M. Ross)

Armistead's Brigade (4th Bde.) (1,600)
Brig. Gen. Lewis A. Armistead
Col. Edward C. Edmonds
Brig. Gen. Lewis A. Armistead

9th Virginia (Lt. Col. James S. Gilliam)
14th Virginia (Col. James G. Hodges)(w on July 1)
38th Virginia (Col. Edward C. Edmonds) (Maj. Joseph R. Cabell) (Col. Edward C. Edmonds)
53rd Virginia (Col. Harrison B. Tomlin) (Major George M. Waddill)(s) (Capt. William R. Aylett)(s) (Capt. Rawley W. Martin) (Capt. John Grammer, Jr.)
57th Virginia (Lt. Col. Waddy T. James)
5th Virginia Battalion (Capt. William E. Alley)
Turner's Goochland (Virginia) Battery (Capt. William H. Turner)
Stribling's Fauquier (Virginia) Battery (Capt. Robert M. Stribling)

Ransom's Brigade (2,500) (attached to Huger)
Brig. Gen. Robert Ransom, Jr. (w on July 1)

24th North Carolina (Col. William J. Clarke)
25th North Carolina (Col. Henry M. Rutledge)(w on July 1)
26th North Carolina (Col. Zebulon B. Vance)
35th North Carolina (Col. Matt W. Ransom)(w on July 1) (Lt. Col. Oliver C. Petway)(mw on July 1)
48th North Carolina (June 25–28) (Col. Robert C. Hill)
49th North Carolina (Col. S. Dodson Ramseur)(w on July 1)

Holmes's Division (6,000–6,700)
Maj. Gen. Theophilus H. Holmes

Daniel's Brigade (3rd Bde.)(1,700)
Brig. Gen. Junius Daniel

43rd North Carolina (Col. Thomas S. Kenan)
45th North Carolina (Col. Junius Daniel)
(Lt. Col. John H. Morehead)
50th North Carolina (Col. Marshall D. Craton)
14th Virginia Cavalry Battalion (Maj. Edgar Burroughs)

Walker's Brigade (4th Bde.)(3,600)

Brig. Gen. John G. Walker (w on July 1)
Col. Van H. Manning

3rd Arkansas (Col. Van. H. Manning)
27th North Carolina (Col. John R. Cooke)
46th North Carolina (Col. E. D. Hall)
48th North Carolina (atch, June 29–July 1) (Col. Robert C. Hill) (Lt. Col. Samuel Walkup)
2nd Georgia Battalion (Maj. George W. Ross)
30th Virginia (Col. Archibald T. Harrison)
Petersburg (Virginia) Cavalry (1 Co.) (Capt. Edward A. Goodwyn)
57th Virginia++
++ served also in Armistead's brigade

Wise's Brigade (atch to Holmes) (1,000)
Brig. Gen. Henry A. Wise

26th Virginia (Col. Powhatan R. Page)
46th Virginia (Col. Richard T. W. Duke)
4th Virginia Heavy Artillery (infantry) (Col. John T. Goode)
Armistead's Mathews (Virginia) Battery (Capt. Andrew D. Armistead)
French's Giles (Virginia) Battery (Capt. David A. French)
Rives' 2nd Nelson (Virginia) Battery (Capt. J. H. Rives)
Andrews' Co. A, Virginia Heavy Artillery (Capt. W. C. Andrews)

Artillery (400)
Col. James Deshler

Branch's Petersburg (Virginia) Battery (Capt. James R. Branch)
Brem's North Carolina Battery (Capt. T. H. Brem) (Capt. Joseph Graham)
French's Stafford (Virginia) Battery (Capt. Thomas B. French)
Graham's Petersburg (Virginia) Battery (Capt. Edward Graham)

Cavalry Brigade (3,600)
Brig. Gen. J. E. B. Stuart

1st Virginia Cavalry (Col. Fitzhugh Lee)
3rd Virginia Cavalry (Col. Thomas F. Goode)
4th Virginia Cavalry(Col. Stephen D. Lee) (Lt. Col. Will T. Martin) (Capt. F. W. Chamberlayne)

9th Virginia Cavalry (Col. W. H. F. Lee)
15th Virginia Cavalry Btn. (Lt. Col. John Critcher)
1st North Carolina Cavalry (3 Co.'s) (Col. Lawrence S. Baker) (Lt. Col. James B. Gordon) (arrived on June 28)
Cobb's (Georgia) Legion Cavalry (Col. Pierce M. B. Young)
Jeff Davis (Mississippi) Legion Cavalry (Lt. Col. William T. Martin)
Hampton's (South Carolina) Legion Cavalry (1 sqdn.) (Capt. Thomas E. Scrivener) (atch. to 5th Virginia Cav.)
Wise's (Virginia) Legion Cavalry (10th Virginia Cavalry) (Col. J. Lucius Davis)
Stuart Horse Artillery (Capt. John Pelham)

Artillery Reserve (2,700)
Brig. Gen. William N. Pendleton

1st Virginia Artillery (600)
Col. J. Thompson Brown

Southall's Albemarle (Virginia) Battery (Capt. William H. Southall)
Garrett's Williamsburg (Virginia) Battery (Capt. John A. Coke)
Brown's Richmond Howitzers, 2nd. Co. (Capt. David Watson)
Macon's Richmond Fayette (Virginia) Battery (Lt. William I. Clopton)

Sumter (Georgia) Battalion (600)
Lt. Col. Allen S. Cutts

Sumter (Georgia) Btn., Battery A (Capt. H. M. Ross)
Sumter (Georgia) Btn., Battery B (Capt. John V. Price)
Sumter (Georgia) Btn., Battery D (Capt. James A. Blackshear)
Sumter (Georgia) Btn., Battery E (Capt. John Lane)
Hamilton's Georgia Regular Battery (Capt. S. P. Hamilton)

Richardson's Battalion (2nd Arty. Btn.)(400)
Maj. Charles Richardson

Ancell's 2nd Fluvanna (Virginia) Battery (Capt. John J. Ancell)
Milledge's (Georgia) Battery (Capt. John Milledge, Jr.)
Masters' Virginia Siege Battery (attached) (Capt. L. Masters)
Davidson's Letcher (Virginia) Battery (attached) (Capt. Greenlee Davidson)
Woolfolk's Ashland (Virginia) Battery (Capt. Pichegru Woolfolk)

Nelson's Battalion (3rd Arty. Btn.)(400)
Maj. William Nelson

Morris Louisa (Virginia) Battery (Capt. Richard C. M. Page)
Huckstep's Fluvanna (Virginia) Battery (Capt. Charles T. Huckstep) (Lt. John L. Massie)
Kirkpatrick's Amherst (Virginia) Battery (Capt. Thomas J. Kirkpatrick)

Jones' Battalion (700)(temp. atch to D. H. Hill)
Maj. Hilary P. Jones

Long Island (Virginia) Battery (Capt. Patrick H. Clark). Clark
Rhett's (South Carolina) Battery (Capt. A. Burnet Rhett)
Orange Richmond (Virginia) Battery (Lt. C. W. Fry)

At Evelington Heights (July 3–4)

Federal

Army of the Potomac
Maj. Gen. George B. McClellan

VI Corps (partial)

2nd Division
Brig. Gen. William F. Smith

1st Brigade
Brig. Gen. Winfield S. Hancock

5th Wisconsin (Col. Amasa Cobb)
6th Maine (Col. Hiram Burnham)
43rd New York (Col. Francis L. Vinton)
49th Pennsylvania (Maj. Thomas M. Hulings)

2nd Brigade
Brig. Gen. William H. T. Brooks

2nd Vermont (Col. Henry Whiting)

3rd Vermont (Lt. Col. Wheelock G. Veazey)
4th Vermont (Col. Edwin H. Stoughton)
5th Vermont (Lt. Col. Lewis A. Grant)
6th Vermont (Col. Nathan Lord, Jr.)

3rd Brigade
Brig. Gen. John W. Davidson

7th Maine (Col. Edwin C. Mason)
20th New York (Col. Francis Weiss)
33rd New York (Col. Robert F. Taylor)
49th New York (Col. Daniel D. Bidwell)
77th New York (Col. James B. McKean)

Kimball's Brigade (attached)
Brig. Gen. Nathan Kimball

4th Ohio (Col. John S. Mason)
14th Indiana (Col. William Harrow)
7th Virginia (U.S.) (Col. James Evans)
8th Ohio (Lt. Col. F. Sawyer)

Artillery

2nd U.S., Battery A (Capt. John C. Tidball)

Confederate

Army of Northern Virginia
Gen. Robert E. Lee

Cavalry Brigade
Brig. Gen. J. E. B. Stuart

1st Virginia Cavalry (Col. Fitzhugh Lee)
3rd Virginia Cavalry (Col. Thomas F. Goode)
4th Virginia Cavalry(Lt. Col. Will T. Martin)
5th Virginia Cavalry(Col. Thomas L. Rosser)
9th Virginia Cavalry(Col. W. H. F. Lee) (absent)
Critcher (Virginia) battalion (Lt. Col. John Critcher)
1st North Carolina Cavalry(Col. Lawrence S. Baker) (arrived on June 28)

Cobb (Georgia) Legion Cavalry (Col. Thomas C. Cobb)
Jeff Davis (Mississippi) Legion Cavalry (Lt. Col. William T. Martin)
Hampton (South Carolina) Legion Cavalry (1 sqdn.) (Capt. Thomas E. Scrivener)
Wise (Virginia) Legion Cavalry (10th Virginia Cavalry) (Col. J. Lucius Davis)
Stuart Horse Artillery (Capt. John Pelham)

APPENDIX B

Casualties

There is a wide range of casualty figures extant, and there are some numbers which are simply not available at all. It is especially difficult to pinpoint casualty figures on the Confederate side. This appendix is an attempt to put the lethality of the campaign in perspective, knowing full well the imperfect nature of the data. Where possible, footnotes have been supplied to explain the source of numbers displayed. In some cases, a range is used, based upon numbers gathered from a number or sources.

FEDERAL CASUALTIES

Battle	Killed	Wounded	Missing/Captured	Totals
Yorktown	38[15]	145[15]	~0	182[13]–183[15]
Williamsburg	456[1,3,5,15]–468[13]	1,410[1,3,5]–1,442[13]	373[1,3,5,13]	2,228[10]–2,283[13]
Eltham's Landing	48[1]–49[15]	104[15]–110[1]	28[1]–41[15]	186[1]–200[15]
Hanover Courthouse	53[15]–62[8]	223[8]–344[15]	70[8]	355[8]–406[15]
Seven Pines (2 days)	790[8]–890[15]	3,594[8]–3,627[15]	647[8]–1,222[15]	5,031[8]–5739[15]
THE SEVEN DAYS	/////////////////	/////////////////	/////////////////	/////////////////
Oak Grove	51[15]–68[7]	401[15]–504[8]	55[8]–64[15]	516[15]–626[8]
Mechanicsville	49[8,9]	207[8,9]	105[8,9]	361[2,8,9]
Gaines' Mill	894[7,8]	3,107[7,8]	2,836[2,7,8]	6,837[2,7,8]
Garnett's & Golding's Farms	37[8]	227[8]	104[8]	368[8]
Savage Station	80[8]	412[8]	1,098[8]	1,590[8]–1,600[11]
Glendale	210–297[8,12]	1,513–1,696[8,12]	1,130–1,804[8,12]	2,853[8,12]
Malvern Hill	397[8]	2,092[8]	725[8]	3,214–3,797[8,12]
SUBTOTALS	1,718–1,822	7,959–8,245	6,053–6,736	15,739–16,442
Evelington Heights	8[15]	32[15]	0*	40[15]
TOTALS	3,111–3,337	13,467–13,945	7,171–8,442	23,721–25,253

* Jeb Stuart claimed to have taken prisoners, but no Federal report admits to having men missing/captured.

CONFEDERATE CASUALTIES

Battle	Killed	Wounded	Missing/Captured	Totals
Yorktown	20[15]	75[15]	~200[15]	295[15]–300[13]
Williamsburg	288[3,8,13]–510[15]	490[15]–753[8,13]	297[3,8,13]	1,503[5]–1,560[3,8,10,13]
Eltham's Landing	8[1,8]	40[1,8]	0[1,8]	48[1,8]
Hanover Courthouse	50[15]–73[8]	150[15]–192[8]	730[15]	265[8]–930[15]
Seven Pines (2 days)	980[8],800[15]	4,749[8]–3,897[15]	405[8]–1,300[15]	6,134[8]–7,997[15]
THE SEVEN DAYS	/////////////////	/////////////////	/////////////////	/////////////////
Oak Grove	65[15]–66[7]	362[7]–465	11[15]–13[7]	441[7,8]–541[15]
Mechanicsville	~250[15]	~1,250[15]	unknown	1,365[8]–1,484[9]
Gaines' Mill	1,483[7]	6,402[7]	108[7]	7,993[7]–9,000[4]
Garnett's & Golding's Farms	>=50	>=229	>=11	438[7]–461[8]
Savage Station	~75[15]	325[15]	>=9	626[8]–700[11]
Glendale	638[12]	2,814[12]	221[12]	3,615–3,673[8,12]
Malvern Hill	870[15]	3,300[15]	~1,130–1,480	>5,300[4]–5,650[8]
SUBTOTALS	3,431–3,432	14,682–16,261	1,490–1,842	19,778–21,509
Evelington Heights	29[15]	71[15]	Unknown	100[15]
TOTALS	4,806–6,872	21,482–21,289	3,122–4,369	28,123–32,444

SOURCES:

1. Alexander, *Military Memoirs of a Confederate*
2. Burton, *Extraordinary Circumstances*
3. OR, Series 1, Vol. XI
4. ABPP
5. Hastings, *A Pitiless Rain*
6. Wheeler, *Sword Over Richmond*
7. Sears, *Gates of Richmond*
8. Fox, *Regimental Losses*
9. Livermore, *Numbers and Losses*
10. Webb, *The Peninsula*
11. Martin, *The Peninsula Campaign*
12. Konstam, *Seven Days Battles - 1862*
13. BL, Vol. II, pp. 200-201
14. *Wikipedia*
15. michiganinthewar.org

APPENDIX C

General Orders No. 75

GENERAL ORDERS,
HDQRS. ARMY OF NORTHERN VIRGINIA,
No. 75. June 24, 1862.

I. General Jackson's command will proceed to-morrow from Ashland toward the Slash Church and encamp at some convenient point west of the Central Railroad. Branch's brigade, of A. P. Hill's division, will also to-morrow evening take position on the Chickahominy near Half-Sink. At 3 o'clock Thursday morning, 26th instant, General Jackson will advance on the road leading to Pole Green Church, communicating his march to General Branch, who will immediately cross the Chickahominy and take the road leading to Mechanicsville. As soon as the movements of these columns are discovered, General A. P. Hill, with the rest of his division, will cross the Chickahominy near Meadow Bridge and move direct upon Mechanicsville. To aid his advance, the heavy batteries on the Chickahominy will at the proper time open upon the batteries at Mechanicsville. The enemy being driven from Mechanicsville and the passage across the bridge opened, General Longstreet, with his division and that of General D. H. Hill, will cross the Chickahominy at or near that point, General D. H. Hill moving to the support of General Jackson and General Longstreet supporting General A. P. Hill. The four divisions, keeping in communication with each other and moving en echelon on separate roads, if practicable, the left division in advance, with skirmishers and sharpshooters extending their front, will sweep down the Chickahominy and endeavor to drive the enemy from his position above New Bridge, General Jackson bearing well to his left, turning Beaver Dam Creek and taking the direction toward Cold Harbor. They will then press forward toward the York River Railroad, closing upon the enemy's rear and forcing him down the Chickahominy. Any advance of the enemy toward Richmond will be prevented by vigorously following his rear and crippling and arresting his progress.

II. The divisions under Generals Huger and Magruder will hold their positions in front of the enemy against attack, and make such demonstrations Thursday as to discover his operations. Should opportunity offer, the feint will be converted into a real attack, and should an abandonment of his intrenchments by the enemy be discovered, he will be closely pursued.

III. The Third Virginia Cavalry will observe the Charles City road. The Fifth Virginia, the First North Carolina, and the Hampton Legion (cavalry) will observe the Darbytown, Varina, and Osborne roads. Should a movement of the enemy down the Chickahominy be discovered, they will close upon his flank and endeavor to arrest his march.

IV. General Stuart, with the First, Fourth, and Ninth Virginia Cavalry, the cavalry of Cobb's Legion and the Jeff. Davis Legion, will cross the Chickahominy to-morrow and take position to the left of General Jackson's line of march. The main body will be held in reserve, with scouts well extended to the front and left. General Stuart will keep General Jackson informed of the movements of the enemy on his left and will co-operate with him in his advance. The Tenth Virginia Cavalry, Colonel Davis, will remain on the Nine-mile road.

V. General Ransom's brigade, of General Holmes' command, will be placed in reserve on the Williamsburg road by General Huger, to whom he will report for orders.

VI. Commanders of divisions will cause their commands to be provided with three days' cooked rations. The necessary ambulances and ordnance trains will be ready to accompany the division and receive orders from their respective commanders. Officers in charge of all trains will invariably remain with them. Batteries and wagons will keep on the right of the road. The chief engineer, Major Stevens, will assign engineer officers to each division, whose duty it will be to make provision for overcoming all difficulties to the progress of the troops. The staff departments will give the necessary instructions to facilitate the movements herein directed.

By command of General Lee:

R. H. CHILTON,

Assistant Adjutant-General.

(Source: *OR*, Ser. I, Vol. XI, pt. 2, pp. 498–499.)

APPENDIX D

Jackson's Dabbs House Conference Memorandum

(from Freeman, *Lee's Lieutenants*, vol. 1, pp. 499–500)

Maj Gen Jackson to be in position on Wednesday night on the Hanover Ct. Ho. Road, or near that road, about half way between Half Sink Bridge, and Hanover Ct. Ho. He will communicate to Maj Gen A. P. Hill, through Brig Gen Branch at Half Sink Bridge his position.

Gen Jackson will commence his movement, precisely at 3 o'clock Thursday morning, and the moment he moves, send messengers to Gen Branch in duplicate, to inform Gen Branch, who will immediately move himself.

Gen Jackson to move from his position down the second road from the Chickahominy, parallel to the first road, and near to it. Major Gen A. P. Hill, as soon as the movement of Jackson or Branch is shown on the other side of the Chickahominy, will push his columns across the Chickahominy at Meadow Bridge, turn to the right and move on Mechanicsville. Maj Gen Jackson will endeavor to come into the Mechanicsville Turnpike in rear of Mechanicsville.

Maj Gen Jacksons [sic] and Hill will unite here, and taking different roads bear down towards Coal [sic] Harbor, and on to York R. R. Maj Gen Longstreet to support Maj Gen A. P. Hill, and Maj Gen Jackson. If practicable, it will be best for the supporting columns to take different roads from, but near to the main columns.

NOTES
Abbreviations Used

BL	*Battles and Leaders of the Civil War*
CV	*Confederate Veteran*
CWTI	*Civil War Times Illustrated*
DUKE	Special Collections Library, Duke University
FLP	Free Library of Philadelphia
LOC	Library of Congress
LVa	The Library of Virginia
MaHS	Massachusetts Historical Society
MoC	Museum of the Confederacy
NA	National Archives
NT	*National Tribune*
OR	*The War of the Rebellion: A Compilation of the Official Records of the Federal and Confederate Armies* (OR citations will denote Volume, Part, and pages cited. All citations are from Series I, unless otherwise noted. e.g. XI, 2, pp. 420–433.)
ORN	*Official Records of the Union and Confederate Navies in the War of the Rebellion* (ORN citations will denote Series, Volume, and pages cited. e. g. I, VII, p. 146.)
OR Supp.	*Supplement to the Official Records of the Union and Confederate Armies*
SHC	Southern Historical Collection, University of North Carolina, Chapel Hill
USAMHI	U. S. Army Military History Institute
USC	South Caroliniana Library, University of South Carolina
UVa	University of Virginia Library
VaHS	Virginia Historical Society

Notes by Chapter

Part I

[1] Blaisdell, *Book of Quotations*, p. 52.

Chapter 1

[1] Burton, *Extraordinary Circumstances*, p.2.
[2] Warner, *Generals in Blue*, pp. 290–292; Eicher & Eicher, *Civil War High Commands*, pp. 271–272].
[3] Fuller, *Military History of Western World*, vol. III, p. 21; Burton, *Extraordinary Circumstances*, p.3.
[4] McClellan, *Report on Campaigns*, pp. 77-82; Donald, Lincoln, pp. 318-319; Dowdey, *Seven Days*, pp. 28–29.
[5] Wert, *Sword of Lincoln*, p. 59; Dowdey, *Seven Days*, p. 29; Sears, *Controversies and Commanders*, pp. 29–30, 37–38, 39–40, 45–46, 47. The Stone affair leads one to the conclusion that "The Great Emancipator" and his Secretary of War were possibly not men of high moral character.
[6] Martin, *Peninsula Campaign*, pp. 13–15.
[7] Martin, *Peninsula Campaign*, p. 15.
[8] Cullen, *Peninsula Campaign*, p. 27.
[9] Wert, *Sword of Lincoln*, p. 55; Miller, ed., *Peninsula Campaign*, vol. 2, p. 82; Swinton, *Campaigns*, pp. 78–80.
[10] Wert, *Sword of Lincoln*, p. 55; Snell, *From First to Last*, pp. 79–81; Sears, *McClellan*, pp. 140–141.
[11] Cullen, *Peninsula Campaign*, p. 27; Wert, *Sword of Lincoln*, p. 55; Boritt, ed., *Lincoln's Generals*, p. 23; Swinton, *Campaigns*, pp. 81–85; Donald, *Lincoln*, p. 331; Snell, *From First to Last*, p. 81.
[12] Martin, *Peninsula Campaign*, pp. 15–16.
[13] Donald, *Lincoln*, pp. 325–326; Wert, *Sword of Lincoln*, p. 56; Donald. *Lincoln*, pp. 325–326.

¹⁴ Wert, *Sword of Lincoln*, p. 56; Donald. *Lincoln*, pp. 333–334.

¹⁵ McClellan, *Report on Campaigns*, pp. 96-97; Wert, *Sword of Lincoln*, pp. 59–60.

¹⁶ McClellan, *Report on Campaigns*, p. 97.

¹⁷ Martin, *Peninsula Campaign*, p. 16.

¹⁸ McClellan, *Report on Campaigns*, pp. 97–107.

¹⁹ Martin, *Peninsula Campaign*, p. 17; McClellan, *Report on Campaigns*, pp. 107–108; Fuller, *Military History of Western World*, vol. III, pp. 21–22.

Chapter 2

¹ Sears, *Gates of Richmond*, p. 5.

² Martin, *Peninsula Campaign*, p. 17.

³ Sears, *Gates of Richmond*, pp. 7–8.

⁴ Wert, *Sword of Lincoln*, p. 61; *OR*, V, pp.18, 50; Donald, *Lincoln*, p. 340; Snell, *First to Last*, pp. 86, 87; Sears, *Gates of Richmond*, pp. 5–7; Michie, *General McClellan*, pp. 204–205; John G. Barnard to Edward D. Townsend, Oct. 3, 1864, Lincoln Papers, LOC.

⁵ Foote, *Civil War - A Narrative*, vol. 1, pp. 252–253.

⁶ Sears, *Gates of Richmond*, p. 9.

⁷ Sears, *Gates of Richmond*, p. 12.

⁸ Sears, *Gates of Richmond*, p. 13; Thomas Bragg Diary, Feb. 20, 1862, SHC; Govan & Livingood, *A Different Valor*, pp. 94–95; *OR*, V, p. 1086; *OR*, XLVII, 2, p. 1305; Johnston, *Narrative*, p. 97; *OR*, V, p. 1079.

⁹ Sears, *Gates of Richmond*, p. 13.

¹⁰ Sears, *Gates of Richmond*, pp. 13–14; Johnston, *Narrative*, pp. 98-99, 102; *OR*, V, pp. 1085, 1091–1092.

¹¹ Sears, *Gates of Richmond*, pp. 15–16.

¹² Sears, ed., *McClellan Papers*, p. 199.

¹³ *OR*, IX, pp. 21–22, 23–24; Nathaniel P. Banks telegram to Marcy, Mar. 8, 1862, Joseph Hooker telegram to Seth Williams, Mar. 9, 1862, Leavitt Hunt telegram to Heintzelman, Mar. 9, 1862, McClellan Papers (A–44:18), LOC; Sears, ed., *McClellan Papers*, p. 200; Sears,

    Gates of Richmond, p. 16; Burton, *Extraordinary Circumstances*, pp. 3–4.

[14] Sears, ed., *McClellan Papers*, p. 200; *OR*, V, p. 741.

[15] McClellan, *Report on Campaigns*, pp. 122–123.

[16] Sears, ed., *McClellan Papers*, p. 201.

[17] Sears, ed., *McClellan Papers*, pp. 201–202.

[18] McClellan, *Report on Campaigns*, p. 124.

[19] McClellan, *Report on Campaigns*, pp. 127–129.

[20] Wheeler, *Sword Over Richmond*, pp. 96–97.

Chapter 3

[1] Donald, *Lincoln*, p. 349.

[2] McClellan, *Report on Campaigns*, pp. 139–140.

[3] Donald, *Lincoln*, pp. 349–350.

[4] McClellan, *Report on Campaigns*, p. 117.

[5] McClellan, *Report on Campaigns*, pp. 110–112.

[6] Foote, *Civil War - A Narrative*, Vol. I, pp. 256–263.

[7] McClellan, *Report on Campaigns*, pp. 132-134; *OR*, V, pp. 57–58; Sears, ed., *McClellan Papers*, pp. 215–216.

[8] McClellan, *Report on Campaigns*, pp. 134–135; Foote, *Civil War - Narrative*, Vol. I, pp. 272–273.

[9] McClellan, *Report on Campaigns*, pp. 155–156.

[10] McClellan, *Report on Campaigns*, pp. 160–164.

[11] McClellan, *Report on Campaigns*, pp. 147–150.

[12] McClellan, *Report on Campaigns*, pp. 119–122.

Part II

[1] Blaisdell, *Book of Quotations*, p. 53.

Chapter 4

[1] McClellan, *Report on Campaigns*, pp. 151–152.
[2] *OR*, XI, 1, p. 5.
[3] Sears, *Gates of Richmond*, p. 23; Wert, *Sword of Lincoln*, p. 65; Swinton, *Campaigns of Army of Potomac*, p. 100.
[4] Martin, *Peninsula Campaign*, p. 57; Cullen, *Peninsula Campaign*, p. 15.
[5] *ORN*, I, VII, p. 146.

Chapter 5

[1] Wheeler, *Sword Over Richmond*, p. 97; Sears, *Gates of Richmond*, p. 21; Wert, *Sword of Lincoln*, pp. 64–65.
[2] Sears, *Gates of Richmond*, p. 22.
[3] McClellan, *Report on Campaigns*, p. 152.
[4] Cullen, *Peninsula Campaign*, p. 15.
[5] Martin, *Peninsula Campaign*, p. 57.
[6] Sears, *Gates of Richmond*, p. 24.
[7] McClellan, *Report on Campaigns*, p. 152; *OR*, XI, 1, p. 6.
[8] McClellan, *Report on Campaigns*, p. 153; *OR*, XI, 1, p. 6.
[9] Alexander, *Memoirs*, p. 63.
[10] *OR*, XI, 3, p. 17.
[11] Johnston, *Narrative*, pp. 108–109.
[12] Johnston, *Narrative*, p. 109.
[13] Johnston, *Narrative*, pp. 109–110.
[14] Johnston, *Narrative*, p. 110.
[15] Wheeler, *Sword Over Richmond*, p. 99.
[16] Wert, *Sword of Lincoln*, p. 53.
[17] Sears, *Gates of Richmond*, pp. 23–24.
[18] Wert, *Sword of Lincoln*, pp. 65–66.
[19] Wheeler, *Sword Over Richmond*, pp. 99–100.

[20] Wheeler, *Sword Over Richmond*, p. 100.

[21] Sears, *Gates of Richmond*, p. 24; Martin, *Peninsula Campaign*, p. 58; Cullen, *Peninsula Campaign*, pp. 15–16.

[22] Sears, *Gates of Richmond*, p. 24.

Chapter 6

[1] Wheeler, *Sword Over Richmond*, p. 102.

[2] Wheeler, *Sword Over Richmond*, p. 102.

[3] Hewett, ed., *OR Supp.*, Part I, Vol. 2, p. 27.

[4] Hewett, ed., *OR Supp.*, Part I, Vol. 2, p. 25; Martin, *Peninsula Campaign*, p. 58.

[5] Hewett, ed., *OR Supp.*, Part I, vol. 2, pp. 315–318.

[6] Hewett, ed., *OR Supp.*, Part I, Vol. 2, p. 25.

[7] *OR*, XI, 1, pp. 158, 160; Swinton, *Campaigns of Army of Potomac*, p. 100; Sears, *Gates of Richmond*, p. 24.

[8] *OR Supp.*, Part I, Vol. 2, p. 24.

[9] Myers, *General George McClellan*, p. 274.

[10] *OR*, XI, 1, p. 8.

[11] Myers, *General George McClellan*, p. 272.

[12] Sears, *McClellan*, p. 173.

[13] Sears, *Gates of Richmond*, pp. 34–35.

[14] *OR*, XI, 1, p. 9; Wert, *Sword of Lincoln*, p. 66; Hewett, ed., *OR Supp.*, Part I, vol. 2, pp. 25, 28, 30, 32, 37.

[15] *OR*, XI, 3, p. 63.

[16] *OR*, XI, 3, p. 64.

[17] *OR*, XI, 1, p. 8; McClellan, *Report on Campaigns*, p. 154.

[18] *OR*, XI, 1, p. 7; McClellan, *Report on Campaigns*, p. 154.

[19] *OR*, XI, 1, p. 7.

[20] Sears, *Gates of Richmond*, pp. 29–30.

[21] Myers, *General George McClellan*, p. 273.

[22] McClellan, *Report on Campaigns*, p. 155.

23 Hewett, *OR Supp.*, Part I, Vol. 2, p. 28.
24 Sears, ed. *McClellan Papers*, p. 225.
25 *ORN*, I, VII, pp. 195–196; Sears, ed., *McClellan Papers*, p. 226.
26 *OR*, XI, 3, p. 65; McClellan, *Report on Campaigns*, pp. 155–156; Martin, *Peninsula Campaign*, p. 58; Dowdey, *Seven Days*, p. 45; Wert, *Sword of Lincoln*, p. 66; Hewett, ed., *OR Supp.*, Part I, Vol. 2, pp. 28, 29, 30; Sneden, *Eye of Storm*, pp. 36, 37; Sears, *McClellan*, p. 172; Webb, *Peninsula*, pp. 33, 42–43.
27 *OR*, XI, 3, p. 64; Sears, ed., *McClellan Papers*, p. 227.
28 *OR*, XI, 1, p. 10.
29 *ORN*, I, VII, p. 199.
30 *ORN*, I, VII, p. 200.
31 Campbell, *McClellan*, p. 143.

Part III

1 Blaisdell, *Book of Quotations*, p. 54.

Chapter 7

1 Wert, *Sword of Lincoln*, p. 66.
2 Alexander, *Military Memoirs*, p. 63; Webb, *Peninsula*, pp. 43–44.
3 *OR*, XI, 1, p. 11; Wert, *Sword of Lincoln*, pp. 66, 68.
4 McClellan, *Report on Campaigns*, pp. 157–159; Webb, *Peninsula*, pp. 43–44.
5 Sears, *Gates of Richmond*, p. 35.
6 *OR*, XI, 1, pp. 10–11; Wert, *Sword of Lincoln*, p. 68; Yoseloff, *Campaigns of Civil War*, p. 45; Sears, *McClellan*, pp. 174, 175.
7 Wert, *Sword of Lincoln*, p. 68.
8 McClellan, *Report on Campaigns*, p. 135; Alexander, *Military Memoirs*, p. 63.
9 Sears, *Gates of Richmond*, p. 40.

¹⁰ *OR*, XI, 1, pp. 10, 11; Joinville, *Army*, pp. 38, 53; Sears, ed., *McClellan Papers*, p. 230; Welcher, *Union Army*, pp. 300, 364; Fuller, *Military History of Western World*, vol. III, p. 23.

¹¹ Yoseloff, *Campaigns of Civil War*, pp. 36–38.

¹² Yoseloff, *Campaigns of Civil War*, pp. 38–42.

¹³ McClellan, *Report on Campaigns*, p. 156.

¹⁴ Alexander, *Memoirs*, p. 63; Warner, *Generals in Gray*, pp. 207–208; Wert, *Sword of Lincoln*, p. 68.

¹⁵ Alexander, *Memoirs*, p. 63; Sears, *Gates of Richmond*, p. 54.

¹⁶ McClellan, *Report on Campaigns*, pp. 172–176; Sears, ed., *McClellan Papers*, p. 228.

¹⁷ *OR*, XI, 1, p. 11; Wert, *Sword of Lincoln*, p. 68; Michie, *General McClellan*, pp. 238–240; Sears, *McClellan*, p. 175; Dubbs, *Defend This Old Town*, pp. 70, 71.

¹⁸ Alexander, *Memoirs*, pp. 63–64.

¹⁹ Sears, *Gates of Richmond*, pp. 49, 52.

²⁰ Alexander, *Memoirs*, p. 64; Smith, *Confederate War Papers*, pp. 41–43; Longstreet, *Manassas to Appomattox*, p. 66; Davis, *Rise and Fall*, vol. II, pp. 87–88; Sears, *Gates of Richmond*, p. 48.

²¹ Alexander, *Memoirs*, p. 64.

²² Sears, *Gates of Richmond*, p. 48; McClellan, *Report on Campaigns*, pp. 175–176.

²³ Wert, *Sword of Lincoln*, pp. 71–73.

²⁴ Alexander, *Memoirs*, p. 64; Donald, *Lincoln*, p. 91; Sears, *Gates of Richmond*, pp. 48–50, 52–53; Alexander, *Fighting for Confederacy*, p. 75.

²⁵ McClellan, *Report on Campaigns*, p. 177; Yoseloff, *Campaigns of Civil War*, pp. 63–65.

²⁶ *OR*, XI, 1, p. 422; Alexander, *Memoirs*, p. 65; Sears, *Gates of Richmond*, pp. 55–56; Yoseloff, *Campaigns of Civil War*, pp. 63–65.

²⁷ Yoseloff, *Campaigns of Civil War*, pp. 65–66.

²⁸ Alexander, *Memoirs*, p. 65.

²⁹ Sears, *Gates of Richmond*, pp. 61–62; Alexander, *Memoirs*, pp. 65–66.

³⁰ Sears, *Gates of Richmond*, pp. 61, 66.

31 Alexander, *Memoirs*, p. 66.
32 Sears, *Gates of Richmond*, p. 65.
33 Alexander, *Memoirs*, p. 66; McClellan, *Report on Campaigns*, p. 178.

Chapter 8

1 Alexander, *Memoirs*, pp. 66–67.
2 Alexander, *Memoirs*, p. 67; Longstreet, *Manassas to Appomattox*, p. 72.
3 *OR*, XI, 1, p. 465; Hastings, *Pitiless Rain*, pp. 63–64.
4 Hastings, *Pitiless Rain*, p. 64.
5 *OR*, XI, 1, pp. 470–473; Hastings, *Pitiless Rain*, p. 64; Wainwright, *Diary of Battle*, pp. 47–52.
6 Hastings, *Pitiless Rain*, p. 66.
7 *OR*, XI, 1, pp. 465–467; Hastings, *Pitiless Rain*, p. 66.
8 *OR*, XI, 1, p. 580; Wert, *General Longstreet*, p. 105; Hastings, *Pitiless Rain*, p. 66.
9 Hastings, *Pitiless Rain*, pp. 66–67.
10 Wainwright, *Diary of Battle*, pp. 51–52; Hastings, *Pitiless Rain*, p. 67.
11 Hastings, *Pitiless Rain*, pp. 68–69.
12 *OR*, XI, 1, p. 463.
13 *OR*, XI, 1, p. 467; Hastings, *Pitiless Rain*, p. 69;.
14 *Report of Joint Committee*, vol. I, pp. 565–569.
15 Hastings, *Pitiless Rain*, p. 71.
16 Hastings, *Pitiless Rain*, p. 72.
17 Blake, *Three Years*, p. 85.
18 Hastings, *Pitiless Rain*, p. 75; Robertson, *A. P. Hill*, p. 53.
19 Hastings, *Pitiless Rain*, p. 80.
20 Hastings, *Pitiless Rain*, p. 81.
21 Alexander, *Memoirs*, p. 67.
22 *OR*, XI, 1, pp. 517, 518–523; Kettenburg, "The Battle of Williamsburg," pp. 62–63.

23 Hastings, *Pitiless Rain*, p. 85.

24 *OR*, XI, 1, pp. 451, 459; Hastings, *Pitiless Rain*, pp. 85–86.

25 Hastings, *Pitiless Rain*, p. 87.

26 *OR*, XI, 1, p. 473; Hastings, *Pitiless Rain*, p. 88; Wainwright, *Diary of Battle*, p. 54.

27 Sears, *Gates of Richmond*, p. 75.

28 Wainwright, *Diary of Battle*, p. 54.

29 *OR*, XI, 1, p. 572; Longstreet, *Manassas to Appomattox*, p. 75.

30 Hastings, *Pitiless Rain*, pp. 89–90.

31 *OR*, XI, 1, pp. 491–495, 498–499, 501–509; Hastings, *Pitiless Rain*, p. 90; Kettenburg, "The Battle of Williamsburg," pp. 66–68.

32 Hastings, *Pitiless Rain*, p. 91.

33 *OR*, XI, 1, pp. 463–464.

34 Hastings, *Pitiless Rain*, p. 97; Jordan, *Hancock*, p. 43.

35 Carroll, *Custer in Civil War*, p. 152.

36 *OR*, XI, 1, pp. 540, 610; Carroll, *Custer in Civil War*, pp. 153–157.

37 *OR*, XI, 1, p. 533; Kettenburg, "The Battle of Williamsburg," pp. 70–71.

38 *OR*, XI, 1, pp. 582–585; Hastings, *Pitiless Rain*, p. 100.

39 *OR*, XI, 1, pp. 582–583.

40 Bratton, "The Battle of Williamsburg," *SHSP*, Vol. 7, pp. 300–301.

41 *OR*, XI, 1, p. 550.

42 Carroll, *Custer in Civil War*, pp. 153–154.

43 *OR*, XI, 1, p. 556.

44 *OR*, XI, 1, p. 538.

45 *OR*, XI, 1, p. 538.

46 Hastings, *Pitiless Rain*, p. 102.

47 Alexander, *Memoirs*, pp. 67–68.

48 *OR*, XI, 1, pp. 554–556, 601–609; Maury, "The Battle of Williamsburg and the Charge of the 24th Virginia of Early's Brigade," *SHSP*, Vol. 8, pp. 281–300; Early, *War Memoirs*, pp. 68–73.

49 Sears, *Gates of Richmond*, pp. 79–80.

50 *OR*, XI, 1, pp. 539–540; Hastings, *Pitiless Rain*, p. 105.

[51] *OR*, XI, 1, pp. pp. 603–604.
[52] Bratton, "The Battle of Williamsburg," *SHSP*, Vol. 7, pp. 299-301. Bratton mistakenly names the regiment emerging from the woods as the 24th Virginia. It was, of course, the 5th North Carolina.
[53] *OR*, XI, 1, p. 610.
[54] Early, *War Memoirs*, p. 71; Gregory, *38th Virginia Infantry*, pp. 14–17.
[55] Hyde, *Following the Greek Cross*, p. 51.
[56] Carroll, *Custer in the Civil War*, p. 157; Hyde, *Following the Greek Cross*, p. 51.
[57] *OR*, XI, 1, p. 569; Hastings, *Pitiless Rain*, pp. 110–111.
[58] *OR*, XI, 1, pp. 606-608, 609, 610–611; Maury, "The Battle of Williamsburg and the Charge of the 24th Virginia of Early's Brigade," *SHSP*, Vol. 8, pp. 281–300.
[59] Yoseloff, *Campaigns of Civil War*, pp. 78–79.
[60] Hastings, *Pitiless Rain*, p. 112.
[61] Hill, *Bethel to Sharpsburg*, Vol. II, p. 35.
[62] Hastings, *Pitiless Rain*, pp. 114–115; Sears, *McClellan*, p. 183.
[63] *OR*, XI, 1, pp. 22–23.
[64] Sears, *Gates of Richmond*, pp. 81–82; Palfrey, "Fall of Yorktown," p. 161.
[65] Hastings, *Pitiless Rain*, p. 117; Alexander, *Memoirs*, p. 69.
[66] McClellan, *Report on Campaigns*, p. 186.
[67] Hastings, *Pitiless Rain*, pp. 115–116.
[68] Longstreet, *Manassas to Appomattox*, p. 77; Hastings, *Pitiless Rain*, pp. 116–117.

Chapter 9

[1] Hastings, *Pitiless Rain*, p. 118.
[2] Kettenburg, "Battle of Williamsburg," p. 104; Hastings, *Pitiless Rain*, p. 121.
[3] Webb, *The Peninsula*, p. 81; Yoseloff, *Campaigns of Civil War*, p. 81.
[4] Alexander, *Memoirs*, p. 66; Sears, *Gates of Richmond*, pp. 85–86.

[5] Sears, *Gates of Richmond*, pp. 84–85; Alexander, *Memoirs*, p. 66.

[6] Adams, *Story of a Trooper*, p. 411.

[7] Wheeler, *Sword over Richmond*, p. 167.

[8] Sears, *Gates of Richmond*, p. 85.

[9] Webb, *The Peninsula*, p. 82; Yoseloff, *Campaigns of Civil War*, p. 82.

[10] Johnston, *Military Operations*, p. 126

[11] Longstreet, *Manassas to Appomattox*, p. 80; McClellan, *Report on Campaigns*, p. 186; Sears, *Gates of Richmond*, p. 86; Newton, *Johnston and Defense*, pp. 147–148.

[12] McClellan, *Report on Campaigns*, pp. 186–187, Alexander, *Manassas to Appomattox*, p. 70.

[13] Sears, *Gates of Richmond*, p. 86.

[14] *OR*, XI, 1, pp. 614, 625; *OR*, XI, 3, p. 184; Newton, *Johnston and Defense*, p. 148.

[15] Hood, *Advance and Retreat*, pp. 21–22; Sears, *Gates of Richmond*, p. 86.

[16] Blake, *Three Years*, p. 87; Marks, *Peninsula Campaign*, p. 164.

[17] Hastings, *Pitiless Rain*, p. 119.

[18] Hastings, *Pitiless Rain*, p. 120; Rouse, *Remembering Williamsburg*, p. 90.

[19] Rouse, *Remembering Williamsburg*, p. 92.

Chapter 10

[1] McClellan, *Report on Campaigns*, p. 205; Sears, *Gates of Richmond*, pp. 113–114; Wheeler, *Sword over Richmond*, pp. 222–223.

[2] *OR*, XI, 1, p. 33; McClellan, *Report on Campaigns*, pp. 205–206.

[3] Sears, ed., *McClellan Papers*, p. 277.

[4] *OR*, XI, 1, pp. 69; Webb, *The Peninsula*, pp. 93–94.

[5] Sears, *Gates of Richmond*, p. 114.

[6] Newton, *Johnston and Defense*, p. 168.

[7] Webb, *The Peninsula*, p. 94.

[8] Sears, *Gates of Richmond*, p. 114.

[9] Sears, *Gates of Richmond*, p. 114.

[10] Clark, ed., *Histories of North Carolina Regiments*, Vol. II, p. 654.
[11] *OR*, XI, 1, pp. 699–700, 705, 709, 731, 741–742, 743–744; Porter to McClellan, May 27, 1862, McClellan Papers (A–59:23), LOC.
[12] *OR*, XI, 1, p. 685.
[13] McClellan, *Report on Campaigns*, p. 209; Webb, *Peninsula*, p. 96; Wheeler, *Sword Over Richmond*, p. 223; Burton, *Extraordinary Circumstances*, p. 10.
[14] *OR*, XI, 1, p. 35; Sears, ed., *McClellan Papers*, pp. 279–280; Sears, *Gates of Richmond*, p. 117.
[15] *OR*, XI, 1, p. 37; McClellan, *Report on Campaigns*, p. 212.
[16] *OR*, XI, 1, pp. 680; Sears, *Gates of Richmond*, p. 117.
[17] Newton, *Johnston and Defense*, p. 168.
[18] Hubbell, "Seven Days of McClellan," in Gallagher, p. 32.
[19] Swinton, *Campaigns of Army of Potomac*, pp. 129, 140–141.
[20] Dowdey, *The Seven Days*, p. 83; Wheeler, *Sword Over Richmond*, p. 223.

Part IV

[1] Blaisdell, p. 55

Chapter 11

[1] Newton, *Seven Pines*, p. 1; Putnam, *Richmond During the Confederacy*, p. 131; Manarin, *Richmond at War*, pp. 176–177.
[2] *OR*, IV, I, p. 605; Newton, *Seven Pines*, p. 2; Richardson, *Messages and Papers of Jeff Davis*, vol. 1, p. 129.
[3] *OR*, V, pp. 884–887, 894, 904–906, 930, 944, 949–950, 990, 1036, 1053, 1057, 1075, 1089; Johnston, *Narrative*, pp. 87–94; Newton, *Seven Pines*, p. 2.
[4] *OR*, V, pp. 526–527, 1063–1064, 1083–1085, 1096, 1099–1100; *OR*, LI, pt. 2, p. 497; Johnston, *Narrative*, p. 97; Newton, *Seven Pines*, p. 3; Rowland, *Jefferson Davis, Constitutionalist*, Vol. VI, pp. 502–504; Newton, "Defense," pp. 167–173.

[5] *OR*, XI, 3, pp. 499; Newton, *Seven Pines*, p. 3.

[6] *OR*, XI, 3, p. 536; Newton, *Seven Pines*, pp. 3–4.

[7] Davis, *Rise and Fall*, vol. 2, p. 121; Newton, *Seven Pines*, p. 4.

[8] Newton, *Seven Pines*, p. 5; Newton, "Defense," pp. 436–439n. Contains order of battle and troop strengths.

[9] Fuller, *Military History of Western World*, vol. III, p. 26; Newton, *Seven Pines*, pp. 5–6; Newton, "Defense," pp. 383–384.

[10] Long, *Memoirs of Lee*, pp. 158-159; Newton, *Seven Pines*, p. 6.

[11] Long, *Memoirs of Lee*, p. 159; Newton, *Seven Pines*, pp. 6–7; Newton, "Defense," pp. 454–455.

[12] Newton, *Seven Pines*, p. 8; Longacre, "Silas Casey," *Historical Times Encyclopedia*, pp. 118–119.

[13] *OR*, XI, 3, p. 198; Newton, *Seven Pines*, pp. 8–9.

[14] *OR*, XI, 3, p. 198; Newton, *Seven Pines*, p. 9.

[15] Newton, *Seven Pines*, pp. 10–11.

[16] Dowdey, *Seven Days*, p. 80; Newton, *Seven Pines*, p. 13.

[17] Newton, *Seven Pines*, p. 13.

[18] Newton, *Seven Pines*, pp. 17–18.

[19] Dowdey, *Seven Days*, pp. 86–87; Newton, *Seven Pines*, p. 19.

[20] Newton, *Seven Pines*, p. 19; Smith, *Battle of Seven Pines*, p. 8.

[21] Newton, *Seven Pines*, p. 20; Johnston to Jefferson Davis, Feb. 16, 1862, in Joseph E. Johnston papers, College of William and Mary; Beverly Johnston to Joseph E. Johnston, Sept. 14, 1867, Beverly Johnston to Joseph E. Johnston, Feb. 23, 1868 (2 letters that date), (Box 26, Folder 14), in Robert Morton Hughes Collection, Old Dominion University; Joseph E. Johnston to Smith, Jan. 21, 1868, in Joseph E. Johnston papers, College of William and Mary.

[22] *OR*, XI, 1, pp. 663–664; *OR*, XI, 3, pp. 537–539; Freeman, *Lee's Lieutenants*, Vol. I, pp. 214–217; Smith, *Battle of Seven Pines*, pp. 7–8; Newton, *Seven Pines*, pp. 20–21.

[23] Newton, *Seven Pines*, p. 21; Smith, *Battle of Seven Pines*, p. 14.

[24] Newton, *Seven Pines*, p. 21; Smith, *Battle of Seven Pines*, p. 15; Longstreet, *Manassas to Appomattox*, pp. 85–86. Page numbers applicable to Da Capo reprint of 1992.

²⁵ *OR*, XI, 1, p. 275; Newton, *Seven Pines*, p. 21.

²⁶ *OR*, XI, 1, p. 943; Newton, *Seven Pines*, p. 21.

²⁷ *ORN*, II, I, pp. 635–636; Newton, *Seven Pines*, p. 22; Longstreet, *Manassas to Appomattox*, p. 82; Newton, "Defense," pp. 394–397.

²⁸ *OR*, XI, 1, p. 938; Newton, *Seven Pines*, p. 22.

²⁹ Newton, *Seven Pines*, p. 22; Smith, "Two Days of Battle at Seven Pines," *BL*, vol. 2, p. 242; Freeman, *Lee's Lieutenants*, vol. I, p. 232n.

³⁰ Newton, *Seven Pines*, pp. 22–23. Newton points out that neither Johnston's report nor his memoirs support this account of the meeting.

³¹ Newton, *Seven Pines*, p. 23; Longstreet, *Manassas to Appomattox*, pp. 77–79; Johnston, *Narrative*, p. 122.

³² *OR*, XI, 1, pp. 939–940; Newton, *Seven Pines*, p. 23.

³³ Newton, *Seven Pines*, p. 23; Smith, *Battle of Seven Pines*, pp. 19–22.

³⁴ *OR*, XI, 1, p. 938; Newton, *Seven Pines*, p. 24.

³⁵ *OR*, XI, 1, p. 938; Newton, *Seven Pines*, p. 24.

³⁶ *OR*, XI, 1, p. 938; Newton, *Seven Pines*, pp. 24–25.

³⁷ Newton, *Seven Pines*, p. 25; Longacre, "Benjamin Huger," in Faust, pp. 118–119.

³⁸ Newton, *Seven Pines*, p. 25; Johnston, "Manassas to Seven Pines," *BL*, Vol. 2, p. 203.

³⁹ Newton, *Seven Pines*, pp. 25–26.

⁴⁰ Longstreet, *Manassas to Appomattox*, p. 32.

⁴¹ Piston, *Lee's Tarnished Lieutenant*, p. 11.

⁴² Newton, *Seven Pines*, p. 27; Sanger, *James Longstreet*, pp. 36–37.

⁴³ Newton, *Seven Pines*, p. 27; Sorrel, *Recollections*, pp. 37–38; Piston, *Lee's Tarnished Lieutenant*, pp. 15–16.

⁴⁴ *OR*, V, pp. 1001–1002; Newton, *Seven Pines*, p. 27.

⁴⁵ Longstreet, *Manassas to Appomattox*, p. 65; Newton, *Seven Pines*, pp. 28–29.

⁴⁶ *OR*, XI, 1, p. 564; Longstreet to Samuel Cooper, May 9, 1862, in *Letters Received*, M-474, Reel 30, NA; Lee to James Longstreet, May 28, 1862, in Lee, "Letters Sent by Gen. Robert E. Lee, March-August 1862," Chapter II, Volume 83 1/2 in Rec. Gp. 109, War Department Collection of Confederate Records, NA; Newton, *Seven Pines*, p. 29.

47 Newton, *Seven Pines*, pp. 29–30; Newton, "Defense," pp. 344–365; Grimsley, "Rear Guard at Williamsburg," *CWTI*, 24:3 (May 1985): pp. 28–30.

48 *OR*, XII, 3, p. 852; Newton, *Seven Pines*, p. 30.

49 Newton, *Seven Pines*, p. 30–31.

50 *OR*, XI, 1, p. 943.

51 Newton, *Seven Pines*, p. 31.

52 Newton, *Seven Pines*, p. 32; Freeman, *Lee's Lieutenants*, vol. I, p. 235.

53 Newton, "Defense," p. 452; Newton, *Seven Pines*, pp. 32–33.

54 *OR*, XI, 1, p. 873; Werstein, *Kearny the Magnificent*, p. 213; Clark, *Histories of Regiments from North Carolina*, vol. 1, p. 237.

55 Johnston, *Narrative*, p. 133.

56 Ward, *106th Pennsylvania*, p. 52.

57 Longstreet, *Manassas to Appomattox*, p. 91; Smith, "Two Days of Battle at Seven Pines," *BL*, vol. 2, p. 229; Newton, *Battle of Seven Pines*, p. 33; Sears, *Gates of Richmond*, p. 123.

58 Smith, *Battle of Seven Pines*, p. 24; Newton, *Seven Pines*, p. 34.

59 *OR*, XI, 1, p. 942; Capt. B. Sloan to Maj. Gen. G. W. Smith, Aug. 17, 1885, in *BL*, vol. 2, p. 228; Rhoades, *Scapegoat General*, pp. 50-51; Newton, "Defense," p. 470; Newton, *Seven Pines*, pp. 34–35.

60 *OR*, XI, 1, pp. 939–942; Longstreet, *Manassas to Appomattox*, p. 92; Smith, "Two Days of Battle at Seven Pines," *BL*, vol. 2, p. 229; Smith, *Battle of Seven Pines*, p. 77; Freeman, *Lee's Lieutenants*, vol. I, p. 239; Newton, *Seven Pines*, p. 35.

61 *OR*, XI, 1, p. 971; Newton, *Seven Pines*, pp. 35–36.

62 Newton, *Seven Pines*, p. 36.

63 Dickey, *85th Pennsylvania*, pp. 67–68; Reed and Dickey, *101st Pennsylvania*, p. 8; Newton, *Seven Pines*, p. 37.

64 Dickey, *85th Pennsylvania*, p. 62; Newton, *Seven Pines*, p. 37.

65 Dickey and Evans, *103rd Pennsylvania*, p. 15; Newton, *Seven Pines*, p. 37.

66 *OR*, XI, 1, p. 914; *Report of Joint Committee on War*, vol. I, p. 433; Newton, *Seven Pines*, p. 37.

67 Newton, *Seven Pines*, p. 37; Dickey and Evans, *103rd Pennsylvania*, pp.

15–16.

[68] *OR*, XI, 1, p. 928; Newton, *Seven Pines*, p. 38; *OR*, Ser. I, Vol. XI, pt. 1, p. 914.

[69] *OR*, XI, 1, p. 928; Dickey and Evans, *103rd Pennsylvania*, pp. 16–17; Newton, *Seven Pines*, pp. 38–39.

[70] *OR*, XI, 1, pp. 961–962; Newton, *Seven Pines*, p. 39.

[71] Dickey, *85th Pennsylvania*, p. 77.

[72] *OR*, XI, 1, p. 928; Newton, *Seven Pines*, p. 39.

[73] *OR*, XI, 1, p. 928; Dickey, *85th Pennsylvania*, p. 77; Newton, *Seven Pines*, p. 39.

[74] *OR*, XI, 1, p. 928; Dickey, *85th Pennsylvania*, p. 77; Dickey and Evans, *103rd Pennsylvania*, p. 16–17; Newton, *Seven Pines*, pp. 39, 41.

[75] *OR*, XI, 1, pp. 961–962; Newton, *Seven Pines*, p. 41; Clark, *North Carolina Regiments*, vol. 2, p. 204.

[76] *OR*, XI, 1, p. 921; Newton, *Seven Pines*, p. 41.

[77] *OR*, XI, 1, p. 914; Newton, *Seven Pines*, p. 41.

[78] *OR*, XI, 1, pp. 914, 921, 926, 929; Newton, *Seven Pines*, pp. 41, 43.

[79] *OR*, XI, 1, pp. 962, 967; Newton, *Seven Pines*, pp. 41, 43.

[80] *OR*, XI, 1, p. 962; Newton, *Seven Pines*, pp. 43–44.

[81] *OR*, XI, 1, pp. 951, 953; Newton, *Seven Pines*, p. 44.

[82] *OR*, XI, 1, p. 971; Newton, *Seven Pines*, p. 44.

[83] *OR*, XI, 1, p. 979; Gordon, *Reminiscences*, p. 56; Newton, *Seven Pines*, pp. 44–45.

[84] *OR*, XI, 1, p. 921; Newton, *Seven Pines*, p. 45.

[85] *OR*, XI, 1, p. 922; Dickey, *85th Pennsylvania*, pp. 128, 171; Newton, *Seven Pines*, p. 45.

[86] *OR*, XI, 1, p. 922; Newton, *Seven Pines*, p. 45; *Report of Joint Committee on War*, vol. 1, p. 444; Clark, *North Carolina Regiments*, vol. 1, p. 238.

[87] *OR*, XI, 1, pp. 916, 922, 951; Newton, *Seven Pines*, p. 46.

[88] *OR*, XI, 1, p. 915; Newton, *Seven Pines*, p. 46.

[89] *OR*, XI, 3, p. 203.

[90] Keyes, *Fifty Years*, pp. 461–462; Newton, *Seven Pines*, p. 47.

[91] Keyes, *Fifty Years*, pp. 41, 174, 334; Newton, *Seven Pines*, pp. 47–48.

[92] Keyes, *Fifty Years*, pp. 433, 438, 446.
[93] Newton, *Seven Pines*, p. 48.
[94] *OR*, XI, 1, pp. 873, 880, 888; Newton, *Seven Pines*, pp. 48–49.
[95] *OR*, XI, 1, pp. 874–875, 880.
[96] *OR*, XI, 1, p. 874.
[97] *OR*, XI, 1, pp. 943, 947.
[98] *OR*, XI, 1, pp. 893–894, 969–970.
[99] *OR*, XI, 1, p. 947.
[100] *OR*, XI, 1, p. 918; Newton, *Seven Pines*, pp. 50, 52; Gallagher, ed., *Fighting for the Confederacy*, pp. 86–87.
[101] *OR*, XI, pt. 1, p. 918.
[102] Newton, *Seven Pines*, pp. 52–53.
[103] *OR*, XI, 1, pp. 918, 929, 972–973; Gallagher, *Fighting for the Confederacy*, p. 87.
[104] Dickey, *85th Pennsylvania*, p. 171.
[105] Clark, *North Carolina Regiments*, vol. 1, p. 238.
[106] Clark, *North Carolina Regiments*, vol. 1, p. 238.
[107] Dickey, *85th Pennsylvania*, p. 171.
[108] *OR*, XI, 1, p. 929.
[109] Clark, *North Carolina Regiments*, vol. 1, p. 239.
[110] *OR*, XI, 1, p. 973.
[111] Dickey, *85th Pennsylvania*, pp. 78, 170–171.
[112] Newton, *Seven Pines*, p. 55.
[113] *OR*, XI, 1, p. 940; Smith, *Battle of Seven Pines*, p. 66.
[114] *OR*, XI, 1, p. 813.
[115] Wert, "Heintzelman," in Faust, *Historical Times Illustrated Encyclopedia*, p. 356.
[116] *OR*, XI, 1, p. 813; Newton, *Seven Pines*, pp. 56–57.
[117] *OR*, XI, 1, p. 813.
[118] *OR*, XI, 1, p. 813.
[119] *OR*, XI, 1, p. 852.

120 *OR*, XI, 1, pp. 816, 852.

121 Newton, *Seven Pines*, p. 58.

122 Werstein, *Kearny the Magnificent*, pp. 13–14.

123 Werstein, *Kearny the Magnificent*, pp. 130–131, 156, 187–189; McClellan, *McClellan's Own Story*, p. 138; Werstein, *Kearny the Magnificent*, pp. 166–167, 207.

124 Sifakis, *Who Was Who in Union*, p. 217; Werstein, *Kearny the Magnificent*, p. 207; Catton, *Glory Road*, p. 3.

125 *OR*, XI, 1, p. 818.

126 *OR*, XI, 1, p. 835.

127 *OR*, XI, 1, pp. 818, 835; *Report of Joint Committee on War*, vol. 1, p. 578.

128 *OR*, XI, 1, pp. 815–816, 838.

129 *OR*, XI, 1, pp. 951–953, 964–967.

130 *OR*, XI, 1, pp. 986–987.

131 *OR*, XI, 1, pp. 970–982; Newton, *Seven Pines*, p. 62.

132 *OR*, XI, 1, p. 888; Smith, "Two Days at Seven Pines," *BL*, vol. 2, p. 240.

133 *OR*, XI, 1, pp. 838, 888.

134 *OR*, XI, 1, pp. 838, 915.

135 *OR*, XI, 1, pp. 838, 867–870; Werstein, *Kearny the Magnificent*, p. 215.

136 *OR*, XI, 1, pp. 888–889, 894–895.

137 Newton, *Seven Pines*, p. 64.

138 *OR*, XI, 1, pp. 969–970, 980; Gordon, *Reminiscences*, p. 57.

139 *OR*, XI, 1, pp. 974, 978.

140 *OR*, XI, 1, p. 843.

141 *OR*, XI, 1, pp. 874–875, 949.

142 *OR*, XI, 1, pp. 876–877, 897.

143 *OR*, XI, 1, pp. 906, 911.

144 *OR*, XI, 1, pp. 906, 911–912.

145 *OR*, XI, 1, p. 906.

146 *OR*, XI, 1, pp. 949.

147 *OR*, XI, 1, pp. 906–907.

148 *OR*, XI, 1, pp. 974, 986.

149 *OR*, XI, 1, pp. 949.

150 *OR*, XI, 1, p. 814.

151 *OR*, XI, 1, p. 944.

152 Freeman, *R. E. Lee*, vol. II, p. 68; Davis, *Rise and Fall*, vol. II, pp. 122–123.

153 Smith, *Confederate War Papers*, p. 170.

154 Smith, *Confederate War Papers*, p. 170; Smith, *Battle of Seven Pines*, pp. 22–23.

155 Smith, *Confederate War Papers*, pp. 162–163; Smith, *Battle of Seven Pines*, pp. 22–23.

156 Freeman, *R. E. Lee*, vol. II, p. 68; Freeman, *Lee's Lieutenants*, vol. I, p. 236.

157 Newton, "Defense," p. 467.

158 Newton, "Defense," pp. 467–468.

159 *OR*, XI, 1, p. 989.

160 Smith, *Confederate War Papers*, p. 174; Davis, *Rise and Fall*, vol. II, pp. 122–123.

161 Sifakis, *Who Was Who in Civil War*, pp. 634–635.

162 Walker, *History of II Corps*, p. 27.

163 Ward, *One Hundred and Sixth Regiment*, p. 52; Winslow, *General John Sedgwick*, p. 15.

164 *OR*, XI, 1, pp. 802, 804, 805; Ward, *One Hundred and Sixth Regiment*, p. 52.

165 *OR*, XI, 1, p. 795; Ward, *One Hundred and Sixth Regiment*, p. 52; Sifakis, *Who Was Who in Civil War*, p. 365.

166 Ward, *One Hundred and Sixth Regiment*, pp. 52–53; Sifakis, *Who Was Who in Civil War*, pp. 92–93.

167 Ward, *One Hundred and Sixth Regiment*, pp. 52–53.

168 *OR*, XI, 1, pp. 879–880.

169 *OR*, XI, 1, p. 880; Sifakis, *Who Was Who in Civil War*, p. 146.

170 Cochrane, *Civil War Memories*, p. 21

171 *OR*, XI, 1, p. 880.

172 *OR*, XI, 1, p. 803.

173 McMurry, *Hood and Southern Independence*, p. 41; Smith, *Confederate War Papers*, pp. 174–175.

174 Smith, *Battle of Seven Pines*, p. 97.

175 *OR*, XI, 1, pp. 904, 992; Newton, "Defense," p. 488; Smith, *Battle of Seven Pines*, p. 98.

176 Smith, *Battle of Seven Pines*, p. 98.

177 *OR*, XI, 1, p. 990; Smith, *Battle of Seven Pines*, p. 98.

178 *OR*, XI, 1, pp. 803, 900, 904; Walker, *History of II Corps*, p. 36; Cochrane, *Civil War Memories*, p. 22.

179 *OR*, XI, 1, pp. 803, 904; Cochrane, *Civil War Memories*, p. 22.

180 *OR*, XI, 1, p. 991.

181 *OR*, XI, 1, p. 991; Hood, *Advance and Retreat*, p. 23.

182 *OR*, XI, 1, p. 881; Walker, *History of II Corps*, p. 36.

183 *OR*, XI, 1, p. 763; Walker, *History of II Corps*, pp. 37–38.

184 Lasswell, *Rags and Hope*, p. 102; Smith, *Battle of Seven Pines*, p. 98.

185 Johnston, *Narrative*, pp. 137–139.

186 Ward, *One Hundred and Sixth Regiment*, p. 53; Howard, *Autobiography*, vol. I, p. 239; Stoeckel, *Correspondence of Sedgwick*, vol. II, p. 59.

187 *OR*, XI, 1, p. 802; Ford, *Story of 15th Massachusetts*, p. 164.

188 Johnston, *Narrative*, p. 138.

189 Armistead, "Battle in Which Johnston Wounded," *SHSP*, vol. 18(Jan.–Dec. 1890): p. 187.

190 Johnston, *Narrative*, p. 139.

191 Benjamin Stoddert Ewell to Joseph E. Johnston, May 4, 1885, in Robert Morton Hughes Collection, (Box 29, Folder 2), Old Dominion University.

192 Smith, *Battle of Seven Pines*, pp. 103–104. This seems to be most objective version of what took place.

193 Sears, *McClellan*, p. 195.

194 *OR*, XI, 1, pp. 793–794.

195 Ford, *Fifteenth Regiment*, p. 163.

196 *OR*, I, XI, 1, p. 749.

[197] Palfrey, "Period Between Yorktown and Seven Days," p. 199–200.

Chapter 12

[1] *OR*, XI, 1, p. 765; *Report of Joint Committee on War*, vol. 1, p. 363.
[2] Smith, *Battle of Seven Pines*, p. 129; Longstreet, *Manassas to Appomattox*, p. 103.
[3] Smith, *Battle of Seven Pines*, p. 128.
[4] *OR*, XI, 1, p. 992; Smith, *Battle of Seven Pines*, pp. 127–129.
[5] Longstreet, *Manassas to Appomattox*, p. 104; Smith, *Battle of Seven Pines*, p. 129.
[6] Smith, *Battle of Seven Pines*, p. 129.
[7] *OR*, XI, 1, p. 940; Longstreet, *Manassas to Appomattox*, pp. 104–104.
[8] Bridges, *Lee's Maverick General*, p. 48.
[9] *OR*, XI, 1, p. 983; Bridges, *Lee's Maverick General*, p. 49.
[10] *OR*, XI, 1, p. 983; Bridges, *Lee's Maverick General*, p. 49; Smith, "Two Days at Seven Pines," *BL*, vol. 2, p. 256.
[11] *OR*, XI, 1, pp. 765, 771, 782.
[12] Smith, *Battle of Seven Pines*, p. 119.
[13] *OR*, XI, 1, p. 785; Smith, *Battle of Seven Pines*, p. 119.
[14] *OR*, XI, 1, p. 775; Smith, "Two Days at Seven Pines," *BL*, vol. 2, p. 258.
[15] *OR*, XI, 1, p. 765; Smith, *Battle of Seven Pines*, pp. 119–120.
[16] *OR*, XI, 1, p. 945; Bridges, *Lee's Maverick General*, pp. 49–50; Smith, *Battle of Seven Pines*, p. 120.
[17] *OR*, XI, 1, pp. 783–791, 984–986.
[18] *OR*, XI, 1, pp. 982–983.
[19] *OR*, XI, 1, pp. 819, 856–857, 982–983.
[20] *OR*, XI, 1, p. 856.
[21] *OR*, XI, 1, p. 818.
[22] *OR*, XI, 1, pp. 982–983.
[23] *OR*, XI, 1, pp. 819, 822–823.
[24] *OR*, XI, 1, pp. 856–858.

25 *OR*, XI, 1, pp. 758–759, 819, 856–858, 983.

26 Palfrey, "Period Between Yorktown and Seven Days," p. 182.

27 Smith, *Confederate War Papers*, pp. 208–209.

28 Smith, *Confederate War Papers*, p. 209; Longstreet, *Manassas to Appomattox*, p. 107.

29 Smith, *Confederate War Papers*, pp. 210–211.

30 Newton, *Seven Pines*, p. 95; Smith, *Confederate War Papers*, pp. 210–211.

31 Smith, *Confederate War Papers*, pp. 211–212.

32 Konstam, *Fair Oaks 1862*, p. 17.

33 Konstam, *Fair Oaks 1862*, p. 85.

34 Dickey, *85th Pennsylvania*, p. 155.

35 Livermore, *Numbers and Losses*, p. 81.

36 *OR*, XI, 1, pp. 749–750.

37 *OR*, XI, 1, p. 916.

38 *OR*, XI, 1, pp. 876–878.

39 *OR*, XI, 1, p. 816.

40 *OR*, XI, 1, pp. 43, 752–756; Warner, *Generals in Blue*, p. 75; Sears, ed., *McClellan Papers*, p. 302.

41 *OR*, XI, 1, pp. 933–941; Smith, *Battle of Seven Pines*, pp. 20–22.

42 *OR*, XI, 1, pp. 936–942.

43 Warner, *Generals in Gray*, p. 144.

44 Newton, *Seven Pines*, pp. 99–100.

Chapter 13

1 Harsh, *Confederate Tide Rising*, p. 50.

2 Von Borcke, "The Prussian Remembers," *CWTI*, 19:10 (Feb. 1981), p. 42; Ware Diary, June 1, 1862, SHC; Constance Cary Harrison in *BL*, vol. 2, pp. 443–445, Putnam, *Richmond During the Confederacy*, pp. 135–136, Hunter, *Johnny Reb and Billy Yank*, p. 157, Fox, *Regimental Losses*, p. 549.

3 *OR*, XI, 1, p. 178; Adams, *Doctors in Blue*, p. 71; *OR*, XI, 1, p. 762.

Wormeley, *The Other Side of the War: With the Army of the Potomac,* pp. 105–106.

⁴ Wainwright, *Diary of Battle,* p. 76; Thomas B. Leaver to mother, June 6, 1862, Leaver Papers, New Hampshire Historical Society.

⁵ McClellan to wife, June 2, 1862, to Army of Potomac, June 2, 1862, telegrams to Stanton, June 2, 1862, to Lincoln, June 4, 1862, Sears, ed., *McClellan Papers,* pp. 287, 286–287, 285, 288–289; Comte de Paris to McClellan, Mar. 13, 1875, McClellan Papers, (A–95:38) LOC.

⁶ *OR,* XI, 1, p. 940; *OR,* XI, 3, p. 580; Huger notes, Sept. 28, 1862, *OR,* XI, 1, pp. 937–938; Davis to wife, June 2, 1862, Rowland, *Jefferson Davis, Constitutionalist,* vol. V, p. 265.

⁷ William Allan conversation with Lee, Dec. 17, 1868, Allan Papers, SHC; Marshall, *Aide-de-Camp of Lee,* ed. Frederick Maurice, p. 77; Longstreet, *Manassas to Appomattox,* pp. 112–113; Jefferson in *SHSP,* vol. 17 (1889), p. 369.

⁸ Boteler telegram To Randolph, June 1, 1862, RG 109 (M–618:10) NA; Lee to Randolph, to Davis, June 5, 1862, Lee, *Papers,* pp. 185, 183–184; Boteler in *SHSP,* vol. 40 (1915), pp. 164–166; *Richmond Dispatch,* May 29, 1862; Jackson telegram to Samuel Cooper, June 10, 1862, Thomas J. Jackson Papers, MoC.

⁹ William Allan conversation with Lee, Dec. 17, 1868, Allan Papers, SHC; Brent, *Memoirs,* pp. 154–155; Marshall, *Aide-de-Camp,* p. 84; Pinkerton to McClellan, June 16, 1862, McClellan Papers (A–64:25), LOC; Porter to Marcy, June 16, 1862, McClellan Papers (A–64:25), LOC; Lee to Randolph, June 11, 1862, Lee, *Papers,* p. 191; King to Shriver, June 18, 1862, *OR,* I, XII, 3, p. 404; Lincoln telegram to McClellan, June 19, 1862, Lincoln, *Works,* Vol. V, p. 277; McClellan telegram to Lincoln, June 19, 1862, Sears, ed., *McClellan Papers,* p. 303.

¹⁰ Harsh, *Confederate Tide Rising,* pp. 18–19.

¹¹ Lee to Davis, June 5, 1862, Lee, *Papers,* pp. 184, 182–183; Davis to Lee, June 2, 1862, *OR,* XI, 3, p. 570; *Charleston Mercury,* Oct. 14, 1861.

¹² Whiting to Lee, June 2, 1862, *OR,* XI, 3, pp. 685–686; G. W. Smith to Johnston, July 18, 1862, *OR,* LI, 2, pp. 593–594.

¹³ *OR,* XI, 3, pp. 530–531; *OR,* XI, 3, p. 645.

¹⁴ Burnside telegram to McClellan, June 13, 1862, McClellan Papers

(A–63:25), LOC; McClellan to wife, June 6 & 11, 1862, McClellan, *Papers,* pp. 289, 296.

[15] *OR,* XVI, 2, pp. 14, 26–27; McClellan telegram to Stanton, June 10, 1862, Sears, ed., *McClellan Papers,* pp. 295–296; McClellan to wife, June 22, 1862, Sears, ed., *McClellan Papers,* pp. 304–305; Halleck telegrams to Stanton, June 12 & 16, OR, XVI, 2, pp. 14, 26–27.

[16] Lincoln to Stanton, June 8, 1862, Lincoln, *Works Supplement,* p. 138; Lincoln telegrams to McClellan, June 15 & 20, 1862, Lincoln, *Works,* Vol. V, pp. 272, 277–278; Lincoln to Fremont, June 15, Lincoln, *Works,* Vol. V, pp. 270–271.

[17] Barnard report, *OR,* XI, 1, pp. 114–116; McClellan telegram to Lincoln, June 20, 1862, Sears, ed., *McClellan Papers,* p. 304; McClellan telegram to wife, June 15, 1862, Sears, ed., *McClellan Papers,* pp. 300–302.

[18] Army of the Potomac S.O. 168, June 2, 1862, S.O. 189, June 23, 1862, *OR,* XI, 3, pp. 210–211, 248; McClellan telegram to Stanton, June 15, 1862, Sears, ed., *McClellan Papers,* pp. 302; McClellan to wife, June 11, 1862, Sears, ed., *McClellan Papers,* p. 296; *McClellan's Own Story* draft, McClellan Papers (D–9:71), LOC.

[19] McClellan to wife, June 9, 1862, Sears, ed., *McClellan Papers,* p. 293; *New York Times,* June 24, 1862; Sears, *Gates of Richmond,* pp. 160–161.

[20] Key to Stanton, June 16, 1862, Stanton to McClellan, June 21, 1862, *OR,* XI, 1, pp. 1052–1056, 1056; McClellan telegram to Lincoln, June 20, 1862, Sears, ed., *McClellan Papers,* p. 304.

[21] J. Ambler Johnston, *Echoes of 1861–1965,* pp. 64–65, W. R. Mason in *BL,* Vol. 2, p. 277, Robert G. Haile diary, June 10, 1862, Swem Library, College of William and Mary.

[22] McClellan to wife, June 22, 1862, McClellan telegrams to Stanton, June 25, 1862, to Lincoln, June 18, 1862, Sears, ed., *McClellan Papers,* pp. 309–310, 303, Pinkerton to A. Porter, June 15, 1862, McClellan to Marcy, June 19, 1862, McClellan Papers (A–64:25), A–65:26), LOC; Pinkerton to McClellan, June 26, *OR,* XI, 1, p. 269, Fishel, "Pinkerton and McClellan," *Civil War History,* vol. 34, no. II, pp. 127–128; Lee to Jackson, June 16, 1862, Lee, *Papers,* p. 194; McClellan telegrams to Burnside, June 20, 1862, to Rodgers, June 24, McClellan to Barlow, June 23, Sears, ed., *McClellan Papers,* pp. 303, 307, 306.

[23] Sears, *Gates of Richmond,* pp. 163–164.

[24] Sears, *Gates of Richmond,* pp. 164–165.

²⁵ Steiner, *Disease in the Civil War*, p. 134; Lane, *Letters from Georgia Soldiers*, p. 153; Sears, *Gates of Richmond*, p. 165.

²⁶ Robert G. Haile diary, June 6, 1862, Swem Library, College of William and Mary; Sears, *Gates of Richmond*, pp. 165–167.

Chapter 14

¹ Warner, *Generals in Gray*, p. 296.

² *OR*, I, V, p. 777; Sears, *Gates of Richmond*, p. 167.

³ Lee to Stuart, June 11, 1862, *OR*, XI, 3, pp. 590–91; *OR*, XI, 1, p. 1038; Von Borcke, *Memoirs of the Confederate War for Independence*, Vol. I, pp. 34–37; Mosby in *SHSP*, vol. 26 (1898), pp. 246–248.

⁴ *OR*, XI, 1, pp. 1036–1038; Von Borcke, *Memoirs*, vol. I, p. 37; Stuart Report, Frayser, "Narrative of Stuart's Raid," *SHSP*, vol. 11 (1883): pp. 506–507; Cooke, *Wearing of the Gray*, pp. 179; Sears, *Gates of Richmond*, pp. 168–170.

⁵ Porter telegrams to Marcy, June 13, 1862, McClellan Papers, (A–62:25), LOC; Cooke, Warren reports, *OR*, XI, 1, pp. 1013, 1029–1031.

⁶ Sears, *Gates of Richmond*, p. 170.

⁷ Cullen, *Peninsula Campaign*, p. 66.

⁸ *OR*, XI, 1, pp. 1032, 1028–1029, 1030, 1039; Frayser in *SHSP*, vol. 11 (1883), pp. 507–511; Cooke, *Wearing of the Gray*, pp. 183–187; Beale, *Lieutenant of Cavalry*, p. 30.

⁹ Alexander, *Military Memoirs of a Confederate*, p. 169.

¹⁰ W.T. Robins in *BL*, Vol. 2, p. 275; Emily J. Salmon, "The Burial of Latane: Symbol of the Lost Cause," *Virginia Cavalcade*, vol. 28 (Winter 1979), pp. 118–129.

¹¹ William Y. Ripley to wife, June 17, 1862, Ripley Papers, Perkins Library, Duke University; Cook, *Siege of Richmond*, pp. 286–287; McClellan telegram to Stanton, June 14, 1862, Sears, ed., *McClellan Papers*, p. 299; McClellan to S.S. Cox, 1884, Charles P. Kingsbury to Marcy, June 17, 1862, McClellan Papers (A–65:26, LOC; Charles P. Kingsbury to Marcy, June 17, 1862, McClellan Papers (A– 65:26), LOC; Clarke, Van Vliet reports, *OR*, XI, 1, pp. 169, 159.

¹² Marshall, *Aide-de-Camp*, pp. 82–83; Lee to Jackson, June 16, 1862, Lee,

Papers, p. 194; Imboden, *BL*, vol. 2, pp. 296–297; Harmon to brother, June 21, 1862, J. William Jones memoir, Hotchkiss Papers (39), LOC; Douglas, *I Rode With Stonewall,* p. 97.

[13] D.H. Hill in *BL,* Vol. 2, pp. 347–348; General Orders No. 75, June 24, 1862, Lee to Davis June 10, 1862, Lee, *Papers,* pp. 198–200, 188; Longstreet, *Manassas to Appomattox,* pp. 121–122; Longstreet to D.H. Hill, Nov. 5, 1877, D.H. Hill Papers, LVa; William Allan conversation with Lee, Dec. 17, 1868, Allan Papers, SHC; Marshall, *Aide-de-Camp,* p. 85.

Part V

[1] Marks, *Peninsular Campaign,* p. 4

Chapter 15

[1] Wheeler, *Sword Over Richmond,* p. 296.
[2] Smith, *Autobiography,* pp. 40-41; *OR,* XI, 1, p. 50; Burton, *Extraordinary Circumstances,* pp. 41–42.
[3] *OR,* XI, 1, p. 50; *OR,* XI, 2, p. 108; *OR,* XI, 3, p. 250; Burton, *Extraordinary Circumstances,* p. 43.
[4] *OR,* XI, 2, pp. 96, 108, 120–121, 134–135.
[5] *OR,* XI, 2, pp. 121, 623, 787, 792, 798–799, 804–805 Burton, *Extraordinary Circumstances,* pp. 44, 45, 418, 419.
[6] *OR,* XI, 2, pp. 135–136, 155–156, 791, 804–805; Burton, *Extraordinary Circumstances,* p. 45.
[7] *OR,* XI, 2, pp. 96, 137, 147, 201, 805; Burton, *Extraordinary Circumstances,* pp. 47–48.
[8] OR, XI, 2, pp. 173–176, 179–182, 184.
[9] *OR,* XI, 2, pp. 173–174, 184, 799, 802; Burton, *Extraordinary Circumstances,* pp. 48–49.
[10] *OR,* XI, 2, pp. 174, 179–180, 184, 792, 799, 803, 806; Burton, *Extraordinary Circumstances,* pp. 49–50.
[11] *OR,* XI, 2, pp. 121–122, 180, 792–793, 806.

12 Sears, *Gates of Richmond*, p. 189; Burton, *Extraordinary Circumstances*, p. 50.

13 Sears, *Gates of Richmond*, p. 189.

14 Burton, *Extraordinary Circumstances*, p. 51; Sears, *Gates of Richmond*, p. 189.

15 Alexander, *Military Memoirs*, pp. 114–115.

16 *OR*, XI, 2, pp. 490, 970; *OR*, XI, 3, pp. 251–252; Lee, *Lee's Dispatches*, pp. 13–14.

17 *OR*, XI, 2, pp. 498–499.

18 Dabney Memorandum, Mar. 31, 1896, Hotchkiss Papers, LOC; Douglas, *I Rode With Stonewall*, p. 99; Davis, *They Called Him Stonewall*, p. 214.

19 Douglas, *I Rode With Stonewall*, p. 100; General Orders No. 75 is reprinted at Appendix D of this book; The text of Jackson's memorandum from the Dabbs House conference is reprinted at Appendix E.

20 *OR*, XI, 2, p. 514; Lee, *Lee's Dispatches*, pp. 14–15

Chapter 16

1 Cullen, *Peninsula Campaign*, p. 78; Burton, *Extraordinary Circumstances*, p. 58.

2 Cullen, *Peninsula Campaign*, pp. 78–79.

3 *OR*, XI, 2, pp. 498–499; Cullen, *Peninsula Campaign*, p. 79.

4 Burton, *Extraordinary Circumstances*, pp. 59, 61.

5 *OR*, XI, 3, p. 247; Smith, *Autobiography*, p. 51; Burton, *Extraordinary Circumstances*, pp. 62–63.

6 *OR*, XI, 1, pp. 51–52; *OR*, XI, 3, p. 258.

7 Burton, *Extraordinary Circumstances*, p. 63.

8 *OR*, XI, 1, p. 59; *OR*, XI, 2, p. 499; Burton, *Extraordinary Circumstances*, pp. 62–63.

9 *OR*, XI, 2, p. 835; Dowdey, *The Seven Days*, p. 190; Cullen, *Peninsula Campaign*, p. 96.

10 *OR*, XI, 2, p. 538; Burton, *Extraordinary Circumstances*, pp. 64–65.

[11] *OR*, XI, 2, pp. 414, 623; *OR*, LI, 1, p. 109; Burton, *Extraordinary Circumstances*, pp. 65–67.

[12] Burton, *Extraordinary Circumstances*, pp. 67–68.

[13] "Purcell Battery," *SHSP* vol. 21, pp. 362–363; OR, XI, 2, pp. 841, 899; *OR*, XI, 2, p. 841.

[14] *OR*, XI, 2, p. 877; Burton, *Extraordinary Circumstances*, p. 69.

[15] *OR*, XI, 2, pp. 289, 385, 411, 419, 835, 841, 877–878; *OR*, LI, 1, pp. 110–111, 117.

[16] *OR*, XI, 2, pp. 289, 385, 411, 419, 835, 841, 877–878; *OR*, LI, 1, pp. 111–112, 117.

[17] *OR*, XI, 2, pp. 201, 399, 411, 841, 897; Burton, *Extraordinary Circumstances*, pp. 70, 71.

[18] *OR*, XI, 2, pp. 261, 399, 409, 899; Burton, *Extraordinary Circumstances*, p. 72.

[19] *OR*, XI, 2, p. 623; Burton, *Extraordinary Circumstances*, p. 73.

[20] *OR*, XI, 2, pp. 623, 648.

[21] OR, XI, 2, pp. 499, 614; Burton, *Extraordinary Circumstances*, pp. 76–77.

[22] Sears, *Gates of Richmond*, p. 208; Burton, *Extraordinary Circumstances*, p. 78.

[23] Sears, *Gates of Richmond*, p. 207; Burton, *Extraordinary Circumstances*, p. 78.

[24] OR, XI, 3, pp. 259–260; Burton, Extraordinary Circumstances, p. 79.

[25] Sears, *Gates of Richmond*, p. 209; Burton, *Extraordinary Circumstances*, pp. 79–80.

Chapter 17

[1] *OR*, XI, 3, pp. 620–621; Burton, *Extraordinary Circumstances*, p. 82.

[2] *OR*, XI, 223; Burton, *Extraordinary Circumstances*, p. 81.

[3] Cullen, *Peninsula Campaign*, p. 111.

[4] Cullen, *Peninsula Campaign*, p. 111.

[5] *OR*, XI, 2, pp. 569–570, 586; Burton, *Extraordinary Circumstances*, p. 83.

[6] *OR*, XI, 2, pp. 491–492, 624; Burton, *Extraordinary Circumstances*, pp.

    83–84.
7 Lee, *Lee's Dispatches*, p. 18; Burton, *Extraordinary Circumstances*, p. 84.
8 *OR*, XI, 2, pp. 853–854; Longstreet, *From Manassas to Appomattox*, p. 125; Freeman, *R. E. Lee*, p. 144.
9 *OR*, XI, 2, pp. 313, 535, 836, 854; Freeman, *R.E. Lee*, p. 144; Burton, *Extraordinary Circumstances*, pp. 84, 86.
10 *OR*, XI, 1, p. 118; *OR*, XI, 2, pp. 224, *OR*, XI, 2, pp. 224, 272–273, 348, 371; Slater, "Fray at Gaines' Mill," p. 1.
11 Burton, *Extraordinary Circumstances*, p. 87.
12 *OR*, XI, 1, pp. 58, 118; *OR*, XI, 2, pp. 224, 348, 429; *OR*, XI, 3, pp. 264–265.
13 *OR*, XI, 2, pp. 313, 348, 492, 853–854, 836; Sears, *George B. McClellan*, p. 211; Sears, *Gates of Richmond*, p. 224.
14 *OR*, XI, 1, pp. 58–59; Burton, *Extraordinary Circumstances*, pp. 90–91.
15 DeMotte, "The Cause of a Silent Battle", *BL*, Vol. 2, p. 365; Burton, *Extraordinary Circumstances*, pp. 91.
16 *OR*, XI, 2, p. 836; *Extraordinary Circumstances*, p. 91.
17 *OR*, XI, 2, pp. 356, 378, 836, 854–856, 861; *OR*, XI, 2, pp. 356, 873–874.
18 *OR*, XI, 2. p. 856; Burton, *Extraordinary Circumstances*, p. 93.
19 *OR*, XI, 2, pp. 361, 367, 369, 372, 856, 858–860, 885–886, 903; Burton, *Extraordinary Circumstances*, pp. 93–94.
20 *OR*, XI, 2, pp. 278, 313, 373, 883, 888, 891, 893, 896; Burton, *Extraordinary Circumstances*, pp. 94–95.
21 *OR*, XI, 2, pp. 883, 900.
22 OR, XI, 2, pp. 296, 847, 849, 878–879; Burton, *Extraordinary Circumstances*, pp. 97.
23 *OR*, XI, 2, pp. 296, 897; Slater, "Fray at Gaines' Mill," *Philadelphia Weekly Times*, Jan. 26, 1884, p. 1.
24 *OR*, XI, 2, pp. 841-842; Slater, "Fray at Gaines' Mill," *Philadelphia Weekly Times*, Jan. 26, 1884, p. 1; Burton, *Extraordinary Circumstances*, pp. 98–99.
25 *OR*, XI, 2, pp. 842, 845, 874, 897, 982–983; Burton, *Extraordinary Circumstances*, pp. 99.

[26] Fox, *Regimental Losses*, p. 562; Burton, *Extraordinary Circumstances*, p. 100.

[27] *OR*, XI, 2, pp. 679, 756–757, 767, 771–772, 868; Longstreet, *Manassas to Appomattox*, p. 127.

[28] Burton, *Extraordinary Circumstances*, pp. 101–102.

[29] *OR*, XI, 2, pp. 553, 624, 757; Burton, *Extraordinary Circumstances*, p. 102; Sears, *Gates of Richmond*, pp. 227–228.

[30] Burton, *Extraordinary Circumstances*, p. 102.

[31] Sears, *Gates of Richmond*, p. 221.

[32] *OR*, XI, 2, pp. 243, 353, 515, 553, 624, 652; Burton, *Extraordinary Circumstances*, pp. 103–104.

[33] *OR*, XI, 2, p. 553; Burton, *Extraordinary Circumstances*, p. 104; Dowdey, *The Seven Days*, p. 217. Dowdey found Jackson's reasoning "uninspired", and noted the poor communication on Jackson's part during the whole of the campaign.

[34] *OR*, XI, 2, p. 605; Burton, *Extraordinary Circumstances*, pp. 104–106.

[35] *OR*, XI, 2, pp. 371, 614–615, 856–857; Nisbet, *Four Years*, pp. 64–65; Oates, *War and Lost Opportunities*, pp. 115, 118–119.

[36] Sears, *Gates of Richmond*, p. 229; Burton, *Extraordinary Circumstances*, p. 107.

[37] Sears, *Gates of Richmond*, pp. 232, 236; Burton, *Extraordinary Circumstances*, p. 108.

[38] Sears, *Gates of Richmond*, p. 123; Burton, *Extraordinary Circumstances*, p. 108.

[39] *OR*, XI, 2, pp. 401–402, 413; Burton, *Extraordinary Circumstances*, pp. 108–109.

[40] Burton, *Extraordinary Circumstances*, p. 109.

[41] *OR*, XI, 2, pp. 313, 456–458, 605, 620; Burton, *Extraordinary Circumstances*, p. 109; Sears, *Gates of Richmond*, p. 229.

[42] *OR*, XI, 2, pp. 457, 560, 606, 614.

[43] Burton, *Extraordinary Circumstances*, pp. 110–111.

[44] *OR*, XI, 2, p. 563; Polley, *Hood's Texas Brigade*, p. 41.

[45] *OR*, XI, 2, pp. 21, 401, 413, 421, 424; *OR*, XI, 3, p. 265; Burton, *Extraordinary Circumstances*, pp. 111–112.

46 *OR*, XI, 2, pp. 420, 433, 438, 444, 445; Burton, *Extraordinary Circumstances*, pp. 112–113.

47 *OR*, XI, 2, pp. 286, 447; Burton, *Extraordinary Circumstances*, p. 113.

48 *OR*, XI, 2, pp. 358, 365, 515, 624, 627, 652; Burton, *Extraordinary Circumstances*, pp. 113–114.

49 Burton, *Extraordinary Circumstances*, p. 114.

50 *OR*, XI, 2, pp. 555, 570, 595, 624–625, 637, 640–641, 837; Burton, *Extraordinary Circumstances*, pp. 114–115.

51 *OR*, XI, 2, pp. 451, 837; Jones, "Reminiscences No. 8," p. 560; Burton, *Extraordinary Circumstances*, p. 116.

52 Burton, *Extraordinary Circumstances*, pp. 116.

53 *OR*, XI, 2, pp. 348–349, 626, 630, 635, 641–642, 644; Sears, *Gates of Richmond*, p. 237; Burton, *Extraordinary Circumstances*, pp. 117–118.

54 Burton, *Extraordinary Circumstances*, pp. 118-120.

55 *OR*, XI, 2, pp. 287, 621, 624, 649; Blackford, *War Years*, p. 75.

56 *OR*, XI, 2, pp. 570, 575, 580, 584; Burton, *Extraordinary Circumstances*, pp. 120–121.

57 *OR*, XI, 2, pp. 362, 365, 367–70; Allen, "Battle of Gaines's Mill", *NT*, May 2, 1901, p. 3.

58 *OR*, XI, 2, pp. 447–448; Burton, *Extraordinary Circumstances*, pp. 121–122.

59 *OR*, XI, 2, pp. 448, 451–452, 625; Burton, *Extraordinary Circumstances*, p. 122.

60 *OR*, XI, 2, pp. 284, 371–372, 375, 401, 424, 447–448, 595–596; Burton, *Extraordinary Circumstances*, p. 123.

61 *OR*, XI, 2, pp. 313, 437–438, 457, 460; Burton, *Extraordinary Circumstances*, pp. 123–124.

62 *OR*, XI, 2, pp. 437, 614–615; Burton, *Extraordinary Circumstances*, p. 124.

63 *OR*, XI, 2, p. 313; Burton, *Extraordinary Circumstances*, p. 124.

64 *OR*, XI, 2, pp. 388, 401–402, 408, 410–412, 438, 615–616; Sears, *Gates of Richmond*, p. 253; Burton, *Extraordinary Circumstances*, pp. 124-125; *OR*, LI, 1, p. 115.

65 *OR*, XI, 2, pp. 563, 757; Longstreet, *Manassas to Appomattox*, pp. 127–

128; Sears, *Gates of Richmond,* p. 240.

[66] *OR,* XI, 2, pp. 563, 757; Hood, *Advance and Retreat,* pp. 25–26; Burton, *Extraordinary Circumstances,* p. 128.

[67] *OR,* XI, 2, p. 563, 503; Burton, *Extraordinary Circumstances,* p. 128.

[68] *OR,* XI, 2, pp. 40, 322–324, 757, 767; Burton, *Extraordinary Circumstances,* p. 129.

[69] *OR,* XI, 2, pp. 273, 282, 302; Burton, *Extraordinary Circumstances,* pp. 129–130.

[70] *OR,* XI, 2, pp. 282, 297, 307, 309, 311; Slater, "Fray at Gaines' Mill," p. 3.

[71] *OR,* XI, 2, pp. 773–774; Burton, *Extraordinary Circumstances,* pp. 130–131.

[72] *OR,* XI, 2, pp. 285, 317, 339–340, 344–345, 421; Terrell, "Gaines's Mills," *NT,* Aug. 8, 1895, p. 3; Burton, *Extraordinary Circumstances,* pp. 131–132.

[73] *OR,* XI, 2, pp. 563–564; Burton, *Extraordinary Circumstances,* p. 132.

[74] *OR,* XI, 2, pp. 41–42, 225–226, 249–250, 273, 282, 408; *OR,* LI, 1, p. 115; Burton, *Extraordinary Circumstances,* pp. 132–133.

[75] *OR,* XI, 2, p. 233, 70-71; McCaleb, "Mississippi Brigade," *SHSP,* vol. 32, (Jan.–Dec.): p. 333; Burton, *Extraordinary Circumstances,* p. 134.

[76] *OR,* XI, 2, pp. 39–40, 76; Powell, *Fifth Army Corps,* p. 121.

[77] Sears, *Gates of Richmond,* p. 240.

[78] *OR,* XI, 2, pp. 39–41, 558–559, 642, 758, 780, 973–991; Livermore, *Numbers and Losses,* pp. 83, 140; Fox, *Regimental Losses,* pp. 543, 550, 562–563.

Chapter 18

[1] See Appendix D.

[2] *OR,* XI, 2, p. 463; Burton, *Extraordinary Circumstances,* pp. 141–142.

[3] *OR,* XI, 2, pp. 462-463; Warner, *Generals in Gray,* pp. 163–164; Burton, *Extraordinary Circumstances,* p. 142.

[4] Sears, *Gates of Richmond,* p. 258; Burton, *Extraordinary Circumstances,* p. 142.

⁵ *OR*, XI, 2, pp. 462–463, 688–689, 706, 831; Burton, *Extraordinary Circumstances*, pp. 144–145.

⁶ *OR*, XI, 2, pp. 237, 689; Smith, *Autobiography*, p. 41; Jones, *Rebel War Clerk's Diary*, vol. 1, p. 139.

⁷ *OR*, XI, 2, pp. 689, 695; Burton, *Extraordinary Circumstances*, pp. 143, 144.

⁸ *OR*, XI, 2, pp. 463, 661, 689, 695, 715; *OR*, XI, 3, pp. 621–622; Burton, *Extraordinary Circumstances*, p. 144.

⁹ *OR*, XI, 2, pp. 88, 467, 476, 695, 699–700; Burton, *Extraordinary Circumstances*, pp. 144, 146.

¹⁰ *OR*, XI, 2, pp. 467, 696, 698, 700, 977; *OR*, XI, 3, p. 238; Burton, *Extraordinary Circumstances*, p. 146; Sears, *Gates of Richmond*, p. 247.

¹¹ *OR*, XI, 3, p. 622; Burton, *Extraordinary Circumstances*, pp. 146–147, 153.

¹² *OR*, XI, 2, p. 690; *OR*, XI, 2, pp. 33–36; *OR*, XI, 2, p. 977; Sears, *Gates of Richmond*, p. 258.

Chapter 19

¹ *OR*, XI, 2, p. 662.

² *OR*, XI, 2, pp. 662, 707; Longstreet, *Manassas to Appomattox*, p. 130; Burton, *Extraordinary Circumstances*, p. 178.

³ *OR*, XI, 2, pp. 726, 744; Longstreet, *Manassas to Appomattox*, pp. 130, 148–149.

⁴ *OR*, XI, 2, pp. 662, 707; *OR*, XI, 2, pp. 726, 744; Burton, *Extraordinary Circumstances*, pp. 179–180.

⁵ Burton, *Extraordinary Circumstances*, pp. 180, 182.

⁶ Sears, *Gates of Richmond*, p. 260–261; *OR*, XI, 2, p. 494.

⁷ *OR*, XI, 2, p. 837; Sears, *Gates of Richmond*, p. 262; Burton, *Extraordinary Circumstances*, pp. 182–183.

⁸ Burton, *Extraordinary Circumstances*, pp. 183–184.

⁹ *OR*, XI, 2, pp. 662, 716, 726.

¹⁰ *OR*, XI, 2, pp. 716, 726, 750.

¹¹ *OR*, XI, 2, p. 257, 463, 468; Burton, *Extraordinary Circumstances*, pp.

185–186.

[12] *OR*, XI, 2, pp. 71, 122, 137, 151, 269.

[13] *OR*, XI, 2, pp. 54.

[14] *OR*, XI, 2, pp. 57, 77; Burton, *Extraordinary Circumstances*, p. 187.

[15] *OR*, XI, 2, pp. 60, 82, 87, 90, 93–94.

[16] Burton, *Extraordinary Circumstances*, pp. 187–188.

[17] *OR*, XI, 2, pp. 63, 82–84, 90–91, 98, 663–664, 726; Fox, *Regimental Losses*, p. 278.

[18] *OR*, XI, 2, pp. 54, 57, 83, 662, 691, 707, 709; *OR*, LI, 1, p. 108.

[19] *OR*, XI, 2, pp. 24–25, 694, 977; Burton, *Extraordinary Circumstances*, pp. 190–191.

[20] *OR*, XI, 2, pp. 574, 663–664, 680; Burton, *Extraordinary Circumstances*, pp. 191–192.

[21] *OR*, XI, 2, pp. 788–789, 808–809; Burton, *Extraordinary Circumstances*, pp. 192–193.

[22] Brent, *Memoirs*, pp. 181–183; *OR*, XI, 2, pp. 680, 788–789, 808–809.

[23] Burton, *Extraordinary Circumstances*, p. 193.

[24] *OR*, XI, 2, pp. 205, 207, 235, 525–527; Averell, "With the Cavalry," *BL*, vol. 2, p. 431.

[25] *OR*, XI, 2, pp. 243, 251–252, 265–266, 269, 274, 292, 350, 389; Burton, *Extraordinary Circumstances*, pp. 195, 197.

[26] *OR*, XI, 2, p. 434.

[27] *OR*, XI, 2, p. 193; Burton, *Extraordinary Circumstances*, p. 198.

[28] *OR*, XI, 2, p. 193; Averell, "With the Cavalry," *BL*, vol. 2, p. 431; Webb, *Peninsula*, p. 141.

[29] Bliss, "No. 1 Narrative," Bancroft-Bliss Family Papers, LOC; *OR*, XI, 1, pp. 118–119; Burton, *Extraordinary Circumstances*, p. 199.

[30] *OR*, XI, 1, pp. 140–141; *OR*, XI, 2, p. 22; *OR*, XI, 3, p. 277; Sears, *Gates of Richmond*, p. 265; Burton, *Extraordinary Circumstances*, pp. 200–201.

[31] Smith, *Autobiography*, pp. 42–43; Franklin, "Rear Guard Fighting," p. 371; Burton, *Extraordinary Circumstances*, p. 201.

[32] *OR*, XI, 2, pp. 50, 99, 161, 162, 170, 465; Cullen, *Peninsula Campaign*, p. 136; Sears, *Gates of Richmond*, p. 267.

33 *OR*, XI, 2, p. 89; Brent, *Memoirs*, pp. 180–181; Marks, *Peninsular Campaign*, p. 245.

34 Burton, *Extraordinary Circumstances*, p. 204.

35 Cook, *Siege of Richmond*, p. 325; Sanborn, "Savage Station," *NT*, Oct. 12, 1905, p. 3.

36 *OR*, IV, p. 798; Marks, *Peninsular Campaign*, pp. 237–248; Sanborn, "Savage Station," *NT*, Oct. 12, 1905, p. 3.

37 *OR*, XI, 2, pp. 663, 789, 809; Burton, *Extraordinary Circumstances*, pp. 205–206.

38 *OR*, XI, 1, pp. 111, 114–115; *OR*, XI, 2, pp. 571, 578, 627, 664, 748, 750; Burton, *Extraordinary Circumstances*, pp. 206–207; Sears, *Gates of Richmond*, p. 269.

39 *OR*, XI, 2, pp. 675, 716, 789; Burton, *Extraordinary Circumstances*, p. 208; Brent, *Memoirs*, p. 182. Brent obscures the timing of events.

40 *OR*, XI, 2, pp. 516–517; Davis, *They Called Him Stonewall*, p.232; Alexander, *Military Memoirs*, p. 136; Longstreet, *Manassas to Appomattox*, p. 131.

41 Blackford, *War Years*, p. 75; Burton, *Extraordinary Circumstances*, pp. 209-210.

42 Long, *Robert E. Lee*, p. 175; *OR*, XI, 2, p. 517, 556, 680; von Borcke, *Memoirs*, vol. 1, p. 67; Blackford, *War Years*, pp. 75–76; Sears, *Gates of Richmond*, p. 268.

43 *OR*, XI, 1, p. 114; *OR*, XI, 2, p. 571; *OR*, LI, 1, p. 688; Dabney, *Life and Campaigns*, pp. 459, 461.

44 Brent, *Memoirs*, p. 182; Doubleday, *"The Seven Days' Battles," NT*, Sept. 14, 1916, p. 7; *OR*, XI, 2, pp. 170, 464, 664, 691, 716, 720, 726, 732, 735.

45 Franklin, "Rear Guard Fighting," p. 373; Burton, *Extraordinary Circumstances*, pp. 213–214.

46 *OR*, XI, 2, pp. 50, 91, 727; *OR*, LI, 1, p. 108; Burton, *Extraordinary Circumstances*, p. 214.

47 *OR*, XI, 2, pp. 56–57, 64–65, 69, 71, 77, 84, 86, 118–119, 464; Burton, *Extraordinary Circumstances*, pp. 215–216.

48 *OR*, XI, 2, pp. 694, 727, 732, 747; Brent, *Memoirs*, p. 188.

49 *OR*, XI, 2, pp. 91–92, 726, 735, 741; Dickert, *Kershaw's Brigade*, pp. 128–

129; Wyckoff, "Kershaw's South Carolina Brigade" pp. 121–124; Burton, *Extraordinary Circumstances*, pp. 216–217.

[50] *OR*, XI, 2, pp. 477, 479; Burton, *Extraordinary Circumstances*, pp. 217–218.

[51] *OR*, XI, 2, pp. 717, 721, 741, Burton, *Extraordinary Circumstances*, p. 219.

[52] *OR*, XI, 2, pp. 733, 744; Brent, *Memoirs*, pp. 184–188; Burton, *Extraordinary Circumstances*, pp. 219–220.

[53] *OR*, XI, 2, pp. 89, 91–92, 737–738, 750; Smith, *Autobiography*, p. 44; Franklin, "Rear Guard Fighting," *BL*, vol. 2, pp. 374–375; Burton, *Extraordinary Circumstances*, pp. 220-221.

[54] *OR*, XI, 2, pp. 25, 35, 37, 721, 731, 978–979; Fox, *Regimental Losses*, pp. 147–148, 150–151, 279, 430; Burton, *Extraordinary Circumstances*, pp. 221.

[55] *OR*, XI, 2, pp. 665, 691, 702, 705, 707, 713, 748, 750; Coward, *South Carolinians*, p. 41; Burton, *Extraordinary Circumstances*, pp. 221–222.

[56] *OR*, XI, 2, pp. 665, 687; Alexander, *Military Memoirs*, p. 138; Freeman, *Lee's Lieutenants*, vol. 1, p. 563; Dowdey, *Seven Days*, pp. 268–269; Cullen, *Peninsula Campaign*, p. 139; Sears, *Gates of Richmond*, p. 274. Various authors have differing opinions of the validity of Lee's criticism of Magruder's performance at Savage Station.

[57] Winslow, *General John Sedgwick*, p. 25; Burton, *Extraordinary Circumstances*, p. 223; Sears, *Gates of Richmond*, p. 271.

[58] Burton, *Extraordinary Circumstances*, p. 223.

[59] *OR*, XI, 2, pp. 162, 181, 185, 789, 797, 809; Werstein, *Kearny the Magnificent*, p. 226.

[60] *OR*, XI, 2, pp. 556, 565, 571, 607, 622, 627, 775, 879; Brown, "Down the Peninsula," p. 57; Burton, *Extraordinary Circumstances*, p. 225.

[61] *OR*, XI, 2, p. 110.

[62] *OR*, XI, 2, pp. 199, 202, 431, 434; Slocum, *Life and Services*, p. 30; Burton, *Extraordinary Circumstances*, p. 226.

[63] Burton, *Extraordinary Circumstances*, pp. 226–227.

[64] Burton, *Extraordinary Circumstances*, p. 227.

[65] *OR*, XI, 2, pp. 227–228, 389; Powell, *Fifth Army Corps*, pp. 133–134; Burton, *Extraordinary Circumstances*, pp. 227–228.

[66] *OR*, XI, 2, pp. 55, 228, 431; Franklin, "Rear Guard Fighting," *BL*, vol. 2, p. 375; Smith, *Autobiography*, pp. 44–45.

[67] Hyde, *Following the Greek Cross*, pp. 72–73; Burton, *Extraordinary Circumstances*, pp. 228–229.

Chapter 20

[1] *OR*, XI, 2, pp. 55, 58; Bruce, *Twentieth Massachusetts*, pp. 118–119; Burton, *Extraordinary Circumstances*, pp. 229–230.
[2] *OR*, XI, 2, pp. 55, 58, 77; Stiles, *Four Years with Marse Robert*, pp. 97–99; Burton, *Extraordinary Circumstances*, p. 231.
[3] Sears, *Gates of Richmond*, p. 277; Burton, *Extraordinary Circumstances*, pp. 231, 234–235.
[4] *OR*, XI, 2, pp. 665–666; Sears, *Gates of Richmond*, pp. 277–278; Burton, *Extraordinary Circumstances*, pp. 231–232, 234.
[5] Burton, *Extraordinary Circumstances*, pp. 232, 234; Brent, *Memoirs*, p. 190; Cullen, *Peninsula Campaign*, p. 140. Cullen maintains that Lee had no confidence in Magruder.
[6] *OR*, XI, 2, pp. 495, 906–907, 916–917; Burton, *Extraordinary Circumstances*, p. 234.
[7] *OR*, XI, 2, pp. 55, 58, 431, 464–465; Smith, *Autobiography*, pp. 45–46.
[8] *OR*, XI, 2, pp. 99, 162–163, 166, 431, 435; Dodge Journal, Dodge Papers, LOC; Burton, *Extraordinary Circumstances*, pp. 236, 237.
[9] *OR*, XI, 2, pp. 81, 111, 389–390; Burton, *Extraordinary Circumstances*, p. 237.
[10] *OR*, XI, 2, p. 111; Burton, *Extraordinary Circumstances*, pp. 237, 239.
[11] *OR*, XI, 2, pp. 99, 389–390, 402, 431; Powell, *Fifth Army Corps*, p. 137.
[12] Martin, *Peninsula Campaign*, p. 196; Burton, *Extraordinary Circumstances*, p. 239.
[13] *OR*, XI, 2, pp. 99, 193; Burton, *Extraordinary Circumstances*, pp. 239-240.
[14] *OR*, XI, 1, p. 64; Sears, *Gates of Richmond*, pp. 282; Burton, *Extraordinary Circumstances*, pp. 240–241.
[15] *OR*, XI, 2, pp. 38–40; *OR*, XI, 3, p. 238; Dowdey, *Seven Days*, pp. 285-286; Franklin, "Rear Guard Fighting," *BL*, vol. 2, p. 377.
[16] Sears, *Gates of Richmond*, pp. 280; Dowdey, *Seven Days*, pp. 286-287; Burton, *Extraordinary Circumstances*, p. 242.
[17] Dowdey, *Peninsula Campaign*, p. 288; Burton, *Extraordinary Circumstances*, pp. 242–243.
[18] *OR*, XI, 1, pp. 65, 141; Sears, *Gates of Richmond*, pp. 280-281; Sears, ed., McClellan *Papers*, pp. 325–326; Lincoln, *Collected Works*, vol. V, pp. 292–295.
[19] Burton, *Extraordinary Circumstances*, p. 244.

20. Taylor, "Savage's Station," *NT,* Jan. 31, 1884, p. 7; Dabney, *Life and Campaigns,* pp. 460–462; Burton, *Extraordinary Circumstances,* pp. 244–245.
21. *OR,* XI, 2, pp. 495, 789, 797, 809–810; Dowdey, *Peninsula Campaign,* pp. 291–292; Burton, *Extraordinary Circumstances,* pp. 245–246.
22. *OR,* XI, 2, pp. 809-810; Burton, *Extraordinary Circumstances,* p. 246; Dowdey, *Seven Days,* p. 292.
23. *OR,* XI, 2, pp. 809–810; Burton, *Extraordinary Circumstances,* pp. 246–247.
24. *OR,* XI, 2, pp. 495, 666; Burton, *Extraordinary Circumstance,* p. 247.
25. *OR,* XI, 2, pp. 495, 666, 718, 838; Longstreet, "'Seven Days,'" *BL,* vol. 2, p. 400; *OR,* XI, 2, pp. 495, 666, 718, 838; Brent, *Memoirs,* p. 192.
26. *OR,* XI, 2, pp. 389–390, 402; Roberts, "Battle of Charles City Crossroads," p.1; Burton, *Extraordinary Circumstances,* p. 249.
27. Sypher, *Pennsylvania Reserve Corps,* pp. 261, 263–264; *OR,* XI, 2, pp. 389–390, 402–403, 420; Meade, *Life and Letters,* p. 285.
28. Longstreet, *Manassas to Appomattox,* p. 134; Burton, *Extraordinary Circumstances,* p. 250.
29. *OR,* XI, 2, pp. 527, 666, 675, 759, 763, 775, 785, 838; Longstreet, *Manassas to Appomattox,* p. 134; Sypher, *Pennsylvania Reserve Corps,* pp. 264–265; Longstreet, "'The Seven Days'", *BL,* vol. 2, p. 400.
30. *OR,* XI, 2, pp. 557, 561, 627, 655; Burton, *Extraordinary Circumstances,* p. 251.
31. *OR,* XI, 2, p. 465; Smith, *Autobiography,* pp. 45–46; Cullen, *Peninsula Campaign,* p. 145.
32. *OR,* XI, 2, pp. 464–465; Smith, *Autobiography,* pp. 45–46; Cullen, *Peninsula Campaign,* p. 145.
33. *OR,* XI, 2, pp. 477, 481; Franklin, "Rear-Guard Fighting," *BL,* vol. 2, p. 379; Smith, *Autobiography,* p. 46.
34. Alexander, *Military Memoirs,* pp. 148–149; *OR,* XI, 2, pp. 58, 466, 557, 594, 627; Hill, "McClellan's Change of Base," *BL,* vol. 2, p. 388; Franklin, "Rear-Guard Fighting," *BL,* vol. 2, p. 378.

[35] *OR*, XI, pt. 2, pp. 58, 466; Dabney, *Life and Campaigns of Jackson*, p. 464; Franklin, "Rear Guard Fighting," *BL*, vol. 2, p. 378; Burton, *Extraordinary Circumstances*, p. 259.

[36] Alexander, *Military Memoirs*, p. 148; *OR*, XI, 2, pp. 55–60, 561, 566; Naisawald, *Grape and Canister*, p. 107; Franklin, "Rear Guard Fighting," *BL*, vol. 2, p. 378.

[37] *OR*, XI, 2, pp. 63, 78–80, 557, 974, 984; Franklin, "Rear-Guard Fighting," *BL*, vol. 2, p. 378; Wise, *Long Arm of Lee*, p. 249.

[38] *OR*, XI, 2, pp. 566, 790, 810–811; Dabney, *Life and Campaigns*, pp. 465–466; Alexander, *Military Memoirs*, p. 149; Franklin, "Rear Guard Fighting," *BL*, vol. 2, p. 381.

[39] *OR*, XI, 2, pp. 89, 94; Burton, *Extraordinary Circumstances*, pp. 258–259.

[40] Alexander, *Military Memoirs*, p. 149; Burton, *Extraordinary Circumstances*, p. 259.

[41] Jackson, *Memoirs of Stonewall Jackson*, p. 297; Dabney, *Life and Campaigns*, p. 467; Alexander, *Military Memoirs*, pp. 150–151; Burton, *Extraordinary Circumstances*, p. 259.

[42] Alexander, *Military Memoirs*, pp. 144, 147; Jackson, *Memoirs of Stonewall Jackson*, p. 302; Davis, *They Called Him Stonewall*, pp. 243-244; Dabney, *Life and Campaigns*, pp. 466–467; Dowdey, *Seven Days*, pp. 307–308; Robertson, *Stonewall Jackson*, p. 490; Sears, *Gates of Richmond*, p. 289; Cullen, *Peninsula Campaign*, pp. 150-151.

[43] Burton, *Extraordinary Circumstances*, pp. 260–261.

[44] Dabney to Hotchkiss, Apr. 22, 1896, Hotchkiss Papers, LOC; Hill, "McClellan's Change of Base," *BL*, vol. 2, p. 388; Burton, *Extraordinary Circumstances*, pp. 261–262.

[45] *OR*, XI, 2, pp. 55, 61. Robertson, *Stonewall Jackson*, p. 498; Burton, *Extraordinary Circumstances*, p. 262.

[46] Dowdey, *The Seven Days*, p. 308; Burton, *Extraordinary Circumstances*, p. 263.

[47] *OR*, XI, 2, pp. 166, 435, 547, 789, 797–798; Burton, *Extraordinary Circumstances*, pp. 264–265.

[48] *OR*, XI, 2, pp. 435, 495, 790; Alexander, *Military Memoirs*, p. 143; Burton, *Extraordinary Circumstances*, p. 265.

[49] Alexander, *Military Memoirs*, p. 143; Dowdey, *Seven Days*, p. 306.

50 Longstreet, *Manassas to Appomattox*, pp. 134–135; Burton, *Extraordinary Circumstances*, p. 266.
51 Longstreet, *Manassas to Appomattox*, p. 134; Longstreet, "'The Seven Days'," *BL*, vol. 2, p. 400; Burton, *Extraordinary Circumstances*, pp. 266-267.
52 Longstreet, "The Seven Days," *BL*, vol. 2, pp. 401; Longstreet, *Manassas to Appomattox*, p. 134; Burton, *Extraordinary Circumstances*, p. 267.
53 *OR*, XI, 2, pp. 410, 532, 759, 838, 907; *OR Supp.*, Part I, Vol. 2, p. 442.
54 *OR*, XI, 2, pp. 119, 202, 227-228, 238, 274, 284, 350, 380; Burton, *Extraordinary Circumstances*, p. 268.
55 *OR*, XI, 2, pp. 354–355, 910, 914–915; Hill, "McClellan's Change of Base," *BL*, vol. 2, p. 390; Porter, "Battle of Malvern Hill," p. 411.
56 *OR*, XI, 2, pp. 354–355, 362, 910, 914–915; *ORN*, Vol. VII, pp. 699, 709; Hill, "McClellan's Change of Base," *BL*, vol. 2, p. 390.
57 *OR*, XI, 2, p. 908; Burton, *Extraordinary Circumstances*, p. 271.
58 *OR*, XI, 2, pp. 495, 667, 908; Longstreet, *Manassas to Appomattox*, p. 139; Porter, "Battle of Malvern Hill," *BL*, vol. 2, p. 411; Alexander, *Fighting for the Confederacy*, p. 106; Hill, "McClellan's Change of Base," *BL*, vol. 2, p. 391. Dowdey, *Seven Days*, pp. 297, 304–306; Alexander, Dowdey and Hill criticize Theophilus Holmes.
59 *OR*, XI, 2, pp. 666–667, 675, 691, 718; Longstreet, *Manassas to Appomattox*, p. 139; Burton, *Extraordinary Circumstances*, pp. 271–273.
60 *OR*, XI, 2, pp. 495, 666–667, 691, 705, 707, 715, 718, 742, 748; Longstreet, *Manassas to Appomattox*, p. 139; Brent, *Memoirs*, pp. 193–194.
61 *OR*, LI, 1, p. 114; *OR*, XI, 2, pp. 171, 255, 403, 421, 423, 425, 428, 759; *OR*, LI, 1, p. 114; Burton, *Extraordinary Circumstances*, pp. 275–276.
62 *OR*, XI, 2, pp. 255, 410, 420, 423; *OR Supp.*, Part I, Vol. 2, p. 442; Sypher, *Pennsylvania Reserve Corps*, p. 264; Alexander, "Records of Longstreet's Corps, A.N.V.," *SHSP*, vol. 1, (Feb. 1876): p. 68.

[63] Jenkins to wife, July 4, 1862, Micah Jenkins papers, USC; Sears, *Gates of Richmond*, p. 296; Burton, *Extraordinary Circumstances*, pp. 277–278.
[64] *OR*, LI, 1, p. 111; Powell, *Fifth Army Corps*, p. 140; Longstreet, *Manassas to Appomattox*, p. 135.
[65] *OR*, XI, 2, pp. 255, 396, 403, 410, 412; *OR*, LI, 1, p. 112; *OR Supp.*, Part I, Vol. 2, pp. 442–443; Sypher, *Pennsylvania Reserve Corps*, pp. 269–270; Burton, *Extraordinary Circumstances*, pp. 279–280.
[66] *OR*, Ser. I, Vol. XI, pt. 2, pp. 32, 38, 40, 980–982; Alexander, "Records of Longstreet's Corps, A.N.V.," *SHSP*, vol. 1, (Feb. 1876): p. 68n; Fox, *Regimental Losses*, p. 563.
[67] *OR*, XI, 2, pp. 138, 265; Burton, *Extraordinary Circumstances*, pp. 281–282.
[68] *OR*, XI, 2, pp. 86, 92, 106–107, 111, 131; Burton, *Extraordinary Circumstances*, pp. 282–283.
[69] *OR*, XI, 2, pp. 123, 425, 428, 759, 763–766, 883, 895; *OR*, LI, 1, pp. 111; Sypher, *Pennsylvania Reserve Corps*, p. 266; Alexander, "Records of Longstreet's Corps, A.N.V.," *SHSP*, vol. 1, (Feb. 1876): p. 67n.
[70] *OR*, XI, 2, pp. 417, 425, 428, 765, 769-770, 883; *OR*, LI, 1, p. 113; Sypher, *Pennsylvania Reserve Corps*, p. 279; Burton, *Extraordinary Circumstances*, pp. 284–285.
[71] Sears, *Gates of Richmond*, p. 299; Burton, *Extraordinary Circumstances*, pp. 285–286.
[72] *OR*, XI, 2, pp. 81, 87, 89–90, 92, 94–95, 417, 770; Burton, *Extraordinary Circumstances*, p. 286.
[73] *OR*, XI, 2, pp. 32, 38, 81, 92, 94–95, 111, 125, 133–134, 893, 895; Sedgwick, *Correspondence*, p. 70.
[74] *OR*, XI, 2, pp. 172, 255–256, 391, 404, 421, 776–778; Powell, *Fifth Army Corps*, pp. 141–143; Sypher, *Pennsylvania Reserve Corps*, p. 279; Burton, *Extraordinary Circumstances*, p. 288.
[75] *OR*, XI, 2, pp. 32, 38, 40, 980; Burton, *Extraordinary Circumstances*, p. 290.
[76] *OR*, XI, 2, pp. 166, 168–171, 175–176, 781; Leach, "Frazier's Farm," *SHSP*, vol. 21 (Jan.–Dec. 1893): pp. 163–164; Burton, *Extraordinary Circumstances*, p. 291.

77 *OR,* XI, 2, pp. 175–177, 179, 786; Longstreet, *Manassas to Appomattox,* p. 137; Burton, *Extraordinary Circumstances,* pp. 291–293.

78 *OR,* XI, 2, pp. 61, 65–66, 163–164, 171–173, 177–178, 186, 188, 786, 842, 844, 862, 865, 867, 870–871, 874; Doubleday, "Seven Days' Battles," *NT,* Oct. 8, 1914, p. 7.

79 *OR,* XI, 2, pp. 100, 163–164, 391, 418, 842, 845, 850; Longstreet, "'The Seven Days'," *BL,* vol. 2, p. 402n; Baquet, *History of the First Brigade,* pp. 30–32; Kearny to wife, July 9, 1862, Kearny Papers, LOC; Burton, *Extraordinary Circumstances,* pp. 295–296.

80 *OR,* XI, pt. 2, pp. 90, 124, 133–134, 769, 901; *OR,* LI, 1, p. 109.

81 *OR,* XI, 2, pp. 838–839, 879–880; Longstreet, *Manassas to Appomattox,* p. 139. Dickert, *Kershaw's Brigade,* p. 130; Schenck, *Up Came Hill,* p. 88; Robertson, *General A. P. Hill,* pp. 91–92; Alexander, "Records of Longstreet's Corps, A.N.V.," *SHSP,* vol. 1 (Feb. 1876): p. 71.

82 *OR,* XI, 2, pp. 24–27, 32–34, 37–40, 979–980, 982–983; Alexander, "Records of Longstreet's Corps, A.N.V.," *SHSP,* vol. 1 (Feb. 1876): p. 71; Alexander, *Military Memoirs,* pp. 154–155.

83 McGuire to Hotchkiss, Apr. 23, 1896, Hotchkiss Papers, UVa; Alexander, "Records of Longstreet's Corps, A.N.V.," *SHSP,* vol. 1, (Feb. 1876): p. 66; Burton, *Extraordinary Circumstances,* p. 299.

84 Freeman, *R. E. Lee,* Vol. II, p. 199; Cullen, *Peninsula Campaign,* p. 149; Dowdey, *Seven Days,* p. 304; Alexander, *Fighting for the Confederacy,* pp. 110–111; Alexander, *Military Memoirs,* pp. 143–144.

85 Brent, *Memoirs,* p. 193; Sears, *Gates of Richmond,* p. 291; Dowdey, *Seven Days,* p. 304.

86 *OR,* XI, 2, pp. 77, 101, 431, 466; Smith, *Autobiography,* pp. 46–47; Franklin, "Rear-Guard Fighting," *BL,* vol. 2, pp. 379–381; *OR Supp.,* Part I, Vol. 2, p. 416; Hyde, *Following the Greek Cross,* p. 76.

87 *OR,* XI, 1, p. 67; *OR,* XI, 2, pp. 101, 436; *OR,* XI, 3, p. 281; Dodge Journal, Dodge Papers, LOC; Burton, *Extraordinary Circumstances,* pp. 302–303.

⁸⁸ *OR*, XI, 2, pp. 51–52, 61, 101, 112, 124, 139, 151, 404; Sypher, *Pennsylvania Reserve Corps*, p. 277.
⁸⁹ *OR*, XI, 2, pp. 557, 622, 667, 790, 908; Burton, *Extraordinary Circumstances*, p. 305.

Chapter 21

¹ Porter, "Battle of Malvern Hill," *BL*, vol. 2, pp. 409–410; Cullen, *Peninsula Campaign*, pp. 151–152; Sears, *Gates of Richmond*, p. 311.
² *OR*, XI, 2, pp. 22, 102; Sears, *Gates of Richmond*, p. 311.
³ Burton, *Extraordinary Circumstances*, pp. 306–307.
⁴ *OR*, XI, 2, pp. 52, 60, 83, 102, 116, 119, 166, 202–203, 208–209, 211, 217, 238, 250, 265–267, 274–275, 279, 284, 293, 319, 350, 431, 971-972; Burton, *Extraordinary Circumstances*, pp. 307–308.
⁵ *OR*, XI, 1, p. 120; *OR*, XI, 2, pp. 22, 102, 228, 496; Porter, "Battle of Malvern Hill," *BL*, 2, pp. 409–410; Freeman, *R. E. Lee*, vol. 2, p.204.
⁶ Sears, ed., *McClellan Papers*, pp. 328, 329; Sears, *Gates of Richmond*, p. 309; Burton, *Extraordinary Circumstances*, pp. 309–310.
⁷ Porter, "Malvern Hill," *BL*, vol. 2, p. 414; *OR*, I, XI, 2, p. 52; Sears, ed., *McClellan Papers*, pp. 328–329; Burton, *Extraordinary Circumstances*, pp. 310–311.
⁸ Longstreet, *Manassas to Appomattox*, p. 142; Burton, *Extraordinary Circumstances*, p. 311.
⁹ Hill, "McClellan's Change of Base," *BL*, vol. 2, p. 391; Longstreet, *Manassas to Appomattox*, p. 142; Brent, *Memoirs*, pp. 197–203.
¹⁰ *OR*, XI, 2, pp. 760, 790, 811, 818; Freeman, *Lee's Lieutenants*, vol. 1, p. 612; Burton, *Extraordinary Circumstances*, pp. 312, 314.
¹¹ Hill, "McClellan's Change of Base," *BL*, vol. 2, pp. 391, 392; Longstreet, *Manassas to Appomattox*, p. 142; Burton, *Extraordinary Circumstances*, p. 314.
¹² Longstreet, *Manassas to Appomattox*, p. 143; Sears, *Gates of Richmond*, pp. 316–317; Burton, *Extraordinary Circumstances*, pp. 314–315.
¹³ Longstreet, *Manassas to Appomattox*, p. 142; Sears, *Gates of Richmond*, pp. 314–315; Burton, *Extraordinary Circumstances*, p. 315.

[14] *OR*, XI, 2, pp. 668, 676–677, 691, 719; Longstreet, *Manassas to Appomattox*, p. 143; G. W. Finley to Hotchkiss, Mar. 17, 1897, Hotchkiss Papers, LOC.

[15] *OR*, XI, 2, p. 628; Alexander, *Military Memoirs*, p. 161; Brent, *Memoirs*, p. 207; Dowdey, *Seven Days*, p. 329.

[16] *OR*, XI, 2, pp. 105, 116, 120, 165, 166, 266, 287, 557, 566, 573, 972; Balthis, "Recollections," Hotchkiss Papers, LOC. There cannot be certainty as to which batteries fired at which targets throughout the day, but this is a reasonable estimate; Burton, *Extraordinary Circumstances*, pp. 316–317.

[17] *OR*, XI, 2, pp. 566, 573–574; Jones, "Reminiscences No. 8," *SHSP*, vol. 9 (Oct.–Dec. 1881): p. 567; Brown, "Down the Peninsula," pp. 61–62; Hill, "McClellan's Change of Base," *BL*, vol. 2, p. 392; L. W. Cox to Hotchkiss, Aug. 3, 1897, Hotchkiss Papers, LOC; Driver, *Staunton Artillery*, pp. 20–22.

[18] *OR*, XI, 2, pp. 64, 81, 83–84, 88, 95, 116, 151, 165, 182, 228, 266–267; Dodge Journal, Dodge Papers, LOC; Gray, "Artillerist's Yarn," *NT*, Aug. 16, 1900, p. 7; Powell, *Fifth Army Corps*, pp. 158–159; Hyde, *Following the Greek Cross*, p. 77.

[19] *OR*, XI, 2, pp. 260, 269–271, 283, 285, 287, 351, 802, 812–814, 818–819, 823, 972; Longstreet, *Manassas to Appomattox*, p. 143; Slater, "Scenes at Malvern Hill," *Philadelphia Weekly Times*, Dec. 11, 1880, p. 1; Burton, *Extraordinary Circumstances*, pp. 319–320.

[20] *OR*, XI, 2, pp. 542, 562, 629, 669, 747, 819, 839, 904, 979–983; McCreery Journal, McCreery Papers, VaHS; G. W. Finley to Hotchkiss, Mar. 17, 1897, Hotchkiss Papers, LOC; Longstreet, *Manassas to Appomattox*, p. 143.

[21] *OR*, XI, 2, pp. 483–489, 533–536, 539, 549; *OR*, XI, 2, pp. 537, 547, 550; *OR*, XI, 3, pp. 612–613; *OR*, LI, 2, pp. 577–578; Alexander, *Military Memoirs*, p. 160; Dowdey, *Seven Days*, pp. 334–335; Freeman, *Lee's Lieutenants*, vol. I, pp. 616, 617; Sears, *Gates of Richmond*, p. 318.

[22] *OR*, XI, 2, pp. 105, 119, 213, 260, 271, 287, 627; Hill, "McClellan's Change of Base," *BL*, vol. 2, p. 392; Burton, *Extraordinary Circumstances*, p. 324.

²³ *OR*, XI, 2, pp. 275, 812–813, 819, 821, 823, 824, 828, 829; Finley to Hotchkiss, Mar. 17, 1897, Hotchkiss Papers, LOC; Again, it is impossible to exactly know which Federal batteries fired at which targets; Burton, *Extraordinary Circumstances*, pp. 324–325.

²⁴ *OR*, XI, 2, p. 677; Longstreet, *Manassas to Appomattox*, pp. 143–144; Brent, *Memoirs*, p. 221.

²⁵ Burton, *Extraordinary Circumstances*, p. 326.

²⁶ *OR*, XI, 2, pp. 628, 669, 883–884; *OR*, XI, 2, p. 760; Hill, "McClellan's Change of Base," *BL*, vol. 2, p. 392; Longstreet, *Manassas to Appomattox*, p. 144; Hood, *Advance and Retreat*, pp. 30–31; Dabney to Hotchkiss, Mar. 10, 1897, Hotchkiss Papers, LOC.

²⁷ *OR*, XI, 2, pp. 496, 668, 749, 790; Brent, *Memoirs*, pp. 211–212; Burton, *Extraordinary Circumstances*, pp. 327–328.

²⁸ *OR*, XI, 2, pp. 88, 95, 105, 119, 120, 209, 211–212, 257–259, 267, 271, 275, 283, 285, 288, 293, 314, 319, 357, 566; Brent, *Memoirs*, p. 215; Alexander, *Memoirs*, p. 162.

²⁹ *OR*, XI, 2, pp. 691–692, 707, 719; Brent, *Memoirs*, p. 196, Burton, *Extraordinary Circumstances*, pp. 329–330.

³⁰ *OR*, XI, 2, pp. 669, 677–678, 747, 751, 794, 800, 839; Brent, *Memoirs*, pp. 215–217; Burton, *Extraordinary Circumstances*, pp. 330–331.

³¹ *OR*, XI, 2, pp. 275, 567, 609, 618, 669–670, 694, 749, 813–814, 819; Brent, *Memoirs*, p. 217; Cox to Hotchkiss, Aug. 1897, Hotchkiss Papers, LOC; Herndon, "Infantry and Cavalry Service," *CV*, vol. 30, no. 5 (May 1922): pp. 173–174; Davis Memoir, Papers of Wilbur Fisk Davis, UVa; James L. Dinwiddie to Bettie, July 3, 1862, Dinwiddie Family Papers, UVa; McCreery Journal, McCreery Papers, VaHS; *OR Supp.*, Part I, Vol. 2, pp. 464–465.

³² *OR*, XI, 2, pp. 270, 275–276, 294, 314, 350–351, 355, 814; Baxter, "Battle Flag of the Third Georgia," *SHSP*, vol. 38, (Jan.–Dec. 1910): p. 211; Bernard, "Malvern Hill," *SHSP*, vol. 18, p. 60.

³³ *OR*, XI, 2, pp. 203, 267, 314, 357, 814, 824, 826; Tuffs, "Malvern Hill," *NT*, Apr. 27, 1893, p. 4; John Shipp diary, Shipp Family Papers, VaHS; Bernard, "Malvern Hill," *SHSP* vol. 18 (Jan.-Dec. 1890): pp. 61–62, 67; Porter, "Battle of Malvern Hill," *BL*, vol. 2, p. 417n.

34 *OR,* XI, 2, pp. 260, 314, 357, 749, 820, 824, 833; B. Wylie Scott to Ella, July 9, 1862, Merryman Papers, VaHS; Gilmore, "With the 4th Mich.," *NT,* July 7, 1910, p. 7; Burton, *Extraordinary Circumstances,* pp. 335–336.

35 *OR,* XI, 2, pp. 294, 320–321, 325, 328–329, 342, 345–346; Porter, "Malvern Hill," *BL,* vol. 2, pp. 425–426; Boies, "Malvern Hill," *NT,* Feb. 13, 1896, p. 1; Burton, *Extraordinary Circumstances,* pp. 336–337.

36 Robert, "Justice to General Magruder," *SHSP,* vol. 5 (May 1878): p. 250; *OR,* XI, 2, pp. 30, 276, 801, 821, 834, 979, 981–982, 985, 987; Evans, *Confederate Military History,* vol. 4, pp. 89–93; Fox, *Regimental Losses,* p. 563.

37 *OR,* XI, 2, pp. 208–209, 634, 643, 650, 659; Sears, *Gates of Richmond,* p. 326; Burton, *Extraordinary Circumstances,* pp. 337–338.

38 *OR,* XI, 2, pp. 212–214, 634, 635, 637; Gordon, *Reminiscences,* p. 74; Burton, *Extraordinary Circumstances,* pp. 338–339.

39 *OR,* XI, 2, pp. 628, 634, 643, 650, 976, 977; Brown, "Down the Peninsula," p. 66; Fox, *Regimental Losses,* pp. 557, 563; Hill, "McClellan's Change of Base," *BL,* vol. 2, p. 394.

40 *OR,* XI, 2, pp. 28–29, 52, 64, 107, 176, 251, 283, 628, 697, 700, 703, 705, 707–709, 712, 713, 715; Coward, *South Carolinians,* p. 43; Stovall, *Robert Toombs,* pp. 254–258; Burton, *Extraordinary Circumstances,* pp. 341–342, 344.

41 *OR,* XI, 2, pp. 52–53, 260, 267, 293–294, 297, 305–308, 311–312, 342, 347, 751–755; Johnson, "Barksdale-Humphreys Mississippi Brigade," p. 206; Averell, "With the Cavalry," *BL,* vol. 2, p. 431.

42 *OR,* XI, 2, pp. 72, 204, 230, 238, 283, 351, 972; Porter, "Battle of Malvern Hill," *BL,* pp. 416n, 422; Porter to commander of gunboats, July 1, 1862, McClellan Papers, LOC; Brown, "Down the Peninsula," p. 61.

43 *OR,* XI, 2, p. 794; Dowdey, *Seven Days,* pp. 318, 342; Freeman, *Lee's Lieutenants,* vol. I, p. 612; Burton, *Extraordinary Circumstances,* p. 345; Sears, *Gates of Richmond,* p. 335. All of the authors rate Huger's performance as poor. Sears alone believes better performance by Huger could have made a real difference in the outcome of the battle.

[44] *OR*, XI, 2, pp. 671, 678, 680, 760, 794, 839, 884; Brent, *Memoirs*, pp. 218, 219; Burgwyn to mother, July 14, 1862, Burgwyn Family Papers, SHC.

[45] *OR*, XI, 2, pp. 558, 571, 585, 587, 597, 607, 611, 618, 620, 622; Longstreet, *Manassas to Appomattox*, p. 144; Alexander, *Military Memoirs*, p. 167; Sears, *Gates of Richmond*, p. 318; Burton, *Extraordinary Circumstances*, pp. 347–348.

[46] *OR*, XI, 2, pp. 629, 672, 908, 914, 915, 917; George Wills to father, July 3, 1862, Wills Papers, SHC; Hill, "McClellan's Change of Base," *BL* vol. 2, p. 391; Freeman, *Lee's Lieutenants*, vol. I, p. 614.

[47] *OR*, XI, 2, pp. 351, 360, 794–795, 984; Evans, "At Malvern Hill," *CWTI*, 6:10 (Dec. 1967): p. 40; Henry Burgwyn to mother, July 14, 1862, Burgwyn Family Papers, SHC; Hager Memoirs, Hager Family Papers, UVa.; Burton, *Extraordinary Circumstances*, pp. 348, 350.

[48] *OR*, XI, 2, pp. 73–74, 245–246, 250, 670–671, 698, 708, 717, 719, 723–724, 749–751, 800, 815, 819, 978; Moore, "Malvern Hill," *SHSP*, vol. 35 (Jan.–Dec. 1907): pp. 122–123; Haw Diary, Haw Papers, VaHS; Porter, "Battle of Malvern Hill," *BL*, vol. 2, p. 421; Fox, *Regimental Losses*, p. 204.

[49] *OR*, XI, 2, pp. 68, 209, 212, 214, 728, 734, 737, 742; Wray, "Malvern Hill," *NT*, Apr. 17, 1890, p. 4; Burton, *Extraordinary Circumstances*, pp. 352–353.

[50] *OR*, XI, 2, pp. 140–141, 698, 700, 705, 728, 734, 737, 738, 742; Wray, "Malvern Hill," *NT*, Apr. 17, 1890, p. 4; Coker, "A Story of the Confederate War," Coker Papers, VaHS; Burton, *Extraordinary Circumstances*, p. 353.

[51] *OR*, XI, 2, pp. 107, 209, 571–572, 576, 582, 587, 598, 601, 612, 620, 622, 729, 973; Jones Journal, Benjamin Anderson Jones Papers, VaHS; Hale, "Recollections of Malvern Hill," *CV*, vol. 30, (Sept. 1922): p. 333; Kearns Diary, Kearns Papers, VaHS; Brown, "Down the Peninsula," p. 65.

[52] *OR*, XI, 2, pp. 238, 240, 567, 598, 618–619, 815; Burton, *Extraordinary Circumstances*, p. 356.

[53] "Horrors of the Battlefield," *CV*, vol. 15 (July 1907): p. 306; *OR*, XI, 2, pp. 24–41, 973–984; Fox, *Regimental Losses*, p. 563; Hill, "McClellan's Change of Base," *BL*, vol. 2, p. 394.

Chapter 22

[1] *OR*, XI, 2, pp. 201, 216, 234, 517–518, 525, 527, 529, 533; Blackford, *War Years*, p. 79; Burton, *Extraordinary Circumstances*, pp. 365–366.

[2] McClellan telegram to Lincoln, July 2, 1862, *Papers*, p. 329; Sears, *Gates of Richmond*, p. 338.

[3] *OR*, XI, 2. p. 23; Averell, "With the Cavalry," *BL*, vol. 2, p. 433; Porter to McClellan, July 1, 1862, McClellan Papers, LOC; Heintzelman Diary, Heintzelman Papers, LOC; Smith, *Autobiography*, pp. 47–48; Burton, *Extraordinary Circumstances*, pp. 366–367.

[4] *OR*, XI, 3, p. 282; Brown, "Down the Peninsula," p. 64; Hyde, *Following the Greek Cross*, p. 80; Le Duc, "McClellan and Richmond," *NT*, July 30, 1914, p. 7; Burton, *Extraordinary Circumstances*, pp. 367–368.

[5] Bliss, "No. 1 Narrative," Bancroft-Bliss Family Papers, LOC; *OR*, XI, 2, pp. 64, 80–81, 90, 103, 124, 141, 144, 151, 165, 182, 186, 189, 204, 217, 235, 246, 250, 276, 294–295, 315, 351, 364, 381, 436, 464; Sypher, *Pennsylvania Reserve Corps*, p. 306; Heintzelman Diary, Heintzelman Papers, LOC; Dodge Journal, Dodge Papers, LOC; Burton, *Extraordinary Circumstances*, pp. 368–370.

[6] Sears, *Gates of Richmond*, p. 337; *OR*, XI, 2, pp. 567, 612–613, 619–620, 643–644, 650, 686, 692, 724, 729, 751, 760, 795, 800, 819, 867, 884; Hands Civil War Memoirs, UVa.; Brown, "Down the Peninsula," p. 67; "General Thomas J. Jackson," *SHSP*, vol. 19 (Jan. 1891): p. 311; Burton, *Extraordinary Circumstances*, p. 370.

[7] Alexander, "Longstreet's Corps, A.N.V.," *SHSP*, vol. 1 (Feb.–Mar. 1883): p. 75; Evans, "At Malvern Hill," *CWTI*, 6:10 (Dec. 1967): p. 40; Bernard, "Malvern Hill." *SHSP*, vol 18 (Jan.–Dec. 1890): p. 69; Burton, *Extraordinary Circumstances*, pp. 370–371.

[8] *OR*, XI, 2, pp. 124, 193, 217; Hyde, *Following the Greek Cross*, pp. 81–82; Evans, "At Malvern Hill." *CWTI*, 6:10 (Dec. 1967): p. 42; Burton, *Extraordinary Circumstances*, pp. 371–372; Sears, *Gates of Richmond*, p. 338.

⁹ *OR*, XI, 1, p. 70; pt. 2, pp. 60, 103, 155, 194, 217–218, 220, 258, 351, 355, 381, 436, 464, 481; Smith, *Autobiography*, p. 48; Burton, *Extraordinary Circumstances*, p. 372.

¹⁰ *OR*, XI, 2, pp. 206, 235–236, 360; Hager Memoir, Hager Papers, UVa.; Averell, "With the Cavalry," *BL*, vol. 2, pp. 431–432; Burton, *Extraordinary Circumstances*, pp. 372, 374.

¹¹ *OR*, XI, 2, pp. 801, 815, 816, 819; Burgwyn to mother, July 14, 1862, Burgwyn Family Papers, SHC; Early, *War Memoirs*, p. 83; Johnson, "Memoir," *SHSP*, vol. 10 (May 1882): p. 218; Blackford, *War Years*, p. 82; Brent, *Memoirs*, pp. 229–230, 232–235; Hands Civil War Memoirs, UVa; Burton, *Extraordinary Circumstances*, pp. 374–376.

¹² *OR*, XI, 2, pp. 519, 760; Dabney, *Life and Campaigns of Jackson*, pp. 474–475; Dabney, undated memorandum for G. F. R. Henderson, Hotchkiss Papers, LOC; McGuire to Hotchkiss, May 28, 1896, Hotchkiss Papers, LOC; Longstreet, *Manassas to Appomattox*, p. 146; Davis, *Rise and Fall*, p. 149; Burton, *Extraordinary Circumstances*, pp. 376–377.

¹³ *OR*, XI, 2, pp. 568, 572, 587, 619, 629, 713, 790, 908; Lee, *Lee's Dispatches*, pp. 23–25; Burton, *Extraordinary Circumstances*, pp. 377–378.

¹⁴ Bliss, "No. 1 Narrative," Bancroft-Bliss Family Papers, LOC; *OR*, XI, pt. 2, pp. 64, 80–81, 88, 103, 147, 160, 246, 259, 262, 276, 283, 310, 383, 436, 464; Averell, "With the Cavalry," *BL*, vol. 2, p. 432; Hager Memoir, Hager Papers, UVa; Burton, *Extraordinary Circumstances*, p. 378.

¹⁵ Smith, *Autobiography*, p. 48. (Quoted from Smith, *Memoirs*, pp. 145–146).

¹⁶ Bliss, "No. 1 Narrative," Bancroft-Bliss Family Papers, LOC; Dodge Journal, Dodge Papers, LOC; Hager Memoir, Hager Papers, UVa; Porter, "Battle of Malvern Hill," *BL*, vol. 2, p. 423; Smith, *Autobiography*, p. 49; Burton, *Extraordinary Circumstances*, pp. 378–379.

¹⁷ *OR*, XI, 2, pp. 218, 220, 299, 334, 530, 531; Sears, ed., *McClellan Papers*, pp. 329–330; Lincoln, *Collected Works*, vol. V, p. 301; Stillwell, "Incidents of McClellan's Retreat," *NT*, Apr. 15, 1909, p. 7; Burton, *Extraordinary Circumstances*, pp. 379–380.

Chapter 23

[1] Lee to Davis, July 2, 1862, Lee, *Papers*, pp. 206–207; Davis, *Rise and Fall*, II, pp. 149–150; Sears, *Gates of Richmond*, p. 339.

[2] Cullen, *Peninsula Campaign*, pp. 164–165.

[3] *OR*, XI, 2, pp. 519–520; Dabney, *Life and Campaigns of Jackson*, pp. 475–476; Freeman, *R. E. Lee*, vol. II, p. 225; Burton, *Extraordinary Circumstances*, pp. 380–381.

[4] *OR*, XI, 2, p. 246, 464, 482, 520, 922; Lee, *General Lee*, p. 165; Smith, *Autobiography*, p. 49; Hager Memoir, Hager Papers, UVa; Sears, ed., *McClellan Papers*, pp. 334–335; Barnard to McClellan, July 2, 1862, McClellan Papers, LOC; Jones, "Reminiscences No. 8," *SHSP*, vol. 9 (Oct.–Dec. 1881): p. 569; Burton, *Extraordinary Circumstances*, pp. 381–383.

[5] Alexander, *Military Memoirs*, p. 169; Cullen, *Peninsula Campaign*, p. 165; Lee, *General Lee*, pp. 165–166; Jones, "Reminiscences No. 8," *SHSP*, vol. 9 (Oct.–Dec. 1881): p. 569; Sears, *Gates of Richmond*, pp. 340–341; "Jackson and Ewell," *SHSP*, vol. 20 (Jan.–Dec. 1892): p. 31; Burton, *Extraordinary Circumstances*, p. 383.

[6] *OR*, XI, 2, pp. 520, 760; Freeman, *Lee's Lieutenants*, Vol. I, p. 643; Dabney, *Life and Campaigns of Jackson*, p. 476; Alexander, *Military Memoirs*, p. 169; Burton, *Extraordinary Circumstances*, p. 383.

[7] *OR*, XI, 2, p. 922.

[8] Alexander, *Military Memoirs*, p. 171.

[9] Alexander, *Military Memoirs*, p. 171; Sears, *Gates of Richmond*, p. 341.

[10] *OR*, XI, 3, pp. 636–637; Sears, ed., *McClellan Papers*, pp. 334–339; *Lee's Dispatches*, pp. 24–32; Dabney, *Life and Campaigns of Jackson*, p. 476; Foote, *Civil War — A Narrative*, vol. I, pp., 517–518; Burton, *Extraordinary Circumstances*, p. 385.

[11] Alexander, *Fighting for the Confederacy*, pp. 117, 572n; Sears, *Gates of Richmond*, p. 342.

Part VI

[1] Sears, *Gates of Richmond*, p. 342

Chapter 24

[1] Smith, *Autobiography*, pp. 48–49.
[2] Konstam, *Seven Days Battles*, p. 83.
[3] Cullen, *Peninsula Campaign*, pp. 170–171.
[4] Sears, *Gates of Richmond*, p. 349.
[5] Dowdey, *Seven Days*, p. 352; Burton, *Extraordinary Circumstances*, pp. 384–385.
[6] Wert, *Sword of Lincoln*, p. 126.
[7] Sears, *Gates of Richmond*, pp. 350–351.
[8] McClellan, *Report on Campaigns*, pp. 280–282.
[9] Wert, *Sword of Lincoln*, p. 127.
[10] Sears, *Gates of Richmond*, p. 351; Cullen, *Peninsula Campaign*, pp. 353-354.
[11] Martin, *Peninsula Campaign*, pp. 236-237; Konstam, *Seven Days Battles*, pp. 84–85; Sears, *Gates of Richmond*, p. 351; Sears, ed., *McClellan Papers*, pp. 333, 344–345, 348, 362–363.
[12] *OR*, XI, 2, pp. 940–942.
[13] Alexander, *Military Memoirs*, pp. 171–172; McClellan, *Report on Campaigns*, p. 285.
[14] Sears, *Gates of Richmond*, p. 344.
[15] Sears, *Gates of Richmond*, p. 343.
[16] Steiner, *Disease in the Civil War*, p. 124; Norton, *Army Letters*, pp. 327–329; Martin, *Peninsula Campaign*, p. 236; Sears, *Gates of Richmond*, pp. 347–348.
[17] Sears, *Gates of Richmond*, pp. 345–346.
[18] Sears, *Gates of Richmond*, p. 348.
[19] Konstam, *Seven Days Battles*, p. 83.

Chapter 25

[1] Burton, *Extraordinary Circumstances*, pp. 387–388.
[2] Sears, *Gates of Richmond*, p. 86.
[3] Sears, *Gates of Richmond*, pp. 116–117.
[4] *OR*, XI, 2, pp. 973–984.
[5] Sears, *Gates of Richmond*, pp. 344–345.

⁶ *OR*, XI, 2, pp. 973-984; Fox, *Regimental Losses*, pp. 556-558.
⁷ *OR*, XI, 2, pp. 501–510; *OR*, XI, 2, pp. 24–37, 40–41, 498, 629, 973–984; Alexander, *Military Memoirs*, p. 174; Sears, *Gates of Richmond*, pp., 342–343; Burton, *Extraordinary Circumstances*, pp. 386–387; Livermore, *Numbers and Losses*, pp. 140–141; Fox, *Regimental Losses*, pp. 556–558; Alexander, *Fighting for the Confederacy*, p. 112.
⁸ Steiner, *Disease in Civil War*, pp. 102–142.
⁹ Sears, *Gates of Richmond*, p. 345.
¹⁰ Blackford, *War Years*, p. 75.

Chapter 26

¹ Konstam, *Seven Days Battles*, p. 85.
² Hansen, *The Civil War*, p. 209.
³ McClellan, *Report on Campaigns*, p. 287.
⁴ McClellan, *Report on Campaigns*, pp. 288–289.
⁵ Hansen, *The Civil War*, p. 209; McClellan, *Report on Campaigns*, p. 289.
⁶ Cullen, *Peninsula Campaign*, p. 178.
⁷ Martin, *The Peninsula Campaign*, p. 240.
⁸ Wheeler, *Sword Over Richmond*, p. 352.
⁹ McClellan, *Report on Campaigns*, pp. 316–318; Coski, *Army of Potomac at Berkeley Plantation*, p. 33.
¹⁰ Coski, *Army of Potomac at Berkeley Plantation*, p. 34; Sears, *Gates of Richmond*, pp. 355–356.
¹¹ *OR*, XI, 1, pp. 87–88; *OR*, XI, 3, pp. 372–373, 378; Sears, ed., *McClellan Papers*, p. 388; Sears, *Controversies and Commanders*, pp. 54, 55; Donald, *Lincoln*, pp. 370–371.
¹² McClellan, *Report on Campaigns*, pp. 290, 295, 297–298, 299–302, 302, 304, 306.
¹³ McClellan, *Report on Campaigns*, pp. 289–290, 292, 293–294, 295, 298, 302–303, 306–307, 309–310.
¹⁴ McClellan, *Report on Campaigns*, pp. 288–290.
¹⁵ McClellan, *Report on Campaigns*, pp. 290–291.
¹⁶ McClellan, *Report on Campaigns*, pp. 290, 293.
¹⁷ McClellan, *Report on Campaigns*, pp. 290, 292.

[18] McClellan, *Report on Campaigns*, p. 302.
[19] Michie, *General McClellan*, p. 382.
[20] McClellan, *Report on Campaigns*, pp. 302–303.
[21] Alexander, *Military Memoirs*, p. 179; McClellan, *Report on Campaigns*, pp. 318–321; Coski, *Army of Potomac at Berkeley Plantation*, pp. 33–34; Martin, *Peninsula Campaign*, p. 238.
[22] Alexander, *Military Memoirs*, p. 179; Wert, *Sword of Lincoln*, p. 130.
[23] Hansen, *The Civil War*, p. 209.

Part VII

[1] Webb, *Peninsula*, p. 34

Chapter 27

[1] Naisawald, *Grape and Canister*, p. 138; Swinton, *Campaigns of Army of Potomac*, pp. 172–173.
[2] Naisawald, *Grape and Canister*, p. 138; Swinton, *Campaigns of Army of Potomac*, p. 173.
[3] Swinton, *Campaigns of Army of Potomac*, pp. 173.
[4] Naisawald, *Grape and Canister*, pp. 139–140.
[5] Sears, ed., *McClellan Papers*, p. 401.
[6] Swinton, *Campaigns of Army of Potomac*, p. 184.
[7] Sears, ed., *McClellan Papers*, p. 402.
[8] Michie, *General McClellan*, pp. 383–384.
[9] Freeman, *Lee's Lieutenants*, p. 264.
[10] Freeman, *Lee's Lieutenants*, pp. 264–265.
[11] Freeman, *Lee's Lieutenants*, p. 264.
[12] Freeman, *Lee's Lieutenants*, pp. 262–263.
[13] Sears, *Gates of Richmond*, pp. 343–344.
[14] McClellan to Mary Ellen McClellan, McClellan Papers (C–7:63), LOC; Wert, *Sword of Lincoln*, p. 138; Sears, *Controversies and Commanders*, pp. 82, 85–87; Sears, ed., *McClellan Papers*, p. 428.
[15] Wert, *Sword of Lincoln*, p. 138; OR, XII, 2, p. 83.
[16] Wert, *Sword of Lincoln*, p. 138; Donald, *Lincoln*, p. 371; Sears, *Controversies and Commanders*, pp. 87–88.
[17] Michie, *General McClellan*, p. 394.

[18] Davis, *Lincoln's Men*, p. 76; Wert, *Sword of Lincoln*, p. 139; Sears, *Controversies and Commanders*, pp. 88–91.
[19] Sears, ed., *McClellan Papers*, pp. 402–403.
[20] Michie, *General McClellan*, p. 398.
[21] Swinton, *Campaigns of Army of Potomac*, p. 194; Martin, *The Peninsula Campaign*, p. 240.
[22] Freeman, *Lee*, p. 250.
[23] Swinton, *Campaigns of Army of Potomac*, pp. 632–633.
[24] Swinton, *Campaigns of Army of Potomac*, pp. 201–202.
[25] Michie, *General McClellan*, p. 406.
[26] Freeman, *Lee*, p. 262.
[27] Freeman, *Lee*, p. 263.
[28] Swinton, *Campaigns of Army of Potomac*, pp. 225–226.
[29] *OR*, XIX, 2, p. 549; McClellan, *Report on Campaigns*, p. 438; Swinton, *Campaigns of Army of Potomac*, p. 227.
[30] Michie, *General McClellan*, pp. 438–439.
[31] Sears, ed., *McClellan Papers*, p. 520.
[32] Sears, ed., *McClellan Papers*, p. 521; *OR*, XIX, 2, p. 551; McClellan Papers (B–12:48), LOC.
[33] Swinton, *Campaigns of Army of Potomac*, pp. 231–232.
[34] Michie, *General McClellan*, p. 443.
[35] Michie, *General McClellan*, p. 452.

Chapter 28

[1] Gallagher, "Civil War Watershed," p. 3, 5–7.
[2] Gallagher, " Civil War Watershed," p. 10.
[3] Gallagher, "Civil War Watershed," p. 3.
[4] Freeman, *Lee*, p. 221.
[5] Burton, *Extraordinary Circumstances*, pp. 391–392.
[6] Freeman, *Lee*, p. 221.
[7] Freeman, *Lee's Lieutenants*, pp. 264–266.
[8] Freeman, *Lee*, pp. 223–224.
[9] Sears, *Controversies & Commanders*, p. 18.
[10] Freeman, *Lee's Lieutenants*, pp. 281–284.
[11] Gallagher, ed., *Fighting for Confederacy*, p. 120.
[12] Burton, *Extraordinary Circumstances*, pp. 388–389.

[13] Sears, *Controversies & Commanders*, p. 15; Sears, ed., *McClellan Papers*, pp. 26, 72.
[14] Dowdey, *Seven Days*, p. 355.
[15] Edge, *McClellan and Campaign on Peninsula*, pp. 202–203.
[16] Foote, *Civil War*, Vol. I, pp. 530–531.
[17] Sears, *Controversies & Commanders*, p. 24.

BIBLIOGRAPHY

Books

Adams, F. Colburn. *The Story of a Trooper.* New York: Dick & Fitzgerald, 1865.

Adams, George W. *Doctors in Blue: The Medical History of the Union Army in the Civil War.* New York: Schuman, 1952.

Aimone, Alan C. and Barbara A. *A User's Guide to the Official Records of the American Civil War.* Shippensburg, PA: White Main Publishing Co., Inc., 1991.

Alexander, Edward Porter. *Military Memoirs of a Confederate: A Critical Narrative.* New York: Da Capo Press, 1993.

____. *Fighting for the Confederacy.* Ed. Gary W. Gallagher. Chapel Hill: University of North Carolina Press, 1989.

Allan, William. *The Army of Northern Virginia in 1862.* Dayton, OH: Morningside Press, 1984. (Reprint).

Amann, William. *Personnel of the Civil War.* 2 vols. New York: Thomas Yoseloff, 1961.

Bailey, Ronald H. *Forward To Richmond: McClellan's Peninsular Campaign.* Alexandria, VA: Time-Life Books, Inc., 1983.

Baquet, Camille. *History of the First Brigade, New Jersey Volunteers from 1861 to 1865.* Trenton: State of New Jersey, 1910.

Barnard, John Gross. *The Peninsula Campaign and its Antecedents, as Developed by the Report of Maj.-Gen. Geo. B. McClellan, and other published documents.* Washington: The Union Congressional Committee, 1864.

Beale, George W. *A Lieutenant of Cavalry in Lee's Army.* Boston: Gorham Press, 1918.

Beale, R. L. T. *History of the Ninth Virginia Cavalry.* Richmond, VA: B. F. Johnson, 1899.

Bearss, Edwin C. *River of Lost Opportunities; The Civil War on the James River, 1861–1862.* Lynchburg, Va.: H. E. Howard, 1986.

Bill, Alfred Hoyt. *The Beleaguered City: Richmond, 1861–1865.* New York: Knopf, 1946.

Birkhimer, William E. *Historical sketch of the organization, administration, matériel and tactics of the artillery, United States Army.* Washington, DC: J. J. Chapman, agent, 1884.

Blackford, W. W. *War Years with Jeb Stuart.* New York: Charles Scribner's Sons, 1945. Reprint Baton Rouge: Louisiana State University Press, 1993.

Blackwell, Samuel M., Jr. *In the Front Line of Battle: The 12th Illinois Cavalry in the Civil War.* DeKalb: Northern Illinois University Press, 2002.

Blaine, James G. *Twenty Years of Congress: From Lincoln to Garfield., 2 vols.* Norwich, CT: The Henry Bill Publishing Co., 1884.

Blaisdell, Bob, ed. *The Civil War: A Book of Quotations.* Mineola, NY: Dover Publications, Inc.

Blake, Henry Nichols. *Three Years in the Army of the Potomac.* Boston: Lee and Shepard, 1865.

Boatner, Mark Mayo. *The Civil War Dictionary.* New York: David McKay Co., Inc., 1959.

Boritt, Gabor S., ed. *Jefferson Davis' Generals.* New York: Oxford University Press, 1999.

_____. *Lincoln's Generals.* New York: Oxford University Press, 1994.

Bowers, John. *Stonewall Jackson: Portrait of a Soldier.* New York: Morrow, 1989.

Brainerd, Wesley. *Bridge Building in Wartime: Colonel Wesley Brainerd's memoir of the 50th New York Volunteer Engineers.* Ed. Ed Malles. Knoxville: University of Tennessee Press, 1997.

Brent, Joseph L. *Memoirs of the War Between the States.* New Orleans: Fontana Printing Co., Inc., 1940.

Bridges, Hal. *Lee's Maverick General: Daniel Harvey Hill.* New York: McGraw-Hill, 1961.

Bruce, George A. *The Twentieth Regiment of Massachusetts Volunteer Infantry.* Boston: Houghton Mifflin, 1906.

Burns, James R. *Battle of Williamsburg and Reminiscences of the Campaign.* New York, 1865.

Burton, Brian K. *Extraordinary Circumstances: The Seven Days Battles.* Bloomington and Indianapolis: Indiana University Press, 2001.

Bushong, Millard Kessler. *Old Jube: A Biography of General Jubal A. Early.* Boyce, VA: Carr Publishing Co., Inc., 1955.

Campaigns of the Civil War. 16 vol. Wilmington, N.C.: Broadfoot Pub. Co., 1989.

Campbell, James H. *McClellan.* New York: Neale Publishing Co., 1916.

Carroll, Jon M., ed. *Custer in the Civil War, His Unfinished Memoirs.* San Rafael, CA: Presidio Press, 1977.

Casdorph, Paul D. *Lee and Jackson: Confederate Chieftains.* Reprint. New York: Paragon House, 1992.

Casler, John O. *Four Years in the Stonewall Brigade.* Girard, KS: Appeal, 1906.

Catton, Bruce. *Glory Road.* Garden City, NJ: Doubleday, 1952.

_____. *Mr. Lincoln's Army.* Garden City, NY: Doubleday, 1962.

Chamberlain, Joshua Lawrence. *The Passing of the Armies.* Dayton, OH: Morningside Press (reprint), 1989.

Clark, Walter, ed. *Histories of the Several Regiments and Battalions from North Carolina in the Great War, 1861–1865*, 5 volumes. Goldsboro, NC: State of North Carolina, 1901.

Cleaves, Freeman. *Meade of Gettysburg.* Dayton, OH: Morningside Press (reprint), 1980.

Cochrane, John C. *American Civil War, Memories of Incidents connected with the origin and culmination of the rebellion that threatened the existence of the national government.* New York: Rogers & Sherwood, 1879.

Coddington, Edwin B. *The Gettysburg Campaign: A Study in Command.* Dayton, OH: Morningside Press (reprint), 1983.

Collins, Darrell. The *46th Virginia Infantry.* Lynchburg, VA: H. E. Howard, 1992.

Cook, Joel. *The Siege of Richmond: A Narrative of the Military Operations of Major-General George B. McClellan During the Months of May and June, 1862.* Philadelphia: George W. Childs, 1862.

Cooke, John Esten. *Wearing of the Gray: Being Personal Portraits, Scenes, and Adventures of the War.* New York: E. B. Treat, 1867.

Coski, John M. *The Army of the Potomac at Berkeley Plantation: the Harrison's Landing Occupation of 1862.* Richmond, VA: J. M. Coski, 1989.

Coulter, E. Merton. *The South During Reconstruction.* Baton Rouge: Louisiana State University Press, 1982.

Coward, Asbury. *The South Carolinians.* Ed. Natalie J. Bond and Osmun L. Coward. New York: Vantage Press, 1968.

Cowley, Robert, ed. *With My Face to the Enemy: Perspectives on the Civil War.* New York: G.P. Putnam's Sons, 2001.

Crute, Jr., Joseph H. *Units of the Confederate States Army.* Midlothian, VA: Derwent Books, 1987.

Cullen, Joseph P. *The Peninsula Campaign 1862: McClellan & Lee Struggle for Richmond.* Harrisburg, PA: Stackpole, 1973.

Dabney, Robert L. *Life and Campaigns of Lieut.-Gen. Thomas Jackson.* New York: Blelock, 1866.

Davis, Burke. *Gray Fox: Robert E. Lee and the Civil War* (reprint). New York: Harry Holt and Co., 1998.

———. *They Called Him Stonewall* (reprint). New York: Harry Holt and Co., 1999.

Davis, Jefferson. *The Rise and Fall of the Confederate Government.* 2 vols. New York: D. Appleton, 1881.

Davis, William C. *The Guns of '62.* Garden City, NY: Doubleday & Co., 1982.

———. *Lincoln's Men: How President Lincoln Became Father to an Army and a Nation.* New York: Free Press, 1999.

Dickert, Augustus. *History of Kershaw's Brigade.* Newberry, SC: E. H. Aull Co., 1899.

Dickey, Luther. *History of the Eighty-fifth Regiment of Pennsylvania Veteran Volunteer Infantry, 1861–1865.* New York: J.C. and W.E. Powers, 1915.

Dickey, Luther S. and Samuel E. Evans. *History of the 103rd Pennsylvania Veteran Volunteer Infantry, 1881–1865.* Chicago: L. S. Dickey, 1910.

Dixon, Thomas. *The Man in Gray: A Romance of the North and South.* New York: D. Appleton & Co., 1921.

Donald, David Herbert. *Lincoln.* New York: Simon & Schuster, 1995.

Dornbusch, Charles E. *Military Biography of the Civil War*, 3 vols. New York: The New York Public Library; Astor, Lenox and Tilden Foundations, 1961, 1967, 1972. Reprint Dayton, OH: Morningside, 1987.

Dougherty, Kevin and J. Michael Moore. *The Peninsula Campaign of 1862: A Military Analysis.* Jackson: university press of Mississippi, 2005.

Douglas, Henry Kyd. *I Rode With Stonewall.* Chapel Hill: UNC Press, 1940.

Dowdey, Clifford. *The Seven Days: The Emergence of Robert E. Lee.* New York: Fairfax Press, 1964.

_____, ed. *The Wartime Papers of Robert E. Lee.* New York: Da Capo, 1987.

Driver, Jr., Robert J. *The 1st and 2nd Rockbridge Artillery.* Lynchburg, VA: H. E. Howard, Inc., 1987.

_____. *The Staunton Artillery – McClanahan's Battery.* Lynchburg, VA: H. E. Howard, Inc., 1998.

_____. 5th Virginia Cavalry. Lynchburg, VA: H. E. Howard, Inc., 1997.

_____. 10th Virginia Cavalry. Lynchburg, VA: H. E. Howard, Inc., 1997.

Dubbs, Carol Kettenburg. *Defend This Old Town: Williamsburg During the Civil War.* Baton Rouge: Louisiana State University Press, 2002.

Dyer, Frederick H. *A Compendium of the War of the Rebellion,* 3 vols., 1908, reprint. New York: Thomas Yoseloff, 1959.

Early, Jubal A. *War Memoirs: Autobiographical Sketch and Narrative of the War Between the States.* Philadelphia: Lippincott, 1912.

Edge, Frederick Milnes. *Major General McClellan and the Campaign on the Yorktown Peninsula.* London: Trübner & Co., 1865.

Eicher, John H. and David J. Eicher. *Civil War High Commands.* Stanford: Stanford University Press, 2001.

Elliot, Joseph Canty. *Lee's Noble Soldier: Lt. Gen. Richard Heron Anderson.* Dayton: Morningside House, Inc., 1985.

Evans, Clement Anselm, ed. *Confederate Military History.* 12 vols. Atlanta: Confederate Publishing Co., 1899. Reprint, 12 vols., New York: Thomas Yoseloff, 1962. Reprint, 17 vols., Wilmington, NC: Broadfoot Publishing Co., 1987.

Farwell, Byron. *Stonewall: A Biography of General Thomas J. Jackson.* New York: Norton, 1992.

Faust, Patricia L., ed. *Historical Times Illustrated Encyclopedia of the Civil War.* New York: Harper and Row, 1986.

Fehrenbacher, Don. E. and Virginia Fehrenbacher. *Recollected Words of Abraham Lincoln.* Stanford: Stanford University Press, 1996.

Fishel, Edwin C. *The Secret War for the Union: the Untold Story of Military Intelligence in the Civil War.* Boston: Houghton Mifflin Co., 1996.

Foote, Shelby. *The Civil War: A Narrative—Fort Sumter to Perryville.* New York: Random House, 1986.

Ford, Andrew E. *The Story of the Fifteenth Regiment of Massachusetts Volunteer Infantry in the Civil War, 1861–1864.* Clinton, MA: W. J. Coulter, 1898.

Fortier, John. *15th Virginia Cavalry.* Lynchburg, VA: H. E. Howard, Inc., 1993.

Fox, William F. *Regimental Losses in the American Civil War 1861–1865.* Albany, NY: Albany Publishing, 1889. Reprint, Gulf Breeze, FL: eBooksonDisk.com, 2002.

Freeman, Douglas Southall. *Lee.* An Abridgement in one volume of the four-volume *R. E. Lee* by Douglas Southall Freeman / by Richard Harwell. New York: Macmillan Publishing Co., 1991.

____. *Lee's Lieutenants: A Study in Command.* 3 vols. New York: Scribner's, 1942–44.

____. *Lee's Lieutenants: A Study in Command;* abridged in one volume by Stephen W. Sears; introduction by James M. McPherson. New York: Scribner, 1998.

____. *R. E. Lee.* 4 vols. New York: Charles Scribner's Sons, 1934–35.

French, Samuel L. *The Army of the Potomac from 1861 to 1863.* New York: Publishing Society of New York, 1906.

Fuller, J. F. C. *Decisive Battles of the U. S. A.* New York, Scribner, 1940.

____, J. F. C. *A Military History of the Western World: From the American Civil War to the End of World War II,* Vol. III. New York: Funk and Wagnalls, 1957.

Furgurson, Ernest B. *Ashes of Glory: Richmond at War.* New York: Alfred A. Knopf, 1996.

Gallagher, Gary W., ed. *Fighting for the Confederacy: The Personal Recollections of General Edward Porter Alexander.* Chapel Hill: The University of North Carolina Press, 1989.

____. *The Richmond Campaign of 1862: The Peninsula & the Seven Days.* Chapel Hill and London: University of North Carolina Press, 2000.

____. *The Shenandoah Valley Campaign of 1862.* Chapel Hill: University of North Carolina Press, 2003.

Giles, Valerius Cincinnatus. *Rags and Hope, The Recollections of Val C. Giles, Four Years with Hood's Brigade, Fourth Texas Infantry, 1861–1865.* Lasswell, Mary, ed. New York: Coward-McCann, 1961.

Gordon, John B. *Reminiscences of the Civil War.* New York, 1903. Reprint, New York: Time-Life, 1984.

Govan, Gilbert E. and James W. Livingood. *A Different Valor: The Story of General Joseph E. Johnston.* New York: Bobbs-Merrill, 1956.

Gregory, G. Howard. *38th Virginia Infantry.* Lynchburg: H. E. Howard, Inc., 1956.

Hall, Charles B. *Military Records of General Officers of the Confederate States of America.* Austin, Texas: The Steck Company, 1963.

Hansen, Harry. *The Civil War: A History.* New York: Penguin Putnam, Inc., 1961.

Hardy, Michael C. *The Battle of Hanover Court House: turning point of the Peninsula Campaign, May 27, 1862*. Jefferson, NC: McFarland & Co., 2006.

Harsh, Joseph J. *Confederate Tide Rising: Robert E. Lee and the Making of Southern Strategy, 1861–1862*. Kent, OH: Kent State University Press, 1998.

_____. *Taken at the Flood: Robert E. Lee and Confederate Strategy in the Maryland campaign of 1862*. Kent, OH: Kent State University Press, 1999.

Harwell, Richard B. *The Union Reader: As the North Saw the War*. New York: Dover, 1989.

Hassler, Warren W. *General George B. McClellan: Shield of the Union*. Baton Rouge, 1957.

Hassler, William Woods. *A. P. Hill. Lee's Forgotten General*. Richmond: Garrett & Massie, 1957.

Hastings, Earl C. And David S. Hastings. *A Pitiless Rain: The Battle of Williamsburg*. Shippensburg, PA: White Mane Publishing Company, 1966.

Hattaway, Herman, and Jones, Archer. *How the North Won: A Military History of the Civil War*. Urbana: University of Illinois Press, 1983.

Hebert, Walter H. *Fighting Joe Hooker*. New York: Indianapolis: Bobbs-Merrill, 1944.

Henderson, G. F. R. *Stonewall Jackson and the American Civil War*. 2 vols. New York: Fawcett, 1962.

Hewett, Janet B. *Supplement to the Official Records of the Union and Confederate Armies.* 100 volumes. Wilmington, NC: Broadfoot, 1994–2001.

Hill, Daniel Harvey. *Bethel to Sharpsburg.* Vol. II. Raleigh: Edwards & Broughton Co., 1926.

Hood, John B. *Advance and Retreat: Personal Experiences in the United States and Confederate States Armies.* New Orleans: Hood Orphan Memorial Fund, 1880. Reprint, Bloomington: Indiana University Press, 1959. Reprint, Secaucus, NJ: Blue and Grey, 1985; reprint of 1880 edition.

Howard, Oliver Otis. *Autobiography of Oliver Otis Howard.* 2 vols. New York: Baker and Troy, 1907.

Hurlbert, William Henry. *The Life of General George Brinton McClellan.* New York: Rand & Avery, 1864.

Hunt, Roger D. and Jack R. Brown. *Brevet Brigadier Generals in Blue.* Gaithersburg: Olde Soldier Books, 1997.

Hunter, *Johnny Reb and Billy Yank.* New York and Washington: Neale Publishing Co., 1905.

Hyde, Thomas W. *Following the Greek Cross, or Memoirs of the VI Army Corps.* Boston: Houghton Mifflin, 1894.

Jackson, Mary Anna. *Memoirs of Stonewall Jackson.* Louisville: Prentice Press, 1895.

Jensen, Les. *32nd Virginia Infantry.* Lynchburg, Va.: H.E. Howard, c1990.

Johnson, Robert U. and Clarence C. Buel, eds. *Battles and Leaders of the Civil War.* 4 vols. New York: 1884.

Johnston, James Ambler. *Echoes of 1861–1961.* Milwaukee: P. J. Hohlbeck, 1971.

Johnston, Joseph E. *Narrative of Military Operations: Its Organization, Its Commander, and Its Campaign.* New York: D. Appleton & Co., 1874. Reprint, Bloomington, IN: Indiana University Press, 1959.

Joinville, Prince de. *The Army of the Potomac.* New York: Anson D. F. Randolph, 1862.

Jones, Archer. *Civil War Command and Strategy: The Process of Victory and Defeat.* New York: Free Press, 1992.

Jones, John B. *A Rebel War Clerk's Diary.* 2 vols. Philadelphia: J. B. Lippincott, 1866.

Jones, J. William. *Life and Letters of Robert Edward Lee, Soldier and Man.* New York: Neale, 1906.

_____. *Personal Reminiscences, Anecdotes, and Letters of Gen. Robert E. Lee.* New York: D. Appleton and Co., 1874. (Reprint) United States Historical Society Press, c1989.

Jones, Terry L. *Lee's Tigers: The Louisiana Infantry in the Army of Northern Virginia.* Baton Rouge: Louisiana State University Press, 1992.

Jordan, David M. *Winfield Scott Hancock: A Soldier's Life.* Bloomington: Indiana University Press, 1988.

Kearny, Philip. *Letters From the Peninsula: The Civil War Letters of General Philip Kearny*. Ed. William B. Styple. Kearny, NJ: Belle Grove Publishing, 1988.

Ketchum, Hiram. *General McClellan's Peninsula Campaign: Review of the Report of the Committee on the Conduct of the War relative to the Peninsula Campaign*. New York: s.n., 1864.

Keyes, Erasmus D. *Fifty Years Observation of Men and Events, Civil and Military*. New York: Charles Scribner's Sons, 1884.

Konstam, Angus. *Fair Oaks: McClellan's Peninsula Campaign*. Oxford: Osprey, 2003.

_____. *Seven Days Battles: Lee's Defense of Richmond*. Osceola, WI: Osprey Publishing, Ltd., 2004.

Krick, Robert K. *The Fredericksburg Artillery*. Lynchburg, VA: H. E. Howard, Inc., 1986.

_____. *9th Virginia Cavalry*. Lynchburg, VA: H. E. Howard, Inc., 1982.

_____. *Lee's Colonels: A Biographical Register of the Field Officers of the Army of Northern Virginia*, 2nd edition. Dayton, OH: Press of Morningside Bookstore, 1984.

Lane, Mills. *Dear Mother, don't grieve about me: if I get killed, I'll only be dead: Letters from Georgia Soldiers*. Savannah: Beehive Press, 1977.

Lee, Fitzhugh. *General Lee*. New York: D. Appleton, 1884. Reprint, Wilmington, NC: Broadfoot, 1989.

Lee, Robert E. *Lee's Dispatches*. Ed. Douglass Southall Freeman. New York: G. P. Putnam's Sons, 1957.

———. *The Wartime Papers of R. E. Lee*. Ed. Clifford Dowdey. Boston: Little, Brown & Co., 1961.

Lee Takes Command: From Seven Days to Second Bull Run. Alexandria, VA: Time-Life Books, Inc., 1984.

Leech, Margaret. *Reveille in Washington, 1861–1865*. New York: Book of the Month Club, 1989. Reprint of 1941 edition.

Lincoln, Abraham. *The Collected Works of Abraham Lincoln*. Ed. Roy P. Basler. New Brunswick, NJ: Rutgers University Press, 1953.

———. *The Collected Works of Abraham Lincoln*. Supplement, 1832–1865. Westport, Conn.: Greenwood Press, 1974.

Livermore, Thomas L. *Numbers and Losses in the Civil War in America 1861–65*. Reprint. Dayton, OH: Morningside House, Inc., 1986.

Long, Armistead L. *Memoirs of Robert E. Lee: His Military and Personal History*. New York: J. M. Stoddard & Co., 1886.

Long, E. B. and Barbara. *The Civil War Day by Day: An Almanac 1861–1865*. Garden City, NY: Doubleday, 1971.

Longstreet, James. *From Manassas to Appomattox*. New York: Konecky & Konecky, 1984.

Manarin, Louis H., ed. *Richmond at War, the Minutes of the City Council, 1861–1865*. Chapel Hill, NC: University of North Carolina Press, 1966.

Marks, James J. *The Peninsular Campaign in Virginia, or Incidents and Scenes on the Battle-fields and in Richmond*. Philadelphia: Lippincott, 1864.

Marshall, Charles. *An Aide-de-Camp of Lee: Being the Papers of Colonel Charles Marshall*. Ed. Frederick Maurice. Boston: Little, Brown, 1927.

Martin, David G. *The Peninsula Campaign: March–July 1862 (Great Campaigns Series)*. Conshohocken, PA: Combined Books, 1992.

Maurice, Major General Sir Frederick. *Robert E. Lee: The Soldier*. Boston and New York: Houghton Mifflin Company, 1925. Reprint (electronic) Oakman, AL: H-Bar Enterprises, 1995.

Maury, Dabney. *Recollections of a Virginian in the Mexican, Indian, and Civil Wars*. New York: C. Scribner's Sons, 1894.

McClellan, George B. *The Civil War Papers of George B. McClellan: Selected Correspondence*. Ed. Stephen W. Sears. New York: Ticknor and Fields, 1989.

_____, *McClellan's Own Story : the war for the Union, the soldiers who fought it, the civilians who directed it and his relations to it and to th*em. 2 vols. New York: C.L. Webster & Company, 1887.

_____. *Report on the Organization of the Army of the Potomac, and of Its Campaigns in Virginia and Maryland*. New York: Sheldon & Co., 1864.

McMurry, Richard M. *John Bell Hood and the War for Southern Independence*. Lexington, KY: University Press of Kentucky, 1982.

Meade, George. *The Life and Letters of George Gordon Meade*. New York: Charles Scribner's Sons, 1913.

Michie, Peter S. *General McClellan.* New York: D. Appleton, 1915.

Military and Historical Society of Massachusetts. *The Peninsular Campaign of General McClellan in 1862.* Boston: James R. Osgood, 1881.

Military Historical Society of Massachusetts. *Campaigns in Virginia, 1861–1862.* Theodore F. Dwight, ed. Wilmington, NC: Broadfoot Publishing Co., 1989.

Miller, Marion Mills, ed. *Life and Works of Abraham Lincoln.* 9 vols. New York: The Current Literature Publishing Co., 1892.

Miller, William J., ed. *The Peninsula Campaign of 1862: Yorktown to the Seven Days.* 2 vols. Campbell, CA: Savas Woodbury, 1903, 1995.

____. *The Peninsula Campaign of 1862: Yorktown to the Seven Days.* vol. 3 Campbell, CA: Savas Publishing Co., 1997.

____. *The Battles for Richmond, 1862.* Eastern National, 1996.

Moore, Alison. *The Louisiana Tigers or the Two Louisiana Brigades of the Army of Northern Virginia, 1861–1865.* Baton Rouge: Louisiana State University Press, 1961.

Moore, Edward A. *The Story of a Cannoneer Under Stonewall Jackson.* New York, 1907. Reprint Alexandria, VA: Time-Life Books, 1983.

Moore, II, Robert H. *The Richmond Fayette, Hampden, Thomas, and Blount's Lynchburg Artillery.* Lynchburg, VA: H. E. Howard, Inc., 1991.

____. *Miscellaneous Disbanded Virginia Light Artillery.* Lynchburg, VA: H. E. Howard, Inc., 1997.

Myers, William S. *General George Brinton McClellan*. New York: D. Appleton Century Co., 1934.

Naisawald, Louis Van Loan. *Grape and Canister: The Story of the Field Artillery of the Army of the Potomac*. New York: Oxford University Press, 1899.

Nanzig, Thomas P. *The Third Virginia Cavalry*. Lynchburg: H. E. Howard, Inc., 1989.

Naval War Records Office. *Official Records of the Union and Confederate Navies in the War of the Rebellion*. 30 vols. Washington, DC: Government Printing Office, 1897–1927.

Nevins, Allan. *The War for the Union*. 4 Vol. New York: Charles Scribner's Sons, 1960.

Newton, Steven H. *The Battle of Seven Pines: May 31–June 1, 1862*. Lynchburg: H. E. Howard, Inc., 1993.

_____. *Joseph E. Johnston and the Defense of Richmond*. Lawrence: University of Kansas Press, c1998.

Nisbet, James C. *Four Years on the Firing Line*. Chattanooga, TN: Imperial Press, 1915.

Norton, Oliver W. *Army Letters, 1861–1865*. Chicago: privately printed, 1903.

Oates, William C. *The War Between the Union and the Confederacy and its Lost Opportunities*. New York: Neale, 1905.

Osborne, Charles C. *Jubal: The Life and Times of General Jubal A. Early*. Algonquin Books of Chapel Hill, 1992.

Page, Thomas Nelson. *Robert E. Lee – Man and Soldier.* New York: Charles Scribner's Sons, 1911. CD-ROM. Oakman, AL: H-Bar Enterprises, 1995.

Paris, Comte de. *History of the Civil War in America,* vol. 2, Philadelphia: Jos. H. Coates & Co., 1876.

Phillips, David. *Maps of the Civil War – The Roads They Took.* New York: MetroBooks, 2001.

Phisterer, Frederick. *Statistical record of the armies of the United States,* Vol. 13. New York: C. Scribner's sons, 1883.

Pinkerton, Allan. *The Spy of the Rebellion.* New York: G. W. Carleton & Co., 1883.

Piston, William Garrett. *Lee's Tarnished Lieutenant, James Longstreet and His Place in Southern History.* Athens, GA: University of Georgia Press, 1987.

Polley, J. B. *Hood's Texas Brigade.* New York, 1908.

Powell, William H. *The Fifth Army Corps (Army of the Potomac): A Record of Operations During the Civil War in the United States of America, 1861–1865.* London: G. P. Putnam's Sons, 1896. Reprint, Dayton, Ohio: Morningside Press, 1984.

Powell, William S. *Dictionary of North Carolina Biography.* 6 Vols. Chapel Hill: University of North Carolina Press, 1979.

Putnam, Sallie A. *In Richmond During the Confederacy.* New York: R. M. McBride, 1961. Original t.p. reads: Richmond during the war; four years of personal observation. By a Richmond lady. New York, G.V. Carlton, 1867. Reprint, New York: Robert M. McBride Co., 1961.

Quarstein, John V. *The Civil War on the Virginia Peninsula.* Charleston, SC: Arcadia, 1998.

Reed, John A., and Luther S. Dickey, *History of the 101st Pennsylvania Volunteer Infantry, 1861–1865.* Chicago: L. S. Dickey, 1910.

Reese, Timothy J. *Sykes' Regular Infantry Division, 1861–1864: a History of Regular United States Infantry Operations in the Civil War's Eastern Theater.* Jefferson, NC: McFarland & Co., 1990.

Report of the Joint Committee on the Conduct of the War. 3 vols. Washington: Government Printing Office, 1863.

Richardson, Albert D. *Personal History of Ulysses S. Grant.* Hartford: American Publishing Co., 1868.

Richardson, James D. *The Messages and Papers of the Confederacy, Including the Diplomatic Correspondence, 1861–1865.* 2 vols. Nashville: United States Publishing Co., 1906. Reprint, New York: R.R. Bowker, 1966.

Rhoades, Jeffrey L. *Scapegoat General: The Story of Major General Benjamin Huger, CSA.* Hamden, CT: Archon Books, 1985.

Robertson, James I., Jr. *General A. P. Hill: The Story of a Confederate Warrior.* New York: Random House, 1987.

____. *Stonewall Jackson: The Man, The Soldier, The Legend.* New York: Macmillan, 1997.

Robinson, Fayette. *An Account of the Organization of the Army of the United States*, 2 vols. Philadelphia: E. H. Butler, 1848.

Rodenbaugh, Theodore F., Robert S. Lanier, and Henry W. Elson, editors. *The Photographic History of the Civil War.* New York: Random House, 1997.

Ropes, John C. *The Story of the Civil War, vol 2: The Campaigns of 1862.* New York: Putnam's, 1905.

Rouse, Parke, Jr. *Remembering Williamsburg: A Sentimental Journal Through Three Centuries.* Richmond: Dietz Press, 1989.

Rowland, Dunbar, LL.D., ed. *Jefferson Davis Constitutionalist: His Letters, Papers and Speeches.* 10 vols. Jackson: Mississippi Department of Archives and History, 1923.

Salmon, John S. *The Official Virginia Civil War Battlefield Guide.* Mechanicsburg, PA: Stackpole Books, 2001.

Sanger, Donald B. and Thomas Robson Hay. *James Longstreet.* Baton Rouge: Louisiana State University Press, 1952.

Schenck, Martin. *Up Came Hill: The Story of the Light Division and Its Leaders.* Harrisburg, PA: Stackpole, 1958.

Sears, Stephen W., ed. *The Civil War Papers of George B. McClellan, Selected Correspondence, 1860–1865.* New York: Ticknor and Fields, 1989.

_____. *Controversies and Commanders: Dispatches from the Army of the Potomac.* New York: Houghton-Mifflin Company, 1999.

_____. *George B. McClellan: The Young Napoleon.* New York: Ticknor and Fields, 1988.

_____. *Landscape Turned Red: The Battle of Antietam.* New York: Mariner Books, 2003.

_____. *To the Gates of Richmond: The Peninsula Campaign.* New York: Houghton Mifflin Company, 2001.

Sedgwick, John. *Correspondence of John Sedgwick, Major General.* N. p.: Privately printed, 1903.

Sherwood, George L. *The Mathews Light Artillery; Penick's Pittsylvania Artillery; Young's Halifax Light Artillery, & Johnson's Jackson Flying Artillery.* Appomattox, VA: H. E. Howard, Inc., 1999.

Sherwood, W. Cullen. *The Nelson Artillery Lamkin and Rives Batteries.* Lynchburg, VA: H. E. Howard, Inc., 1991.

Sibley, Jr., F. Ray. *The Confederate Order of Battle.* Shippensburg, PA: White Mane Publishing Company, 1996.

Sifakis, Stewart. *Compendium of the Confederate Armies: Alabama.* Facts on File, c1992.

_____. *Compendium of the Confederate Armies: Florida and Arkansas.* Facts on File, c1992.

_____. *Compendium of the Confederate Armies: Kentucky, Maryland, Missouri, the Confederate Units and the Indian Units.* Facts on File, c1995.

_____. *Compendium of the Confederate Armies: Louisiana.* New York : Facts on File, c1995.

_____. *Compendium of the Confederate Armies: Mississippi.* Facts on File, c1995.

_____. *Compendium of the Confederate Armies: Tennessee.* Facts on File, c1992.

_____. *Compendium of the Confederate Armies: Texas.* New York : Facts on File, c1995.

_____. *Compendium of the Confederate Armies: South Carolina and Georgia.* Facts on File, c1995.

_____. *Compendium of the Confederate Armies: Virginia.* Bowie, MD: Willow Bend Books, 2003.

_____. *Who Was Who in the Civil War.* New York: Facts on File, 1988.

_____. *Who Was Who in the Confederacy.* New York: Facts on File, 1989.

_____. *Who Was Who in the Union.* New York: Facts on File., 1989.

Simpson, Harold B. *Hood's Texas Brigade: Lee's Grenadier Guard.* Dallas: Alcor Publishing, 1983.

Slocum, Charles E. *The Life and Services of Major-General Henry Warner Slocum.* Toledo, OH: Slocum, 1913.

Smith, Gustavus W. *Confederate War Papers: Fairfax Courthouse, New Orleans, Seven Pines, Richmond, and North Carolina.* 2nd edition. New York: Atlantic Publishing and Engraving, 1884.

_____. *The Battle of Seven Pines.* New York: C. G. Crawford, 1891.

Smith, William F. *Autobiography of Major General William F. Smith 1861–1864.* Ed. Herbert M. Schiller. Dayton, OH: Morningside, 1990.

Sneden, Robert Knox. *Eye of the Storm: a Civil War Odyssey.* Edited by Charles F. Bryan, Jr. and Nelson D. Lankford. New York: Free Press, 2000.

Snell, Mark A. *From First to Last: The Life of Major General William B. Franklin.* New York: Fordham University Press, 2002.

Sorrel, G. Moxley. *Recollections of a Confederate Staff Officer.* New York: Neale, 1905. Reprint, New York: Konecky & Konecky, 1994.

Southern Historical Society Papers. 52 vols. Richmond: 1876–1953.

Spruill, Matt. *Echoes of Thunder: a guide to the Seven Days Battles.* Knoxville: University of Tennessee Press, c2006.

Starr, Stephen Z. *The Union Cavalry in the Civil War.* 3 vols. Baton Rouge: Louisiana State University Press, 1979–1985.

Steiner, Paul E. *Disease in the Civil War: Natural Biological Warfare in 1861–1865.* Springfield, IL: C.C. Thomas, 1968.

Stiles, Kenneth L. *4th Virginia Cavalry.* Lynchburg, VA: H. E. Howard, Inc., 1985.

Stiles, Robert. *Four Years Under Marse Robert.* New York: Neale, 1903. Reprint, Dayton, OH: Morningside Press, 1988.

Stine, J. H. *History of the Army of the Potomac.* Washington, DC: Gibson Brothers, 1893.

Stoeckel, Carl, ed. *Correspondence of John Sedgwick, Major General,* 2 vols. N.P.: DeVinne Press, 1903.

Stovall, Pleasant A. *Robert Toombs: Statesman, Speaker, Soldier, Sage.* New York: Cassell, 1892.

Strong, George Templeton. *The Diary of George Templeton Strong: The Civil War, 1860–1865.* 4 vols. Eds. Allan Nevins and Milton H. Thomas. New York: Macmillan, 1952.

Swinton, William. *Campaigns of the Army of the Potomac.* Revised edition. New York: University Publishing Co., 1884.

Sword, Wiley. *Southern Invincibility – A History of the Confederate Heart.* New York: St. Martin's Press, 1999.

Symonds, Craig L. *Joseph E. Johnston: A Civil War Biography.* New York: Norton, 1992.

Sypher, Josiah R. *History of the Pennsylvania Reserve Corps.* Lancaster, PA: Elias Barr, 1865.

Taylor, Richard. *Destruction and Reconstruction.* Edited by Richard Harwell. (New edition) New York, 1954.

Taylor, Walter H. *Four Years With General Lee.* New York: D. Appleton, 1877. Reprint, Bloomington: Indiana University Press, 1962.

Thomas, Emory M. *Bold Dragoon, The Life of Jeb Stuart.* New York: Vintage Books, 1986.

____. *Richmond: The Peninsula Campaign.* New York: Eastern Acorn Press, 1985.

Trobriand, Regis de. *Four Years with the Army of the Potomac.* Boston: Ticknor, 1889.

The Union Army: a History of Military Affairs in the Loyal States, 1861–65: Records of the Regiments in the Union Army, Cyclopedia of Battles, Memoirs of Commanders and Soldiers. 9 vols. Wilmington, NC: Broadfoot Pub. Co., 1997.

von Borcke, Heros. *Memoirs of the Confederate War for Independence.* 2 vols. New York: Peter Smith, 1938.

Wainwright, Charles S. *Diary of a Battle: The Personal Journal of Colonel Charles S. Wainwright, 1861–1865.* Ed. Allan Nevins. New York: Harcourt, Brace & World, 1962.

Wakelyn, Jon L. *Biographic Dictionary of the Confederacy.* Westport, CT: Greenwood Press, 1977.

Walker, Francis A. *History of the Second Army Corps in the Army of the Potomac.* 2nd edition. New York: Charles Scribner's Sons, 1891.

Wallace, Jr., Lee A. *The Richmond Howitzers.* Lynchburg, VA: H. E. Howard, Inc., 1993.

War Department. *The War of the Rebellion: A Compilation of the Official Records of the Union and Confederate Armies.* 128 vols. Washington, DC: Government Printing Office, 1880–1901.

Ward, Joseph R. C. *History of the 106th Regiment Pennsylvania Volunteers.* Philadelphia: F. McManus, Jr., 1906.

Warner, Ezra J. *Generals in Blue: Lives of the Union Commanders.* Baton Rouge: Louisiana State University Press, 1999.

_____. *Generals in Gray: Lives of the Confederate Commanders.* Baton Rouge: Louisiana State University Press, 2000.

Weaver, Jeffrey C. *Brunswick Rebel, Johnston, Southside, United, James City, Lunenburg Rebel, Pamunkey Heavy Artillery and Young's Harborguard.* Lynchburg, VA: H. E. Howard, Inc., 1996.

Webb, Alexander Stewart. *Campaigns of the Civil War, III. The Peninsula - McClellan's Campaign of 1862.* New York: Charles Scribner's Sons, 1881. Reprint. Edison, NJ: Castle Books, 2002.

Welcher, Frank J. *The Union Army, 1861–1865: Organization and Operations, Volume I: The Eastern Theater.* Bloomington and Indianapolis: Indiana University Press, 1989.

Werstein, Irving. *Kearny the Magnificent.* New York: John Day Co., 1962.

Wert, Jeffrey. *General James Longstreet.* New York: Simon and Schuster, 1993.

_____. *The Sword of Lincoln: The Army of the Potomac.* New York: Simon & Schuster, 2005.

Wheat, Thomas Adrian. *A Guide to Civil War Yorktown.* Knoxville, TN : Bohemian Brigade Bookshop and Publishers, 1997.

Wheeler, Richard. *Sword Over Richmond: An Eyewitness History of McClellan's Peninsula Campaign.* New York: Harper and Row, 1986.

Wilkes, George. *McClellan: From Ball's Bluff to Antietam.* New York: Sinclair Tousey, 1863.

Williams, T. Harry. *Lincoln and his Generals.* New York: Gramercy Books, 2000.

Winslow, Richard Elliott III. *General John Sedgwick: The Story of a Union Corps Commander.* Novato, CA: Presidio Press, 1982.

Wise, Jennings Cropper. *The Long Arm of Lee – The History of the Artillery of the Army of Northern Virginia.* (New Edition) New York, 1959.

Wood, W. J. *Civil War Generalship – The Art of Command (reprint).* New York: Da Capo Press, 2000.

Wormeley, Katharine P. *The Other Side of War on the Hospital Transports: With the Army of the Potomac: Letters from the Headquarters of the U. S. Sanitary Commission During the Peninsular Campaign.* Boston: Ticknor & Co., 1888.

Wright, Marcus J. *General Officers of the Confederate Army.* New York: Neale Publishing Co., 1911.

Wycoff, Mac. "Joseph B. Kershaw's South Carolina Brigade in the Battle of Savage Station." In *Peninsula Campaign of 1862: Yorktown to the Seven Days.* Vol. 2. Ed. William J. Miller. Campbell, CA: Savas Woodbury, 1993.

Dissertations & Theses

Chapman, Anne W. "Benjamin Stoddert Ewell: A Biography". Thesis for the College of William and Mary, 1984.

Kettenburg, Carol A. "The Battle of Williamsburg." Thesis for the College of William and Mary, 1980.

Newton, Steven H. "Joseph E. Johnston and the Defense of Richmond." Ph. D. Dissertation. The College of William and Mary, 1989.

Riedel, Leonard W., Jr. "John Bankhead Magruder and The Defense of the Virginia Peninsula 1861–1862". Thesis for the Old Dominion University, Norfolk, Va., 1991.

Settles, Thomas Michael. "The Military Career of John Bankhead Magruder." Ph.D. diss., Texas Christian University, 1972.

Siciliano, Stephen N. "Major General William Farrar Smith: Critic of Defeat and Engineer of Victory." Ph. D. Dissertation, College of William and Mary, 1984.

Articles and Monographs

Alexander, Edward Porter. "Records of Longstreet's Corp, A.N.V." *Southern Historical Society Papers*, vol. 1 (Feb. 1876): pp. 61–76.

Allen, James. "The Battle of Gaines's Mill" *National Tribune*, May 2, 1901, p. 3.

Anderson, Joseph R. Jr. "Anderson's Brigade in the Battles Around Richmond." *Confederate Veteran* (Dec. 1923): pp. 448–451.

Armistead, Drury. "The Battle in Which General Johnston was Wounded," *Southern Historical Society Papers*. vol. 18 (Jan.-Dec. 1890): pp. 185-188.

Averell, William W. "With the Cavalry on the Peninsula." *Battles and Leaders of the Civil War*, vol. 2, pp. 429–433.

Baxter, Alice. "Battle Flag of the Third Georgia." *Southern Historical Society Papers*, vol. 38 (Jan.–Dec. 1910): pp. 210–216.

Bearss, Edwin C. "Jeb Stuart's Ride around McClellan." In *The Peninsula*

Campaign of 1862: Yorktown to the Seven Days. vol. 1. Ed. William J. Miller. Campbell, CA: Savas Woodbury, 1993.

Bernard, George S. "Malvern Hill." *Southern Historical Society Papers* vol. 18 (Jan.–Dec. 1890): pp. 56–71.

Blair, William A. "The Seven Days and the Radical Persuasion: Convincing Moderates in the North of the Need for a Hard War." In *The Richmond Campaign of 1862: The Peninsula & the Seven Days*, edited by Gary W. Gallagher. Chapel Hill and London: University of North Carolina Press, 2000.

Bohannon, Keith S. "One Solid Unbroken Roar of Thunder: Union and Confederate Artillery at the Battle of Malvern Hill." In *The Richmond Campaign of 1862: The Peninsula & the Seven Days*, edited by Gary W. Gallagher. Chapel Hill and London: University of North Carolina Press, 2000.

Boies, A. H. "Malvern Hill." *National Tribune*, Feb. 13, 1896, pp. 1–2.

Bratton, John. "The Battle of Williamsburg." *Southern Historical Society Papers*, vol. 7 (Jan.–Dec. 1879): pp. 299–302.

Brown, Campbell. "Down the Peninsula with Richard Ewell: Capt. Campbell Brown's Memoirs of the Seven Days Battles." Ed. Terry Jones. In *Peninsula Campaign of 1862: Yorktown to the Seven Days*. vol. 2. Ed. William J. Miller. Campbell, CA: Savas Woodbury, 1993. Reprint ed. by Gary W. Gallagher. Chapel Hill and London: University of North Carolina Press, 2000.

Carmichael, Peter S. "The Great Paragon of Virtue and Sobriety: John Bankhead Magruder and the Seven Days." In *The Richmond Campaign of 1862: The Peninsula & the Seven Days*, edited by Gary W. Gallagher. Chapel Hill and London: University of North Carolina Press, 2000.

Cooke, Philip St. George. "The Charge of Cooke's Cavalry at Gaines's Mill." *Battles and Leaders of the Civil War*, vol. 2, pp. 344–346.

DeMotte, John B. "The Cause of a Silent Battle." *Battles and Leaders of the Civil War*, vol. 2, p. 365.

Doubleday, J. M. "Oak Grove." *National Tribune*, Oct. 8, 1914, p. 7.

_____. "The Seven Days' Battles." *National Tribune*, Sept. 14, 1916, p. 7.

Dunn, William E. "On the Peninsula Campaign: Civil War Letters from William E. Dunn." *Civil War Times Illustrated*, 14:1 (July 1975), pp. 14–19.

Dutcher, Salem. "Williamsburg; A Graphic Story of the Battle of May 5, 1862." *Southern Historical Society Papers*, vol. 17 (Jan.-Dec. 1889): pp. 409–419.

Evans, Thomas. "At Malvern Hill." *Civil War Times Illustrated*, Dec. 1967, pp. 38–43.

Fishel, Edwin C. "Pinkerton and McClellan: Who Deceived Whom?" *Civil War History*, 34:2 (June 1988), pp. 115–142.

Foltermann, Miles. "Opportunities Lost: Military Blunders of the Seven Days Campaign." Agora no. 1, issue 1 (Summer 2000).

Franklin, William B. "Rear-Guard Fighting During the Change of Base." *Battles and Leaders of the Civil War*, vol. 2, pp. 366–382.

Frayser, Richard E. "Stuart's Raid in the Rear of the Army of the Potomac." *Southern Historical Society Papers*, vol. 11 (Nov 1883): pp. 505–517.

Frye, C. J. "Savage Station." *National Tribune*, Mar. 6, 1913, p. 5.

Gallagher, Gary W. "A Civil War Watershed: The 1862 Richmond Campaign in Perspective." In *The Richmond Campaign of 1862: The Peninsula & the Seven Days*, edited by Gary W. Gallagher. Chapel Hill and London: University of North Carolina Press, 2000.

Garnett, James M. "Personal Reminiscences of Seven Days' Battles Around Richmond." *Southern Historical Society Papers* vol. 30 (Jan.–Dec. 1902): pp. 147–151.

"General Thomas J. Jackson." *Southern Historical Society Papers* vol. 19 (Jan. 1891): pp. 298–318.

Gilmore, J. F. "With the 4th Mich." *National Tribune*, July 7, 1910, p. 7.

Grimsley, Mark. "Rear Guard at Williamsburg." *Civil War Times Illustrated*, vol. XXIV (May 1985), no. 3: pp. 28–30.

Hale, G. W. B. "Recollections of Malvern Hill." *Confederate Veteran*, vol. 30 (Sept. 1922): pp. 332–333.

Harman, George D. "General Silas Casey and the Battle of Fair Oaks." *The Historian*, 4:1 (Autumn 1941), pp. 84–101.

Herndon, John G. "Infantry and Cavalry Service." *Confederate Veteran*, vol. 30 (May 1922): pp. 297–310.

Hill, Daniel H. "Lee's Attacks North of the Chickahominy." *Battles and Leaders of the Civil War*, vol. 2, pp. 347–362.

_____. "McClellan's Change of Base and Malvern Hill." *Battles and Leaders of the Civil War*, vol. 2, pp. 383–395.

"Horrors of the Battlefield," *Confederate Veteran*, vol. 15 (July 1907): p. 306

Hubbell, John T. "The Seven Days of George Brinton McClellan." In *The Richmond Campaign of 1862: The Peninsula & the Seven Days*, edited by Gary W. Gallagher. Chapel Hill and London: University of North Carolina Press, 2000.

"Jackson and Ewell." *Southern Historical Society Papers* vol. 20 (Jan.–Dec. 1892): pp. 26–33.

Jeffreys, Thomas D. "The 'Red Badge' Explained." *Southern Historical Society Papers* vol. 36 (Jan.–Dec. 1908): pp. 248–249.

Johnson, W. Gart. "Barksdale-Humphreys Mississippi Brigade." *Confederate Veteran* vol. 1, no. 7 (July 1893): pp. 206–207.

Johnston, Joseph E. "Manassas to Seven Pines," *Battles and Leaders of the Civil War*, vol. 2, p. 203.

Jones, J. William. "Reminiscences of the Army of Northern Virginia No. 8." *Southern Historical Society Papers* vol. 9 (Oct.–Dec. 1881): pp. 557–570.

Kent, William C. "Sharpshooting with Berdan: William C. Kent's Eyewitness Account of the Seven Days' Battles." *Civil War Times Illustrated*, 15:2 (May 1976), pp. 4–9, 42–48.

Krick, Robert E. L. "The Battle of Gaines' Mill." *Civil War* Issue 51 (June 1995), pp. 61–63).

_____. "The Men Who Carried This Position Were Soldiers Indeed: The Decisive Charge of Whiting's Division at Gaines's Mill." In *The Richmond Campaign of 1862: The Peninsula & the Seven Days*, edited by Gary W. Gallagher. Chapel Hill and London: University of North

Carolina Press, 2000.

Krick, Robert K. "Sleepless in the Saddle: Stonewall Jackson in the Seven Days." In *The Richmond Campaign of 1862: The Peninsula & the Seven Days*, edited by Gary W. Gallagher. Chapel Hill and London: University of North Carolina Press, 2000.

Lash, Gary G. "No Praise Can Be Too Good for the Officers and Men: The 71st Pennsylvania Infantry in the Peninsula Campaign." In *The Peninsula Campaign of 1862: Yorktown to the Seven Days*. vol. 3, edited by William J. Miller. Campbell, CA: Savas Publishing Co., 1997.

Law, Evander M. "The Fight for Richmond in 1862." *Southern Bivouac*, 2 (1886–87), pp. 649–60, 713–23.

Leach, John W. T. "The Battle of Frazier's Farm." *Southern Historical Society Papers* vol. 21 (Jan.–Dec. 1893): pp. 160–165.

LeDuc, William G. "McClellan and Richmond." *National Tribune*, July 30, 1914, p. 7.

Lee, Baker P. "Magruder's Peninsula Campaign in 1862." *Southern Historical Society Papers,* vol. 19, pp. 60–65.

Long, A. L. "Memoirs of John Bankhead Magruder," *Southern Historical Society Papers*. vol. 12, (Mar. 1884): pp. 105–110.

Longacre, Edward G. "Silas Casey," In *The Historical Times Illustrated Encyclopedia of the Civil War*, edited by Patricia L. Faust. New York: Harper and Row, 1986.

Longstreet, James. "'The Seven Days,' Including Frayser's Farm." *Battles and Leaders of the Civil War*, vol. 2, pp. 396–405.

Marten, James. "A Feeling of Restless Anxiety: Loyalty and Race in the Peninsula Campaign and Beyond." In *The Richmond Campaign of 1862: The Peninsula & the Seven Days*, edited by Gary W. Gallagher. Chapel Hill and London: University of North Carolina Press, 2000.

Maury, Richard L. "The Battle of Williamsburg and the Charge of the 24th Virginia of Early's Brigade." *Southern Historical Society Papers*, vol. 8, (Jan.-Dec.1880): pp. 281–300.

McCaleb, Howard. "Featherstone-Posey-Harris Mississippi Brigade." *SHSP* vol. 32 (Jan.–Dec. 1904): p. 333.

McClellan, George B. "The Peninsula Campaign." *Battles and Leaders of the Civil War* vol. 2, New York: Castle Books, 1956.

Miller, James C. "Serving Under McClellan on the Peninsula in '62." *Civil War Times Illustrated*, 8:3 (June 1969), pp. 24–30.

Miller, William J. "I Only Wait for the River: McClellan and His Engineers on the Chickahominy." In *The Richmond Campaign of 1862: The Peninsula & the Seven Days*, edited by Gary W. Gallagher. Chapel Hill and London: University of North Carolina Press, 2000.

____. "The Battle of Oak Grove." *Civil War*, June 1995, pp. 55–56.

____, editor. "To Alleviate Their Suffering: A Report of Medical Personnel and Activity at Savage's Station During and After the Seven Days Battles." In *The Peninsula Campaign of 1862: Yorktown to the Seven Days*. vol. 3, edited by William J. Miller. Campbell, CA: Savas Publishing Co., 1997.

____, "Weather Still Execrable: Climatological Notes on the Peninsula Campaign March through August, 1862." In *The Peninsula Campaign of 1862: Yorktown to the Seven Days*. vol. 3, edited by William J. Miller. Campbell, CA: Savas Publishing Co., 1997.

Newton, Steven H. "He Is a Good Soldier: Johnston, Davis and Seven Pines: The Uncertainty Principle in Action." In *The Peninsula Campaign of 1862: Yorktown to the Seven Days*. vol. 3, edited by William J. Miller. Campbell, CA: Savas Publishing Co., 1997.

O'Neill, Robert. "What Men We Have Got Are Good Soldiers & Brave Ones Too: Federal Cavalry Operations in the Peninsula Campaign." In *The Peninsula Campaign of 1862: Yorktown to the Seven Days*. vol. 3, edited by William J. Miller. Campbell, CA: Savas Publishing Co., 1997.

Palfrey, Francis W. "The Period Which Elapsed Between the Fall of Yorktown and the Seven Days," in *Campaigns in Virginia, 1861–1862: Papers of the Military Historical Society of Massachusetts*. Theodore F. Dwight, ed. Wilmington, NC: Broadfoot Publishing Co., 1989.

Park, Robert E. "Sketch of the Twelfth Alabama Infantry." *Society Historical Society Papers* vol. 33 (Jan.–Dec. 1905): pp. 193–296.

____. "Diary of Robert E. Park, Macon, Georgia, Late Captain Twelfth Alabama Infantry." *Southern Historical Society Papers* vol. 1 (May 1876): pp. 370–386.

Porter, Fitz John. "The Battle of Malvern Hill." *Battles and Leaders of the Civil War*, vol. 2, pp. 406–427.

____. "Hanover Court House and Gaines's Mill." *Battles and Leaders of the Civil War*, vol. 2. New York: Castle Books, 1956.

"The Purcell Battery." *Southern Historical Society Papers*, vol. 21 (Jan.–Dec. 1893): pp. 362–365.

Robert, Rev. P. G. "Justice to General Magruder." *Southern Historical Society Papers* vol. 5 (May 1878): pp. 249–250.

Roberts, R. Biddle. "The Battle of Charles City Crossroads." *Philadelphia Weekly Press,* Mar. 3, 1886, p.1.

Robins, W. T. "Stuart's Ride Around McClellan." *Battles and Leaders of the Civil War,* vol. 2, pp. 271–275.

Salmon, Emily J. "The Burial of Latane: Symbol of a Lost Cause," *Virginia Cavalcade,* vol. 28 (Winter 1979): pp. 118–129.

Sanborn, Lucius. "Savage Station." *National Tribune,* Oct. 12, 1905, p. 3.

Slater, J. S. "At Gaines' Mill." *National Tribune,* Sept. 17, 1881, p. 3.

____. "The Fray at Gaines' Mill." *Philadelphia Weekly Times,* Jan. 26, 1884, p.1.

____. "Malvern." *National Tribune,* Sept. 10, 1881, p. 3.

____. "Scenes at Malvern Hill." *Philadelphia Weekly Times,* Dec. 11, 1880, p. 1.

Smith, Gustavus W. "Two days of Battle at Seven Pines," in Robert U. Johnston and Clarence C. Buel, eds. *Battles and Leaders of the Civil War.* 4 vols. Secaucus, NJ: Castle, 1980; reprint of 1887 edition.

Sneden, Robert Knox. "Pen and Sword at Savage's Station." *Civil War Times Illustrated,* Oct. 2000, pp. 42–51.

Taylor, P. H. "Savage's Station." *National Tribune,* Jan. 31, 1884, p. 7.

Terrell, J. G. "Gaines's Mill." *National Tribune,* Aug. 8, 1895, p. 3.

Tuffs, Richard W. "Malvern Hill." *National Tribune*, Apr. 27, 1893, p. 4.

Von Borcke, Heros. "The Prussian Remembers," *Civil War Times Illustrated*, 19:10 (Feb. 1981): pp. 40–43.

Weller, Jac "The Field Artillery of the Civil War," *Military Collector & Historian*, vol. 5, (1953).

Wert, Jeffrey. "Samuel Peter Heintzelman." In Faust, *Historical Times Illustrated Encyclopedia of the Civil War*. New York: Harper and Row, 1986, p. 356.

Woodworth, Steven E. "Dark Portents: Confederate Command at the Battle of Williamsburg." In *The Peninsula Campaign of 1862: Yorktown to the Seven Days*. vol. 3, edited by William J. Miller. Campbell, CA: Savas Publishing Co., 1997.

Wray, William J. "Malvern Hill." *National Tribune*, Apr. 17, 1890.

Wright, J. A. "Rear Guard Fighting at Savage Station." *National Tribune*, Nov. 7, 1912, p. 5.

Wyckoff, Mac. "Joseph B. Kershaw's South Carolina Brigade in the Battle of Savage Station." In *Peninsula Campaign of 1862: Yorktown to the Seven Days*. Vol. 2. Ed. William J. Miller. Campbell, CA: Savas Woodbury, 1993.

Manuscript Collections

Manuscripts Division, Library of Congress, Washington, D.C.

Judah P. Benjamin diary
Theodore A. Dodge papers
Douglass Southall Freeman papers

Jedediah Hotchkiss papers
Samuel P. Heintzelman papers
Henry J. Hunt papers
Philip Kearny papers
Abraham Lincoln papers
George B. McClellan papers
Fitz John Porter papers
Alexander Hugh Holmes Stuart papers

National Archives, Washington

Robert Edward Lee Letterbook, 1862–1864
Letters Received, Confederate Adjutant and Inspector-General, 1861–1865: M–474.
Record Group 94: U.S. Generals' Reports
Record Group 109: War Department Collection of Confederate Records

Southern Historical Collection, Wilson Library, University of North Carolina, Chapel Hill

Edward Porter Alexander papers
William Allan papers
Barnsley Family papers
Berry G. Benson papers
Burgwyn Family papers
J.F.H. Claiborne papers
George C. Gordon papers
Alexander Cheeves Haskell papers
John Cheeves Haskell papers
Hatrick Family papers
William J. Hoke papers

James Longstreet papers
William Nelson Pendleton papers
William H. Wills papers

Manuscript Division, South Caroliniana Library, University of South Carolina

Micah Jenkins papers

Archives, Mariners Museum

William Moneghan Papers: 1861–1862

Archives Division, Library of Virginia, Richmond

Fairfax Family papers
Samuel P. Heintzelman papers
D. H. Hill papers
Dabney-Jackson Collection
Valentine Wood Southall papers
J. E. Whitehorne papers

Special Collections, Earl Gregg Swem Library, College of William and Mary

Benjamin Stoddert Ewell papers
John Buchanan Floyd papers
Robert G. Haile diary
Robert Morton Hughes papers
Daniel Harvey Hill papers, 1861–1865

Joseph E. Johnston papers, 1825–1891
Stephen Russell Mallory papers

Vermont Historical Society

Smith, William F. "Memoirs," Typescript., William Farrar Smith papers

Manuscripts Department, University of Virginia Library, Charlottesville

Lawrence O'Bryan Branch papers
Wilbur Fisk Davis papers
Dinwiddie Family papers
Z. Lee Gilmer diary
Jonathan B. Hager papers
Washington Hands Civil War Memoirs
Jedediah Hotchkiss papers
John B. Wise papers

Virginia Historical Society, Richmond

Bagby Family papers
Blanton Family papers
Hannah (Lide) Coker papers
Cooke Family papers
Edward S. Duffey diary
Richardson Wallace Haw papers
Hobson Family papers
Benjamin Anderson Jones papers
Watkins Kearns papers
Keith Family papers
John Gottfried Lange papers

Robert E. Lee Headquarters papers
John McAnerney papers
John Van Lew McCreery papers (Recollections)
David Gregg McIntosh papers (Reminiscences)
Meade Family papers
Ella Merryman papers
William W. Sherwood papers
Shipp Family papers
William Barrett Sydnor papers
Fanny W. Gaines Tinsley papers
John Steele Tyler papers
Gilbert Jefferson Wright papers

New Hampshire Historical Society

Leaver papers

Museum of the Confederacy

R. H. Chilton papers
Thomas J. Jackson papers

Old Dominion University

Robert Morton Hughes Collection

Cartographic Materials

Johnson, Alvin Jewett. *Johnson's map of the vicinity of Richmond and Peninsular Campaign in Virginia: showing also the interesting localities along the James, Chickahominy, and York Rivers / compiled from the official maps of the War Dept. by Johnson and Ward.* New York : Johnson and Ward, [1864 or 1865], c1862.

Johnson, Alvin Jewett. *Johnson's map of the vicinity of Richmond and Peninsular Campaign in Virginia: showing also the interesting localities along the James, Chickahominy, and York Rivers / compiled from the official maps of the War Dept. by A. J. Johnson.* New York: A. J. Johnson, [1868], c1862.

Sheppard, Edwin. *Map showing the battle grounds of the Chickahominy: and the positions of the subsequent engagements in the retreat of the Federal Army towards James River and all other points of interest in connection with the siege of Richmond / from the most reliable information to be obtained by Edwin Shepard.* Richmond: Hoyer & Ludwig, 1862.

Electronic Sources

The 1862 Peninsula Campaign
<http://www.peninsulacampaign.org/>
[Accessed 19 May 2005]

The American Civil War Research Database
<http://www.civilwardata.com/>
[Accessed 3 January 2006]

The complete Civil War DVD-ROM [electronic resource]: official records and more. Version 1.02. Zionsville, IN: Guild Press, 2002.
[Accessed 27 Jun 2006]

Civil War Battles Pages
<http://www.fortunecity.com/victorian/pottery/1080/a_battles.htm/>

[Accessed 19 May 2005]

Civil War Field Fortifications
<http://www.civilwarfortifications.com/dictionary/dictionary.html/>
[Accessed 19 May 2005]

Confederate Military History [CD-ROM]: H-Bar Enterprises, 1996.
[Accessed 14 October 2006]

Official Records of the Union and Confederate Armies in the War of the Rebellion
< http://cdl.library.cornell.edu/moa/moa_browse.html>
[Accessed 06 January 2008]

Official Records of the Union and Confederate Navies in the War of the Rebellion
<http://cdl.library.cornell.edu/moa/moa_browse.html>
[Accessed 06 January 2008]

eHistory.osu.edu
<http://eHistory.osu.edu/>
[Accessed 2 January 2008]

findagrave.com
<http://findagrave.com/>
[Accessed 18 June 2006]

Mississippi Division, S.C.V.
<http://www.mississippiscv.org/>
[Accessed 15 April 2007]

GLOSSARY

This brief glossary is provided simply to assist the reader in more fully understanding this book and others on similar topics. Realizing that our language has changed in the years since this great conflict, some of the terms included are not military or technical, but simply no longer in common use.

abatis
(also abattis). An obstacle created by felling trees in the direction of the enemy.

ambuscade
Ambush.

antiscorbutics
Remedies for scurvy.

barbette
A platform in a fort or ship from which guns fire over a parapet, etc. and not through an embrasure.

bastion
A projecting part of a wall, rampart, or other fortification, consisting of two faces forming a salient angle and two flanks.

brevet
The conferring of nominal military rank without corresponding pay.

buck and ball
A musket round consisting of one lead ball and several buckshot.

butternut

Confederate. Pertaining to the color of some Confederate uniforms.

caisson

An ammunition wagon for artillery.

canister

A type of artillery projectile consisting of a number of pellets, usually 27, in a cylindrical container. Canister is especially effective against infantry at ranges of 300 yards or less.

cascabel

Knob at breech end of a cannon.

case shot

A thin spherical or oblong cast-iron shell containing musket balls and a bursting charge, with a time fuse.

celerity

Swiftness, speed.

chevaux-de-frise

Obstructions to attacking infantry or cavalry created by implanting sharpened stakes in a central timber.

Coehorn mortar

The smallest member of the mortar family, which could be carried by two to four men. All other Civil War mortars had limited mobility.

coffee-mill gun

Ager's Coffee-Mill Gun, designed by Wilson Ager, was a multi-cylinder, hopper-fed rapid fire weapon of small–arm caliber. It was not, strictly speaking, a machine gun, as it was powered by an external hand crank.

Confederate lemonade
A drink made of sorghum or vinegar and water.

Copperheads
Peace Democrats. A political faction opposed to Lincoln and the prosecution of the war.

corps de chasseurs
Body of troops trained and equipped for rapid movement.

cottonclad
A vessel using bales of cotton placed on the deck to provide some protection from enemy fire.

coup de main
A surprise attack.

curtains
Trenches of lesser strength which connect the salients of fortifications.

debouches
Openings in a fortification where troops may enter or leave.

destruction in detail
Destruction of an opposing force one small part at a time.

embrasure
An opening in a parapet that widens towards the outside, made to fire a gun through.

encomium

A formal or high-flown expression of praise.

enfilade

The situation of a position that it commands a line from end to end.

epaulement

A parapet or breastwork, especially one protecting the flank.

fascine

A long bundle of sticks or twigs used to line a trench.

flank attack

An attack upon an enemy force's side or rear, where it is less capable of defending itself.

flanks in the air

Term used to describe the ends of a line of troops which have no protection, either by adjacent friendly troops or natural obstacles.

floating battery

A battery of artillery mounted upon a barge or raft. They were towed into desired firing positions inaccessible by land.

gabions

A.K.A. baskets. Large open-ended wicker-work frames, filled with earth, used to protect soldiers while they were digging trenches. They served as a retaining wall or bracing to hold the sides of trenches in place and to keep breastworks from caving in.

gill

A measure of liquids equal to a quarter of a pint.

glacis

A gently sloping natural or artificial bank sloping down from the covered way of a fort so as to expose attackers to the defenders' missiles, etc.

grape

An artillery projectile consisting of small cast iron balls grouped together to make a scattering charge.

grayback

Confederate.

hard tack

A hard bread-like ration issued to troops in the field.

haversack

A leather bag used to carry rations. Also used by artillerymen to carry powder to the gun.

in defilade

Shielded from observation or enemy file by natural obstacles or fortifications.

ironclad

An armored ship designed to resist cannon fire.

kepi

A hat worn by both armies, originally of French design. It had a circular flat top, sloping toward the front, and a horizontal peak.

lamp posts

Ten-inch projectiles fired by Federal gunboats.

limber

A detachable forepart of a gun carriage. It has two wheels on an axle, a pole for horses, and one or two ammunition boxes.

"Lincoln shinplasters"

Derogatory Confederate term for U.S. paper currency.

line of contravallation

The chain of redoubts and breastworks constructed by besiegers for protection against sorties of the garrison under siege.

lunette

A raised firing platform built into the perimeter of a fort to allow guns to fire directly at an attacking force. Also, a towing ring for a field piece.

mantelet

A kind of loose sleeveless cape, cloak, or mantel.

marplot

A person who spoils a plot or hinders an undertaking.

meeting engagement

A firefight resulting from the accidental convergence of opposing forces.

parapet

A protective wall at the top of a fortification, around the outer side of the wall-walk.

pendulum-hausse

A sighting device for field artillery.

plank road

A road made more passable in wet weather by planking it with trunks of saplings.

point d'appui

A fulcrum, a strategic point.

portmanteau

A case or bag for carrying clothing, etc. when traveling, often made of stiff leather and hinged at the back.

prolonge

A cable that can be attached to the trail of a cannon and used to withdraw it without exposing its limber or horses to direct enemy fire.

provost duty

Military police duty, often in an army's camp.

Quaker guns

Dummy cannons constructed from a length of log painted black. Designed to deceive an enemy from a great distance.

Radical Republicans

A faction of Republicans who believed in total emancipation and that freed slaves should have equality with all other citizens. In addition, they believed that punitive measures should be taken against the Southern states for seceding from the Union. They desired the total destruction of South's power, both economic and political. Lincoln had three in his Cabinet: Chase, Stanton and Speed.

ready finders

Civilian scavengers who moved in the wake of a maneuvering army, gleaning for profit items left in their wake.

redan

A pair of parapets that form a V-shaped projection from the wall of a fortification. It is open at the rear.

redoubt

A temporary fortification built to defend a position such as a hilltop.

refuse the line

To maneuver a regiment or larger to cause the front to change direction by 90 degrees.

salients

Projecting portions of a line of trenches, often placed on higher ground.

sap

An approach trench, dug by besieging forces, always zigzagged, which connects old and new parallel trenches.

scaling ladders

Ladders carried by infantry units to cross a wall of a position under siege.

Scott's Anaconda

Plan by Union General Winfield Scott to strangle the Confederacy by blockading their ports and controlling the Mississippi River.

shabraque

A saddle cover.

soft tack

Bread, as opposed to hard tack.

straggler

A soldier who has allowed himself to be separated from his unit, either by being physically unable to keep up, or through mere shirking of his duty.

sutlers

Civilians who sell provisions to troops in the field or in garrison.

terminus ad quem

The finishing-point of an argument, policy, period, etc.

terre-plein

A level platform behind a parapet, rampart, etc., where guns are mounted.

thunder barrels

Powder-filled hogsheads, fused at the bung and rolled downhill into enemy trenches.

tinclad

A ship with armor no more than musket-proof.

tirailleurs

Skirmishers.

torpedoes

Land mines. Usually artillery shells buried in opportune places and fitted with pressure fuses or concealed trip wires. First used by Confederate defenders at Yorktown in 1862.

traverses

Raised mounds of earth designed to defilade the interior spaces of field works and to limit the area affected by explosions occurring within gun positions.

turning movement

A campaign strategy in which a commanding general employs a part of his army to conduct a wide sweeping movement around his adversary, hazarding a position critical to the adversary. The result expected is for the adversary to respond by abandoning his prepared positions and fight in the open on more or less equal terms. Alternative beneficial results would be for the adversary to give up gained ground or force him to go on the offensive.

vidette (*also* vedette)

A mounted sentry placed in advance of an army's position to observe enemy movements and warn of possible danger.

War Democrats

A political group of Northern Democrats who supported the War.

water battery

A battery located as closely as possible to water level. It was either sited on the shore or mounted on a barge or raft and towed to and anchored in a favorable position inaccessible by land. Firing from water level allowed the gunners to use a very flat trajectory, thus skipping solid shot off the water into the target vessel. This technique took the range variable out of the firing solution.

Whigs

Antecedents of Republicans. Believers in protective tariffs and a strong central government.

INDEX

A

Abercrombie, John J.
    at Malvern Hill, 359, 377, 385, 395
    at Oak Grove, 201
    at Seven Pines, 102, 130, 138–139, 142–143, 149
Aiken, D. Wyatt, 292
Alexander, Barton S., 279–280
    and Washington defense, 24
    at Glendale, 314–315
Alexander, E. Porter, 132, 339, 420, 439
    at Malvern Hill, 377
    at Savage Station, 285
Allen, E. J. (see Pinkerton, Allan), 24, 184
Allen, George D., 91
Allen, James W., 243
Allen, Rev. L. W., 364
Allen's Farm, 271–273
Ames, Adelbert, 259, 277, 370, 373, 381, 386, 388
Amsden, Frank P., 338–339
Anaconda Plan, 3
Anderson, George B.
    at Gaines' Mill, 240, 242
    at Malvern Hill, 373, 383
Anderson, George T.
    at Garnett's & Golding's, 256
    at Malvern Hill, 387
    at Savage Station, 264
Anderson, Joseph R., 95
    at Glendale, 352
Anderson, Richard H., 468
    at Gaines' Mill, 232, 249
    at Seven Pines, 114, 170
    at Williamsburg, 58
Aquia (Acquia) Creek, 35, 443, 448–450
Aquia (Acquia) Landing, 21, 446–447, 450, 453
Armistead, Drury, 153
Army of Northern Virginia, 173, 179, 186, 205, 268, 403, 425, 427, 431, 435, 437, 457, 458, 459, 466–467, 469, 471
    at Gaines' Mill, 228, 231, 236, 249, 253
    at Garnett's & Golding's, 255
    at Glendale, 307, 328
    at Malvern Hill, 374, 390, 400
    at Mechanicsville, 208, 216–218
    at Oak Grove, 204
    at Savage Station, 297
    at Seven Pines, 158
    retreat to Harrison's, 408
Army of the Potomac, 4, 7, 15, 16–17, 24–25, 28, 30, 33, 41, 174, 181, 183, 403–404, 415, 417, 419, 425, 427, 432, 433–434, 438, 440, 453, 456, 466, 473–474
    and deployment, 36
    and maps, 40
    and redeployment, 443, 444–445, 449
    at Eltham's Landing, 83
    at Gaines' Mill, 223, 253–254
    at Glendale, 303, 308, 310, 313, 340, 353, 356
    at Hanover Court House, 90, 95
    at Harrison's Landing, 425
    at Harrison's Landing, 411, 441, 443
    at Malvern Hill, 358–359, 361, 365, 369, 376, 378–379, 383
    at Mechanicsville, 208, 212, 220–221
    at Oak Grove, 196, 204
    at Savage Station, 263, 265–266, 275, 277–278, 280, 283, 298, 302
    at Seven Pines, 100, 104–105, 168
    retreat to Harrison's, 408
Army of Virginia, 426–427, 449, 452–453, 457
Averell, William W., 402, 405, 408, 411, 413, 433, 444, 445
    at Savage Station, 275–277, 300
    at Yorktown, 46
    retreat to Harrison's, 407–408
Ayres, Romeyn B., 309, 322–323, 356

B

Badham, John C., 79
Bailey, Guilford D., 132

Baine, David W., 347
Baker, Laurence S., 275
Balthis, William L., 321, 367, 369, 371
Banks, Nathaniel P., 2, 11, 16, 178, 452
Barhamsville, 86, 90
Barksdale, William, 406
    at Malvern Hill, 363, 376, 388, 394
    at Savage Station, 284, 292, 294–296
Barlow, Francis C., 349
Barlow, Samuel, 184
    and McClellan, 425
Barnard, John G., 12, 21, 49, 51, 222, 227, 279, 358, 360, 416
    and Urbanna Plan, 11
Barnum, Henry, 383
Bartlett, Joseph J.
    at Gaines' Mill, 237
Batteries, Confederate, artillery
    Georgia
        Sumter (Georgia), 258, 318, 329
    Louisiana
        Madison (Louisiana), 87
    Virginia
        Ashland (Virginia), 258
        Danville (Virginia), 323, 369
        King William (Virginia), 133
        Lynchburg (Virginia) Battery, 134, 139, 342
        Lynchburg Beauregard (Virginia), 329
        Richmond Howitzers, 1st Co., 304
        Virginia Light, 201
        Wise (Virginia), 256, 258
Batteries, Federal, artillery
    Connecticut
        1st Connecticut Heavy, 91, 256
    Massachusetts
        1st Massachusetts, 86
    New Jersey
        1st New Jersey, Battery B, 202
    New York
        1st New York Independent Light, 71
        1st New York Light, Battery A, 125, 132
        1st New York Light, Battery B, 271
        1st New York Light, Battery D, 59, 389
        1st New York Light, Battery H, 125
        3rd New York Independent Light, 323
        4th New York Independent Light, 69
        6th New York Independent Light, 59
        7th New York Independent Light, 125, 132
        8th New York Independent Light, 125, 132–133
    Pennsylvania
        1st Pennsylvania Light, Battery A, 248
        1st Pennsylvania Light, Battery B, 216–217, 248, 345
        1st Pennsylvania Light, Battery G, 216
        1st Pennsylvania Light, Battery H, 148, 150–151
    Rhode Island
        1st Rhode Island Light, Battery A, 258, 271
        1st Rhode Island Light, Battery E, 309
    U. S.
        1st U. S., Battery E, 277
        1st U. S., Battery H, 59
        1st U. S., Battery I, 148, 271
        2nd U. S., Batteries B & L, 251
        2nd U. S., Battery D, 239, 248
        2nd U. S., Battery E, 256
        2nd U. S., Battery M, 91, 277
        4th U. S., Batteries A & C, 271
        4th U. S., Battery K, 201, 398
        5th U. S., Battery A, 256
        5th U. S., Battery D, 91
        5th U. S., Battery K, 216–217
Baylor, William S. H., 243–244, 398
Beam, John E., 332, 367, 369
Beauregard, Pierre G. T., 102, 181, 184
Beaver Dam Creek, 100, 104, 106–108, 192, 204, 208, 214–219, 227, 364, 439
Beckham, Robert, 119
Benson, Henry, 277, 300, 386, 404–405
Berdan, Hiram
    at Fort Monroe, 37
    at Gaines' Mill, 230, 236
    at Garnett's & Golding's, 258, 259
    at Hanover Court House, 91
    at Malvern Hill, 359, 373, 380, 381, 382, 388

at Mechanicsville, 215
at Yorktown, 54
Berkeley Plantation, 311, 445
Berry, Hiram G.
   at Glendale, 309, 348–349
   at Oak Grove, 198
   at Savage Station, 270, 298–299
   at Seven Pines, 138, 140, 144, 202–203
   at Williamsburg, 69, 71
Bethesda Church, 226, 234
Beulah Church, 235, 242
Birney, David B., 348
   at Glendale, 309
   at Malvern Hill, 369, 385
   at Oak Grove, 198, 201–203
   at Savage Station, 270, 298–299
   at Seven Pines, 136, 138, 142, 144, 162, 164
   at Williamsburg, 69, 71
Black, Samuel W., 237
Blackford, Eugene, 403
Blackford, W. W., 286
Blaisdell, William E., 62
Blenker, Louis, 23, 24, 43, 47
   and Urbanna Plan, 11
Bondurant, James W., 234
Botts, Lawson, 398
Bramhall, Walter M., 59, 68, 367, 373, 377
Branch, Lawrence O'B., 187, 437
   at Gaines' Mill, 230–231, 236
   at Glendale, 321, 333, 341–344, 348, 351
   at Hanover Court House, 91–95
   at Malvern Hill, 375, 390
   at Mechanicsville, 209, 211, 213, 218–219
   at Oak Grove, 205, 207
Bratton, John, 73–74, 77–78
Braxton, Carter M., 216, 231
Brem, T. H., 333
Brent, Joseph L., 274, 335, 363, 376, 409
   at Glendale, 319, 335
   at Malvern Hill, 378–379, 390
   at Savage Station, 289, 292
Brick Chimney, 201
Bridges
   Alexander's Bridge, 222, 237, 284, 287, 299
   Bottoms Bridge, 90, 235, 268, 270, 286, 289, 308–309, 403
   Forge Bridge, 188–190, 445
   Grapevine Bridge, 148–149, 156, 182, 197, 222, 227, 239–240, 245, 268, 270, 281, 284, 287, 304, 327, 402
   Howard's Bridge, 42
   Jones' Bridge, 268, 286, 315, 403
   Long Bridge, 268, 315, 402
   Lower Bridge, 270
   Meadow Bridge(s), 184, 205, 209, 213, 289
   Mechanicsville Bridge, 193, 205, 209–210, 213, 215, 243
   New Bridge, 92, 197, 208–209, 217–218, 222, 232, 261, 266, 269, 286
   Turkey Island Creek Bridge, 278, 300, 310, 313, 359, 375, 376, 405, 407–408, 410
   White Oak Swamp Bridge, 278–279, 298, 300, 308–309, 311–312, 314, 318, 321, 324–327, 330, 343, 355–357, 362
   Woodbury's Bridge, 222, 237
Briggs, Henry S., 142–143
Britton farm, 275–276, 279
Brockenbrough, James B., 238
Brockenbrough, John M., 349
Brooks, William T. H., 55, 74
   at Garnett's & Golding's, 256, 259
   at Glendale, 317
   at Savage Station, 270–271, 280, 290–295, 297
   at Williamsburg, 64
Brown, Campbell, 235–236, 406
Brown, J. Thompson, 372
Buchanan, Robert C.
   at Gaines' Mill, 230, 239–242, 245
   at Glendale, 311, 334
   at Malvern Hill, 359, 389, 393–394
   retreat to Harrison's, 405, 407
Buckner, Simon B., 2
Burns, William W., 151
   at Glendale, 341, 343–344
   at Malvern Hill, 377
   at Savage Station, 271–272, 289–292, 294–295, 297
   at Seven Pines, 148, 152
Burnside, Ambrose E., 2, 181, 184, 427, 432, 445–448, 450, 464
   at Newport News, 426
Butterfield, Daniel, 37–38, 434

at Gaines' Mill, 233, 237, 239, 248–249, 250
at Hanover Court House, 91
at Harrison's Landing, 412
at Malvern Hill, 359, 380–383, 385, 388, 400
at Mechanicsville, 215
Byrnes, Richard, 189

C

Caldwell, John
  at Glendale, 349, 357
  at Malvern Hill, 359, 385–386, 395
  at Savage Station, 271–272, 290, 294–295
  retreat to Harrison's, 405
Cameron, Simon, 7, 8
Campbell, Reuben P., 92, 231
Carlisle, J. Howard, 270, 277, 332, 370, 381
Carlton, Henry H., 272
Carpenter, John C., 369
  at Malvern Hill, 380
Carr, Joseph B.
  at Glendale, 310
  at Oak Grove, 198, 200
  at Savage Station, 270
  retreat to Harrison's Landing, 405
Carrington, James M., 379
Carter, Thomas H., 133
Carter's Mill road, 264, 313, 330
  at Malvern Hill, 363, 365–366, 373, 375–380, 387, 395, 397, 406
Casey, Silas, 46, 182
  and McClellan, 182
  at Fort Monroe, 40, 43
  at Gaines' Mill, 223
  at Seven Pines, 102–106, 108, 121–122, 125, 127–128, 130–138, 140, 144, 148, 152, 156–157, 162, 168–171, 177
  at White House Landing, 286
  at Williamsburg, 63, 74
  at Yorktown, 57
Cass, Thomas, 383
Chambliss, William P., 94
Chandler, Zachariah
  and Scott, 6
Chapman, Edmund G., 338
Chapman, William

at Gaines' Mill, 227
Charles City Court House, 415
Charles City Crossroads, 303
Charles City road, 106, 108–111, 117–118, 120, 135, 139, 161, 198, 200, 202, 264, 268–269, 273–275, 277, 285, 296–299, 304, 309, 311, 313–314, 317, 325, 328, 330, 346, 363, 370
Chase, Salmon
  and Lincoln, 6
Chilton, Robert H., 286–287, 335–336, 366, 383, 385
  at Malvern Hill, 374
  at Savage Station, 263, 287
City Point, 314
Clark, A. Judson, 202
Clitz, Henry B., 245
Cobb, Amasa, 76
Cobb, Howell, 55, 100, 183
  at Malvern Hill, 376–379, 381–383, 387–388, 393–394
  at Savage Station, 269, 284–285, 289, 296
Cochrane, John, 151
Coggins Point, 432–433
Coker, James L., 345
Collins, Joseph B., 240
Colquitt, Alfred H.
  at Gaines' Mill, 240, 243
  at Malvern Hill, 385–386
Colston, Raleigh E.
  at Seven Pines, 120, 139, 162, 164
  at Williamsburg, 58, 70
Conner, James, 231
Cooke, John E.
  at Stuart's ride, 188
Cooke, Philip St. G.
  at Gaines' Mill, 251
  at Stuart's ride, 188–189
Cooper, James, 178, 248, 310, 320, 332, 337–340, 344–346, 349, 351
Cooper, Samuel, 98, 114
Couch, Darius N.
  at Fort Monroe, 40
  at Glendale, 310, 332
  at Harrison's Landing, 411
  at Malvern Hill, 359–360, 377, 382, 385–386, 388–389, 395, 398–400
  at Oak Grove, 201
  at Savage Station, 275, 277

    at Seven Pines, 102, 105, 128, 130–131, 134–138, 142, 144, 148–151, 156, 171
    at Williamsburg, 63, 66–68, 81
    at Yorktown, 46, 57
    retreat to Harrison's, 403, 405
Courtney, Alfred R., 238, 379
Cowan, Andrew, 71, 73, 309
Cowan, Robert H., 92
Cowdin, Robert, 168
Crenshaw, William G., 230, 372
Cross Keys, 178
Crumpler, Thomas N., 275
Crutchfield, Stapleton
    at Glendale, 316, 321, 324
    at Malvern Hill, 371
Cumming, Alfred, 393
Cunningham, Richard H., Jr.
    at Gaines' Mill, 226, 241
    at Malvern Hill, 399
Cutshaw, Wilford E., 369
Cutts, Allen S., 329

D

Dabbs house, 426
Dabney, C. W., 206
Dabney, Rev. Robert L., 205–206, 238, 284–286, 327
Dam No. 1 (Yorktown), 54
Dana, Napoleon J. T., 152
    at Eltham's Landing, 86
    at Glendale, 325, 343–344
    at Malvern Hill, 376
    at Oak Grove, 200
    at Savage Station, 271, 281, 294–295
Daniel, John, 144
Daniel, Junius
    at Glendale, 307, 333
Darbytown road, 264, 269, 299, 304, 306, 318–319, 335–336, 372
Davidson, Delozier, 240
Davidson, Greenlee, 380
Davis, Jefferson, 3, 34, 52, 101, 107, 177, 179, 467
    and Johnston, 12, 52, 106
    and Lee, 98, 179, 207, 455
    at Evelington Heights, 420
    at Garnett's & Golding's, 258, 261
    at Glendale, 307, 330, 333, 338, 352

    at Mechanicsville, 217–218
    at Poindexter house, 410
    at Savage Station, 299
    at Seven Pines, 100, 144, 146, 154, 167, 172
De Russy, Gustavus A., 201, 329, 386
Dearing, James G., 134, 139, 342
Deep Run, 309
DeHart, Henry V., 248
Deshler, James, 333–334
Devens, Charles, Jr.
    at Seven Pines, 102, 130, 138–139, 142–143
Dickinson, Andrew G., 378–379
Diederich, Otto, 277, 310, 320, 337, 340, 342, 344
Dispatch Station, 287
Doles, George P., 200, 318
Douglas, Beverly B., 92
Douglas, Marcellus, 398
Duane, James C., 445
Dudley farm, 270
Duryea, Hiram, 91, 230

E

Early, Jubal A., 34, 406, 408, 437
    at Malvern Hill, 362, 391, 397
    at Williamsburg, 66, 70, 75–82
Easton, Hezekiah, 248
Elder, Samuel S., 270, 277, 377
Elzey, Arnold, 246
    at Gaines' Mill, 235–236
Emory, William H.
    at Hanover Court House, 91
    at Williamsburg, 61, 68–71, 81
Enroughty farmhouse, 365
Evelington Heights, 415–420
Ewell, Benjamin S.
    at Seven Pines, 154
Ewell, Richard S., 34, 116, 406, 409, 426, 452–453
    at Evelington Heights, 420
    at Gaines' Mill, 235, 238, 241
    at Glendale, 303
    at Malvern Hill, 362, 367, 371, 379, 386, 390–391, 397
    at Mechanicsville, 211, 218–219
    at Oak Grove, 207
    at Savage Station, 264, 268, 282, 286–

287, 299, 300
  at Seven Pines, 154
Excelsior Brigade, 198, 200

F

Fair Oaks Station, 148–149, 156, 158, 165, 171, 255, 264, 269–270, 272, 282
Faison, Franklin J., 245
Featherston, Winfield S., 438
  at Gaines' Mill, 232–233, 250
  at Glendale, 321, 347–348
  at Williamsburg, 66
Ferry, Orris A., 412
Fisher house, 325, 329
Fitch, Butler, 132
Fort Donelson, 2, 99
Fort Macon, 2
Fort Magruder, 57–62, 65, 67–68, 70, 73–74, 81
Fort Monroe, 11, 14–15, 29, 31, 34, 36–37, 46, 49, 453
Fort Pulaski, 3
Fox, Gustavus V., 39, 48
  and C.S.S. *Virginia*, 15
  and Goldsborough, 29
  and Lincoln, 11
Frank, John D., 408
Franklin, William B., 7, 52
  and Lincoln, 6, 7
  and Urbanna Plan, 11
  at Eltham's Landing, 83–87
  at Glendale, 325, 327–328, 343, 355–356
  at Malvern Hill, 359, 361, 375
  at Williamsburg, 81
  at Yorktown, 47
  retreat to Harrison's, 403
French, William H.
  at Gaines' Mill, 252
Fulkerson, Samuel V.
  at Gaines' Mill, 241, 250

G

Galena, USS (ironclad gunboat), 280, 314–315, 334, 361, 403, 412
Garland, Samuel, Jr., 127
  at Gaines' Mill, 225, 240, 242
  at Glendale, 317
  at Malvern Hill, 383, 385–387
  at Oak Grove, 200
  at Seven Pines, 118, 120, 123–127, 131–132, 138, 142
Garnett house, 256
Garnett, James, 255
Gazzam, Audley W., 122, 124, 126–127
General Orders No. 75, 196, 204–207, 209, 219, 235, 255, 269
Getty, George W., 277
Glendale, 266, 269, 273, 275, 278, 298, 300, 306, 308–310, 329, 336–337, 340–341, 343, 353, 355–356, 371, 438–439
Glorieta Pass, 3, 465
Gloucester Point, 38–39, 43, 56
Goldsborough, Louis M., 38, 39, 42, 43, 49, 212
  and Fox, 29
  and McClellan, 39, 49
Goode, Thomas F., 320
Gordon, John B., 127, 383, 385
  at Seven Pines, 141, 143
Gorman, Willis A., 148
  at Seven Pines, 147–148
Gosline, John M., 246
Gove, Jesse A., 91, 250
Grant, Ulysses S., 2
Grapevine Bridge road, 182
Gregg, Maxcy
  at Gaines' Mill, 226, 229
  at Glendale, 348
Griffin, Charles
  at Gaines' Mill, 231, 247
  at Malvern Hill, 359
  at Mechanicsville, 215–216
Griffith, Richard, 439
  at Garnett's & Golding's, 258
  at Savage Station, 264, 269, 273, 284
Grigsby, Andrew J., 398
Grimes, Bryan, 133
Grimes, Carey F., 202, 370
Grover, Cuvier
  at Glendale, 310, 341, 344
  at Oak Grove, 198, 200–203
  at Savage Station, 270
  at Seven Pines, 168
  at Williamsburg, 60, 65, 67, 69
  retreat to Harrison's, 405

H

Hairston, Peter, 79
Half Sink, 209
Halleck, Henry W., 181, 184, 431, 443–444, 446–447, 449, 454, 456
    and Lincoln, 432, 456
    and McClellan, 181, 443, 446–449
    at Harrison's Landing, 432
Hampton Legion, 151
Hampton road, 59–60, 62, 66, 69
Hampton Roads, 14–15, 21–22, 35, 49
Hampton, VA, 37
Hampton, Wade, 406
    at Eltham's Landing, 87
    at Glendale, 326–327
    at Malvern Hill, 375, 377
    at Seven Pines, 146, 150–152, 154, 326
Hancock, Winfield S.
    at Garnett's & Golding's, 256, 258–259
    at Savage Station, 270, 290
    at Williamsburg, 62, 64, 71, 73–82
    at Yorktown, 55
Hanover Court House, 90–95, 187, 437, 439
Hardaway, Robert A., 321
Hardeman, Thomas, 92
Harvey, Elisha B., 346
Hass Creek, 329
Hatton, Robert, 437
    at Seven Pines, 146, 150–154
Hay, John, 456
Hayden, Horace, 245
Hays, Alexander, 348
Hays, William, 277
Hazzard, George W., 271, 273, 290, 303, 309, 323–324
Heintzelman, Samuel P., 11, 29, 33–34, 445–446, 453
    and deployment, 31
    and McClellan, 31
    and Urbanna Plan, 11
    At Evelington Heights, 419
    at Fairfax council, 17
    at Fort Monroe, 33, 37–40, 42
    at Gaines' Mill, 228
    at Glendale, 309, 311, 314, 329, 351, 356–357
    at Hanover Court House, 90, 95
    at Harrison's Landing, 411, 428
    at Malvern Hill, 358–361, 377, 389
    at Oak Grove, 196, 197–198, 201, 204
    at Savage Station, 270–271, 280–281, 282–283, 288–289, 295, 297–298
    at Seven Pines, 101–102, 104–105, 135–142, 144, 149, 156, 164–165, 169–171, 176
    at Williamsburg, 62–63, 66, 68–70, 80
    at Yorktown, 46, 56–57
    retreat to Harrison's, 405, 407
Henderson, Tome, 201
Herring Creek, 416
Hexamer, William, 86, 239, 247, 309, 329
Hill, Ambrose P., 180, 406, 410, 426–427, 438, 452
    at Dabbs House, 193
    at Evelington Heights, 419–420
    at Gaines' Mill, 223, 225–227, 229–231, 234–236, 238, 240, 242
    at Glendale, 304, 306–307, 313, 318–319, 321, 330–331, 335, 348, 352–355
    at Hanover Court House, 95
    at Malvern Hill, 364, 370–371, 375, 379, 390
    at Mechanicsville, 208–213, 215, 218
    at Oak Grove, 205
    at Poindexter house, 410
    at Savage Station, 266, 269, 286, 299
    at Seven Pines, 101, 108, 110, 114, 145, 159
    at Williamsburg, 58, 61, 65–66, 68
Hill, Daniel H., 34, 177, 180, 193, 303, 406, 410, 434, 437– 439, 458, 468
    at Dabbs House, 193
    at Gaines' Mill, 223, 225, 229, 234–235, 240, 242–243, 245
    at Glendale, 316–317, 321, 323–324
    at Malvern Hill, 362, 364, 366–367, 371, 373, 375–376, 383, 385–387, 390, 392–393, 395, 397, 399, 400
    at Mechanicsville, 208–210, 213, 215, 217–218
    at Oak Grove, 200, 205
    at Savage Station, 266, 268, 299
    at Seven Pines, 107–112, 114–126, 130, 132, 134, 136, 139, 144, 147, 149, 158, 160–162, 165, 167, 170–171
    at Williamsburg, 66, 70, 75–80, 82
Hill, Daniel H..

at Glendale, 317
Hogan house, 226
Hoke, Robert F., 92
Hoke, William J., 217
Holmes, Theophilus H., 180, 193, 410, 425, 455
   at Glendale, 307, 319, 332, 333, 334, 335, 336, 337, 354, 357
   at Malvern Hill, 360, 364–365, 371, 379, 392–393
   at Oak Grove, 198
   reassigned, 427, 455
Hood, John B.
   at Gaines' Mill, 248–249
Hooker, Joseph, 20–21, 31, 65, 340, 437–438, 444, 447, 464
   at Glendale, 309–310, 313, 341, 344, 351–352, 357
   at Malvern Hill, 358, 363, 369, 377
   at Oak Grove, 197–198, 201–203
   at Savage Station, 270, 289, 299
   at Seven Pines, 136–140, 142, 144, 164–165, 168, 176
   at Williamsburg, 58–63, 65–71, 81–82
   at Yorktown, 57
   retreat to Harrison's, 403
Howard, Oliver O., 161
Howe, Albion P.
   at Malvern Hill, 359, 369, 377, 385–386, 395
   at Oak Grove, 201
Howell, Joshua B., 124, 134
Howland, Joseph, 245
Hubbs, William B., 246
Huger, Benjamin, 42, 455
   at Glendale, 313
   at Oak Grove, 198
   at Savage Station, 263
   at Seven Pines, 101, 165
Huger, Benjamin:, 217
Huger, Frank, 201
Humphreys, Benjamin G., 360
Hunton, Eppa
   at Gaines' Mill, 250
   at Glendale, 321, 341–342, 345
Hyllested, W., 390

I

Ingalls, Rufus, 432
Irish Brigade (N.Y.), 294, 394, 445
Iverson, Alfred, 242, 245

J

Jackson, Thomas J., 3, 100, 178, 182, 196, 206, 403, 406, 409–410, 427, 434, 439, 452–453, 456, 465, 468
   and General Orders No. 75, 206
   and Lee, 192
   at Dabbs House, 193–194
   at Gaines' Mill, 234–235, 238, 241–242
   at Glendale, 304, 306, 316, 323–328
   at Malvern Hill, 363, 367, 375, 392
   at Mechanicsville, 208, 219
   at Oak Grove, 206
   at Savage Station, 268, 270, 287
   in Shenandoah, 178
James River road, 279
Jameson, Charles D.
   at Seven Pines, 138, 141, 144
Jenkins, Micah
   at Glendale, 320–321, 332, 337–339, 340–342, 344–345, 353
   at Seven Pines, 126, 131–132, 142–144
   at Williamsburg, 61, 67–68, 70, 73–74, 78
Johnson, Bradley T., 243
Johnson, Charles A., 91
Johnson, Marmaduke, 211
Johnston, Joseph E., 18, 33, 45, 403, 437, 467
   and retreat, 12
   and Stuart, 186
   at Richmond, 52
   at Seven Pines, 159
   at Yorktown, 52
Joint Committee on the Conduct of the War, 5–6, 30
Joinville, Prince de, 247, 277
Jones, David R., 107
   at Garnett's & Golding's, 256, 261
   at Savage Station, 264, 272
Jones, William G., 272
Jordan, Tyler C., 318

K

Kearny, Philip, 57, 171, 438
  at Glendale, 304, 309–310, 317–318, 329, 337, 346–347, 349, 351, 356–357
  at Malvern Hill, 358, 369, 386, 395
  at Oak Grove, 197–198, 201–203
  at Savage Station, 270, 281, 288–289, 298–299
  at Seven Pines, 135–141, 143–144
  at Williamsburg, 63, 66, 69–71, 81
  retreat to Harrison's, 403, 405
Keim, William H., 185
Kemper, Del, 272, 288, 290, 292, 294
Kemper, James L.
  at Gaines' Mill, 232, 234, 248
  at Glendale, 321, 340–341
  at Seven Pines, 120, 139, 143
Kennedy, John D., 264
Kerns, Mark, 310, 320
Kershaw, Joseph B., 58, 406
  at Garnett's & Golding's, 258
  at Malvern Hill, 378, 393, 395, 397
  at Savage Station, 264, 269, 270, 272–273, 288–289, 291–295
  at Seven Pines, 272
Keyes, Erasmus D., 11, 419, 428, 438, 446, 453
  and McClellan, 183
  and Urbanna Plan, 11
  at Evelington Heights, 419
  at Fairfax council, 17
  at Fort Monroe, 40
  at Gaines' Mill, 228
  at Glendale, 311, 314
  at Hanover Court House, 90, 95
  at Malvern Hill, 361, 375
  at Oak Grove, 196
  at Savage Station, 266, 275, 277–300
  at Seven Pines, 101–103, 105, 109–110, 127, 128–130, 134–139, 142–144, 148, 157, 169–171, 176
  at Williamsburg, 63, 66, 71, 73–74, 80
  at Yorktown, 46–47
  retreat to Harrison's, 403, 407
Kimball, John W., 294
Kimball, Nathan, 417
  at Evelington Heights, 420
King, Rufus, Jr., 324

Kingsbury, Henry W., 243, 367, 370, 373, 377
Kirby, Edmund, 148, 151–153, 156, 271–272, 290, 341, 343, 369
Knieriem, John, 277, 310, 320, 337, 340, 342, 344, 351

L

Labor-in-Vain Swamp, 272
Lane, James H., 92
Lane, John, 258
Langley, Samuel G., 272
Lansing, Henry S., 91
Latham, A. C., 92
Law, Evander M.
  at Gaines' Mill, 248–249
  at Malvern Hill, 399
Lawton, Alexander R.
  at Gaines' Mill, 240
Lawton, Edward P., 244
Lee, Charles C., 92
Lee, Fitzhugh, 287
Lee, Robert E., 173, 402, 410, 417, 427, 439, 455, 464, 466–469
  and Davis, 98, 179
  and Holmes, 455
  and Mahone, 318
  and Stuart, 186, 190
  and Stuart's ride, 187
  at Evelington Heights, 420
  at Gaines' Mill, 223, 234, 238, 248, 254
  at Garnett's & Golding's, 255, 261
  at Glendale, 304, 328, 330, 332, 353, 355
  at Malvern Hill, 363, 365, 372, 374, 378, 390
  at Mechanicsville, 217
  at Oak Grove, 196, 203, 207
  at Poindexter house, 409
  at Poindexter House, 419
  at Richmond, 52
  at Savage Station, 266, 285, 287
  at Seven Pines, 102, 144, 146, 154, 167–168, 172
Lee, Rooney, 287
Lee, William R.
  at Glendale, 325
Lincoln, Abraham, 3, 6, 15–17, 20, 22, 48, 100, 129, 183–184, 431, 444, 456–457,

693

465–466, 469
and C.S.S. *Virginia*, 14
and Cameron, 8
and Gen. War Order No. 1, 8
and Halleck, 181, 432, 456
and Jackson, 182
and McClellan, 7, 10, 18–20, 23, 24, 43, 48, 51–52, 94–95, 101, 105, 179, 181, 315, 428, 454
and McDowell, 20
and Pope, 456
and Seven Pines, 105
and Spec. War Orders No. 1, 8
and Stanton, 8
and Stone, 6
and Urbanna Plan, 9, 11, 28
and Washington defense, 20
at Harrison's Landing, 427
Livingston, LaRhett L., 370, 373, 377
Lomax, Tennant, 161
Long Bridge road, 269, 275, 278, 300, 304, 306–307, 309–310, 313, 319–321, 330, 332, 334, 336–337, 341–342, 345, 347, 349–350, 352, 359, 363, 365, 372, 375, 406, 416
Long, Armistead L., 144
and Johnston, 101
at Gaines' Mill, 253
Longstreet, James, 34, 193, 406, 410, 425, 427, 438, 453, 461, 468
and Johnston, 169
at Dabbs House, 193
at Evelington Heights, 416–420
at Gaines' Mill, 223, 226, 229–230, 232–235, 238, 242, 248–250, 253
at Glendale, 304, 306, 313, 318–321, 326, 327, 330–332, 335–338, 340, 346–348, 352–355
at Malvern Hill, 363–367, 369, 370–371, 373–378, 390, 401
at Mechanicsville, 209–210, 213, 217–218
at Oak Grove, 205
at Poindexter house, 409–410
at Richmond, 52–53
at Savage Station, 263–264, 266, 269, 286, 299, 301
at Seven Days, 170
at Seven Pines, 106–109, 111–112, 114–120, 129, 134–135, 138–139,
144–146, 152–154, 158–161, 165–166, 170–171, 177
at Williamsburg, 58, 61, 66–70, 73, 75, 82
at Yorktown, 53
Lord, Nathan, Jr., 56
Lovell, Charles S.
at Gaines' Mill, 230, 236, 246
at Glendale, 311
at Malvern Hill, 359, 389
retreat to Harrison's Landing, 405
Lowe, Thaddeus
at Gaines' Mill, 228
Luckie, Lorenzo F., 318

M

Magill, William J., 272–273
Magruder, John B.
at Garnett's & Golding's, 255–256, 258
at Glendale, 306, 335, 337
at Malvern Hill, 363, 365–366, 376, 379, 388–390
at Savage Station, 263, 272
at Yorktown, 49
Mahone, William, 376, 405, 408
at Glendale, 317–318, 328–329
at Malvern Hill, 363, 370, 378–381, 383, 387–388, 394
at Oak Grove, 198, 200, 202–203
at Savage Station, 274, 298–299
at Seven Pines, 160–162, 164
Malvern Hill, 265, 313, 315, 330, 332, 334, 358, 360–361, 371, 379, 383, 387, 389, 392, 394, 406, 420, 440, 447, 455, 468
Manassas, VA, 4, 7, 9, 15, 19, 28, 30, 56, 186, 434, 457
Maratanza USS (gunboat), 420
Marcy, Randolph B., 201, 277, 416
and McClellan, 16, 315
and Urbanna Plan, 10–11
at Mechanicsville, 219
Marks, James J., 195
Marshall, Elisha G., 91
Marshall, John, 249
Martin, Augustus P., 91
Martin, William T., 187
Martindale, John H., 382, 388
at Gaines' Mill, 231, 237, 248, 250
at Hanover Court House, 91, 93

    at Harrison's Landing, 412
    at Malvern Hill, 359, 380–381, 388, 400
    at Mechanicsville, 215–216
    at Savage Station, 277
    retreat to Harrison's, 404
Mason, C. R., 284
Matheson, C. Roderick, 237
Maurin, Victor, 232
Maury, Richard L., 79–80, 126
Mayo, Robert M., 349
McAlester, Miles D., 16, 61–62, 66, 71
McAllister, Robert, 246–247
McCall, George A., 181, 183, 310, 438–439, 445
    and McClellan, 181
    and Urbanna Plan, 11
    at Gaines' Mill, 237, 239, 246
    at Glendale, 309–310, 313–314, 319–321, 337–342, 344, 346–347, 349, 351–353
    at Malvern Hill, 358
    at Mechanicsville, 213–215, 219
    at Oak Grove, 204
    at Savage Station, 277, 300–301
McCarter, James M., 131
McClellan, George B., 18–19, 34, 45, 177–179, 193, 431–432, 435, 438, 444–446, 449, 453–454, 456, 466–467, 469, 471
    and C.S.S. *Virginia*, 14
    and demotion, 16
    and deployment, 31, 33
    and flotilla, 21, 28–29
    and Goldsborough, 42–43, 49
    and Halleck, 181, 432, 443, 446–449
    and Hallleck, 184
    and Harrison's Bar Letter, 431
    and Heintzelman, 31, 33, 38
    and Keyes, 129
    and Lee, 432
    and Lincoln, 6–7, 10, 18–20, 24, 43, 48, 52, 101, 179, 181, 183–184, 315, 427–428, 456
    and Lorenzo Thomas, 24
    and Marcy, 16
    and Old Tavern, 197
    and Pinkerton, 51
    and President Buchanan, 8
    and Stanton, 15, 16, 22, 43–44, 48, 424
    and Stone, 5
    and Stuart's ride, 190, 192
    and U. S. Navy, 403
    and U.S.S. *Monitor*, 15
    and Urbanna Plan, 4, 9–13, 21, 23, 28
    and Washington defense, 20, 24–25
    and wife, 42, 182, 315
    andLincoln, 179
    at Britton farm, 276
    at Eltham's Landing, 83–89
    at Evelington Heights, 418–419
    at Fairfax council, 17
    at Fort Monroe, 38, 39–43
    at Gaines' Mill, 222–223, 227–228, 232, 239, 252–254
    at Garnett's & Golding's, 256, 261–262
    at Glendale, 304, 307–317, 325, 332–333, 353–354, 356–357
    at Hanover Court House, 90–91, 93–95
    at Harrison's Landing, 420, 424–426, 432
    at Malvern Hill, 358–362, 364, 366, 377–378, 400–401
    at Manassas, 15
    at Mechanicsville, 208–213, 215, 217–221
    at Oak Grove, 196–197, 201, 204, 207
    at Savage Station, 263–266, 268–269, 271, 273–275, 277–280, 286, 288, 290, 297–298, 301–302
    at Seven Pines, 102–105, 111, 114, 118, 129, 135–137, 143, 147, 156, 158–159, 165, 167–169, 171, 174, 176
    at White House Landing, 286
    at Williamsburg, 58, 62, 80–82
    at Yorktown, 46–49, 51–57
    Little Mac, 277, 428, 432, 434
    retreat to Harrison's, 403, 405
McDowell Creek, 340, 342
McDowell, Irvin, 11, 47, 95
    and Lincoln, 6
    and Urbanna Plan, 11
    at Fairfax council, 17
McGehee house, 239–240, 245
McGowan, Samuel
    at Glendale, 348
McIntosh, David G., 216
McIntosh, William M., 259
McKinney, Robert M., 55
McLane, John W., 91, 250, 382
McLaws, Lafayette, 58, 427

at Garnett's & Golding's, 258
at Glendale, 319, 336
at Malvern Hill, 366, 375, 378, 390
at Savage Station, 264, 269, 272–273, 285
at Seven Pines, 107–110, 116, 145, 158–159, 165–166
McQuade, James, 91, 381
at Hanover Court House, 91
Meade, George G., 439
at Gaines' Mill, 237, 248, 250
at Glendale, 320, 337, 346
at Savage Station, 300–301
Meadow road, 268, 271, 297
Meagher, Thomas F.
at Gaines' Mill, 239, 252–253
at Garnett's & Golding's, 261
at Glendale, 322, 349
at Malvern Hill, 359, 389, 394
at Savage Station, 270, 280, 289–290, 294–295
Meares, Gaston, 385
Mechanicsville, 204–205, 207, 209, 215, 219, 436, 438–440
Mechanicsville Turnpike, 205–206, 210, 234
Merritt, Wesley, 251
Mexican War, 4, 280
Miles, Nelson A., 16, 61
Miller, James, 161
Miller, Ozro, 143, 385
Mink, Charles E., 128
Moorman, Marcellus N., 329, 370
Morehead, John H., 333
Morell, George W., 37, 411
at Gaines' Mill, 226–227, 237, 239, 246, 248–249, 252
at Glendale, 310, 332
at Hanover Court House, 91
at Malvern Hill, 359–360, 373, 380–382, 388–389
at Mechanicsville, 215, 219
at Savage Station, 275, 277, 300–301
retreat to Harrison's, 403–404
Morgan, Charles M., 377
Mott, Christopher H., 62
Mott, Thaddeus P., 309, 322–323
Munford, Thomas T., 316, 323, 409
at Glendale, 316, 323–324, 326–327

N

Naglee, Henry M., 80, 300, 413
and Urbanna Plan, 11
at Glendale, 308, 310, 323, 356
at Harrison's, 405
at Malvern Hill, 358
at Savage Station, 270, 289
at Seven Pines, 102, 125–128, 130–132
retreat to Harrison's, 407, 419
Nairn, Joseph E., 281, 289–290, 332, 334, 381
Nance, James D., 292
Neff, John F., 398
Neill, Thomas H., 131
Nelson, William, 2
Nelson, George W., 321
New Bern, 2
New Bern, NC, 91
New Cold Harbor, 206, 209, 226, 234–235, 240
New Kent Court House, 90
New Market, 300, 303–304, 447
New Market road, 264, 300, 307
Newton, John
at Eltham's Landing, 86–87
at Gaines' Mill, 237–239, 246, 248
Nine Mile road, 102, 106, 108–109, 111, 116–117, 119– 121, 125, 130, 144–146, 149–150, 153–154, 160, 177, 193, 197, 258, 269
Norfolk, 22, 31, 33, 38, 42, 44, 52–53, 57
North Carolina, Department of, 200, 307, 427, 449
Norton, Oliver, 434
Nugent, Robert
at Glendale, 349, 357
at Savage Station, 290

O

Oak Grove, 196, 199, 204, 207, 284, 438, 473
Olcott, Egbert W., 337–338, 345, 399
Old Church, 187–188
Old Cold Harbor, 206, 226–227, 234, 240, 245
Old Tavern, 196
Orchard Station, 288
Osborn, Thomas W., 59, 281, 289–290,

333, 367, 373, 377

P

Palmer, Innis N.
   at Oak Grove, 201
Palmetto Sharpshooters, 439
Pamunkey River, 84, 87, 94, 183, 186–187, 223, 286
Paris, Comte de
   at Gaines' Mill, 251
Patterson, Francis E., 60, 137
   at Seven Pines, 138, 162
   at Williamsburg, 65
Pea Ridge, 3
Peck, John J., 182, 403, 410, 413, 446
   at Glendale, 308, 310
   at Harrison's Landing, 412
   at Malvern Hill, 358–359, 361, 392
   at Savage Station, 270
   at Seven Pines, 102, 130, 139–141, 144
   at Williamsburg, 66–68, 73
   retreat to Harrison's, 407, 413
   retreat to Harrison's Landing, 405
Pegram, William J., 231, 240, 370, 372, 409
Pegues, Christopher C., 243
Pelham, John, 235, 286, 402, 413, 415–417
   at Stuart's ride, 187
Pender, W. Dorsey
   at Gaines' Mill, 225, 231, 236
   at Glendale, 351–352
   at Mechanicsville, 217–218
   at Seven Pines, 146, 149–153
Pendleton, William N., 432, 455, 468
   at Malvern Hill, 371–372
   at Seven Pines, 106
Petersburg, 101, 178, 184, 307, 426, 432, 473
Petherbridge, Edward R., 277
Pettigrew, James J.
   at Seven Pines, 146, 149–152, 154
Pettit, Rufus D., 271, 273, 290, 323–324, 369
Petway, Oliver C., 390
Phillips house, 420
Pickett, George E., 469
   at Gaines' Mill, 232–234, 248–250
   at Glendale, 321, 341
   at Seven Pines, 120, 160–162, 164–165
   at Williamsburg, 58, 61, 65, 68

Pinkerton, Allan, 25, 42, 473–474
   and McClellan, 24, 51, 184, 404
Pleasonton, Alfred, 444–445
   at Savage Station, 279
Poague, William T., 367, 369
Poe house, 118
Poe, Orlando M., 35, 70
Poindexter field, 367, 370, 375, 377
Poindexter house, 409–410, 415, 419
Pole Green Church, 205–207, 211
Pope, John, 426–428, 432, 434, 443–444, 446–447, 449, 452–454, 456–457, 469, 474
   and Lincoln, 456
Port Republic, 178
Porter, Andrew
   and Urbanna Plan, 11
Porter, Fitz John, 187, 193, 431, 437–438
   and deployment, 31
   and Urbanna Plan, 11
   at Gaines' Mill, 228, 252
   at Hanover Court House, 91, 94
   at Malvern Hill, 358, 394, 401
   at Mechanicsville, 209
   at Savage Station, 300
   at Seven Pines, 137
Porter, Josiah, 86, 239, 329
Potomac River, 10, 14, 29, 33, 461–462
Powhite Creek, 226, 229, 232–233, 251
Pratt, Calvin, 300
Price house, 256
Price, Mrs., 256
Pryor, Roger A., 438
   at Gaines' Mill, 232–233, 250
   at Glendale, 321, 346–348
   at Seven Pines, 120, 160
   at Williamsburg, 58, 61

Q

Quaker road, 264, 300–301, 363, 365–366, 378, 383, 415

R

Radical Republicans, 5, 6, 30, 434, 465–466
Railroads
   Orange & Alexandria, 12–13, 452
   Richmond & York River, 104, 106, 174, 189, 192, 197, 206, 212, 271, 289

Richmond, Fredericksburg & Potomac, 94–95
Virginia Central, 90–91, 94, 192, 206–207, 209, 211, 426
Rains, Gabriel J.
  at Seven Pines, 118, 121, 131–132, 139–141
  at Williamsburg, 66, 75
Randol, Alanson M., 277, 301, 310, 320, 337–339, 345–346, 349–350, 399
Randolph, George W.
  at Mechanicsville, 217
  at Richmond, 52
Randolph, John M., 309, 329, 346, 367
Ransom, Matt W., 390
Ransom, Robert, Jr., 180, 405–406, 411, 425
  at Glendale, 307, 317
  at Malvern Hill, 363, 376, 378, 379, 389–390, 393–394
  at Oak Grove, 198, 200–201
  at Savage Station, 274, 284, 299
Rapidan River, 15, 34, 434, 452–453
Rappahannock River, 4, 13, 17, 19, 34, 99, 450, 453, 464
Rectortown, 463
Regan, Peter C., 132
Regiments, Confederate, cavalry
  Mississippi
    Jeff Davis (Mississippi) Legion Cavalry, 187, 206, 413
  North Carolina
    1st North Carolina Cavalry, 275
  Virginia
    1st Virginia Cavalry, 186–187, 287, 402, 415
    2nd Virginia Cavalry, 316
    3rd Virginia Cavalry, 275, 299, 320
    4th Virginia Cavalry, 59, 92, 187, 206, 234, 413
    5th Virginia Cavalry, 300, 332
    9th Virginia Cavalry, 92, 187–188, 415
Regiments, Confederate, infantry
  Alabama
    3rd Alabama, 161, 386, 439
    4th Alabama, 249
    5th Alabama, 141, 231
    6th Alabama, 127, 141, 383, 437
    8th Alabama, 345–346

9th Alabama, 68, 339
10th Alabama, 339, 345–346
11th Alabama, 139, 345–346, 439
12th Alabama, 140–141, 385
14th Alabama, 61, 74, 347
15th Alabama, 236, 238, 248
26th Alabama, 243, 385
44th Alabama, 299
Florida
  2nd Florida, 70, 124
Georgia
  2nd Georgia, 259, 395
  3rd Georgia, 200, 318, 325, 380–381, 383
  4th Georgia, 200, 202, 274, 318, 380, 383
  6th Georgia, 386
  7th Georgia, 259
  8th Georgia, 261, 387
  10th Georgia, 289, 293–295, 393
  11th Georgia, 256, 387
  12th Georgia, 397
  13th Georgia, 398
  14th Georgia, 216, 352
  15th Georgia, 259
  16th Georgia, 382
  17th Georgia, 259, 387
  18th Georgia, 86, 248–249, 251
  19th Georgia, 87, 231
  20th Georgia, 256, 259, 395, 397
  21st Georgia, 236, 238, 248
  22nd Georgia, 200, 203, 380
  24th Georgia, 376, 381
  26th Georgia, 397
  27th Georgia, 126
  28th Georgia, 126, 142
  31st Georgia, 245
  35th Georgia, 216
  38th Georgia, 244, 253
  44th Georgia, 218, 243, 386, 439–440
  45th Georgia, 92, 352
  48th Georgia, 218, 243
  49th Georgia, 352
  53rd Georgia, 394
Louisiana
  1st Louisiana, 200, 203, 325, 380, 383
  1st Louisiana Special Battalion, 236
  2nd Louisiana, 376, 381

3rd Louisiana Battalion, 216, 352
5th Louisiana, 295, 394
6th Louisiana, 236
8th Louisiana, 398
9th Louisiana, 236, 238, 398
10th Louisiana, 394
14th Louisiana, 61, 68, 347

Maryland
1st Maryland, 243

Mississippi
2nd Mississippi, 249
2nd Mississippi Battalion, 124, 126
11th Mississippi, 249
12th Mississippi, 70, 127, 141
16th Mississippi, 236, 246
19th Mississippi, 62, 68, 143
21st Mississippi, 292, 294–295, 363

North Carolina
1st North Carolina, 218, 243, 246, 275, 385, 439, 440
2nd North Carolina, 383
3rd North Carolina, 218, 243, 385, 397
4th North Carolina, 126, 128, 133–134, 317, 437
5th North Carolina, 75, 77–79, 81, 126, 317
6th North Carolina, 249
7th North Carolina, 92, 211, 230–231
12th North Carolina, 92
13th North Carolina, 162
14th North Carolina, 373
15th North Carolina, 55–56, 376, 381
16th North Carolina, 87
18th North Carolina, 92, 93
20th North Carolina, 242–243, 245, 253
21st North Carolina, 236, 246
22nd North Carolina, 217, 231
23rd North Carolina, 70, 75, 77–79, 124, 126, 386
24th North Carolina, 203, 389–390
25th North Carolina, 200
26th North Carolina, 203, 390
28th North Carolina, 92, 230–231
30th North Carolina, 385
33rd North Carolina, 92
35th North Carolina, 390, 393
37th North Carolina, 92, 231, 439
38th North Carolina, 217
45th North Carolina, 333
48th North Carolina, 202–203
49th North Carolina, 200–201, 394, 405
50th North Carolina, 307

South Carolina
1st South Carolina, 230, 236, 348
1st South Carolina Rifles, 230, 253, 348, 439
2nd South Carolina, 264, 291, 337, 397
3rd South Carolina, 288, 291–292, 294–295
5th South Carolina, 143, 250, 337
6th South Carolina, 68, 73, 78–80, 126, 142, 332, 345, 437
7th South Carolina, 291–292
8th South Carolina, 258, 264, 291–292, 295
12th South Carolina, 226, 230
13th South Carolina, 230, 236, 348
14th South Carolina, 230, 348
Palmetto Sharpshooters (South Carolina), 68, 126, 142, 250, 337, 339, 439

Texas
4th Texas, 152, 249, 251, 253
5th Texas, 86, 248

Virginia
2nd Virginia, 243, 349
2nd Virginia Hvy. Arty. Btn. (as 22nd Inf. Btn.), 349
4th Virginia (4th Va. Hvy. Arty. as inf.), 141
5th Virginia, 240, 243, 398
5th Virginia Battalion, 200
6th Virginia, 203
7th Virginia, 65
12th Virginia, 161–162, 203, 383
13th Virginia, 236, 367
14th Virginia, 162, 370
15th Virginia, 393
17th Virginia, 340
19th Virginia, 164, 342
24th Virginia, 75–79, 126, 437
27th Virginia, 398
28th Virginia, 70
30th Virginia, 333

31st Virginia, 397
32nd Virginia, 289, 295, 394
33rd Virginia, 243, 397–398
38th Virginia, 75, 77–80, 124, 126, 365, 373
40th Virginia, 349
41st Virginia, 161
46th Virginia, 307
47th Virginia, 231, 349
49th Virginia, 126, 200, 203, 379
52nd Virginia, 242
53rd Virginia, 162, 255, 373
56th Virginia, 351
57th Virginia, 200, 381, 382
58th Virginia, 236
60th Virginia, 215, 349, 351

Regiments, Federal, cavalry
  Illinois
    8th Illinois Cavalry, 61, 206, 211, 252, 278
  New York
    1st New York Cavalry, 449
  Pennsylvania
    3rd Pennsylvania Cavalry, 40, 46, 61, 275–277, 300, 388, 402, 405, 408, 411, 433
    4th Pennsylvania Cavalry, 251, 319–320, 338, 340
    5th Pennsylvania Cavalry, 83
    6th Pennsylvania Cavalry, 91, 235, 251, 279
    8th Pennsylvania Cavalry, 279, 413
  U. S.
    1st U. S. Cavalry, 40, 186, 251
    2nd U. S. Dragoons, 279
    5th U. S. Cavalry, 40, 46, 188, 251
    6th U. S. Cavalry, 91, 94

Regiments, Federal, infantry
  Delaware
    2nd Delaware, 271
  Indiana
    20th Indiana, 202–203, 281, 288–289, 347–348
  Maine
    2nd Maine, 91, 93, 231, 250, 388
    3rd Maine, 136, 164, 299, 385
    4th Maine, 69, 202–203, 298, 385
    5th Maine, 86, 231, 239, 245
    6th Maine, 71, 73, 77
    7th Maine, 71, 73, 77, 79, 322

    11th Maine, 125, 127–128
  Massachusetts
    1st Massachusetts, 341, 344, 351
    7th Massachusetts, 81, 130, 142–143, 148, 275, 310, 359
    9th Massachusetts, 91, 226, 231, 237, 251, 253, 381, 382, 383
    10th Massachusetts, 134, 142–143, 385
    11th Massachusetts, 61–62, 168, 198, 341
    15th Massachusetts, 151, 259, 271, 280, 282, 294–295, 343, 351
    16th Massachusetts, 198, 203, 341, 344
    18th Massachusetts, 412
    19th Massachusetts, 200, 343, 344
    20th Massachusetts, 152, 271, 273, 294–295, 303, 343, 344
    22nd Massachusetts, 91, 216, 250, 388
    29th Massachusetts, 394, 405
  Michigan
    1st Michigan, 69, 250, 388
    2nd Michigan, 35, 70, 348
    3rd Michigan, 69, 140–141, 348
    4th Michigan, 91, 216, 231, 237, 248, 381–383
    5th Michigan, 69–70, 140, 202–203, 348
    7th Michigan, 151, 259, 271, 294–295, 343–344
    16th Michigan, 37–38, 91, 249–250, 382
  Minnesota
    1st Minnesota, 149, 151, 271, 273, 290–291, 294, 343, 352, 405
  New Hampshire
    2nd New Hampshire, 198, 341
    5th New Hampshire, 161, 271–273, 294–295, 349, 386, 405, 411, 437
  New Jersey
    1st New Jersey, 246–247, 300
    2nd New Jersey, 259
    3rd New Jersey, 246
    4th New Jersey, 239, 248, 438
    5th New Jersey, 68, 137
    6th New Jersey, 137, 164
    7th New Jersey, 200
    8th New Jersey, 137, 198, 203

New York
- 1st New York, 203, 438
- 5th New York, 91, 230
- 7th New York, 290, 395, 398
- 10th New York, 230, 246
- 12th New York, 38, 91, 250, 383, 388
- 13th New York, 91, 216, 250, 381
- 14th New York, 91, 216, 231, 247, 380–381, 393
- 16th New York, 239, 245, 253
- 17th New York, 91, 412
- 20th New York, 322
- 25th New York, 91, 93, 250, 388, 437
- 27th New York, 86, 239, 245
- 31st New York, 237–238, 246, 300
- 32nd New York, 86, 237, 239, 246–247
- 33rd New York, 71, 73, 77–79
- 34th New York, 343
- 36th New York, 143, 395, 405
- 37th New York, 35, 70, 140, 202, 348
- 38th New York, 136, 164
- 40th New York, 70, 203
- 42nd New York, 271, 281, 343–344
- 44th New York, 37, 91, 93, 233, 250, 382, 388, 437
- 49th New York, 294–295, 297
- 52nd New York, 161
- 55th New York, 67–68, 130
- 56th New York, 125, 419
- 61st New York, 271, 349, 395
- 62nd New York, 130, 148
- 63rd New York, 273, 394
- 65th New York, 148, 151, 377, 395
- 66th New York, 271
- 67th New York, 130, 142, 377, 395
- 70th New York, 81, 437
- 71st New York, 200, 395, 405, 408
- 72nd New York, 395, 398, 437
- 73rd New York, 201, 395
- 74th New York, 66, 164, 395
- 82nd New York, 151, 271, 294–295, 343
- 85th New York, 125, 133, 413, 419
- 87th New York, 141, 202–203, 309, 325, 386
- 88th New York, 290, 294–295, 394
- 92nd New York, 133
- 93rd New York, 104
- 96th New York, 122, 125
- 98th New York, 125
- 100th New York, 121, 125, 128
- 101st New York, 202–203

Pennsylvania
- 1st Pennsylvania Reserves, 216, 320, 338–339
- 2nd Pennsylvania Reserves, 248
- 3rd Pennsylvania Reserves, 216, 320–321, 338
- 4th Pennsylvania Reserves, 337
- 7th Pennsylvania Reserves, 237, 250, 301, 346
- 9th Pennsylvania Reserves, 237, 337
- 10th Pennsylvania Reserves, 237, 337, 341–342, 357
- 11th Pennsylvania Reserves, 237, 248, 337, 345–346, 438
- 12th Pennsylvania Reserves, 217, 237, 337, 340
- 23rd Pennsylvania, 131, 377, 385, 395
- 26th Pennsylvania, 61, 198, 341, 344, 351
- 31st Pennsylvania, 148, 377, 395
- 49th Pennsylvania, 71, 73, 77, 261
- 52nd Pennsylvania, 125
- 53rd Pennsylvania, 271–273
- 57th Pennsylvania, 347–348
- 61st Pennsylvania, 142, 148, 377, 395, 437
- 62nd Pennsylvania, 91, 231, 237, 381–382
- 63rd Pennsylvania, 202, 347–349, 386, 405
- 69th Pennsylvania, 341, 344, 351
- 71st Pennsylvania, 271–273, 294–295, 341, 344
- 72nd Pennsylvania, 148, 151–152, 294, 295, 341, 343, 352
- 81st Pennsylvania, 161, 271, 290, 349, 395
- 83rd Pennsylvania, 37–38, 91, 250, 382, 388
- 85th Pennsylvania, 122, 124, 128, 133–134
- 8th Pennsylvania Reserves, 237, 277, 300, 342, 398

701

93rd Pennsylvania, 67, 130–131
95th Pennsylvania, 86, 237–239, 246
96th Pennsylvania, 86, 239, 245
98th Pennsylvania, 67
101st Pennsylvania, 121, 132
102nd Pennsylvania, 67–68, 140, 385
103rd Pennsylvania, 122, 124–127
104th Pennsylvania, 125, 127–128, 419, 437
105th Pennsylvania, 141, 143, 202, 347
106th Pennsylvania, 148, 152, 289, 291, 294–295, 341, 376
Rhode Island
  2nd Rhode Island, 142, 202, 275, 310, 359
U. S.
  1st U. S. Sharpshooters, 54, 91, 215, 236, 258
  3rd U. S., 230, 245, 334
  4th U. S., 240, 352, 394
  10th U. S., 246
  11th U. S., 246, 359
  12th U. S., 245
  14th U. S., 230, 240, 245, 393, 408
  17th U. S., 230, 245–246
Vermont
  2nd Vermont, 291
  3rd Vermont, 55, 80, 291
  4th Vermont, 56, 259
  5th Vermont, 291, 295, 317
  6th Vermont, 55–56, 259, 291, 295
Wisconsin
  5th Wisconsin, 71, 73, 76–78, 259
Reilly, James, 321, 367, 369, 371
Reynolds, John F.
  at Gaines' Mill, 237, 246
  at Mechanicsville, 215–216, 219
Rhett, A. Burnet, 321
Richardson, Robert M., 383
Richmond, VA, 22, 135, 158, 358, 426, 445, 462
Ripley, Roswell S., 180, 439
  at Gaines' Mill, 240, 243
  at Malvern Hill, 385, 397
  at Mechanicsville, 215, 217–218
  at Seven Pines, 101, 165–166
Ripley, William Y.
  and Stuart's ride, 192

River road, 278, 304, 307, 310, 313, 319, 332, 334, 336, 357–360, 364–365, 375, 380, 392, 407, 415–416, 418–419, 455
Roberts, Charles W., 91
Roberts, R. Biddle, 320
Robertson, James M., 252
Robinson, John C.
  at Glendale, 309, 325, 346, 348
  at Malvern Hill, 386
  at Oak Grove, 198, 202–203
  at Savage Station, 270
  retreat to Harrison's, 405
Rodes, Robert E.
  at Gaines' Mill, 240, 242
  at Malvern Hill, 383
  at Seven Pines, 108–111, 117–120, 126, 127, 132–134, 139–141, 143
  at Williamsburg, 66, 70
Rodgers, John, 280, 314
  and McClellan, 315, 361, 404
Ross, H. M., 318
Rossell, Nathan, 245
Rosser, Thomas L., 332
Royston, Young L., 345
Rush, Richard H., 91
Rutledge, Henry M., 390

S

Savage Station, 135, 138, 266, 268, 270–271, 273, 278–284, 288–290, 294–299, 301, 307, 316, 335, 439, 444
Scales, Alfred M., 162
Scott, Eben G., 248
Scott, Winfield, 3
  and Chase, 6
Sedgwick, John, 259, 411, 444, 447
  at Eltham's Landing, 84–86
  at Fort Monroe, 40
  at Glendale, 310, 314, 325, 328, 343–344, 352, 357
  at Malvern Hill, 369, 376, 392
  at Oak Grove, 200
  at Savage Station, 271, 281, 289–290, 297, 298, 302
  at Seven Pines, 147, 152–153, 158
  at Yorktown, 46, 47
Seeley, Francis W., 343, 386, 397–398
Selwyn plantation, 234
Semmes, Paul J., 58, 406

at Glendale, 317, 335–336
at Malvern Hill, 378, 393–394
at Savage Station, 269, 289–295, 297
Seven Days, 87, 170, 172, 183, 196, 208, 216, 253, 327, 330, 359, 433, 438–439, 468, 469
Seven Pines, 90, 95, 117, 120, 129, 134–136, 140, 144, 146, 148, 150, 152, 154, 156, 159, 167, 169, 170–172, 176, 182, 255, 284–285, 371, 437, 467
Seward, William H., 7, 315, 465
Seymour, Isaac G.
   at Gaines' Mill, 236–238
Seymour, Truman, 246, 445
   at Gaines' Mill, 237
   at Glendale, 320, 337–338, 341–342, 346, 356–357
   at Malvern Hill, 358
   at Mechanicsville, 215, 217, 219
   retreat to Harrison's, 404
Shady Grove Church, 211
Shenandoah Valley, 25, 91, 100, 178, 196, 204, 209, 417, 426, 452, 458, 465
Shiloh, TN, 168
Shirley Plantation, 279, 280
Sickel, Horatio G., 321
Sickles, Daniel E.
   at Glendale, 310
   at Malvern Hill, 389, 395, 398
   at Oak Grove, 198, 200–201
   at Savage Station, 270
   at Seven Pines, 164
   at Williamsburg, 65
   retreat to Harrison's, 405
Simmons, Seneca G., 343
   at Glendale, 320, 337, 341–342
   at Savage Station, 300–301
Skillen, Charles H., 91
Slash Church, 205–206
Slocum, Henry W., 239, 438
   at Eltham's Landing, 86
   at Evelington Heights, 419
   at Gaines' Mill, 223, 228, 235, 237, 239, 245, 253
   at Glendale, 309–310, 313–314, 317, 325, 328–330, 346, 351, 356
   at Harrison's Landing, 411
   at Malvern Hill, 358
   at Savage Station, 278, 280, 288, 300
   retreat to Harrison's Landing, 405

Smead, John R., 332
Smith, Gustavus W., 34, 173, 180
   at Eltham's Landing, 84, 86
   at Richmond, 52
   at Seven Pines, 100, 106–108, 110, 114, 144–146, 158–159, 165–166, 170
Smith, William F., 410
   and Old Tavern, 197
   and Urbanna Plan, 11
   at Evelington Heights, 417
   at Fort Monroe, 40
   at Gaines' Mill, 250
   at Garnett's & Golding's, 256, 261
   at Glendale, 308, 321–323
   at Harrison's Landing, 411
   at Savage Station, 270, 281, 288–289, 291, 294, 301
   at Williamsburg, 59, 61, 63, 67, 73–74, 80–81
   at Yorktown, 54–57
   retreat to Harrison's, 407
   retreat to Harrison's Landing, 405
Sorrel, G. Moxley, 409
Special War Orders, No. 1, 8
Spratt, Joseph, 125, 127–128, 132
Stafford, Leroy A., 406
   at Gaines' Mill, 238
   at Malvern Hill, 391, 398
Stanton, Edwin M., 8, 14–16, 19, 22, 425, 434, 444, 469
   and C.S.S. *Virginia*, 14
   and Lincoln, 181, 424
   and McClellan, 15–16, 22, 43–44, 48, 94–95, 169, 204, 220, 227, 315, 428, 431
   and Stone, 5
   and Urbanna Plan, 11
   and Washington defense, 20
   and Wool, 33
Staples, Henry G., 164
Starke, William E., 351
Starr, Samuel H.
   at Seven Pines, 137
Steiner, Paul E., 440
Stevens, Walter H.
   at Seven Pines, 166
Stiles, Robert, 304
Stockton, Thomas B. W., 91, 250
Stone, Charles P., 5
Stone, Valentine H., 402

Stoneman, George, 57
   at Yorktown, 46
Stonewall Brigade, 226, 243, 367, 392
   at Gaines' Mill, 240
Stoughton, Edwin H., 56
stragglers, 100, 136, 252, 265, 269, 300, 309–310, 316– 317, 388, 394, 413, 415, 437, 440
Strange, John B., 351
   at Glendale, 342, 344
Strong, George Templeton, 315
Stryker, Stephen, 91, 250
Stuart, James E. B., 58, 95, 100, 402, 417
   at Evelington Heights, 421
   at Gaines' Mill, 235
   at Glendale, 332
   at Savage Station, 275
   at Stuart's ride, 186–190
   at White House Landing, 441
Sturtevant, Edward E., 405
Suiter, James A.
   at Glendale, 325
Sully, Alfred, 149, 151
   at Glendale, 325, 343, 351
   at Malvern Hill, 377
   at Savage Station, 271, 290, 294–295
Sumner, Edwin V., 11, 19, 446, 453–454, 456, 464–465
   and McClellan, 183
   and Urbanna Plan, 11
   at Fairfax council, 17
   at Gaines' Mill, 228
   at Garnett's & Golding's, 259
   at Glendale, 309, 314, 325, 341, 343, 351, 357
   at Harrison's Landing, 411
      at Harrison's Landing, 428
   at Malvern Hill, 358–359, 361, 369, 389
   at Oak Grove, 196, 198
   at Savage Station, 270–271, 273, 280–282, 288, 289, 290, 294, 296–297, 301
   at Seven Pines, 104–105, 118, 136, 146–149, 151–153, 156, 158–160, 165, 170–171, 176
   at Williamsburg, 62–63, 65–67, 69, 74, 77, 79–80, 82
   at Yorktown, 47, 57
   retreat to Harrison's, 403
   retreat to Harrison's Landing, 405
supplies, 3, 6, 12–13, 15, 21, 36–38, 42, 94, 104, 173, 184, 212, 226, 240, 280–281, 302, 317, 404, 412, 425, 432, 441, 449, 453, 473
Sycamore Creek, 433
Sydnor, Lincoln, 205
Sykes, George, 411
   at Gaines' Mill, 227, 230, 234, 236–237, 239, 246, 252
   at Glendale, 310, 332
   at Malvern Hill, 358–360, 370, 377, 389, 393
   at Mechanicsville, 215
   at Savage Station, 277, 300–301
   at Stuart's ride, 188
   at Yorktown, 46–47
   retreat to Harrison's, 403
   retreat to Harrison's Landing, 405

T

Taylor, George W.
   at Gaines' Mill, 237, 246, 248
Taylor, John G., 124
Taylor, Nelson, 66
Taylor, Richard
   at Gaines' Mill, 235–236
Taylor, Robert F.
   at Savage Station, 290
Taylor, William H., 127
teamsters, 148, 279, 311, 322
Teaser, CSS (gunboat), 420
Terry, Henry D., 140
Tew, Charles C., 383, 385–386
   at Malvern Hill, 385
Thomas, George, 2
Thompson, James, 281, 288, 309, 337, 345–346, 348, 367
Tidball, John C., 234, 388, 394, 417
Timberlake, John H., 234–335
Tomlin, Harrison B., 162
Tompkins, John A., 271
Toombs, Robert A., 409
   at Garnett's & Golding's, 256, 258–259, 261
   at Malvern Hill, 377, 386–387, 394–395, 397
   at Savage Station, 264, 288, 296
Torbert, Alfred T. A., 246

Totopotomoy Creek, 186–187, 190, 211
Trent house, 182, 222, 228, 270, 278, 288, 297
Trimble, Isaac R., 391, 406
  at Gaines' Mill, 235, 236, 238, 246
  at Malvern Hill, 377, 399
  at Savage Station, 282
Trumbull, Senator
  and Scott, 6
Tucker, John, 28, 36, 40
Turkey Island Creek, 359, 375
Tyler, Robert O., 91

U

Upton, Emory, 237, 239, 329
Urbanna Plan, 16

V

Valley Army, 180, 196
Van Vliet, Stewart, 33, 42, 212
Vest house, 65, 83
Voegelee, Adolph, 332, 370, 381

W

Wade, Benjamin O., 92
Waggaman, Eugene, 394
Wainwright, Charles S., 59, 61–62, 67–70
Walker, James A., 367
  at Gaines' Mill, 246
Walker, John G., 34
Walker, Thomas W., 334
War Department (US), 17, 20, 24
Ward, John H. H.
  at Seven Pines, 164
Warren, Gouverneur K.
  and Stuart's ride, 188
  at Gaines' Mill, 230
  at Hanover Court House, 91
Warwick River, 40–41, 47, 51, 54
Warwick, Bradfute, 249
  at Gaines' Mill, 251
Washington, DC, 3, 14–15, 18–19, 25, 39, 81, 95, 122, 128, 192, 420, 428, 446, 449–450, 454
Washington, J. Barrol, 121
Washington, William D., 190
Waterman, Richard, 377

Watt house, 227, 252
Webb, Alexander S., 451
Webber, Charles H., 59
Weed, Stephen H., 234, 240, 332, 334, 381
Weeden, William B., 91, 250, 252, 377, 381, 386, 389
Weeks, Henry A., 91
Wessells, Henry W.
  at Seven Pines, 102, 125–126, 128, 134
  retreat to Harrison's, 413, 419
  retreat to Harrison's Landing, 405
West Point, VA, 22
Wheat, C. Roberdeau, 236
Wheeler, Charles C., 73, 309
White House Landing, 88, 90, 174, 183, 186, 189–190, 192–193, 212, 223, 253, 261, 268, 286, 315, 402–403, 412, 415, 441
White House, the (Lee), 183
White Oak road, 264–266, 268, 306, 309, 322–324, 326
White Oak Swamp, 118, 265–266, 273, 275, 277, 279–281, 288–289, 298, 300–301, 303, 306, 307–310, 312–313, 316, 318, 322, 326–328, 343, 349, 354, 356, 362, 371, 402, 406
White Oak Swamp Bridge, 278, 300
White, J. Claude, 402
Whiting, Charles J., 251
Whiting, Jasper, 206
Whiting, William H. C., 192
  at Eltham's Landing, 86
  at Gaines' Mill, 235
  at Malvern Hill, 371, 373
  at Seven Pines, 108–110, 147, 150
Whitlock farm, 320, 337, 340
Whittle, Powhatan B., 78
Wickham, William C., 187
Wilcox, Cadmus M., 34
  at Gaines' Mill, 232, 250
  at Williamsburg, 58
Williamsburg, 57, 61, 65, 81, 90, 362
Williamsburg road, 102, 106, 108–109, 111, 116–118, 120, 123, 125–127, 135, 139–145, 160–162, 167, 198, 200–201, 264, 268, 269–270, 274, 281, 285, 289–291, 294, 296, 304, 306
Willis Church, 275, 308, 320, 357, 367, 376, 392, 397, 410, 419
Willis Church road, 264, 278, 300, 304,

307, 309–311, 313, 318–319, 339–340,
  343–344, 353, 355–357, 359, 363– 365,
  373, 377, 382, 385–386, 390, 392–394,
  397–399, 406
    at Malvern Hill, 375
Wilson, Joseph H., 121
Winder, Charles S., 406, 409, 426
    at Gaines' Mill, 235, 238, 240–241, 243
    at Glendale, 326
    at Malvern Hill, 362, 392, 397–398
    at Oak Grove, 206–207
    at Savage Station, 284, 288
Wise, Henry A., 410
    at Glendale, 307, 336
    at Malvern Hill, 392
Wolcott, John W., 367, 369
Woodbury, Dwight A., 91
Wooding, George W., 323, 369
Wool, John E., 14, 24, 31, 38, 40–43, 181
    and C.S.S. *Virginia*, 14
    and Stanton, 33
Woolfolk, James, 258
Wright, Ambrose R., 304
    at Malvern Hill, 381
    at Oak Grove, 198, 200, 202
    at Savage Station, 285

Y

York River, 13, 17, 31, 39–42, 47–48, 58,
  84, 86, 90, 120, 135, 188, 209, 446

Z

Zollicoffer, Felix K., 2

Printed in Great Britain
by Amazon.co.uk, Ltd.,
Marston Gate.